QURAN: THE FINAL SCRIPTURE
(Authorized English Version)

Translated from the Original
by
Rashad Khalifa, Ph.D.

Imam, Mosque of Tucson
Tucson, Arizona

> *A prophet like me will the Lord, your God, raise up for you from among your own kinsmen; to him you shall listen.*
>
> *(Moses in Deuteronomy 18:15)*

> *I will raise up for them a prophet like you from among their kinsmen, and will put my words into his mouth; he shall tell them all that I command him. If any man will not listen to my words which he speaks in my name, I myself will make him answer for it.*
>
> *(Deuteronomy 18:18-19)*

> *I will ask the Father, and He will give you another Paraclete — to be with you always: THE SPIRIT OF TRUTH.*
>
> *(Jesus in John 14:16-17)*

> *When THE SPIRIT OF TRUTH comes to you, he will guide you to all truth, and will announce to you the things to come.*
>
> *(Jesus in John 16:13)*

ISBN 0-934894-19-1
Library of Congress Card No. 81-80923

COPYRIGHT © 1981 by ISLAMIC PRODUCTIONS

For information address
ISLAMIC PRODUCTIONS, 739 E. 6TH STREET, TUCSON, AZ 85719
PRINTED IN THE UNITED STATES OF AMERICA

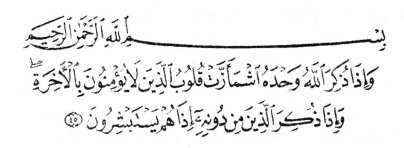

When God ALONE is advocated, the hearts of those who do not believe in the hereafter shrink with aversion. But when idols are mentioned besides Him, they rejoice (39:45).

You may be Jewish, Christian, Muslim, or anything else. But you can fulfill the purpose of your life, attain perfect happiness, and achieve salvation, ONLY if you submit to God; the omnipotent, omniscient, omnipresent, Lord, cherisher, and sustainer of the universe.

Over the times, our creator has pointed out for us the path to perfect happiness. But we have a formidable enemy who is bent on diverting us from the path of God.

Over the times, our creator has sent messages aiming at directing us towards the path of happiness, and alerting us to avoid the paths of misery.

Unfortunately, our enemy has succeeded in duping us en masse.

Our creator gave the Jews the Torah. But Satan diverted them to the Mishnah (oral) and Gemarah (traditions) of Talmud.

Our creator sent Jesus to save the world, but his followers were duped into worshiping him against his will.

Our creator sent this Quran to guide all humanity. But the Muslims were equally duped into following the Hadith (oral) and Sunna (traditions), which are falsely attributed to the messenger.

On the 27th night of Ramadan of the year 13 B.H. (Before Hijra) (610 AD), the prophet Muhammad was summoned to the highest possible point, and this Quran was placed into his heart (see 2:97, 17:1, 44:3, 53:1-18, and 97:1-5). Subsequently, the Quran was released, through Muhammad's mouth, over a period of 23 years, namely, between 610 and 632 AD (see 17:106). At the moment of release, it was scrupulously written down, and divinely guarded since then (see footnote 1:1 and Appendix 1).

INDEX OF SURAS

INDEX OF SURAS (Continued)

Sura 1: The Opener (Al-Fatihah)

---

1. In the name of God, most gracious, most merciful.*
2. Praise be to God, Lord of the Universe;
3. most gracious, most merciful;
4. master of the day of judgment.
5. You alone we worship; and You alone we ask for help.
6. Guide us in the right path;
7. the path of those whom You blessed; not of those who deserve wrath, nor the strayers.

1:1. This opening statement of Quran is the foundation upon which a miraculous numerical code is built. This code, which remained a divinely guarded secret for 1400 years, presents to the world the first physical, touchable, and utterly indisputable proof that this Quran is a divine scripture. The Quran's miraculous numerical code is so intricate that it leaves no doubt that the Quran is the word of God, and that it has been perfectly protected from the slightest distortion, addition, or loss. Yet it is so simple that any person can fully appreciate its significance. There is no greater acknowledgement than God's own description of this Quranic code as "one of the greatest miracles" (74:35). It was the will of the Almighty to bless this very translation with the exclusive discovery of this profound miracle, as a clear sign of divine approval and authorization.

The opening statement (verse 1 of sura 1) consists of 19 Arabic letters, and this is the number upon which the Quran's numerical code is based (see Appendix 1 for details). Every word in the opening statement is mentioned throughout the Quran a number of times which is consistently a multiple of 19. Thus, the first word (Ism=name) is found in the Quran exactly 19 times; the second word (Allah=God) is mentioned 2,698 times (19x142); the third word (Al-Rahman=most gracious) is mentioned 57 times (19x3); and the last word (Al-Raheem=most merciful) is mentioned 114 times (19x6). The reader, therefore, is handed at the outset physical proof that Quran is God's message to humanity. Of the millions of books in existence, how many will exhibit this elaborate phenomenon; that the opening statement consists of an "X" number of letters, and every word in the statement is mentioned throughout the book a multiple of "X"? Although this unique phenomenon is a minute portion of the Quran's numerical miracle, the renowned journal "SCIENTIFIC AMERICAN" described it as "an ingenious study of Quran." (September 1980, pp 22-24).

Sura 2: The Heifer (Al-Baqarah)

In the name of God, most gracious, most merciful

1. A.L.M.*

Three Categories of People

1. The Righteous

2. This scripture is infallible; a beacon for the righteous,
3. who believe in the unseen,* observe the **salat** prayers,* and from our provisions to them, they give;
4. and they believe in what was revealed to you, and in what was revealed before you; and they are positively certain about the hereafter.
5. They have followed the guidance from their Lord; they are the winners.

2. The Disbelievers

6. As for those who disbelieve, it will be the same for them; whether you warn them or not, they can not believe.
7. (That is because) God seals their hearts, and their hearing, and places veils upon their eyes. They have deserved terrible retribution.

3. The Hypocrites

8. Then there are those who say, "We believe in God and the last day," while they are not believers.
9. In attempting to deceive God and the believers, they only deceive themselves without perceiving.
10. In their hearts is a disease, and consequently, God augments their disease. They have deserved painful retribution for their lying.

2:1. *The meaning or significance of these Quranic initials remained unknown for 1400 years, since the revelation of Quran. Now we recognize them as a part of the Quran's numerical miracle. These letters, as it turned out, provide the proof that this scripture is the infallible word of God (see Appendix 1).*

2:3. *Such as God, the hereafter, the angels, the jinns, and satan.*

2:3. *The word* **"salat"** *designates a specific set of actions, including bowing, prostrating, and reciting specific words. The* **salat** *prayers must be observed at five specific times each day. The word "prayer" alone is not sufficient to describe this important religious duty.*

11. When they are told, "Do not corrupt the earth," they say, "But we are righteous."
12. In fact, they are corruptors, but they do not perceive.
13. When they are told, "Believe as the people have believed," they say, "Shall we believe as the fools have believed?" In fact, it is they who are fools, but they do not know.
14. When they meet the believers, they say, "We believe," but when alone with their devils, they say, "We are with you. We were only mocking."
15. God mocks them, by allowing them to continue their transgressions, blundering.
16. They have chosen the straying instead of guidance and thus, their trade never prospers, nor are they ever guided.
17. Their allegory is that of one who starts a fire, then, as it begins to shed light around him, God takes away their light, leaving them in total darkness, unable to see.
18. Deaf, dumb, and blind; they can never return.
19. Or like a storm from the sky, with darkness, thunder, and lightning. They place their fingers in their ears as if to evade death by lightning. God thus encompasses the disbelievers.

The Light of Faith

20. The lightning is so bright, it almost blinds them. Whenever it lights for them, they move forward. And when it turns dark, they stand still. Had God willed, He* could have taken away their hearing and their eyesight. God is omnipotent.
21. O people, you shall worship your Lord, who created you and those before you, that you may attain salvation.
22. He is the one who made the earth habitable for you; He is the one who constructed the sky. He sends down water from the sky to produce fruits for your sustenance. Therefore, you shall not set up idols besides God, despite this knowledge.
23. If you have any doubts concerning this revelation to our servant, then produce one sura like these, and ask your idols, whom you set up besides God, to do the same, if you are truthful.

Heaven and Hell Allegorically Described

24. If you fail to do this, and most certainly you will fail, then beware of the hellfire whose fuel is people and rocks; it awaits the disbelievers.

2:20. "He" does not imply gender in the Arabic language. God Almighty is neither male nor female. Is this why Arabic was chosen for the final scripture? See Appendix 3.

25. And give good news to those who believe and work righteousness that they have deserved gardens with flowing streams. When given a fruit therein, they would say, "This is what was given to us before." They will be given the same kind. They will have pure spouses therein, and abide therein forever.

26. Thus, God does not shy away from any kind of allegory, from down to a mosquito and higher. Those who believe know that it is the truth from their Lord, while the disbelievers would say, "What did God mean by such an allegory?" He misleads many thereby, and guides many thereby; but He never misleads except the wicked;

27. who violate God's covenant after pledging to keep it, disregard what God has ordered upheld, and corrupt the earth. These are the losers.

Two Deaths and Two Lives

28. How could you disbelieve in God, when you were dead and He gave you life, then He will put you to death, then bring you back to life? To Him is your ultimate return.

Creation of the Heavens and the Earth

29. He is the one who created for you everything on earth, then turned to the sky and designed seven heavens therein.* He is fully aware of all things.

Creation of Man

30. Then your Lord said to the angels, "I am placing a representative on earth." They said, "Shall you place therein one who would corrupt therein, and shed blood, while we praise Your glory and hold You sacred?" He said, "I know what you do not know."*

31. And He taught Adam all the names, then presented them to the angels, saying, "Tell Me the names of these, if you are right."

2:29. Our immediate universe includes 100 billion galaxies and a billion trillion stars, at distances of millions of light years. All this incredible vastness is only part of the lowest and smallest "heaven." Six more larger heavens surround our innermost, small heaven, and all seven heavens are within God's "right hand." (see Appendix 5, and 39:67). Yet some people are ignorant enough to idolize such minute and powerless mortals as Jesus, Muhammad, and various saints.

2:30. What is the purpose behind our creation? Why are we here? See Appendix 6.

32. They said, "Glory be to You. We have no knowledge, except that which
     You taught us. You are the omniscient, the wise."
33. He said, "O Adam, tell them their names." When he told them their
     names, He said, "Did I not tell you that I know the secrets of the heavens
     and the earth, and I know everything you declare and everything you
     conceal?*
34. Then we said to the angels, "Fall prostrate before Adam." They fell
     prostrate, except Iblis (satan); he refused, turned arrogant, and thus, he
     became a rebel.
35. Then we said, "O Adam, live with your wife in paradise, and eat
     generously therefrom as you please. But do not approach this one tree,
     lest you become sinners."
36. But the devil duped them out of it, causing their eviction therefrom. We
     said, "Go down as enemies to each other, and on earth will be your
     habitation and sustenance for awhile."
37. Then Adam received from his Lord words, whereby He redeemed him.
     He is the redeemer, the merciful.
38. We said, "Go down therefrom, all of you; and when guidance comes to
     you from Me, those who follow My guidance have nothing to fear, nor
     will they grieve."
39. As for those who disbelieve and reject our* revelations, they have
     deserved hell; they abide therein forever.

The Children of Israel*

40. O children of Israel, appreciate the blessings I have bestowed upon you,
     and uphold My covenant, that I uphold your covenant; and reverence
     Me.
41. And believe in what is revealed herein confirming what you have, and do
     not be the first to reject it. Do not trade away My revelations for a cheap
     price; and observe Me.

2:33. See Appendix 6 for the details of satan's fall from angelhood.

2:39. God speaks frequently in the plural. This invariably indicates
participation of the angels, and God's will to give them credit for their
participation. For example, God's revelations to us were brought down by the
angel Gabriel, hence the statement "our revelations." On the other hand, God
speaks in the singular where the action is exclusively His, such as worship (see
20:14, 21:25, 21:92, 29:56, and 36:61). When God spoke to Moses (20:12-14)
without the mediation of any angels, we find that God speaks in the singular.

2:40-123. Why are the children of Israel so frequently mentioned throughout
the Quran? See footnote 4:153 for the parallel between the followers of Moses
and the followers of Muhammad.

42. Do not confound the truth with falsehood, nor shall you conceal the truth knowingly.

43. You shall observe the **salat** prayers and **zakat** charity; you shall bow down with those who bow down.*

44. Would you enjoin righteousness upon the people, and forget yourselves, though you read the scripture? Do you not understand?

45. Seek help through steadfastness and **salat**; this is difficult indeed, but not for the reverent;

46. who realize that they will meet their Lord; that to Him they ultimately return.

47. O children of Israel, appreciate the blessings I have bestowed upon you, and that I set you apart from all the people.

48. Beware of the day when no one can avail another, no intercession will be accepted,* and no one can be helped.

49. Recall that we delivered you from Pharaoh's people who inflicted disastrous persecution upon you, slaughtering your sons and sparing your daughters. It was an exacting trial from your Lord.

50. Recall that we parted the sea for you; we thus saved you and drowned the Pharaoh's people before your eyes.

51. Recall that we summoned Moses for forty nights, then you idolized the calf in his absence and turned wicked.

52. Yet we pardoned you thereafter, that you may be thankful.

53. Recall that we gave Moses the scripture and the statute book, that you may be guided.

54. Recall that Moses said to his people, "O my people, you have wronged your souls by idolizing the calf. You shall repent to your initiator." God did redeem you, for He is the redeemer, the merciful.

55. And when you said, "O Moses, we will not believe unless we see God physically," the lightning struck you as you looked.

56. Then we resurrected you from death, that you may be appreciative.

---

*2:43. Just as the **salat** prayers are a specific set of practices, the **zakat** charity is a specific proportion of one's properties to be given to the needy on regular basis. In Islam, **zakat**, is 2% of one's capital possessions annually.*

2:48. The myth of "intercession" is prevalent in both Christianity and Islam. The Christians claim that Jesus will intercede on their behalf, and the Muslims claim that Muhammad will intercede on their behalf. The divine truth, as shown throughout the Quran, is that neither Jesus nor Muhammad, nor anyone else, will possess the power of intercession. See Appendix 7 for details.

In Sinai

57. We shaded you with clouds, and sent down to you manna and quails. Eat from the good things we provided for you. They did no harm to us (by rebelling); it is their own souls that they harmed.
58. Recall that we said, "Enter this village and eat therefrom as you please, generously. Enter the gate humbly, and speak amicably. We will then forgive your sins, and increase the reward for the righteous."
59. But the wicked distorted the commandments given to them, and consequently, we sent down upon them a curse from the sky; because of their wickedness.
60. And when Moses sought water for his people, we said, "Strike the rock with your staff." Whereupon, twelve springs gushed out therefrom, and thus, each tribe had their own water. Eat and drink from God's provisions, and do not corrupt the earth.
61. Then you said, "O Moses, we can no longer tolerate one kind of food, so call upon your Lord to produce for us such earthly crops as beans, cucumber, garlic, lentils, and onions." He said, "Do you wish to substitute that which is inferior for that which is good? Maybe you should go back to Egypt where you had such things!" They were condemned to humiliation and poverty, and they incurred wrath from God. That is because they rejected God's revelations, and slew the prophets unjustly; they disobeyed and transgressed.

Minimum Requirement for Salvation

62. Those who believe, those who are Jewish, the Christians, and the converts; any of them who believe in God and the last day, and lead a righteous life, have nothing to fear, nor will they grieve.

The Covenant

63. Recall that we made a covenant with you, as we raised Mount Sinai over you. You shall uphold this covenant strongly, and remember its tenets, that you may attain salvation.
64. You turned back thereafter, and if it were not for God's indulgence towards you, and His mercy, you would have been destroyed.
65. You have known about those among you who desecrated the Sabbath; we said to them, "Be you despicable apes."
66. We thus made them an example for their generation, as well as subsequent generations, and an enlightenment for the righteous.

The Heifer*

67. When Moses said to his people, "God commands you to sacrifice a heifer," they said, "Are you kidding us?" He said, "God forbid that I should be so foolish."

68. They said, "Call upon your Lord to show us which one." He said, "He says that she should be a heifer that is neither too old, nor too young; of an intermediate age. This is the command you shall carry out."

69. They said, "Call upon your Lord to show us her color." He said, "He says that she shall be a yellow heifer; bright colored; pleases the beholders."

70. They said, "Call upon your Lord to point her out for us. The heifers look alike to us, and with God's help we will find her."

71. He said, "He says that she shall be a heifer that was never humiliated in plowing the soil, or watering the crops; perfectly safe from any blemish." They said, "Now you are telling the truth." They finally sacrificed her, though with great reluctance.

72. You murdered someone and disputed among yourselves, then God revealed what you tried to conceal.

73. Thus, we said, "Strike the murder victim with part of the heifer." God thus resurrects the dead, and shows you His signs, that you may understand.

74. Yet, your hearts hardened thereafter and became like rocks, or even harder. For there are rocks from which streams gush out; others crack and release water; while others even cringe out of reverence for God. God is never unaware of anything you do.

75. Do you expect them to believe as you do, even though some of them distort the word of God after hearing it, with full understanding thereof, and maliciously?

76. When they meet the believers they say, "We believe." But when alone with each other they say, "Do you tell them of God's revelations to you, and thus provide them with support for their argument? Do you not understand?"

77. Do they not realize that God knows everything they conceal and everything they declare?

78. Among them are illiterates who do not know the scripture except through hearsay and conjecture.

79. Therefore, woe to those who distort the scripture with their own hands then say, "This is from God," seeking a cheap gain. Woe to them for distorting the scripture, and woe to them for their illicit earnings.

2:67-74.   See the Bible's book of Numbers, Chapter 19.

Heaven and Hell are Eternal

80. They said, "We will not suffer in hell, except for a few days." Say, "Did you take such a promise from God, and God never breaks His promise; or do you say about God what you do not know?"
81. Indeed, anyone who works evil, and becomes surrounded by his sin, these have deserved hell; they abide therein forever.
82. As for those who believe and work righteousness, they have deserved heaven; they abide therein forever.

The Children of Israel Rebel

83. We made a covenant with the children of Israel; you shall not worship except God; you shall regard the parents, the relatives, the orphans, and the poor; you shall speak amicably to the people; you shall observe the **salat** prayers and the **zakat** charity. But you turned away, except a few of you, and you became averse.
84. We made a covenant with you, that you shall not shed each others blood, nor shall you evict each other from your homes. You agreed and bore witness.
85. Yet, here you are slaying each other, and evicting some of you from their homes, banding against them sinfully and maliciously. When they came to you as captives, you ransomed them, though evicting them was forbidden in the first place. Do you believe in part of the scripture and disbelieve in part? What should be the retribution for those who do this except humiliation in this life, and a harsher retribution on the day of resurrection? God is never unaware of anything you do.
86. It is they who gave preference to this life over the hereafter, and consequently, their retribution will not be commuted, nor will they find help.
87. We gave Moses the scripture, and subsequent to him we sent messengers. And we gave Jesus the son of Mary profound signs, and supported him with the holy spirit. Whenever a messenger came to you with commandments contrary to your wishes you turned arrogant; you rejected some, and killed some.
88. They said, "Our hearts are shielded." Rather, it is a curse from God, because of their disbelief, that prevents them from ever believing.
89. Thus, when a scripture came to them from God, and even though it confirms what they have, and even though they used to predict its coming to the idolaters, when their own predictions came true, they disbelieved. Thus does God's curse affect the disbelievers.

90. Miserable indeed is what they sold their souls for; rejecting these revelations of God, out of sheer resentment that God should bestow His blessings upon whomever He wills. Consequently, they incurred wrath upon wrath; they will suffer humiliating retribution.

91. When they are told, "Believe in these revelations of God," they say, "We believe only in what was revealed to us." They thus reject all subsequent scripture, even though they know it is the truth, and even though it confirms their own scripture. Say, "Why did you slay God's prophets in the past, if you were really believers?"

92. Moses had come to you with profound miracles, yet you idolized the calf in his absence and turned wicked.

93. We made a covenant with you, as we raised Mount Sinai above you. You shall strongly uphold the commandments we gave you, and hearken. They said, "We heard, but we will not obey." Their hearts were filled with adoration for the calf, as a consequence of their disbelief. Say, "Miserable indeed is what your convictions dictate upon you, if you do have any convictions."

94. Say, "If the hereafter is reserved for you alone at God, to the exclusion of all others, then you should long for death, if you are truthful."

95. They will never long for it, because of what their hands have committed. God is fully aware of the wicked.

96. In fact, you will find them the most covetous of life; even more so than the pagans. The one of them wishes to live a thousand years, though this will never spare him the retribution, should he survive. God sees everything they do.

Gabriel Mediated the Revelation

97. Say, "Anyone who opposes Gabriel should know that he revealed this scripture into your heart with God's permission, confirming previous scriptures, and providing guidance and good news for the believers."

98. Anyone who opposes God, His angels, His messengers, Gabriel, and Michael, should know that God opposes the disbelievers.

99. We have revealed to you* profound revelations, and only the wicked will disbelieve therein.

2:99. *Like all previous scriptures, the Quran addresses all the people in the second person singular, as though all the people were one man. Thus, when God says, "We have revealed to you this Quran," the word "you" here refers to all the people. See for example 18:27-28. Certain verses are specifically addressed to the prophet to serve as examples and lessons for the rest of us, or to address a specific incident.*

100. Is it not a fact that whenever they made a covenant, some of them would violate it? Indeed, most of them do not believe.

101. And when a messenger came to them from God, confirming their own scripture, some of those who follow previous scripture disregarded this new scripture as if they did not know.

Sorcery Prohibited

102. They also followed what the devils narrated concerning the kingdom of Solomon. Solomon, however, never abused his powers, but the devils did. They taught the people sorcery that was revealed to the world through the two angels Haroot and Maroot. But these two did not teach anyone without pointing out that such knowledge is revealed as a test, and should not be abused. Yet, they practiced such evil schemes as breaking up marriages, though they can never harm anyone against the will of God. They learn from sorcery what harms, not what benefits, and they knew well that anyone who practices sorcery will have no share in the hereafter. Miserable indeed is what they sold their souls for, if they only knew.

103. Had they believed and led a righteous life, the recompense from God would have been better for them, if they only knew.

Playing on Words

104. O you who believe, do not say, **"Ra'ina*** (be our shepherd)," but say, **"Unzurna** (watch over us)," and hearken. The disbelievers have deserved painful retribution.

Superceding Previous Revelations

105. Those who disbelieve among the followers of previous scriptures, as well as the idol-worshipers, dislike to see any blessing come down to you from your Lord. But God chooses for His mercy whomever He wills. God possesses unlimited bounty.

106. Whenever we abrogate any revelation, or cause it to be forgotten, we bring a better one or at least a similar one. Do you not know that God is omnipotent?

107. Do you not know that to God belongs the kingship of the heavens and the earth, and that you have none besides God as master and sustainer?

108. Would you demand of your messenger what was demanded of Moses before? Anyone who substitutes disbelief for belief has indeed strayed off the right path.

*2:104. The word **Ra'ina** sounds like a dirty word in one of the old languages.*

109. Many followers of previous scripture wish to revert you back to paganism, due to jealousy on their part, now that the truth has been manifested to them. You shall forgive and forget them, for God is the one who will judge them. God is omnipotent.

110. You shall observe the **salat** prayers and **zakat** charity. Any righteous work you send forward on behalf of your souls, you will find it at God. God is seer of everything you do.

Submission: Key to Salvation

111. They said, "No one will enter heaven unless he is Jewish, or Christian." Such is their wishful thinking. Say, "Show us your proof, if you are right."

112. Indeed, whoever submits to God, while leading a righteous life, these have nothing to fear, nor will they grieve.

113. And the Jews said, "The Christians have no basis," while the Christians said, "The Jews have no basis," though both of them recite the scripture. Those who received no scriptures have uttered similar utterances. God will judge them on the day of resurrection regarding their disputes.

114. Who is more evil than one who forbids others from attending the mosques of God, where His name is commemorated, and seeks to have them deserted? These ought not to enter therein except fearfully. These have deserved humiliation in this life, and terrible retribution in the hereafter.

115. To God belong the East and the West; wherever you might be there will be the presence of God. God is omnipresent, omniscient.

116. And they said, "God has begotten a son!" Glory be to Him; nay; to Him belongs everything in the heavens and the earth; all subservient to Him.

117. He is the initiator of the heavens and the earth; to have anything done He simply says to it, "Be," and it is.

118. Those who do not know said, "If only God could speak to us, or some profound miracle come to us (we will then believe)." Others before them have uttered similar utterances; their hearts are all the same. We do manifest the signs for those who have attained certainty.

119. We have sent you, truthfully, as a bearer of good news as well as a warner, and you are not answerable for those who deserve hell.

120. Neither the Jews, nor the Christians, will accept you, unless you follow their creed. Say, "God's guidance is the perfect guidance," and if you ever acquiesce to their wishes despite this knowledge, you will find no one to help you against God.

121. Those who received previous scripture, and truly uphold it, will believe in this.* As for those who disbelieve, they are the losers.

2:121.   See the Biblical teachings on the inside front cover, and Appendix 19.

122. O children of Israel, remember the blessings I bestowed upon you, and that I set you apart from all the people.
123. Beware of the day when no one can benefit another, no ransom will be accepted, no intercession will be useful, and no one can receive help.

Abraham Passes the Test

124. When Abraham was put to the test by his Lord, through certain commandments, he carried them out. God then said, "I am appointing you an imam for the people." He said, "Will this include my descendants?" God said, "My promise does not include the wicked."
125. We then designated the shrine (of Mecca) as a focal point for the people, and a sacred sanctuary. You shall use this abode of Abraham as a place of worship. We directed Abraham and Ishmael to sanctify My shrine for those who encircle it, retreat in it, and bow and prostrate.
126. Abraham said, "My Lord, make this a peaceful land, and provide its people with fruits; provide for those who believe in God and the last day." God said, "I will also provide for the disbeliever; I will let him enjoy for awhile, then commit him to the retribution of hell, and a miserable destiny."
127. As Abraham raised the foundations of the shrine (of Mecca), together with Ishmael, they prayed, "Our Lord, accept from us, for You are the hearer, the omniscient.
128. "Our Lord, make us Muslims (submitters) to You, and from our descendants let there be a Muslim nation (submitting) to You. Teach us how to practice our religious duties,* and redeem us; You are the redeemer, the merciful.
129. "Our Lord, and raise among them a messenger who would recite for them Your revelations, and teach them the scripture and wisdom, and sanctify them. You are the Almighty, the wise."
130. Thus, who would then forsake the religion of Abraham, except those who fool themselves? We have chosen him in this life, and in the hereafter he will be with the righteous.
131. When his Lord said to him, "Submit," he said, "I submit to the Lord of the universe."

2:128.   Many Muslims entertain the erroneous idea that Muhammad was the source of religious practices in Islam, namely, **salat, zakat,** *fasting, and* **hajj** *pilgrimage. However, the Quran teaches us that all religious duties were revealed to us through Abraham. See also 2:183, 2:187, 16:123, 21:73, 22:27, 22:78, and Appendix 8.*

132. Moreover, Abraham exhorted his children to submit to God, and so did Jacob, saying "O my children, God has pointed out the religion for you; you shall not die except as Muslims (submitters)."

133. Had you witnessed Jacob on his death bed; he said to his children, "What will you worship after me?" They said, "We will continue to worship your God, and the God of your fathers Abraham, and Ishmael, and Isaac; the one God; to Him we are Muslims (submitters)."

134. This is a community from the past. They are responsible for their own works; you are responsible for your own works; and you are not answerable for anything they did.

Islam is the Religion of Abraham*

135. They said, "You have to be Jewish, or Christian, to be guided." Say, "We follow the religion of Abraham, the monotheist; he never was an idol worshiper."

136. Say, "We believe in God, and in what was revealed to us, and in what was revealed to Abraham, Ishmael, Isaac, Jacob, and the Patriarchs, and in what was given to Moses and Jesus, and in what was given to all the prophets from their Lord; we make no distinction among any of them; we submit to God."

137. If they believe as you believe, then they are rightly guided. But if they turn away, then they have joined the opposition. God will spare you their opposition; He is the hearer, the omniscient.

138. Such is God's mode, and whose mode is better than God's? We worship Him alone.

139. Say, "Do you argue with us concerning God, though He is our Lord and your Lord; and we are responsible for our works, while you are responsible for your works? We are devoted to Him alone."

140. Would you say that Abraham, Ishmael, Isaac, Jacob, and the Patriarchs were Jewish or Christian? Say, "Who is more knowledgeable, you or God?" Who is more evil than one who conceals a testimony concerning God? God is never unaware of anything you do.

141. This is a community from the past. They are responsible for their own works, and you are responsible for your own works. You are not answerable for anything they did.

2:135. *Those who idolize the prophet Muhammad against his will try to promote the idea that he is the source of all religious guidance in Islam. The Quranic truth teaches us that God Almighty is the source, and that all religious practices in Islam came to us generation after generation through Abraham, not Muhammad. See 2:128.*

Abolition of Prejudice and Bigotry

142. The fools among the people may ask, "Why did they change the direction of **Qiblah** (direction faced during **salat** prayers)?* Say, "To God belong the East and the West. He directs whomever He wills to the right path."

143. We thus made you an unbiased congregation,* that you may serve as witnesses among the people, just as the messenger serves as witness among you. We only changed the **Qiblah** as a test, in order to distinguish those who would follow the messenger from those who would turn back on their heels. Indeed, it was a difficult test, but not for those guided by God. God never puts your worship to waste (regardless of direction). God is compassionate towards the people, most merciful.

144. We have seen your face (O Muhammad) turning about the sky. Therefore, we now appoint for you a **Qiblah** that pleases you. Henceforth, you shall turn your face (during **salat**) towards the sacred mosque (of Mecca). Wherever you may be (O believers), you shall turn your faces towards it. Even those who received previous scripture recognize that this is the truth from their Lord. God is never unaware of anything they do.

145. However, even if you show the followers of previous scripture every kind of miracle, they will not follow your **Qiblah**, nor should you follow their **Qiblah**; they do not even follow each others' **Qiblah**. If you ever acquiesce to their wishes, despite the knowledge you have received herein, you will be a sinner.

146. Those who received previous scripture recognize this, just as they recognize their own children.* But many of them conceal the truth, knowingly.

147. This is the truth from your Lord; do not harbor any doubts.

2:142. This is another proof that the **salat** *prayers were practiced before Muhammad.*

2:143. The Arabs were fanatically prejudiced towards the Ka'ba in Mecca, and when the **Qiblah** *was changed towards Jerusalem, many people who had followed Muhammad were overcome with prejudice and reverted to idolatry. The Muslims, however, learned to overcome their traditional bigotry and prejudice, and submitted to the will of God. After the first Muslims learned to abolish bigotry and fanaticism, the Ka'ba was restored as the eternal direction of* **Qiblah**.

2:146. Both the Old testament and the New testament clearly predict the coming of the "final paraclete" to "show you all truth." See the inside cover of this book, and Appendix 19 entitled, "The Bible's Preview of Muhammad."

148. To each is his own direction; therefore, you shall race towards righteous works. Wherever you might be, God will bring you all; God is omnipotent.

149. Wherever you may go, you shall turn your face (in **salat**) towards the sacred mosque (of Mecca). This is the truth from your Lord. God is never unaware of anything you do.

150. Wherever you may go, you shall turn your face (during **salat**) towards the sacred mosque (of Mecca). Wherever you may be, you shall turn your faces towards it. Thus, the people will have no argument against you, except the wicked among them. Do not fear them, and fear Me instead, that I may complete My blessings upon you, that you may be guided.

151. Such blessings as the sending of a messenger from among you, to recite for you our revelations, and to sanctify you, and to teach you the scripture and wisdom, and to teach you what you never knew.

152. Therefore, you shall remember Me, that I may remember you, and be thankful to Me; do not be unappreciative.

Steadfastness Required

153. O you who believe, seek help through steadfastness and **salat**; God is with those who steadfastly persevere.

154. Do not say about those who are killed in the cause of God, "They are dead," for they are alive, but you do not perceive.*

155. We will surely put you to the test, by means of some fear, hunger, and loss of money, lives, and crops. Give good news to those who steadfastly persevere.

156. If a disaster should strike them, they say, "We belong to God, and to Him is our ultimate return."

157. These have deserved blessings from their Lord, and mercy; they are the guided ones.*

Hajj Pilgrimage

158. The knolls of Safa and Marwah are part of the worship practices decreed by God. Thus, whoever observes the **Hajj** pilgrimage or the **Umrah** pilgrimage commits no error by traversing the distance between them. If one volunteers more righteous works, then God is appreciative, fully aware.

159. As for those who conceal what we send down of profound revelations and guidance, after declaring them for the people in this scripture, they have deserved God's curse, and should be cursed by all who curse.

2:154.   *See footnote 3:170.*

2:157.   *Compare the Arabic text of this verse with 33:43 and 33:56.*

160. But those who repent, reform, and clarify, I redeem them; I am the redeemer, the merciful.
161. Those who disbelieve and die as disbelievers have deserved the curse of God, and the angels, and all the people.
162. Eternally they will abide therein; their retribution is never commuted, nor are they reprieved.
163. Your God is one God; there is no god except He, the gracious, the merciful.

Overwhelming Signs of God

164. In the creation of the heavens and the earth, the alternation of night and day, the ships that roam the sea for the benefit of mankind, the water that God sends down to revive dead lands and spread all kinds of creatures therein, the manipulation of the winds, the clouds placed between the heaven and the earth; all these are signs for people who understand.

The Idol Worshipers Disowned by Their Idols

165. Yet, some people set up idols besides God and adore them as if they were God. However, the believers love God more than anything else. If only the wrong doers could envision themselves when they face the retribution; they will find out that all power belongs to God alone, and that God is very strict in imposing retribution.
166. Those who were followed will disown their followers; they will suffer the retribution, and all help to them will be severed.
167. The followers will then say, "If we could live our first life again, we will then disown them as they disown us now." Thus will God show them the consequences of their works as nothing but sorrow; they will never exit from hell.

Free Mind Prerequisite for Salvation

168. O people, eat from everything that is lawful and good, and do not follow the steps of satan; he is your ardent enemy.
169. He directs you towards vice and evil, and to invent lies and attribute them to God.*

2:169.   *Therefore, it must be satan's work that led many people to invent long lists of prohibitions, then attribute them to God and/or His messenger. The Quran consistently lists four specific dietary prohibitions (see 2:173, 6:145, 16:115). Furthermore, the Quran teaches that those who worship God alone follow the laws decreed by God alone. Specifically, those who follow dietary regulations dictated by other than the Quran are called "idol-worshipers." See 6:121.*

170. Then, when they are told, "Follow only God's commandments," they say, "We follow what we found our parents doing." What if their parents lacked the understanding and guidance?

171. The example of such disbelievers is that of a parrot; they repeat what they heard without understanding. Deaf, dumb, and blind; they fail to understand.

Dietary Regulations

172. O you who believe, eat from the good things we provide for you, and be thankful to God, if you do worship Him alone.

173. He only prohibits for you animals that die of themselves, blood, the meat of pigs, and animals sacrificed in any name other than God's.* However, if one is forced (to eat these), without being malicious or deliberate, then he incurs no sin. God is forgiver, merciful.

174. Those who conceal God's revelations in the scripture, seeking a lowly material gain, are eating fire into their bellies. God will not speak to them on the day of resurrection, nor will He sanctify them. They will suffer painful retribution.

175. It is they who chose the straying instead of guidance, and the retribution instead of forgiveness. Consequently, they will have to endure the hellfire.

176. That is because God has sent down the scripture truthfully, and those who dispute the scripture are in manifest defiance.

Righteousness Defined

177. Righteousness is not the turning of your faces towards the East or the West. But righteousness is to believe in God, the last day, the angels, the scriptures, and the prophets; and to donate the money despite one's love thereof to the relatives, the orphans, the needy, the alien, the beggars, and to free the slaves, and to observe the **salat** and **zakat**, and to keep the promises that are made, and to remain steadfast in the face of adversity, hardship, and war. These are the truthful; these are the righteous.

Equivalence is the Law

178. O you who believe, equivalence is decreed herein as the law when dealing with murder; the free for the free, the slave for the slave, and the woman for the woman. However, if the guilty is pardoned by the victim's kin, then a gracious response is in order, and an equitable compensation shall be offered. This is leniency from your Lord and mercy. Whoever transgresses henceforth will suffer painful retribution.

2:173. Before sacrificing an animal, we must take permission from the creator.

179.   Equivalence shall be a life-saving law, O you who possess intelligence, that you may attain salvation.

Leave a Will Before Death

180.   Decreed for you is the dictation of a will when death approaches the one of you, for the benefit of your parents and relatives. This is an incumbent duty upon the righteous.
181.   If anyone alters a will he had witnessed, he incurs the sin of such distorting. God is hearer, omniscient.
182.   However, if one senses obviously sinful partiality on the part of a testator, and alters the will to restore justice, then he incurs no sin. God is forgiver, merciful.

Fasting Reinforced and Revised*

183.   O you who believe, fasting is decreed for you, as it was decreed for those before you, that you may attain salvation.
184.   You shall fast during the specified days. Those who are ill or travelling may fast an equal number of other days. And those who find it too difficult may substitute the feeding of a poor person for each day of fasting; if they volunteer to feed more people, it would be better. But fasting is the best for you, if you only knew.
185.   Ramadan is the month during which the Quran was revealed, bringing guidance, clear guidelines, and the statute book. Anyone who witnesses this month shall fast. Those who are ill or travelling may fast an equal number of days. God wishes convenience for you, rather than hardship; He wishes to enable you to fulfil your duty, and to glorify God for guiding you, and to show your appreciation.
186.   And when My servants ask you about Me, I am always near. I respond to the call of any caller who calls on Me.* Therefore, they shall respond to Me, and believe in Me, that they may attain guidance.

2:183-187.   Like all religious practices in Islam, fasting was decreed through Abraham (see 2:128, 3:68, 16:123, 21:73, 22:27, 22:78, and Appendix 8). The injunction prohibiting intercourse throughout the month of fasting is revised here to allow intercourse during the nights of fasting.

2:186.   This verse refers especially to the "night of power," (see sura 97).

187. Permission is granted to you herein to have intercourse with your spouses during the nights of fasting. They are your confidantes, and you are their confidants. God knew that you used to violate the previous injunction (revealed to Abraham), and He has redeemed you and pardoned you. Henceforth, you may have intercourse with them, seeking what God has permitted for you. You may eat and drink until the white thread becomes distinguishable from the dark thread at dawn. Then fast until the following night. You may not have intercourse if you decide to retreat to the mosques (during the last ten days of Ramadan). These are God's Laws; you shall not violate them. God thus clarifies His revelations for the people, that they may attain salvation.

Dishonesty and Bribery Prohibited

188. You shall not take each others' monies dishonestly, nor shall you bribe the officials in order to take other people's monies sinfully and knowingly.

Do Not Beat Around the Bush*

189. They ask you about the phases of the moon; say, "They provide a timing device for the people, and determine the time of **Hajj** pilgrimage." It is not righteous to beat around the bush (by asking such irrelevant questions), but the righteous thing is to be straightforward, and to observe God, that you may succeed.

Rules of War

190. You shall fight in the cause of God against those who fight you, but do not aggress, for God does not love the aggressors.
191. You may kill them if they attack you, and evict them whence they evicted you; oppression is worse than murder. Do not fight them at the Sacred Mosque, unless they attack you therein. If they attack you, then you may kill them, and this would be their just retribution.
192. However, if they refrain, then God is forgiver, merciful.
193. You may fight them to prevent oppression, and to practice God's religion in complete freedom. Once they refrain, there shall be no aggression, except against the wicked.

2:189. The Arabic proverb says, "Do not enter the homes from the back door." The equivalent English proverb is used here.

194. If they attack you during the sacred months, then you may fight during the sacred months, and sacrileges may be met by equivalent responses. If they attack you, you may attack them to inflict an equivalent retribution. You shall observe God, and know that God is with those who observe Him.

195. And spend in the cause of God; do not throw yourselves with your own hands into disaster. You shall be charitable, for God loves the charitable.

Hajj Pilgrimage*

196. You shall complete the **Hajj** and **Umrah** observance for God. If you are prevented, then offer a sacrifice and do not resume cutting your hair until your offering has reached its destination. But if you are ill or suffering some head injury, then you may cut your hair, and expiate by fasting, or giving a charity, or some other form of worship. During the normal times of peace, if you break the state of sanctity between **Umrah** and **Hajj**, then expiate by offering a sacrifice. Those who cannot afford it may fast three days during **Hajj** and seven when they return home, thus completing ten, provided they do not live at the sacred mosque. You shall observe God, and know that God is strict in enforcing judgment.

197. **Hajj** shall be observed during the specified months. Thus, whoever sets out to observe **Hajj** shall abstain from sexual intercourse, evil deeds, and arguments throughout **Hajj**. Whatever good you do, God is fully aware thereof. As you take provisions for the journey, remember that the best provision is righteousness. You shall observe Me, O you who possess intelligence.

198. You commit no sin by seeking commercial benefits during **Hajj**. When you file from Arafat, you shall commemorate God at the sacred shrine (of Muzdalifah). Commemorate Him for guiding you; before such guidance, you were really straying.

199. You shall file together with the rest of the people, and seek God's forgiveness. God is forgiver, merciful.

200. Once you complete your duties of worship, you shall continue to remember God, just as you remember your own parents, or even better. Some people may say, "Our Lord, give us in this life," while they have no share in the hereafter.

201. Others would say, "Our Lord, let us be righteous in this life, and righteous in the hereafter, and spare us the agony of hell."

202. Each of these will reap the fruits of their work, and God is most efficient at reckoning.

2:196. Originally decreed through Abraham, like all religious practices in Islam (See 22:27).

203. You shall commemorate God during the specified days after **Hajj** (2-3 days at Mina). Thus, if you complete this in two days, you commit no error, and if you stay longer, you commit no error, so long as you maintain righteousness. You shall observe God, and know that you will be gathered before Him.

Appearances May Be Deceiving

204. Among the people, one may impress you with his rhetoric, and may even call upon God to witness his intentions, though he is a most ardent opponent.
205. When he turns away, he roams the earth corruptingly, ruining properties and lives. God dislikes corruption.
206. Then, when told to observe God, sinful pride overtakes him. Consequently, his only destiny is hell and a miserable abode.
207. Then there are those who readily devote themselves to attain God's pleasure, and God is most compassionate towards such people.
208. O you who believe, you shall submit totally to God, and do not follow the steps of satan; he is your ardent enemy.
209. If you regress, despite these profound revelations, then know that God is almighty, wise.
210. Are they waiting until God Himself comes to them in dense clouds, together with the angels? If this happens, the whole matter will be terminated, and all things will be referred to God (for judgment).
211. Ask the children of Israel how many profound miracles have we manifested for them. For those who disregard God's favors, after receiving them, God is most strict in enforcing judgment.

The Hereafter is the Real Life

212. This life is adorned in the eyes of the disbelievers, and thus, they ridicule those who believe. However, the righteous will rank high above them on the day of resurrection. God blesses whomever He wills without limits.
213. The people used to be one homogeneous congregation, until God sent the prophets as preachers and warners, and sent with them the scripture as a statute book. Ironically, it is those who received the scripture and the knowledge that disputed among themselves, out of sheer resentment for one another. As for those who believe, God guides them to the truth, in accordance with His will, while leaving the others in dispute. God guides whomever He wills to the right path.

Hardship: A Mandatory Test

214.   Do you expect to enter Paradise without undergoing the same test as those before you? They suffered hardship and adversity, and were so shaken up that the messenger and those who believed with him said, "Where is God's victory?" Indeed, God's victory is always near.

Recipients of Charity

215.   They ask you about charity; say, "Charity shall go to the parents, the relatives, the orphans, the poor, and the alien." Any righteous work you do, God is fully aware thereof.

Submit to the Omniscient

216.   Fighting may be forced upon you, though you dislike it. But you may dislike something which is actually good for you, and you may like something which is actually bad for you. God knows while you do not know.

217.   They ask you about the desecration of the sacred months by fighting therein. Say, "Fighting during the sacred months is sacrilege. But repelling the people from the path of God, and disbelieving in Him and in the sacredness of the sacred mosque, and evicting the people therefrom, are all worse sacrileges in the sight of God. Oppression is worse than murder. They will continue to fight you, until they revert you from your religion, if they could. Those who revert from their religion, and die as disbelievers, have wasted their works in this life and in the hereafter; they have deserved hell, wherein they abide forever.

218.   As for those who believe, immigrate, and strive in the cause of God, they have deserved God's mercy. God is forgiver, merciful.

Intoxicants and Gambling Prohibited

219.   They ask you about intoxicants and gambling; say, "There is gross evil in them, and some benefits for the people. However, their evil outweighs their benefit." They ask you what to give as charity; say, "The excess." God thus clarifies the revelations for you, that you may reflect

220.   upon this life and the hereafter. They ask you about the orphans; say, "The best thing is to bring them up as righteous individuals. If you mix their property with yours, you shall treat them as members of your family." God is fully aware who the wicked are, and who the righteous are. Had God willed, He could have decreed harsher rules. God is almighty, wise.

Do Not Marry Pagans*

221. You shall not marry pagan women, unless they believe. A believing woman is better than the pagan, even if you like her. Nor shall you permit your women to marry pagans, unless they believe. A believing man is better than the pagan, even if you like him. They invite to hell, while God invites to heaven, and forgiveness, in accordance with His will. He clarifies the revelations for those who take heed.

Menstruation

222. They ask you about menstruation; say, "It is harmful; you shall avoid intercourse with the women during menstruation, until they are clean. Once they are clean, you may have intercourse with them in the manner designated by God. God loves the repenters, and He loves those who are clean."

223. Your women are assets for you, and you may enjoy your assets however you like, so long as you maintain righteousness. You shall observe God, and know that you will ultimately meet Him. Give good news to the believers.

Do Not Take the Name of God in Vain

224. You shall not subject God's name to your casual swearing, seeking to appear righteous, virtuous, and conciliators among the people. God is hearer, omniscient.

225. God does not hold you responsible for the mere utterance of your oaths. He holds you responsible for your actual intentions. God is forgiver, clement.

Divorce Laws

226. Those who estrange their wives shall wait a period of four months. Thereafter, if they reconcile, then God is forgiver, merciful.

227. But if they insist on divorce, then God is hearer, fully aware.

2:221.   *Pagans include those who are not Jewish, Christian, or Muslim (see 5:5). Jews, Christians, and Muslims share the common belief in God, the hereafter, the angels, satan, heaven, and hell, and all suffer from various distortions (see 4:153).*

228.   The divorcees shall wait an interim of three menstruations (before remarriage), and they shall not conceal what God creates in their wombs, if they truly believe in God and the last day. In case of pregnancy, their husbands shall be given priority to remarry them, if they so desire. The women have their rights equitably, and they also have obligations. In case of pregnancy, the man's wishes shall be given priority over the women's wishes. God is almighty, wise.

229.   Divorce may be retracted twice. Thereafter, you shall allow them to stay in your home amicably (if they so desire), or allow them to go amicably. You shall not take back anything you had given them, unless the couple fears the violation of God's law. If they fear the violation of God's law, then they incur no sin if the wife forfeits anything voluntarily. These are God's laws; you shall not transgress them. If anyone trangresses God's laws, then these are the wicked.

230.   If he divorces her for the third time, then he cannot marry her, unless she marries another man and he divorces her. If the second husband divorces her, then she and the first husband may remarry, so long as they uphold God's law, these are God's laws; He clarifies them for people who know.

231.   If you divorce the women, once they have fulfilled their interim, you shall allow them to live in your homes amicably, or let them go amicably. Do not force them to stay against their will. Anyone who does this wrongs his own soul. You shall not take God's revelations in vain. You shall be appreciative of God's blessings upon you, and the scripture and wisdom He has sent down to enlighten you. You shall observe God, and know that God is fully aware of all things.

232.   If you divorce the women, once they have fulfilled their interim, you shall not prevent them from remarrying their husbands, if they wish to reconcile. This will be heeded by those among you who truly believe in God and the last day. This is more righteous, and more sanctifying for you. God knows, while you do not know.

233.   The divorced mothers shall nurse their infants two full years, if the father so requires. The father shall provide sustenance and clothing, equitably. No one shall be burdened beyond his means; the mother shall not be harmed on account of her infant, nor the father shall be harmed. If the father dies, the inheritor shall assume his responsibilities. If the parents decide to end the nursing agreement, after mutual consultation and consent, they incur no sin. If you hire a nursing mother, you incur no sin, provided you pay them equitably. You shall observe God, and know that God is seer of everything you do.

234.   Those of you who die and leave wives behind, their widows shall wait an interim of four months and ten days (before remarriage). Once they have fulfilled the interim, you commit no sin by letting them do whatever they want, so long as they maintain righteousness. God is fully cognizant of everything you do.

235.   You commit no sin if you declare your wish to marry the widows, or keep it secret. God knows that you may be interested in them. However, you shall not meet them secretly, unless you have something righteous to discuss, nor shall you consummate the marriage before the interim has been fulfilled. You should realize that God knows your innermost intentions; beware of Him, and know that God is forgiver, clement.

236.   You commit no sin if you divorce the women before you touch them, and before setting the dowry for them. In this case, you shall pay them a compensation in accordance with your means; the rich as he can afford, and the poor as he can afford: an equitable compensation. This is an incumbent duty upon the righteous.

237.   If you divorce them before you touch them, but after you had set the dowry, the compensation shall be half the dowry, unless they willingly forfeit the compensation, or the groom forfeits the whole dowry. To forfeit is more righteous. Do not abandon the amicable relations among you, for God is seer of everything you do.

You Shall Observe the Salat Prayers

238.   You shall constantly observe the **salat** prayers, especially the middle **salat**, and steadfastly maintain your obedience to God.

239.   Under abnormal circumstances, you may pray while walking or riding, but in the normal times you shall commemorate God according to His teachings.*

Alimony For Widows and Divorcees

240.   Those among you who die and leave widows behind shall bequeath enough support for their widows to last them one full year, provided they choose to stay in the husband's household. If they choose to leave, then you incur no sin by letting them do whatever they wish, so long as they maintain righteousness. God is almighty, wise.

241.   For the divorcees, equitable alimony shall be provided. This is an incumbent duty upon the righteous.

242.   God thus explains the revelations for you, that you may understand.

---

*2:239. The original teachings of **salat** were revealed to Abraham, then transmitted to us generation after generation (see 2:128, 16:123, 21:73, and 22:78).*

You Shall Courageously Struggle for the Cause of God

243. What do you think of those who fled their homes, though they numbered in the thousands, because they feared death? Consequently, God said to them, "Die," then revived them. God is gracious towards the people, but most people are not appreciative.

244. You shall courageously fight for the cause of God, and know that God is hearer, fully aware.

245. Would you not loan God a righteous loan that He multiplies for you many fold?

The Believers Always Victorious

246. Have you noted the elders of Israel, after the time of Moses, who said to their prophet, "Appoint a king for us, if you want us to fight for the cause of God?" He said, "Is it your intention that when fighting is decreed for you, you will not fight?" They said,"Why should we not fight for the cause of God, when we were forcibly evicted from our homes and deprived of our children?" Yet, when fighting was decreed for them, they turned away, except a few. God is fully aware of the wrongdoers.

247. Then their prophet said to them, "God has appointed Talut (Saul) to be your king." They said, "How could he be our king, when we are more worthy of kingship that he is, and he is not rich?" He said, "God has chosen him, and endowed him with abundance in both mind and body. God grants kingship to whomever He wills. God is bounteous, omniscient.

248. Their prophet said to them, "The sign of his kingship is that the ark of the covenant will come to you, bringing assurance from your Lord, and relics from the time of Moses and Aaron. The angels will bring it to you. This should be a convincing sign for you, if you are really believers."

249. When Saul took command of the troops, he said, "God will put you to the test by means of a river; anyone who drinks from it does not belong with me. And anyone who refrains from ingesting it, except for a single taste, belongs with me." They drank from it, except a few of them. Thus, when he crossed with those who believed, they said, "Now we lack the power to face Goliath and his troops." But those who were conscious of meeting God said, "Many a small army can defeat a formidable army by God's leave. God is with those who steadfastly persevere."*

250. And when they encountered Goliath and his troops they said, "Our Lord, grant us steadfastness, and strenghten our foothold, and make us victorious against the disbelievers."

2:249.   See the Bible's book of Judges, 7:5-8.

251. They defeated them by God's leave, and David killed Goliath. God then bestowed upon him kingship and wisdom, and taught him in accordance with His will. If it were not for God's setting up of some people against others, the earth would be corrupted. God is gracious towards the people.

252. These are the revelations of God; we recite them for you, truthfully, for you are one of the messengers.

253. Some of the messengers we honored more than others; God spoke to some, and raised others to higher ranks, and we endowed Jesus the son of Mary with profound miracles, and supported him with the holy spirit. Had God willed, their followers would not have fought each other when the clear scriptures came to them. But they differed; some believed, and some disbelieved. Had God willed, they would not have fought each other. Whatever happens is in accordance with God's will.

254. O you who believe, you shall give to charity from our provisions to you, before a day comes wherein there will be no trade, no favoritism, and no intercession.* It is the disbelievers who chose wickedness.

God

255. Allah; the one God. There is no god except He; the living; the eternal. Not a moment of unawareness or slumber ever overtakes Him. To Him belong everything in the heavens, and everything on earth. Who can intercede with Him, except in accordance with His will?* To Him belong the past and the future, and no one attains any of His knowledge except in accordance with His will. His dominion encompasses the heavens and the earth, and ruling them never burdens Him. He is the most high, the great.

No Compulsion in Religion

256. There shall be no compulsion in religion. The truth is now distinguishable from falsehood. Thus, those who reject idol-worship and believe in God alone have grasped the strongest bond that never breaks. God is hearer, omniscient.

257. God is the Lord of those who believe; He leads them out of the darkness into the light. While those who disbelieve, their lords are their idols; they lead them out of the light into the darkness. They have deserved hell as their eternal abode.

2:254-255. The Christians claim that Jesus will possess the power to intercede at God on the day of judgment, and the Muslims claim that Muhammad will have such power. Our creator, however, teaches us in the Quran that there will be no intercession on the day of judgment, unless such intercession happens to agree with God's decision (see also 2:48, 2:123, 6:51, 6:70, 19:87, 20:109, 21:28, 39:44 and Appendix 7).

258. Have you noted the one who argued with Abraham concerning his Lord, though God is the one who granted him kingship? When Abraham said, "My Lord grants life and death," he said, "I too grant life and death." Abraham said, "God brings the sun from the East, can you bring it from the West?" The disbeliever was stumped. God does not guide the wicked.

No Time Between Death and Resurrection*

259. Or the one who passed by a deserted town, then said, "How could God revive this from death?" God then put him to death for one hundred years, then resurrected him and asked, "How long have you been here?" He said, "One day, or part of the day." He said, "You have been here one hundred years. Yet, look at your food and drink; they did not spoil; and look at your donkey. We thus set you up as a lesson for the people. Look at the bones and see how we construct them, and cover them with flesh." When he realized what had happened, he said, "Now I know that God is able to do anything."

Even Believers Need Reassurance*

260. When Abraham said, "My Lord, show me how You revive the dead," He said, "Do you not believe?" He said, "Yes indeed; but I wish to reassure my heart." God said, "Take four birds, and identify their marks, then place a piece from each bird on top of a hill, then call them, and they will come to you flying. You should realize that God is almighty, wise."

The Great Investment

261. The parable of those who spend their monies for the cause of God is like a seed that grows into seven ears, with one hundred seeds in each ear. God multiplies the reward manyfold for whomever He wills. God is bounteous, omniscient.

262. Those who spend their monies in the cause of God, and do not follow their charity with reproach or insult, will receive their recompense from their Lord. They have nothing to fear, nor will they grieve.

2:259.   The period between death and resurrection will seem like one night of sleep, complete with dreams. In fact, most people never realize that they had died. See 6:60, 18:19, and Appendix 14.

*2:260.   Those with disease in their hearts (see 74:31) claim that their faith is so strong that they do not need the Quran's miraculous numerical code to augment their faith (See Appendices 1 & 2). But here is Abraham, God's beloved messenger, requesting a sign to reassure his heart. Abraham is a good example (**Uswah Hasanah**) for all of us, as stated in 60:4 and 60:6.*

263. Kind words and compassion are better than a charity which is followed by insult. God is bounteous, clement.

264. O you who believe, do not nullify your charity by reproach and insult. If you do, you will be like one who spends his money only to show off, while disbelieving in God and the last day. His parable is like a useless rock covered with a thin layer of soil; when heavy rain falls, it leaves it solid. They harvest nothing from their efforts. God does not guide the disbelievers.

265. And the parable of those who spend their monies seeking God's pleasure, and through their own convictions, is that of a garden on high and deep soil; when heavy rain falls it gives double the crop; if heavy rain is not available, a light rain would suffice. God is seer of everything you do.

266. Would any of you wish to own a garden of date palms and grapes with flowing streams and all kinds of fruits; then, as he gets old and his children are still weak, the garden gets stricken with a holocaust that burns it up? God thus explains the revelations for you, that you may reflect.

267. O you who believe, you shall spend in charity from the good things you earn, and from what we produce for you from the earth. Do not pick out the inferior thereof to give away, when you would not accept it for yourselves unless your eyes are closed. You should realize that God is rich, worthy of all praise.

268. The devil promises you only poverty and exhorts you to commit evil works, while God promises you forgiveness from Him and blessings. God is bounteous, omniscient.

269. He bestows wisdom upon whomever He wills, and whoever is endowed with wisdom is endowed with a great bounty. That is because those who possess intelligence are the ones who take heed.

Secret Charities Recommended

270. Whatever charity you give, or a vow you make, God is fully aware thereof. The wicked will find no helpers.

271. If you declare your charities, they are still good. But if you conceal them and give them secretly to the poor, it would be better for you, and would remit more of your sins. God is fully cognizant of everything you do.

Only God Guides*

272. You can never guide anyone; God is the only one who guides in accordance with His will. Any charity you give away is for your own good. Any charity you give shall be purely for the sake of God. Any charities you give will be repaid to you without the least injustice.

273. Charity shall go to the poor who are persecuted because of their belief, and trapped. Those who are unaware may think that they are rich, due to their honorable character. But you can recognize them by certain signs. They never annoy the people by begging. Any charity you give, God is fully aware thereof.

274. Those who give to charity by night and by day, secretly and publicly, their recompense is with their Lord. They have nothing to fear, nor will they grieve.

Usury Prohibited*

275. Those who earn from usury stand only like one who is struck by the devil's touch. That is because they claim that usury is a form of trade. But God permits trade, and prohibits usury. Whoever heeds this admonition from his Lord, and abstains from usury, may keep his past earnings, and his judgment rests with God. As for those who return to usury, they will deserve hell, wherein they abide forever.

276. God diminishes usury and augments charities, and God dislikes the guilty disbelievers.

277. Those who believe and work righteousness, and observe the **salat** and **zakat**, their recompense is with their Lord. They have nothing to fear, nor will they grieve.

278. O you who believe, beware of God, and refrain from all forms of usury, if you are really believers.

279. If you do not refrain, then expect a war from God and His messenger. But if you repent, then you may keep your capital, without inflicting injustice, or suffering injustice.

280. If the debtor is unable to pay, then wait for a better time. If you give up the debt as a charity, it would be better for you, if you only knew.

281. Beware of the day when you return to God, and each soul is repaid for whatever it earned. No one will suffer injustice.

2:272. The sole mission of the prophet was to deliver the Quran, the whole Quran, and nothing but the Quran. He could not guide his most beloved uncle; the majority of his nine uncles were disbelievers, and one of them is condemned in Quran. Similarly, no saint can ever guide you; God is the one who guides you. We do not owe anyone anything for guiding us; we owe everything to our creator, God almighty.

2:275. Usury is any "fixed" percentage of earnings in return for deposited or loaned money. Earnings that fluctuate with investment profits and losses do not constitute usury. It should be noted that the Quran condemns only those who "take" usury (see 3:130 and 4:161), while those who are forced by circumstance to "pay" usury are considered victims, rather than sinners (see 2:280).

Write Down Monetary Transactions

282. O you who believe, when you carry out a loan transaction for any period, you shall write it down. Let a scribe write it down equitably, and no scribe shall refuse to write as God has taught him. Let him write, while the debtor dictates. He shall observe God his Lord, and never cheat. If the debtor were mentally incompetent, or incapable, or for some reason unable to dictate, his agent shall dictate equitably. You shall have two witnesses from among your men, or one man and two women, whom you accept as witnesses. Thus, if one woman is biased, the other would remind her. The witnesses shall not refuse to give their testimony whenever asked. Do not neglect to write down all the details, no matter how small or extensive, including the time of repayment. This is more equitable in the sight of God, it insures the accuracy of testimony, and minimizes your doubts. If the transaction is a trade on the spot, you commit no sin by not writing it down; but you may have witnesses thereof. No hardship shall befall any scribe or witness; if you cause any hardship to them, it would be wicked on your part. If you observe God, God will teach you. God is omniscient.

283. If you are travelling, and no scribe is available, then a bond shall be posted. If you trust each other in this manner, the one entrusted with the bond shall return it when due, and observe God his Lord. You shall not conceal anything you had witnessed. Anyone who conceals a testimony is guilty at heart. God is fully aware of everything you do.

284. To God belong everything in the heavens and the earth, and whether you declare your thoughts, or conceal them, God will hold you answerable for them. He will then forgive whomever He wills, and punish whomever He wills. God is omnipotent.

Make No Distinction Among the Prophets

285. The messenger believes in what was revealed to him from his Lord; and so do the believers. They believe in God, His angels, His scriptures, and His messengers. They say, "We make no distinction among any of His messengers. We hearken, and we obey. Forgive us, our Lord. To You is the ultimate return."

286. God never burdens any soul beyond its means. Credit is earned for any righteous work, and discredit is incurred for any sin. Our Lord, do not punish us when we forget or err. Our Lord, and let it not be Your will that we violate the covenant, like those before us who violated the covenant. Our Lord, do not obligate us beyond our abilities; pardon us, forgive us, and shower us with mercy. You are our Lord, so grant us victory against the disbelievers.

Sura 3: Ali-Imran (The Family of Imran)

In the name of God, most gracious, most merciful

1. A.L.M.*
2. Allah; the one God; there is no god except He, the living, the eternal.
3. He revealed to you this scripture, truthfully, confirming previous scripture, just as He revealed the Torah and the Gospel
4. previously, to guide the people. He revealed the statute book. Those who disbelieved in God's revelations have deserved terrible retribution. God is almighty, avenger.
5. Nothing is ever concealed from God, on earth or in the heavens.
6. He is the one who shapes you inside the womb as He wills. There is no god except He, the almighty, the wise.
7. He is the one who revealed to you this scripture, with perfect verses that must be taken literally, for they constitute the essence of the scripture. Other verses are allegorical.* Those who harbor doubts in their hearts dwell on the allegorical verses, to create confusion and misrepresentation thereof. No one knows the correct interpretation thereof except God and those well founded in knowledge. They say, "We believe in all the revelations; they all come from our Lord." Indeed, only those who possess intelligence will take heed.
8. "Our Lord, let not our hearts falter after being guided by You, and shower us with Your mercy; You are the grantor.
9. "Our Lord, you will surely gather all the people on a day that is inevitable, for God never breaks His promise."
10. Those who disbelieve, neither their monies, nor their children, will avail them against God. They will be fuel for hell.
11. Like the people of Pharaoh and others before them who rejected our revelations; God punished them for their sins. God is strict in enforcing retribution.
12. Say to those who disbelieve, "You will be defeated, then end up in hell and a miserable abode."

3:1. See footnote 2:1 and Apendix 1 for the miraculous significance of these Quranic initials. After 1400 years, the mystery of these letters is now unveiled.

3:7. Things beyond our imagination and comprehension, such as heaven and hell, are presented in allegorical terms. See Appendix 4.

13. An example has been set for you by two armies who clashed; one was fighting in the cause of God, while the other consisted of disbelievers. They saw each other twice as many (for different reasons).* God supports with His victory whomever He wills. This is a lesson for those who can see.

14. Adorned in the eyes of the people is the love of lusts, such as women, children, the piles upon piles of gold and silver, trained horses, livestock and crops. These are the materials of this world, but the best abode is with God.

15. Say, "Shall I inform you of far better materials? Those who work righteousness will enjoy Paradise at their Lord, with flowing streams. Forever they abide therein, with pure spouses, and blessings from God." God is seer of His true servants.

16. who say, "Our Lord, we believe; forgive our sins and spare us the agony of hell."

17. They are steadfast, truthful, obedient, charitable, and they pray for forgiveness at dawn.

18. God bears witness that there is no god except He, and so do the angels and those who possess knowledge. He is the only master; there is no god except He, the almighty, the wise.

19. The only religion in the sight of God is Islam (submission).* The followers of previous scripture have disputed this Quran, even after realizing that it is divine truth, due to sheer resentment. Those who reject God's revelations have deserved God's severe retribution.

20. If they argue with you, then say, "I have simply submitted to God, and so do my followers." And say to the followers of previous scriptures, as well as the gentiles, "Have you submitted?" If they submit, then they are guided; but if they turn away, then your sole mission is to deliver the message. God is seer of His true servants.

21. Those who reject God's revelations, and slay the prophets unjustly, and slay those who preach righteousness, promise them painful retribution.

22. It is these whose works have been nullified, in this life and in the hereafter. No one can help them.

3:13. *See also 8:44.*

3:19. *All God's messengers delivered one and the same message, namely, submission to the one God. Thus, the first commandment in the Bible's Old Testament, the New Testament, as well as the Quran, is "You shall not worship except the one God." See Deuteronomy 6:4, Mark 12:29, and the Quran 21:92.*

The Danger of Ignorance

23. Have you noted those who know only part of the scripture, and when invited to adopt God's scripture as their law, they turn away in aversion?
24. That is because they have said, "Hell is not eternal," and thus, they are deceived in their religion by their own inventions.*
25. How terrible will it be for them when we gather them on a day that is inevitable, and each soul is repaid for its works, without the least injustice.
26. Say, "Our God, You are the possessor of all kingship; You grant kingship to whomever You will, and remove kingship from whomever You will. You bestow dignity upon whomever you will, and humiliate whomever You will. All bounty is in Your hand. You are omnipotent."
27. "You merge the night into the day, and merge the day into the night. You evolve the live from the dead, and evolve the dead from the live. You provide for whomever You will without limits."

Do Not Befriend Disbelievers

28. The believers shall not take disbelievers as friends, instead of believers. Whoever does this is not following God's commandments, unless he is forced to avoid their tyranny. God alerts you that you should fear only Him. To God is the ultimate destiny.
29. Say, "Whether you conceal your innermost thoughts, or declare them, God is fully aware thereof." He is fully aware of everything in the heavens and the earth; God is omnipotent.
30. The day will come when each soul will find everything righteous it had done brought forth; as for the evil works, it will wish if it were sent as far away from it as possible. God alerts you that you should fear Him alone. God is compassionate towards His creature.

The Prophet Preaches Quran*

31. Say, "If you love God, then follow me; God will then love you, and forgive your sins. God is forgiver, merciful."

3:24. *Relying on wishful thinking, Satan succeeded in convincing multitudes of people that hell is not eternal. Many Muslims are conned into believing that the mere utterance of* **"La Ilaha Illa Allah**=*There is no god except God" will assure them heaven. The Quran states clearly that heaven and hell are eternal, and that the assignment to either place is irreversible (see 2:81-82, 2:167, and Appendix 10).*

3:31. *To follow and obey the prophet is to uphold the Quran, the whole Quran, and nothing but the Quran (see 6:112-116, and Appendix 11).*

32. Say, "Obey God and the messenger." If they turn away, then God does not love the disbelievers.

The Family of Imran

33. God has chosen Adam, Noah, the family of Abraham, and the family of Imran as messengers to all the people.
34. They are related to each other. God is hearer, omniscient.

Mary

35. The wife of Imran said, "My Lord, I pledge to You the infant in my womb, so accept from me. You are the hearer, the omniscient."
36. Then, when she gave birth to a girl, she said, "My Lord, I have given birth to a girl," and God was fully aware of what she bore. "The boy is not the same as the girl. I have named her Mary, and I invoke Your protection for her and her progeny from Satan the rejected."
37. Her Lord accepted her a gracious acceptance, and brought her up a gracious upbringing. Zachariah cared for her, and whenever Zacariah entered her sanctuary, he found provisions therein. He would say, "O Mary, where did you get this?" She would say, "It is from God. God provides whomever He wills without limits".

John

38. Zachariah then prayed to his Lord, saying, "My Lord, grant me righteous descendants. You are the hearer of all prayers."
39. The angels called him as he prayed in the sanctuary, saying, "God gives you good news; a son to be named Yahya (John), believing in the word of God, and honorable and chaste, and a righteous prophet."
40. He said, "My Lord, will I have a son despite my old age, and my wife's sterility?" He was told, "God does whatever He wills."
41. He said, "My Lord, grant me a sign." He was told, "Your sign is that you will not speak to the people for three days, except by signal. You shall commemorate your Lord frequently, and glorify Him night and day."

Jesus

42. The angels said, "O Mary, God has chosen you, and sanctified you; He has chosen you over all the women.
43. "O Mary, obey your Lord, fall prostrate, and bow down with those who bow down."
44. This is history from the past that we reveal to you. You were not present when they threw their raffles to decide who cares for Mary. You were not present when they feuded with each other.

45. The angels said, "O Mary, God gives you good news: a word from Him to be called Messiah, Jesus the son of Mary. He will be honorable in this life and in the hereafter, and one of those who are close to God.

46. "He will speak to the people as an infant, and as a man, and he will be righteous."

47. She said, "My Lord, how could I have a son, when no man has touched me?" She was told, "God thus creates whatever He wills. To have anything done, He simply says to it, 'Be,' and it is."

48. God endowed him with the scripture, wisdom, the Torah, and the Gospel.

49. And He sent him to the children of Israel, saying, "I have come to you with miracles from your Lord: I create from clay the form of a bird, then blow into it, and it becomes a live bird by God's leave. I heal the blind and the leprous, and I revive the dead by God's leave. I can tell you what you ate, and what you left in your homes. These shoud be convincing signs for you, if you are really believers.

50. "I come to confirm previous scripture, the Torah, and to revoke certain prohibitions. I have come to you with miracles from your Lord; you shall observe God, and obey me.

51. "God is my Lord and your Lord; you shall worship Him. This is the right path."*

52. When Jesus sensed disbelief from them, he said, "Who will support me towards God?" The disciples said, "We are the supporters of God. We believe in God, and bear witness that we are Muslims (submitters).

53. "Our Lord, we have believed in Your revelations, and we have followed the messenger, so count us among the witnesses."

54. The others plotted and schemed; but so did God. God is the best schemer.

55. Thus, God said, "O Jesus, I am terminating your life, and raising you to Me, and ridding you of the disbelievers. I will exalt those who follow you above those who disbelieve, until the day of resurrection. To Me is the ultimate return, then I will judge between you concerning your disputes."

56. Those who disbelieve, I will punish them severely, both in this life and the hereafter, and no one can help them.

57. As for those who believe and lead a righteous life, I will recompense them generously. God is never unjust.

58. These are the revelations and the message of wisdom that we recite to you.

59. The creation of Jesus, as far as God is concerned, is the same as the creation of Adam. God created Adam from dust, then said to him, "Be" and he was.

3:51. See Deuteronomy 6:4, and the Gospel of Mark 12:29-33.

60. This is the truth from your Lord; you shall not harbor any doubts.
61. Should anyone dispute with you, after this knowledge has come to you, then say, "Let us call upon our children and your children, our women and your women, ourselves and yourselves, then let us pray that the curse of God befalls the liars."
62. Indeed, this is the truthful narration; indeed, there is never any god besides the one God; and indeed, God is the almighty, the wise.
63. If they turn away, then God is fully aware of the wicked.

The Great Commandment: You Shall Not Worship Except God*

64. Say, "O people of the scripture, let us come to a reasonable agreement between us and you: that we shall not worship except God, and shall never set up any idols to rank with Him, nor shall we set up lords from among ourselves." If they turn away, then say, "Bear witness that we are Muslims (submitters)."

Abraham: The Founder of Islam*

65. O people of the scripture, why do you dispute about Abraham, when the Torah and the Gospel were not revealed until after him? Do you not understand?
66. You have disputed previously about things you knew, but why do you dispute about things you do not know? God knows, while you do not know.
67. Abraham was neither a Jew, nor a Christian; he was a monotheist Muslim, and never an idol-worshiper.
68. The people most worthy of Abraham are those who followed him, and this prophet, and the believers in this message. God is the Lord of the believers.
69. Some followers of the previous scriptures may wish to mislead you, but they only mislead themselves without perceiving.

3:64. This is "the First Commandment" of the Old Testament, the New Testament, and the Quran (see footnote 3:19). It should be noted that this is a "negative" commandment (You shall NOT worship except God), since people can worship God, and still go to hell (see 11:2, 11:26, 23:84-90, 29:61-63, 41:14, and 46:21).

*3:65-68. Many people are under the erroneous impression that Muhammad is the founder of Islam. The Quran, however, teaches that Abraham is the founder, and that all religious practices, i.e., **salat, zakat,** fasting, and **hajj** pilgrimage, were revealed through Abraham, then transmitted to us generation after generation. See also 2:135, 2:183, 3:95, 16:123, 21:73, 22:27, and 22:78.*

70. O people of the scripture, why do you reject these revelations of God, even when you bear witness that they are truth.

71. O people of the scripture, why do you confound the truth with falsehood, and conceal the truth knowingly?

72. Some among the people of the scripture even said, "Let us pretend that we believe in what was revealed to the Muslims during the day, and disbelieve by the day's end, in order to keep them away.

73. "Do not trust except those who follow your creed." Say, "God's guidance is the right guidance." If others claim to have similar guidance, or dispute with you about your Lord, then say, "All grace belongs to God, and He endows whomever He wills. God is bounteous, omniscient.

74. "He showers His mercy upon whomever He wills; God possesses unlimited grace."

You Shall Act Righteously With All The People

75. Among the people of the scripture there are some you can trust with a whole lot, and they would pay it back. And you may trust others with one Dinar, but they would not pay it back unless you keep after them. That is because they say, "We do not have to observe the commandments when dealing with the Gentiles." Thus, they invent lies about God knowingly.

76. In fact, whoever keeps his vows, and leads a righteous life, then God loves the righteous.

77. As for those who disregard God's covenant, and violate their own vows for a cheap material gain, they will have no share in the hereafter. God will neither speak to them, nor look at them on the day of resurrection, nor will He sanctify them. They have deserved painful retribution.

78. Some of them even twist their tongues to simulate the scripture, to make you think that it is from the scripture, when it is not from the scripture; and claim that it is from God, when it is not from God. They invent lies and attribute them to God, knowingly.

79. It is not possible for a human whom God had blessed with the scripture and wisdom, and prophethood, that he should tell the people to idolize him besides God. Rather, he would say, "You shall devote your worship to the Lord, in accordance with the scripture that you study and preach."

80. Nor will he ask you to idolize the angels or the prophets. Would he exhort you to disbelieve, after becoming Muslims?

Before Genesis*

81. God has made a covenant with the prophets that He will give them the scripture and wisdom: then, when a messenger comes to you (O people), confirming the scripture, you shall believe in him and support him. God said, "Do you agree and make a covenant with Me?" (The people) said, "We agree." God said, "You have thus borne witness and I bear witness with you."

82. If anyone turns away thereafter, then these are the wicked.

83. Would they seek other than God's religion, when everything in the heavens and the earth have submitted to Him, willingly or unwillingly? To Him they will all return.

Islam Preached By All Messengers

84. Say, "We believe in God, and in what was sent down to us, and in what was sent down to Abraham, Ishmael, Isaac, Jacob, and the Patriarchs, and in what was given to Moses and Jesus, and to all the prophets from their Lord. We make no distinction among any of them. We have submitted to God."

85. Anyone who seeks other than Islam (submission) as a religion, it will not be accepted from him, and in the hereafter he will be a loser.

86. Why should God guide people who disbelieve after having believed, and after bearing witness that the messenger is truthful, and after profound miracles have come to them? God does not guide the wicked people.

87. They have deserved the curse of God, and the angels, and all the people.

88. Eternally they abide therein; the retribution will never be commuted for them, nor will they be reprieved.

89. However, those who repent thereafter, and reform, will find God forgiving, merciful.

90. Those who disbelieve after having believed, then plunge deeper into disbelief, their repentance will never be accepted, and they will be the real strayers.

91. Those who disbelieve, and die as disbelievers, an earthful of gold will not be accepted from them as ransom. They have deserved painful retribution, and no one can help them.

3:81. *This was part of the "pre-creation" pact that God made with all the people (see 7:172). Note the distinction between a "prophet" and a "messenger;" the prophet is one who was given a scripture, while the messenger merely confirms and preaches existing scriptures. Since Quran is the last scripture, Muhammad is the last prophet.*

You Shall Be Charitable

92. You can never attain righteousness, unless you give to charity from the things you love. Anything you give to charity, God is fully aware thereof.

Unauthorized Prohibition of Foods Is Wickedness

93. All food used to be lawful for the children of Israel, until Israel initiated prohibitions against themselves, before the revelation of the Torah. Say, "Bring the Torah, and read it, if you are truthful."
94. Anyone who invents lies about God, after this, these are the wicked.*
95. Say, "The truth has come from God, and you shall follow the religion of Abraham; monotheism; he never was an idol-worshiper."
96. The first shrine designated for the people is the one in Becca;* a blessed beacon for all the people.
97. In it, there are profound signs, such as the footprints of Abraham.* Anyone who enters it shall be guaranteed safety. The people owe it to God, that they shall observe the **Hajj** pilgrimage to the shrine, whenever they can afford it. As for those who disbelieve. God is in no need for anyone.
98. Say, "O people of the scripture, why do you reject these revelations of God, knowing that God witnesses everything you do?"

3:94. Many Muslims have fallen into Satan's trap, and invented a long list of unauthorized prohibitions, based on the great blasphemy known as **"hadith"** *and/or* **"sunna."** *See 2:173, 5:87, 6:112-116, 6:145, 16:115, 16:116, and Appendix 13.*

3:96. There is no doubt that the word "Becca" refers to the famous Arabian city "Mecca." Although the Quran was revealed through a Meccan man, and all the people around him knew the city as "Mecca," the mandatory Quranic spelling came down as "Becca." This deliberate and profound alteration, as it turned out, serves to prove the divine source of Quran, and that every word, indeed every letter, in the Quran has been divinely designed and divinely preserved. The reader will note that this sura is initialed with the letters "A.L.M." (verse 1). Therefore, the count of the letter "M" in this sura must conform to the Quran's secret numerical code (see Appendix 1). Had the word "Becca" been written down as "Mecca", the frequency of occurrence of the letter "M" would have increased by 1, the total will no longer be divisible by 19, and the Quran's secret numerical code would have simply disappeared.

3:97. Abraham's footprints were miraculously imprinted on a rock, and can be viewed by all visitors of the Sacred Mosque in Mecca.

99. Say, "O people of the scripture, why do you repulse the people from the path of God, and defame it, though you bear witness that it is the truth? God is never unaware of anything you do."

100. O you who believe, if you obey some people of the scripture, they would revert you from believers to disbelievers.

101. And how could you revert after God's revelations have been recited to you, and the messenger had come to you? The one who holds fast to God, has been guided in the right path.

You Shall Be United

102. O you who believe, you shall observe God as He should be observed, and do not die except as Muslims (submitters).

103. You shall hold fast to the rope of God, all together, and do not be divided. Be appreciative of God's favors upon you; you used to be enemies, and He reconciled your hearts. By His grace, you became brethren. God thus explains His revelations for you, that you may be guided.

104. Let there be a community among you who preach goodness, advocate righteousness, and forbid evil. These are the winners.

105. Do not be like those who became divided, and disputed among themselves, despite the profound revelations that had come to them. They have deserved severe retribution.

106. The day will come when some faces are brightened (with joy), while other faces are darkened (with misery). Those whose faces are darkened (will be told), "Did you not revert to disbelief, after having believed? Therefore, you have deserved the retribution for your disbelief."

107. As for those whose faces are brightened, they have deserved God's mercy; they abide therein forever.

108. These are the revelations of God; we recite them to you, truthfully. God does not wish injustice for anyone.

109. To God belongs everything in the heavens and everything on earth. God is in full control of all things.

110. You are the best congregation ever established on earth; you advocate righteousness, forbid evil, and believe in God. If the people of the scripture believe in this, it will be better for them. Among them are believers, but the majority are wicked.

111. They can never harm you, beyond insult, and if they fight you, they will turn around and flee; they can never attain victory against you.*

*3:111. Historically, for as long as the Muslims upheld the Quran, and nothing but the Quran, they were victorious. When they turned to the invented sources of jurisprudence, such as **"Hadith"** and **"Sunna,"** they lost their scientific, social, and military leadership. Compare the history of the first 250 years of Islam, with the Arab-Israeli wars.*

112.   They are condemned to humiliation wherever they are encountered (in war), unless they make a treaty with God and you. They have incurred God's wrath, and they are condemned to disgrace. That is because they used to disregard God's revelations, and slew the prophets unjustly. That is because they disobeyed and transgressed.

Righteous Jews and Christians

113.   They are not all alike; among the people of the scripture there are those who are righteous. They recite God's scripture throughout the night, and they fall prostrate.

114.   They believe in God and the last day; they advocate righteousness and forbid evil; and they are eager to work righteousness; they are pious.

115.   Whatever good they do will never go unrewarded. God is fully aware of those who are devout.

116.   As for those who disbelieve, neither their money, nor their children, will help them against God. They have deserved hell, wherein they abide forever.

117.   The parable of their spending in this life is that of a violent storm that hits the harvest of people who had wronged their souls, and wipes it out. God is not the one who wronged them; it is they who wronged themselves.

118.   O you who believe, do not trust and befriend outsiders who never cease to wish you harm and detriment. Hatred shows through their mouths, and what their hearts conceal is even worse. We thus explain the revelations for you, that you may understand.

119.   Here you are loving them, while they do not love you, and you believe in all the scripture. When they meet you, they say, "We believe,", but when alone, they bite their fingers, due to rage towards you. Say, "Die in your rage." God is fully aware of the innermost thoughts.

120.   When you are blessed with something good, they grieve, and when disaster afflicts you, they rejoice. If you steadfastly persevere and maintain righteousness, their schemes will never harm you. God is fully aware of everything they do.

The Battle of Badr

121.   Recall that you were preparing the believers for battle, and God is hearer, knower.

122.   Two groups among you almost failed, but God supported them. In God the believers shall trust.

123.   Thus, God granted you victory in the battle of Badr, despite your weakness. Therefore, you shall observe God, as a token of your appreciation.

124. You (Muhammad) had said to the believers, "Is it not enough that God supports you with three thousand angels descending?"
125. Indeed, if you steadfastly persevere and work righteousness, then they attack you, your Lord will support you with five thousand well-trained angels.
126. God gave you this good news, in order to reassure your hearts. For victory comes only from God, the almighty, the wise.
127. God thus eliminates some disbelievers, and confuses the rest, and defeats them.
128. It is not up to you (Muhammad); God may redeem them, or He may punish them if they are wicked.
129. To God belongs everything in the heavens and everything in the earth. He forgives whomever He wills, and punishes whomever He wills. God is forgiver, merciful.

Usury Prohibited

130. O you who believe, you shall not eat from usury, compounded manyfold, and observe God, that you may succeed.
131. And beware of hell that awaits the disbelievers.

Attributes of the Righteous

132. You shall obey God and his messenger, that you may attain mercy.
133. And race towards forgiveness from your Lord, and a paradise that encompasses the heavens and the earth; it awaits the righteous.
134. who are charitable during the times of prosperity and the times of hardship. They control their anger, and they pardon the people. God loves those who are charitable.
135. When they fall into gross sin, or wrong their souls, they remember God and ask forgiveness for their sins; and who forgives the sins except God? They never persist in sinfulness, knowingly.
136. Their recompense is forgiveness from their Lord, and gardens with flowing streams. They abide therein forever; what a beautiful recompense for the workers.
137. Many generations have passed before you, so roam the earth and see the consequences for those who disbelieved.
138. This is a declaration for the people, and a beacon and enlightenment for the righteous.
139. You shall not waver, nor shall you worry; you are guaranteed victory for as long as you are believers.

140. If hardship afflicts you, your enemies are similarly afflicted. We alternate the days of war and peace among the people, in order to distinguish those who really believe, and to grant martyrdom to some of you. God is never unjust.

141. God thus cleanses the believers, and annihilates the disbelievers.

142. Did you expect to enter Paradise without God distinguishing those among you who struggle and steadfastly persevere?

143. You had longed for death before you faced it, and now you have faced it before your eyes.

144. Muhammad is no more than a messenger like the messengers before him. Should he die or get killed, would you then turn back on your heels? Whoever turns back on his heels never hurts God, while those who are appreciative will be rewarded.

Time of Death Predetermined

145. No one will die except by God's leave, at a predetermined moment. Thus, whoever seeks the materials of this world, we will give him therefrom, and whoever seeks the rewards of the hereafter, we will give him therefrom. We will generously reward the appreciative.

146. Many a prophet was supported by devoted people. They never wavered when afflicted in the cause of God, nor did they weaken or falter. God loves the steadfast.

147. Their only utterance was, "Our Lord, forgive us our sins and transgressions, and strengthen our foothold, and grant us victory over the disbelievers."

148. Consequently, God blessed them with the rewards of this world, and the better rewards of the hereafter. God loves the good doers.

149. O you who believe, if you obey those who disbelieve, they will turn you back on your heels, then you become losers.

150. God is your Lord; and He is the best supporter.

The Disbelievers Invariably Lose

151. We will throw terror into the hearts of the disbelievers, because they set up powerless idols to rank with God. Their ultimate destiny is hell, the wicked's miserable abode.

152. God has fulfilled His promise to you, and you defeated them by His leave. Then, when you became negligent, and disputed among yourselves, and disobeyed despite the blessings He had bestowed upon you; some of you seeking this world, while others seeking the hereafter; He diverted you from them as a trial. He has pardoned you, for God is compassionate towards the believers

153. You then fled, paying no attention to anyone; not even to the messenger who was calling you as you fled. Consequently, God afflicted you with a greater affliction that distracted you from the previous affliction. God is cognizant of everything you do.

154. After the affliction, He sent down upon you peaceful slumber to pacify some of you. Others, however, were more concerned about their own lives. They harbored thoughts about God that were not right, similar to those of the days of ignorance. They said, "Are we not supposed to control everything?" Say, "Everything is controlled by God." Thus, they harbored wrong thoughts, and concealed them from you. They said, "If it were really up to us, none of us would have been killed here?" Say, "Had you stayed in your homes, those destined to die would have crawled into their own death beds." God thus examines your intentions, and thoroughly exposes your innermost convictions. God is fully aware of the innermost thoughts.

155. Those of you who turned around and fled when the two armies clashed were simply duped by the devil, as a consequence of their sins. God has pardoned them, for God is forgiver, clement.

156. O you who believe, do not be like those who disbelieved and said of their comrades who mobilized for war, "Had they stayed with us, they would not have died or gotten killed," God repaid them with sorrow in their hearts. God is the one who decides life and death, and God is seer of everything you do.

157. Whether you get killed in the cause of God, or die, God's forgiveness and mercy are far better than anything the others can hoard.

158. Whether you die or get killed, you will ultimately be gathered before God.

159. It was mercy from God that you (Muhammad) treated them compassionately. Had you been harsh and mean hearted, they would have abandoned you. Therefore, you shall pardon them, ask forgiveness for them, and consult them. Once you reach a decision, then carry it out, putting your trust in God. God loves those who trust in Him.

The Believers Never Defeated

160. If God supports you, who can defeat you? And if He abandons you, who can support you? In God the believers shall trust.

161. No prophet shall take more than his rightful share of the spoils. Whoever takes more than his rightful share, will be held responsible for such earnings on the day of resurrection. That is when every soul will be repaid for whatever it has done, without the least injustice.

162. Is one who complies with God's wishes, equal to one who incurs God's wrath and his inevitable destiny is hell?

163. Certainly, they attain different ranks at God. God is seer of everything they do.

164. It is a blessing from God upon the believers, that He has sent a messenger from among them, to recite His revelations to them, and sanctify them, and to teach them the scripture and wisdom. Before this, they had gone astray.

165. Yet, when a disaster afflicts you, even though you inflicted twice as much upon your enemy, you said, "Why did this happen to us?" Say, "Whatever happens is due to your own actions. God is omnipotent."

166. What afflicted you, when the two armies clashed, was in accordance with God's will, in order to distinguish the true believers;

167. and to expose the hypocrites. Thus, they were told, "You shall fight for the cause of God, or contribute." But they said, "If we knew how to fight, we would have gone with you." They were closer to paganism then, than they were to belief. They utter with their mouths, what is not in their hearts, and God is fully aware of everything they conceal.

168. It is they who said of their comrades, as they stayed behind, "Had they obeyed us, they would not have been killed." Say, "Then prevent death from coming to you, if you are right."

Martyrdom: A Great Honor

169. You shall not think of those who are killed in the cause of God as dead. Indeed, they are alive and well at their Lord.

170. They rejoice in what God bestows upon them from His grace, and rejoice as well for their comrades who were not martyred with them; they too have nothing to fear, nor will they grieve.*

171. They rejoice in God's blessings and grace, for God never neglects to reward the believers;

172. who respond to God and the messenger, despite their afflictions. Those among them who maintained piety and led a righteous life have deserved a great recompense.

173. When the people tell them, "The people have mobilized to fight you, and you should fear them," their faith becomes even stronger, and they say, "God suffices us, and He is the best protector."

174. Consequently, they were rewarded with blessings from God, and grace. No harm even touched them. They have followed God's commandments. God possesses unlimited grace.

3:170. *The period between death and resurrection passes on each one of us like one night of sleep (see 2:259 & Appendix 14). Since the martyrs occupy a special position in the hereafter, we should not think of them as dead. As pointed out in all the scriptures, the righteous attain eternal life (see Psalm 37:29, Matthew 22:32, Luke 10:25, and John 17:3).*

175. It is the devil who instills fear into his friends. Do not fear them, and fear Me instead, if you are really believers.

176. Do not be saddened by those who rush to disbelief; they can never harm God in the least. Instead, God will deprive them of any share in the hereafter, and they will suffer terrible retribution.

177. Those who choose disbelief, instead of belief, can never harm God in the least. They have deserved painful retribution.

178. Those who disbelieve should not think that we respite them because they are good; we only respite them to affirm their sinfulness. They will suffer humiliating retribution.

You Must Be Put To The Test

179. God never leaves the believers in the condition you are in, until the bad and the good are distinguished. Nor does God inform you of the future (regarding your ultimate rank), except for those whom He chooses as messengers. Therefore, you shall believe in God and His messengers. If you believe and lead a righteous life, you will merit a great recompense.

180. The stingy who hoard God's provisions to them should not think that hoarding is good for them. In fact, it is bad for them; for they will carry what they hoard around their necks on the day of resurrection. God is the one who ultimately inherits the heavens and the earth. God is fully cognizant of everything you do.

181. God has heard the utterances of those who said, "God is poor, while we are rich." We will record everything they say, just as we recorded their killing of the prophets unjustly, and we will say, "Suffer the retribution of hell.

182. "This is the retribution for what your hands have sent forth. God is never unjust towards the creatures."

183. They also said, "God has enjoined us from believing any messenger, unless he shows us an offering consumed by holocaust." Say, "Messengers did come before me with profound signs, including what you just demanded; why did you slay them, if you are truthful?"

184. If they disbelieve you, the messengers before you have been similarly disbelieved, despite the profound signs they brought, and the Psalms, and the enlightening scripture.

185. Everyone will taste death; then you get paid fully on the day of resurrection. Thus, the one who barely misses hell, and gets admitted into Paradise, has attained a great triumph. This life is no more than temporary illusion.

186. You will have to undergo tests, by means of your properties and your lives, and you will hear from the people of previous scriptures, and from the idol worshipers, a lot of abuse. If you steadfastly persevere, and lead a righteous life, you will prove the strength of your faith.

187. God has made a covenant with the people of the scripture, that they shall declare it to the people, and never conceal it. But they disregarded it behind their backs, and traded it away for a cheap price; what a miserable trade.

188. Those who are proud because of their charity givings, and wish to be praised for what they did not actually do (God is the one who provided them), will never evade the retribution; they have deserved a painful punishment.

189. God is the one who possesses the dominion of the heavens and the earth. God is omnipotent.

Overwhelming Signs of God

190. In the creation of the heavens and the earth, and the alternation of night and day, there are signs for those who possess intelligence;

191. who commemorate God while standing up, sitting down, and lying on their sides. And they reflect upon the creation of the heavens and the earth. "Our Lord, You did not create all this in vain; glory be to You; so spare us the agony of hell.

192. "Our Lord, whomever You commit to hell is the real loser, and no one can help the wicked."

193. "Our Lord, we have hearkened to the caller who called to faith, saying, 'You shall believe in your Lord,' and we did believe. Therefore, forgive us our transgressions, our Lord, and remit our sins, and count us among the righteous when we die."

194. "Our Lord, grant us what you promised through Your messengers, and do not forsake us on the day of resurrection. Surely, You never break Your promise."

Equality of Men and Women

195. Their Lord responds to these by saying, "I never neglect to recompense any worker among you, male or female; you are equal to each other. Thus, those who leave their homes, and those who are driven out of their homes, and those who suffer because of Me, and those who fought and got killed, I wil certainly remit their sins, and admit them into gardens with flowing streams." Such is the reward from God; God possesses the best rewards.

196. Do not be deceived by the apparent material successes of the disbelievers.

197. They only attain a temporary material pleasure, then end up in hell and a miserable abode.

198. As for those who observe their Lord, they have deserved gardens with flowing streams. They abide therein forever; in a glorious abode from God. God reserves better things for the righteous.

199. Among the Jews and the Christians, there are those who believe in God, and in this scripture, as well as their own scriptures. They are devoted to God, and they do not forsake the revelations of God for a cheap material gain. They have deserved their full recompense from their Lord, and God is most efficient in reckoning.

200. O you who believe, you shall be steadfast; you shall persevere; you shall be ready; you shall observe God, that you may succeed.

Sura 4: Women (Al-Nisaa')

In the name of God, most gracious, most merciful

1. O people, you shall observe your Lord, who created you from one person, then created from him his mate, then from the two of them He spread many men and women. You shall observe God, whom you swear by, and regard the relatives. God is watching over you.

The Orphans

2. You shall give the orphans their due properties, and do not substitute the bad for the good, nor shall you consume their money by mixing their properties with yours. This would be a gross injustice.
3. If you deem it in the best interest of the orphans (to give them a home), you may marry their mother if you like; you may marry two of them , or three, or four.* However, if you feel that you may not be equitable, then one is enough, or be content with what you already have. This may be easier for you to afford.
4. You shall give such women their due dowry equitably, but if they willingly forfeit any part of it, then you may take it graciously and amicably.
5. You may not give the mentally incapable orphans the money that God has entrusted to you. You shall provide for them therefrom, and clothe them, and treat them righteously.
6. You shall test the orphans when they reach puberty, and as soon as you sense from them rationality, you shall hand their money over to them. Do not consume their properties extravagantly and wastefully before they grow up. If the guardian is rich, he shall not take any compensation for managing their properties. But if he is poor, he may take a reasonable compensation. When you give them their money, you shall have witnesses. God suffices as a reckoner.

4:3.   *This is the only mention of polygamy in Quran, and it has to do with giving orphans a home with two parents. Due to ignorance, misunderstanding, and the invention of "Hadith," many Muslims are under the false impression that Islam limits polygamy to four wives. The fact is that the Quran, while recommending only one wife, does not place any limit on polygamy (see 4:3, 129). Ironically, those who claim that Islam, and specifically "Hadith," limits polygamy to four, seem to forget that the prophet left nine wives when he died.*

Women's Rights Decreed

7. The men shall get a share of what the parents and the relatives leave, and the women shall get a share of what the parents and the relatives leave, be it small or large; a decreed share.

8. During the distribution of an estate, if relatives, orphans, and poor people are present, you shall give them therefrom, and speak to them amicably.

9. Those of you who have small children, and are concerned about their welfare in case they die and leave them behind, shall observe God and treat the orphans equitably.

10. Indeed, those who consume the orphans' properties illicitly, are consuming fire into their bellies, and they have deserved hell.

11. God decrees what you shall bequeath for your children: the male shall get the share of two females.* If the children are all females, more than two, they shall get two-thirds of the estate. If there is only one daughter, she gets one-half. As for the parents, each gets one-sixth of the estate, if the deceased had children. If he left no children, and his parents are the only inheritors, then the mother gets one-third. If the deceased had brothers and sisters, then the mother gets one-sixth. Any special will, or debt, shall be deducted first.** Of your parents and your children, you never know which one is really closer to you, and more beneficial. This is God's decree, and God is knower, wise.

12. You shall get one-half of what your wives leave, if they have no children. If they have children, then you get one-fourth of the estate, after deducting any special will, or debts. And they get one-fourth of your estate, if you have no children. If you have children, then they get one-eighth of what you leave, after deducting any special will, or debts. If the deceased is an unmarried man or woman, and he has a brother or a sister, then he or she shall get one-sixth of the estate. If there are more brothers and sisters, then they equally share one-third, after deducting any special will that does not infringe on their rights, or debt. This is the will decreed by God, and God is omniscient, clement.

13. These are God's statutes; those who obey God and His messenger will be admitted into gardens with flowing streams. They abide therein forever, and this is the greatest triumph.

4:11. Generally, the man supports a family, while the woman is being supported by a husband; hence, the designation of a double share for the male.

4:11. One may wish to bequeath a share of his or her estate to needy person(s) or a favorite charity. These donations should be set aside before dividing the estate according to God's law.

14. As for those who disobey God and His messenger, and transgress His laws, God will admit them into hell forever; they have deserved humiliating retribution.

Punish the Adulterers

15. If any woman commits adultery, you shall first obtain four witnesses against her. If you do find four witnesses, then you shall keep her in her home until she dies, or until God provides an outlet for her.*
16. The two who commit adultery shall be punished. Once they repent and reform, you shall pardon them, for God is redeemer, merciful.

Conditions For Acceptable Repentance

17. Repentance is accepted by God from those who fall in sin due to ignorance, then repent immediately. God redeems these, and God is knower, wise.
18. But repentance is not acceptable from those who continue to commit sins until death comes to them, then say, "Now I repent." Nor is it acceptable from those who die as disbelievers. We have prepared for these a painful retribution.

Protection For Women

19. O you who believe, you are not permitted to inherit your wives against their will, nor shall you force them to give up anything you had given them, unless they commit a proven adultery. You shall live with them amicably. If you dislike your wife, it may be that you dislike something wherein God has placed a lot of good.
20. If you wish to substitute one wife in place of another, and you had given the first wife a great deal, you shall not take anything back. Would you take it illicitly and sinfully?
21. How could you take it after you had been united in marriage, and after they had taken from you a solemn covenant?

4:15. A woman who can be witnessed by four persons, at four different occasions or at the same occasion, is obviously a corrupting influence on the society, and should be isolated. If she sincerely repents, and God knows our innermost thoughts, then God will create the circumstances that ensure her release from isolation, as stated in 4:16. The punishment for adultery is spelled out in 24:1-2.

Marriage Laws

22. You shall not marry women who were previously married to your fathers, with the exception of current marriages. Such practice is abominable, and in bad taste.

23. Prohibited for you in marriage are your mothers, your daughters, your sisters, your father's sisters, your mother's sisters, your brother's daughters, your sister's daughters, your foster mothers who nursed you, the girls who nursed from the same woman as you, your mothers-in-law, stepdaughters from wives with whom you consummated the marriage; if the marriage had not been consummated by sexual intercourse, then you may marry the daughter instead. Also prohibited are women previously married to your genetic sons, and to be married to two sisters simultaneously, with the exception of current marriages. God is forgiver, merciful.

24. Also prohibited are women who are still legally married, unless their estranged husbands are pagans at war with you.* This is God's decree for you, and you are permitted to marry any woman beyond these categories, provided you pay them their due dowry. You commit no sin if you mutually agree to anything beyond the dowry. God is knower, wise.

25. Those who cannot afford to marry free believing women, may marry believing slave women. God is fully aware of your beliefs, and you are all equal as far as believing is concerned. You may marry them with permission from their guardians, and pay their due dowry to them, equitably, and maintain chastity. Do not commit adultery, nor take secret lovers. Once the slave woman is freed through marriage, if she commits adultery, her punishment shall be half of that for the free woman.* If you resort to such marriage because you cannot stand the hardship of waiting, it would be better for you to wait. God is forgiver, merciful.

26. God wishes to clarify things for you, and to guide you as He guided those before you, and to redeem you. God is omniscient, wise.

27. God wishes to redeem you, while those enslaved by their lusts wish to see you deviate greatly.

28. God wishes to make things easier for you, since the human being is weak by nature.

4:24.   *See 60:10.*

4:25.   *Obviously, the punishment for a married woman who commits adultery could not possibly be death, as claimed by the inventors of "**Hadith**" and/or "**Sunna.**" Otherwise, what is half of the death penalty? See 24:1-2.*

You Shall Not Confiscate Properties

29. O you who believe, you shall not consume each other's properties illicitly. Any transaction shall be carried out with mutual consent. Nor shall you kill each other. God is full of mercy towards you.

30. Anyone who commits these sins maliciously and deliberately, we will burn him in hell. This is easy for God to do.

31. But if you refrain from the gross offenses forbidden for you, we will remit your sins, and admit you an honorable admittance.

Men and Women Shall Not Covet Each Other's Qualities

32. You shall not covet what God has bestowed upon each of you; the men are endowed with certain qualities, and the women are endowed with certain qualities. You may ask to increase your blessings. God is fully aware of all things.

33. We have decreed for everyone what they deserve from the estates left by the parents, the relatives, and the spouses. Therefore, you shall give each one his due share. God witnesses all things.

34. The men are placed in charge of the women, since God has endowed them with the necessary qualities, and made them the bread earners. Thus, the righteous women will accept this arrangement obediently, and will honor their husbands in their absence, in accordance with God's commandments. As for the women who show rebellion, you shall first enlighten them, then desert them in bed, and you may beat them as a last resort.* Once they obey you, you have no excuse to transgress against them. God is high above you, and more powerful.

35. When a couple experience difficulty in their marriage, you shall appoint a judge from his family, and a judge from her family. If the couple reconcile, God will bring them back together. God is knower, cognizant.

The Great Commandment: You Shall Not Worship Except God

36. You shall worship God, and never idolize anything besides Him; you shall honor your parents, and regard the relatives, the orphans, the poor, the related neighbor, the unrelated neighbor, the close associates, the aliens, and your servants. God does not love the proud boasters;

37. who hoard, and exhort the people to hoard, and conceal God's blessings to them. We have prepared for the disbelievers a humiliating retribution.

4:34.   *This is in fact a Quranic admonition to enjoin the men from beating their wives. In many regions, wife beating is almost a way of life. This verse prohibits wife beating by ordering the men to enlighten the wife first, then using some negative incentives.*

38. They spend their money only for show, while disbelieving in God and the last day. Whoever chooses the devil as his companion, has picked out the worst companion.

39. What is wrong with believing in God and the last day, and giving to charity from God's provisions? God is fully aware of everyone.

40. God never inflicts an atom's weight of injustice. In fact, He pays manyfold for the righteous work, and adds more rewards from Him.

41. What will they do when we bring a witness from every group, and bring you as a witness over your group?

42. On that day, those who disbelieved, and disobeyed the messenger, will wish they were level with the ground.

Tayammum: The Waterless Ablution

43. O you who believe, do not perform the **salat** prayers while intoxicated, that you may know what you are saying; nor after sexual activity, unless you bathe. If you are ill, or travelling, and you have fecal excretion, or sexual intercourse, and no water is available for ablution, you shall make **Tayammum** with high, dry, and clean soil: wipe your hands and faces therefrom. God is pardoner, forgiver.

44. Have you noted those who know only part of the scripture, and how they follow the wrong path, then wish that you too follow the wrong path?

45. God knows best who your real enemies are, and God suffices as your ally; God suffices as a supporter.

46. Also among the Jews there are those who distort the scripture, and say, "We have heard you, and we reject; your invitation is falling on deaf ears," They also said, "**Raa'ina**, (be our shepherd)," as a play on words, and to ridicule the religion.* Had they said, "We have heard, and obeyed and hearkened," and had they said, "**Unzurna** (watch over us)," it would have been better for them, and more righteous. But because of their disbelief, God has placed a curse upon them that prevents them from ever believing, except rarely.

47. O people of the scripture, you shall believe in these revelations, which confirm what you have, before we condemn certain faces, and turn them back, or place a curse on them, as we did to those who desecrated the Sabbath. God's will is always done.

Idol Worship: The Only Unforgivable Offense

48. God never forgives the idolization of anything besides Him, and He forgives all lesser offenses for whomever He wills. Anyone who sets up any idol besides God, has forged a gross blasphemy.

---

*4:46. Apparently, the word "**Raa'ina**" sounded like a dirty word in the Hebrew language, and some Hebrew speakers abused this relationship.*

49. Have you noted those who exalt themselves? God is the one who exalts whomever He wills, without the least injustice.
50. Note how they invent lies, then attribute them to God.* This is a gross sin.
51. Have you noted those who know only part of the scripture, and how they believe in falsehood and idol worship? They even said that the pagans are better than the believers!
52. It is these who are really cursed by God, and whomever God curses will find no one to help him.
53. Should they ever own a share of the dominion, they will not give the people as much as a seed.
54. Are they resenting what God had bestowed upon the people from His grace? We have bestowed upon Abraham's family the scripture and wisdom, and we endowed them with a great kingdom.
55. Then some of his descendants believed, and some repulsed therefrom, and for these, hell suffices as a retribution.

Allegorical Descriptions of Heaven and Hell*

56. Those who reject our revelations, we will burn them in hell. Whenever their skin is burned up, we will substitute new skin to let them suffer the retribution. God is almighty, wise.
57. As for those who believe and work righteousness, we will admit them into gardens with flowing streams. They abide therein forever, and they will have pure spouses therein. We will admit them into abundant shade.

You Shall Be Trustworthy

58. God orders you to give back anything entrusted to you, and when you judge between the people, you shall judge equitably. Excellent indeed are God's commandments to you. God is hearer, seer.
59. O you who believe, you shall obey God, and you shall obey the messenger and those in charge among you.* If you dispute in any matter, you shall refer it to God and the messenger, if you truly believe in God and the last day. This is better for you, and provides you with the best solution.

4:48-51. *The half-educated who know only part of the Quran, or part of the previous scriptures, are not aware that the Quran clearly states that it is complete, perfect, and shall be the sole source of jurisprudence (5:48-51, 6:38, 6:112-116, 17:73-75). Consequently, they blasphemed against God and the prophet by inventing "**Hadith**" and "**Sunna**" then claimed that these Satanic inventions were divine revelations! Futhermore, they used such inventions to abrogate God's law, and substitute their own traditions (see 24:1-2).*
4:56-57. *See also 2:26, and Appendix 4.*
4:59. *The messenger and those in charge shall be obeyed, because they uphold and apply the Quran, the whole Quran, and nothing but the Quran.*

60. Have you noted those who claim that they believe in what was revealed to you, and what was revealed before you, and then apply the statutes of idols? They were enjoined from idol worship, but the devil misleads them completely.

61. When they are told, "Come to what God has revealed, and to the messenger," you see the hypocrites snubbing you completely.

62. Why then, when a disaster strikes them as a consequence of their own deeds, they come to you swearing by God that they meant well, and intended righteousness?

63. God is fully aware of their innermost intentions. You shall disregard them, and enlighten them, and give them valuable advice concerning their souls.

All Messengers Preached the Word of God*

64. We did not send any messenger except to be obeyed by God's leave. Had the people come to you when they wronged their souls, and asked God for forgiveness, and the messenger prayed for their forgiveness, they would have found God a merciful redeemer.

65. Never, by your Lord, will they be considered believers, unless they ask you to judge between them, then find no hesitation whatsoever in their hearts regarding your judgment, and unless they submit completely.

Submission Must Be Total

66. Had we decreed for them that they shall give their lives, or leave their homes, they would not have done it, except a few of them. Had they done whatever is enjoined upon them, it would have been better for them and more strengthening.

67. And we would have blessed them with a great recompense

68. And we would have guided them in the straight path.

69. Those who obey God and the messenger have deserved to be with those blessed by God, such as the prophets, the saints, the martyrs, and the righteous; what a great company.*

4:64. *See Deuteronomy 18:18-19, John 5-24, 8:42, and 13:49.*

4:69. *Those who idolize the messengers refuse to believe this Quranic statement. They cannot believe that any human being possesses the God-given capability to be equal to, or even better than, any of God's messengers and prophets. They have to be freed from slavery to their idols, and from Satan's influence, before submitting and believing the word of God. By simply obeying God, and upholding His message, anyone of us will be with the prophets, the saints, the martyrs, and the righteous. See 18:65-78.*

70. This is the real grace from God, and God is the best knower.

71. O you who believe, you shall be prepared, and mobilize yourselves for war, either in groups, or in one group.

72. Some of you will surely drag their feet. Then, if a disaster afflicts you, they would say, "God has blessed me, that I was not martyred with them."

73. But when victory comes to you from God, he would say, as if no friendship was lost between you and him, "I wish I was with them to share in this great victory."

74. Let those fight in the cause of God who choose the hereafter in preference to this life. Whoever fights in the cause of God, then either gets killed, or wins, we will certainly bless him with a great recompense.

75. Why should you not fight in the cause of God, when the oppressed men, women, and children are crying out, "Our Lord, deliever us from this community whose people are unjust, and make us worthy of having You as our protector, and make us worthy of having You as our supporter.

76. Those who believe are fighting in the cause of God, while those who disbelieve are fighting in the cause of idols. Therefore, you shall fight the devil's allies, for surely, the devil's power is feeble.

You Shall Be Courageous

77. Have you noted those who were told, "Do not fight, and observe the **salat** prayers and give the **zakat** charity," then, when fighting was decreed for them, some of them feared the people the same as fearing God, or even more? They said, "Our Lord, why did You decree fighting for us? Would You postpone this to another time?" Say, "The material of this world is nil, while the hereafter is far better for those who lead a righteous life. No one will suffer the least injustice."

78. Wherever you may be, death will catch up with you, even if you are in formidable castles. When something good happens to them, they say, "This is from God," and when something bad happens to them, they say, "This is because of you." Say, "All things come from God." What is wrong with these people, that they can hardly understand any preaching?

79. Whatever good that happens to you, is from God. Whatever bad that happens to you is a consequence of your own work. We have sent you to the people as a messenger. God suffices as witness.

80. Whoever obeys the messenger is obeying God.* As for those who turn away, we have not appointed you as their guardian.

4:80 *Throughout the Bible and the Quran, we are told that the messengers "do not speak on their own." Thus, when we uphold the message given to us through the messengers (Moses, Jesus, David, Muhammad), we will be upholding the word of God. Muhammad is fully represented by Quran, the whole Quran, and nothing but the Quran.*

81. They claim obedience, then, as soon as they leave you, some of them harbor intentions contrary to what they say. God records their innermost intentions. Therefore, you shall disregard them, and trust in God; God suffices as trustee.

Proof Of Divine Revelation

82. Why do they not study the Quran carefully? If it were from other than God, they would have found many contradictions therein.

You Shall Verify Any Rumors

83. When a matter of security or insecurity comes their way, they spread it. Had they first referred it to the messenger and those in charge among them, the knowledgeable among them would have dealt with it. If it were not for God's indulgence towards you, and His mercy, you would have followed the devil, except rarely.
84. Therefore, you shall fight in the cause of God, and although you are answerable only for yourself, you shall exhort the believers to fight. God will then check the disbeliever's power, and God is more powerful, and more forceful.
85. Whoever mediates a righteous work, receives a share thereof; and whoever mediates an evil work, suffers the consequences thereof. God is counting all things.
86. When you are greeted with a greeting, you shall return a better greeting, or at least an equally courteous one. God takes account of all things.
87. Allah; the one God; there is no god except He. He will surely gather you on the day of resurrection which is inevitable. Who is more truthful than God?

The Hypocrites Condemned

88. Why should you divide yourselves into two groups, and dispute because of the hypocrites? God is the one who cursed them, as a consequence of their work. Do you want to guide those who are misguided by God? Whomever God misguides, you will never find a way to guide him.*

4:88   *God is fully aware of our innermost intentions, and anyone who harbors disbelief while professing belief is known to God. Such hypocrites are consequently blocked out, and deliberately misguided by God. Even though they look like believers to us, we should not feel sorry for them when all signs point at them as hypocrites, and consequences of their hypocrisy are manifested. God, therefore, guides or misguides, depending on our innermost beliefs. See Appendix 12.*

89. They wish that you disbelieve, as they have disbelieved, then you become equal. Therefore, do not consider them allies, unless they mobilize in the cause of God. But if they turn away, then capture them, and kill them when you encounter them. You shall not take them as allies or supporters.

90. Exempted are those who join people with whom you have a treaty, and those who come to you lacking the heart to fight you, or fight their relatives. Had God willed, He could have set them up against you. Therefore, so long as they leave you alone, refrain from fighting you, and offer you peace, God does not permit you to fight them.

91. You will find others who want to have peace with you, and peace with their people, but whenever war erupts, they become aggressors. Therefore, unless they leave you alone, and offer you peace, and refrain from aggression, you shall capture them and kill them whenever you encounter them. It is these against whom we give you a definite permission.

The Grossness of Murder

92. No believer kills another believer, except by mistake. Whoever kills a believer by mistake shall expiate by freeing a believing slave, and paying compensation to the victim's family, unless they forfeit it. If the victim belonged to people who are enemies, though he was a believer, then the expiation shall be by freeing a believing slave. If the victim belonged to people with whom you have a treaty, then you shall pay the compensation, and free a believing slave. Those who cannot afford it may expiate by fasting two consecutive months, as a token of repentance and atonement towards God. God is omniscient, wise.

93. As for the one who kills a believer deliberately, his retribution is hell, wherein he abides forever, and God is angry with him, curses him, and has prepared for him a terrible retribution.

94. O you who believe, you shall be absolutely sure before you strike in the cause of God. Do not say to one who offers you peace, "You are not a believer," just to capture some material of this world; God possesses far better spoils. Remember that you yourselves used to be disbelievers, and God blessed you. Therefore, you shall be absolutely sure, for God is fully cognizant of what you do.

95. Not equal are the believers who are not handicapped and stay behind, and those who struggle with their money and their lives in the cause of God. God exalts those who strive with their money and their lives, over those who sit behind, to higher ranks. God promises salvation for all believers; but He distinguishes those who strive, over those who stay behind, with a great recompense.

96. He bestows upon them higher ranks, and forgiveness, and mercy. God is forgiver, merciful.

Do Not Yield to Oppression

97. Those whose lives are terminated by the angels in a state of unrighteousness, will be asked by the angels, "What was the matter with you?" They would say, "We have been weak and oppressed." The angels would say, "Was not God's earth spacious enough for you to move about?" The destination for these is hell, and a miserable abode.

98. Exempted are the weak men, women, and children who are hopelessly trapped, with no way out.

99. These are the ones to be pardoned by God; and God is pardoner, forgiver.

100. Whoever emigrates in the cause of God, will find many bounties on earth, and richness. And whoever leaves his home, emigrating in the cause of God and His messenger, then death catches up with him, his recompense has been reserved with God. God is forgiver, merciful.

101. While you are on the move, you commit no sin by shortening the **salat** prayers, if you fear lest the disbelievers may attack you. Certainly, the disbelievers are your manifest enemies.

102. If you are with them, and lead the **salat** for them, let some of you stand guard, and hold their weapons. Thus, while you are prostrating, they will protect your backs. Then let another group, who did not pray, take their turn praying with you, while the first group stands guard, and hold their weapons. The disbelievers wish that you neglect your weapons and equipment, in order to attack you once and for all. You commit no sin, if you are hampered by rain or illness, by putting down your weapons, so long as you stay alert. God has prepared for the disbelievers a humiliating retribution.

Salat Decreed at Specific Times

103. If you observe **salat** under these circumstances, then you may worship God while sitting, standing, or laying on your sides. Once the war is over, you shall observe the regular **salat**. The **salat** prayers are decreed for the believers at specific times.*

104. You shall not waver in going after the enemy. If war is painful to you, it is equally painful to them. However, you expect from God what they can never expect. God is omniscient, wise.

4:103.   *The five times of* **salat** *prayers per day, as well as the specific method of carrying out* **salat** *were revealed to Abraham, then transmitted to us generation after generation (2:128, 3:67-68, 16:123, 21:73, and 22:78). The Quran instructs us to uphold such revelations (2:4), and ordered us to observe* **salat** *in one of the first revelations. (73:20).*

105. We have revealed to you this scripture, truthfully, in order that you judge between the people in accordance with God's teachings to you. Do not defend the betrayers.

106. And turn to God for forgiveness; God is forgiver, merciful.

107. Do not argue on behalf of those who wrong their own souls, for God loves not any betrayer, guilty.

108. They hide from the people, and do not care to hide from God, who is with them as they scheme and conspire against His wishes. God is fully aware of everything they do.

109. You may defend them, and argue on their behalf now; but who would defend them before God on the day of resurrection? Who would be their advocate?

110. Anyone who falls in sin, or wrongs his soul, then turns to God for forgiveness, he will find God forgiving, merciful.

111. Anyone who commits sin, commits it against his own soul. God is omniscient, wise.

112. Anyone who commits a transgression, or a sin, then accuses an innocent person thereof, has incurred a blasphemy, and a profound sin.

113. If it were not for God's grace toward you, and His mercy, some of them would have succeeded in misleading you, though they only mislead themselves. They can never harm you. God has revealed to you the scripture and wisdom, and taught you what you never knew. Indeed, God's grace towards you has been generous.

114. There is nothing good in their private discussions, unless they advocate charity, or righteousness, or conciliation among the people. Whoever does this, in compliance with God's wishes, we will endow him with a great recompense.

You Shall Follow The Messenger, But Do Not Idolize Him

115. Anyone who opposes the messenger, after the guidance has been clarified to him, and follows other than the believers' path, we will direct him toward the direction he chose, and burn him in hell; a miserable abode.*

116. God does not forgive the idolization of any idols besides Him, and He forgives all lesser offenses for whomever He wills. Anyone who idolizes any idol besides God, has gone far astray.

4:115. When you tell the average Christian that Jesus is not God, nor son of God, he will accuse you of opposing Jesus. Similarly, when you tell the average Muslim that Muhammad preached the Quran, the whole Quran, and nothing but the Quran, and that following the inventions of **"Hadith"** and **"Sunna"** is an act of opposing the prophet, he will accuse you of opposing Muhammad. Thus, the Muslims appear to have fallen in the same satanic trap as the Christians; they idolize Muhammad against his will.

117. They even set up female idols, and, in fact, they idolize the rebellious devil.

118. God has cursed him, and he vowed, "I will surely take a definite share of Your creatures.

119. "I will surely mislead them, and entice them, and order them to prohibit certain meats by marking the ears of certain animals, and I will order them to distort the creation of God." Whoever takes the devil as his ally, instead of God, has incurred a profound loss.

120. He promises them, and entices them; whatever the devil promises is an illusion.

121. The final abode for these will be hell; they can never evade it.

122. As for those who believe and work righteousness, we will admit them into gardens with flowing streams. They abide therein forever. This is the truthful promise of God, and whose utterance is more truthful than God's?

123. It is not according to your wishes, or the wishes of the people of the scripture; anyone who works evil will be punished therefor, and will find no one to protect him, or support him, against God.

124. On the other hand, anyone who works righteousness, be it male or female, while being a believer, these will enter Paradise, and never suffer a grain of injustice.

This Is The Religion of Abraham

125. Whose religion is better than one who submits himself to God, works righteousness, and follows the creed of Abraham the monotheist? God has chosen Abraham as a beloved friend.

126. To God belongs everything in the heavens and the earth, and God is in full control of all things.

You Shall Regard The Women And The Orphans

127. They consult you concerning the women; say, "God instructs you in this scripture about them, and about the orphan girls whom you wish to marry, but refuse to give them their due dowry. God also instructs you about the small children, and that you shall treat the orphans equitably. Whatever good you do, God is fully aware thereof."

128. And when a woman fears desertion or neglect by her husband, the couple should try to reconcile, for conciliation is better. Since selfishness is a human instinct, if you work righteousness and observe God, then God is fully cognizant of everything you do.

129. In polygamy, you can never be equally attentive towards your wives, no matter how hard you try. However, you shall not be so partial that you neglect one wife so completely that she is left hanging, neither married, nor free to marry someone else. If you correct this situation, and observe righteousness, then God is forgiver, merciful.

130. If they decide to part, God will enrich them from His bounty, for God is bounteous, wise.

131. To God belongs everything in the heavens and the earth, and we have given commandments to those who received previous scriptures, and to you, that you shall observe God. If you disbelieve, then to God belongs everything in the heavens and the earth, and God is in no need, worthy of all praise.

132. To God belongs everything in the heavens and the earth, and God suffices as guardian.

133. If He wills, He can get rid of you, O people, and substitute others in your place, God is certainly able to do this.

134. If you want the materials of this world, to God belongs the material of both this world and the hereafter. God is hearer, seer.

You Shall Not Bear False Witness

135. O you who believe, you shall be perfectly honest, and observe God, when you serve as witnesses; even if it is against yourselves, your parents, or your relatives. Whether the defendant is rich or poor, God will deal with him equitably. You shall not follow your personal desires, lest you deviate. If you bear false witness, or refuse to testify, then God is fully cognizant of what you do.

136. O you who believe, you shall believe in God, and His messenger, and the scripture He revealed through His messenger, and the scriptures He revealed previously. Anyone who disbelieves in God, His angels, His scriptures, His messengers, and the last day, has indeed strayed far away.

The Hypocrites

137. Those who believe, then disbelieve, then believe, then disbelieve, then plunge deeper into disbelief, God will not forgive them, nor will He guide them to any path.

138. Promise the hypocrites that they will suffer painful retribution.

139. They are the ones who choose the disbelievers as allies, instead of believers. Are they seeking dignity through them? To God belongs all dignity.

140. He has revealed to you in the scripture that if you hear the revelations of God being rejected and ridiculed, you shall not sit with them, unless they change the subject. Otherwise, you will be as guilty as they are. God will gather the hypocrites together with the disbelievers in hell.

141. They watch you and wait. Then, if God blesses you with victory, they would say, "Were we not with you?" And if the disbelievers win, they would say to them, "Did we not protect you by hindering the believers?" God will judge between you on the day of resurrection, and God will never permit the disbelievers to overcome the believers.

142. The hypocrites are trying to deceive God, but He is the one who deceives them. When they get up for the **salat** prayers, they get up lazily, for they only do it to show off, and they never think of God but rarely.

143. They waver between this and that; they neither belong to this group, nor to that group. Whomever God misguides, you will find no way to guide him.

144. O you who believe, do not choose the disbelievers as allies, instead of believers. Do you wish to provide God with a manifest proof against you?

145. The hypocrites will occupy the lowest pit of hell, and no one can help them.

146. Only those who repent, reform and hold fast to God, and devote their religion to God, will be counted as believers. God will endow the believers with a great recompense.

147. What will God gain from punishing you, if you are appreciative believers? God is appreciative, omniscient.

Do Not Utter Bad Language

148. God dislikes the utterance of bad language, unless you suffer injustice. God is hearer, knower.

149. Whether you declare a righteous work, or conceal it, or pardon an offense, God is pardoner, omnipotent.

No Distinction Among the Messengers*

150. Those who disbelieve in God and His messengers, and make distinctions among God and His messengers, and say, "We believe in some, and reject some," and try to follow an inbetween path;

151. these are really disbelievers, and we have prepared for the disbelievers a humiliating retribution.

152. As for those who believe in God and His messengers, and make no distinction among any of them, God will recompense them. God is forgiver, merciful.

4:150-151. *A common practice among the Muslims is the description of Muhammad as "the most honorable messenger" or "the imam of the messengers," in defiance of God's commandments.*

Lessons From Israel*

153. The people of the scripture ask you to show them a scripture coming down from the sky! They have asked Moses for more than that, saying, "Show us God, physically." The lightning struck them as a consequence of their wickedness. Then, they idolized the calf inspite of the profound miracles they had witnessed, and we still pardoned them. We gave Moses profound authority.

154. We raised Mount Sinai above them, as we made a convenant with them, and we said to them, "Enter the gate humbly," and we said to them, "Do not desecrate the Sabbath." We took from them a solemn pledge.

155. Therefore, because they violated their covenant, and discarded God's scripture, and killed the prophets unjustly; and because they said, "Our hearts are shielded," though God is the one who sealed their hearts, as a consequence of their disbelief. That is why they do not believe, except rarely.

156. And because of their rebellion, and because of accusing Mary of a terrible falsehood;

157. And because they said, "We killed the Messiah, Jesus the son of Mary," the messenger of God. Indeed, they never killed him; they never crucified him; but they were led to believe that they did. Those who dispute in this matter are doubtful thereof; they have no real knowledge; they follow only conjecture. They never killed him, for certain.

158. Instead, God raised him towards Him, and God is almighty, wise.

159. Everyone among the people of the scripture shall believe in him before his death, and on the day of resurrection, he will serve as a witness over them.

160. Thus, because of all their wicked actions, we prohibited for the Jews good things that were previously permitted for them. Also, because they repulsed many people from the way of God.

161. And because they charged usury, though they were forbidden therefrom, and because they cheated the people out of their money. We have prepared for the disbelievers among them a painful retribution.

---

*4:153-161. The reader will note that the children of Israel are frequently mentioned throughout the Quran. Obviously, God wants to alert us against the pitfalls that Israel fell in. The parallel between the Muslims and Jews is noteworthy. Although God gave the Jews His scripture, the Torah, the Jews eventually invented the **Mishnah** (oral) and the **Gemarah** (traditions), and used them as sources of jurisprudence. Similarly, the Muslims abandoned God's message to them, the Quran, and invented the "**Hadith**" (oral) and "**Sunna**" (traditions), and used them as sources of jurisprudence (See 6:112-116 and 25:30-31).*

162. As for those well founded in knowledge among the Jews, as well as the Muslims, they believe in what was revealed to you, and what was revealed before you; they observe the **salat** prayers and give the **zakat** charity; and they believe in God and the last day. We will bestow upon these a great recompense.

No Excuse For Disbelieving

163. We inspired you, as we inspired Noah and the prophets after him. And we inspired Abraham, Ishmael, Issac, Jacob, the Patriarchs, Jesus, Job, Jonah, Aaron, and Solomon. And we endowed David with the Psalms.

164. We inspired messengers whom we mentioned to you previously, and messengers we never mentioned to you. And God spoke to Moses directly.

165. Messengers who served as preachers and warners, in order that the people may not protest before God, for lack of messengers. God is almighty, wise.

166. God bears witness that these revelations are given to you with His knowledge, and so do the angels; God suffices as a witness.

167. Those who disbelieve, and prevent others from believing, have gone totally astray.

168. Those who disbelieve and work evil, God does not forgive them, nor guides them to any path.

169. Except the path to hell. They abide therein forever, and this is easy for God to do.

170. O people, the messenger has come to you with the truth from your Lord, and you shall believe for your own good. But if you disbelieve, then to God belongs everything in the heavens and the earth, and God is omniscient, wise.

Jesus: A Messenger of God*

171. O people of the scripture, do not transgress the limits of your religion, and do not say about God other than the truth. The Messiah, Jesus the son of Mary, is no more than a messenger of God, and His word that He threw unto Mary, and a spirit from Him. Therefore, you shall believe in God and His messengers, and do not say, "Trinity." You shall refrain for your own good. God is only one God, much too glorious to have a son. To Him belongs everything in the heavens and the earth, and God suffices as a guardian.

4:171. See the Bible's Book of Revelation 1:1.

172. Never will the Messiah disdain from being a slave of God, nor will the closest angels. Those who disdain, and are too arrogant to worship Him, God will gather them all before Him.

173. Those who believe and lead a righteous life, God will fully recompense them, and shower them with His grace. But those who disdain, and are too arrogant, He will punish them severely, and they will find no one to help them or support them against God.

The Proof Is Right Here

174. O people, a proof is given to you herein from your Lord, and we have sent down to you a profound beacon.

175. As for those who believe in God, and hold fast to Him, He will admit them into mercy from Him and grace, and will guide them towards Him in a straight path.

More Inheritance Statutes

176. They consult you about the lone person who dies; say, "The loner who dies, and leaves no children, his sister inherits half of his estate. And he inherits all her estate, if she leaves no children. If the deceased has two sisters, they share two-thirds of the estate. If he leaves many brothers and sisters, then the male gets the share of two females. God thus explains things for you. lest you go astray, and God is fully aware of all things.

Sura 5: The Feast (Al-Maa'idah)

In the name of God, most gracious, most merciful

1. O you who believe, you shall fulfill your convenants. You are permitted to eat the meat of any livestock, except those specified for you. And do not allow hunting while observing **Hajj** pilgrimage. God decrees whatever He wills.

2. O you who believe, you shall not violate God's shrines, nor the sacred months, nor the offerings, nor the garlands marking them, nor those who are heading for the Sacred Mosque, seeking the grace and pleasure of their Lord. Once you end the pilgrimage, you may hunt. Do not be provoked by enmity of those who prevent you from reaching the Sacred Mosque into aggression. You shall cooperate with one another in matters of righteousness and piety, but do not cooperate in sin and aggression. You shall observe God, for God's punishment is severe.

Only Four Kinds of Meat Prohibited*

3. Prohibited for you are the meats from animals that die of themselves, blood, the meat of pigs, and animals dedicated to other than God. (Animals that die of themselves include) the animal that was strangled to death, the animal that was struck dead by an object, the animal that dies by falling from height, the animal that was gored to death, and the animal that was partially eaten by a beast, unless you rescue it alive. Also prohibited are animals sacrificed on an idol's altar, and to divide your meats by throwing arrows. These are abominations. Today, the disbelievers have despaired regarding your religion; do not fear them, and fear Me instead. Today, I have perfected the religion for you and completed My favors upon you, and I decreed Islam (submission) as the religion for you. If anyone is forced to eat any of these, because of famine, and without malice, then God is forgiver, merciful.

5:3. *The Quran consistently and repeatedly lists these four kinds of meats as the only prohibitions (see 2:173, 6:145, 16:115-116, and Appendix 13). It should be noted that if God wants to prohibit "meat," He clearly prohibits "meat," and when He wants to prohibit "fat," He clearly prohibits "fat" (see 2:173, 5:3, 6:145, 16:115, and also 6:146). God is extremely displeased with those who make up prohibitions not specifically mentioned in Quran (see 3:93-94, 5:87, 6:143-146, 10:59-60, 16:116, 7:32, and Appendix 13).*

4. They ask you what is permitted for them; say, "Permitted for you are the good things, including what you train your falcons and dogs to catch. You train them in accordance with God's designs. Thus, you may eat what they catch for you, and mention God's name thereupon. You shall observe God, for God is most strict in reckoning.

5. Today, all good things are permitted for you, and the food of those who were given previous scriptures is permitted for you, and your food is permitted for them. Also, you are permitted to marry the chaste Muslim women, as well as the chaste women who are Jewish or Christian, provided you pay them their due dowry, and maintain chastity, not committing adultery, nor taking secret lovers. Anyone who rejects faith, has nullified his work, and will be a loser in the hereafter.

Ablution and Tayammum Detailed

6. O you who believe, when you get up to pray, you shall wash your faces, your arms to the elbows, wipe your heads, and wash your feet to the ankles. If you were unclean due to sexual activity, you shall bathe. If you are ill, or travelling, or had fecal excretion, or had intercourse with women, and no water is available, then you shall perform the waterless ablution (tayammum), by touching high clean soil, then wiping your faces and hands. God wishes no hardship for you; He wishes to cleanse you, and to complete His favors upon you, that you may become appreciative.

7. You shall be appreciative of God's blessings upon you, and uphold the covenant He has made with you, when you said, "We hearken and obey." You shall observe God, for God is fully aware of the innermost intentions.

You Shall Not Bear False Witness

8. O believers, you shall be absolutely equitable, and observe God, when you serve as witnesses. Do not be provoked by the enmity of anyone into bearing false witness. You shall be equitable, for it is righteous, and observe God. God is fully cognizant of everything you do.

9. God promises those who believe and work righteousness, that they have deserved forgiveness, and a great recompense.

10. But those who disbelieve and reject our revelations, have deserved hell.

God Defends the Believers

11. O you who believe, you shall be appreciative of God's favors upon you; when some people extended their hands to strike you, He withheld their hands. You shall observe God; in God the believers shall trust.

12. God has taken a covenant from the children of Israel, and we appointed for them twelve patriarchs; God said, "I will be with you for as long as you observe the **salat** prayers and give the **zakat** charity, and believe in My messengers and support them, and lend God a loan of righteousness. I will then remit your sins, and admit you into gardens with flowing streams. Anyone who disbelieves after this, has indeed strayed off the right path.

13. Because they violated their covenant, we put a curse on them, and we hardened their hearts. Consequently, they distort the scripture given to them, and disregard parts thereof. You will always see betrayal from them, excepting a few. You shall forgive and forget them, for God loves the compassionate.

14. As for those who said, "We are Christian," we made a covenant with them, but they too disregarded parts thereof. Consequently, we condemned them to enmity and hatred among themselves, until the day of resurrection. God will inform them of everything they did.*

15. O people of the scripture, our messenger has come to you to disclose many things in the scripture that you are concealing,* and to overlook many others. A beacon has come to you from God, and a profound scripture.

16. With it, God will guide those who seek His pleasure to the paths of peace, and will lead them out of the darkness, into light, by His leave. He will guide them in a straight path.

---

*5:13-14. Obviously, our creator is showing us how the Jews violated their covenant, and the Christians violated their covenant, in order to warn us against falling in the same trap. However, the Muslims, being humans with the same weaknesses as the Jews and the Christians, have fallen in the same trap. They broke their covenant with God, by abandoning their scripture, the Quran, and adopting the satanic inventions known as "**Hadith**" and "**Sunna**" in flagrant defiance of God and His messenger (see 6:19, 38, 112-116, 15:91, 20:114, 24:1-2, 25:30, 75:19, and Appendix 11, 15, & 16).*

5:15. See Appendix 19, and the inside front cover of this book.

5:17. Those who idolize Jesus, and claim to love him, are in fact his enemies. They are obviously prevented by God from understanding and following their own Bible, for Jesus clearly exhorted them to worship the one God, the Lord of Jesus and all the people (see Mark 10:17-18, 12:39-30, Luke 4:18, John 4:33, 5:24, and 8:40-41).

The Great Blasphemy*

17. Pagans indeed are those who say that Christ, the son of Mary, is God. Say, "Who then can do anything, if God willed to annihilate Christ, the son of Mary, and his mother, and all the people on earth?" To God belongs the kingdom of the heavens and the earth, and everything between them. He creates whatever He wills. God is omnipotent.

18. The Jews and the Christians said, "We are the children of God, and His beloved ones." Say, "Why then does He punish you for your sins? Indeed, you are no more than human beings like the rest." He forgives whomever He wills, and punishes whomever He wills. To God belongs the kingdom of the heavens and the earth, and everything between them. To Him is the ultimate destiny.

19. O people of the scripture, our messenger has come to you, following a succession of messengers, lest you say, "We have not received any preacher or warner." A preacher and warner has now come to you. God is omnipotent.

Lessons From Israel*

20. Recall that Moses said to his people, "O my people, you shall appreciate God's favors upon you. He appointed for you prophets, and made you kings. He endowed you as He never endowed anyone else.

21. "O my people, you shall enter the holy land that God has designated for you, and do not turn back, lest you become losers."

22. They said, "O Moses, there are powerful people therein, and we will not enter it unless they get out therefrom. If they get out, we will enter."

23. Two men whom God had blessed with reverence said, "If you just enter the gate, you will be victorious. You shall trust in God, if you are really believers."

24. They said, "O Moses, we will not enter it, so long as they are therein, so go with your Lord and fight; we are sitting right here."

25. He said, "My Lord, I can only control myself and my brother. Therefore, separate us from the wicked people."

26. He said, "Then it is prohibited for them; for forty years, they will wander in the land. Do not grieve over the wicked people."

The First Murder

27. Recite for them the story of Adam's two sons, truthfully. They made offerings, but it was accepted from one of them, not the other. He said, "I will kill you." He said, "God accepts only from the righteous.

5:20-26. *See footnote 4:153 and Appendix 11.*

28. "If you extend your hand to kill me, I will not extend my hand to kill you, for I fear God, Lord of the universe.

29. "I want you, not me, to bear my sins in addition to yours, then you end up in hell. This is the retribution for the sinners."

30. His ego provoked him into killing his brother, and thus, he became a loser.

31. God then sent a raven digging in the ground, to show him how to bury his brother's corpse. He said, "Woe to me, I failed to be like this raven, and bury my brother's corpse." He became ridden with sorrow and remorse.

32. Because of this, we decreed for the children of Israel that the killing of one person, who did not commit murder or vast corruption, is the same as killing all the people; and the sparing of one life is the same as sparing the lives of all the people. Indeed, our messengers went to them with profound messages, but most of them continued to transgress.

33. Only those who actively fight God and His messenger, and commit gross corruption, may be punished by execution or crucifixion, or by cutting their hands and feet on alternate sides, or by banishing them. They have deserved humiliation in this life, and far worse retribution in the hereafter.

34. As for those who repent before you overcome them, you should know that God is forgiving, merciful.

35. O you who believe, you shall observe God, and seek the ways and means towards Him, and struggle in His cause, that you may succeed.

36. If the disbelievers owned everything on earth, and even twice as much, and offered it all as ransom, to spare them the agony on the day of resurrection, it will not be accepted from them. They have deserved painful retribution.

37. They will want to exit from hell, but they can never exit therefrom. They have deserved eternal retribution.

Criminal Justice

38. The thief, male or female, shall be punished by cutting their hands as a punishment for their crime, as well as a deterrent from God. God is almighty, wise.*

39. If one repents after his offense, and reforms, God will redeem him. God is forgiver, merciful.

40. Do you not realize that to God belongs the kingdom of the heavens and the earth? He punishes whomever He wills, and forgives whomever He wills, and God is omnipotent

41.   O you messenger, do not be saddened by those who hasten to disbelieve, among those who said, "We believe," with their mouths, while their hearts disbelieved. Nor by the Jews who listen to lies, listen to other people who never met you, and distort the original scripture, then say, "If you are given this, you may accept it. But if you are not given this, then beware." Whomever God wills to misguide, there is nothing you can do for him. God does not want to cleanse their hearts. They have deserved humiliation in this life, and they have deserved terrible retribution in the hereafter.

42.   They listen to lies, and make their living dishonestly. If they come to you to judge between them, you may judge between them, or you may disregard them. If you disregard them, they can never harm you, but if you judge between them, you shall judge equitably. God loves the equitable.

43.   Why should they seek your judgment, when they have the Torah, with God's law therein? It is they who turned away thereafter, for they are not really believers.

44.   We have revealed the Torah, containing guidance and light. With it, the prophets who submitted judged between the Jews, and so did the rabbis and the priests. They judged in accordance with God's scripture given to them, and witnessed by them. Therefore, you shall not fear the people, and fear Me instead, and do not trade away My scripture for a cheap material gain. Those who do not rule according to God's scripture are the disbelievers.

5:38.   This is the Quranic law abused most frequently by the enemies of God. They ignore the fact that God created us, and knows best how our minds work, and what is best for all of us. Real life experiences confirm that God's law is far superior to the man-made laws. For example, the people of U.S.A. were shocked by the thief who entered a house, stole the valuables, then gouged the eyes of the baby sitter to prevent her from serving as witness against him. In this incident, the innocent lost her eyes. The incident took place in St. Louis, Missouri, and the famous victim's name was Wilma. We have to ask ourselves, "Is it justice to have the innocent lose his eyes, or the thief be deterred in the first place by fear of losing his hand?" On the other hand, in the countries where God's law is applied, the crime of theft is virtually non-existent, and thus, no one loses his properties through theft, nor his hand. Additionally, the Quranic law defines the thief as one who is not driven by hunger or the survival instinct to steal. According to this definition, thousands of prisoners should be set free, and the officials responsible for their poverty should be tried.

God's Statutes: The Only Just Law

45. We decreed for them therein that: the soul for the soul, the eye for the eye, the nose for the nose, the ear for the ear, the tooth for the tooth, and an equivalent injury for any injury. However, any one who pardons and forfeits as a charitable act will have his sins remitted. Those who do not rule according to God's scripture are the unjust.

46. Subsequent to them, we sent Jesus the son of Mary, confirming the previously revealed Torah. We gave him the Gospel, containing guidance and light, and confirming the Torah, as well as providing guidance and enlightenment for the righteous.

47. The people of the Gospel shall judge according to God's teachings therein. Those who do not rule according to God's scripture are the wicked.

Muhammad's Mission: Deliver Quran, and Nothing But Quran*

48. Then we revealed to you this scripture, truthfully, confirming all previous scriptures, and superseding them. You shall judge among them according to this scripture, and follow not their ideas instead of the truth that has come to you. We have decreed statutes and methods for each of you, although, had God willed, He could have made you one congregation. But He thus puts you to the test, according to what He has given you. You shall compete towards righteous works. To God is your ultimate return, then He will inform you of everything you disputed.

49. You shall judge among them according to God's scripture, and do not follow their ideas, and beware lest they divert you from some of God's revelations to you. If they turn away, then you should know that God wants to punish them for their sins. Indeed, many people are wicked.

50. Is it the laws of the days of ignorance that they want to apply? Whose laws are better than God's, for those who are firm believers?*

4:48-50. *These verses clearly define the prophet for us: a man who preaches the Quran, the whole Quran, and nothing but the Quran. Therefore, those who invent lies and use them as sources of jurisprudence besides the Quran are enemies of God and His messenger (see Appendix 11).*

5:50. *A perfect example of applying the laws of the days of ignorance, instead of God's law, is the stoning of adulterers. Although God's law clearly states the punishment for adulterers, stoning has been forced on many Muslims through the invention of "**Hadith**" and "**Sunna**." See 24:1-2.*

Historical Fact of Life

51. O you who believe, do not consider the Jews and the Christians as your allies. Instead, they are allies of one another. Anyone of you who allies himself with them is one of them. God does not guide the wicked.

52. You will see those with disease in their hearts hasten to ally themselves with them, saying, "We fear lest we may be defeated some day." May God bring victory from Him, or certain blessings, then they will regret the ideas they had harbored.

53. The believers will then say, "Look at these people who swore by God solemnly that they were with you. Their works have been nullified, and now they are losers."

54. O you who believe, if any of you reverts from his religion, then God will bring people whom He loves as they love Him; and humble themselves towards the believers, while being stern towards the disbelievers; and strive in the cause of God; and never worry about any blamer who might blame them. Such is God's grace that He bestows upon whomever He wills. God is bounteous, omniscient.

55. Your true ally is God, and His messenger, and the believers who observe the **salat** and **zakat,** and bow down.

56. Those who ally themselves with God, and His messenger, and the believers, are the party of God; these are the winners.

57. O you who believe, do not take the people of previous scriptures who mock and ridicule your religion, nor the disbelievers, as allies, and observe God, if you are really believers.

58. When you call for the **salat** prayers, they mock and ridicule. That is because they do not understand.

59. Say, "O people of the scripture, do you not resent us simply because we have believed in God, and in what was revealed to us, and in what was revealed before, and because most of you are wicked?"

60. Say, "Let me tell you who are really in bad shape. Those who are cursed by God, and displeased Him, until He made them monkeys and pigs, and those who worship idols. It is these who are really evil, and farthest from the right path."

61. When they come to you, they say, "We believe," although they have entered as disbelievers, and left as disbelievers. God is fully aware of everything they conceal.

62. You will see many of them hasten into sinfulness and transgression, and earning dishonestly. Evil indeed is what they do.

63. If only the rabbis and the priests would enjoin them from sinful utterances and dishonest earnings. Evil indeed is what they commit.

64. The Jews said, "God's hand is tied down!" It is their hands that are tied down, and they incurred a curse for such utterance. Instead, His hands are wide open, freely providing as He wills. Indeed, most of them plunge deeper into transgression and heathenism, because of resenting the revelation to you from your Lord. We have cast among them enmity and hatred until the day of resurrection. Whenever they ignite the fires of war, God puts it out. They roam the earth corruptingly, and God dislikes the corruptors.

Salvation For Jews and Christians

65. If only the people of the scripture believe and work righteousness, we will then remit their sins, and admit them into blissful Paradise.
66. If they uphold the Torah, the Gospel, and what is revealed herein from their Lord, they would be provided from above them, and from beneath their feet. Some of them are righteous, but most of them are evildoers.

The Messenger Delivers Everything Revealed to Him*

67. O messenger, you shall deliver everything revealed to you from your Lord. If you do not, then you have failed in your mission. God will protect you from the people. God does not guide the disbelievers.
68. Say, "O people of the scripture, you have no basis until you uphold the Torah, the Gospel, and what is revealed herein from your Lord." Indeed, many of them will plunge deeper into transgression and heathenism, because of resenting the revelation to you from your Lord. Do not be saddened by the disbelievers.

Three Requirements For Salvation

69. Surely, the followers of this scripture, and the Jews, and the converts, and the Christians; any of them who believe in the one God, and believe in the last day, and work righteousness, will have nothing to fear, nor will they grieve.
70. We made a covenant with the children of Israel, and we sent to them messengers; whenever a messenger went to them with commandments they did not like, they either rejected him, or killed him.
71. And they expected no retribution. Consequently, they turned blind and deaf, then God redeemed them, but many of them still turned blind and deaf. God fully sees everything they do.

5:67. *This verse indicates that the Quran's secret numerical code was not revealed to the prophet Muhammad, since he did not deliver it to us (see Appendix 1).*

The Great Blasphemy

72. Pagan indeed are those who say that Christ, the son of Mary, is God. Christ himself said, "O children of Israel, you shall worship God, my Lord and your Lord."* Indeed, if anyone sets up an idol besides God, then God has forbidden him from Paradise, and his inevitable destiny is hell. The wicked will have no helper.

73. Pagan indeed are those who say that God is one third of a trinity. There is absolutely no god except the one God. Unless they refrain from such utterances, these disbelievers will suffer painful retribution.

74. Would they not repent to God, and implore for His forgiveness? God is forgiver, merciful.

75. Christ, the son of Mary, was no more than a messenger like the messengers before him, and his mother a saint. Both of them used to eat the food. Note how we explain the revelations for them, then note how they still deviate.

76. Say, "Would you worship besides God idols who possess no power to harm you or benefit you? God is the one who hears, and knows.*"

77. Say, "O people of the scripture, do not exceed the limits of your religion beyond the truth, and do not follow the ideas of people who had gone astray, and caused many people to go astray."

78. Those who deviated among the children of Israel are cursed by the tongue of David and Jesus the son of Mary. That is because they rebelled and transgressed.

79. They did not enjoin one another from evildoing. Wicked indeed is what they did.

80. You will see many of them allying themselves with those who disbelieve. Evil indeed is what their souls have sent forward. God is displeased with them, and they have deserved eternal retribution.

81. Had they believed in God and the prophet, and the scripture revealed to him, they would not have allied themselves with them. But most of them are wicked.

5:72. *See the Gospel of Mark 12:29, John 5:24, 8:40-41, 9:4, & 12:49.*

5:76. *The fact is that Mary, Jesus, Muhammad, and all the dead saints, are totally unaware of anything at this time (see 16:20-21), while only God hears and sees everything. The blasphemy is obvious when a religious leader proclaims, "May the holy mother protect you!"*

An Historical Fact

82. You will find that the most ardent opponents of those who believe are the Jews and the idolaters. And you will find that the closest friends of the believers are those who say, "We are Christians." That is because there are among them priests and monks, and because they are not arrogant.

83. And when they hear what is revealed to the messenger, you would see tears flooding their eyes, because they recognize the truthfulness thereof. They say, "Our Lord, we believe; so count us among the witnesses.

84. "Why should we not believe in God, and in the truth that has come to us, and hope that God may count us among the righteous?"

85. Consequently, God has rewarded them with gardens and flowing streams, wherein they abide forever. Such is the reward for the pious.

86. As for those who disbelieved and rejected our revelations, they have deserved hell.

Do Not Prohibit Lawful Foods*

87. O you who believe, do not prohibit the good things that God has permitted for you, nor shall you transgress; God dislikes the transgressors.

88. You shall eat from God's provisions to you, that which is good and lawful, and observe God, in whom you believe.

Keep Your Vows

89. God does not hold you responsible for the vain utterances of oaths, but He holds you responsible for your actual intentions. You shall expiate for breaking an oath by feeding ten poor people from the same food that you offer to your family, or clothing them, or by freeing a slave. Those who cannot afford it shall fast three days. This is the expiation for breaking your vows. You shall keep your vows. God thus explains His revelations to you, that you may be appreciative.

Intoxicants and Gambling Prohibited

90. O you who believe, intoxicants, gambling, the dedication of offerings (and candles) to idols, the dividing of meat by throwing arrows, are all satanic abominations. You shall abstain therefrom, that you may succeed.

5:87. *Traditions, myths, superstitions, and the inventions of "Hadith" and "Sunna" have established a long list of dietary prohibitions, beyond the four decreed by God (see 2:173, 5:3, 6:145, 16:115-116, and Appendix 13). Throughout the Quran, God is extremely displeased by those who prohibit lawful food (see 3:93-94, and 10:59).*

91. The devil wants to instill enmity and hatred among you, through intoxicants and gambling, and wants to divert you from remembering God, and from the **salat** prayers. Will you then abstain?

Sole Function of the Messenger*

92. You shall obey God, and obey the messenger, and beware. If you turn away, then you should know that the sole function of our messenger is to deliver the message.

93. Those who believe and lead a righteous life commit no sin by eating any food, so long as they observe righteousness and faith, and work righteousness; then continue to grow in piety, faith, and righteous works. God loves the pious.

Do Not Hunt During Pilgrimage

94. O you who believe, God may put you to the test through placing game within reach of your hands and arrows. God thus will distinguish those who reverence Him in their privacy. Anyone who transgresses after this, has deserved painful retribution.

95. O you who believe, do not kill any game during pilgrimage. If anyone kills it on purpose, he shall expiate by offering an equivalent livestock, as judged by two equitable people. The offering shall go to the Kaaba.* Otherwise, the expiation may be by feeding some poor people, or by an equivalent fast as an atonement for his sin. God has pardoned all past offenses, but whoever reverts to this sin, God will avenge from him. God is almighty, avenger.

96. Permitted for you is fishing the sea, and eating therefrom, as a provision for you and your caravan. But you are forbidden from hunting on land, for as long as you are observing pilgrimage. You shall observe God, before whom you will be gathered.

97. God has decreed that the Kaaba shall be sacred for all the people, as well as the holy months, the offerings to Kaaba,* and the garlands marking them. You should realize that God knows everything in the heavens and the earth. God is fully aware of all things.

5:92 & 99.   The idol worshipers who idolize the prophet Muhammad against his will, ascribe to the prophet other functions besides delivering Quran, the whole Quran, and nothing but the Quran. Unfortunately, the majority of Muslims have fallen in this trap, just like the Christians before them (5:100, 12:106). The only difference is, while the Christians declare their idolization of Jesus, the Muslims will deny their idolization of Muhammad, all the way through the day of judgment (see 6:22-24).

98. You should realize that God is strict in enforcing retribution, and that God is forgiver, merciful.

Sole Function of the Messenger*

99. The sole function of the messenger is to deliver the message, and God knows what you declare, and what you conceal.

100. Say,"The bad is never the same as the good, even if you are impressed by the abundance of the bad. Therefore, you shall observe God, O you who possess intelligence, that you may succeed."

101. O you who believe, do not ask about things if revealed to you, you will be hurt. If you consider them in light of the Quran, you will realize that God left them out as an alleviation. God is forgiver, clement.*

102. Others before you have asked similar questions, then rejected the answers given to them.

103. God never prohibited the **Baheerah** (female that gives birth to a certain sequence of males), nor the **Saa'ibah** (animal liberated by an oath), nor the **Waseelah** (female that gives birth to consecutive males), nor the **Ham** (male that fathers ten). It is the disbelievers who invented such lies, and most of them do not understand.

104. When they are told, "Come to what God has revealed, and to the messenger," they say, "Sufficient for us is what we found our parents doing." What if their parents lacked the knowledge, and the guidance?

105. O you who believe, you shall worry only about yourselves; you are not harmed by those who go astray, so long as you are guided. To God is the ultimate return of all of you, then He will inform you of everything you did.

5:95 & 97:   *The offerings "to the Kaaba" are designed to provide for the people who come to Kaaba for pilgrimage. These people are usually aliens from all parts of the world, and often short on funds. The offerings are God's way for providing for them (see 28:57).*

*5:101.   God teaches us that we have everything we need in the Quran (see 6:19, 38, 114, and Appendix 15). Anything not mentioned specifically in the Quran is left to our freedom of choice. For example, the Quran does not specify a method for sleeping. Therefore, we can sleep any way we like; on the right side, on the left side, on the back, or on the belly. Similarly, we can eat with our right hand, or the left hand, with or without forks and knives. The idol-worshipers have invented a most unreasonable set of behaviors, and termed them "*Sunna.*"*

Witnessing a Will

106. O you who believe, you shall have witnesses, to witness the will, when death comes to any of you. You shall appoint two equitable persons from among you or two outsiders if death strikes while you are travelling. Following the **salat** prayer, let the two witnesses swear by God, if you have any doubts, that they will not take advantage and distort the will in their favor, even if the deceased is related to them, nor will they conceal the testimony. Otherwise, they will be sinners.

107. If they are found guilty of bias, then appoint two others who suffered injustice by the first two. Let them swear by God that their testimony will be more honest and truthful, and that if they transgress, they will be wicked.

108. This will persuade them to give an accurate testimony, and guard against bias and exposure as bearers of false witness. You shall observe God, and hearken, for God does not guide the wicked.

109. The day will come when God gathers all the messengers and asks them, "How was the response to you?" They will say, "We do not know; You are the knower of all secrets."

110. That is when God will say, "O Jesus, son of Mary, recall the favors I bestowed upon you and your mother. I supported you with the holy spirit, causing you to speak to the people as an infant, as well as a grown-up, and I taught you the scripture and wisdom, the Torah, and the Gospel. And recall that you fashioned birds from clay, then blew into it, and it became a live bird by My leave. You healed the blind and the leprous by My leave, and you revived the dead by My leave. And recall that I protected you from the children of Israel: when you went to them with profound miracles, the disbelievers among them said, 'This is obviously magic.'

111. "And recall that I inspired the disciples, 'Believe in Me and My messengers.' They said, 'We believe, and bear witness that we are Muslims.' "

The Feast

112. The disciples said, "O Jesus, son of Mary, can your Lord bring down to us a feast from the sky?" He said, "Fear God, if you are really believers."

113. They said, "We want to eat therefrom, reassure our hearts, and know that you have told us the truth. We want to see for ourselves."

114. Jesus, the son of Mary, said, "O God, our Lord, send down to us a feast from the sky. Let it be a celebration for each and everyone of us, and a sign from You. Provide for us; You are the best provider."

115. God said, "I am sending it down to you, and if anyone disbelieves thereafter, I will punish him as I never punish anyone else."

Jesus Disowns His Worshipers

116. And God will say, "O Jesus, son of Mary, did you tell the people to consider you and your mother idols besides God?" He will say, "Glory be to you, it is not right for me to say what is not true. Had I said it, You would have known about it. You know my innermost thoughts, while I do not know Your innermost thoughts. You are the knower of all secrets.

117. "I did not tell them except what you commanded me to say: that you shall worship God, my Lord and your Lord. I was a witness among them, for as long as I lived with them. When You terminated my life, You became the watcher over them. You are the witness of all things.

118. "If You punish them, they are Your servants, and if You forgive them, You are the almighty, the wise."

119. It will be said, "This is the day when the truthfulness of the truthful will benefit them. They have deserved gardens with flowing streams, wherein they abide forever. God is pleased with them, and they are pleased with Him. This is the great triumph."

120. To God belongs the kingdom of the heavens and the earth, and everything in them, and He is omnipotent.

Sura 6: Livestock (Al-An'aam)

In the name of God, most gracious, most merciful

1. Praise be to God, who created the heavens and the earth, and devised the darkness and the light. Yet, the disbelievers set up idols to rank with their Lord.
2. He is the one who created you from clay, then appointed the life spans, and a predetermined end that is known only to Him. Yet, you still harbor doubts.
3. And He is the one God of the heavens and the earth. He knows your secrets, and your declarations, and He knows everything you earn.

The Disbelievers

4. Whenever a sign comes to them from their Lord, they turn away therefrom.
5. Because they rejected the truth when it came to them, they have deserved the consequences thereof.
6. Did they not see how many generations we annihilated before them? We had established them on earth, even more than we did for you, and we sent the sky pouring on them generously, and provided them with flowing rivers. Then, because of their sins, we annihilated them and substituted other generations.
7. Even if we sent down to you a physical book, written on paper, so that they could touch it with their hands, the disbelievers would have said, "This is no more than clever magic."
8. And they said, "Why does he not have an angel come down with him?" If we send down an angel, the whole matter would be terminated, and no one would be respited.
9. Even if we sent an angel, we would send him as a man, and would confuse them as they are confused.
10. Messengers before you have been ridiculed, and those who ridiculed them were subsequently condemned.
11. Say, "Roam the earth, and note the consequences for the rejectors."

God Alone Worthy of Worship

12. Say, "To whom belongs everything in the heavens and the earth?" Say, "To God." He has decreed mercy as one of His attributes, and He will gather you on the inevitable day of resurrection. It is the disbelievers who lose their souls.

13. To Him belongs everything that inhabits the night and the day, and He is the hearer, the omniscient.

14. Say, "Shall I seek a Lord other than God, when He is the initiator of the heavens and the earth, and He feeds and needs no food?" Say, "I am commanded to be the first to submit, and never to set up any idol."

15. Say, "I fear, if I disobey my Lord, the retribution of a profound day."

16. Anyone who is spared the retribution on that day, God has showered him with mercy, and this is the great triumph.

Only God Benefits and Harms

17. If God afflicts you with adversity, there is none who can relieve it except He. And if He blesses you with something good, He is omnipotent.

18. He is the supreme master over His creatures, and He is the wise, the cognizant.

Quran: The Only Divine Revelation to Muhammad

19. Say, "Whose testimony is greater?" Say, "God is the witness between me and you. This Quran has been revealed to me in order to preach to you therewith, and whomever it reaches. Indeed, you bear witness that there are other gods besides God." Say, "I do not bear such witness." Say, "There is only one God, and I disown the idols you set up."

20. Those who received previous scripture recognize this (Quran), as they recognize their own children. Those who lost their souls are the ones who disbelieve.

Hadith and Sunna: Imperceptible Idolatry*

21. Who is more wicked than those who invent lies, then attribute them to God, or reject His revelations? Indeed, the wicked never succeed.

22. On the day when we gather them all together, we will say to the idol worshipers. "Where are the idols you had fabricated?"

6:21-24. *These profound verses identify those who advocate "**Hadith**" and "**Sunna**" as idolaters who have set up Muhammad as an idol against his will. They invented lies and claimed that they were divine revelations to the prophet (6:21). They vehemently deny that they idolize the prophet, all the way through the day of judgment, even as they face God almighty (6:22-23). They use their invented lies as sources of jurisprudence, to suit their own traditions and superstitions, in total defiance of God and the prophet (see 6:19). On the day of judgment, Muhammad will disown those who idolize him, just as Jesus and the saints will disown those who idolize them (see 6:24, 16:86, 19:81, 36:74, and the Gospel of Matthew 7:23). The true believers uphold the Quran, the whole Quran, and nothing but the Quran. (see 6:114).*

23. Their only pretense will be, "By God our Lord, we were not idolaters!"

24. Note how they lied to themselves, and that the idols they made up abandon them.

25. Some of them may listen to you; but we place shields on their hearts to prevent them from understanding (the Quran), and deafness in their ears. Thus, no matter what kind of miracle they see, they will not believe. Then, when these disbelievers come to debate with you, they would say, "These are simply tales from the past."

26. And they divert others from the Quran, as they themselves stay away from it. Thus, they only destroy themselves, without perceiving.

27. If you could only envision them as they face hell; they would say, "Oh, we wish if we could be sent back, then never reject the revelations of our Lord, and be perfect believers!"

28. However, they will only say this after their true identity has been exposed. If they are given a second chance, they will revert right back to what was forbidden them; they are liars.

29. They had said, "We only live this life, and will not be resurrected."

30. If you could only envision them as they face their Lord; He will say, "Is this not the truth?" They would say, "Yes, by our Lord." He will say, "Then suffer the consequences of your disbelief."

31. Losers indeed are those who deny the meeting with God, until the hour comes to them suddenly, then say, "What a disaster it was that we wasted the first life." They will carry their sins on their backs; what a miserable load.

32. This first life is no more than illusions and vanity, while the abode of the hereafter is far better for the righteous, Would you not understand?

God's Messengers Persecuted

33. We realize that you are saddened by what they say. However, it is not you that they reject; it is God's revelations that the wicked disregard.

34. The messengers before you have been rejected, and they steadfastly persevered in the face of rejection, and they were persecuted until our victory came to them. And this will always be the case; God's system is unchangeable. I have narrated to you some history of the messengers.

35. You may find it too much that they disregard you. However, even if you dig a tunnel through the earth, or erect a ladder into the sky, and produce a miracle for them, (they still will not believe). Had God willed, He could have guided all of them. Therefore, do not be like the ignorant ones.

36. Only those who can hear will respond. As for the dead, God will resurrect them, and they will be returned to Him.

37. And they said, "If only a miracle could come down to him from his Lord!" Say, "God is certainly able to send down a miracle." However, the majority do not know.

Quran: All the Commandments We Need

38. Any creature on earth, and any bird that flies with wings, are all nations like you. We did not leave anything out of this scripture.* To their Lord, they will all be gathered.

39. Those who reject our revelations are deaf, dumb, and in total darkness. Whomever God wills, He sends astray; and whomever He wills, He places on a straight path.

40. Say, "What if God's retribution came to you, or the hour came to you, would you implore other than God, if you are truthful?"

41. Indeed, you would implore Him alone, then He relieves your problem, if He wills; you would forget your idols.

The Standard Method

42. We have sent to nations before you, and we afflicted them with hardship and adversity, that they may implore.

43. If only, when our affliction came to them, they implored. But instead, their hearts were hardened, and the devil adorned their works in their eyes.

44. Consequently, because they discarded the message given to them, we opened for them the gates of everything. Then, just as they rejoiced with such givings, we seized them suddenly, and they became stunned.*

45. Thus, the wicked are wiped out, and praise be to God, Lord of the universe.

6:38. *The connection between the Quran's miraculous numerical code, and the rejection of "Hadith" and "Sunna" as satanic inventions, becomes obvious when we realize that this statement (We have left nothing out of this scripture) consists of 19 Arabic letters, the verse number is 38 (19 × 2), and that verse 19 states that the Quran is the only divine revelation to Muhammad, and that the statement, "He revealed the Quran fully detailed," also consists of 19 letters, and is found in verse 114 (19 × 6) of this sura. See also Appendix 16.*

6:44. *The Muslims of today have abandoned the Quran, and adopted the inventions of "Hadith" and "Sunna" in complete defiance of God and the prophet (see 24:1-2, 25:30, Appendices 7, 11, 13, & 15). Therefore, it appears that the vast oil wealth given to Saudi Arabia, the Arabian Gulf states, Kuwait, Iraq, Iran, Indonesia, and North Africa is in fact a curse that leads to the inevitable retribution predicted in this verse. Before the guilty is thrown out the window, he is taken to the tenth floor.*

God Alone Omnipotent, While the Messengers Powerless

46. Say, "What if God took away your hearing and your eyesight, and sealed your hearts, which god, other than God, can restore them to you?" Note how we explain the revelations, then they still deviate.
47. Say, "What if God's retribution came to you suddenly, or after a warning. is it not the wicked who are destroyed?"
48. We do not send the messengers except as preachers and warners. Then, whoever believes and leads a righteous life will have nothing to fear, nor will they grieve.
49. As for those who reject our revelations, they have deserved the retribution for their wickedness.
50. Say (O Muhammad), "I do not claim that I possess the treasures of God, nor do I know the future, nor do I claim to be an angel. I simply follow what is revealed to me." Say, "Is the blind the same as the seer? Can you not reflect?"
51. You shall preach with the Quran to those who reverence the gathering before their Lord. They have none besides Him as Lord; nor do they have an intercessor. Perhaps they will attain salvation.

First Believers: The Poor and Oppressed

52. Do not dismiss those who implore their Lord day and night, seeking only Him. You are not accountable for anything they do, nor are they accountable for anything you do. If you dismiss them, you will be a wrongdoer.
53. We thus put the people to the test by each other. Thus, some would say, "Are these the ones blessed by God?" Is God not fully aware of the deserving ones?
54. Thus, when those who believe in our revelations come to you, you shall say, "Peace be upon you. Your Lord has decreed mercy as His attribute. Thus, if anyone falls in sin due to ignorance, then repents thereafter, and reforms, then God is forgiver, merciful."
55. We thus explain the revelations, and expose the ways of the wicked.
56. Say, "I have been stopped from worshiping the idols you had set up besides God."* Say, "I will not follow your ideas, lest I go astray and never find guidance."
57. Say, "I have a profound sign from my Lord, and you disbelieve therein. I have no power to afflict you with the doom you challenge me to bring. Judgment is absolutely God's; He exacts the truth, and He is the best judge."

6:56. *Before being guided and blessed by God, Muhammad worshiped idols like the rest of his pre-Islamic community (see also 40:66 and 93:7).*

58. Say, "If I had the power to bring judgment, the whole matter between me and you would have been finished already. God knows best who the wicked are."

59. At Him are the keys to all secrets; no one knows them except He. He knows everything on land and in the sea; not a single leaf falls without His knowledge, nor a seed in the darkness of the soil, nor anything that is wet or dry, all in a profound record.

60. And He is the one who puts you to death during the night,* and knows everything you do during the day. He resurrects you therein, until your predetermined life span is fulfilled, then you are returned to Him, then He informs you of everything you have done.

61. He is the supreme being above His creatures, and He appoints guards to protect you. Then, when death comes to the one of you, our messengers put him to death without delay.

62. Then they are returned to God, their true Lord. Indeed, judgment belongs to Him alone, and He is the most efficient reckoner.

63. Say, "Who saves you from the darkness of land and sea?" You implore Him publicly and secretly, "If He only saves us from this one, we will be appreciative."

64. Say, "God saves you from that one, and from all kinds of disasters, then you set up idols."

65. Say, "He is able to pour upon you retribution from above you, and from beneath your feet. Or He may divide you into sects, and let you suffer the tyranny of one another." Note how we explain the revelations, that they may comprehend.

66. Your people have rejected this (Quran), although it is the truth! Say, "I am not your protector.

67. "Everything will be ultimately known, and you will surely find out."

Stay Away From the Wicked

68. When you see those who mock our revelations, do not stay with them, unless they change their subject. If the devil causes you to forget, then you shall leave the wicked people as soon as you remember.

69. Those who maintain righteousness are not accountable for anything those people do, but this may serve as a reminder; perhaps they observe righteousness.

6:60. The period between death and resurrection passes on each one of us like one night of sleep, complete with dreams (see also 2:259, 18:19 & 25, and Appendix 14). Since each one of us did in fact experience the first death (see 2:28 and 40:11), we should know exactly how the second and final death will feel like.

70. And stay away from those who take their religion in vain and play, and were distracted by this life. Admonish them with the Quran, lest a soul may suffer the retribution, and finds none to protect it from God or intercede therefor. Even if it offered any kind of ransom, it will not be accepted therefrom. They have deserved boiling drinks, and painful retribution for their disbelief.

71. Say, "Shall we idolize besides God what possesses no power to benefit us, or harm us, and turn back on our heels after being guided by God?" That would be like one duped by the devils, and rendered totally perplexed, while his friends plead with him to be guided, saying, "Come along with us." Say, "God's guidance is the true guidance, and we are commanded to submit to the Lord of the universe.

72. "And we are commanded to observe the **salat** prayers, and to observe God; He is the one before whom you will be gathered."

73. And He is the one who created the heavens and the earth, truthfully, and whenever He says, "Be," it is. His word is the truth, and absolute kingship belongs to Him on the day the trumpet is blown. He is the knower of all secrets and declarations, and He is the wise, the cognizant.

Abraham Discovers God

74. Recall that Abraham said to his father Azar, "How could you consider these statues to be gods? I see that you and your people have gone astray."

75. Because of this, we decided to show Abraham the marvels of the heavens and the earth, and to endow him with certainty.

76. Thus, when the night fell, he saw a planet, and said, "This is my Lord." But when it set, he said, "I dislike anything that sets."

77. When he saw the moon rising, he said, "This is my Lord." Then, when it set, he said, "Unless my Lord guides me, I will be one of the strayers."

78. When he saw the sun rising, he said, "This must be my Lord; this is the biggest." But when it set, he said, "O my people, I disown your idolatry.

79. "I have turned my face towards the one who initiated the heavens and the earth, worshiping Him alone, and never worshiping idols."

80. When his people argued with him, he said, "Do you argue with me about God, after He has guided me? I have no fear from the idols you set up. Only what my Lord wills shall prevail. The knowledge of my Lord encompasses all things. Would you not take heed?

81. "How could I possibly fear your idols, when you do not fear that you idolize powerless gods. Which side is worthy of security, if you know?"

82. Those who believe, and do not adulterate their belief with wickedness, are worthy of security, and they are guided.

83.   We supported Abraham's argument against his people for we raise
      whomever we choose to higher ranks. Your Lord is wise, omniscient.

.84.   And we granted him Isaac and Jacob, and we guided them as we had
      guided Noah previously. And from his descendants, (we guided) David,
      Solomon, Job, Joseph, Moses, and Aaron. We thus reward the
      righteous.

85.   And Zachariah, John, Jesus, and Elias; they were all pious.

86.   And Ishmael, Elija, Jonah, and Lot; each we set apart from the rest.

87.   Also others among their ancestors, their descendants, and their siblings;
      we chose them, and guided them in a straight path.

88.   Such is God's guidance that He bestows upon whomever He wills from
      among His servants. Had they ever set up any idol besides God, all their
      works would have been nullified.

89.   Those are they to whom we gave the scripture, wisdom, and
      prophethood. If these people disbelieve therein, we will entrust it to
      others who would not reject it.

90.   Those are they whom God has guided; you shall follow their guidance.
      Say, "I do not ask you for any wage. I simply deliver this message for all
      the people."

91.   They never understood God as He should be when they said, "God does
      not send down anything to a human being." Say, "Who then sent down
      the scripture that Moses brought, with light and guidance for the people?
      You wrote it down on paper, though you concealed much thereof, and
      you learned things that neither you nor your parents ever knew." Say,
      "God sent it down," then leave them in their confusion, playing.

True Believers of all Religions Will Accept Quran

92.   Similarly, this is a blessed scripture that we reveal, confirming all
      previous scriptures, and to preach the central community and all around
      it. Those who truly believe in the hereafter will believe in this, and will
      observe their **salat** prayers.

93.   Who is more evil than one who invents lies then attribute them to God, or
      claim to have received divine revelations, when nothing has been revealed
      to him, or say, "I can write the same things as God?" If you could only
      envision the wicked at the time of death: the angels extend their hands to
      them, saying, "Let go of your souls. Today you suffer humiliating
      retribution for uttering untruths about God, and for being too arrogant
      to accept His revelations.

94. "Now, you come back to us as individuals, just as we created you the first time, and you left behind everything we had provided for you. We do not see any of your intercessors that you invented and idolized. All ties among you are now severed, and the idols you invented have disowned you."

God Alone Worthy of Worship

95. God is the one who germinates the grains and the seeds; He produces the live from the dead, and the dead from the live. Such is God; how could you deviate?

96. He generates the morning break, and designed the night for your rest, and the sun and moon as timing devices. Such is the design of the almighty, the omniscient.

97. And He is the one who designed the stars to guide you through the darkness of land and sea. We have explained the revelations for those who know.

98. And He is the one who created you from one person, then reproduced you generation after generation. We have explained the revelations for those who comprehend.

99. And He is the one who sends down water from the sky, to produce all kinds of plants, and from the green vegetation we produce compounded grains. From the palm trees, we produce hanging fruit from their sheaths. And we produce gardens of grapes, olives, and pomegranate: fruit that are similar yet dissimilar. Look at the fruits thereof as they develop, and note their freshness. All these are proofs for people who believe.

100. They even set up idols from among the jinns, though He created them. And they invented sons and daughters for Him, without knowledge. Most glorified and most exalted He is, over and above anything they describe.

101. He is the designer of the heavens and the earth. How could He need a son? Nor did He need a wife. Instead, He created all things, and He is fully aware of all things.

102. Such is God your Lord. There is no god except He; the creator of all things. Therefore, you shall worship Him Alone. He is in full control of all things.

103. No vision can ever encompass Him, while He encompasses all vision. He is the compassionate, the cognizant.

104. Proofs have come to you from your Lord; if anyone sees, it will be for his own good, and if anyone turns blind, it will be to his detriment. I am not a guardian over you.

105. We thus explain the revelations to let them realize that you have learned. We clarify the revelations for those who know.

106. You shall follow what is revealed to you from your Lord; there is no god except He; and disregard the idol-worshipers.
107. Had God willed, they would not have worshiped idols. We did not appoint you as their guardian, nor are you their advocate.

Do Not Berate Their Idols

108. Do not curse the idols they set up besides God, lest they curse God maliciously due to ignorance. We have adorned for every community their works in their eyes, then they will be returned to their Lord to inform them of everything they did.
109. They swore by God solemnly that if a miracle came to them, they would believe. Say, "Miracles come only from God." What makes you think that even if a miracle came to them, they will not continue to disbelieve?
110. We control their minds and their visions, as a consequence of their initial decision to disbelieve, and we keep them in their transgression blundering.
111. Thus, even if we send the angels down to them; even if the dead spoke to them; even if we gather before their eyes all kinds of miracles, they can never believe except in accordance with God's will. Indeed, the majority of people are unaware.

Hadith and Sunna: The Great Test to Distinguish True Muslims From False Muslims

112. Additionally, we have appointed for every prophet enemies from among the human devils and jinn devils, who invent and narrate to each other fancy words in order to deceive. Had your Lord willed, they would not have done it. You shall disregard them and their inventions.
113. (This is God's will) in order that the minds of those who do not really believe in the hereafter may listen thereto, and accept it, and to have them commit what they are supposed to commit.*
114. Shall I seek other than God as a source of law, when He revealed to you this book fully detailed? Even those who received previous scripture recognize that it came down from your Lord, truthfully. Therefore, you shall not harbor any doubt.

6:113. *One may grow up in an environment that equates goodness with belief in God and the hereafter. Consequently, this person may profess belief, in order to be good, while in fact his innermost convictions are contrary. God teaches us in these verses that the inventions of "Hadith" and/or "Sunna" was designed to distinguish the true Muslims from the false Muslims. The true Muslims uphold the Quran, the whole Quran, and nothing but the Quran, as we see in 6:114.*

115.   The word of your Lord is complete, in truth and justice. Nothing shall abrogate His words. He is the hearer, the knower.

116.   If you obey the majority of people on earth, they will divert you from the path of God. They only follow conjecture, and they only guess.*

117.   Indeed, your Lord knows best who has strayed from His path, and He knows best who are the guided ones.

Permission From the Creator Before Killing Animals

118.   You shall eat from that upon which the name of God has been pronounced, if you are really believers in His revelations.

119.   Why should you not eat from that upon which the name of God has been pronounced? God has detailed for you everything that is prohibited, unless you are forced. Many people mislead others with their own opinions, without knowledge. Indeed, your Lord is fully aware of the transgressors.

120.   You shall forsake both obvious and hidden sins, for those who commit sins will pay for their evil works.

121.   Do not eat from that upon which the name of God has not been pronounced, for it is an abomination. The devils will inspire their allies to argue with you, and, if you obey them, you will be idol worshipers.*

122.   Is one who used to be dead, then we granted him life, and provided him with a beacon with which he walks among the people; is he equal to one eternally committed to darkness? We have adorned for the disbelievers their works in their eyes.

123.   And we have appointed in every community prominent criminals who plot and scheme therein. However, they plot and scheme against their own souls, without perceiving.

124.   And when a revelation comes to them, they say, "We will not believe, unless we are given what is given to God's messengers." God knows best who is worthy of delivering His message. These criminals will suffer debasement at God, and a severe retribution for their scheming.

6:116   Unfortunately, the majority of Muslims have flunked the **"Hadith"** test. Instead of following the proven revelations of God, they follow what is conjectured to be the prophet's utterances and/or actions. Thus, they disobey God and the prophet by following the **"Hadith"** guesswork (see Appendix 11).

6:121.   Most people underestimate the seriousness of making up lists of prohibitions. We are told here that following the dictates of unauthorized prohibitions, beyond the four Quranic prohibitions, is idolatry. See 5:3, and Appendix 13.

Scientific Miracle*

125. When God wants to guide someone, He opens his heart to Islam, and when He wants to send someone astray, He makes his chest straightened, like one who climbs towards the sky. God thus afflicts with unholiness those who do not believe.

126. This is the straight path of your Lord. We have explained the revelations for those who take heed.

127. They have deserved the abode of peace at their Lord, and He is their savior because of their works.

The Majority of People Heedless

128. On the day when we gather them all, "O you Jinns, you have claimed a majority of the humans." Their followers among the humans will say, "Our Lord, we enjoyed each other, until the life span You had appointed for us came to an end." God will say, "You have deserved hell, wherein you abide forever, in accordance with God's will. Your Lord is wise, omniscient."

129. We thus match the wicked as friends of each other, and let them suffer the company of each other, because of their deeds.

130. O you Jinns and humans, did you not receive messengers from among you, who narrated for you My revelations, and warned you about this day? They will say, "We bear witness against ourselves." They were distracted by this life, and they bore witness against themselves that they were disbelievers.

131. Thus, your Lord never destroys any community unjustly, without forewarning its people (through the messengers).

132. Everyone will be assigned a rank, in accordance with their works, and your Lord is never unaware of anything they do.

133. Your Lord needs no one; He is full of mercy. If He wills, He can get rid of you and substitute others, just as He established you from the progeny of other people.

134. What is promised to you herein will surely come to pass, and you can never escape.

135. Say, "O my people, do what you think is right, and I will. You will surely find out who the ultimate winner will be." Surely, the wicked will never succeed.

6:125.   At the time of Quran's revelations, no one knew that the proportion of oxygen becomes less and less as we climb towards the sky, causing one to gasp for breath.

Ancient Traditions

136. They even assigned for God a share of the crops and livestock He has provided for them, saying, "This is for God," according to their claims, "and this is for our idols." However, what was assigned to their idols never reached God, while that assigned to God invariably ended up at their idols. Evil indeed is their judgment.
137. Additionally, many idol worshipers were duped by their idols into killing their own children. Thus, they cause disasters, and confuse their religion for them. Had God willed, they would not have done it. You shall disregard them and their inventions.

Do Not Prohibit Lawful Things

138. They said, "These livestock and crops are prohibited; no one shall eat them, except whomever we will," according to their claims. Other livestock were forbidden from work, while others they did not pronounce God's name on them. All these are blasphemies against God, and He will punish them for such fabrications.
139. And they said, "What is in the wombs of these animals shall be reserved for our men, and prohibited for our women." However, if born still, they all shared therein. God will punish them for their claims. He is wise, omniscient.
140. Losers indeed are those who killed their own children foolishly,* due to ignorance, and those who prohibited God's provisions to them. They have gone astray, and were never guided.

Follow the Teachings of God Alone

141. God is the one who created gardens, trellised and untrellised, and palm trees, and vegetations of various tastes, and olives, and pomegranate; fruits that are similar yet dissimilar. Eat from the fruits thereof, and give the due proportion thereof to charity, on the day of harvest. And do not be wasteful, for God is displeased with the wasteful
142. And (He created) the livestock to carry your loads, and to provide clothes. Eat from God's provisions, and do not follow the steps of Satan, for he is your ardent enemy.

6:137 & 140. A famous recent example is the 1978 execution of a Saudi Arabian princess accused of adultery. God's law, as clearly stated in 24:1-2, calls for whipping, while the law of the idol-worshipers specifies death for the adulterers. See appendices 11 and 15 for the details.

143. (He created) eight kinds of livestock, two kinds of sheep, and two kinds of goats. Say, "Is it the two males that He prohibited, or the two females, or the contents of the wombs of the two females? Inform me, knowledgeably, if you are truthful."

144. And two kinds of camels, and two kinds of cattle. Say, "Is it the two males that He prohibited, or the two females, or the contents of the wombs of the two females? Did you witness God as He issued such prohibitions?" Who is more evil than one who invents lies, then attribute them to God, causing many people to stray without knowledge? Indeed, God never guides the wicked people.

Only Four Things Prohibited

145. Say, "I do not find in what is revealed to me anything prohibited for any eater except the animals that die of themselves, running blood, the meat of pigs,* for it is unclean, or animals dedicated to other than God. However, if one is forced to eat these, without being malicious or deliberate, then your Lord is forgiver, merciful."

146. For the Jews we prohibited animals with undivided hoofs, and the fat of cattle and sheep, except fat which is on the back, or the entrails, or mixed with bones. We did this as punishment for their transgression, and we are truthful.

147. If they disbelieve you, then say, "Your Lord is full of mercy, but His punishment cannot be evaded by the guilty."*

148. The idol worshipers would say, "Had God willed, we would not have idolized anything, nor our ancestors, and we would not have prohibited anything." Thus did those before them disbelieve, until they suffered our retribution. Say, "Do you have any knowledge that you can show us? You only follow conjecture, and you only guess."*

149. God possesses the most convincing proof; had He willed, He could have guided all of you.

6:145-146. *Note that when God wants to prohibit "meat," He specifically prohibits "meat," and when He wants to prohibit "fat," He specifically prohibits fat (6:146). Unfortunately, most Muslims have gone too far in prohibiting everything remotely related to the pig, including such things as soaps, tooth pastes, and even hair brushes. We must remember that God shows a great deal of displeasure at those who prohibit perfectly lawful things.*

6:147. *It is not mercy or justice when a teacher gives top grades to all the students.*

6:148. *Long lists of unauthorized prohibitions are found in the inventions called "**Hadith**" and/or "**Sunna**," which are not more than conjecture and guesswork.*

150.   Say, "Summon your witnesses who can testify that God prohibited this or that." Even if they do testify, do not testify as they do, and do not follow the opinions of those who reject our revelations, disbelieve in the hereafter, and set up idols to rank with their Lord.*

Do Not Bicker Over Minor Issues

151.   Say, "Come let me tell you what is really prohibited for you: you shall not set up any idol besides God; you shall honor your parents; you shall not kill your infants from fear of poverty, for we provide for you and for them; you shall not approach gross sins, obvious or hidden; you shall not kill, for God has made life sacred, except in the course of justice. These are God's commandments to you, that you may understand.

152.   You shall not approach the orphan's money, except in a righteous manner, until he reaches maturity. When you trade, you shall give full measure and weight, equitably. We never burden any soul beyond its means. When you bear witness, you shall be just, even against your own relatives. You shall fulfill your vows to God. These are God's commandments, that you may take heed.

153.   This is My straight path; you shall follow it, and do not follow any other paths, lest they take you away from the path of God. These are God's commandments, that you may attain salvation.

154.   We have given the scripture to Moses, detailing what is right, and explaining everything, and providing guidance and mercy, that they may believe in meeting their Lord.

155.   Similarly, this is a blessed scripture that we sent down; you shall follow it and work righteousness, that you may attain mercy.

156.   Thus, you cannot say, "The scripture was sent down for two previous groups, and we were unaware of their teachings."

157.   Nor can you say, "Had the scripture been sent down to us, we would have been better guided than they." A profound message has come to you from your Lord, and guidance and mercy. Consequently, who is more evil than one who rejects the revelations of God, and disregards them? We will punish those who disregard our revelation, a terrible punishment, for their heedlessness.

158.   Are they waiting until the angels, or your Lord, or some profound signs come to them? The day some profound signs come from your Lord, it will be too late for anyone to believe who has not believed already and gained righteousness. Say, "Keep waiting, and we too will wait."

6:150.   Accepting any prohibitions not specifically mentioned in Quran is idolatry. Although they confess belief in the hereafter, verse 113 tells us otherwise.

One Quran; One Islam

159. Those who divide their religion into sects do not belong with you (O Muhammad). Their judgment rests with God, and He will inform them of everything they did.*

160. Whoever does one righteous work, will be rewarded for ten; while the one who commits a sin is punished for only one. No one will suffer injustice.

Muhammad: A Follower of Abraham*

161. Say (O Muhammad), "My Lord has guided me in a straight path; the perfect religion of Abraham, the devoted monotheist; never was he an idol worshiper."

162. Say, "My **salat** prayers, my worship, and my life and death, belong to the Lord of the universe.

163. "He has no partner. These are the commandments given to me, and I am the first to submit."

6:159.   The only reason behind the existence of several Islamic sects today is that the Muslims have abandoned the Quran in favor of the human opinions of their leaders, who are in fact their idols. The single most important factor contributing to this unholy division is the invention of "**Hadith**" and "**Sunna**." Ironically, the prophet Muhammad will be the first to disown those who follow "**Hadith**" and/or "**Sunna**" on the day of judgment, just as those who idolize Jesus will be disowned by him. Those who obey God and the prophet are those who uphold the Quran, the whole Quran, and nothing but the Quran (see Appendix 15). Since there is only one Quran, there should be one Islam, and one Islamic congregation. As we learned from verses 19, 38, and 114 of this sura, the Quran is fully detailed, and needs no further explanation. Moreover, God Himself has informed us that only He will explain the Quran, as He puts it in the hearts of those worthy of it (see 40:44 and 75:19).

6:161.   When the false Muslims (see footnote 6:112-116) who follow "**Hadith**" and "**Sunna**" are faced with the Quranic reality that the Quran shall be the sole source of religious knowledge (6:19, 38, &114), their favorite argument is, "If the Quran is complete (see 6:114), where is the description of **salat** prayers?" This famous question reveals their ignorance and isolation from Quran. They are obviously unaware of the Quran's statements that **salat** was originally revealed to Abraham, then transmitted to us generation after generation, and that Muhammad prayed according to the religion of Abraham, Islam, before he, Muhammad, was appointed a messenger (see 2:128, 2:135, 3:67-68, 3:95, 4:125, 16:123, 21:73, 22:27, 22:78, and Appendix 8).

164. Say, "Shall I seek other than God as a Lord, when He is the Lord of all things?" Whatever anyone earns is for his own account. No burdened soul will bear the burdens of another. To your Lord is your ultimate return, then He will inform you of everything you disputed.

165. He is the one who made you inherit the earth, and He raised some of you above others, in order to put you to the test. Your Lord is swift in imposing retribution, and He is forgiver, merciful.

Sura 7:   The Purgatory (Al-A'raaf)

In the name of God most gracious, most merciful

1. A. L. M. S.*

Quran: The Only Source of Islamic Knowledge

2. This scripture is God's revelation to you; let not any doubt enter your heart. It is sent down to you, to preach therewith, and to serve as a message to the believers.

3. You shall follow what is sent down to you from your Lord, and do not follow any idols besides Him.* Only a few of you take heed.

4. We have annihilated many communities, and our retribution came to them as they slept, or wide awake.

5. They had no discourse, when our retribution came to them, but to say, "We have been wrong indeed."

6. Certainly, we will question those who received the message, and certainly, we will question the messengers.

7. We will then inform them with real knowledge, for we were never absent.

8. The weighing on that day will be equitable. As for those whose weights are heavy, they are the winners.

9. Those whose weights are light will be the losers; they have lost their souls as a consequence of discarding our revelations.

10. We put you in control of the earth, and established for you provisions therein. Only a few of you are appreciative.

Satan: The Great Challenge*

11. We created you, then shaped you, then said to the angels, "Fall prostrate before Adam." They fell prostrate, except Iblis (Satan); he was not with the prostrators.

12. God said, "What prevented you from prostrating, when I ordered you?" He said, "I am better than he; You created me from fire, and created him from clay."

13. God said, "Therefore, go down therefrom, for you are not to be proud therein. Get out; you are debased."

7:1.   See Appendix 1 for details of the Quran's secret numerical code, and the meaning of these Quranic initials.

7:3.   Those who worship God alone, follow God's scripture alone. Those who follow anything else as a source of jurisprudence are idol worshipers, as defined by this verse.

14. He said, "Respite me till the day of resurrection."
15. God said, "You are respited."
16. He said, "Since You willed that I go astray, I will always skulk on Your straight path, and mislead them.
17. "Then I will come to them from their front, from behind them, from their right, and from their left, and You will find most of them unappreciative."
18. God said, "You are evicted therefrom, despised and debased. Those who follow you, will join you in hell.
19. "As for you, Adam, dwell with your wife in Paradise, and eat therefrom as you please. But do not approach this one tree, lest you become wrongdoers."
20. But the devil whispered to them, in order to expose what was hidden from them, namely, their bodies. He said, "Your Lord did not prohibit you from this tree, except to prevent you from becoming angels, or becoming immortal."
21. And he swore to them, "I am sincerely advising you."
22. He thus duped them, and when they tasted the tree, their bodies became visible to them, and they started to cover themselves with the leaves of Paradise. Their Lord called upon them, "Did I not forbid you from this tree, and tell you that the devil is your ardent enemy?"
23. They said, "Our Lord, we have wronged our souls and unless you forgive us, and have mercy on us, we will be losers."
24. God said, "Go down therefrom, as enemies of one another. On earth will be your habitation and provision for a while."
25. God said, "You will live therein, die therein, and get resurrected thereon."
26. O children of Adam, we have sent down to you garments to cover your bodies, and to serve as luxury. The garment of righteousness is the best. These are God's revelations to you, that you may take heed.
27. O children of Adam, let not the devil mislead you, as he evicted your parents from Paradise, and removed their garments in order to show them their bodies. He and his tribe can see you, while you cannot see them. We have assigned the devils as companions to those who do not believe.

7:11-25.   Why were we created? Although the angels saw God, and knew that He was the absolute master, Satan entertained rebellious ideas inside his head, and God knew about these ideas (see 2:30). In order to expose Satan's rebellious ideas, God created Adam, and ordered the angels to bow down to him. The other reason for creating us is to show the angels that a creature who never sees God can reach God and worship Him alone. (See Appendix 6 for details).

God Never Advocates Evil

28. They commit evil, then say, "We found our parents doing this, and God commanded us to do it." Say, "God never advocates evil. Do you say about God what you do not know?"

29. Say, "My Lord advocates justice, and to devote yourselves completely to the worship of God alone, at every place of worship. He is the one who created you, and He is the one who resurrects you."

30. He guides some people, while others are committed to straying. They have chosen the devils as masters, instead of God, and they think they are guided.*

31. O children of Adam, you shall dress nicely when you go to the mosque. And eat and drink moderately, for God loves not the gluttonous.

Do Not Prohibit Lawful Things*

32. Say, "Who has forbidden the nice things that God produces for His creatures, and the good provisions?" Say, "For those who believe in this life, these things will be exclusively theirs on the day of resurrection." We thus explain the revelations for those who know.

33. Say, "My Lord prohibits only evil works, be them obvious or hidden, and sinfulness, and aggression without justification, and to set up powerless idols besides Him, and to invent lies then attribute them to God."

34. Each community has a predetermined life span; once their end comes, they cannot delay it by one hour, nor advance it.

Follow the Teachings of God Alone

35. O children of Adam, when messengers from among you come to you preaching My revelations, those among you who observe righteousness and reform, will have nothing to worry about, nor will they grieve.

36. As for those who reject our revelations, and are too arrogant to accept them, they have deserved hell; they abide therein forever.

7:30. *Those who follow and advocate "**Hadith**" and/or "**Sunna**" firmly believe that they are righteous, and that they are duely honoring and obeying the prophet! Thus, they are exactly like the Christians who firmly believe that they are duely honoring and obeying Jesus. The Quranic fact, however, is that these people have fallen in Satan's formidable trap, as indicated by this verse (see also 6:112-116).*

7:32. *If it is not SPECIFICALLY prohibited in Quran, it must not be prohibited.*

37. Who is more wicked than one who invents lies then attribute them to God, or rejects His revelations?* These will attain their due share in this life, then, when our messengers come to terminate their lives, they will say, "Where are those idols that you set up besides God?" They will answer, "They have abandoned us." They will bear witness against themselves, that they were disbelievers.

What Happened on the Day of Judgment*

38. God said, "Join the previous generations of Jinns and humans in hell." As each generation entered, they cursed each others. When all of them were gathered therein, the last one said of the first, "Our Lord, these people misguided us, so double the punishment for them." God said, "Each is suffering double, but you do not know."

39. And the first one said of the last, "Since you had an advantage over us, suffer the retribution for your own works."

40. Indeed, those who reject our revelations, and were too arrogant to accept them, the gates of heaven will never open for them, until the camel can pass through the needle's eye. We thus requite the guilty.

41. Hell will be their abode, with barriers above them. We thus punish the wicked.

42. As for those who believe and lead a righteous life, and we never burden any soul beyond its means, they have deserved Paradise; they abide therein forever.

43. We remove all traces of hatred from their hearts. Rivers will flow beneath them, and they will say, "Praise be to God, who guided us towards this; we were not to be guided without His guidance. Indeed, the messengers of our Lord have brought the truth." They were told,"This is the Paradise you have deserved for your works."

7:37.   *The followers of "**Hadith**" are committing both evils; they invent lies then claim that they are divine inspiration, and they reject God's revelations in this Quran stating clearly that the Quran is complete, perfect, needs no explanation, and shall be the sole source of jurisprudence (see 6:19, 38, 112-116, and 75:19).*

7:38-51.   *These verses are written in the past tense, like the vast majority of the Quran's statements. They narrate events that actually took place on the day of judgment, as witnessed by God. Of course, the day of judgment is still in the future for us, but not so for God.*

Initially, there will be four distinct groups in the hereafter, namely, the high heaven, the lower heaven, the purgatory, and hell. Later, the purgatory will be merged into the lower heaven (see suras 55 and 56, and Appendix 10 for details).

44. The dwellers of Paradise called upon the dwellers of hell, saying, "We have found exactly what our Lord had promised us; have you found what your Lord had promised you?" They answered, "Yes," then an announcer announced that the curse of God had befallen the wicked.

45. They are those who divert others from the path of God, seek to distort it, and disbelieve in the hereafter.

46. Between the two sides there will be a barrier, while the purgatory will be occupied by people who recognize each group by their marks. They called the dwellers of Paradise, saying, "You have really attained peace." They did not enter it by wishful thinking.

47. Then, they turn their eyes towards the dwellers of hell, and say, "Our Lord, do not put us with these wicked people."

48. The dwellers of the purgatory will call upon the dwellers of hell, whom they recognize by their marks, saying, "Your great number did not help you, nor did your pride.

49. "Are those not the people you swore will never attain God's mercy? Indeed, it is they who were told. 'Enter Paradise; you have nothing to worry about, nor will you grieve.' "

50. The dwellers of hell called upon the dwellers of Paradise, saying, "Would you pour upon us some water, or some of God's provisions to you?" They said "God has forbidden them for the disbelievers."

51. They took their religion in vain and play, and were distracted by the worldly life. Therefore, we forget them today, because they forgot this day, and ignored our revelations.

52. We had given them a fully detailed scripture, with knowledge, guidance and mercy for those who believe.*

53. Are they waiting for the full interpretation thereof? The day its final interpretation comes, those who had ignored it in the past would say, "Indeed, the messengers of our Lord have brought the truth. Now, can we find intercessors to intercede on our behalf? Or, can we get another chance, in order to live differently?" Indeed, they have lost their souls, and their own inventions did not help them.

7:52.   *This is another clear verse stating that the Quran is "fully detailed" (see also 6:19, 38, and 114). Those who invent and advocate other sources of religious knowledge, such as Hadith, Sunna, and the works of various "scholars," flagrantly defy God and His messenger, and refuse to submit to the truth of the Quran. The true believers, on the other hand, uphold the Quran, the whole Quran, and nothing but the Quran (see footnote 6:112-116).*

God Alone Worthy of Worship

54.   Indeed, your Lord is God; the one God who created the heavens and the earth in six days, then assumed all responsibility. The night overtakes the day, as it pursues it persistently, and the sun, the moon, and the stars are all subservient to His command. All creation and all authority belong to Him. Most exalted is God, the Lord of the universe.

55.   Implore your Lord publicly and secretly; He does not love the aggressors.

56.   And do not corrupt the earth after setting it in order. Implore Him out of reverence, and out of hope. Indeed, God's mercy is readily attainable by the righteous.

57.   And He is the one who sends the winds with good omen as a mercy from Him. Then, when they gather loaded clouds, we drive them to dead lands where we send down water, and produce all kinds of fruits. We will thus resurrect the dead, that you may take heed.

58.   The good land readily produces its plants, by the will of its Lord, while the bad soil produces only with great difficulty. We thus explain the revelations for those who are appreciative.

Believers: The Ultimate Winners

Noah

59.   We have sent Noah to his people, saying, "O my people, you shall worship God. You have no other god besides Him. I fear for you the retribution of a profound day."

60.   The leaders among his people said, "We see that you have gone astray."

61.   He said, "O my people, I have not gone astray; I am a messenger from the Lord of the universe.

62.   "I deliver my Lord's messages to you, and I care about you. I have learned from God what you do not know.

63.   "Is it such a wonder that a message from your Lord should come to you through a man like you? This is to alert you, and to make you righteous, that you may attain mercy."

64.   They disbelieved him, and consequently, we saved him and his followers in the ark, and we drowned those who rejected our revelations; they had turned blind.

Hūd

65.   To the people of 'Aad, we sent their brother Hūd. He said, "O my people, you shall worship God. You have no other god besides Him. Would you not work righteousness?

66. The leaders who disbelieved among his people said, "We see that you are foolish, and we believe that you are a liar."

67. He said, "O my people, I am not foolish; I am a messenger from the Lord of the universe.

68. I deliver to you my Lord's messages, and I honestly care about you.

69. "Is it such a wonder that a message from your Lord should come to you through a man like you, in order to alert you? Remember that He made you successors after the people of Noah, and multiplied you in number. Be appreciative of God's blessings, that you may succeed."

70. They said, "Do you want us to worship God alone, and discard what our parents have worshiped? Bring the doom you threaten us with, if you are truthful."

71. He said, "You have deserved debasement from your Lord, and displeasure. Do you argue with me on behalf of idols that you made up; you and your ancestors? God never placed any authority therein. Therefore, just wait, and I too shall wait."

72. Subsequently, we saved him and his followers with our mercy, and we wiped out those who rejected our revelations and refused to believe.

Saalih

73. To Thamud (we sent) their brother Saalih, saying, "O my people, worship God; you have no other god besides Him. A profound sign has come to you from your Lord. Here is God's camel as a miracle for you; you shall allow her to eat in God's earth, and do not touch her with any harm, lest you incur a painful retribution.

74. "Remember that He made you successors after the people of 'Aad, and put you in control of the earth, building mansions in its valleys, and carving homes out of the mountains. Remember God's favors, and do not roam the earth corruptingly."

75. The arrogant elders among his people said to their subjects who believed. "Are you sure that Saalih is sent by his Lord?" They said, "We believe in the message he brought."

76. The arrogant ones said, "We reject what you believe in."

77. Subsequently, they slaughtered the camel, and rebelled against the order of their Lord, and said, "Saalih, bring the doom you threaten us with, if you are really a messenger."

78. The quake then destroyed them, leaving them dead in their homes.

79. As he left them, he said, "O my people, I have delivered my Lord's message to you, and advised you, but you dislike anyone who advises you."

Lot

80. Lot said to his people. "You commit such an abomination; no one ever has done it before.
81. "You practice sex with the men, instead of the women! Indeed, you have transgressed."
82. The only answer his people gave him was, "Evict these people from your town; they wish to be holy."
83. Consequently, we saved him and his family, but not his wife, for she was doomed.
84. We showered them with a miserable shower. Note the consequences for the guilty.

Shu'aib

85. And to Midyan (we sent) their brother Shu'aib, saying, "O my people, worship God; you have no other god besides Him. A profound sign has come to you from your Lord. Therefore, you shall give full measure and weight, and do not cheat the people out of their rights, and do not corrupt the earth after it has been set in order. This is better for you, if you are believers.
86. "Do not practice highway robbery, and do not divert others from the path of God, seeking the crooked ways. And recall that you used to be few, and He multiplied you in number, and note the consequences for the wicked.
87. "Now that some of you have believed in the message I bring, while others disbelieved, wait until God judges between us. He is the best judge."
88. The arrogant elders among his people said, "We will banish you, O Shu'aib, and those who follow you, from our community, unless you revert to our religion." He said, " Are you going to force us?
89. "We will be inventing lies against God, if we ever revert to your religion, after God has saved us therefrom. We will never revert, unless it is the will of God our Lord. Our Lord is fully aware of all things. We trust in God. Our Lord, judge between us and our people with the truth. You are the best judge."
90. The elders who disbelieved among his people said, "If you follow Shu'aib, you will be losers."
91. Consequently, the quake destroyed them, leaving them dead in their homes.
92. It was as though those who disbelieved Shu'aib never existed. Those who disbelieved Shu'aib were the losers.
93. As he moved away from them he said, "O my people, I have delivered to you the messages of my Lord, and advised you. How could I grieve over disbelieving people?"

God's System

94. Whenever we sent a prophet to any community, we afflicted its people with hardship and adversity, that they may implore.

95. Then we substituted prosperity in place of the hardship, until they forget and say, "It was our ancestors who underwent adversity and prosperity." Consequently, we seized them suddenly, when they least expected.

96. Had the people of those communities believed and worked righteousness, we would have showered them with blessings from the heaven and the earth. But they disbelieved, and consequently, we punished them for their works.

97. Do the people of the the present communities guarantee that our affliction will not come to them at night while they sleep?

98. Do the people of the present communitees guarantee that our affliction will not come to them in the forenoon, as they play?

99. Have they taken God for granted? Indeed, no one takes God for granted, except the losers.

100. Did it ever occur to those who inherit the earth from previous generations that, if we will, we can punish them for their sins, and seal their hearts, so they cannot hear?

101. We narrate to you the history of those communities, who received messengers with profound signs. They refused to believe in what they had rejected before. God thus seals the hearts of disbelievers.

102. We find that most of them break their covenants; we found most of them wicked.

Moses

103. Subsequent to them, we sent Moses with our miracles to Pharaoh and his people, but they turned heedless. Note the consequences for the wicked.

104. Moses said, "O Pharaoh, I am a messenger from the Lord of the universe.

105. "My duty is never to say about God except the truth. I have come to you with a profound message from your Lord; let the children of Israel go."

106. He said, "If you brought a miracle, let us see it, if you are truthful."

107. He then threw down his staff, and it turned into a manifest serpent.

108. And he took out his hand, and it was white to the beholders.

109. The elders among Pharaoh's people said, "He is no more than an experienced magician.

110. "He wants to take you out of your land; so what do you think?"

111. They said, "Respite him and his brother, and send delegates to every town.

112. "Let them summon every experienced magician."

113. The magicians came to Pharaoh and said, "Do we get a reward, if we are the winners?"
114. He said, "Yes, and you will become close to me."
115. They said, "O Moses, either you throw, or we will throw."
116. He said, "You throw." When they threw, they bewitched the people's eyes, and intimidated them, and produced a profound magic.
117. We then inspired Moses to throw down his staff, whereupon it swallowed everything they fabricated.
118. Thus, the truth prevailed, and everything they did was nullified.
119. They were defeated right there, and became totally stumped.
120. And the magicians fell prostrate.
121. They said, "We believe in the Lord of the universe.
122. "The Lord of Moses and Aaron."
123. Pharaoh said, "Do you believe in him without my permission? This must be a plot you conspired in the city, in order to take its people therefrom. Surely, you will find out.
124. "I will cut your hands and feet on alternate sides, then I will crucify all of you."
125. They said, "We will then return to our Lord.
126. "You are enraged simply because we believed in the signs of our Lord when they came to us." "Our Lord, give us strength and steadfastness, and let us die as Muslims (submitters)."
127. The elders among Pharaoh's people said, "Will you leave Moses and his people to corrupt the earth, and discard you and your gods?" He said, "Let us kill their sons and spare their daughters. We have power over them."
128. Moses said to his people, "Turn to God for help, and maintain your steadfastness. The whole earth belongs to God, and He gives it to whomever He chooses. The ultimate victory belongs to the righteous."
129. They said, "We were persecuted before you showed up, and after you came to us." He said, "May your Lord destroy your enemy, and establish you as rulers of your land; He will see how you behave."
130. We afflicted Pharaoh's people with famine, and loss of crops, that they might take heed.
131. Whenever something good happened to them, they said, "We deserved this," but when adversity struck them, they blamed it on Moses and his people. They should have thought of God, but most of them do not know.
132. And they said, "No matter what kind of plague you bring on us, in order to bewitch us, we will never believe."
133. We then afflicted them with the flood, the locusts, the lice, the frogs, and the blood; profound signs. But they were too arrogant, and really wicked.

134. Whenever a plague afflicted them, they said, "Call upon your Lord, with whom you have connections. If you relieve this plague, we will believe, and will let the children of Israel go with you."

135. But as soon as we relieved their plague, temporarily, they broke their promise.

136. Consequently, we avenged from them, and drowned them in the sea, because they rejected our signs, and disregarded them.

137. And we blessed the oppressed people, and made them inherit the blessed land, East and West. Thus, the good promises of your Lord to the children of Israel were fulfilled, in return for their patience, and we nullified the works of Pharaoh and his people.

Idol Worship: A Perennial Human Disease

138. We delivered the children of Israel across the sea, and they passed by people who worshiped idols. They said, "O Moses, erect an idol for us, like the idols they have." He said, "You are foolish indeed.

139. "These people are disasterously afflicted, and abominable is what they do.

140. "Shall I seek other than God as deity, after He has set you apart from all the people?

141. "And after we delivered you from Pharaoh's people, who severely persecuted you; killing your sons and sparing your daughters? That was an exacting trial from your Lord."

142. We summoned Moses for thirty nights, and added to them ten, thus making the total audience with his Lord forty nights.* Moses said to his brother Aaron, "Stay behind with my people, maintain righteousness, and do not follow the ways of the wicked."

7:142. *This unique and deliberate way of stating these numbers is directly related to the Quran's secret numerical code. Since this Quranic miracle is based on numbers, it is only natural that any number mentioned in Quran must be involved. Thus, we find that the Quran contains 285 numbers, and this number is a multiple of 19 (19x15), and the total sum of the 285 numbers is 174,591 which is also a multiple of 19. Even if we remove all repetitions, we find that the remaining total is 162,146 which is a multiple of 19 as well. While other verses state that God summoned Moses for forty nights, this verse contains three numbers, which is necessary to conform with the Quran's miraculous code (see also 2:51, 2:196, and Appendix 1).*

God is Not Here*

143.   When Moses came to our audience, and his Lord spoke to him, he said, "My Lord, let me look at You and see You, " He said, "You cannot see Me, but look at the mountain; if it stays in its place, then you can see Me." Then, when his Lord manifested Himself to the mountain, He caused it to crumble, and Moses fell unconscious. When he came to, he said, "Glory be to You; I repent to You, and I am the first to believe."

144.   God said, "O Moses, I have chosen you over the rest of the people with My messages and by speaking with you. You should take what I bestowed upon you, and be appreciative."

145.   And we wrote for him on the tablets all kinds of enlightenments, and details of everything. "You shall firmly uphold these, and order your people to uphold the good teachings therein. I will point out for you the destiny of the wicked."

The Curse of Pride

146.   I will divert from My revelations those who commit pride on earth, without justification. Consequently, even if they see all kinds of miracles, they will not believe therein, and when they see the path of guidance they will not accept it as their path, and when they see the path of evil they will accept it as their path. That is because they have rejected our revelations, and disregarded them.

147.   Those who reject our revelations, and the meeting of the hereafter, their works are nullified. Have they not deserved the retribution by their actions?

148.   During his absence, the people of Moses sculpted from their jewelry a calf that produced a sound. Did they not see that it could not speak to them, nor help them in any way? They worshiped it and turned wicked.

149.   When they finally wised up, and realized that they had deviated, they said, "Unless our Lord has mercy on us, and forgives us, we will be losers indeed."

150.   And when Moses returned to his people, angry and disappointed, he said, "Evil indeed is what you did in my absence. Were you in such a hurry to rebel against your Lord?" And he threw down the tablets, and took hold of his brother's head, dragging him. Aaron said, "Son of my mother, the people took advantage of my weakness, and almost killed me. Please do not let my enemies rejoice over my predicament, and do not count me with the wicked."

7:143.   While God controls everything in the universe to the extent that not even a leaf falls without His knowledge (6:59), our world cannot stand the "physical" presence of God (see also 56:4-6, 69:13-16, suras 81, 82, & 84, and Appendix 10).

151.   Moses said, "My Lord, forgive me and my brother, and admit us into Your mercy. Of those who are merciful, You are the most merciful."

152.   Indeed, those who idolized the calf have deserved wrath from their Lord, and disgrace in this life. We thus requite the fabricators.

153.   As for those who fall in sin, then repent thereafter, and believe, your Lord is then forgiving, merciful.

154.   When Moses' anger subsided, he picked up the tablets, wherein guidance was written down, and mercy for those who reverence their Lord.

155.   Then Moses chose seventy men to have an audience with us. When the quake shook them, Moses said, "My Lord, had You willed, You could have annihilated them and me. Would You annihilate us because of what the fools among us had done? It was only Your test, whereby You send astray whomever You will, and guide whomever You will. You are our master, so forgive us, have mercy on us, and You are the best forgiver.

156.   "And grant us righteousness in this life, and in the hereafter, for we have submitted to You." God said, "My retribution afflicts whomever I will, and My mercy encompasses all things. However, I will designate it for those who work righteousness, and give to charity, and believe in our revelations.

Quran: God's Message to the Jews and the Christians*

157.   "Also for those who follow the messenger, the Gentile prophet, whom they find written in their Torah and Gospel. He exhorts them to work righteousness and to refrain from evil, and he permits for them the good things and prohibits the bad, and he unloads the burdens of their covenant and removes the chains that bind them. Thus, those who believe in him, honor him, support him, and follow the light that was sent down with him, they are the winners."

Muhammad: God's Messenger to ALL the People

158.   Say, "O people, I am God's messenger to all of you. To Him belongs the kingdom of the heavens and the earth. There is no god except He. He grants life and death." Therefore, you shall believe in God and His messenger, the Gentile prophet, who believes in God and His words, and follow him, that you may be guided.

The Example of Israel*

159.   Among the followers of Moses, there are those who guide by the truth and judge accordingly.

7:157.   *See the inside front cover of this book.*

160. We divided them into twelve tribal communities, and when his people asked for water, we inspired Moses to strike the rock with his staff. Whereupon, twelve springs gushed out therefrom; one for each tribe. And we shaded them with clouds, and sent down to them manna and quails. Eat from the good things we provided for you. They did not harm us (by rebelling); they only harmed themselves.

161. They were told, "Live in this town, and eat therefrom as you please. If you speak humbly, and enter the gate in peace, we will forgive your sins, and reward the pious."

162. But the wicked among them listened to commandments other than the commandments given to them, and consequently, we afflicted them with a curse from the sky because of their wickedness.

163. And ask them about the town by the sea shore. Because they desecrated the Sabbath, the fish came to them abundantly on the Sabbath day, but not so on the other days. We thus put them to the test, as a consequence of their wicked actions.

164. And recall that some of them said, "Why should you preach to people whom God is supposed to destroy or punish severely?" They answered, "Perhaps you can apologize to your Lord, and then attain salvation."

165. When they neglected the message given to them, we saved those who spoke up against evil, and punished the wrongdoers severely because of their wicked actions.

166. Because they transgressed the laws of prohibition, we said to them, "Be you despicable apes."

167. (Because of their transgressions,) your Lord has decreed that tyrants will rise up against them, and persecute them, until the day of resurrection. Indeed, your Lord is most strict in imposing retribution, and He is forgiving, merciful.

168. And we scattered them throughout the earth, into many communities. Some of them are righteous, while others are less than righteous. We tested them with prosperity, as well as adversity, that they may return.

7:159-171.   There is a great parallel between the followers of Moses, and the followers of Muhammad. This explains the fact that the history of Israel is narrated in such detail, and in such frequency throughout the Quran. The parallel becomes incredibly manifest when the reader notes that the followers of Moses invented the Mishnah (oral) and Gemarah (traditions) to overtake God's scripture, the Torah. The Muslims invented **hadith** *(oral) and* **sunna** *(traditions) to overtake Quran (see 24:1-2). Thus, both groups fell into idol worship in an almost identical manner.*

169. Then God replaced them with new generations who inherited the scripture. But they preferred the materials of this world, saying, "We will be forgiven." Then again, they became attracted to similar materials. Did they not covenant that they will uphold the scripture, and never to say about God except the truth? Did they not study the scripture? Indeed, the abode of the hereafter is far better for those who work righteousness. Do you not understand?

170. Those who strictly adhere to the scripture, and observe the **salat** prayers, we never neglect to recompense the righteous.

171. As we raised the mountain above them like a canopy, and they thought it was about to fall with them, we said, "You shall uphold what we have given you, strongly, and study the contents thereof, that you may attain salvation."

Knowledge of God: Our Natural Instinct

172. Recall that your Lord gathered all the descendants of Adam (before creation), and had them bear witness on themselves, saying, "Am I not your Lord?" They said, "Yes indeed, we bear witness." Therefore, you cannot say on the day of resurrection, "We never knew about this!"

173. Nor can you say, "It was our parents who set up idols, and we followed in their footsteps. Would you punish us for what the falsehood inventors have done?"*

174. We thus explain the revelations; perhaps they come back.

175. And recite for them the example of one who received our revelations, but disregarded them. Consequently, the devil pursued him, and he became lost.

176. Had we willed, we could have elevated him with the scripture, but he insisted on sticking to the ground, and following his own opinions. His example is that of the dog; if you give him attention he pants, and if you ignore him he pants. Such is the example of those who reject our revelations. You shall narrate these narrations, that they may reflect.

177. Miserable indeed is the example of those who reject our revelations; they only hurt themselves.

7:172-173. *A frequently asked question is, "What is the fault of one who grew up in a pagan society, or an atheistic environment?" These verses teach us that we have all witnessed our creator before the creation of Adam, and thus, we are born with the knowledge about God as a natural instinct. We also learn from these verses that no one is excused for not reaching and worshiping God. A prominent Quranic example is Abraham; he grew up in a pagan society, and his own father was the maker of idols. But he observed the world around him, and independently reached God (see 6:74-79).*

178. Whomever God guides is the truly guided one, and whomever He sends astray, these are the losers.

179. We have assigned to hell multitudes of jinns and humans. They are the ones who have hearts that do not understand, eyes that do not see, and ears that do not hear. They are like animals; no, they are even worse. They are unaware.*

180. To God belong the most beautiful names, so call upon Him therewith, and disregard those who distort His names.* They will be punished for their work.

181. Among our creation, there are those who guide with the truth, and live accordingly.

182. As for those who reject our revelations, we will lead them on, without them ever realizing it.

183. I will even encourage them; indeed, My scheming is formidable.

184. Have they not reflected on their friend? He is not crazy; he is simply a manifest warner.

Quran is the Only "**Hadith**"

185. Have they not seen the dominion of the heavens and the earth, and all the things that God created? Does it ever occur to them that the end of their life may be near at hand? In which **"hadith"** (narration), other than this, do they believe in?

186. Whomever God sends astray, will find none to guide him, and He leaves them in their transgression, blundering.

Do Not Idolize Muhammad

187. They ask you (O Muhammad) about the Hour, and when it will come! Say, "Only my Lord possesses such knowledge. None can reveal its time except He. Heavy indeed is such an event, in the heavens and the earth, and it will not come to you except suddenly." They ask you as if you are cognizant thereof. Say, "The knowledge thereof is with God alone, but most people do not know."

7:179. *See the Gospel of Matthew 13:13-16.*

7:180. *Among the common inventions are the so-called "99 names of God," many of which are not mentioned in Quran. Not to be outdone, those who idolize the prophet Muhammad against his will have invented 201 names of Muhammad. These names, dutyfully engraved on the walls of the prophet's mosque in Medina, include some of God's own exclusive names, such as "Al-Muhaymin = the Supreme Being," and "Al-Shaafee = The Healer."*

188.   Say (O Muhammad), "I possess no power to either benefit, or harm myself. Only what God wills takes place. Had I known the future, I would have increased my wealth, and no harm would have afflicted me. I am no more than a warner and preacher for those who believe.

Various Kinds of Idols*

189.   God is the one who created you from one person, then created his mate from him to keep him company. When a man gets together with his wife, she first carries a light load that she hardly notices. Then, when the load becomes heavier, they implore God their Lord, "If You give us a good healthy baby, we will be appreciative."

190.   However, when He gives them a good healthy baby, they set up an idol out of God's gift to them. Most exalted is God, over and above anything they idolize.

191.   How could they idolize idols that create nothing, and are themselves created?

192.   They are too powerless to help them, or even help themselves.

193.   And when you invite them to the right guidance, they refuse to follow you. It is the same for them, whether you invite them, or remain silent.

194.   Indeed, the idols you idolize besides God are servants like you. Therefore, pray to them, and see if they can answer your prayers, if you are truthful.

195.   Do they have legs with which they walk; do they have hands with which they strike; do they have eyes with which they see; do they have ears with which they hear? Say, "Implore your idols to destroy me, without delay.

196.   "My only master is God, the one God who revealed this scripture. He protects the righteous.

197.   "While the idols you set up besides Him cannot protect you, nor protect themselves."

198.   When you invite them to the right guidance, they do not hear. And you see them looking at you, but they do not see.

199.   You shall resort to pardon, maintain compassion, and be tolerant of the ignorant.

200.   And when the devil approaches you with any idea, seek refuge in God. He is hearer, omniscient.

201.   Whenever the righteous are touched by the devil's ideas, they remember; whereupon they become seers.

202.   Their comrades ceaselessly entice them to fall in sin.

7:189-197.   *Idols can be your children as shown here, or your spouse, or your leader, or your supervisor, or your own properties (see 18-42). Anything that takes priority over your creator's commandments is an idol.*

Muhammad Could Not Utter the Quran on His Own*

203. When you do not produce a certain revelation that is acceptable to them, they say, "Make it up!" Say, "I only follow what is revealed to me from my Lord. This Quran provides insight from your Lord, and guidance and mercy for those who believe."

204. When the Quran is recited, you shall listen to it, and hearken, that you may attain mercy.

205. And commemorate your Lord within yourself, publicly, secretly, and quietly, day and night. Do not be like those who are unaware.

206. Even those who are at your Lord are never too arrogant to worship Him, and they glorify Him, and fall prostrate for Him.

7:203. *See the Bible's Deuteronomy 18:18, John 12:49 & 16:13.*

Sura 8: The Spoils of War (Al-Anfaal)

In the name of God, most gracious, most merciful

1. They ask you about the spoils of war. Say, "The spoils of war belong to God and the messenger." You shall observe God, maintain righteousness among yourselves, and obey God and His messenger, if you are really believers.

2. The true believers are those whose hearts cringe upon remembering God, their faith intensifies upon hearing His revelations, and they trust in their Lord.

3. They observe the **salat** prayers, and from our provisions to them, they give to charity.

4. These are the true believers; they have deserved high ranks at their Lord, and forgiveness, and a generous recompense.

5. When your Lord willed that you leave your homes, some believers were exposed as reluctant believers.

6. They argued with you, even after the truth had become evident to them, as if they were driven to certain death.

7. And when God promised you victory over one group, they wanted to face the weaker group instead. But God wanted to establish the truth with His words, and punish the disbelievers (at your hands).

8. The truth is to be established, and falsehood is to be nullified, despite the evildoers.

9. Recall that you implored your Lord for help, and He answered your prayers, saying, "I will support you with one thousand angels, in succession."

10. God thus provided you with good news, and reassured your hearts. Victory comes only from God. God is almighty, wise.

11. He causes slumber to pacify you, and sends down water from the sky to clean you therewith, and removes the devil's curse from you, and reassures your hearts, and strengthens your footholds.

12. Your Lord instructed the angels, saying, "I will be with you as you support the believers, and I will throw terror in the hearts of the disbelievers. Therefore, strike above the necks, and strike every finger of them."

13. They have deserved this, because they oppose God and His messenger. For those who oppose God and His messenger, God is most strict in imposing retribution.

14. Suffer the war, O disbelievers, then end up in the retribution of hell.

15. O you who believe, when the disbelievers attack you, do not turn around and flee.

16. Anyone who turns his back to them, except in the course of fighting, or to support another group, has deserved wrath from God, and his destiny is hell, and a miserable abode.

17. It was not you who killed them; God is the one who killed them. It was not you who threw, when you threw; God is the one who threw. He just wanted to grant the believers a good test.* God is hearer, fully aware.

18. God thus frustrates the plans of the disbelievers.

19. You have sought victory, and victory has come against you. Thus, it would be best for you if you refrain. If you ever return (to aggression), we will repeat, and your numbers will never help you, no matter how great. God is always with the believers.

20. O you who believe, obey God and His messenger, and do not turn away from Him while you hear.

21. Do not be like those who say, "We hear," when they really do not.

22. Indeed, the worst creatures in the sight of God are the deaf and dumb, who have no common sense.

God Knows Which Among Us Deserve to Hear

23. If God knew of any good in them, He would have made them hear. Even if He made them hear, they still would turn away in aversion.

24. O you who believe, you shall hearken to God and the messenger when He invites you to that which gives you life. You should realize that God stands between you and your heart, and that you will be gathered before Him.

25. Beware lest a punishment may come and afflict not only the wicked in particular, and know that God is most strict in imposing retribution.*

26. Remember that you used to be few and oppressed, fearing that the people may snatch you, and He gave you refuge, supported you with His victory, and provided for you generously. You should be appreciative.

27. O you who believe, do not betray God and the messenger*, and do not betray those who trust you, while you know.

28. Remember that your money and children are a test, and that God possesses great rewards.

8:17. See Deuteronomy 20:4.

8:25. Therefore, if the righteous are too passive to preach the word of God, prohibit evil, and advocate righteousness, they will suffer along with their corrupt community.

*8:27. The greatest betrayal of Muhammad is the invention of "**Hadith**" and "**Sunna**" against his own instructions and the divine teachings of Quran (see Appendix 11).*

29.　O you who believe, if you observe God, He will enlighten you, remit your sins, and forgive you. God possesses unlimited grace.

The Believers Persecuted

30.　The disbelievers schemed to neutralize you, or kill you, or banish you. But they plot and scheme, and so does God; and God is the best schemer.
31.　And when our revelations are recited to them, they say, "We have heard and, if we wish, we can write the same. These are tales from the past."
32.　They even said, "Our God, if this is really the truth from You, then shower us with stones from the sky, or strike us with a terrible disaster."
33.　However, God was not to strike them while you were still with them; God was not to strike them while they had a chance to repent.
34.　Have they not deserved retribution from God, when they repelled from the Sacred Mosque, as if they were the keepers thereof? The true keepers thereof are the righteous, but most people do not know.

Salat Prayers Observed Before Muhammad

35.　Their prayer at the shrine was no more than deceit and alienation. They have deserved the retribution for disbelieving.*
36.　The disbelievers are spending their money on repelling others from the path of God. Thus, they will spend it, and it will return nothing but sorrow for them, and defeat, then they will be gathered in hell.
37.　God separates the bad from the good, piles up the bad on each other, then casts them in hell. These are the losers.
38.　Tell those who disbelieve that if they repent, their past transgressions will be forgiven. But if they revert, then the examples of the past should be remembered.
39.　You shall fight them to prevent persecution, and to practice God's religion in total freedom. Once they refrain, then God sees everything they do.
40.　If they turn away, then you should realize that God is your master; the best master, and the best supporter.

8:35. *Many Muslims erroneously believe that the* **salat** *prayers were first revealed through Muhammad. The Quran, however, teaches us that* **salat** *was first revealed to Abraham, then transmitted to us generation after generation (see for example 2:4, 2:128:, 2:135, 2:142, 3:67-68, 3:95, 4:125, 16:123, 21:73, 22:27, 22:78, and 73:20). Those who refuse to believe God's statements that the Quran is complete and perfect (6:19, 38, 114), as well as the ignorant, frequently ask the question, "If the Quran is complete, where is the description of* **salat**?"

Distribution of the Spoils of War

41.   Whatever you win as spoils of war, you shall set aside one fifth thereof for God and the messenger, and donate it to the (poor) relatives, the orphans, the needy, and the alien, if you truly believe in God and in what we revealed to our servant on the day of decision; the day the two armies clashed. God is omnipotent.

42.   You were on this side of the valley, while they were on the far side, and the caravan down beneath you. Had you deliberately planned it this way, you could not have done it. But God was to conclude a matter already decided, in order to destroy those who deserved destruction, and to save those who deserved to be saved. God is hearer, knower.

43.   God made them appear in your dream as few in number. Had He shown them to you as multitudes, you would have been discouraged, and you would have disputed among yourselves. But God spared you all this. God knows the innermost secrets.

44.   And when you clashed, He made them appear few in your eyes, and made you appear few in their eyes, in order for God to conclude a matter already decided. God fully controls all things.

45.   O you who believe, whenever you encounter the enemy, you shall be steadfast, and commemorate God frequently, that you may succeed.

46.   And obey God and His messenger,* and do not dispute among yourselves, lest you fail and scatter your strength. You shall steadfastly persevere, for God is with those who steadfastly persevere.

47.   Do not be like those who left their homes grudgingly, and to show off, while alienating others from the path of God. God knows everything they do.

48.   The devil has adorned their works for them, and said, "You can never be defeated by any people, and I will protect you." Then, when the two armies clashed, he turned back on his heels, saying, "I have nothing to do with you. I see what you do not see, and I fear God. God's retribution is very severe."

The Disbelievers Always Losers

49.   The hypocrites and those with disease in their hearts may say, "The believers are fooled by their religion!" Indeed, when you trust in God, you trust in the almighty, the wise.

---

*8:46. Those who obey God and His messenger uphold the Quran, the whole Quran, and nothing but the Quran (see 5:48-50, 17:73-75). On the other hand, those who advocate "**Hadith**" and/or "**Sunna**" disobey God and disobey the prophet and idolize him against his will, just like the Christians who idolize Jesus and claim that they love him.*

50. If you could only see the disbelievers at the time of death; the angels will beat them on the faces and the rear ends (saying), "You have deserved the retribution of hell.

51. "This is what your own hands have advanced for you, and God is never unjust towards His creatures."

52. The people of Pharaoh and others before them have also rejected God's revelations. Consequently, God punished them for their sins. God is powerful, and strict in imposing retribution.

53. That is because God does not change the blessings He had bestowed upon any people, unless they themselves change. God is hearer, knower.

54. Just like the people of Pharaoh and others before them; when they rejected the revelations of their Lord, we destroyed them as a consequence of their sins, and we drowned Pharaoh's people; they were all wicked.

55. Indeed, the worst creatures in the sight of God are those who are unappreciative and consequently, fail to believe.

56. It is they who enter into agreements with you, then violate their agreements every time, and they do not work righteousness.

Believers Are Stern and Alert

57. Therefore, when you encounter them in war, you shall make them a deterrant example for the disbelievers who come after them, that they may get the message.

58. And when you are betrayed by any group, you shall mobilize against them, and inflict an equivalent punishment. God loves not the betrayers.

59. Let not the disbelievers think that they will ever win. Nor will they evade the retribution.

60. You shall prepare for them all the force and equipment you can muster, in order to deter the enemies of God, and your enemies, as well as others you are not aware of, while God knows them. Anything you expend in the cause of God will be repaid to you without the least injustice.

61. If they resort to peace, you shall resort to peace, and trust in God; He is the hearer, the knower.

62. And if they try to deceive you, God will take care of them. He is the one who supported you with His victory, and with the believers.

63. He is the one who harmonized their hearts, at a time when you could have spent all the money on earth to harmonize their hearts, and fail. But God created harmony among them. He is almighty, wise.

64. O you prophet, sufficient for you is God, and the believers who follow you.

65. O you prophet, you shall exhort the believers to fight. If there are only twenty of you who steadfastly persevere, they can defeat two hundred, while one hundred of you can defeat one thousand disbelievers, for they do not comprehend.

66. But in view of your weaknesses at this stage, God has reduced your burden. Henceforth, one hundred of you who are steadfast can defeat two hundred, and one thousand can defeat two thousand by God's leave. God is with those who steadfastly persevere.

The Prophet Subject to the Same Tests

67. No prophet shall acquire captives, unless he actually fights in battle. You may care about the material of this world, but God cares about the hereafter. God is almighty, wise.

68. If it were not for God's knowledge about your future repentance, you would have suffered a terrible retribution for the spoils you acquired.

69. You may take from the spoils of war that which is lawful and good, and beware of God. God is forgiver, merciful.

70. O you prophet, tell the captives who fell in your hands that if God knew of any good in their hearts, He would have given them better than that which was taken from them, and would have forgiven them. God is forgiver, merciful.

71. If they want to betray you, they have already betrayed God, and He has condemned them. God is knower, wise.

72. Those who believe, and leave their homes, and struggle with their money and their lives in the cause of God, and those who give them refuge and support them, are natural allies for one another. As for those who believe, but refuse to leave their homes along with you, you owe them no obligations until they do emigrate. However, if they need your support to defend their religion you shall support them, unless you have a peace treaty with their opponents. God sees everything you do.

73. Those who disbelieve are allies of one another, and unless you check them, there will be chaos on earth, and terrible corruption.

74. Those who believe, and emigrate, and struggle in the cause of God, as well as those who give them refuge, and support them, these are the true believers. They have deserved forgiveness and a generous reward.

75. And those who believe afterwards, and emigrate, and struggle along with you, they belong with you. Those who are related to each other shall give refuge and take care of each other, in accordance with God's commandments. God is fully aware of all things.

Sura 9: Repentance (Al-Tawbah)*

1. Reprieve is herein granted from God and His messenger to those among the idol worshipers who sign a peace treaty with you.
2. Thus, you may roam the earth freely for four months, and know that you can never escape from God, and that God will inevitably defeat the disbelievers.
3. And a declaration is herein issued from God and His messenger, on the great day of pilgrimage, that God disowns the idol worshipers, and so does His messenger. If you repent, it would be best for you. But if you turn away, then know that you can never escape from God. Warn the disbelievers of a painful retribution.
4. As for the idol worshipers who sign a peace treaty with you, then abate none of your rights, nor ally themselves with your enemy, you shall fulfill their treaty to the end of its term. God loves the righteous.
5. Once the sacred months are over, you shall kill the idol worshipers whenever you encounter them, and capture them, and besiege them, and keep after them. However, if they repent, and observe the **salat** prayers and **zakat** charity, then you shall pardon them. God is forgiver, merciful.
6. If one of the idol worshipers seeks protection from you, you shall grant such protection and give him a chance to hear the word of God, then send him back in safety. That is because they are people who do not know.

9:1. *This is the only sura that does not begin with the opening statement, "In the name of God, most gracious, most merciful." This fact puzzled the students of Quran throughout the last 14 centuries, and many theories were advanced to explain the absence of "Basmalah" from this sura. As it turned out, this is an integral part of the Quran's miraculous code that remained a divinely guarded secret until this very translation came into existence, and represented God's authorization of this translation. As the reader already knows (from Appendices 1 & 2), the Quran's code is based on the number 19, and its foundation is the opening statement "In the name of God, most gracious, most merciful," which consists of 19 Arabic letter. Since the Quran consists of 114 suras (19x6), and since the absence of "Basmalah" will violate the code by having only 113 opening statements, we find that this deficiency is compensated in sura 27, which contains two "Basmalahs" (see 27:30). Not only do we find that the additional statement in 27:30 perfecting the frequency of the opening statement, but also providing additional proof that the order of suras is divinely designed, and should never be tampered with. To find out this additional proof, the reader is requested to count the suras starting here at sura 9, and ending at sura 27. Glory be to God, the almighty, most exalted.*

7. How could the idol worshipers expect peace from God and His messenger, unless they sign a peace treaty with you at the sacred mosque? Whenever they keep their treaty with you, you shall keep your treaty with them. God loves the righteous.

8. How could they expect peace, when, if they ever prevail, they do not observe any ties of relationship or treaty towards you? They appease you with their words, while their hearts are concealing otherwise, and most of them are wicked.

9. They have traded away God's revelations for a cheap price, and repelled from His path. Evil indeed is what they did.

10. They never observe towards any believer any tie of relationship or treaty, and they are the aggressors.

11. However, if they repent, and observe the **salat** prayers and **zakat** charity, then they are your brethren in faith. We thus explain the revelations for those who know.

12. And if they violate their vows as spelled out in their treaty, and attack your faith, then you shall fight the leaders of paganism, who have violated their vows, until they refrain.

13. Would you not fight people who violated their vows, and conspired to banish the messenger, and initiated the aggression against you? Are you afraid of them? God is the one to be feared, if you are really believers.

14. You shall fight them, for God will punish them at your hands, and humiliate them, while giving you victory, and please the hearts of those who believed;

15. And remove the rage of their hearts. God redeems whomever He wills, and God is fully aware, wise.

16. Did you expect to be left alone, without distinguishing those among you who strive, and give no priority to anything over God, His messenger, or the believers? God is fully cognizant of everything you do.

God Guards His Mosques

17. The idol worshipers are not to frequent the mosques of God, while professing heathenism. They have nullified their works, and in hell they will abide.

18. The only people to frequent the mosques of God are those who believe in God and the last day, and observe the **salat** and **zakat**, and fear no one except God. These are the truly guided ones.

19. Did you think that watering the pilgrims, and keeping the sacred mosque, is a substitute for believing in God and the last day, and striving in the cause of God? These are never the same in the sight of God. God does not guide the wicked people.

20. Those who believe, and leave their homes, and strive in the cause of God with their money and their lives, occupy a greater rank at God; they are the winners.

21. Their Lord promises them mercy from Him, and approval, as well as gardens with eternal bliss.

22. They abide therein forever. Indeed, God possesses great rewards.

God: The Only Priority

23. O you who believe, do not ally yourselves with your parents, and your siblings, if they choose paganism instead of faith. If any of you side with them, then these are the wrongdoers.

24. Say, "If your parents, your children, your siblings, your spouses, your tribe, your money, your business, and the homes that you love, are more beloved to you than God, and His messenger, and the striving in His cause, then just wait until God brings His judgment. God does not guide the wicked people.

25. God has supported you with many victories in many situations. But in the battle of Hunain, your number impressed you. Consequently, it did not help you at all, and the wide earth became so straitened for you, that you turned around and fled.

26. Then God sent down a sense of security upon His messenger and the believers, and He sent down invisible soldiers, who tormented the disbelievers. This is what the disbelievers deserve.

27. Yet, God redeems whomever He wills, for God is forgiver, merciful.

28. O you who believe, the idol worshipers are unholy. Henceforth, let them not come close to the sacred mosque. If you fear loss of business, God will enrich you from His bounties, if He so wills. God is omniscient, wise.

29. You shall fight those who do not believe in God and the last day, nor abide by the prohibitions decreed by God and His messenger, nor uphold the religious truth among the followers of previous scripture, unless they pay the expiation willingly, and without a grudge.*

Quran Rectifies Previous Deviations

30. The Jews said that Ezra was the son of God, while the Christians said that Christ was the son of God. Such is their utterance with their mouths, resembling the utterances of the pagans. God has condemned them; how could they deviate!

9:29. *Since Islamic law forbids non-Muslims from enlisting in the military, this expiation is designed as a substitute for military service. In this way, the non-Muslims who live in a Muslim society equitably contribute towards the cost of defending them.*

31. They have taken their priests and rabbis as lords besides God, as well as Christ the son of Mary. They were commanded not to worship but the one God; there is no god except He, much too glorious to have partners.

32. They want to put out God's light with their mouths, but God insists upon perfecting His light, inspite of the disbelievers.

33. He is the one who sent His messenger, with the guidance and truthful religion, and will make it prevail over all other religions, inspite of the idolaters.

34. O you who believe, many priests and monks cheat the people out of their money, and divert them from the path of God. Those who hoard the gold and silver, and spend it not in the cause of God, promise them a painful retribution.

35. The day will come when their money will be heated in the fire of hell, and then used to burn their foreheads, their sides, and their backs. This is what you hoarded for yourselves, so suffer the consequences of your hoarding.

Conservation

36. The count of months according to God is twelve, as decreed in God's scripture, since the day He created the heavens and the earth; four of them are sacred. This is the perfect religion. Therefore, you shall not wrong your souls during these months (by hunting or fighting).* However, you may fight the pagans at any time, if they attack you at any time, and know that God is with the righteous.

37. The alteration of the sacred months is a blasphemy indeed. With it, those who disbelieved mislead the people, and alter the sacred months from year to year, though they preserve the same number of God's sacred months. They thus violate what God has decreed as sacred. Their evil works are adorned in their eyes, for God does not guide the disbelieving people.

You Shall Eagerly Struggle

38. O you who believe, why is it that when you are told to mobilize in the cause of God, you become heavily attached to the ground? Have you chosen this life over the hereafter? Indeed, the materials of this life are nil, compared with the hereafter.

39. Unless you eagerly mobilize, God will punish you severely, and substitute others in your place, and you do not harm Him in the least. God is omnipotent.

9:36.   See also 5:1, 2, 94, 95, & 96.

40. When you did not support (the messenger), God supported him when the disbelievers banished him. He was one of two people in the cave, when he said to his companion, "Do not worry; God is with us." God then sent down calm upon him, and supported him with invisible soldiers, and made the word of the disbelievers lowly, while God's word prevailed. God is almighty, wise.

41. You shall readily mobilize, light or heavy, and struggle with your money and your lives in the cause of God. This is better for you, if you only knew.

42. If it were a quick gain, or a short journey, they would have readily followed you. But the hardship seems too much for them, and they would swear by God, "If we could, we would have gone with you." They thus destroy themselves, and God knows well that they are liars.

43. God has pardoned you (O Muhammad) for permitting them to stay behind. You thus deprived yourself of distinguishing those who are sincere, from those who are liars.

44. The sincere believers in God and the last day never ask you to exempt them from struggling with their money and their lives. God is fully aware of the righteous.

45. The only ones who do this are those who do not believe in God and the last day, and their hearts are full of doubt. It is their doubt that makes them hesitate.

46. If they were readily willing to mobilize, they would have thoroughly prepared for it. But God disliked their participation, and He deliberately discouraged them. They were told, "Stay behind with the sedentary."

47. Had they mobilized with you, they would have only confused you, and discouraged you, especially that some of you would listen to them. God is fully aware of the wicked.

48. They had tried previously to confuse you, and turned things around for you. However, the truth finally prevailed, and God's will was done, inspite of them.

49. Some of them would say, "Allow me to stay behind, and spare me the hardship." Indeed, they have already incurred hardship by saying this, and hell is their inevitable destiny.

50. When something good happens to you, they hurt; and when something bad happens to you, they rejoice and say, "We were wise not to participate with them."

51. Say, "Nothing will happen to us, except that which is decreed for us by God. He is our master." In God the believers shall trust.

52. Say, "You can only expect for us one of two things (victory or martyrdom), while we expect that God afflicts you with a retribution from Him, or at our hands. Therefore, just wait, and we will wait along with you."

53. Say, "Whether you spend your money willingly or unwillingly, nothing will be accepted from you, because you are wicked."

54. The reason their charities are not acceptable is that they have disbelieved in God and His messenger, and do not observe the **salat** except unenthusiastically, and do not give to charity except grudgingly.

55. Do not be impressed by their money and their children. For God punishes them therewith in this life, and then they die as disbelievers.

56. They swear by God that they belong with you, when they do not really belong with you; they have deviated.

57. If they could find a refuge, or caves, or any place of hiding, they would go to it running.

58. And some of them criticize your charity distributions; if they are given therefrom, they are satisfied, but if not given therefrom, they complain.

59. They should be content with whatever God and His messenger have bestowed upon them, and should have said, "God will suffice us, and will endow us from His bounty, and so will His messenger. We only seek God."

Distribution of Charities

60. Charities shall go to the poor, the needy, those who administer them, the new converts, the freeing of slaves, those afflicted with hardship, in the cause of God, and to the alien. This is God's decree, and God is knower, wise.

61. And some used to hurt the prophet by saying, "He is all ears." Say, "Being all ears is better for you. He believes in God, trusts the believers, and he brought mercy for those among you who believe. As for those who hurt the messenger of God, they have deserved painful retribution."

62. They swear by God to please you, when it is God and His messenger that they should be pleasing, if they were really believers.

63. Did they not know that any one who opposes God and His messenger has deserved the fire of hell, wherein he abides forever? This is the worst humiliation.

64. The hypocrites are afraid lest a sura may expose what they hide in their hearts. Say, "Keep on scoffing; God will surely expose what you fear."

65. If you ask them then, they would say, "We were only kidding." Say, "Do you take God, and His revelations, and His messenger, as objects of your kidding?

66. "Do not apologize now, for you have reverted to paganism after believing. We may pardon some of you, but some have deserved retribution for their crime."

67. The hypocrite men and women are equally guilty. They advocate evil, forbid righteousness, and refrain from charity. They disregarded God, so He disregarded them. Indeed, it is the hypocrites who are wicked.

68. God promises the hypocrite men and women, as well as the disbelievers, the fire of hell, wherein they abide forever. It is their only destiny, and God has cursed them; they have deserved eternal retribution.

69. Like those before them who were stronger, and possessed more money and children. They became distracted by their material share, just as you became distracted by your material share. You even utter the same utterances as they did. Such people waste their works in this life and in the hereafter, and they are the losers.

70. Do they not learn from the examples before them? The people of Noah, Aad, Thamud, the people of Abraham, the dwellers of Midyan, and the evildoers (of Sodom and Gomorrah), received messengers with profound signs. It was not God who wronged them; it was they who wronged themselves.

The Winners

71. The believing men and women are allies of one another. They advocate righteousness, forbid evil, observe the **salat** prayers, give the **zakat** charity, and obey God and His messenger. God will shower them with His mercy. God is almighty, wise.

72. God promises the believing men and women gardens with flowing streams. They abide therein forever, and enjoy beautiful homes in the gardens of Eden, and God's gratification is even greater. This is the greatest triumph.

73. O Prophet, strive against the disbelievers and the hypocrites, and be stern with them. Their final abode is hell, and a miserable destiny.

74. They swear by God that they never uttered the word of disbelief, when in fact they did. They reverted to disbelief after embracing Islam, and turned away when no material gains were attained. They became averse, even after God and His messenger brought to them many blessings. If they repent, it would be better for them. But if they turn away, God will punish them severely, both in this life and in the hereafter. They will find no helper on earth, nor a supporter.

75. Some of them had vowed to God that if He bestowed upon them from His bounty, they would be charitable and righteous.

76. Then, when He did bestow upon them from His bounty, they became stingy, and turned away in aversion.

77. Consequently, He committed their hearts to hypocrisy, until the day they meet Him, since they broke their vows to God, and because of their lying.

78. Do they not know that God knows their secrets and their declarations, and that God is the knower of all secrets?

79. Those who ridicule the poor believers who give to charity, simply because they cannot afford but a bare minimum, will be ridiculed by God, and will suffer painful retribution.

80. You may ask forgiveness for them, or you may not ask forgiveness for them. Even if you ask forgiveness for them seventy times, God will never forgive them.* That is because they have disbelieved in God and His messenger, and God does not guide the wicked people.

The Sedentary

81. The sedentary rejoiced for staying behind the messenger of God, and hated to struggle with their money and their lives in the cause of God. They said, "Let us not mobilize in this heat." Say, "The fire of hell is a lot hotter," if they could comprehend.

82. Let them laugh a little, and cry a lot, as a consequence of their work.

83. When God returns you to a situation where some of them ask your permission to mobilize with you, then say, "You will never mobilize with me again, nor will you be allowed to fight an enemy. You have accepted to be with the sedentary the first time. Therefore, stay with the sedentary."

84. And do not observe the funeral prayer for any of them, nor shall you stand at his grave. They have disbelieved in God and His messenger, and died in a state of wickedness.

85. Do not be impressed by their money and children. God wants only to torment them therewith in this life, and their life expires as disbelievers.

86. When a sura comes down that you shall believe in God, and struggle with His messenger, the healthy among them ask you to exempt them, and say, "Let us stay with the sedentary."

87. They accept to stay with the sedentary, and consequently, God seals their hearts, so they never comprehend.

88. As for the messenger and those who believed with him, they struggle with their money and their lives. They have deserved the best rewards, and they are the winners.

89. God has prepared for them gardens with flowing streams, wherein they abide forever. This is the greatest triumph.

---

*9:80. Another proof that Muhammad does not possess the power of intercession, and that intercession is accepted only if it happens to coincide with God's decision (see 21:28, and Appendix 7).

90. Those among the bedouins who ask permission to stay behind, and those who stay behind because they disbelieve in God and His messenger, these are the real disbelievers. They have deserved painful retribution.

91. Not to be blamed are those who are weak, or ill, or have nothing to offer, provided they observe God and His messenger. The righteous among them have nothing to fear. God is forgiver, merciful.

92. Also excused are those who come to you offering themselves, but you tell them, "I have nothing to carry you on." They then go back with tears in their eyes, sincerely disappointed because they had nothing to offer.

93. The blame is on those who wish to stay behind, even though they are rich. They accept to stay with the sedentary, and consequently, God seals their hearts, so they do not know.

94. They apologize to you when you return. Say, "Do not apologize, for we no longer trust you. God has informed us about you, and God will see your works, as well as His messenger. Then you will be returned to the knower of all secrets and declarations, and He will inform you of everything you had done.

95. They will swear by God when you return to them, in order to disregard them. You should disregard them, for they are unholy, and their inevitable abode is hell because of their actions.

96. They implore you to be gracious towards them. Even if you turn gracious towards them, God does not like the wicked people.

97. The nomads are deeper in disbelief and hypocrisy, and more likely to be ignorant of God's laws as revealed to His messenger. God is omniscient, wise.

98. Thus, some nomads consider charity a loss, and can hardly wait for you to incur defeat. It is they who incur the worst defeat. God is hearer, knower.

99. Other nomads, however, do believe in God and the last day, and consider their charities a means of drawing nearer to God, and responding to the messenger. Indeed, it will bring them nearer to God, and God will admit them into His mercy. God is forgiver, merciful.

100. Similarly, the first vanguards who emigrated, as well as those who gave them refuge, and those who followed them in righteousness. God is pleased with them, and they are pleased with Him. God has prepared for them gardens with flowing streams, wherein they abide forever. This is the greatest triumph.

101. Among the nomads around you there are hypocrites, and among the city dwellers as well. They persist in hypocrisy, and while you may not know them, we know them. We will double the punishment for them, then they will be returned for a terrible retribution.

Repentance

102. There are others who confess their sins, and mix righteous work with evil work. May God redeem them, for God is forgiver, merciful.

103. Take from their money a portion for charity, in order to cleanse them thereby, and sanctify them; and pray for them, for your prayer pacifies them. God is hearer, knower.

104. Do they not know that God accepts the repentance of His servants, and accepts the charities, and that God is the redeemer, the merciful?

105. Say, "You shall work, for God will see your work, as well as His messenger and the believers, then you will be returned to the knower of all secrets and declarations, then He will inform you of everything you had done."

106. There are others who await God's decision; He may punish them, or He may redeem them. God is fully aware, wise.

Mosques Abused*

107. And some abuse the mosque, creating dissent, disbelief, and dividing the believers, while providing aid and comfort to those who had fought God and His messenger. Yet, they swear that their intentions are good, and God bears witness that they are liars.

108. Do not worship in such a mosque. A mosque that is founded on righteousness from the first day is more worthy of your worship therein. It is a mosque where the people wish to purify themselves, and God loves those who purify themselves.

109. Is one who builds upon foundations of righteousness and gratification from God better, or one who builds on the brink of a crumbling ledge that falls with him into the fire of hell? God does not guide the wicked people.

110. Such building will only provide them with doubt in their hearts, unless their hearts are torn asunder. God is omniscient, wise.

Most Profitable Trade

111. God has bought from the believers their lives and their properties, in exchange for Paradise. They readily fight in the cause of God, willing to kill or get killed. This is the truthful promise of God, as stated in the Torah, the Gospel, and the Quran. Who fulfills promises better than God? Therefore, rejoice in the trade you have made; this is the greatest triumph.

*9:107. *Those who use the mosque to preach anything besides Quran, are abusing the mosque, disobeying God and His messenger, and creating divisiveness. It is the preaching of other than the Quran that caused division and sectarianism in Islam.*

112. The repenters, worshipers, praisers, devout, bowing and prostrating, advocators of righteousness and forbidders of evil, and observers of God's law; give good news to these believers.

God: The Only Priority

113. It is not right for the prophet, nor the believers, to ask forgiveness for the idol worshipers, even if they were their relatives, once they find out that they have deserved hell.
114. Abraham did not ask forgiveness for his father, except to fulfill a promise he had made to him. But when he found out that he was an enemy of God, he disowned him. Indeed, Abraham was compassionate, clement.
115. God never sends any people astray without first pointing out the consequences for them. God is fully aware of all things.
116. To God belongs the kingship of the heavens and the earth; He grants life and death; and you have none besides God as master and supporter.
117. God has redeemed the prophet, and the emigrants, and their supporters, who stayed with him throughout the difficult times. The hearts of some of them almost waivered; but God redeemed them. He is compassionate towards them, merciful.
118. Even the three who were left behind, then the vast earth became straitened around them, their remorse intensified, and they finally realized that there was no escape from God, except to Him. God then redeemed them, that they may repent. God is the redeemer, the merciful.
119. O you who believe, observe God, and be sincere.
120. Neither the dwellers of the city, nor the nomads, should seek to stay behind the messenger of God when he mobilizes for war, nor should they place their lives ahead of his life. This is because no thirst afflicts them, or any effort, or any hardship in the cause of God, nor do they make a single step that discourages the disbelievers, nor do they strike an enemy, without having this credited to them as a righteous work. God never fails to reward the righteous.
121. Nor do they spend anything, small or large, nor travel any distance, without being credited, in order that God rewards them generously for their work.

The Importance of Religious Knowledge

122. It is not right that all the believers should mobilize for war; a few from each group shall stay behind in order to study the religion, then preach to their people when they come back from battle, that they may beware.

123.   O you who believe, you shall fight those who actively oppose you among the disbelievers, and let them find you stern, and know that God is always with the righteous.
124.   Whenever a sura is revealed, some of them said "Did this augment the faith of anyone?" As for those who believed, it does augment their faith, and they rejoice.
125.   As for those with disease in their hearts, it only augments their unholiness, and they die as disbelievers.
126.   Do they not see that they are struck every year once or twice, then they fail to repent or take heed?
127.   When a sura is revealed, they look at each other, as if to say, "Does anyone see you?" Then they turn away, for God has turned their hearts away, since they refuse to comprehend.
128.   A messenger has come to you from among you, who is careful not to impose any hardship on you, and cares about you, and is tolerant and merciful towards the believers.
129.   If they turn away, then say, "God suffices me; there is no god except He; I trust in Him; and He is the Lord of the great dominion.

Sura 10: Jonah (Yoonus)

In the name of God, most gracious, most merciful

1. A. L. R. These (letters) constitute the miracle of this book of wisdom.*
2. Is it too much of a wonder for the people that we inspired a man like them, saying, "Warn the people, and give good news to the believers, that they have deserved an honorable rank at their Lord?" The disbelievers said, "This is indeed a clever magician!"
3. Your Lord is the one God who created the heavens and the earth in six days, then assumed all authority. He controls all things. There is no intercessor, except in accordance with His will.* Such is God your Lord; you shall worship Him. Would you not take heed?
4. To Him is your ultimate return, all of you, and this is the truthful promise of God. Just as He initiated the creation, He will repeat it, in order to reward the believers who work righteousness, equitably. As for those who disbelieve, they have deserved lava drinks, and painful retribution because they disbelieved.

Overwhelming Signs of God

5. God is the one who made the sun luminescent, and the moon a light; and He designed its phases to provide you with a timing device. God did not create all this in vain. He explains the revelations for people who know.
6. The alteration of the night and day, and the things that God created in the heavens and the earth, provide signs for the righteous.

10:1 *These letters participate in the Quran's miraculous numerical code that remained a divinely guarded secret for 14 centuries, pending the preparation of this translation (see Appendix 1). Thus, we find the total frequency of occurrence of these three letters a multiple of 19 in every single sura that is initialed with them. This sura contains 2527 of the Arabic letters A, L, and R; sura 11 contains the same total of A, L, and R; sura 12 contains 2413; sura 14 contains 1216; and the last A.L.R.- initialed sura, namely, sura 15, contains 931. Each of these totals is a multiple of 19. This miraculously flawless numerical code explains the expression, "These letters constitute the miracle of Quran." It should be noted that this particular expression appears exclusively in conjunction with Quranic initials (see also 12:1, 13:1, 15:1, 26:1, 27:1, 28:2, and 31:2).*

10:3. *Intercession on the day of judgment will be accepted only if it happens to coincide with God's decision (see 21:28 and Appendix 7). In effect, there is no such thing as intercession (see 2:254).*

7. Yet, there are those who are oblivious of meeting us, are satisfied and content with this life, and are heedless of our revelations.

8. These have deserved hell, as a consequence of their work.

The Initial Decision is Ours

9. Those who believe and work righteousness, their Lord guides them, as a reward for their faith. Rivers will flow beneath them in the gardens of bliss.

10. Their prayer therein will be, "Glory be to You, our God," and their greeting therein will be, "Peace." Their ultimate prayer will be, "Praise be to God, Lord of the universe."

11. If God is to hasten the retribution to the people, the way they hasten in hoarding material things, their life would be terminated immediately. But we leave those who are oblivious of meeting us, blundering in their transgression.

12. When the human being is afflicted with hardship, he implores us while lying on his side, or sitting, or standing. But as soon as we relieve his hardship, he goes on as if he never implored us. Thus are the works of the transgressors adorned in their eyes.

13. We destroyed generations before them, when they turned wicked. Their messengers went to them with manifest signs, but they refused to believe. We thus punish the guilty people.

14. Then we made you inherit the earth after them, to see what you do.

Quran: Muhammad's Sole Mission

15. When our revelations are recited to them, those unmindful of meeting us say, "Produce a Quran other than this, or change it." Say, "I cannot change it on my own. I simply follow what is revealed to me. I fear, if I disobey my Lord, the retribution of a terrible day."

16. Say, "It is completely up to God; had He willed, I would not have recited it to you, nor would you ever know about it. I have lived among you for a long time before this. Do you not understand?"

17. Who is more evil than one who invents lies, then attributes them to God, or rejects His revelations? Indeed, the wicked never succeed.

Do Not Idolize Anyone

18. They idolize besides God idols that are too powerless to harm them, or benefit them, then say, "These are our intercessors at God." Say, "Are you informing God of something He does not know in the heavens or the earth?" Most glorified He is, and exalted, over and above any idols.

19. The people used to be one congregation, but they differed. If it were not for a predetermined decision by your Lord, they would have been judged concerning their disputes.

Muhammad's Miracle Revealed Centuries Later*

20. They say, "How come no miracle came down to him from his Lord?" Say, "Only God knows the future. Therefore, just wait, and I will wait along with you."

Do Not Waiver With Circumstances

21. When we bestow mercy on the people, following adversity, they plot and scheme against our revelations. Say, "God's scheming is most efficient, and our messengers write down everything you scheme."
22. God is the one who moves you on land and sea. Thus, when they ride the sea, and the ships are driven with good wind, they rejoice. But when violent wind blows, and the waves surround them, and they think they lost all hope, they remember God and sincerely implore Him alone, "If You save us from this one, we will be appreciative."
23. However, as soon as He saves them, they transgress throughout the land. O people, your transgression is only against yourselves. You temporarily live in this world, then you return to us, then we inform you of everything you did.
24. The allegory of this life is that of water that we send down from the sky, produce earthly plants for the people and the animals, then, just as the earth is beautified and perfected, and its people think that they are in full control thereof, our judgment comes to them by night, or by day. Thus, it becomes barren land, as if nothing existed the previous day. We thus clarify the revelations for those who reflect.
25. God invites to the abode of peace, and guides whomever He wills in a straight path.
26. For those who do good, even better rewards. No misery, nor humiliation, will ever cover their faces. They have deserved Paradise; they abide therein forever.
27. As for those who commit sins, they get punished once for each sin, and humiliation covers them. They have no protector from God. It will be as if their faces were covered with dark pieces of night. They have deserved hell; they abide therein forever.

10:20. The Quran is Muhammad's only miracle (see 29:50-51), and the miracle of the Quran was not revealed until this translation was done (see Appendices 1 & 2, and 13:43).

Idols Disown Their Idolizers

28. The day will come when we gather them all, then say to the idol worshipers, "Here you are together with your idols." Then we will have them face each other, and the idols will say, "It was not us that you worshiped."

29. "God suffices as witness between us and you. We were totally unaware of your idolizing us."

30. That is when every soul will examine everything it did. They are returned to God, their rightful master, and all the idols they invented have disowned them.

31. Say, "Who provides for you from the heaven and the earth? Who controls the senses of hearing and sight? Who produces the living from the dead, and the dead from the living? Who is in control?" They would say, "God." Say, "Would you then work righteousness?"

32. Such is God, your rightful Lord. After the truth, what else but falsehood? How could you deviate?

33. It is predetermined by your Lord's decision that the wicked will not believe.

34. Say, "Can any of your idols initiate creation, then repeat it?" Say, "God initiates creation, then repeats it," How could you deviate?

35. Say, "Can any of your idols guide to the truth?" Say, "God guides to the truth." Is one who guides to the truth worthy of being followed or one who needs the guidance himself? What is wrong with you? How do you make your decisions?

"Hadith" is Conjecture, While Quran is Flawless*

36. The majority follows only conjecture, and conjecture is no substitute for the truth. God is fully aware of everything they do.

37. But the Quran can never be invented by other than God. It confirms all previous scripture, and consummates them. There is absolutely no doubt that it comes from the Lord of the universe.

38. If they ever say, "He made it up," then say, "Produce a sura like these, and invite whomever you like, other than God, if you are truthful."

10:36-37. *Even the most enthusiastic advocates of* **"Hadith"** *and/or* **"Sunna"** *admit that they follow only conjecture; that they are never sure whether the source of* **"Hadith"** *or a* **"Sunna"** *is actually the prophet or some inventor. On the other hand, the reader of Quran is handed physical, indisputable proof that it is God's message to the world (see Appendix 1).*

39. Indeed, they have rejected the Quran without even studying it, and without knowing its secrets. Thus did those before them disbelieve, and note the consequences for the wicked.

40. Some of them believe therein, and some disbelieve. Your Lord knows best which are the wicked.

41. If they disbelieve you, then say, "I have my work, and you have your work. You are not answerable for my work, and I am not answerable for your work."

42. Some of them may listen to you; but can you make the deaf hear, even if they do not understand?

43. Some of them look at you; but can you guide the blind, even if they do not see?

44. God is never unjust towards the people; it is the people who are unjust to themselves.

45. When the day comes, and God gathers them all, they will feel as if they lived only one hour, during which they met. Losers indeed are those who disbelieve in meeting God; they are not guided.

46. Whether we show you the doom we promise them, or terminate your life, their ultimate return is to us. God witnesses everything they do.

47. To every community (we send) a messenger. After their messenger comes to them, they are judged equitably; no one suffers injustice.

48. They say, "Where is the doom you are threatening, if you are truthful?"

49. Say (O Muhammad), "I possess no power to harm or benefit myself, except in accordance with God's will. Every community has a predetermined end. Once their end comes, they cannot delay it by one hour, nor advance it."

50. Say, "What will you do when His doom comes to you by night or by day? Why are the guilty in such a hurry?

51. "Would you believe when it afflicts you? Now you believe, after your challenging and questioning it?"

52. The wicked will be told, "Suffer the eternal retribution. Do you not get what you deserved?"

53. They question you, "Is this the truth?" Say, "Yes, by my Lord, this is the truth, and you can never escape."

One Chance to Develop Our Souls

54. If any wicked soul possessed everything on earth, it would readily offer it as ransom. They will suffer severe remorse when they see the retribution. They will be judged equitably, without the least injustice.

55. Absolutely, everything in the heavens and the earth belong to God, and absolutely, God's promise is truth, but the majority do not know.

56. He grants life and death, and to Him you ultimately return.

57. O people, this is an enlightenment from your Lord, and a healing for the hearts, and a guide and mercy for the believers.
58. Say, "With this grace from God, and His mercy, they should rejoice. This is far better than anything they hoard."

Only Four Meats Specifically Prohibited*

59. Say, "Do you note how God provides for you, then you render some provisions "**haram**" (prohibited), and render others "**halal**"(permitted)? Say, "Did God give you permission to do this, or do you invent lies about God?"
60. What do those who invent lies about God expect on the day of resurrection? God is most gracious towards the people, but the majority are thankless.
61. There is not any condition that you may be in, nor any reading of Quran that you may do, nor anything you do, that is not witnessed by us, as you engage therein. Nothing is concealed from your Lord, as small as an atom, in the earth or in the heaven; not even smaller that that, or larger except in a manifest record.

Heaven Begins Here

62. Absolutely, God's allies have nothing to fear, nor will they grieve.
63. Those who believe and work righteousness.
64. They have deserved happiness in this life, as well as in the hereafter. God's decisions are never changeable. This is the greatest triumph.
65. Do not be saddened by their utterances. All power belongs to God. He is the hearer, the omniscient.
66. To God belong everyone in the heavens and the earth, and those who follow idols besides God are following powerless idols. They follow only conjecture, and they totally deviate.
67. God is the one who made the night for your rest, and the day visible. These are signs for people who hear.
68. They said, "God has begotten a son!" God be glorified; He needs no one. To Him belong everything in the heavens and everything on earth. You have absolutely no evidence for this. Do you say about God what you do not know?
69. Say, "Those who invent lies about God never succeed."
70. A temporary life in this world, then to us is their final return, then we afflict them with terrible retribution for their disbelief.

---

*10:59-60. God is extremely displeased with those who prohibit perfectly lawful provisions. Unless something is "specifically" prohibited in Quran, it must never be considered "**haram**" (prohibited). Please see footnote 6:145 and Appendix 13.*

Noah

71. Narrate for them the history of Noah. He said to his people, "O my people, if you find it too much that I persistently remind you of God's signs, I have put my trust in God. Therefore, get together with your masters, and make a final decision, then inform me without delay.

72. "If you decide to turn away, I have not asked you for any wage. My wage comes from God, and I am ordered to be a Muslim (submitter)."

73. They disbelieved him, and consequently, we saved him and his followers in the ark, and made them inheritors, while drowning those who rejected our revelations. Note the consequences for those who were warned.

74. Then we sent after him messengers to their people, and they went to them with profound signs. But they were not to believe in what they had rejected before. We thus seal the hearts of the transgressors.

Moses

75. Subsequent to them, we sent Moses and Aaron, with our signs, to Pharaoh and his elders. But they were too arrogant, and sinful people.

76. When he showed them the truth from us, they said, "This is no more than clever magic."

77. Moses said, "Is this what you say about the truth when it comes to you? Is this magic? Magicians can never prevail."

78. They said, "Did you come to divert us from the ways of our parents, and to claim leadership on earth? We will never believe with you.

79. Then Pharaoh said, "Let us summon all experienced magicians."

80. When the magicians came, Moses said to them, "Throw what you wish to throw."

81. When they threw, Moses said, "What you produced is magic, and God will expose it as falsehood. God does not support the corruptors.

82. "God supports the truth with His words, no matter how averse the guilty might be."

83. Only a small group of his people believed with Moses, while fearing the tyranny of Pharaoh and his elders. Indeed, Pharaoh was a tyrant on earth; he was a transgressor.

84. Moses said, "O my people, if you truly believe in God, then put your trust in Him, and totally submit (be Muslims)."

85. They said, "We have put our trust in God." "Our Lord, let us not be victimized by the oppressive people.

86. "Deliver us with Your mercy from the disbelievers."

87. We inspired Moses and his brother, "Let your people confine themselves to their homes in Egypt, and let them consider their homes temples, and let them observe the **salat** prayers therein, and give good news to the believers."

88. Moses said, "Our Lord, You have endowed Pharaoh and his elders with luxury and wealth in this life. Our Lord, they only use this to repel from Your path. Our Lord, neutralize their wealth, and seal their hearts so that they fail to believe until the painful retribution comes to them."

89. God said, "Your prayers have been answered. Therefore, you shall remain steadfast, and do not follow the ways of those who do not know."

90. We then delivered the children of Israel across the sea. Pharaoh and his troops, blinded by hatred and transgression, pursued them. When Pharaoh realized that he was drowning, he said, "I believe that there is no god except the one in which the children of Israel believe, and I am a Muslim (submitter)."

91. "Now (you believe)? After you had rebelled in the past, and worked evil?*

92. "Today, we will only preserve your body, to set you up as a sign for subsequent generations." Indeed, most people are heedless of our signs.*

93. We have exalted the children of Israel to a place of honor, and provided for them generously. Ironically, they deviated only after the knowledge came to them. Your Lord will judge between them on the day of resurrection, regarding their deviations.

Muhammad the Man vs Muhammad the Messenger*

94. If you (Muhammad) have any doubts concerning what we reveal to you, then ask those who studied the previous scriptures. The truth has come to you from your Lord, and you should not be with the doubters.

10:91. Although Pharaoh actually believed in God as he was drowning, this was not sufficient for his salvation (see 2:62, 32:29, & 40:85). Believing in God is only the first, though the most important, step. We need to nourish, sustain, and develop our souls through the acts of worship and righteous works. Following his sincere belief, Pharaoh did not have time to grow and develop (see 7:8, 23:102, 101:6, and Appendix 10).

10:92. This is another profound Quranic miracle. Pharaoh's body was indeed preserved, and can be viewed today in the Mummies Room of the Cairo Museum. The ancient Egyptians were exclusively gifted with the science of mummification.

10:94-95. Muhammad the man is instructed here to follow Muhammad the messenger, and the distinction becomes even clearer in 33:37, where Muhammad the man actually disobeys Muhammad the messenger. The Quran teaches us that Muhammad the messenger is infallible, because he utters only the Quran. On the other hand, Muhammad the man is a human being like you and me, who is required to uphold the Quran, the whole Quran, and nothing but the Quran (see 6:50, 10:49, 18:110, and 41:6).

95. Nor shall you be with those who reject God's revelations, lest you become a loser.

96. Those who have deserved condemnation from your Lord can never believe.

97. Even if every miracle comes to them, (they will not believe) until they see the painful retribution.

98. When any community believes, it does so for its own good. Thus, when the people of Jonah believed, we relieved their humiliating retribution in this life, and we endowed them for a while.

God Blocks Out the Skeptics*

99. If your Lord wills, He can make all the people on earth believe. Would you force the people to believe?

100. No soul can believe except with God's leave, for He deliberately blocks out those who defy common sense.

101. Say, "Look at all the marvels in the heavens and the earth." All these marvels, and all these warnings, can never help those who disbelieve.

102. Should they expect anything but the same fate as those before them? Say, "Wait, and I will wait along with you."

103. We always save our messengers and those who believe, for it is our duty to save the believers.

104. Say, "O people, if you have any doubt about my religion, I do not idolize those whom you idolize besides God. I worship the one God who puts you to death, and I was commanded to be with the believers.

105. "And (I was told,) 'Devote yourself to the religion of absolute oneness of God, and never be with the idol worshipers.

106. 'Do not idolize besides God those who can neither benefit you, nor harm you. If you do, then you are wicked.' "

107. If God afflicts you with adversity, only He can relieve it for you. And if He blesses you with something good, none can repel His grace. He bestows it upon whomever He chooses, and He is the forgiver, the merciful.

108. Say, "O people, the truth has come to you from your Lord. Thus, whoever is guided, is guided for his own good; and whoever goes astray, does so to his own detriment. I am not your advocate."

109. You shall follow what is revealed to you, and be patient until God issues His judgment; He is the best judge.

10:99-100. See Appendix 12.

Sura 11: Hood

In the name of God, most gracious, most merciful

1. A.L.R.* A scripture whose verses were perfectly designed, then elucidated, from One who is wise, cognizant.
2. That you shall not worship except God. I come to you, from Him, as a warner, as well as a bearer of good news.*
3. And, that you shall ask forgiveness from your Lord, then repent to Him. He will then endow you with a happy life, for a finite period, and bestow grace upon every one who deserves it. But if you turn away, then I fear for you the retribution of a terrible day.
4. To God is your ultimate return, and He is omnipotent.
5. They try to hide their thoughts from God. However, no matter how they cover themselves, He knows everything they conceal, and everything they declare. He is fully aware of the innermost thoughts.
6. There is not a creature on earth that is not guaranteed its provision from God, and He knows its course, and its final destiny. All is recorded in a manifest record.
7. And He is the one who created the heavens and the earth in six days, and His dominion was initially over water. This, in order to test you and show which of you is the most righteous. Yet, when you say, "You will be resurrected after death," the disbelievers would say, "This is obviously magic."
8. Because we delay their retribution to a specific time, they say, "What is holding him?" Indeed, when it comes to them, they can never evade it, and the very thing they ridicule will overwhelm them.
9. When we bless the human being with mercy from us, then remove it, he turns desperate, unappreciative.
10. And when we endow him with a blessing, after adversity, he says, "Hardship is gone from me," and he turns joyful and proud.

11:1. See footnote 10:1. This verse states that the Quranic initials bear the proof that the verses of Quran are perfectly designed by the almighty.

11:2. This is the "First Commandment," and it is a "negative" commandment stating that "You shall NOT worship other than God." This is because a "positive" commandment stating that "You shall worship God," does not necessarily guarantee salvation; one can worship God, and still go to hell. Those who worship God, and idolize Jesus, or Muhammad, or the saints, will inevitably end up in hell (see footnote 41:14 and verses 23:84-89). Note that it is the Quran that says, "I come to you as a warner."

11. As for those who remain steadfast (under any circumstance), and work righteousness, they have deserved forgiveness and a generous reward.

Muhammad's Role: Deliver the Message

12. You may wish to discard some of God's revelations to you (Muhammad), and you may be annoyed therewith. For they say, "If only a treasure could come down to him, or an angel comes with him!" You are no more than a warner, while God is in full control of all things.
13. Or, they may say, "He made it up!" Say, "Then produce ten suras like these, fabricated; and invite whomever you can besides God, if you are truthful."
14. If they fail to respond, then know that this is revealed with God's knowledge, and that there is no god except He. Would you then submit?
15. Those who prefer this life and its vanities, we will pay them for their works therein, without the least reduction.
16. It is these who get nothing in the hereafter except hell. Everything they had done is nullified, and all their work is in vain.
17. On the other hand, those who see the clear proof from their Lord, as recited in this message, and as predicted by the scripture of Moses which served as an example and mercy, they are the true believers. As for the parties who reject this, hell is their only destiny. You shall have no doubt about this. This is the truth from your Lord, but most people do not believe.
18. Who is more evil than those who invent lies, then attribute them to God?* They will face their Lord, and the witnesses will testify, "These are the ones who lied about their Lord." Indeed, God's curse befalls the wicked.
19. They have repelled from the path of God, and seek to distort it; and they do not believe in the hereafter.*
20. They will never escape from God, nor will they find any allies against God. The retribution is doubled for them, for they failed to hear, and failed to see.
21. It is these who have lost their souls, and the very inventions they fabricated have caused their doom.*
22. No doubt, they will be the worst losers in the hereafter.
23. As for those who believe, work righteousness, and totally submit to their Lord, they have deserved Paradise, wherein they abide forever.
24. The allegory of the groups is that of the blind and deaf, compared to the seer and hearer; are they equal? Would you not take heed?

11:18-22. These verses describe vividly those who have invented the "Hadith" and/or "Sunna" and claim that they are "divine revelations."

11:19. See verse 6:113, and footnote 6:112-116.

The First Commandment*

You Shall NOT Worship Except God

25. We sent Noah to his people, saying, "I am a manifest warner to you.

26. "That you shall not worship except God. I fear for you the retribution of a painful day."

27. The elders who disbelieved among his people said, "We see that you are a human being like us, and that the worst among us were the first to follow you. We do not see any advantage for you over us, and, in fact, we think you are liars."

28. He said, "O my people, what if I have proof from my Lord, and mercy from Him that is concealed from you? We cannot force it upon you, against your will.

29. "And, O my people, I do not ask you for any money; my wage comes from God. I cannot dismiss those who believe; they will face their Lord, and He is the one to judge them. Indeed, I see that you are ignorant people.

30. "And, O my people, who would support me against God, if I dismiss them? Would you not be reasonable?

31. "I do not say that I possess the treasures of God, nor do I know the future, nor do I say that I am an angel, nor can I say that the people you despise will attain no mercy from God; God knows their true convictions. If I do, I would be unjust."

32. They said, "O Noah, you argued with us too much. Bring us the doom you are threatening, if you are truthful."

33. He said, "God is the only one who can bring it, if He so wills, then you can never escape.

34. "My concern for you, even if I do care about you, will be useless, if God's will is to send you astray. He is your Lord, and to Him is your final return."

35. If they say, "He made it up," then say, "If I made it up, then I am responsible for my crime, and I am innocent of your crimes."

36. It was revealed to Noah that, "No more of your people will believe. Do not be saddened by their actions."

37. "And build the ark under our eyes, and with our inspiration. And do not defend the evildoers; they will be drowned."

38. As he built the ark, his people mocked him whenever they passed by him. He said, "You may mock us, but we mock you, just as you are mocking us.

39. "You will find out which of us will deserve a humiliating retribution, and abide in everlasting misery."

11:26. See footnote 11:2.

40. When our judgment came, and the water fountains gushed out, we said, "Carry a pair of each kind, and your family, except those who have been condemned, and those who believed;" only a few believed with him.
41. He said, "Ride therein, in the name of God shall be its running, and its mooring. Indeed, my Lord is forgiver, merciful."
42. As it moved with them on waves like hills, Noah called upon his son, who was isolated, "O my son, ride with us, and do not be with the disbelievers."
43. He said, "I will take refuge on top of a hill, to protect me from the water." He said, "There is no protector today from God's judgment, except for those who attain His mercy." The waves separated them, and he drowned with the others.
44. Then it was said, "O earth, swallow your water, and O sky, halt." The water subsided, and the judgment was done, and the ark rested on the Joodiy. It was said, "The wicked have perished."
45. Noah called upon his Lord, saying, "My Lord, my son is from my family, and Your promise is truth, and You are the wisest of the wise."
46. God said, "O Noah, he is not from your family. It is unrighteous (to ask forgiveness for him).* Therefore, do not ask me for what you do not know. I enlighten you, lest you be ignorant."
47. He said, "My Lord, I seek refuge in You, lest I ask You for what I do not know. Unless You forgive me, and have mercy on me, I will be a loser."
48. It was said, "O Noah, disembark with peace and blessings from us, upon you and generations that will come from those with you. As for the others (who do not deserve our blessings), we will let them enjoy temporarily, then afflict them with painful retribution."
49. This is history from the past that we reveal to you. Neither you, nor your people knew any of this before. Therefore, you shall steadfastly persevere, for the ultimate victory belongs to the righteous.

Hood

50. To Aad we sent their brother Hood. He said, "O my people, worship God; you have no other god besides Him. You are only inventing.
51. "O my people, I do not ask you for any wage; my wage comes only from the one who created me. Would you not understand?
52. "And, O my people, ask forgiveness from your Lord, then repent to Him. He will then send the sky pouring generously for you, and add strength to your strength. Do not turn away as sinners."
53. They said, "O Hood, you have not shown us any proof, and we will never abandon our gods for what you say; we will not believe with you.

11:46. See 9:113-114

54. "We only say that our gods have afflicted you with a curse." He said, "I call upon God to bear witness, and you bear witness, that I disown the idols you set up

55. "besides Him. Thus, you may plot and scheme against me, all of you, without delay.

56. "I have put my trust in God, my Lord and your Lord. There is not a creature on earth that He does not control. My Lord is on the right path.

57. "If you turn away, I have delivered to you what was entrusted to me. God will substitute others in your place, and you can never harm Him in the least. My Lord is in full control of all things."

58. When our judgment came, we saved Hood and those who believed with him, by mercy from us; we saved them from a terrible disaster.

59. Thus was Aad, they discarded their Lord's signs, and disobeyed His messengers, and followed the orders of the stubborn tyrants.

60. Consequently, they incurred a curse in this life, as well as in the hereafter. Indeed, Aad have rejected their Lord. Indeed, Aad, the people of Hood, have perished.

Saalih

61. To Thamud we sent their brother Saalih. He said, "O my people, worship God, you have no other god besides Him. He initiated you from the earth, and settled you therein. Therefore, you shall ask His forgiveness, then repent to Him. My Lord is near, responsive."

62. They said, "O Saalih, you used to be popular among us. Do you forbid us from idolizing what our parents have idolized? We are doubtful of what you tell us; very doubtful."

63. He said, "O my people, what if I have a proof from my Lord, and mercy? Who would support me against God, if I disobeyed Him. You can only increase my problems."

64. "And, O my people, here is God's camel as a sign for you. You shall let her graze on God's land, and do not touch her with any harm, lest you incur an immediate disaster."

65. But they slaughtered her, and he said, "You will live only three days in your homeland; this is a promise that will never fail."

66. When our judgment came, we saved Saalih and those who believed, by mercy from us, from the humiliation of that day. Your Lord is the most powerful, the almighty.

67. And the disaster struck the wicked, leaving them dead in their homes.

68. It was as though they never existed. Behold! Thamud have rejected their Lord. Behold! Thamud have perished.

Abraham

69. When our messengers went to Abraham, carrying good news, they said, "Peace," and he said, "Peace." Soon, he brought a roasted calf.

70. When he saw that they did not reach for it, he feared them. They said, "Have no fear; we are being sent to the people of Lot."

71. His wife stood there and laughed, when we gave her the good news about Isaac, and, after Isaac, Jacob.

72. She said, "How can I bear a child at my old age, and my husband is an old man? This is really strange."

73. They said, "Do you find God's command strange? God's mercy and blessings are upon you, O people of the shrine. He is praiseworthy, glorious."

74. When Abraham's fears subsided, and he received the good news, he started to defend the people of Lot.

75. Indeed, Abraham was clement, compassionate, and obedient.

76. O Abraham, refrain from this; your Lord's judgment has come. They have deserved unavoidable retribution.

Lot

77. When our messengers went to Lot, they were mistreated, and he was embarrassed by them. He said, "This is a difficult day."

78. His people came rushing, hoping to practice their evil ways. He said, "O my people, take my daughters instead; they are purer for you. Observe God, and do not embarrass me with my guests. Is there any reasonable man among you?"

79. They said, "You know well our rights to your daughters, and you know well what we want."

80. He said, "I wish I had power over you, or find a mighty ally."

81. (The angels) said, "O Lot, we are messengers from your Lord, and they can never harm you. Move during the night with your family, and do not look behind, except your wife; she is doomed with the others. Their appointed time is the morning; is not the morning soon enough?"

82. When our judgment came, we turned it upside down, and showered them with a barrage of solid rocks.

83. Trained by your Lord, (the rocks) struck directly at the wicked.

Shu'aib

84. To Midyan (we sent) their brother Shu'aib. He said, "O my people, worship God; you have no other god besides Him, and do not cheat when you measure or weigh. I see that you are prosperous, and I fear lest you suffer the retribution of an overwhelming day.

85. "O my people, give full measure, and full weight, equitably. Do not cheat the people out of their things, and do not corrupt the earth.

86. "A smaller provision from God would be better for you, if you are really believers. I am not a guardian over you."

87. They said, "O Shu'aib, does your faith enjoin us from idolizing what our parents have idolized, and from doing whatever we want with our money? Surely, you are too clement, and too wise!"

88. He said, "O my people, what if I have proof from my Lord, and good blessings? I do not wish to impose any hardship upon you, through my prohibitions; I only seek to reform as much I can. My success depends completely on God; I trust in Him, and I submit to Him.

89. "And, O my people, let not your hatred of me provoke you into suffering the same fate as the people of Noah, or the people of Hood, or the people of Saalih; and the people of Lot are not too far from you.

90. "You shall ask forgiveness from your Lord, then repent to Him. Indeed, my Lord is merciful, kind."

91. They said, "O Shu'aib, we do not comprehend most of what you say, and we see that you are feeble. If it were not for your tribe, we would have stoned you; we do not care about you."

92. He said, "O my people, is my tribe more respectable to you than God? Is this why you disregard Him? Indeed, my Lord is fully aware of everything you do.

93. "And, O my people, do what you wish, and so will I. You will find out which of us suffers humiliating retribution, and which of us is the liar. Keep watching, and I am a watcher with you."

94. When our judgment came, we saved Shu'aib and those who believed, with mercy from us, and the wicked were struck by disaster; they were left dead in their homes.

95. It was as though they never existed. Behold, Midyan perished, just as Thamud had perished.

Moses

96. And we sent Moses with our miracles and manifest authorization;

97. to Pharaoh and his elders. But they followed Pharaoh's orders; and Pharaoh's orders were not wise.

98. He will lead his people on the day of resurrection, plunging them into hell, what a miserable abode to plunge in.

99. They were accursed in this life, as well as on the day of resurrection; what a miserable fate to be attained.

100. This is history from the past communities that we narrate to you; some of them are still standing, while others were wiped out.

101. We were not unjust towards them; it was they who were unjust to themselves. The idols they had set up besides God never helped them, when God's judgment came. They only augmented their plight.
102. Thus does your Lord punish the wicked communities; indeed, His punishment is painful, severe.
103. This should be a lesson for any one who dreads the retribution of the hereafter. This is a day on which all the people will be gathered; this is a day that will be witnessed (by all).
104. We have it delayed until a predetermined time.
105. The day it comes, no one will speak, except with God's permission; some will be miserable, and (some will be) happy.
106. As for those destined for misery, they abide in hell, wherein they sigh and wail.
107. Eternally they stay therein, for as long as the heavens and the earth endure, in accordance with the will of your Lord. Your Lord's will is done.
108. As for those destined for happiness, they abide in Paradise. Eternally they stay therein, for as long as the heavens and the earth endure, in accordance with the will of your Lord; an everlasting gift.
109. You should have no question about the idol worship that these people practice; they are following their parents' footsteps. We will pay them their full share, without the least reduction.
110. We have given Moses the scripture, and it was disputed. If it were not for a predetermined decision by your Lord, they would have been judged. Similarly, these people are doubtful about the Quran.
111. And surely, God will pay each of them fully for their works; He is fully cognizant of everything they do.

Important Commandments

112. You shall follow the straight path pointed out to you, along with those who have repented with you, and do not transgress. God is seer of everything you do.
113. And do not ally yourselves with those who wrong their souls, lest you deserve hell, and find no allies besides God, nor any help.
114. You shall observe the **salat** prayers at both ends of the day, and during the night. The righteous works nullify the evil works. This is a message for those who take heed.
115. You shall be steadfast; for God never fails to reward the righteous.
116. If only the previous generations had some intelligent people who enjoined them from corruption, they would have been saved. But we saved a few of them, while the rest pursued their material things, and became sinners.

117. Your Lord never destroys any community unjustly, while the people are righteous.
118. Had your Lord willed, He could have made all the people one congregation. But they will always dispute.
119. Only those endowed with mercy from your Lord (will not dispute), and this is what He created them for. Your Lord's decision has already been made; that I will fill Gehenna of both jinns and humans.
120. We have narrated to you the history of previous messengers, in order to strengthen your heart. The truth has come to you herein, and enlightenment, and a reminder for the believers.
121. And say to those who do not believe, "Keep doing what you are doing, and we will.
122. "Then wait, and we will wait."
123. To God belongs the future of the heavens and the earth. He is in full control of all things. You shall worship Him, and trust in Him. Your Lord is never unaware of anything you do.

Sura 12: Joseph (Yusuf)

In the name of God, most gracious, most merciful

1. A.L.R. These (letters) are the miracles of this manifest scripture.*
2. We have sent it down, an Arabic Quran, that you may understand.*
3. We narrate to you the best narrations by revealing this Quran to you. Before this, you were unaware.
4. Recall that Joseph said to his father, "O my father, I saw eleven planets and the sun and the moon, prostrating before me."
5. He said, "O my son, do not mention your dream to your brothers, lest they become jealous of you. Surely, the devil is man's most ardent emeny."
6. "Your Lord thus chooses you, and teaches you the correct interpretation of things, and fulfills His favors upon you, and upon the family of Jacob, as He had fulfilled them upon your forefathers Abraham and Isaac. Your Lord is omniscient, wise."
7. Surely, in Joseph and his brothers there are lessons for those who seek.
8. They said, "Joseph and his brother are more beloved by our father than we are, and there are more of us. Our father is making a big mistake.
9. "Let us kill Joseph, or banish him to gain your father's undivided attention. Later, you can be righteous people."
10. One of them said, "Do not kill Joseph. Instead, throw him in the darkness of the well. Some caravan may pick him up if you do this."

12:1.   See Appendix 1 for details of the Quran's miraculous secret numerical code involving these letters. One of the miraculous features of Quran is the use of multiple-meaning words. One such word is "Ayat." This word has at least three different meanings, namely, "sign" (see for example 2:164), "verse" (see for example 2:99), and "miracle" (see for example 17:101). In this way, various generations of people can derive the meaning that perfectly suits each one of them. Before the discovery of the Quran's secret numerical code, the word "ayat" in verse 12:1 was understood to mean "verses" and to apply to the verses of Quran in general. However, now that the significance of these letters is unveiled, we find that the suitable meaning of the word "ayat" is "miracles." Two facts pin down the meaning of this verse to what you see in this translation:

(1) this expression is used **exclusively** with Quranic initials such as these A.L.R. (see also 13:1, 15:1, 26:2, 27:1, 28:2, & 31:2), and

(2) the Arabic word commonly used for "miracle," namely, "Mu'jizah" is never mentioned in the Quran.

12:2   The word "you" in this verse applies to all the people of the world, regardless of their mother tongue. See Appendix 3 for details.

11. They said, "O our father, why do you not trust us with Joseph? We will take care of him.

12. "Send him with us tomorrow to run and play. We will protect him."

13. He said, "It worries me to see you go away with him; I worry that the wolf may eat him while you are not watching him."

14. They said, "If the wolf eats him while there are so many of us, then we are really losers."

15. Then, when they took him away, they unanimously agreed to place him in the darkness of the well. Meanwhile, we inspired him that, "You will remind them someday of all this, when they least expect it."*

16. They came to their father in the evening weeping.

17. They said, "Our father, we went racing, leaving Joseph with our things, and the wolf ate him. You will never believe us, even if we are telling the truth."

18. They produced his shirt with false blood thereon. He said, "No, it is you who carried out some conspiracy. I can only resort to a quiet patience. God is the only helper against your claims."

19. When a caravan came, they sent their waterer to the well, and he sent down his bucket. He said, "What a good fortune. This is a boy." They took him as part of their merchandise. God was fully aware of everything they did.

20. They sold him for a cheap price -- a few dirhams. They were eager to get rid of him.

21. The one from Egypt who bought him said to his wife, "Take good care of him. Perhaps he may help us, or we may adopt him." We thus provided Joseph with a home in the new land, and we taught him the interpretation of dreams. God's commands are always carried out, but most people do not know.

22. When he grew up, we endowed him with wisdom and knowledge. We thus reward the righteous.

23. The lady of the house tried to seduce him. She closed the doors and said, "I am all yours." He said, "God forbid. He is my Lord who took good care of me.* Surely, the wicked never succeed."

12:15. This is a classic example of the perfect happiness and contentment of God's sincere servants. In this example, Joseph appears to the outsiders to be in deep trouble. But inside, he had received his Lord's assurances that everything will be allright.

12:23. Note the incredibly clever answer that bears a double meaning. To the lady, it sounded as if Joseph was talking about her husband. But Joseph was talking about God. This is one example of the Quran's superb and extraordinary literary style.

24. She almost succumbed to him, and he almost succumbed to her, if it were not that he saw a sign from his Lord. We thus diverted from him evil and vice. For he was one of our devoted servants.

25. As they raced towards the door, she grabbed and tore his shirt from behind; and they found her husband by the door. She said, "What is the punishment for one who wanted to hurt your family, except imprisonment or a painful punishment?"

26. He said, "She is the one who tried to seduce me." A witness testified from her family saying, "If his shirt is torn from the front, then she has told the truth and he is a liar.

27. "And if his shirt is torn from the back, then she has lied, and he is truthful."

28. Thus, when he saw that his shirt was torn from the back, he said to her, "This is deceit on your part, and the women's deceit is mighty indeed.

29. "As for you Joseph, you can forget the whole thing. And you, my wife, shall ask forgiveness for your sin. You are certainly wrong."

30. Some women in the city gossiped, "The governor's wife is trying to seduce her servant. She is madly in love with him. What she is doing is really gross."

31. When she heard of their gossip, she sent for them and prepared a feast. After she gave each one of them a knife, she said to him, "Go out to them." When they saw him, they so admired him that they cut their hands and said, "By God, this is not a human being; he is a handsome angel."

32. She said, "This is the one about whom you blame me, and I did try to seduce him, but he refused. Unless he does what I command him to do, he will be imprisoned, and debased."

33. He said, "My Lord, the prison is better for me than what they invite me to do. Unless you divert their evil from me, I may desire them and behave like the ignorant."

34. His Lord answered his prayer and diverted their evil from him. He is the hearer, the omniscient.

35. They later decided, in spite of all the signs, to imprison him for awhile.

36. Two young men entered the prison with him. One of them said, "I saw myself in a dream pressing wine." The other one said, "I saw myself carrying bread on my head, from which the birds were eating. Tell us the interpretation of these dreams. We see that you are a righteous person."

37. He said, "I have been telling you of every food that came to you as provision, even before it came to you. This is what my Lord has taught me, for I have forsaken the religion of people who disbelieve in God and the hereafter.

38. "I follow the religion of my fathers, Abraham, Isaac and Jacob. We never worship anything besides God. This is but grace from God upon us, and upon the people, but most people are not appreciative.

39. "O my prison companions, is it better to have several idols, or one God, the most powerful?

You Shall Not Worship Except God*

40. "You only idolize besides Him idols that you make up, you and your parents. God never places any power in them. Kingship belongs only to God. He commanded that you shall not worship except Him. This is the perfect religion, but most people do not know.
41. "O my prison companions, one of you will be the king's wine butler. As for the other, he will be crucified, and the birds will eat from his head. This is the opinion concerning your inquiry."
42. He then said to the one to be saved, "Remember me at your lord." But the devil made him forget to remember him at his lord, and Joseph remained in prison a few more years.

The King's Dream

43. The king said, "I saw seven fat cows being devoured by seven skinny cows; and seven green spikes of wheat, and seven dry spikes. O you elders, explain my dream to me if you can interpret the dreams."
44. They said, "This is probably a nonsense dream. We know nothing about the interpretation of dreams."
45. Then the one who had been saved remembered after such a long time and said, "I can tell you the interpretation thereof if you send me."
46. "Joseph, my friend, explain to us seven fat cows being devoured by seven skinny ones; and seven green spikes of wheat and seven dry spikes, that I may return to the people, and let them know."
47. He said, "You will produce good crops for seven consecutive years. When you harvest, you should store them in their spikes, except for a minimum that you eat."
48. "Then seven bad years will follow, and will exhaust what you had advanced for them, except for a little that may be left.
49. "After that, a year will come in which the people will prosper, and will again press (wine and oil)."
50. The king said, "Bring him to me." When the messenger went to him, Joseph said, "Go back to your lord and ask him about the women who cut their hands. My Lord is fully aware of their schemes."

12:40. See footnote 11:2.

51. The king said, "What happened when you tried to seduce Joseph?" They said, "God forbid, we have not known of anything bad about him." The governor's wife said, "Now the truth is manifest. I am the one who tried to seduce him. He had told the truth.

52. "Now he should know that I did not betray him in his absence. God does not bless the schemes of the betrayers.

53. "I claim no innocence for myself. Surely, the self advocates evil, except for those blessed by my Lord. My Lord is forgiver, merciful."

54. The king said, "Bring him to me, to have him work for me." When he talked to him he said, "As of now, you are our trusted confidant."

55. He said, "Put me in charge of the treasury. I am an experienced treasurer."

56. We thus established Joseph in the land, ruling therein as he pleases. We endow with our mercy whomever we will, and we never neglect to reward the righteous.

57. The reward of the hereafter is even better for those who believe and maintain righteousness.

58. Joseph's brothers came to obtain grain. When they entered, Joseph recognized them, while they did not recognize him.

59. After he provided them with their provisions he said, "Next time bring your step brother with you. Do you not see that I give you generous measures, and I am being a charitable host?

60. "If you do not bring him next time, you will get no grain, nor will you even come close."

61. They said, "We will try to induce his father to part with him. We will surely do this."

62. Joseph said to his assistants, "Put their goods back in their bags. When they find them upon arrival to their home, this will encourage them to come back."

63. When they returned to their father they said, "O our father, we are prevented from any future shares, unless you send with us our brother. We will take care of him."

64. He said, "Shall I trust him to you any more than I trusted his brother to you previously? God is the best protector; He is the most merciful."

65. When they opened their bags, they found their goods returned to them. They said, "O our father, what more can we wish for? Here are our goods returned to us. We will thus provide for our family, and protect our brother. We can get one more camel load on account of our brother. This will be an easy share to get."

66. He said, "I will not send him with you unless you give me a solemn pledge before God that you will bring him back to me, unless you are completely overwhelmed." When they gave him their pledge, he said, "God is witness to what we say."

67. He said, "O my sons, do not enter from one door; you shall always enter from separate doors. However, I cannot avail you at all against God's will."*

68. They entered as their father had instructed them, though this could not avail them at all against God's will. But it was a personal wish that Jacob had expressed. He possessed certain knowledge from us, but most people do not know.

69. When they entered to Joseph, he confided to his brother, saying, "I am your brother, so do not be saddened by their actions."

70. When he supplied them with their grains, he slipped the cup into his brother's bag. Then an announcer announced that "You, the people of this caravan, are thieves."

71. They said, as they returned, "What did you lose?"

72. They said, "We lost the king's cup; anyone who recovers it will get a camel's load; I guarantee this."

73. They said, "By God, you know well that we did not come to corrupt the earth; we are not thieves."

74. They said, "What then should be the punishment if you are liars?"

75. They said, "If you find the cup in any person's bag, then this person becomes your slave. This is our law."

76. He started looking in their bags, before his brother's bag, then he took it out of his brother's bag. We thus planned for Joseph, for he could not take his brother according to the king's law. This was God's will. We raise whomever we will to higher ranks. Over any possessor of knowledge, there is one who knows more.

77. They said, "If he has stolen, a brother of his had committed the same crime." Joseph noted this remark, and concealed it in himself, saying, "You are far worse, and God knows the falsehoods you utter."

78. They said, "O you honorable one, his father is an old man. Would you take one of us in his place? We see that you are charitable."

79. He said, "God forbid that we should take other than the guilty person. We would then be unjust."

80. When they gave up on him, they conferred with each other. The oldest one said, "Did you not give your father a solemn pledge before God? Also, you have lost Joseph previously. I will not leave this land until my father gives me permission, or until God rules for me. He is the best ruler.

12:67.   *A myth that still dominates the Middle East is that known as "the evil eye." Jacob was afraid that if his eleven sons entered from one door, they may be stricken by the "evil eye." According to this legend, the "evil eye" can kill its victim. Tourists who visit certain areas of the Middle East may be aware of the natives' wariness of people who admire or praise their children and/or properties.*

81. "Go back to your father, and say, 'O our father, your son has stolen and we bear witness to what we know for sure. We could not foretell the future.

82. 'You may ask the community where we were, and the caravan in which we came. We are telling the truth.' "

83. He said, "It is you who plotted a conspiracy. I can only resort to quiet patience. May God bring them back to me. He is the omniscient, the wise."

84. He turned away from them saying, "How do I grieve for Joseph!" His eyes became white from weeping, and he became depressed.

85. They said, "By God, you will continue to think of Joseph until you ruin your health or until you die."

86. He said, "I only complain of my sorrow and my grief to God, and I know from God what you do not know.*

87. "O my sons, go fetch Joseph and his brother, and never despair of God's grace; only the disbelievers despair of God's grace."

88. When they later returned to Joseph they said, "Your honor, we have suffered hardship, our whole family, and we bring with us humble goods. Give us a generous share and treat us kindly. God rewards those who are charitable."

89. He said, "Are you aware of what you have done to Joseph and his brother, when you were ignorant?"

90. They said, "You must be Joseph." He said, "I am Joseph, and this is my brother. God has been gracious to us. If anyone works righteousness and steadfastly perseveres, then God never neglects to reward the righteous."

91. They said, "Indeed, God has preferred you over us, and we were really wrong."

Israel's Family Moves to Egypt

92. He said, "There is no blame on you today. May God forgive you. Of those who are merciful, He is the most merciful.

93. "Take this shirt of mine, and throw it on my father's face; he will then recover his eyesight, and bring all your family to me."

94. When the caravan arrived, their father said, "I sense the smell of Joseph. Can you deny?"

95. They said, "By God, you are still in your old imaginations."

96. Then, when the bearer of good news came, he threw the shirt on his face, whereupon he recovered his eyesight. He said, "Did I not tell you that I knew from God what you do not know?"*

12:86. Jacob knew from Joseph's dream in 12:4 that the family will be reunited some day.

12:96. See footnote 12:86.

97. They said, "O our father, pray for forgiveness of our sins; we have been really wrong."
98. He said, "I will ask my Lord to forgive you. He is the forgiver, the merciful."
99. When they arrived at Joseph, he hugged his parents and said, "You will live in Egypt, God willing, in peace."
100. He honored his parents by hosting them in the mansion, and they fell prostrate all together before him. He then said, "O my father, this is the realization of my old dream; my Lord has made it come true. He has been most gracious to me, by saving me from the prison, and bringing you from the desert, after the devil interfered between me and my brothers. My Lord is kind towards whatever He wills; He is the knower, the wise."
101. "My Lord, you have bestowed some kingship on me, and taught me the interpretation of dreams. O creator of the heavens and the earth, You are my master in this life, and in the hereafter. Let me die as a Muslim, and count me with the righteous."
102. This is history from the past that we narrate to you. You were not present when they made their unanimous decision, or when they plotted and schemed.

The Majority of People Will Not Believe

103. The majority of people, no matter what you do, will not believe.
104. Even though you do not ask them for any wage; for this is a message to all the people.
105. (And even though) the heavens and the earth are full of signs. They pass by them totally heedless.

Minority of the Minority Attain Salvation

106. And the majority of those who believe, fall into idol worship.*
107. Have they guaranteed that overwhelming retribution will not come to them from God? Have they guaranteed that the Hour will not come to them suddenly, when they least expect it?
108. Say, "This is my way; I invite to God on the basis of positive knowledge; me and those who follow me. God be glorified; I will never set up idols."
109. We have not sent before you except humans from among the communities, whom we inspired. Do they not travel the earth, and see the fate of those before them? Indeed, the abode of the hereafter is far better for those who observe piety. Do you not understand?

12:106. The majority of Jews follow the Talmud instead of the Torah; the majority of Christians idolize Jesus instead of God; and the majority of Muslims follow **"Hadith"** instead of the Quran.

110. Just as the messengers reach the point of despair, and imagine that they have failed, our victory comes to them. We then save whomever we will, while the guilty can never evade our retribution.

111. Their history offers lessons for those who possess intelligence. This is not fabricated **"Hadith"** (narration). It is a confirmation of previous scriptures; it details everything; it is a guide and mercy for those who believe.

Sura 13: Thunder (Al-Ra'd)

In the name of God, most gracious, most merciful

1. A.L.M.R.* These (letters) constitute the miracles of this scripture. They prove that these revelations from your Lord are the truth, but most people do not believe.
2. God is the one who raised the heavens without visible pillars, then assumed all authority. He committed the sun and the moon (in your service), each running for a specified period. He controls everything. He explains the revelations,* that you may be certain about meeting your Lord.
3. And He is the one who constructed the earth, and placed stabilizers and rivers therein. Of all the fruits, He designated two kinds. The night covers the day. In all these, there are signs for people who reflect.*
4. And on earth, adjoining pieces of land produce gardens of grapes, crops, date palms, dioecious and non-dioecious. Although they are watered with the same water, we prefer some of them over others in eating. In all these, there are lessons for people who understand.
5. If you ever wonder, you should wonder about their saying, "After we are dust, are we going to be recreated?" These are the ones who disbelieve in their Lord; these are the ones whose necks will be chained; these are the ones who have deserved hell; they abide therein for ever.

13:1.   The initials A.L.M.R. participate in the Quran's miraculous numerical code that proves the divine source of Quran (see Appendix 1). Thus, when we count the Arabic alphabets A, L, M & R in this sura, we find 624 A's, 480 L's, 260 M's, and 137 R's. The total sum is 1501, and this total is a multiple of 19. This extremely sensitive index (the alteration of a single letter destroys the system), illustrates how every letter in the Quran is divinely designed and counted beyond human ability. Hence the statement that these letters constitute the miracles of Quran.

13:1-4.   The word "Ayat" is used in each one of these verses to illustrate another miraculous feature of Quran, namely, the use of multi-meaning words. In 13:1, the word "Ayat" means "miracles; in 13:2, it means "revelations or verses," and in 13:3-4 it means "signs or lessons." Thus, the generations of people who lived before the discovery of the Quran's secret numerical code, were content with the meaning "verses" for the word "Ayat." This makes the Quran suitable for all generations. Please see also footnote 10:1, and note that the standard word for "miracle," namely, "Mu'jizah" is NEVER used in Quran.

6. They challenge you to bring doom upon them, instead of following the righteous path, even though the examples have been set before them. Indeed, your Lord is full of forgiveness towards the people, despite their wickedness; and indeed, your Lord is most strict in imposing retribution.

7. Those who disbelieved say, "How come no miracle came down to him from his Lord?" You are no more than a warner; for every community, we appoint a guide.

God Only Worthy of Worship

8. God knows what any female bears, and whatever comes out of the wombs, and whatever grows inside them. Everything is designed by Him in exact measure.

9. The knower of all secrets and declarations; the magnificent, the most exalted.

10. Thus, it is the same whether you conceal your thoughts or declare them, and whether you hide in the darkness of night, or appear during the day.

11. Each of you has a succession of angels, in front of you and behind you, who guard you in accordance with God's decision. God does not change the condition of any people, unless they change themselves. And if God wills an adversity for any people, none can repel it, and they have none besides Him as a protector.

12. He is the one who shows you the lightning as a source of both fear and hope, and He initiates the loaded clouds.

13. Thunder glorifies His praises, as well as the angels, out of reverence for Him. And He sends the lightning bolts to strike whomever He wills. Yet, they debate about God, while His power is awesome.

14. His message is the truth, while the idols they set up besides Him can never respond to them; they are like one who reaches for the water with a stretched hand; nothing reaches his mouth. Indeed, the prayers of the disbelievers are in vain.

15. And to God prostrates everyone in the heavens and the earth, willingly or unwillingly, and so do their shadows, day and night.

16. Say, "Who is the Lord of the heavens and the earth?" Say, "God." Say, "Would you accept besides Him masters who possess no power to even benefit themselves or harm themselves?" Say, "Is the blind the same as the seer? Or, is the darkness the same as the light?" Have they found idols who created like the creations of God, then the creations looked alike to them? Say, "God is the creator of all things, and He is the One, the supreme."

17. He sends water from the sky, causing valleys to overflow therewith, and the rapids carry abundant foam. Similarly, foam is formed when they melt metal in the fire to make jewelry or equipment. God thus cites the example of the truth and falsehood. The foam goes to nothing, while that which benefits the people stays down to earth. God thus cites the examples.

18. For those who respond to their Lord is happiness. As for those who do not respond to Him, if they owned everything on earth, or even twice as much, they would readily offer it as ransom. They have deserved the worst reckoning, and their destiny is hell, and a miserable abode.

19. Is one who recognizes that the revelation given to you is the truth, equal to one who is blind? Only those who possess intelligence will take heed.

20. They fulfill their vows to God, and do not violate the covenant.

21. And they uphold what God has commanded to be upheld, they reverence their Lord, and they fear the dreadful reckoning.

22. They steadfastly persevere in seeking their Lord, observe the **salat** prayers, and give to charity from our provisions to them, secretly and publicly. They counter evil with good. They have deserved the ultimate abode.

23. Gardens of Eden that they enter, together with the righteous among their ancestors, their spouses, and their descendants. The angels enter to them from every gate.

24. You have attained peace, because of your steadfastness, so enjoy the ultimate abode.

25. As for those who violate their covenant with God, after pledging it, and sever what God had commanded to uphold, and corrupt the earth, they have deserved the curse, and the miserable abode.

26. God increases the provision for whomever He wills, and withholds it. They have rejoiced in this life, although this life is nil, compared to the hereafter.

Muhammad Performed No Miracles*

27. The disbelievers say, "How come no miracle came down to him from his Lord?" Say, "God misleads whomever He wills,* and guides towards Him those who submit.

28. "Those who believe and their hearts exult in the remembrance of God. Surely, the remembrance of God causes the hearts to exult.

13:27. See 29:50-51 about Muhammad's miracle. God deliberately misleads those who made a decision not to seek Him, and guides those who decide to believe in Him (see Appendix 12 for details).

29. "Those who believe and work righteousness have deserved good fortune, and an honorable destiny."

30. We have sent you to this congregation, just as we sent messengers to previous congregations, in order that you deliver to them what we reveal to you. Yet, they disbelieve in the gracious God. Say, "He is my Lord; there is no god except He; I trust in Him, and to Him is my ultimate return."

The Disbelievers Hopelessly Blocked Out

31. Even if the Quran caused mountains to move, or the earth to shatter, or the dead to speak, (they will not believe). That is because the whole matter is up to God. Is it not time for the believers to give up on the disbelievers? If God wills, He can guide all the people. However, those who disbelieve will continue to suffer disasters, as a consequence of their work, or have them strike close to them, until God's judgment comes. Surely, God never breaks His promise.

32. Messengers before you have been ridiculed, and I first encouraged those who disbelieved, then I punished them. How awesome was My retribution!

33. Is there any equal to the one who calls everyone to account for everything they do? Yet, they set up idols to rank with God. Say, "Name them. Are you informing Him of something He does not know on earth? Or, do you follow some fanciful utterances?" Indeed, the schemes of the disbelievers are adorned in their eyes, and thus, they are repelled from the path. And whomever God misleads will find none to guide him.

34. These have deserved misery in this life, and the misery of the hereafter is far worse; they have no protector against God.

35. The allegory of Paradise, which is promised to the righteous, has rivers flowing beneath it; its food and its shade are eternal. Such is the destiny for those who observe righteousness, while the destiny for the disbelievers is hell.*

Quran Recognized and Appreciated by Jews and Christians

36. Those to whom we gave the scripture rejoice in what is revealed to you, although some congregations may reject some of it. Say, "I was simply commanded to worship God, and never associate any idols with Him. To Him alone I pray, and to Him alone is my final return."

37. We have sent this as an Arabic statute book, and if you ever follow their opinions, despite the knowledge you receive herein, then you will find no ally, nor a protector, against God.

13:35. *See Appendix 4 for details.*

38. We have sent messengers before you, and we made them men with wives and children. No messenger was ever allowed to produce a miracle except by God's leave. Everything will be manifested at its appointed time.*

39. God erases whatever He wills, and affirms (whatever He wills), and with Him is the master record.

40. And whether we show you some of the doom we promise them, or terminate your life, your sole mission is the delivery, and the reckoning is up to us.

41. Do they not see that we bring them closer to the end, with every passing day on earth, and that God rules without anyone appealing His rule? God's reckoning is instantaneous.

42. Those before them have also schemed, but to God belongs all the scheming. For He knows whatever everyone does, and the disbelievers will find out who wins in the final abode.

43. Those who disbelieve say, "You are not a messenger." Say, "God suffices as witness between me and you, and those who possess knowledge of the scripture."*

13:38 and 43.   This is an obvious reference to the Quran's numerical code (see Appendices 1 & 2). This miraculous code proves that Muhammad was a messenger of God.

Sura 14: Abraham (Ibrahim)

In the name of God, most gracious, most merciful

1. A.L.R.* This is a scripture that we reveal to you, in order that you lead the people out of the darkness, into the light, with the will of their Lord; in the path of the almighty, the praiseworthy.
2. The one God, to whom belong everything in the heavens and the earth. And woe to the disbelievers from an awesome retribution.
3. Those who prefer this life over the hereafter, and repel from the path of God and seek to distort it; they have gone totally astray.
4. Every messenger we sent spoke the tongue of his people, in order to clarify for them. Thereafter, God misleads whomever He wills, and guides whomever He wills, and He is the almighty, the wise.*
5. Thus, we sent Moses with our revelations, saying, "Lead your people out of the darkness, into the light, and remind them of God's days." These are lessons for every patient and appreciative person.
6. Moses said to his people, "Remember God's favor upon you, when He delivered you from Pharaoh's people who persecuted you severely, slaughtering your sons and sparing your daughters. Indeed, it was an exacting trial from your Lord."
7. Your Lord has decreed that: if you are appreciative, I will increase (the blessings) upon you, and if you are unappreciative, then My retribution is severe.
8. And Moses said, "If you disbelieve, you and all the people on earth, then God is in no need for anyone; He is praiseworthy."
9. Have you not received the news about those before you? The people of Noah, and Aad, and Thamud, and others after them known only to God, received messengers with clear revelations, but their works were reflected into their mouths, and they said, "We reject what you bring, and we are doubtful of what you invite us to; really doubtful."
10. Their messengers said to them, "Are you doubtful about God, the creator of the heavens and the earth? He invites you to forgive your sins, and He respites you for a specific time." They said, "You are no more than humans like us, who want to divert us from the way our ancestors have worshiped. Show us a manifest proof."

14:1. *See footnote 10:1 for the meaning of these Quranic initials.*

14:4. *Does God mislead? See Appendix 12 for the answer.*

11. Their messengers said, "Indeed, we are no more than humans like you. But God endows whomever He chooses from among His servants. We cannot show you any proof, except in accordance with God's will. In God, the believers shall trust.

12. "Why should we not trust in God, when He has guided us in our paths? We will resort to patience in the face of your persecution. In God the trusting shall trust."

13. The disbelievers said to their messengers, "We will banish you from our land, unless you revert to our religion." But their Lord inspired them, saying, "We will certainly destroy the wicked.

14. "And we will let you inhabit the land after them. This is for those who reverence My majesty, and reverence My omens."

15. They implored for victory, but every stubborn tyrant is doomed to failure.

16. Awaiting him is hell, where he drinks stagnant water.

17. He would swallow it, though he could not stand it, and death will come at him from every direction, though he never dies. Awaiting him is a gross retribution.

18. This is the similitude of those who disbelieve in their Lord; their works are like ashes in the wind. They reap nothing from their efforts. This is the real loss.

19. Do you not see that God created the heavens and the earth, truthfully? If He wills, He can eliminate you, and substitute a new creation.

20. This is not too difficult for God.

The Future That Already Took Place*

21. All came forward before God, and the meek said to their leaders, "We used to follow you, can you spare us any of God's retribution?" They answered, "Had God guided us, we would have guided you. Now it is all the same; whether we resort to despair or patience; there is no exit for us."

22. And the devil said after the judgment had come, "God promised you the truth, and I broke my promise to you. I never had any power over you; I simply invited you, and you responded to my invitation. Therefore, do not blame me; blame yourselves. My cries will not help you, nor will your cries help me. I have always disbelieved in your idolizing me. Indeed, the wicked have deserved painful retribution."

23. As for those who believed and worked righteousness, they were admitted into gardens with flowing streams. They abide therein forever, by the leave of their Lord. Their greeting therein is, "Peace."

14:21-23. The Quran's consistent past tense indicates that what we consider "future" is "past" as far as God is concerned.

24. Do you not see how God cites the example of a good word, as a tree whose roots are firm, and branches high in the sky?

25. It produces its crop every season, by the leave of its Lord. God cites the examples for the people, that they may take heed.

26. And the example of the bad word is that of a bad tree that was chopped above the soil; it has no foundation.

God Misleads the Wicked*

27. God strengthens those who believe with the proven words, both in this life and in the hereafter. And God misleads the wicked. God does whatever He wills.

28. Have you noted those who responded to God's favors with disbelief, and led their people to the abode of misery?

29. That is hell, where they burn and abide in misery.

30. They set up idols besides God, in order to divert others from His path. Say, "Enjoy yourselves; your final destiny is hell."

31. Tell My servants who believe that they shall observe the **salat** prayers, and give to charity from our provisions to them, secretly and publicly, before a day comes where there is no trade or favoritism.

32. God is the one who created the heavens and the earth, and He sends down water from the sky to produce fruits for your sustenance. He placed in your service the ships that roam the sea by His command, and He placed in your service the rivers.

33. He placed in your service the sun and the moon, continuously, and He placed in your service the night and day.

34. And He bestowed upon you everything you asked for; if you count God's blessings you could not possibly encompass them. Indeed, the human being is unappreciative; unjust.

Abraham

35. Recall that Abraham said, "My Lord, make this a peaceful place, and protect me and my children from idol-worship.

36. "My Lord, the idols have led too many people astray. Therefore, whoever follows me belongs with me, and if anyone disobeys me, then You are forgiver, merciful.

37. "My Lord, I have settled some of my family in this plantless valley, at Your sacred shrine. Our Lord, this is to let them observe the **salat** prayers, so make throngs of people come to them, and provide them with fruits, that they may be appreciative.

14:27.   See Appendix 12.

38. "Our Lord, You know everything we conceal, and everything we declare. Nothing is hidden from God in the earth, nor in the heaven.
39. "Praise be to God, who granted me, despite my old age, Ishmael and Isaac. Indeed, my Lord is the hearer of all prayers.
40. "My Lord, make me an observer of **salat**, and also some of my descendants. Our Lord, and accept my prayers.
41. "Our Lord, forgive me, and my parents, and the believers, on the day the reckoning takes place."

The Day of Reckoning*

42. Do not think that God is ever unaware of what the wicked are doing. He respites them until a day wherein the eyes will stare in horror.
43. They will rise instantaneously, looking upward, and their eyes will not even blink; their minds will be terrified.
44. You shall warn the people of the retribution. When it comes, the evildoers will say, "Our Lord, if You give us another chance, we will respond to Your invitation, and follow the messengers." Did you not act previously as if you will never pass away?"
45. And you dwelt in the dwellings of those before you who wronged their souls, and you found out what we did to them; we set the examples for you.
46. They schemed their schemes, and God recorded their schemes. Indeed, their scheming was enough to wipe out mountains.
47. Do not ever think that God will break His promise to His messengers. God is almighty, avenger.
48. On that day, a new earth will replace this earth, and also the heavens will be replaced, and all will rise up before God, the One, the supreme.
49. And you will see the guilty on that day chained in shackles.
50. Their garments will be made of tar, and fire will envelope their faces.
51. For God repays every soul for whatever it earned; God's reckoning is swift.
52. This is a declaration for the people, in order to be forewarned, and to know that there is only one God, and to let those who possess intelligence take heed.

14:42-52.   See Appendix 10 for details.

Sura 15: Al-Hijr Valley (Al-Hijr)

In the name of God, most gracious, most merciful

1. A.L.R.* These (letters) constitute the miracles of this scripture; the profound Quran.
2. Perhaps those who disbelieved should wish to be Muslims.
3. Let them eat and enjoy themselves, and get distracted by wishful thinking, for they will ultimately find out.
4. We have not destroyed any community without fulfilling a specific system.
5. No community can hasten its end, nor can they delay it.
6. They said, "O you who received the message, you are crazy.
7. "Why do you not bring the angels, if you are truthful?"
8. We do not send down the angels, except for specific functions. Otherwise, no one will be respited.

God's Promise

9. Surely, we sent down this message, and surely, we will preserve it.*

The Disbelievers Hopelessly Blocked

10. We have sent (messengers) before you, to previous groups.
11. When a messenger went to any group, they ridiculed him.
12. We thus control the hearts of the guilty.
13. This is why they cannot believe in this; just like their previous counterparts.
14. Even if we opened a gate into heaven, through which they keep on climbing;
15. they would say, "Our eyes are dazed. We are duped by magic."
16. We created constellations in the sky, and adorned it for the beholders.
17. And protected it from every rejected devil.
18. If any of them tries to sneak, a mighty projectile strikes at him.
19. And we constructed the earth, and placed stabilizers therein. And we planted all kinds of things therein, in perfect balance.

15:1. See footnote 10:1 for the meaning of these letters.

15:9. The Quran's miraculous numerical code, a divinely guarded secret for the last 1400 years, proves the two components of this verse: (1) that the Quran is a divine scripture, and (2) that it has been perfectly protected from the slightest distortion. See Appendices 1 and 2 for details.

20. We placed therein your means of survival, and the survival of other creatures.

21. There is nothing that we do not own treasures thereof. But we send it down in exact measure.

22. And we send the winds as pollinators, causing water to pour down for you to drink; you can never store it (in a fresh condition).

23. And it is we who grant life and death, and we are the inheritors.

24. And we already know which of you are ahead, and which are behind.

25. Your Lord will gather them all; He is wise, omniscient.

The Humans and the Jinns*

26. We created the human being from pre-shaped potter's clay.

27. And the jinns we created before that from blazing fire.

28. Your Lord said to the angels, "I am creating a human being from pre-shaped potter's clay.

29. "When I perfect him, and blow into him from My spirit, you shall fall prostrate before him."

30. The angels fell prostrate; all of them,

31. except Iblis (Satan); he refused to be with the prostrators.

32. God said, "O Iblis, why are you not with the prostrators?"

33. He said, "I was not to fall prostrate before a human being You created from pre-shaped potter's clay."

34. God said, "Then get out of here; you are rejected.

35. "You have deserved the curse, until the day of judgment."

36. He said, "My Lord, respite me till the day of resurrection."

37. God said, "You are respited.

38. "Till the day of the appointed time."

39. He said, "My Lord, since it is Your will that I go astray, I will entice them on earth, and will mislead them all.

40. "Except Your servants among them, who are totally devoted."

41. God said, "This will be My irrevocable law.

42. "You will have no power over My servants; only over the strayers who follow you."

43. Hell awaits them all.

44. It has seven gates; for each gate, an assigned number of them.

15:26-38. The humans are descendants of Adam, while the jinns are decendants of Satan. The Quran teaches clearly that Satan is a fallen angel. Therefore, a jinn is a fallen angel. Certain parts of the Muslim world, especially where Arabic is not the native tongue, fail to recognize Satan as a fallen angel. The order to fall prostrate was directed "to the angels" (see 2:30, 15:28, and Appendix 18).

45. As for the righteous, they enjoy gardens and springs.
46. Enter therein, in safety and peace.
47. We remove all hatred from their hearts; they will be brethren in adjacent areas.
48. No fatigue will ever afflict them, nor will they ever be evicted therefrom.
49. Inform My servants that I am the forgiver, the merciful.
50. And that My retribution is the most painful retribution.

Sodom and Gomorrah

51. And inform them about Abraham's guests.
52. They went to him saying, "Peace," and he said, "We are wary of you."
53. They said, "Do not be wary. We bring good news; a knowledgeable son."
54. He said, "Do you bring such good news, despite my old age? How can you bring this news?
55. They said, "This is the truth, so do not despair."
56. He said, "Who despairs of his Lord's mercy, except the strayers?"
57. Then he said, "What else are you doing, O messengers?"
58. They said, "We are being dispatched to wicked people.
59. "But Lot's family will be saved.
60. "Not so his wife, she is destined to be doomed."
61. When the messengers went to Lot's house,
62. he said, "You are strange people."
63. They said, "We bring to you what they have always doubted.
64. "We bring the truth to you; we are truthful.
65. "Thus, you shall move with your family in the darkness of night, with you in the rear, and let not anyone look behind. Go as commanded."
66. We informed him about the judgment, and that the wicked will be wiped out in the morning.
67. The people came from the city with joy.
68. But he said, "These are my guests; do not scandalize me.
69. "Beware of God, and do not embarrass me."
70. They said, "Did we not forbid you from (contacting) the people?"
71. He said, "Here are my daughters, if you wish."
72. But alas, they were blundering in their intoxication.
73. Consequently, the disaster struck them at sun rise.
74. We turned it upside down, and we showered them with hard rocks.
75. These are lessons for the intelligent.
76. And will consistently be the system.
77. This is a lesson for the believers.
78. The people of the woods were also wicked.
79. Consequently, we avenged from them, and both groups are duly documented.

Al-Hijr

80. The dwellers of Al-Hijr Valley also disbelieved the messengers.
81. We showed them our revelations, but they turned away therefrom.
82. They used to carve secure homes out of the mountains.
83. But the disaster struck them in the morning.
84. And their secure homes did not help them.

The Seven Pairs*

85. We did not create the heavens and the earth, and everything between them, except for a purpose. The hour is surely coming, so treat them with benign neglect.
86. Your Lord is the omniscient creator.
87. And we have given you (O Muhammad) seven pairs, and the great Quran.
88. Do not covet what we bestowed upon the other groups, and do not be saddened by them, and humble yourself for the believers.
89. And declare that you are the profound warner.
90. We will also send down retribution upon the dividers,
91. who accept the Quran only partially.
92. By your Lord, we will question them all.
93. About everything they did.
94. Therefore, abide by the orders given to you, and pay no attention to the idol worshipers.
95. We will take care of the scoffers;
96. who set up another god with God; they will surely find out.*
97. We know that you may be annoyed by what they say.
98. Therefore, praise the glory of your Lord, and fall prostrate.
99. And worship your Lord, so that certainty will come to you.*

15:85-88. The seven pairs refer to the 14 sets of Quranic initials. As decoded by computers, the 14 sets of initials are indeed 14 sets of numbers that add up to 1709, the number of years from the time of this Quranic revelation to the end of the world. See the book, "The Computer Speaks" for details.

*15:99. This verse explains the function of the worship rituals, i.e., the **salat** prayers, the fasting of Ramadan, the **zakat** charity, and the pilgrimage. These religious duties are the means to attain certainty.*

Sura 16:   The Bee (Al-Nahl)

In the name of God, most gracious, most merciful

1. God's judgment is already predetermined; do not challenge Him to bring it. God be glorified, and most exalted, over anything they idolize.
2. He sends down the angels, carrying the spirit (revelation) of His commands.* They descend upon His servants, whom He chooses, that: "You shall preach that there is no god except Me; you shall observe Me."
3. He created the heavens and the earth, truthfully. Most exalted He is, over anything they idolize.
4. He created the human being from a drop; yet he turns into a manifest opponent.
5. And the livestock He created to provide you with warmth, benefits, and food.
6. They also provide you with luxury, in your leisure, and your travels.
7. And they carry your loads to distant lands that you cannot reach, except with great hardship. Your Lord is kind, merciful.
8. And He created the horses, the mules, and the donkeys for you to ride, as well as for luxury. And He creates what you do not know.*
9. God is the one who points out the paths for you, including the wrong ones. Had He willed, He could have guided all of you.
10. He is the one who sends down from the sky water, from which you drink and grow plants for pasture.
11. With it, He grows for you crops, olives, date palms, grapes, and all kinds of fruits. This is a lesson for those who reflect.
12. He placed in your service the night and day, and the sun and moon. The stars are similarly committed, by His command. These are lessons for people who understand.
13. All the things He created for you on earth, in various colors, should be a lesson for those who take heed.
14. And He is the one who placed the ocean in your service, in order to eat tender meat therefrom, and extract jewels for you to wear. And you see the ships roaming therein, as you seek God's bounties. You should be appreciative.
15. And He placed stabilizers on earth, lest it tumbles with you, as well as rivers and roads to guide you.
16. Also, landmarks, and the stars to guide them.

16:2.   *The word "spirit" frequently refers to God's revelations, including this Quran as stated in 42:52. See also 4:171, 17:85-89, 26:193, 40:15, 58:22.*

16:8.   *A clear reference to the automobile, the train, the plane, etc. (see 37:96).*

God vs the Idols

17. Is one who creates equal to one who does not create? Would you not take heed?
18. If you count God's blessings, you can never encompass them. God is forgiver, merciful.
19. And God knows everything you conceal, and everything you declare.
20. And the idols they set up besides God create nothing; they themselves are created.
21. They are dead, not alive, and they have no idea how or when they will be resurrected.*
22. Your God is one god; but those who do not believe in the hereafter, their hearts are denying, and they are arrogant.*
23. Undoubtedly, God knows whatever they conceal, and whatever they declare; He does not love the arrogant.
24. When they are told, "What did your Lord send down," they say, "Tales of the past."
25. Because of this, they will carry their sins complete on the day of resurrection, as well as some sins of those misled by them and their ignorance. What a miserable load!
26. Others before them have similarly schemed. Consequently, God destroyed their building at the foundation, causing the roof to fall on them. The retribution came to them whence they never expected.

16:21. When the idol worshipers call upon Jesus, or Mary, or Muhammad, or any saint, they are not only wasting their breath, but also committing themselves to doom. These idolized individuals are servants of God who are dead, and completely unaware of their idolizers (see also 17:56-57, 19:81-82, and 72:21-22). Their souls exist somewhere far from our world, as stated in 23:100.

*16:22. What we utter with our mouths does not necessarily reflect our innermost convictions. The Quran teaches us here that some disbelievers do not know that they are disbelievers; they say that they are believers merely because they grew up in a society that praises the believers and condemns the disbelievers. This verse states that such people have "denying hearts." The test we are put through is designed to show us on the day of judgment whether we were really believers, or merely deceived ourselves (6:22-24). One profound test for the Muslims is described in 6:112-116; those who are attracted to the blasphemy known as "**Hadith**" and/or "**sunna**" are false believers, while those who uphold the Quran, the whole Quran, and nothing but the Quran are true believers.*

27. Then on the day of resurrection He will disgrace them, and say, "Where are the idols for whose sake you became opponents?" Those who had acquired knowledge would say, "Today, disgrace and misery are the share of the disbelievers."

28. Whom the angels put to death while they are in a state of wickedness. They will then submit and say, "We did nothing wrong!" Indeed, God is fully aware of everything you did.

29. Therefore, enter the gates of hell forever; what a miserable abode for the arrogant.

30. And when the righteous are asked, "What do you think of your Lord's revelations," they answer, "(They are) good." For those who work righteousness, happiness in this world; and the abode of the hereafter is even better. Blissful indeed is the abode of the righteous.

31. They have deserved the gardens of Eden, where rivers flow, and where they find anything they wish for. God thus rewards the righteous.

32. The angels put them to death in a state of righteousness, saying, "Peace be upon you; you have deserved Paradise, in return for your works."

33. Are (the disbelievers) waiting for the angels, or God's judgment, to come to them? Others before them have done the same thing. It is not God who wrongs them; it is they who wrong themselves.

34. Consequently, the evils they did afflict them, and the very things they ridicule cause their doom.

35. Those who practice idol worship would say, "If it is God's will, we would not idolize anything, nor would our parents, and we would not prohibit anything besides His prohibitions." Others before them have done the same thing. Is it not the sole duty of the messengers to deliver the message?

36. We have sent to every community a messenger, saying, "Worship God, and beware of idol-worship." Subsequently, some are guided by God, while others are committed to straying. Roam the earth and see the consequences for the disbelievers.

37. No matter what you do to guide them, God will never guide those who deserve the straying; no one can help them.

38. Others swear by God solemnly, that God will not resurrect the dead. Yes indeed; this is His truthful promise, but most people do not know.

39. In order to resolve everything they disputed, and to let the disbelievers know that they were liars.

40. All we need to say, for anything to take place, is, "Be," and it is.

41. Those who have to leave their homes in the cause of God, due to persecution, we will honor them in this world; their reward in the hereafter is even greater, if they only know.

42. They steadfastly persevere, and trust in their Lord.

All the Messengers Humans Like You and Me

43. All the messengers we sent before you were no more than humans who were inspired by us. Ask those who know, if you do not know.

44. They carried manifest revelations, such as the Psalms. Similarly, we reveal to you this message, to show the people what is revealed to them, and to let them reflect.

45. Have the evil doers guaranteed that God will not wipe them off the earth, or that the doom will not come to them when they least expect it?

46. Or that He will not punish them as they sleep, and thus cannot escape?

47. Or punish them after a warning? Indeed, your Lord is compassionate, merciful.

48. Have they not seen all the things created by God, with their shadows all around them, right and left? All submissive to God, and subservient.

49. To God prostrate everything in the heavens and every creature on earth, as well as the angels; they are never too arrogant.

50. They reverence their Lord above them, and do what they are commanded.

One God

51. God says, "Do not set up two gods; there is only one God; you shall reverence Me."

52. To Him belong everything in the heavens and the earth, and the religion shall be absolutely devoted to Him. Would you observe other than God?

53. Any blessing you enjoy is from God, and when adversity hits you, you complain to Him.

54. Yet, when He relieves your adversity, some of you set up idols besides their Lord!

55. Let them reject what we have given them. Enjoy yourselves, you will surely find out.

56. And they set aside for what they do not even know a share of our provisions to them. By God, you will be questioned about your fabrications.

57. They also assigned for God daughters, God be glorified, while assigning for themselves what they like.

58. When any of them begets a daughter, his face becomes darkened with sadness and rage.

59. He even hides from the people; ashamed of the bad news. Should he keep the daughter, or bury her in the soil? Miserable indeed is their judgment.

60. Those who disbelieve in the hereafter set the worst example; while God sets the most exalted example. He is the almighty, the wise.

61.   If God punished the people for their actions, He would not leave a single creature on earth. But He respites them for a predetermined time. Once their end comes, they can neither delay it by one hour, nor advance it.

62.   They ascribe to God what they themselves do not like. Yet their tongues claim that they are righteous. No doubt, they have deserved hell; they have deviated.

63.   By God, we have sent messengers to communities before yours, and the devil adorned their works in their eyes. Consequently, he is their leader today; they have deserved painful retribution.

64.   We did not send this scripture down to you, except to show them what they dispute, and to provide guidance and mercy for those who believe.

Overwhelming Signs of God

65.   God sends down water from the sky, whereby He revives dead land. This should be a sign for those who hear.

66.   And the livestock offer you another lesson; we let you drink from their bellies, from the midst of waste and blood, pure and delicious milk.

67.   And from the fruits of date palms and grapes you make intoxicants, as well as good provisions. This should be a sign for those who understand.

68.   And your Lord inspires the bee : "build homes in the mountains, the trees, and what the people build for you.

69.   "Then eat from all kinds of crops, and obediently follow the designs of your Lord." Out of their bellies comes a liquid of various colors, wherein there is healing for the people. This should be a sign for those who reflect.

70.   And God is the one who created you, then puts you to death. Some of you are allowed to live to the oldest age, in order to find out that there is a limit to their knowledge. God is omniscient, omnipotent.

71.   God bestows provisions upon you in various degrees; those of you endowed with plenty never give back their provisions to their servants, to the extent of equality. Would they reject God's blessings?

72.   And God created for you spouses from among yourselves, then creates from your spouses children and grand children, and He provided for you. Would they then believe in falsehood, and disbelieve in God's blessings?

73.   Yet, they idolize besides God what possesses no provisions in the heavens or the earth, nor can provide them with anything.

74.   Therefore, do not cite any examples for God; God knows, while you do not know.

The Strong Believer Better Than The Weak Believer

75. God cites the example of a slave who is owned and possesses nothing, compared to one whom we provided generously, and he gives to charity secretly and publicly; are they equal? Praise be to God; most of them do not know.

76. And God cites the example of two men; one is dumb and helpless, and totally dependent on his master; wherever he directs him, he produces nothing good. Is he equal to one who rules with justice, and follows a straight path?

77. To God belongs the future of the heavens and the earth, and the Hour is only a matter of an eye's blinking; or even closer. God is omnipotent.

78. And God is the one who got you out of your mothers' wombs knowing nothing, and He gave you the hearing, the eyes, and the minds, that you may be thankful.

79. Do they not see the birds assigned to fly in mid air, none can catch them except God? This should provide signs for those who believe.

80. And God provided you with homes to settle in, as well as portable homes made of animal hides. And from their wool, fur, and hair, you make furnishings and materials for a while.

81. God made for you creations that provide you with shade, and mountains that provide you with shelter. He made for you garments that protect you from the heat, as well as garments that shield you in war. He thus perfects His provisions to you, that you may submit.

82. If they still turn away, then your sole mission is to deliver the message.

83. Although they recognize God's blessings, they disregard them, and most of them disbelieve.

The Idols Disown Their Idolizers

84. The day will come when we raise a witness from each community, and the disbelievers will not be permitted to speak, nor will they be excused.

85. Once the wicked see the retribution, it will never be commuted for them, nor will they be respited.

86. And when the idol worshipers see their idols, they will say, "Our Lord, these are the idols that we idolized besides You." But the idols will shock them with the utterance, "You are indeed liars."*

87. They will then offer the total submission to God, and the idols they fabricated will disown them.

88. Those who disbelieve and repel from the path of God, we will double the retribution for them, because of their wickedness.

16:86. This verse proves that the idols are not only stone statues, but also human beings such as Muhammad, Jesus, Mary, and the saints.

89. The day will come when we raise a witness from each community, and bring you as a witness against these people. We have sent down to you this scripture to explain all things, and to provide guidance and mercy, and good news, for the Muslims.

90. Indeed, God commands justice, righteousness, and regarding the relatives. And He prohibits evil, vice and transgression. He enlightens you, that you may take heed.

91. You shall fulfill the vows you make to God. Do not break your oaths, after pledging to keep them, and after using God's name as surety. God knows everything you do.

92. Do not be like one who rips out her tight knitting into piles of flimsy yarn. Do not use your oaths as a means of deceit amongst yourselves. This shall distinguish your community from any other community. God thus puts you to the test. He will surely explain to you, on the day of resurrection, everything you disputed in.

93. Had God willed, He could have made you one community. But He misleads whomever He wills, and guides whomever He wills. You will surely be questioned about everything you did.*

94. Do not use your oaths as a means of deceit amongst yourselves. Otherwise, your foothold may slip after being firm, and you incur misery for deviating from the way of God; then deserve a terrible retribution.

95. Nor shall you violate your vows to God, in exchange for a cheap price. What God possesses is far better for you, if you only knew.

96. Whatever you possess runs out, and what God possesses is eternal. We will surely reward the steadfast for their righteous works.

97. Whoever works righteousness, be it male or female, while being a believer, we will grant him a happy life, and reward them generously for their righteous works.

Satan Prevents People From Reading Quran

98. When you read the Quran, seek refuge in God from the rejected devil.

99. He has no power over those who believe and trust in their Lord.

100. His power is limited to those who ally themselves with him, and fall into idol worship.

101. When we substitute a revelation in place of a previous revelation, and God is fully aware of everything He sends down, they would say, "You have invented this." Indeed, most of them do not know.

16:93. God does mislead those who deserve to be misled, after making their free-will decision to disbelieve (see Appendix 12 for details).

102. Say, "This was brought down by the Holy Spirit, truthfully from your Lord, in order to strengthen the believers, and to provide guidance and good news for the Muslims.

103. We are fully aware that they say, "A human being has taught him this." The source they hint at is non-Arabic, while this is a perfect Arabic tongue.

The Advocates of "Hadith" and/or "Sunna"

104. Those who refuse to believe God's revelations, God will never guide them, and they have deserved painful retribution.

105. Those who make up religious regulations do not believe God's revelations;* they are the real liars.

106. Anyone who disbelieves in God after having believed, unless forced while the heart is content with faith; such persons whose hearts are willingly open to disbelief, invoke wrath from God and terrible retribution.

107. That is because they preferred this life over the hereafter, and because God does not guide the disbelieving people.

108. God seals their hearts, their hearing, and their visions. Consequently, they are totally unaware.

109. No doubt, they will be losers in the hereafter.

110. However, your Lord regards those who leave their homes, due to persecution in the cause of God, then continue to strive and persevere. For these people, your Lord is forgiving, merciful.

111. The day will come when each soul defends itself, and each soul will be paid for whatever it did. No one will suffer injustice.

Do Not Prohibit Lawful Foods

112. God cites the example of a community that enjoyed peace and security, with abundant provisions from everywhere. Then they prohibited some of God's givings, and consequently, God afflicted them with hunger and fear.

113. A messenger had come to them, from among them, but they rejected him. Subsequently, the retribution afflicted them, because of their wickedness.

114. Therefore, you shall eat from God's lawful and good provisions, and be appreciative of God's blessings, if you do worship Him alone.

16:105. Those who blasphemed against the prophet, and disobeyed him by inventing "Hadith" and/or "Sunna" commit such lies because they obviously reject the Quran's repeated assertions that it is complete, perfect, and shall be the sole source of religious regulations (6:19, 38, 114, 20:114, and 75:19).

Only Four Prohibited Foods*

115. He only prohibits for you animals that die of themselves, blood, the meat of pigs, and animals dedicated to other than God. However, if. one is forced (to eat these) without being deliberate or malicious, then God is forgiver, merciful.

116. And do not make lies with your own tongues, rendering this food permissible and that food prohibited; thus inventing lies about God. Surely, those who invent lies about God never succeed.

117. A temporary enjoyment, then they suffer painful retribution.

118. We had prohibited for the Jews what we already narrated herein. It was not we who wronged them, it was they who wronged themselves.

119. Yet, your Lord regards those who fall in sin out of ignorance, then repent and reform; your Lord thereafter is forgiving, merciful.

Abraham: The Source of Religious Practice
Muhammad: A Follower of Abraham

120. Indeed, Abraham was a vanguard; submitting to God alone, and never regarding any idol.

121. Because he was appreciative of God's blessings, God chose him, and guided him in a straight path.

122. We endowed him with piety in this life, and in the hereafter he will be with the righteous.

123. Then we inspired you (Muhammad) to follow the religion of Abraham, monotheism; he never fell into idol worship.

The Sabbath Law Modified

124. The Sabbath observance was decreed only for those who disputed it, and your Lord is the one who will judge them on the day of resurrection.

125. You shall invite to the path of your Lord with wisdom and compassionate enlightenment, and debate with them in the best possible manner. Your Lord knows best who is deviating from His path, and He knows best who are the guided ones.

126. And when you avenge any aggression against you, you shall inflict an equivalent punishment. But if you resort to patience, it would be best for the patient.

127. You shall resort to patience; and your patience will be aided by God. Do not grieve over them, and do not be annoyed by their schemes.

128. Surely, God is with those who observe righteousness, and those who are pious.

16:115.   All food prohibitions must fall under these four categories. Upholding any other prohibitions is a form of idol worship.

Sura 17: The Children of Israel (Bani Israel)

In the name of God, most gracious, most merciful

1. Glory be to the One who summoned His servant during the night from the Sacred Mosque to the faraway mosque, which is located in blessed surroundings, in order to give him our revelations. God is the hearer, the seer.*

2. Similarly, we revealed the scripture to Moses, and made it a beacon for the children of Israel, instructing them that: "You shall not set up any idol beside Me."

3. They are descendants of those whom we carried with Noah; our appreciative servant.

4. And we decreed for the children of Israel in the scripture that: "You will transgress on earth twice, and will be gross tyrants.

5. "When the first time takes place, we will set up against you servants of ours who possess great might; they will invade your homeland. This is a promise that will come to pass.

17:1.   Two hundred years after Muhammad, some story tellers with limited knowledge, and a lot of imagination, fabricated a story alleging a night journey by the Prophet from Mecca to Jerusalem, followed by ascension to heaven and an audience with God. The story was designed to both entertain the masses who had no other means of entertainment, and to idolize and glorify the prophet against his will. The truth is that there was no "Aqsa Mosque" during the lifetime of Muhammad, and that this verse refers to the manner of Quranic revelation. The truth is plainly obvious throughout the Quran. Verses 2:185, 17:1, 44:3, and 97:1 inform us in a straightforward manner that the Quran was revealed into Muhammad's heart in one night. Verse 17:106, informs us that the Quran was to be "released" from Muhammad's heart to us over a long period (23 years). The process of revealing the Quran into Muhammad's heart, all at once, is described in 53:1-18. Thus, the manner of Quran revelation can be likened to the manner whereby God taught the human being at creation (see 2:31 and 7:173).

*The word "**Masjid**", translated here as "mosque," means "a place of worship." Throughout the Quran, "**Al-Masjid Al-Haram**" refers to the area of Mecca where the shrine (Ka'ba) was built by Abraham and Ishmael. Thus, "**Al-Masjid Al-Aqsa**" refers to a "faraway holy area," described in more detail in 53:1-18. The mosque that was established in Jerusalem after Muhammad's death, and named "Aqsa Mosque" has nothing to do with 17:1.*

6. "Then we will turn the tide in your favor, and supply you with wealth and children, and will make you more powerful.

7. "When you work righteousness, you do so for your own good; and when you work evil, you do so to your own detriment. Then, when the second time comes to pass, they will defeat you, and enter the mosque, just as they entered it the first time." They will completely neutralize your tyranny.

8. May your Lord have mercy on you. Whenever you return to transgression, we return to retribution, and we made Gehenna the disbelievers' final abode.

Quran: The Only Reliable Source

9. Indeed, this Quran presents the most reliable (information), and delivers good news to the believers who work righteousness, that they have deserved a great recompense.

10. And states that those who do not believe in the hereafter, we have prepared for them a painful retribution.

11. The human being invokes evil, the way he should invoke righteousness. Indeed, the human being is hasty.

12. We made the night and the day two signs; we darkened the sign of night, and made the sign of day lighted, that you may seek God's bounties therein, and to provide you with a system of timing and calculation. Everything we explained in detail.

The Video Record*

13. We have the record of every human being tied to his neck. Then, on the day of resurrection, we will give him a record that he will find accessible.

14. Read your record. Today, you suffice as reckoner for yourself.

15. Whoever is guided, is guided for his own good; and whoever goes astray, does so to his own detriment. No burdened soul will bear the burden of another soul. We do not punish without sending a messenger.

16. Before we destroy any community, we send our commandments to the leaders thereof. If they rebel and refuse to honor our message, they invoke our retribution, and we utterly annihilate them.

17. We have thus annihilated many a generation after Noah. Your Lord suffices as knower and seer of His creatures' sins.

17:13-14. We learn from this verse that we are born with our life already recorded, from birth to death. The closest analogy to our minds is the video tape of any event, such as historical narration, a football game, or a boxing match. See also 57:22.

18. If anyone prefers this fleeting life, we will hasten whatever we will for whomever we choose therein. Then we commit him to hell, wherein he burns despised and disgraced.
19. As for the one who prefers the hereafter, and strives to fulfill the requirement thereof, while believing, these will be rewarded for their work.
20. For both kinds of people, we provide from your Lord's bounties. The bounties of your Lord are not restricted.
21. Note how we provide more for some people than others, in this life. However, the differences are far greater in the hereafter, and far more profound.

The Commandments

22. You shall not set up besides God any other god, lest you end up despised and disgraced.
23. And your Lord has decreed that you shall not worship except Him,* and honor your parents. For as long as they live, one of them or both of them, you shall not speak harshly to them, nor mistreat them; you shall speak to them amicably.
24. And lower for them the wings of humility and kindness, and say, "My Lord, have mercy on them, for they brought me up from infancy."
25. Your Lord is fully aware of your innermost thoughts; if you are righteous, whenever you turn to Him, you will find Him forgiving.
26. And you shall regard the relative, equitably, and the needy, and the poor, and the alien, without extravagance.
27. For the extravagant are brethren to the devils, and the devil is unappreciative of his Lord.
28. If you have to break up with any of them, in the cause of seeking your Lord's mercy, you shall continue to speak to them amicably.
29. And do not keep your hand tied to your neck, nor open it completely, in excessive charity, lest you end up blamed and remorseful.
30. Your Lord increases the provision for whomever He wills, and withholds it. He is fully aware of His creatures, cognizant.
31. You shall not kill your children from fear of poverty; we provide for them along with you. Indeed, killing them is a gross offense.
32. You shall not commit adultery, for it is a vice, and a wicked path.
33. You shall not kill anyone, for life is made sacred by God, except in the course of justice. Anyone who is killed unjustly, we give his kin authority to avenge; thus, he shall not avenge excessively; he will then be helped.

17:23. This is the first, and most important commandment. It is a negative commandment, because people can worship God and still end up in hell (see footnote 11:2).

34. You shall not touch the orphan's money, except for his own good, until he grows up. You shall fulfill your covenants; you are responsible for your covenants.

35. You shall give full measure when you trade, and weigh with an equitable balance. This is better, and more righteous.

36. Do not accept anything that you yourself cannot ascertain. You are given the hearing, the eyes, and the mind, in order to examine and verify.*

37. Do not walk on earth proudly, for you can never rend the earth, nor become as tall as the mountains.

38. All the evil things are disliked by your Lord.

39. This is part of the wisdom that your Lord reveals to you. Most important, you shall not set up any idol besides God. If you do, you will be cast into hell, blamed and disgraced.

40. Did your Lord bless you with sons, while taking the angels as daughters? This is one of the gross blasphemies that you utter.

41. We cite (all kinds of examples) in this Quran, that they may take heed. But it only increases their aversion.

42. Say, "If there were any other gods besides Him, as they claim, they would have competed with Him for authority.

43. God be glorified; He is much too exalted above anything they say.

44. Glorifying Him are the seven heavens, and the earth, and everyone in them. There is nothing that does not praise His glory, but you do not understand their glorification. He is clement, forgiver.

Quran: An Uncommon Book

45. When you read the Quran, we place between you and those who do not believe in the hereafter an invisible barrier.*

17:36.   This commandment teaches us that we shall not accept anything without first examining it with our God-given senses and mind. Following the elders, the scholars, the sages, or the saints, without verifying what they give us, often leads to hell (see 14:21).

17:45.   Those who refuse to accept the Quran as the sole source of religious regulations are consistently characterized as disbelievers in the hereafter. They may confess belief in the hereafter, but their hearts inside are denying (see 16:22-24). They reject the Quran's repeated assertions that it is perfect, and they resort to the inventions of "**hadith**" and "**sunna**" as alternative sources (see 6:113, 150, 7:147, 11:18-19, 17:9-10, 27:4-6, 34:6-8, 39:45, and especially 41:6-7).

46. And we place on their hearts shields to prevent them from understanding it, and in their ears deafness. And when you mention your Lord (alone), in the Quran alone,* they run away in aversion.

47. We are in full control of what they hear, when they listen to you. In their private conversations, the wicked say, "You are following a bewitched man."

48. Note the kinds of examples they cite for you. This is what causes them to go astray, and never find the path.

Resurrection Closer Than You Think*

49. They said, "After becoming bones and fragments, are we resurrected as new creation?"

50. Say, "Even if you become rocks, or iron.

51. "Even if you turn into anything that you deem impossible." They will then say, "Who recreates us?" Say, "The One who created you the first time." They will then shake their heads and say, "When will that be?" Say, "It may be closer than you think."

52. The day He calls you, you will respond as you praise Him, and realize that you lasted only briefly.

Satan Divides You

53. Tell My servants to treat each other in the best possible manner, for the devil will always try to divide them. Indeed, the devil is man's most ardent enemy.

54. Your Lord is fully aware of you, and thus, He showers you with mercy, if He so wills, or punishes you, if He so wills. We did not send you as guardian over them.

55. Your Lord is fully aware of everyone in the heavens and the earth. (Based on this knowledge,) we endowed some prophets more than others; we endowed David with the Psalms.

The Idols Themselves Need God's Help*

56. Say, "Pray to your idols, whom you invent besides Him; they have no power to relieve your hardships, nor avert them."

17:46. When you exhort the idol worshipers who advocate "**hadith**" and "**sunna**" to follow the Quran "alone," as stated in this verse, they run away in aversion (see 39:45 & 40:12).

17:49-51. The period between death and resurrection passes like one night of sleep (see Appendix 14 for details).

57. In fact, the idols themselves seek the ways and means to their Lord, whichever is fastest. They need God's mercy, and dread His retribution. Surely, the retribution of your Lord should be dreaded.

58. There is not a community that we will not annihilate before the day of resurrection, or afflict it with severe retribution. This is already predetermined in the book.

Muhammad Performed No Miracles*

59. What stopped us from manifesting any more miracles, is that the previous generations rejected them. For example, we sent the camel to Thamud, a profound miracle, but they turned wicked thereby. We sent the miracles to instill reverence.

60. Then we informed you that your Lord is in full control of the people. We made the vision that we showed you a test for the people, as well as the tree that is accursed in Quran. We exhort them to reverence, but they increase in sinfulness.

The Beginning of Satan

61. When we said to the angels, "Bow down to Adam, they bowed down, except Iblees (Satan). He said, "Shall I bow down to one You created from clay?"

62. Satan said, "Just watch this one, whom You exalt above me; if You respite me till the day of resurrection, I will possess his descendants, except a few."

63. God said, "Go ahead; if any of them follow you, then hell will be sufficient as retribution.

64. "Entice whomever you can with your voice, and mobilize your horses and men against them, and share their wealth and children, and promise them. The devil's promises are no more than illusions.

65. "As for My servants, you will have no power over them. Your Lord suffices as guardian."

17:56-57. The Quran lists various kinds of idols, such as statues (21:52), property (18:42), children (7:190), and people (16:86). Here we learn that some idols are righteous people who are idolized against their will. This category includes Jesus, Mary, Muhammad, and the saints. When the leader of a prominent church prayed to Mary to bring peace to Ireland, he was not only wasting his breath, but also committing a gross blasphemy.

17:59. The only miracle manifested through Muhammad, namely, the Quran, was not unveiled until the preparation of this very translation. See 29:50-51 for details.

66. Your Lord is the one who causes the ships to float in the sea, that you may seek His bounties. He is merciful towards you.

67. And when adversity touches you at sea, all your idols abandon you, but God does not. Then, when He saves you to the shore, you turn away. Indeed, man is unappreciative.

68. Have you guaranteed that He will not destroy you on shore, or send a hurricane against you? You will then find no protector.

69. Or, have you guaranteed that He will not send you back into the sea, then afflict you with a storm, and drown you for your disbelief? You will then have no ally against us.

70. We honored the children of Adam, and we carried them on land and in the sea, and we provided them with good provisions, and we endowed them more than many other creations, generously.

71. The day will come when we summon all the people with their records. Thus, whoever is given his record in his right hand, these will read their records, and will not suffer misery in the least.

72. As for him who was blind in this life, he will be blind in the hereafter, and in worse shape.

The Quran, the Whole Quran, and Nothing But the Quran

73. They almost diverted you (Muhammad) from our revelations to you, and pressured you to invent something else. In that case, they would have considered you a friend.

74. If it were not that we strengthened you, you almost leaned towards them a little bit.

75. Had you done so, we would have doubled the punishment for you in this life, and after death, and you would have found no helper against us.

76. They also wanted to banish you from the land, in order to revert freely to their old ways.

77. This has been the case with all the previous messengers, and you will find that our system is never changeable.

Attainment of the Highest Ranks

78. You shall observe the **salat** prayers from sunrise to the darkness of night. And recite the Quran at dawn; the recitation of Quran at dawn is witnessed.

79. During the night, you shall worship and meditate for extra credit, that your Lord may resurrect you in an exalted rank.

80. And say, "My Lord, grant me an honorable entry, and an honorable exit, and provide me with Your powerful support."

81. And say, "The truth has come, and falsehood has vanished. Surely, falsehood is destined to vanish."

82. We reveal in the Quran healing and mercy for the believers. As for the wicked, it only augments their wickedness.

83. When we endow the human, he turns away, prevented by his independence. And when adversity afflicts him, he turns desperate.

84. Say, "Each will work according to his circumstances. Your Lord is fully aware which of you are the guided ones."

Quran: God's Miraculous Revelation*

85. They ask you about this revelation. Say, "This revelation is from my Lord, and the knowledge given to you herein is minute."

86. If we will, we can take back what we revealed to you, then you will find no way to reach us.

87. This is but mercy from your Lord; indeed, His grace has been abundant towards you.

88. Say, "If all the humans and all the jinns banded together to produce a Quran like this, they can never produce one like it, no matter how much assistance they lend one another."

89. And we cited for the people in this Quran all kinds of examples. But most people insist on disbelieving.

90. They said, "We will not believe, unless you cause a spring to gush out of the ground.

91. "Or unless you acquire a garden of date palms and grapes, with rivers gushing generously therein.

92. "Or unless you cause the sky to fall on us, as you claim, in masses; or bring God and the angels in a group.

93. "Or unless you possess a luxurious mansion, or climb into the sky. Even if you climb, we will not believe, unless you bring down a book that we can read." Say, "God be glorified; am I any more than a human messenger?"

94. Thus, what prevented the people from believing, when the guidance came to them, is their saying, "How could God send a human messenger?"

17:85-89. Previous translations, and interpretations, have erroneously referred to the word "Rooh" as "soul." The Quran, however, consistently uses this word to refer to divine revelations (see 16:2, 40:15, 58:22, and 97:4). Specifically, the Quran is described as "Rooh" in 42:52. The whole context clearly refers to God's revelation, and the interpretation of "Rooh" as "soul" will be taking it out of context.

Verse 88 is a direct reference to the Quran's miraculous numerical code that this translation was exclusively blessed with unveiling. While many human beings did produce literary works as excellent as the Quran, no power on earth can duplicate the Quran's intricate numerical code (see Appendices 1 and 2 for details).

95. Say, "If the earth were inhabited by angels, we would have sent down from the sky an angel messenger."

96. Say, "God suffices as witness between me and you; He is fully cognizant of His servants, seer."

97. Whomever God guides is the truly guided one. As for those whom He sends astray, you will find no allies to help them against Him, and we gather them forcibly on the day of resurrection, blind, dumb, and deaf. Their final abode is hell; whenever it cools down, we re-ignite their fire.

98. This is their just retribution, for they rejected our revelations and said, "After we become bones and fragments, do we get created anew?"

99. Do they not realize that God, who created the heavens and the earth, is able to create the same? And He predetermined an inevitable end for their life; but the wicked insist upon disbelieving.

100. Say, "If you take possession of my Lord's treasures of mercy, you would be too stingy to spend therefrom; the human being is parsimonious."

Muslims and Jews: the Great Parallel*

101. We gave Moses nine miracles, so ask the children of Israel. When he went to them, Pharaoh said to him, "I think you are bewitched, Moses."

102. He said, "You know well that none can manifest these profound miracles except the Lord of the heavens and the earth. I think you are doomed, Pharaoh."

103. He then wanted to oppress them throughout the land, but we drowned him and all his troops.

104. And we said to the children of Israel after him, "Inhabit the land, and when the second prophecy* comes to pass, we will gather you together."

105. Similarly, we reveal this truthfully, and we reveal the truth herein. We send you (O Muhammad) as no more than a preacher and warner.

17:101-106.   The frequency of mentioning Moses and his followers throughout the Quran is noteworthy, and points out the great parallel between the followers of Moses and the followers of Muhammad. God gave the Torah to the followers of Moses, and asked them to uphold it strongly (2:63). But around A.D. 200, the "scholars and sages" of Judaism invented the Mishnah and the Gemara, which make up the Talmud, and eventually replaced the Torah. Similarly, God gave the Muslims the Quran and asked them to uphold it. But 250 years after Muhammad, the "scholars and sages" of Islam invented the "Hadith" and "Sunna" which replaced and abrogated the Quran (see 24:1-2). This amazing parallel explains the frequency of narration of Israel's history.

17:104.   Could this be the gathering of the Jews into the state of Israel? See 17:4-7.

106. This is a Quran that we decreed to be released to the people by you, over a long period, though we sent it down all at once.*

107. Say, "Believe therein, or disbelieve. Those who possess knowledge before it, when it is recited for them, fall down to their chins prostrating."

108. And they say, "Glory be to our Lord; the promise of our Lord has come true."*

109. They fall down to their chins, weeping, for it increases their reverence.

110. Say, "Call Him God, or call Him Al-Rahman (the most gracious); whichever name you call Him by, He possesses the most beautiful names." And do not be too loud when you say your **salat** prayers, nor too low; but use a moderate tone.

111. And say, "Praise God; who has never taken a son for Himself, nor does He have a partner in kingship, nor does He need any ally out of weakness;" you shall magnify Him constantly.

17:106.   Muhammad's soul was summoned, and the Quran was given to him all at once, in the same manner as Adam's acquisition of knowledge (2:31). The process of revelation to Muhammad is described in 53:1-18. This verse teaches us that, although the Quran was revealed into Muhammad's heart all at once (16:102), God decreed that it shall be "released" from Muhammad's heart to the people over a long period of time. Please see 2:185, 17:1, 44:3, and 97:1.

17:108.   See Deuteronomy 18:15 and 18:18-19, John 14:16-17, and John 16:13.

Sura 18:   The Cave (Al-Kahf)

In the name of God, most gracious, most merciful

1.   Praise be to God, who sent down the scripture to His servant, and made it flawless.
2.   (He made it) perfect, in order to warn of severe retribution from Him, and to bear good news for the believers who work righteousness, that they have deserved a delightful recompense.
3.   They abide therein forever.
4.   And to warn those who claimed that God has taken a son for Himself.
5.   They have no real knowledge thereof, nor did their ancestors. Gross indeed is such an utterance, coming out of their mouths. What they utter is a lie.
6.   Yet, you may blame yourself on their account, that they do not accept this **hadith** (message), and you may be saddened.
7.   We created everything on earth, as adornment, in order to test them therewith and distinguish the good doers.
8.   Inevitably, we will wipe out everything therein, making it a barren land.

The Seven Sleepers of Ephesus*

9.   You may consider the people of the cave, and their number, among our wondrous marvels.

18:9-26.   Many variations of this story are found in the various encyclopedias, and the world literature. The Quran sets the record straight. The "Christian" literature generally claims that these youth were running away from the Romans' persecution. But the divine truth herein teaches us that they actually ran away from the Christians who deviated from the teachings of Christ, and idolized him against his will; they wanted to worship God alone, and recognized Jesus as a great teacher. Note that the history of these righteous Ephesians coincides with the period of turmoil that resulted in convening the Councils of Nicene, and permanent distortion of Christianity through the Nicene Creed. This is the Creed that invented the Trinity doctrine, according to all recognized encyclopedias, and the Vatican's own encyclopedia. The seven sleepers of Ephesus wanted to practice the true Christianity, and rejected the false doctrines, such as the Trinity.

Ephesus was an ancient Turkish city, 35 miles south of today's Izmir, and was famous for its Temple of Artemis, one of the ancient seven wonders of the world. It later became the leading Christian community of Asia. In 1928, an Austrian archeologist called Franz Miltner found a tomb near Ephesus which proved that the Seven Sleepers of Ephesus actually existed, and that their story is a historical fact. The ultimate truth, of course, is narrated here by the almighty creator of the universe.

10. Thus, some youths took refuge in the cave, saying, "Our Lord, grant us mercy from You, and direct us rightly in our affairs."

11. We then sealed their ears in the cave, for a number of years.

12. Then we resurrected them, in order to see which party will accurately estimate the length of their stay.

13. We narrate to you herein the truth of their history. They were youths who believed in their Lord, and we increased them in guidance.

14. We strengthened their hearts, for they stood up for their Lord, saying, "Our only Lord is the Lord of the heavens and the earth. We will never call on any other god besides Him; if we do, we will be far astray.*

15. "Here are our people setting up idols besides Him; idols that possess absolutely no power. Who is more wicked than one who invents lies against God?

16. "If you wish to isolate yourselves from them, and their idol worship, then take refuge into the cave. Your Lord will shower you with His mercy, and direct you in your affairs."

17. You see the sun, when it rises, moving to the right of their cave; and when it sets, it shines on them from the left; as they laid down in the hollow thereof. This is one of God's signs; whomever God guides is the truly guided one, and whomever He sends astray, you will never find for him a guiding teacher.

18. You would think that they were awake, when they were actually asleep. We turned them to the right side and the left side, while their dog stretched his arms in their midst. Had you looked at them, you would have fled therefrom, stricken with fear.

---

*18:14.   This story is certainly relevant to our lives today, for the same thing is happening right now on a large scale. Any Christians who discover the great Satanic trick, whereby their religion has been distorted, and who wish to worship God alone, follow the true teachings of Christ, and recognize Jesus as a great teacher and messenger of God, these people are immediately outcast by the "Christian" masses. This is exactly what happened when a group of enlightened Christian scholars declared the truth in a book entitled, "The Myth of God Incarnate." Similarly, any Muslims who try to worship God "alone" and uphold His message, the Quran, the whole Quran, and nothing but the Quran, are immediately outcast by the "Muslim" masses. Unfortunately, the common human plague of idol worship has afflicted the Muslims in much the same manner as it afflicted the Christians, and the Jews before that. Most Muslims today follow an invented set of traditions, known as "**Hadith**" and/or "**Sunna**" that abuse the name of the Prophet as the original source thereof. Satan used these inventions to divert the Muslims from the Quran, and the Prophet will be the first to disown them on the day of judgment (see 25:30).*

19. We then resurrected them, and they questioned one another; one of them said, "How long have you been here?" They answered, "One day, or part of the day." They said, "Your Lord knows best how long you stayed here; let us send one of us with this silver money to the city. Let him find out where the clean food is, in order to bring some of it for you. Let him be gentle and discreet.

20. "If they find out about you, they would stone you, or force you back into their religion, then you never succeed."

21. We thus allowed the people to find them, in order for them to realize that God's promise is truth, and that the hour is inevitable. They then conferred with each other about them, and some of them said, "Let us erect a building over them, their Lord knows best about them." Their leaders finally said, "Let us build a place of worship to commemorate them."*

22. People will say, "They were three; their dog being the fourth." Others will say, "They were five; their dog being the sixth," as a guess. Others yet will say, "They were seven," and the dog was the eighth. Say, "My Lord knows best how many they were. Only a few know their real number. Thus, do not waste your time guessing their number, and do not bother to consult about them.

23. (You should learn from this that you) do not say, "I will do this thing tomorrow."

24. Not without saying, "God willing." You shall turn to your Lord, if you forget to do this, and say, "May my Lord guide me to do better the next time."

25. They stayed in their cave three hundred years, plus nine.*

26. Say, "God knows best how long they stayed therein." He knows the secrets of the heavens and the earth. He is the best seer and the best hearer. The people have no other master besides Him, nor does He allow anyone to share in His kingship.

Quran Revealed to All of Us Through Muhammad*

27. You shall recite what is revealed to you from your Lord; nothing shall abrogate His words, and you shall not find any other source besides it.

18:21. The recognized encyclopedias state that Emperor Theodsius II believed a miracle had taken place, and had a great church built to mark the spot where the seven sleepers of Ephesus had slept.

18:25. Another valuable lesson we learn is that the period of our death will pass like one night of sleep (see Appendix 14 for details, and 2:259).

18:27. See also 42:51.

28. You shall force yourself to stay with those who worship their Lord day and night, seeking only Him, and do not divert your eyes from them, seeking the vanities of this life. And do not obey anyone whose heart we render unaware of our message, and follows his own opinions, and thus his efforts are in vain.

Freedom to Believe or Disbelieve

29. You shall say, "This is the truth from your Lord," then whoever wishes let him believe, and whoever wishes let him disbelieve. We have prepared for the wicked a fire that surrounds them completely. When they plead for water, they get a drink like lava, that burns their faces. What a miserable drink, and a miserable abode!

30. As for those who believe and lead a righteous life, we never fail to reward the good doers.

31. These have deserved the gardens of Eden, where rivers flow beneath them. They will be adorned with bracelets of gold, and wear green garments of silk and velvet. They relax therein on comfortable furnishings. What a beautiful reward, and a beautiful abode!*

Do Not Idolize Your Material Properties

32. Cite for them the parable of two men; one of them we endowed with two orchards of grapes, surrounded them with date palms, and interspersed them with crops.

33. Both orchards produced generously, and never failed. We had a river gush through them.

34. As he noted the fruits therein, he said to his friend who debated with him, "I am richer than you are and have more children."

35. And he entered his orchard in a state of wickedness, saying, "I do not think that this can ever vanish.

36. "Nor do I believe that the hour will come to pass. Even if I am returned to my Lord, I am clever enough to possess a better one."

37. His friend said to him, as he debated him, "Do you disbelieve in the one who created you from dust, then from a drop, then perfected you as a man?

38. "As for me, God is my Lord, and I will never associate any idol with Him.

39. "Whenever you enter your orchard, you should say, 'This is God's giving; I can never possess anything, except by God's leave.' You may see me poorer than you are, with fewer children.

40. "But my Lord may endow me with better orchards than yours, and wipe out your orchards with a storm from the sky, making it a barren land.

18:31.   See Appendix 4 for details of this allegorical description of heaven.

41. "Or its water may sink deeper, beyond your reach."
42. Subsequently, his crops were wiped out, and he become deeply sorrowful over the efforts he wasted therein, and he said, "Oh I wish I did not idolize my property besides my Lord."
43. There was no army to support him against God, nor was he ever destined to win.
44. The true mastership belongs only to God; He provides the best reward, and the best destiny.

Property and Children Can be Distracting Idols

45. Cite for them the parable of this life as a crop watered from the rain, then it turns into hay, and gets blown away by the wind. God is supreme over all things.
46. Money and children are the vanities of this life, and the eternal righteous works are rewarded by your Lord; they are your only hope.
47. The day will come when we remove the mountains, and you see the earth level. We will gather them all, leaving out not a single one of them.
48. They will be presented before your Lord in a row. Now you have come to us as we created you the first time. Did you not claim that this audience will never take place?
49. The record will then be opened, and you will see the guilty frightened from the contents thereof and say, "Woe to us; this record does not leave out anything small or large, without counting it." They will find everything they had done presented to them. Your Lord never inflicts injustice.

Satan Turns From Angel to Jinn

50. When we said to the angels, "Bow down to Adam," they bowed down, except Iblees (Satan). He became a jinn, as he violated the command of his Lord. Would you then accept him, and his descendants, as masters besides Me, even though they are your enemies? What a miserable substitute for the wicked!
51. I never even allowed them to witness the creation of the heavens and the earth; nor the creation of themselves. I never accept the misleaders as assistants.
52. The day will come when He says, "Call upon the idols you set up besides Me." They will call upon them, but they will not respond; we will place a barrier between them.
53. The guilty will see hell, and realize that they are doomed therein; they will have no way of evading it.

Quran is Truth; Other Sources Are Falsehood

54. We have cited in this Quran all kinds of parables for the people, but the human being is the most contentious.
55. What prevented the people from believing when the guidance came to them, and from seeking forgiveness from their Lord, is that they demand to see miracles like previous generations, or challenge the retribution to afflict them in advance.
56. We do not send the messengers except as preachers and warners. Then the disbelivers argue with falsehood, in order to refute the truth. They take My scriptures and warnings in vain.

The Curse

57. Who is more evil than one who is reminded of his Lord's revelations, then he turns away therefrom, paying no attention to what he commits. Consequently, we place on their hearts shields, to prevent them from understanding this Quran, and in their ears deafness. Therefore, when you invite them to the guidance, they can never be guided
58. Your Lord is forgiving, full of mercy. If He punishes them for their deeds, He would immediately afflict them with retribution. Instead, they have a specific appointment that they can never evade.
59. Thus, those communities we destroyed when they turned wicked, and we set a specific time for their destruction.

A Good Reason For Everything

60. Recall that Moses said to his servant, "I have to reach the point where the two rivers meet, even if it takes me ages."
61. When they reached the point where they meet, they neglected their fish, and it sneaked back into the river.
62. Then, after they passed that point, he said to his servant, "Bring our lunch; we are certainly exhausted from this travelling."
63. He said, "Do you recall when we took refuge by the rock back there? That is where I neglected the fish, and it is the devil that made me forget it. Strangely, it found its way back to the river."
64. Moses said, "That is exactly the place we are seeking." They traced their footsteps back.
65. They found a servant of ours whom we endowed with mercy from us, and taught him from our own knowledge.
66. Moses said to him, "Can I follow you, so that you teach me from the wisdom you learned?"
67. He said, "You will not bear to stay with me.
68. "How can you bear with things you do not understand?"

69.   He said, "You will find me, God willing, patient; and I will not disobey
      any order you give me."
70.   He said, "Then, if you wish to follow me, do not ask me about anything,
      unless I talk to you about it."
71.   The two of them set out. When they embarked the ship, he bored a hole
      therein. Moses said, "Did you bore a hole therein to drown the people?
      You have committed something terrible."
72.   He said, "Did I not say that you cannot bear it with me.?"
73.   He said, "Please excuse me, for I have forgotten. Do not be too harsh on
      me."
74.   So they set out. When they met a young boy, he killed them. Moses said,
      "Why did you kill this innocent soul, who did not kill anyone? You have
      committed something horrendous."
75.   He said, "Did I not tell you that you will not bear it with me?
76.   He said, "If I ask you about anything else, then you have the right to send
      me away; I have no more excuses to stay in your company."
77.   So they set out. When they reached a town, they asked the people there
      for food, but they refused to host them. Then they found a wall therein
      that was about to fall down, and he straightened it. Moses said, "You
      could have charged a wage for this."
78.   He said, "Now, you and I have to part. I will explain to you all the things
      you could not bear.
79.   "As for the ship, it belonged to poor fishermen, and I wanted to create a
      defect therein. A king was coming after them, who confiscated every ship
      forcibly.
80.   "As for the boy, his parents were believers, and we expected him to cause
      them a great deal of misery through rebellion and disbelief.
81.   "We wanted that their Lord substitutes a better son, who would be
      righteous and more considerate.
82.   "As for the wall, it belonged to two orphan boys in the city, and a treasure
      was hidden beneath it. Their father was a righteous man, so your Lord
      wanted them to grow up and excavate their treasure. All these were
      merciful decisions of your Lord, and I did nothing on my own. This
      explains all the things you could not bear."

Gog and Magog

83.   And they ask you about the one with two horns. Say, "I will tell you about
      him."
84.   We granted him authority on earth, and we gave him the means to do all
      kinds of things.
85.   Then, he pursued one way.

86. When he reached the far West, he found the sun setting in a vast ocean, and he found people there. We said, "You can rule as you please, either punishing them, or treating them kindly."

87. He said, "As for him who works evil, we will punish him, then he will be returned to his Lord for an even worse retribution.

88. "As for him who believes and works righteousness, he has deserved a good reward, and we will treat him amicably."

89. Then he pursued another way.

90. When he reached the far East, he found the sun rising upon people who had no cover to protect them therefrom.

91. We have already known about the things he just discovered

92. Then he pursued another way.

93. When he reached the two palisades, he found people who spoke a different language.

94. They said, "O you with the two horns, Gog and Magog are tyrants; can we pay you to build a barrier between us and them?"

95. He said, "God has blessed me with great abilities, so help me sufficiently, and I will build an obstruction between you and them.

96. "Bring me blocks of iron." He filled the gap between the two cliffs, then said, "Blow." When it became red hot, he said, "Let us pour tar over it."

97. They could neither surmount it, nor could they bore a hole therein.

98. He said, "This is mercy from my Lord, and it will last until my Lord's promise comes to pass. That is when He wipes it out, for my Lord's promise is truth."

99. On that day, we will let them mingle with each other; the horn will be blown, and we will gather them all together.

100. On that day, we will present hell to the disbelievers face to face.

101. Their eyes were blind to My message, and they could not hear.

Idolizing God's Servants

102. Did the disbelievers think that they can get away with idolizing My servants besides Me? We prepared hell for the disbelievers as an abode.

103. Say, "Shall we inform you of the worst losers?

104. "It is those who go astray in this life, yet believe that they are right."

105. They rejected the scriptures of their Lord, and disbelieved in meeting Him. Consequently, their works are in vain, and they have no weight with us on the day of resurrection.

106. Their just requital is hell, because they disbelieved and scoffed at My scriptures and My messengers.

107. As for those who believe and work righteousness, the gardens of bliss will be their abode.

108. Forever they abide therein, and they will want no substitute.

Quran Encompasses Everything We Need

*Uphold the Words of God, Not the Words Attributed to Muhammad**

109.   Say, "If the ocean was ink for the words of my Lord, the ocean would run
       out before the words of my Lord run out, even if we double the ink
       supply."
110.   Say (O Muhammad), "I am no more than a human being like you. It was
       revealed to me that your God is one God. Therefore, whoever looks
       forward to meeting his Lord shall lead a righteous life, and never idolize
       anyone besides his Lord.

---

*18:109-110.   These two verses teach us that there is no shortage of words as
far as God is concerned, and therefore, the Quran contains everything we
need. Anything left out, such as the way to sleep, or the way to eat, etc. is
therefore up to us and our personal preference. We also learn that Muhammad
is no more than a human being like us, and that following the inventions
attributed to him, or even his personal opinions, is idol worship. Note that the
only two verses in Quran describing Muhammad as a human being end up by
enjoining us from idolizing him (see also 41:6).*

Sura 19: Mary (Maryam)

In the name of God, most gracious, most merciful

1. K. H. Y. 'A. S.*
2. This is a reminder of your Lord's mercy towards His servant Zechariah.
3. He called upon his Lord, a secret call.
4. He said, "My Lord, my bones have become brittle, and my head aflame with gray hair. I am confident, my Lord, You will not let me down.
5. "I worry about my folk after my death, for my wife is sterile. Grant me a successor, as a gift from You.
6. "Let him inherit of me, and of the house of Jacob; and make him, my Lord, acceptable."
7. O Zechariah, we give you good news; a boy to be named John; a name we never gave to anyone previously.
8. He said, "My Lord, will I have a boy despite my wife's sterility, and my old age?"
9. (The angel) said, "Thus said your Lord, 'It is easy for Me; I created you previously, and you were nothing.' "
10. He said, "My Lord, give me a sign." He said, "Your sign is that you do not speak to the people three consecutive nights."
11. He came out of the sanctuary, and signaled to his folk, "Glorify God day and night."
12. O John, uphold the scripture strictly. We endowed him with wisdom in his youth.
13. And we blessed him with kindness from us, and sanctity, for he was righteous.
14. He honored his parents, and was never a disobedient rebel.
15. He deserved peace the day he was born, the day of his death, and the day he is resurrected.

Mary

16. And mention in the scripture Mary, when she isolated herself in an Eastern chamber.

19:1. *These five Quranic initials are part of the Quran's miraculous numerical code that proves to the world the divine source of Quran, and the perfect preservation of every single letter therein. As detailed in Appendix 1, the common denominator of all the Quranic initials is the number 19. As it turned out, this sura contains 137 K's (Kaf), 175 H's (Ha), 343 Y's (Ya), 117 'A's ('Ayn), and 26 S's (Sad) in the Arabic text. The total sum of these 5 Arabic alphabets, in this sura, comes to 798 which is a multiple of 19.*

17. While secluded from her folk, we sent to her our Spirit (Gabriel), and he appeared to her as a perfect human.
18. She said, "I seek refuge in God from you, in case this means anything to you."
19. He said, "I am sent by your Lord, to grant you a pious child."
20. She said, "How can I have a child, when no man has touched me, and I am not unchaste?"
21. He said, "Thus said your Lord, 'It is easy for me,' in order to make him a miracle among the people, and a mercy from us; this is the way it will be people, and a mercy from us; this is the way it will be done."
22. She bore him, and isolated herself to a faraway place.
23. When the birth pangs surprised her by the palm tree, she said, "Oh I wish I was dead before this happened, and was completely forgotten."
24. But (the child) called her from under her, saying, "Do not worry, your Lord has provided you with a running stream.
25. "And if you shake the palm tree, it will drop on you ripe dates.
26. "So eat and drink and be happy, and when you see anyone, then say, 'I have pledged to God a fast; I will not talk to anyone.' "
27. She went to her family, carrying him. They said, "O, Mary, you have committed something unbelievable.
28. "O sister of Aaron; your father was not unrighteous, nor was your mother unchaste."
29. She pointed at him; they said, "How can we speak with a child in the crib?"
30. (The child) said, "I am a servant of God. He endowed me with the scripture, and appointed me a prophet.
31. "And He made me blessed whenever I go, and enjoined upon me the **salat** prayers and **zakat** charity, for as long as I live.
32. "I am to honor my mother, for He did not make me a disobedient rebel.
33. "And I have deserved peace the day I was born, the day I die, and the day I am resurrected."

The True Story of Jesus

34. This is the truthful story of Jesus, the son of Mary, about whom they guess.
35. God is never to take a son for Himself; God be glorified. To have anything done, He simply says to it, "Be," and it is.
36. (Jesus preached) that: "God is my Lord and your Lord; you shall worship Him. This is the right path."
37. But the various parties disputed among themselves. Therefore, woe to those who disbelieve from the witnessing of a terrible day.
38. Listen and look at them, on the day they come to us. On that day, the wicked will discover that they had gone astray.

39. You shall warn them of the day of sorrow, when the whole matter is terminated while they are unaware, and while they do not believe.
40. It is us who inherit the earth and everyone thereon, and to us they will be returned.

Abraham

41. And mention in this scripture Abraham. He was a saintly prophet.
42. He said to his father, "O my father, why do you worship what neither hears, nor sees, nor helps you in anything?
43. "O my father, I have attained knowledge you have not attained, so follow me and I will show you the right way.
44. "O my father, do not be a servant to the devil, for the devil has rebelled against God most gracious.
45. "O my father, I fear lest a retribution from the gracious God may afflict you, then you become an ally of the devil."
46. He said, "Are you forsaking my idols, O Abraham? Unless you refrain, I will stone you. Leave me alone."
47. He said, "Peace be upon you; I will ask my Lord to forgive you. He has been gracious towards me.
48. "I will avoid you, and the idols that you set up besides God. I will implore my Lord, and I am confident that my Lord will answer my prayers."
49. Because he avoided them and their idol worship, We granted him Isaac and Jacob, and We made them both prophets.
50. And We blessed them with Our mercy, and endowed them with an honorable and truthful history.

Other Prophets

51. And mention in the scripture Moses; he attained salvation, and he was a messenger prophet.
52. We called him from the right side of Mount Sinai, and We conferred with him privately.
53. And We granted him, out of Our mercy, his brother Aaron as a prophet (to assist him).
54. And mention in the scripture Ishmael; he was truthful whenever he made a promise, and he was a messenger prophet.
55. And he used to order his family to observe the **salat** prayers and **zakat** charity; he was acceptable to his Lord.
56. And mention in the scripture Idris; he was a saintly prophet.
57. And We exalted him to an honorable position.

58. These are some prophets whom God blessed from the descendants of Adam, and those whom We carried with Noah (in the Ark), and from the descendants of Abraham and Israel, and from those whom we guided and chose. Whenever God's revelations are recited to them, they fall prostrate, weeping.

59. Then He established generations after them who lost the **salat** prayers,* and pursued their lusts. Consequently, they have deserved to stray.

60. Only those who repent, believe, and work righteousness will enter Paradise, and will not be deprived of anything.

61. (They enter) the gardens of Eden promised by God in the future, for His servants. Surely, His promise will come to pass.

62. They hear no nonsense therein; only peace, and their provisions are guaranteed therein day and night.

63. Such is Paradise that We offer to the righteous among Our creatures.

The Words of Quran Speaking

64. We (the words of Quran) are not revealed except in accordance with the command of your Lord. To Him belong our past, and our future, and everything between them; and your Lord is never forgetful.*

65. He is the Lord of the heavens and the earth, and everything between them. You shall worship Him and persist in worshiping Him; do you know of any equal to Him?

66. The human being may say, "After I die, how could I be brought back to life?"

67. Does the human not remember that we created him before, and he was nothing?

68. By your Lord, we will indeed gather them all, together with the devils. Then we will bring them around Gehenna, kneeling.

69. Then, we will pick out from each group, the most ardent opponent of the gracious God.

70. For we are fully aware of those who are most worthy of burning therein.

Initially, We All Go To Hell

71. Every single one of you will initially enter therein.* This is an inevitable matter, decreed by your Lord.

19:59.   *This verse informs us that the Jews, Christians, and Muslims were enjoined to observe the* **salat** *prayers, but they have "lost" it. Today, there is a diminishing proportion of Muslims who still observe this divine commandment (see 2:43, 83, 110, 10:87, 14:37, 19:31, 55, 20:14, 31:17, and 35:8).*

19:64.   *A reminder to those who see wisdom in the words of other than God.*

19:71.   *Your appreciation and enjoyment of heaven doubles after seeing what hell is like.*

72. Then, we save those who worked righteousness, leaving the wicked therein humiliated.

73. (That is because) when our revelations are recited to them, clearly explained, the disbelievers ask the believers, "Which side is more powerful, and greater in number?"

74. We annihilated many generations before them, who were better equipped, and better endowed.

75. Say, "Those who choose the straying, the gracious God will lead them on, and even encourage them, until they see what is awaiting them; either the retribution or the hour. That is when they discover who are really in worse shape, and weaker in power.

76. As for those who choose the guidance, God augments their guidance. and their recorded righteous works bring them better rewards from your Lord, and better returns.

77. Have you noted the one who rejects our revelations, then says, "I will attain wealth and children"?

78. Has he seen the future, or did he make such a covenant with God most gracious?

79. Nay, we will write everything he says, and afflict him with more retribution.

80. We will let him inherit whatever he says, then he comes to us as an individual.

The Idols Disown Their Idolizers*

81. They set up idols besides God, to be of help to them.

82. Instead, the idols will disown their idol worship, and become their enemies.

83. Do you not note how we unleash the devils on the disbelievers to stir them up?

84. Therefore, do not be impatient; we are preparing for them some preparation.

19:81-82.   By their own admission, the people who idolize Muhammad, Jesus, Mary, or the saints believe that these idols will help them. However, we learn here that the idols will disown their idolizers, and abhor their idol worship. Those who idolize Muhammad and pursue the words and actions attributed to him, will be terribly embarrassed and ashamed when Muhammad disowns them on the day of judgment. Those who call upon Mary, who is dead, powerless, and totally unaware, to bring peace to Ireland for example, will be similarly doomed. Idol worship is the only unforgivable offense, and the idols themselves enjoined us from falling in such sin (see Deuteronomy 6:4, Mark 12:29, and Quran 17:23).

85. The day will come when we gather the righteous before God most gracious, in a group.
86. And herd the guilty to Gehenna as their stockade.
87. None will have the power of intercession, unless it agrees with the covenant of God most gracious.

The Great Blasphemy

88. They said, "God most gracious has begotten a son!"
89. Indeed, you have uttered a gross blasphemy.
90. The heavens are about to shatter, the earth is about to burst, and the mountains are about to crumble,
91. Upon hearing such a claim about God most gracious.
92. It is utterly improper that God most gracious should take for Himself a son.
93. Every single one in the heavens and the earth is no more than a slave of God most gracious.
94. He has counted every single one of them.
95. And each will come before Him as an individual, on the day of resurrection.
96. Surely, those who believe and lead a righteous life, God most gracious will shower them with love.
97. Thus, we have elucidated this scripture in your tongue, to deliver good news to the righteous, and to warn therewith those who oppose.
98. We annihilated many generations in the past; do you perceive any of them, or hear from them any sound?

Sura 20: Ṭ. H. (Ṭa Ha)

In the name of God, most Gracious, most Merciful

1.   Ṭ. H.*
2.   We did not reveal this Quran to you (O Muhammad) to cause you any hardship.
3.   Only to remind the reverent.
4.   A revelation from the One who created the earth, and the high heavens.
5.   God most gracious; He has assumed all authority.
6.   To Him belong everything in the heavens and everything in the earth, and everything between them, and everything beneath the soil.
7.   And whether you declare your thoughts, (or not,) He knows the secrets, and even what is better hidden.
8.   The one God; there is no god except He; to Him belong the most beautiful names.

Moses

9.   Has the history of Moses come to you?
10. When he saw a fire, he said to his family, "Wait here; I have seen a fire. Maybe I can bring you some of it, or find some guidance at the fire."
11. When he came to it, he was called, "O Moses,
12. "I am your Lord, so take off your shoes. You are in the sacred valley Tuwa.*
13. "And I have chosen you, so listen to what is revealed.
14. "I am the one God; there is no god except Me. You shall worship Me, and observe the **salat** prayers to commemorate Me.
15. "The hour is sure to come; I keep it almost hidden, to repay each soul for whatever it did.*
16. "So, do not be distracted therefrom by those who disbelieve therein and follow their own opinions, lest you perish.
17. "And what is that in your right hand, Moses?"

20:1.   Like all the other Quranic initials, these letters participate in the Quran's miraculous numerical code. They present the reader with physical, examinable, and indisputable proof that the Quran is God's message to the world (see Appendix 1).

20:12.   Note that God speaks here in the first person singular, because the angels are not involved. Wherever the plural is used, the angels are involved and given credit for their participation.

20:15.   Go to sura 15 to find the Quranic statement regarding the end of the world.

18. He said, "This is my staff. I lean on it, herd my sheep therewith, and use it for other purposes."
19. He said, "Throw it down, Moses."
20. He threw it down, and it turned into a live serpent.
21. He said, "Pick it up, and do not be afraid; we will return it to its original state.
22. "And put your hand under your wing, and it will come out white without a blemish; another miracle.
23. "We will give you some of our great revelations.
24. "Go to Pharaoh, for he has transgressed."
25. He said, "My Lord, cool my temper,
26. "And make this matter easy for me,
27. "And untie a knot in my tongue,
28. "To let them understand my speech.
29. "And appoint an assistant for me from my family,
30. "Aaron my brother.
31. "Strengthen my mission with him,
32. And make him my partner in this matter,
33. "That we may glorify You frequently,
34. "And commemorate You frequently.
35. "Surely, You are seer of us."
36. He said, "You are granted your request, Moses.
37. "And we have bestowed other blessings upon you before,
38. "When we inspired your mother certain inspirations.
39. "That: 'You shall throw him into the box, then throw him into the river, and the river will cast him to the bank. An enemy of Mine and his will get hold of him.' And I showered you with love from Me, and I had you made under My watchful eyes.
40. "Your sister then followed you, and said, 'Let me tell you about one who can nurse him.' We thus returned you to your mother, in order to keep her happy, and to remove her worries. And you killed someone, but we saved you from disaster, and tested you thoroughly. Then you lived years in Midian, and now you have come according to plan, Moses.
41. "I have made you just for Me.
42. "Go, you and your brother, with My revelations to Pharaoh, and do not waver in commemorating Me.
43. "Go to Pharaoh, for he has transgressed.
44. "Talk to him gently, that he may take heed, or become reverent."
45. They said, "Our Lord, we fear lest he persecutes us, or transgresses."
46. He said, "Have no fear; I will be with you, listening and watching.
47. "Go to him and say, 'We are messengers from your Lord, so let the children of Israel go with us, and stop persecuting them. We bring miracles to you, and peace be upon those who follow the guidance.'

48. " 'It has been revealed to us that retribution is inevitable for those who disbelieve and turn away.' "

49. Pharaoh said, "Who is your Lord, Moses?"

50. He said, "Our Lord is the one who gave everything its existence, then provided guidance."

51. He said, "What about the previous generations?"

52. He said, "The knowledge thereof is with my Lord in a record; my Lord never errs, nor does He forget."

53. "He is the one who made the earth for your habitation, and erected for you roads therein, and sends down water from the sky, to produce therewith all kinds of plants."

54. Eat and herd your livestock. These are lessons for those who possess intelligence.

55. From it We created you, and into it We return you, and from it We bring you out again."

56. We showed Pharaoh all Our miracles, but he disbelieved and refused.

57. He said, "Did you come to evict us from our land with your magic, Moses?

58. "We will surely show you similar magic, so set up an appointment that neither we nor you shall break, and let us meet on neutral grounds."

59. He said, "Your appointment is the day of festival, and let the people gather at forenoon."

60. Pharaoh then went and mobilized his forces, and came.

61. Moses said to them, "Woe to you; do not fabricate lies against God, lest He smites you with retribution. The fabricators never succeed."

62. They conferred with each other, and secretly decided.

63. They said, "These two are simply magicians who want to evict you from your land with their magic, and destroy your good way of life.

64. "Thus, mobilize your forces, and come united. Whoever wins today will be exalted."

65. They said, "O Moses, either you throw, or we throw first."

66. He said, "You go ahead," whereupon their ropes and sticks appeared to him, because of their magic, to be moving.

67. Fear crept into Moses.

68. We said, "Have no fear; you are the winner.

69. "Throw what is in your right hand, and it will swallow everything they fabricated. What they fabricated is a magicians's trick, and the magician can never succeed in this manner.

70. The magicians fell prostrate, saying, "We believe in the Lord of Aaron and Moses."

71. Pharaoh said, "Did you believe in him before I give you permission? He must be your leader who taught you magic. I will cut off your hands and feet on alternate sides, and crucify you on the palm trunks. You will find out which of us can inflict a severe and lasting retribution."

72. They said, "We will not give you preference over the one who created us, and the profound miracles shown to us. So issue whatever judgment you wish; you only rule in this lowly life.

73. "We have believed in our Lord, that He may forgive us our sins, and the magic you forced us to commit. God is far better, and ever lasting."

74. Indeed, whoever comes guilty to his Lord, has deserved Gehenna, wherein he neither dies, nor lives.

75. And whoever comes to Him as a believer who had worked righteousness, then these have deserved the highest ranks.

76. They abide forever in gardens of Eden, with flowing streams. This is the reward for the pious.

The Children of Israel Delivered

77. We inspired Moses that: "You shall move out with My servants, and strike a dry path across the sea. Do not fear capture, or oppression."

78. Pharaoh pursued them, with his troops, but the sea overwhelmed them.

79. Thus, Pharaoh misled his people, and never guided them.

80. O children of Israel, we saved you from your enemy, summoned you to the right side of Mount Sinai, and provided you with manna and quails.

81. Eat from the good things we provided for you, and do not transgress, lest you incur My wrath. Whoever incurs My wrath is doomed to failure.

82. Yet, I forgive those who repent, believe, work righteousness, and maintain the guidance.

83. And why did you rush away from your people, Moses?

84. He said, "They are close behind me, and I rushed to You, my Lord, that You may be pleased."

85. God said, "We have tested your people during your absence, and the Samarian led them astray."

86. Moses returned to his people, angry and disappointed. He said, "O my people, did you not receive a good promise from your Lord? Has it been too long for you, or were you anxious to incur wrath from your Lord? Is this why you violated your agreement with me?"

87. They said, "We did not violate your agreement on our own accord. We wanted to get rid of our loads of jewelry, so we threw them in, and so advised the Samarian."

88. He produced for them a sculpted calf, complete with sound, so they said, "This is your god, and the god of Moses." He certainly forgot.

89. Did they not see that it could not answer them, nor possess any power to harm them or benefit them?

90. And Aaron said to them repeatedly, "O my people, you are being put to the test therewith. Your true God is the most gracious God, so follow me, and obey my order."

91. They said, "We will continue to worship it, until Moses returns."

92. Moses said, "O Aaron, what prevented you, when you saw them go astray,

93. "From following me? Have you disobeyed my orders?"

94. He said, "O son of my mother, do not pull my beard and my hair. I feared lest you say, 'You divided the children of Israel, and did not observe my instructions.' "

95. He said, "What is the matter with you, O Samarian?"

96. He said, "I saw what they failed to see. So, I picked up a trace from the (angel) messenger, and used it (to make the calf). It was my own idea."

97. He said, "Then go; throughout your life, do not come close. You have incurred an inevitable retribution. As for your god, whom you worshiped, we will burn it up, then throw it into the bottom of the sea."

98. Your only God is the one God; there is no god except He; His knowledge encompasses all things.

99. We thus narrate to you some history from the past, and we have given you a message from us.

100. Anyone who disregards it will bear a terrible burden on the day of resurrection.

101. They abide therein forever; what a miserable load on the day of resurrection!

102. That is the day when the horn is blown, and the guilty are summoned blue.

103. As they whisper to each other, they would say, "You lasted only ten days."

104. We are fully aware of whatever they say, and the closest to the truth among them would say, "You lasted no more than one day."

105. And they ask you what will happen to the mountains. Say, "My Lord will completely wipe them out."

106. He will thus leave the earth perfectly level.

107. "Not even a crookedness, or a terrain, will you see therein."

108. On that day, they will follow the summoner, without the least deviation, and all voices will yield to God most gracious; you will not hear but whispers.

No Intercession For the Wicked

109.   On that day, intercession will be useless, except for those permitted by God most gracious, and whose intercession happens to agree with God's decisions.

110.   He knows their past, and their future, while their knowledge never encompasses Him.

111.   All faces will submit to the living, the eternal God, and thus, those burdened by sin will be doomed.

112.   As for those who worked righteousness, while believing, they fear no hardship, nor humiliation.

113.   Thus, we send it down as an Arabic Quran, and we cite in it all kinds of admonitions, that they may turn to righteousness or take heed.

114.   Most exalted is God, the true king. Do not hasten to utter the Quran (O Muhammad), before you are ordered to reveal it, and say, "My Lord, increase my knowledge."*

115.   We have made an agreement with Adam previously, but he forgot, and we found him lacking in strength.

Adam Fails

116.   When we said to the angels, "Fall prostrate before Adam, they fell prostrate, except Iblis (Satan); he refused.

117.   So we said, "O Adam, this is an enemy of you and your wife; let him not evict you from heaven, lest you become miserable.

118.   "You are guaranteed that you do not hunger therein, nor go naked.

119.   "And that you do not thirst therein, nor suffer any heat."

120.   But the devil whispered to him, saying, "O Adam, let me show you the tree of eternity, and ever lasting kingship."

121.   They ate from it, whereupon their bodies became visible to them, and they tried to cover themselves with the leaves of Paradise. Thus, Adam disobeyed his Lord, and lost.

122.   Then his Lord chose him; He redeemed and guided him.

123.   God said, "Go down therefrom, all of you, as enemies of one another. When guidance comes to you from Me, those who follow My guidance will never go astray, nor suffer misery.

124.   "As for him who disregards My message, he will have a miserable life, and we raise him, on the day of resurrection, blind."

125.   He would say, "My Lord, why did you raise me blind, when I was a seer?"

20:114-115.   *Muhammad was given the Quran in one night, to be released over a period of 23 years, in a manner similar to the teaching of Adam (see 17:1 and 106).*

126. God will say, "Because our revelations came to you, but you discarded them. Consequently, you are discarded today."

127. We punish those who transgress and refuse to believe in the revelations of their Lord. Additionally, the retribution of the hereafter is even worse, and ever lasting.

128. Did it ever occur to them that we annihilated many generations before them? They are walking in the dwellings left by them. This should be a lesson for those who possess understanding.

129. If it were not for your Lord's decision to predetermine their end, they would have been judged immediately.

130. Therefore, be patient in the face of their utterances, and praise the glory of your Lord before sunrise and before sunset; also during parts of the night, and at both ends of the day, that you may attain happiness.

131. Do not covet what we bestow upon the various kinds of people, for these are temporary vanities of this life; we only test them therewith. Your Lord's blessings are far better, and everlasting.

Important Commandment

132. You shall exhort your family to observe the **salat** prayers, and persist in doing so. We do not ask you for any provisions; it is us who provide for you. The final victory belongs to the righteous.

133. They said, "How come he does not show us any miracle from his Lord?" Did they not know how many miracles we manifested in the previous missions?*

134. Had we afflicted them with retribution without this message, they would have said, "Our Lord, had You sent a messenger to us, we would have honored Your message, and would have evaded this humiliation and disgrace."

135. Say, "Everyone is waiting, so wait along. You will find out who are following the right path and the true guidance."

20:133.   See 17:59 and 29:50-51.

Sura 21:   The Prophets (Al-Anbyaa')

In the name of God, most gracious, most merciful

1. The reckoning for the people is fast approaching, while they are totally unaware, heedless.
2. Whenever a new reminder comes to them from their Lord, they listen to it thoughtlessly.
3. Their hearts are distracted, and the wicked confide to each other, "Is he not just a human being like you? Would you accept magic while you see?"
4. He said, "My Lord is fully aware of all the utterances in the heaven and the earth; He is the Hearer, the Omniscient.
5. They even said, "He dreamt this up; he invented it; he is a poet. Let him show us a miracle like the past messengers."*
6. Any community that disbelieved in the past was annihilated; would these people believe?
7. We did not send before you except men whom we inspired, so ask those who know, if you do not know.
8. We did not give them bodies that required no food, nor were they immortal.
9. We always fulfilled our promise to them; we saved them, together with those whom we chose, and we destroyed the transgressors.
10. We send down to you this book, containing your message. Do you not understand?
11. Many a community we punished in the past because of their wickedness, and we established after them other people.
12. When they sensed our punishment coming, they started to run.
13. Do not run, and return to your material luxuries and your homes, that you may be held accountable.
14. They said, "Woe to us, we were really wrong."
15. This continued to be their utterance, until we completely wiped them out.
16. We did not create the heavens and the earth, and everything between them, for amusement.
17. If we wanted to make up an amusement, we could have done it on our own.
18. But we want to set up the truth against falsehood, in order to expose it and render it obsolete. Woe to you from your claims.
19. To Him belongs everyone in the heavens and the earth, and those at Him are never too arrogant to worship Him, nor do they ever regret it.
20. They glorify (Him) day and night without tiring.

21:5.   See 17:59, 20:133, and 29:50-51.

Do Not Idolize the Prophets

21. Have they found gods on earth who can resurrect the dead?

22. If there were gods (in the heavens and the earth) besides God, they would have been corrupted. Therefore, God be glorified; He is the Lord with total authority; high above any description.

23. He is never questioned about anything He does, while they are questioned.

24. Have they found gods besides Him? Say, "Show us your proofs. This Quran is my proof; it encompasses the present and the past." Indeed, most of them fail to recognize the truth; this is why they turn away.

25. We did not send any messenger before you, except with the message, "There is no god except Me; therefore, you shall worship Me."

26. But they said, "God most gracious has taken for Himself a son!" God be glorified; nay, the prophets are no more than honored servants.

27. Their utterances shall never supercede His;* instead, they follow His orders.

28. He knows their past and their future, and they do not possess the power of intercession, except on behalf of those already saved by Him. The prophets themselves worry about their own fate.

29. Furthermore, if any of them ever claims to be an idol besides God, we will throw him in Gehenna. We thus punish the wicked.

The "Big Bang Theory" Confirmed*

30. Do the disbelievers not realize that the heavens and the earth used to be one entity; then we parted them? And we made water a requisite for every living organism. Therefore, would they not believe?

31. And we placed stabilizers on earth, lest it swerves with them, and we placed valleys therein to serve as roads, that they may travel.

32. And we made the sky a protected ceiling; they are heedless of all the marvels therein.

33. And He is the one who created the night and day, and the sun and moon, each floating in its own orbit.

---

*21:27. In defiance of God and His messenger Muhammad, multitudes of Muslims have turned to the utterances attributed to Muhammad for wisdom and religious regulations. Many of them uphold these inventions, known as "**Hadith**," so strongly that it abrogates the Quran (see footnote 24:1-2). See also 6:112-116.*

21:30. A prominent theory among the scientific community dealing with the origin of the universe

34. We never made any human before you immortal; if you die, are they immortal?

35. Everyone will taste death; you are now being tested through adversity, as well as prosperity, then you will be returned to us.

36. When the disbelievers see you, they scoff at you, saying, "Is this the one who attacks your idols?" Meanwhile, they reject the message of God most gracious.

37. The human being is hasty by nature; I will afflict you (disbelievers) with My judgments; do not be in a hurry.

38. They say, "When will that threat come to pass, if you are truthful?"

39. If only the disbelievers realize how they will try to ward off the fire from their faces and their backs! They will have none to help them.

40. Indeed, judgment will afflict them suddenly; it will overwhelm them, so they can neither evade it, nor will they be respited.

41. Messengers before you have been ridiculed, and those who mocked them were doomed because of their ridiculing.

All Power Belongs to God

42. Say, "Who can protect you during the night and day besides God most gracious?" Indeed, they are neglecting the message of their Lord.

43. Have they found gods who can help them besides us? They cannot even help themselves, nor can they band together against us.

44. Indeed, we allowed these people, and their parents, to go on for a long life. Do they not realize that every day on earth brings them closer to the end? Can they alter this?

45. Say, "I only warn you according to the revelations." However, the deaf cannot hear the call, when they are warned.

46. Only when afflicted with a touch of your Lord's retribution do the wicked admit, "Woe to us; we were indeed wrong."

47. We will set up the equitable scales on the day of resurrection. Thus, not a soul will be wronged in the least. Even the equivalent of a mustard seed will be brought by us. We suffice as reckoners.

Moses and Aaron

48. We have given Moses and Aaron the statute book, and enlightenment, and a message for the righteous;

49. Who reverence their Lord in their privacy, and worry about the hereafter.

50. Similarly, this is a blessed message that we send down; are you going to deny it?

Abraham

51. And we gave Abraham his guidance before that; we were fully aware of him.
52. He said to his father and his people, "What are these statues that you worship?"
53. They said, "We found our ancestors worshiping them."
54. He said, "Indeed, you and your ancestors are totally astray."
55. They said, "Have you brought the truth, or are you just playing?"
56. He said, "Nay, your Lord is the Lord of the heavens and the earth, who created them. This is what I testify to.
57. "By God, I will do something about your statues, as soon as you leave."
58. He broke them into pieces, leaving the biggest among them, that they may refer to it.
59. They said, "Who did this to our gods? He is really wicked."
60. They said, "We heard a youth threaten them; his name is Abraham."
61. They said, "Then bring him in front of all the people, that they may bear witness."
62. They said, "Did you do this to our gods, Abraham?"
63. He said, "It must be the biggest one who did it. So ask them, if they do speak."
64. They conferred and said to each other, "Indeed, it is you who are wrong."
65. Yet, they reverted, against their own common sense, (and said), "You know well that these cannot speak."
66. He said, "Do you then worship besides God what is too powerless to benefit you or harm you?
67. "Shame on you and whatever idols you set up besides God. Do you not understand?"
68. They said, "Burn him in support of your gods; this is what you should do."
69. We said, "O fire, be cool and safe for Abraham."
70. They wanted to oppress him, but we made them the losers.
71. And we saved him, together with Lot, to the land that we blessed for all the people.

The Origin of **Salat** Prayers and **Zakat** Charity

72. We granted him Isaac and Jacob as a gift, and we made them righteous.

73. We made them imams who guide according to our commandments, and we taught them how to work righteousness, and how to observe the **salat** prayers and **zakat** charity.* To us, they were worshipers.

Lot

74. As for Lot, we endowed him with wisdom and knowledge, and we saved him from the community that committed vice. Indeed, they were evil and wicked people.
75. And we admitted him into our mercy, for he was righteous.

Noah

76. And when Noah called before that, we responded to him, and saved him and his family from the great disaster.
77. And we supported him against the people who rejected our revelations. Because they were evil people, we drowned them all.

David and Solomon

78. And when David and Solomon issued their judgments regarding the sheep that ate some people's crops, we were witnessing their judgments.
79. We endowed Solomon with the correct understanding, though we endowed both of them with wisdom and knowledge. And we subjugated the mountains to David; they submitted, and so did the birds. This is what we did.
80. And we taught him the manufacture of shields that protect you from each other's aggression. Would you be thankful?
81. For Solomon, we subjugated the winds, gusting and blowing at his command to the land that we blessed. We are fully aware of all things.
82. Also the devils were subjugated to dive for him, and do all kinds of work; we kept them in his service.

Job

83. And when Job called upon his Lord, saying, "Adversity has afflicted me, and You are the most merciful,"

---

*21:73.   Those who refuse to believe God's repeated assertions that the Quran is complete and perfect (see 6:38, 114, 17:89, 18:54, 30:58, & 39:27), frequently pose a favorite question. They ask, "If the Quran is complete and perfect, where can we find details of **salat** prayers?" This question obviously reveals their ignorance of the Quran. We learn from this verse, as well as many other verses, that **salat** and **zakat** were given originally to Abraham and his family, then transmitted to us generation after generation (see 2:128, 187, 3:68, 16:123, 22:27, 78, and Appendix 8).*

84. we answered his prayer, and relieved his adversity. We restored his family for him, and multiplied them, as mercy from us, and a reminder for the worshipers.

Many Prophets; One Message

85. Similarly, Ishmael, Idris, and Dhal-kifl; each was steadfastly patient.
86. We admitted them into our mercy, for they were righteous.
87. And when Dhan-noon (Jonah) left in anger, and thought that we could not reach him, he ended up calling from the darkness (of the fish): "There is no god except You; glory be to You; I was wrong indeed."
88. We then answered his prayer, and saved him from the disaster; we thus save the believers.
89. And when Zechariah called upon his Lord: "My Lord, leave me not childless, though You are the ultimate inheritor,"
90. we answered his prayer, and granted him John; we fixed his wife for him. They used to hasten into righteous works, and turn to us in need, as well as in reverence; to us, they were humble.
91. And the one who guarded her chastity, we blew into her from the spirit, and we made her and her son a sign for the whole world.
92. Such is your religion: one religion, and I am your Lord, so worship Me.
93. However, they divided themselves into different religions; all are returning to us.
94. Whoever works righteousness, while a believer, his works will never go in vain; we are recording them.
95. Never will a community that we annihilated return back (to this world).
96. Not until Gog and Magog are opened; that is when they will come from every direction.
97. The truthful promise comes to pass, and those who disbelieved in our revelations will look in horror: "Woe to us, we were totally heedless of this. Indeed, we were wrong."
98. Surely, you and the idols you set up besides God will be fuel for Gehenna; you will be thrown therein.
99. If these were really gods, they would not have gone therein; they will abide therein forever.
100. They wail loudly therein, and they will be isolated from hearing anything.
101. As for those who have deserved our blessings, they will be protected therefrom.
102. Not even its hissing will be heard by them, and they will abide forever in everything they desire.
103. The great horror will not worry them, and the angels receive them, saying, "This is your day, that has been promised to you."

104. On that day, We will fold the heavens like the folding of a book. Then, as We initiated the first creation, We will initiate a new creation. This is a promise that We will carry out.

105. We already recorded in the Psalms, as We do in this message, that the earth will be inherited by My righteous servants.

106. This is a declaration for the people who worship.

107. We did not send you, except out of mercy towards the whole world.

108. Say, "It has been revealed to me that your God is one God; will you then submit to Him?"

109. If they turn away, then say, "I have given you the announcement exactly as given to me, and I have no idea how soon or far is what is promised to you.

110. "Only He knows your declared utterances, as well as whatever you conceal.

111. "For all that I know, this is a test, and a temporary life for you."

112. He said, "My Lord, your judgment is equitable. Our Lord most gracious is the helper against your claims."

Sura 22: Pilgrimage (Al-Hajj)

In the name of God, most gracious, most merciful

1. O People, observe your Lord, for the shock of the Hour is a tremendous thing.

2. The day you see it, even a nursing mother will discard her infant, and the pregnant will abort her fetus. And you will see the people intoxicated, not from intoxicants, but because God's retribution is severe.

3. Some people argue against God without knowledge, and follow every rebellious devil.

4. It has been decreed that anyone who allies himself with him, he will mislead him, and guide him only to the agony of hell.

Do You Doubt Resurrection?

5. O people, if you have any doubt concerning resurrection, then (reflect on this): We created you from dust, then from a drop, then from a clot, then from a fetus that is given life or deemed lifeless in order to show you. Then we settle in the wombs what we will for a specific period, then we bring you out as an infant, then you attain full maturity; some of you die, while others attain the oldest age, only to realize that their knowledge is limited. Also, you see the land lifeless, then we send down water, whereupon it moves with life, and produces all kinds of beautiful plants.

6. This proves that God is the truth, and that He can resurrect the dead, and that He is omnipotent.

7. And that the Hour is coming; there is no doubt about it, and that God resurrects those in the graves.

8. Yet, some people argue about God without knowledge, without guidance, and without an enlightening scripture.

9. Turning away in arrogance, he causes others to deviate from the path of God. He has deserved humiliation in this life, and we commit him on the day of resurrection to the agony of burning.

10. This is what your own hands have advanced for you; God is never unjust towards the creatures.

11. And there is the one who worships God conditionally; if something good happens to him, he is content, but when a tribulation afflicts him, he reverts. Thus, he loses both this life and the hereafter. This is the real loss.

12. He idolizes besides God what neither harms him, nor benefits him. This is the farthest straying.

13. He idolizes one who is more likely to hurt him than benefit him; what a miserable master; what a miserable companion!

14.   As for those who believe and work righteousness, God admits them into gardens with flowing streams. God does what He wills.

Relevance of Faith to This Life*

15.   If any one thinks that God cannot support him in this life, as well as in the hereafter, let him turn totally to God and sever (his idolization towards anyone else). He will then find out that this plan eliminates his worries.

16.   We thus reveal these clear revelations, then God guides whomever He wills.

17.   Those who believe, those who are Jewish, the converts, the Christians, the Magi, and the idol worshipers; God will judge them all on the day of resurrection. God is witnessing all things.

18.   Do you not realize that to God prostrate those in the heavens, and those in the earth, and the sun, and the moon, and the stars, and the mountains, and the trees, and the animals, and many people? Other people are committed to doom. Whomever God commits to humiliation, you will find none to honor him. God does what He wills.

19.   Of the two opposing sides, with regard to their Lord, those who disbelieve have deserved garments of fire, and lava being poured on their heads.

20.   Even their insides melt therefrom, and their skins.*

21.   They will be confined in iron cells.

22.   Whenever they try to flee from the agony thereof, they will be returned therein: "Taste the retribution of burning."

23.   As for those who believe and work righteousness, God will admit them into gardens with flowing streams. They are adorned therein with bracelets of gold, and their clothes are silk.

24.   They have been guided to the right message; they have been guided in the path of God most praised.

25.   Those who disbelieve and repel others from the path of God, and from the Sacred Mosque that we appointed for all the people to retreat therein or just visit, and those who introduce any wickedness therein, we will commit them to painful retribution.

22:15.   The problem with most people is that they do not realize the direct relevance of religion to their lives. The fact is that our happiness in this world, our success in all our worldly affairs, as well as our happiness in the eternal real life, depend on following God's law. The vast majority of people, unfortunately, are unaware that God runs every minute detail in this world (see 10:61-64).

22:20-23.   These are allegorical descriptions of heaven and hell (see Appendix 4).

Hajj Pilgrimage, Like All Religious
Practices, Decreed Through Abraham*

26. We pointed out for Abraham the location of the shrine: "You shall never idolize anything besides Me, and purify My shrine for those who encircle it, retreat in it, and those who bow and prostrate therein.

27. "And announce that the people shall observe the **hajj** pilgrimage. They will come to you walking and riding; they will come from the farthest valleys.

28. "They will reap many benefits, commemorate God's name during the specified days, and show their appreciation for the livestock He provides for them. Eat therefrom, and feed the poor and the needy.

29. "They shall carry out the religious duties, fulfill their vows, and encircle the grand shrine."

30. Indeed, for those who respect the sacred duties decreed by God, it will be better for them at their Lord. All livestock are permitted for you as food, except what is already stated. You shall avoid the abomination of idol worship, and avoid false regulations.*

31. You shall devote your worship to God alone; do not set up any idols besides Him. Anyone who idolizes anything besides God is like one who falls from the sky, and gets snatched away by the vultures, or gets blown away by the wind into a bottomless pit.

32. Indeed, those who honor the offerings decreed by God, demonstrate the righteousness of their hearts.

33. After reaping benefits from the livestock for awhile, they offer it as charity at the grand shrine.

34. We decreed certain rituals for each congregation, whereby they show their appreciation of God's provision of livestock. However, your God is the same God; you shall submit to Him. Give good news to the reverent;

35. whose hearts cringe upon remembering God, remain steadfast in the face of adversity, observe the **salat** prayers, and give to charity from our provisions to them.

---

*22:26. Many people erroneously assume that all religious practices in Islam were originally decreed through Muhammad. The Quran, however, consistently teaches that Abraham was the original source of **salat**, **zakat**, fasting, and **hajj** (see 2:128, 135, 3:67-68, 95, 16:123, 21:73, and 22:78).*

*22:30. This verse alerts us that following false regulations regarding food prohibitions is tantamount to idol worship; following religious regulations not decreed by God is idol worship. The major source of false regulations is "**hadith**" and "**sunna**."*

36. The livestock offerings are part of the religious duties decreed by God, for your own good. Thus, you shall mention God's name as you sacrifice them. Once they fall on their sides, you shall eat therefrom, and feed the poor and needy. That is what we created them for, that you may be appreciative.

37. None of their meat or blood reaches God; what reaches Him is your righteousness. That is what He created them for; that you may magnify God for guiding you; give good news to the good doers.

God Defends the Believers

38. God surely defends those who believe; and God loves not any betrayer, unappreciative.

39. Sanction is given to those who suffer aggression, because of the injustice that befalls them. God certainly is able to give them victory.

40. They are evicted from their homes unjustly; for no reason other than saying, "Our Lord is God." If it were not for God's setting up of some people against others, synagogues, churches, and mosques; where God's name is commemorated frequently; would have been destroyed. Most certainly, God will support those who support Him. God is powerful, almighty.

41. (God supports) those who, upon assuming control on earth, establish the **salat** prayers and **zakat** charity, and advocate righteousness and prohibit evil. The ultimate victory belongs with God.

The Disbelievers Consistently Doomed

42. If they disbelieve you, others before them have disbelieved, such as the people of Noah, 'Ad, and Thamood.

43. And the people of Abraham, and the people of Lot.

44. And the inhabitants of Midyan; even Moses was disbelieved. I consistently allowed the disbelievers to carry on for awhile, then I punished them. How devastating was My retribution!

45. Every community that we destroyed because of their wickedness, ended up in ruins, stilled wells, and empty mansions.

46. Did they not travel the land, then have hearts that understand, and ears that hear? Indeed, it is not the eyes that go blind; it is the hearts inside the chests that go blind.

47. They challenge you to bring doom upon them! God never breaks His promise, and a day at your Lord is like one thousand years of your count.

48. Many a community I allowed to carry on their wickedness for awhile, then I punished them; to Me is the final destiny.

49. Say, "O people, I am no more than a manifest warner for you."

50. As for those who believe and work righteousness, they have deserved forgiveness and a generous reward.

51. As for those who challenge our revelations, they have deserved Gehenna.

Messengers Surrounded By Tests

52. Every messenger and prophet before you, did not preach the message without having the devil interfere to frustrate his wishes. God then nullifies the devil's works, and establishes His revelations. God is omniscient, wise.

53. God thus sets up the devil's work as a test, to expose those with disease in their hearts, and those whose hearts are hardened. Indeed, the wicked are thus blocked out.*

54. At the same time, those who have attained knowledge recognize the truth from your Lord, then believe therein, and fill their hearts thereof. God will always guide those who believe to the right path.

55. As for those who disbelieve, they will continue to harbor doubts, until the Hour comes to them suddenly, or the retribution of a miserable day.

56. On that day, all kingship belongs to God, and He will judge them. Then, those who believed and led a righteous life, will be in the gardens of bliss.

57. As for those who disbelieved and rejected our revelations, they have deserved humiliating retribution.

58. Those who flee their homes in the cause of God, then are killed or die, God will certainly reward them generously; God is the best provider.

59. He will certainly admit them into a position that pleases them. God is omniscient, clement.

60. If anyone avenges the persecution against him with an equitable punishment, then is attacked again, God will certainly protect him and grant him victory. God is pardoner, forgiver.

Tokens of God's Power

61. God is the one who merges the night into the day, and merges the day into the night. God is hearer, seer.

22:52-55. *As part of the tests to distinguish the true believers from the insincere ones, the devil is permitted to impart some suspicious or immoral accusations against those who serve God's message. While the believers recognize the devil's work, and steadfastly uphold God's message, the others are driven away by the devil's plan, and thus reject God's path on account of the messenger's apparent fault. As stated in verse 54, the sincere believers worship God, not the messenger, and uphold God's message, regardless of the messenger's personal characteristics. While the murder committed by Moses and his speech defect (see 43:52-54) drove away the unfortunate, the believers followed him and were saved.*

62. God is the truth, and whatever else they set up as idols besides Him is falsehood. God is the most high, the great.
63. Do you not see that God sends down water from the sky, causing the earth to turn green? God is kind, fully cognizant.
64. To Him belong everything in the heavens and everything on earth. God is bounteous, most praised.
65. Do you not see how God placed in your service everything on earth, as well as the ships that roam the sea? And He prevents the sky from crashing with the earth, except in accordance with His command. God is compassionate towards the people, most merciful.
66. He is the one who gave you life, then He puts you to death, then brings you back to life. Indeed, the human being is unappreciative.
67. We decreed religious duties for each congregation, so let them not dispute with you. And continue to invite them to the path of your Lord, for you are in the right guidance.
68. If they argue with you, then say, "God is fully aware of everything you do."
69. God is the one who will judge between you on the day of resurrection, regarding your disputes.
70. Do you know that God knows everything in the heavens and the earth? This is already in a record; this is easy for God.
71. Yet, they idolize besides God powerless idols, and idols they do not even know. The wicked will never be helped (by their idols).
72. And when our clear revelations are recited, you recognize denial on the faces of those who disbelieve. They almost attack those who simply recite our revelations to them. Say, "Shall I tell you what is worse? That is the hellfire which is promised by God for those who disbelieve. What a miserable destiny!"

Can Your Idols Create A Fly?

73. O people, here is an example for you to ponder: the idols you set up besides God can never create a fly; even if they banded together. Furthermore, if the fly steals anything from them, they cannot recover it. Weak is the seeker, and the sought after.
74. Never did they value God as He should be valued. God is the most powerful, the almighty.
75. God chooses messengers from among the angels, and from among the people. God is hearer, seer.
76. He controls their past and their future; God is in full control of all things.
77. O you who believe, you shall bow and prostrate; you shall worship your Lord; and you shall work righteousness, that you may succeed.

Islam: The Religion of Abraham

78.   And strive in the cause of God, as you should strive for Him. He is the one who selected you, and imposed no hardship on you in observing the religion. This is the religion of your father Abraham; he is the one who named you "Muslims." Thus, the messenger will be a witness among you, and you will be witnesses among the people. So observe the **salat** prayers and **zakat** charity, and hold fast to God; He is your Lord, the best Lord, and the best supporter.

Sura 23:   The Believers (Al-Mu'minoon)

In the name of God, most gracious, most merciful

1. Successful indeed are the believers;
2. who stand reverent in their **salat** prayer;
3. and avoid vain talk;
4. and carry out the **zakat** charity;
5. and guard their chastity;
6. only with their spouses, or those who rightfully belong to them, do they have sexual relations, without blame.
7. Those who transgress beyond this limit are sinners.
8. And they are trustworthy when it comes to deposits entrusted to them, or the promises they make.
9. And they consistently observe their **salat** prayers.
10. These are the inheritors;
11. who inherit paradise; they abide therein forever.

Evolution of the Human Being

12. We created the human from a certain kind of clay.
13. Then we made him a drop into a protected repository.
14. Then we created the drop into a clot; then we created the clot into a cartilage; then we created the cartilage into bones; then we covered the bones with flesh; then we turned him into a new creation. Most exalted is God, the best creator.
15. Then you will die;
16. Then on the day of resurrection, you will be raised.

Creation of the Heavens and the Earth

17. We created above you seven layers; we are never unaware of anything we create.
18. We send down water from the sky, in exact measure, and store it underground. If we will, we can surely take it away.
19. We establish therewith orchards of date palms, grapes and many fruits, from which you eat.
20. And desert trees, native to Sinai, which produce oil as well as relish for the eaters.
21. And the livestock represent another illustration for you; we provide you with a drink from their bellies, and you enjoy many benefits therefrom, including food.
22. And on them, and on the ships, you are carried.

Noah

23. We sent Noah to his people, saying, "O my people, you shall worship God; you have no other god besides Him. Would you not be righteous?"
24. The elders who disbelieved among his people said, "This is no more than a human being like you, who wants to gain honor among you. Had God willed, He could have sent down angels. We never heard of this before.
25. "He is simply a crazy man, so just ignore him for awhile."
26. He said, "My Lord, grant me victory, for they have disbelieved me."
27. We then inspired him: "Build the ark under our eyes, and with our inspiration. When our judgment comes, and the pot boils over, place a pair of each kind therein, and your family, except those who are doomed. Do not intercede on behalf of the wicked; they will be drowned.
28. "Once you board the ark, together with those who followed you, then say, 'Praise God; He has delivered us from the wicked people.'
29. "And say, 'My Lord, let us disembark into a blessed place; You are the best deliverer.' "
30. These are valuable lessons. We will surely put you to the test.

Similar Conditions Face Every Messenger

31. Then we established after them another generation.
32. And we sent to them a messenger from among them, saying that: "You shall worship God; you have no other god besides Him. Would you not be righteous?"
33. The elders among his people, who disbelieved and denied the meeting of the hereafter, though we endowed them generously in this life, said, "This is no more than a human being like you, who eats as you eat and drinks as you drink.
34. "Indeed, if you obey a human being like you, you would be losers.
35. "Is he promising you that, after you die and turn into dust and bones, you will be resurrected?
36. "Impossible, impossible, is such a promise.
37. "We only live this life; we die and live, no resurrection for us.
38. "He is simply a man who invented a lie about God; we will never believe him."
39. He said, "My Lord, support me, for they have disbelieved me."
40. (God) said, "Soon, they will be sorry."
41. The disaster struck them, justly, and turned them into ruins. Doomed are the wicked people.
42. Then we established after them other generations.
43. No community could advance its end, nor could they delay it.

44. Then we sent our messengers in succession. Every time a community received their messenger, they rejected him. Consequently, we annihilated them one after the other, and we turned them into history. Doomed are the people who do not believe.

45. Then we sent Moses and his brother Aaron with our miracles and profound authority;

46. to Pharaoh and his elders, but they turned arrogant, and were tyrant people.

47. They said, "Shall we believe in two humans like us, while their people are our slaves?"

48. They rejected them, and consequently they were doomed.

49. We have given the scripture to Moses, that they may be guided.

50. And we set up the son of Mary and his mother as a miracle, and we gave them refuge on a mesa with shelter and water.

51. O you messengers, eat from the good provisions, and work righteousness; I am fully aware of everything you do.

All Messengers Preached One Religion

52. The religion you preach is one religion and I am your Lord, so observe Me.

53. But the people divided themselves into sects; each happy with what they have.

54. Thus, leave them in their blunder for awhile.

55. Do they think that, just because we do provide them with money and children,

56. We are rewarding them for their actions? Nay, they do not perceive.

57. As for those who are concerned about their relationship with their Lord;

58. And in the revelations of their Lord they believe;

59. And never set up idols besides their Lord;

60. And give whatever charity they give, while their hearts are conscious that they ultimately return to their Lord;

61. It is these who readily work righteousness, and are far ahead of all others therein.

62. We never burden any soul beyond its means, and we have a record that utters the truth; no one will be wronged.

The Unfortunate Disregard These Revelations

63. Regrettably, the hearts of the people are too busy to study this (Quran), and they remain preoccupied with lesser works.

64. Then, when we strike their leaders with the retribution, they scream.

65. Do not scream now; you cannot be helped against us.

66. My revelations have been recited to you, but you used to turn back on your heels.

67. You were too arrogant, so you disregarded them, with contempt.

68. Why do they not study this message? Is this different from the previous messages?

69. Or, did they not recognize their messenger? Is this why they rejected him?

70. Or, do they say that he is crazy? Indeed, he has come to them with the truth, and most of them hate the truth.

71. If the truth is to conform to their opinions, corruption would have pervaded the heavens and the earth, and everyone in them. Indeed, we have given them their message, but they are disregarding their message.

72. Are you asking them for any recompense? The recompense from your Lord is far better, and He is the best provider.

73. And certainly, you are inviting them to the right path.

74. And those who do not believe in the hereafter are deviating from the path.

75. Had we showered them with mercy, and relieved their afflictions, they would have plunged deeper into transgression.

76. We afflicted them with the retribution, but they did not turn to their Lord, nor did they implore.

77. Then, when we open the gates of severe retribution against them, they become stunned.

Belief in God Nullified by Idol Worship*

78. God is the one who gave you the hearing, the eyes, and the brains; rarely do you appreciate.

79. And He is the one who established you on earth, and before Him you will be gathered.

80. And He is the one who grants life and death, and alternates the night and day; do you not understand?

81. Yet, they utter what the previous generations have uttered.

82. They said, "After we die and turn into dust and bones, do we get resurrected?

23:78-92. *These verses teach us that worshiping God alone is the prime commandment. Worshiping God does not guarantee salvation. Millions of people worship God, but are destined for hell; in fact, the majority of believers will go to hell as stated in 12:106. The reason is that these millions of believers who worship God, fall into idol worship whereby they idolize Jesus, Muhammad, the saints, their properties, their children, or some other forms of idols. Idol worship is the only unforgivable offense, and the absolute devotion of worship to God ALONE is the minimum requirement for salvation.*

83. "We have been promised this before, and so were our ancestors. This is no more than tales from the past."

84. Say, "To whom belongs the earth, and everyone therein, if you know?"

85. They will say, "To God." Say, "Would you then take heed?"

86. Say, "Who is the Lord of the seven heavens, and the Lord of the mighty throne?"

87. They will say, "God." Say, "Would you then be righteous?"

88. Say, "In whose hand is the sovereignty over all things; and is capable of providing help, while none can find help against Him, if you know?"

89. They will say, "God." Say, "What then bewitched you?"

90. Indeed, we have given them the truth, while they are liars.

91. God has never taken for Himself a son, nor was there ever any god besides Him. Otherwise, each god would have declared independence for himself and his creations, and they would have fought with each other. God be glorified; over and above their utterances.

92. He is the knower of all secrets and declarations; most exalted above their idol worship.

93. Say, "My Lord, if you show me the judgment promised to them;

94. "My Lord, then do not include me with the wicked people."

95. Indeed, we are able to show you the judgment that is awaiting them.

96. Meanwhile, repel with compassion and tolerance their evil work. We are fully aware of everything they utter.

97. And say, "My Lord, I seek refuge in You from the devils' suggestions.

98. "And I seek refuge in You, my Lord, lest they be present with me."

Only One Chance

99. Finally, when death comes to the one of them, he says, "My Lord, return me back

100. "And I will lead a righteous life." Nay, this is just an utterance that he utters. Once death comes, a barrier is placed behind them (between the soul and this world) until the day of resurrection.*

101. Then, when the horn is blown, no relationship among them will exist on that day, nor will they even ask about it.

102. Those whose weights are heavy will be the winners.

103. While those whose weights are light are the ones who lost their souls; they abide in Gehenna forever.

104. The fire will burn their faces; they will be miserable therein.

105. Were not My revelations recited to you, and you rejected them?

23:100. The souls of all the people, including those of Muhammad, Jesus, Mary, and the saints are sent away and a barrier is placed behind them. Thus, they are totally unaware of anything that goes on on earth. See Appendix 14.

106. They would say, "Our Lord, we were overcome by our wickedness, and we were totally astray.

107. "Our Lord, deliver us out of this; if we return (to evil work), then we are really wicked."

108. God said,*"Parch therein, and do not speak to Me.

109. "For there was a group of My servants who used to say, 'Our Lord, we have believed, so forgive us, and have mercy on us; You are the most merciful.' "

110. "Then you ridiculed and mocked them, until they caused you to disregard My message. You used to laugh at them.

111. "I have rewarded them today for their steadfastness, by making them the winners."

112. He said, "How many years have you lasted on earth?"

113. They said, "We lasted one day or part of the day, so ask those who count."

114. He said, "Indeed, you lasted only a short while, if you only knew."

115. Did you think that we created you in vain, and that you will not be returned to us?

116. Most exalted is God, the true king. There is no god except He, the Lord of the honorable throne.

117. Anyone who implores any other idol besides God, possesses no proof thereof. His reckoning is at his Lord. Surely, the disbelievers never succeed.

118. And say, "My Lord, forgive and bestow Your mercy; You are the best bestower of mercy."

23:108. *This frequently used past tense teaches us that the Quran informs us of events that actually took place in the future. What is future to us is past, as far as God is concerned.*

Sura 24: Light (Al-Noor)

In the name of God, most gracious, most merciful

1. This is a sura that we send down, and decree as law. We send down in it verses that are perfectly clear, that you may take heed.*

2. The adulteress and the adulterer, you shall whip each of them one hundred lashes, and do not be swayed by pity from carrying out God's law, if you truly believe in God and the last day. And let a group of believers witness their punishment.

3. The adulterer marries only an adulteress or an idolatress, and the adulteress marries only an adulterer or an idolater. This is forbidden for the believers.

4.. And those who accuse married women of adultery, then produce not four witnesses, you shall whip them eighty lashes, and never again accept any testimony from them; they are wicked.

5. Only if they repent thereafter and reform, then God is forgiver, merciful.

6. As for those who accuse their own wives, without producing any witnesses besides themselves, the testimony of the husband is equal to four, if he swears by God four times that he is telling the truth;

7. The fifth oath by him shall be to incur God's curse upon him, if he was lying.

8. The wife shall be exempted from the punishment, if she swears four times by God that he is lying;

9. And a fifth oath to incur God's curse upon her, if he was telling the truth.

10. This is but grace from your Lord and mercy; God is redeemer, wise.

Historical Accusation of the Prophet's Wife

11. Those who produced the big lie are an evil band among you; do not think that it is bad for you, for it is actually good for you. Each person is responsible for the sins he commits. And anyone among them who bears the greater share thereof has deserved a terrible retribution.

24:1-2. *These verses* **expose** *the most vivid example of Satan's work against the Quran. Through the invention of* **"hadith"** *and* **"sunna"** *Satan succeeded in abrogating God's law, and enforcing human prejudices and strong traditions. Although verse 24:1 states that these verses are perfectly clear, the advocates of* **"hadith"** *and/or* **"sunna"** *refuse to believe it, and claim that the prophet clarified and instituted death for the married men and women (especially women) who commit adultery. This satanic law is the predominant law in most so-called Muslim countries, in total defiance of God and His prophet.*

12. When you heard it, the believing men and women should have trusted themselves as righteous people, and should have said, "This is a terrible falsehood."

13. They should have produced four witnesses thereof. Since they failed to produce the witnesses, then they are, in the sight of God, real liars.

14. If it were not for God's indulgence towards you, and His mercy, you would have suffered terrible retribution for what you did.

15. You reiterated the accusation with your tongues, thus uttering with your mouths what you did not know for sure. You also thought it was a simple matter, when it is a gross offense in the sight of God.

16. When you heard it, you should have said, "We will not reiterate such a thing. God be glorified; this is a profound falsehood."

17. God enlightens you, that you may never again do this, if you are really believers.

18. And God clarifies the revelations for you; God is omniscient, wise.

19. Surely, those who wish to see the believers accused of vice, have deserved painful retribution in this life and in the hereafter. God knows, while you do not know.

20. God showers you with His grace and mercy; God is compassionate, merciful.

21. O you who believe, do not follow the steps of Satan. If anyone follows the steps of Satan, he would advocate evil and vice. If it were not for God's indulgence towards you, and His mercy, none of you would have been saved. But God saves whomever He wills; for God is hearer, knower.

22. And let those who are endowed with bounty and richness never hesitate in helping the relatives, the poor, and those who migrate in the cause of God. Let them pardon and forgive. Do you not wish to be forgiven by God? God is forgiver, merciful.

23. Surely, those who slander the virtuous, unaware, and believing women, incur a curse in this life and the hereafter; they have deserved painful retribution.

24. The day will come when their own tongues, hands, and feet, will bear witness against them, regarding everything they had done.

25. On that day, God will repay them equitably, and they will find out that God is the manifest truth.

26. The bad women for the bad men, and the bad men for the bad women; and the good women for the good men, and the good men for the good women. The latter are innocent of the accusations uttered; they have deserved forgiveness and a generous reward.

27. O you who believe, do not enter homes that are not yours, until you announce yourselves and greet the people thereof. This is better for you, that you may take heed.

28. If you find no one therein, do not enter without permission. If you are told to go back; go back. This is purer for you. God is aware of everything you do.

29. You commit no error by entering uninhabited homes, wherein there is something that belongs to you. God knows what you declare, and what you conceal.

30. Tell the believing men to subdue their eyes and keep chaste. This is purer for them. God is fully cognizant of everything they do.

31. And tell the believing women to subdue their eyes, keep chaste, and not to show off their beauty beyond that which is necessarily visible. They shall cover their chests with their garments, and they shall not show their beauty except to their husbands, or their parents, or the parents of their husbands, or their sons, or the sons of their husbands, or their brothers, or the sons of their brothers, or the sons of their sisters, or their women, or their servants or employees who have not attained puberty, or the children who are not mindful of the women's beauty. Let them not strike their feet as they walk, in order to show off the jewelry they may be wearing on their ankles. You shall all repent to God, O believers, that you may succeed.

32. You shall allow the needy singles among you to marry your righteous servants, men and women. If they are poor, God will provide for them from His grace. God is bounteous, omniscient.

33. As for those who cannot find a match, they shall keep chaste until God provides for them from His grace. Those who wish to free any of your slaves in order to marry them, you shall grant their wish if you feel that they are righteous. And give them some of God's money that He bestowed upon you. You shall not force your girls into prostitution, when they wish to keep chaste, seeking the materials of this world. If anyone forces them, then, because they are forced, God is forgiver, merciful.

34. We thus send down to you clarifying revelations, and examples from the past, and enlightenment for the righteous.

35. God is the light of the heavens and the earth. The analogy of His light is that of a concave mirror behind a lamp; the lamp is placed inside glass; the glass is radiating like a star made of pearls; and the fuel thereof comes from a blessed olive tree that is neither Eastern nor Western; its oil is self-radiating without flame. Light upon light; God guides to His light whomever He wills. God cites the examples for the people. God is omniscient.

36. (God's light is) in buildings exalted by God, for His name is commemorated in them. Glorifying Him therein, day and night,

37. people who are never distracted by trade or business from commemorating God, and observing the **salat** prayers and **zakat** charity. They fear the day when the hearts and the eyes will be terrified.

38. God will reward them for their righteous works, and shower them with His grace. God endows whomever He wills without limits.

39. As for those who disbelieve, their works are like a mirage in the wilderness. The thirsty person thinks it is water, until he reaches it and finds nothing. Instead, he finds God there to hold him accountable. God's reckoning is instantaneous.*

40. Another allegory is that of being in the darkness of rough seas, and being overwhelmed by waves upon waves, and clouds above them; darkness upon darkness. If he takes his hand out, he cannot even see it. Whomever God deprives of light can never find light.

41. Do you not see that God is glorified by everyone in the heavens and the earth? Even the birds in their flight. Each in his own way practices his prayer and glorification. God is fully aware of everything you do.

42. And to God belongs the kingship of the heavens and the earth, and to God is the final destiny.

43. Do you not see that God initiates clouds, then combines them, then places them in one layer, and you see the rain pouring therefrom? And He sends down from the sky enormous hailstones, causing them to strike whomever He wills, and diverts them from whomever He wills. The brightness of the snow therefrom is almost blinding.

44. God controls the night and day; this should be a lesson for those who see.

45. And God created every creature from water; some of them walk on their bellies, some walk on two feet, and some walk on four. God creates whatever He wills; God is omnipotent.

46. We thus reveal clarifying revelations, and God guides whomever He wills in a straight path.

Submission to God Must be Total

47. They say, "We believe in God and in the messenger, and we obey," then some of them turn away thereafter; these are not believers.

48. When invited to heed God and His messenger and uphold His laws, some of them become averse.

49. However, if the law is in their favor, they accept it readily.

50. Do they have disease in their hearts? Or, are they doubtful? Or, do they fear lest God and His messenger may be unjust towards them? It is they who are unjust.

51. The only thing the believers utter when invited to heed God and His messenger and uphold His law is: "We hear, and we obey." These are the winners.

24:39. *See Appendix 10 for details.*

52. Whoever obeys God and His messenger, and reverences God and observes Him, these are the triumphant.
53. They swore solemnly by God that if you order them to mobilize, they would. Say, "Do not swear; obedience is a duty, and God is fully cognizant of everything you do."
54. Say, "Obey God and obey the messenger." If you turn away, then the messenger is responsible for his actions, and you are responsible for your actions. If you obey him, you will be guided. The messenger's sole mission is to deliver the message.

The Great Promise

55. God promises those among you who believe and work righteousness, that He will make them kings on earth,* as He did for those before them, and that He will establish for them their religion that He chose for them, and that He will substitute security in place of their fears. All this because they worship Me alone, without idolizing anything besides Me. If anyone disbelieves after this, then these are the wicked.
56. You shall observe the **salat** prayers and **zakat** charity, and obey the messenger,* that you may attain mercy.
57. As for those who disbelieve, do not think that they will ever escape. Their final abode is hell; what a miserable destiny!

Etiquette

58. O you who believe, permission shall be requested by your servants and the children before entering your rooms, at three specific times: before the dawn prayer, and when you change your clothes for the noon rest, and after the night prayer. Other than these times, they commit no error by going or coming around you, for you belong to the same family. God thus clarifies the revelations for you. God is omniscient, wise.

---

*24:55. If you are not king (or queen) of your surroundings, then your worship of God is still marred by some form of idol worship. God's promise is truth, and you can use this verse as a criterion of your faith. The believers who devote their worship to God alone, and successfully rid themselves of all forms of idol worship, are kings on earth; the whole world is at their fingertips, and the whole world is not good enough as one of their possessions. If you are not a king (or queen) on earth, you are not following the Quran, the whole Quran, and nothing but the Quran; you are probably following also some human inventions such as "**Hadith**," "**Sunna**," and/or the works of saints and sages (see also 16:97, 20:112, 22:38, 37:171-173, 41:30-31, and 65:2-4).*

24:56. The messenger is fully represented by the Quran, the whole Quran, and nothing but the Quran, as stated in 24:54 and 5:48-50.

59. When the children reach puberty, they shall be asked permission before entering their rooms, just like their elders. God thus clarifies His revelations for you, and God is omniscient, wise.

60. As for the women who have reached old age, they commit no error by reducing their clothes without excessive revelation. And it is better to maintain modesty in dress. God is hearer, fully aware.

61. There shall be no blame upon the blind, the handicapped, the sick, or yourselves for eating from your homes, or the homes of your fathers, or the homes of your mothers, or the homes of your brothers, or the homes of your sisters, or the homes of your fathers' brothers, or the homes of your fathers' sisters, or the homes of your mothers' brothers, or the homes of your mothers' sisters, or the homes whose keys belong to you, or the homes of your friends. And you do not commit any error by eating in a group, or as individuals. When you enter any home, you shall greet each other with a greeting from God, blessed and good. God thus clarifies the revelations for you, that you may understand.

62. The true believers are those who believe in God and His messenger; and when they confer with him concerning a community matter, they do not leave without his permission. Those who ask permission are the ones who believe in God and His messenger. Therefore, when they ask your permission to tend to some of their affairs, you may grant permission to whomever you will, and pray God to forgive them; God is forgiver, merciful.

63. Do not take the messenger's requests as lightly as you take each others' requests. God knows those of you who sneak out. Those who disregard his requests shall beware; they may be afflicted, or suffer painful retribution.

64. Certainly, to God belong everything in the heavens and the earth. He is fully aware of your condition, and when they are returned to Him, He will inform them of everything they had done. God is fully aware of all things.

Sura 25:   The Statute Book (Al-Furqan)

In the name of God, most gracious, most merciful

1. Most exalted is the One who revealed the statute book through His servant, to serve as a warner for all the people.

2. The One who possesses the heavens and the earth, and has never taken for Himself a son, nor does He have a partner in kingship; He created everything in exact measures.

3. Yet, they set up gods besides Him, who create nothing and are themselves created, and possess no power to harm or benefit themselves, and possess no power to cause death, or life, or resurrection.

4. As for the disbelievers, they said, "This is an invention that he has fabricated, with the help of some people." Indeed, they have uttered a blasphemy and falsehood.

5. They also said, "These are tales from the past that he has written down, and were dictated to him day and night."

6. Say, "The One who knows the secrets of the heavens and the earth has revealed it. He is forgiving, merciful."

7. And they said, "How come this messenger eats the food, and walks in the markets? How come he has no angel with him, preaching?

8. "How come he has no treasure, or an orchard from which he can eat?" The wicked also said, "You follow only a bewitched man."

9. Note how they drew various analogies for you, causing them to go astray and find no path.

10. Most exalted is the One who could, if He wills, grant you better than that: gardens with flowing streams, and grant you mansions.

11. Indeed, they disbelieve in the Hour, and we have prepared for those who disbelieve in the Hour a hellfire.

12. When it sees them from afar, they will hear its rage and fuming.

13. And when they are thrown into it through a narrow place, and become confined, they will declare their sorrow.

14. Declare not one sorrow, but declare many sorrows.

15. Say, "Is that better, or the eternal Paradise that is promised for the righteous?" That is the recompense and the final abode they deserve.

16. In it they will have anything they wish, and they abide therein forever. This is your Lord's promise that is sure to come.

The Righteous Idols*

17. The day will come when God gathers the people, together with the idols they had set up besides God, then says (to the idols), "Did you mislead these servants of Mine, or did they go astray on their own?"

18. They will answer, "Be You glorified, we would never idolize any idols besides You. But while You endowed these people and their ancestors, they disregarded the message, and turned into losers."

19. Indeed, they have rejected your preaching, and now you can neither divert the retribution from them, nor can you help them. Even you; if any of you commits evil, he will be subject to terrible retribution.

20. All the messengers we sent before you used to eat the food and walk in the markets. We set you up as a test for each other; will you remain steadfast? God is seer.

21. Those who are not mindful of meeting us would say, "How come no angels come down to us, nor do we see our Lord?" Indeed, they have uttered a gross blasphemy, and transgressed a gross transgression.

22. The day they see the angels, there will be no joy for the guilty. They will be told, "There is absolutely no other chance for you."

23. We will turn to the works they had done, and render them null and void.

24. As for those who have deserved Paradise, they will be in a better position on that day, and will hear better words.

25. On that day, the heaven will break up, and through the fog, the angels will descend and descend.

26. All kingship on that day rightfully belongs to God most gracious. It will be a difficult day for the disbelievers.

Choose Your Friends Carefully

27. On that day, the wicked will bite his hands and say, "Oh I wish I followed the path with the messenger.

28. "Oh, woe to me, I wish I never chose that person for a friend.

29. "He has diverted me away from the message when it came to me. Indeed, the devil misleads, then abandons the human being."

25:17-19. The righteous idols are those righteous people who are idolized against their will, such as Muhammad, Jesus, Mary, and the saints. Verse 19 teaches us that these idols do not possess the power of intercession, and that they themselves are held accountable for their actions (see also 21:25-29).

Muhammad's Mission and Wish*

30. The messenger will say, "My Lord, my people have deserted this Quran."
31. We thus appointed for every prophet enemies from among the guilty, and God suffices as guide and protector.
32. The disbelievers said, "How come the Quran was not revealed through him all at once?" We thus released it gradually, in order to fix it in your memory.
33. Whatever argument they come up with, we provide you with the truth, and a better argument.
34. They will be gathered forcibly into Gehenna, since they adopted a wicked stand, and strayed far away from the path.

The Disbelievers Consistently Doomed

35. We gave Moses the scripture, and appointed his brother Aaron as his deputy.
36. We dispatched them to people who subsequently rejected our revelations. Consequently, we utterly destroyed them.
37. Similarly, when Noah's people disbelieved the messengers, we drowned them and set them up as a lesson for the people. We prepare for the wicked painful retribution.
38. Also, 'Ad, Thamood, the inhabitants of Rass, and many other communities;
39. we cited the examples for them, before we condemned and annihilated them.
40. They had passed by the community (Sodom) that we showered with a miserable shower. It is not that they failed to see it; they simply disbelieved in resurrection.
41. And when these people see you, they ridicule you: "Is this the man whom God sent as messenger?

25:30-31.   Muhammad's mission and real wish was to deliver the Quran, the whole Quran, and nothing but the Quran. The Muslims, however, fell in the same satanic trap as the Jews and invented the "hadith" and "sunna" as additional sources of jurisprudence that can be made to conform to the various traditions, customs, and superstitions. The Jewish Mishnah corresponds to "hadith" and the Gemara corresponds to "sunna." Many Muslim scholars and their followers today have gone as far as stating that "hadith" abrogates the Quran (see 24:1-2)! Hence, the prophet Muhammad's disappointment on the day of judgment, as stated in verse 30. It is extremely significant that the words of verse 31 are identical to those dealing with the inventors of "hadith" in 6:112.

42. "He almost diverted us from our idols, if it were not that we steadfastly perservered." They will certainly find out, when they face the retribution, as to who really strayed from the path.

43. What about the one who idolizes his own ego? Can you do anything for him?

44. Do you suppose many of them hear or understand? Indeed, they are just like animals; nay, they are even worse.

45. Do you not see how your Lord designed the shadow? Had He willed, He could have made it constant. Then we would have designed the sun accordingly.

46. Then we would have withdrawn it towards us gradually.

47. And He is the one who made the night to cover you, and the sleep to provide you with rest; and He made the day a resurrection.

48. And He is the one who sends the winds with good omen, as mercy from His hands, then we send down from the sky pure water.

49. With it, we revive dead land, and provide drink for our many creatures, both animals and humans.

50. We thus explain the Quran for them, that they may take heed, but most people insist upon disbelieving.

51. If we will, we can send to every community a preacher.

52. Therefore, do not obey the disbelievers, and struggle against them with this Quran, a great struggle.

53. And He is the one who merges the two seas; one is fresh and sweet, while the other is salty and repulsive. He places between them a barrier (evaporation) they can never break.

54. And He is the one who created from water a human being, then made him reproduce through mating. Your Lord is omnipotent.

Do Not Idolize Muhammad

55. Yet, they idolize besides Him what possesses no power to benefit them or harm them. Indeed, the disbeliever is an opponent of his Lord.*

56. We did not send you (O Muhammad) except as a mere bearer of good news, as well as a warner.

57. Say, "I am not asking you for any wage. All I ask is that those of you who so choose may follow the path to their Lord."

Muhammad Dies; God Does Not

58. You shall trust in the living God who never dies, and praise His glory. Your Lord is fully cognizant of His creatures' sins.

25:55.   See 7:188, 10:49, and 72:21.

59. He created the heavens and the earth, and everything between them, in six days, then ascended the throne. God most gracious; ask about Him those who know.

60. Yet, when told, "You shall fall prostrate for God most gracious," they say, "Who is God most gracious? Shall we fall prostrate for the one you advocate?" It only increases their aversion.

61. Most exalted is the one who placed constellations in the sky, as well as a lamp and a lighted moon.

62. And He is the one who designed the night and the day to alternate, for those who choose to take heed, or choose to be appreciative.

63. And for the servants of God most gracious who walk on earth humbly, and when the ignorant speak to them, they only utter peace.

64. And who spend the night before their Lord, prostrating and standing.

65. And who say, "Our Lord, spare us the agony of Gehenna; surely, its retribution is agonizing.

66. "It is a miserable abode; a miserable destiny."

67. And when they spend, they are neither extravagant, nor stingy; they are moderate.

68. And they never set up besides God any idol, nor do they kill anyone except in the course of justice, nor do they commit adultery. Anyone who does these is wicked.

69. The retribution will be doubled for him on the day of resurrection; he abides therein in eternal humiliation.

70. As for those who repent, believe, and work righteousness, then God will change their sins into credits, for God is forgiving, merciful.

71. Whoever repents and works righteousness, God redeems him a complete redemption.

72. And they do not bear false witness, and when they encounter vain talk, they readily evade it.

73. And when they are reminded of their Lord's revelations, they do not turn deaf and blind.

74. And they say, "Our Lord, let our spouses and children be a source of happiness for us, and make us in the forefront of the righteous."

75. These are the ones who are rewarded the high ranks for their steadfastness; they will be received therein with greetings and peace.

76. Eternally they abide therein; what a beautiful abode and destiny!

77. Say, "My Lord could care less about you, if it were not for your blasphemous allegations. Since you disbelieved, the retribution is inevitable."

Sura 26:   The Poets (Al-Shu'araa')

In the name of God, most gracious, most merciful

1. T.S.M.*
2. These (letters) constitute the miracles of this profound scripture.*
3. You may blame yourself for their disbelief.
4. However, if we will, we can send to them a miracle from the sky that forces their necks to bow.
5. Whenever a new reminder comes to them from God most gracious, they turn away in aversion.*
6. Since they chose to disbelieve, they will surely suffer the consequences.
7. Do they not see how many beautiful kinds of plants have we grown on earth?
8. This alone should be a lesson, but most of them are not believers.
9. Surely, your Lord is the almighty, the most merciful.

Moses

10. Recall that your Lord called upon Moses, saying, "Go to the wicked people;
11. "Pharaoh's people; would they not be righteous?"
12. He said, "My Lord, I fear lest they disbelieve me.
13. "I may also lose my temper, and my tongue may become tied. So send with me my brother Aaron.
14. "They hold a grudge against me, and I fear that they may kill me."
15. God said, "Do not worry; just go, the two of you. We will be with you, listening."
16. "Go to Pharaoh and tell him, 'We are sent by the Lord of the universe."
17. " 'Let the children of Israel go.' "
18. Pharaoh said, "Did we not bring you up from infancy, and raised you among us for many years?"

26:1.   These letters, along with the Quranic initials that prefix 28 other suras are part of the Quran's miraculous numerical code. They prove that the Quran can never be man made; that it is the unaltered word of God (see Appendices 1 and 2).

26:2.   This expression is used exclusively in conjunction with Quranic initials throughout the Quran (see 10:1, 12:1, 13:l, 15:1, 27:1, 28:2, 31:1).

26:5.   The Quran's miraculous numerical code, discovered exclusively in the course of this very translation, is a perfect example of God's "new" reminders.

19. "Yet, you committed the crime that you committed, thus showing your thanklessness."
20. Moses said, "So I did it, when I was astray.
21. "Then I fled because I feared you, then God bestowed upon me wisdom, and made me a messenger.
22. "Is it any favor for me that you enslaved the children of Israel?"
23. Pharaoh said, "What is the Lord of the universe?"
24. Moses said, "The Lord of the heavens and the earth, and everything between them, if you could only attain certainty."
25. He said to those around him, "Did you hear this?"
26. Moses said, "Your Lord, and the Lord of your ancestors."
27. Pharaoh said, "Your messenger who is sent to you is crazy."
28. Moses said, "The Lord of the East and the West, and everything between them, if you could only understand."
29. Pharaoh said, "If you accept any other god besides me, I will imprison you."
30. Moses said, "What if I showed you something profound?"
31. Pharaoh said, "Then show us, if you are truthful."
32. He then threw down his staff, and it turned into a profound serpent.
33. And he took his hand out; it was white to the beholders.
34. Pharaoh said to the people around him, "This man is an expert magician.
35. "He wants to drive you out of your land with his magic. What do you suggest?"
36. They said, "Respite him and his brother, and send delegates to every town.
37. "Let them summon every experienced magician."
38. Thus, the magicians were gathered for the big day.
39. And the people were told, "Would you all gather?
40. "Let us follow the magicians, when they end up winners."
41. Then, when the magicians came, they said to Pharaoh, "Do we get paid if we are the winners?"
42. He said, "Yes, and you become close to me."
43. Moses said to them, "Throw whatever you want to throw."
44. They then threw their ropes and sticks, saying, "By the majesty of Pharaoh, we will be the winners."
45. Moses then threw his staff, whereupon it swallowed what they fabricated.
46. The magicians fell prostrate.
47. They said, "We believe in the Lord of the universe.
48. "The Lord of Moses and Aaron."
49. Pharaoh said, "Did you believe him before I give you permission? He must be your leader who taught you magic. You will certainly find out; I will cut your hands and feet on alternate sides; I will crucify you all."
50. They said, "No harm done; we simply return to our Lord.

51. "We hope that our Lord may forgive us our sins, since we are the first to believe."
52. And we inspired Moses: "Move away with My servants; you will be pursued."
53. Pharaoh sent delegates to the various towns;
54. announcing that these are a rebellious few;
55. and that: "They are our opponents;
56. "beware of them."
57. Consequently, we deprived them of their gardens and springs;
58. the treasures and the great mansions.
59. We made the children of Israel inherit (the earth).
60. The Egyptians pursued them towards the East.
61. When the two groups could see each other, Moses' companions said, "We will get caught."
62. He said, "No way; my Lord is with me; He will guide me."
63. We then inspired Moses: "Strike the sea with your staff." Whereupon, it parted; each part like a great hill.
64. We let them pass through.
65. We delivered Moses and all those with him.
66. And we drowned the others.
67. This should be a lesson, but most people are not to believe.
68. Surely, your Lord is the almighty, the merciful.

Abraham

69. Recite for them the history of Abraham.
70. He said to his father and his people, "What do you worship?"
71. They said, "We worship statues; we are totally devoted to them."
72. He said, "Do they hear you when you implore?
73. "Can they benefit or harm you?"
74. They said, "We found our parents doing this."
75. He said, "Indeed, whatever you worship:
76. "you and your parents before you;
77. "are enemies to me. I only worship the Lord of the universe.
78. "The one who created me and guides me.
79. "The one who feeds me and waters me.
80. "When I get sick,* he is the one who heals me.
81. "The one who puts me to death, then resurrects me.
82. "He is the one I hope will forgive my sins on the day of judgment.
83. "My Lord, grant me wisdom, and count me with the righteous.
84. "Make me a truthful guide for the generations after me.

27:80. Note that Abraham attributed sickness to himself, and not to God.

85. "Make me one of the inheritors of blissful Paradise.
86. "And forgive my father, for he is one of the strayers.
87. "Do not forsake me on the day they are resurrected."
88. That is the day when money and children will be useless.
89. Only those who come to God with a whole heart, will be saved.
90. Paradise will be offered to the righteous.
91. And hell will be forced upon the transgressors.
92. They will be told, "Where now are your idols;
93. "that you set up besides God? Can they help you, or help themselves?"
94. They will be thrown therein, together with their deceivers.
95. As well as all of Satan's recruits.
96. They will then say, as they feud with their idols,
97. "By God, we were really wrong;
98. "when we set you up to rank with God, Lord of the universe.
99. "It was but the criminals who misled us.
100. "Now we have no intercessors;
101. "nor a close friend.
102. "If only we could get another chance, we will then become believers."
103. This should be a lesson, but most people are not to believe.
104. Surely, your Lord is the almighty, the most merciful.

Noah

105. The people of Noah disbelieved the messengers.
106. Their brother Noah said to them, "Would you not be righteous?
107. "I am an honest messenger to you.
108. "Observe God and obey me.
109. "I do not ask you for any pay; my pay comes from God, Lord of the universe.
110. "Observe God and obey me."
111. They said, "Shall we believe you, when the worst among us have followed you?"
112. He said, "I have no idea what kind of works they do.
113. "Their judgment belongs with my Lord, if you could only perceive.
114. "I will never dismiss any believers.
115. "I am no more than a manifest warner."
116. They said, "Unless you abstain, O Noah, you will be stoned."
117. He said, "My Lord, my people have disbelieved me.
118. "So grant me victory over them; a decisive victory; and save me and those who believed with me."
119. We then saved him, and those who followed him, in the loaded ark.
120. And we drowned the others.

121. This should be a lesson, but most people are not to believe.
122. Surely, your Lord is the almighty, the most merciful.

Hood

123. 'Ad disbelieved the messengers.
124. Their brother Hood said to them, "Would you not be righteous?
125. "I am an honest messenger to you.
126. "Observe God, and obey me.
127. "I do not ask you for any pay; my pay comes from God, Lord of the universe.
128. "You build a great mansion on every hill, just for vanity;
129. "and establish castles as if you will last forever.
130. "When you strike, you strike with tyranny.
131. "Observe God, and obey me.
132. "Observe the One who provided you with everything you know.
133. "He provided you with livestock and children.
134. "And gardens and springs.
135. "I fear for you the retribution of a terrible day."
136. They said, "It is the same whether you admonish us, or stop admonishing.
137. "This has been going on since the ancient times.
138. "We will never be punished."
139. They disbelieved him, and consequently we destroyed them. This should be a lesson, but most people are not to believe.
140. Surely, your Lord is the almighty, the most merciful.

Saalih

141. Thamood disbelieved the messengers.
142. Their brother Saalih said to them, "Would you not be righteous?
143. "I am an honest messenger to you.
144. "Observe God, and obey me.
145. "I am not asking you for any pay; my pay comes from God, Lord of the universe.
146. "Do you think you will be left alone in peace;
147. "enjoying your gardens and springs,
148. "and crops, and the date palms with their ripe fruits,
149. "and carve luxurious mansions out of the mountains?
150. "Observe God and obey me.
151. "Do not obey the transgressors;
152. "who corrupt the earth, instead of reforming."
153. They said, "You are simply bewitched.

154. "You are no more than a human being like us. Show us a miracle, if you are truthful."

155. He said, "Here is a camel that will drink only on a certain day, while your animals will drink on a certain day.

156. "You shall not touch her with any harm, lest you incur the retribution of a terrible day."

157. They then slaughtered her, and consequently, they became sorry.

158. The retribution destroyed them. This should be a lesson, but most people are not to believe.

159. Surely, your Lord is the almighty, the most merciful.

Lot

160. The people of Lot disbelieved the messengers.

161. Their brother Lot said to them, "Would you not be righteous?

162. "I am an honest messenger to you.

163. "Observe God and obey me.

164. "I do not ask you for any pay; my pay comes from God, Lord of the universe.

165. "How could you practice sex with the males;

166. "instead of your wives that your Lord created for you: You are really wicked."

167. They said, "Unless you refrain, O Lot, you will be banished."

168. He said, "I condemn your actions."

169. "My Lord, deliver me and my family from their works."

170. We saved him and all his family;

171. except a condemned old woman.

172. And we destroyed the others.

173. We showered them a miserable shower, after having warned them.

174. This should be a lesson, but most people are not to believe.

175. Surely, your Lord is the almighty, the most merciful.

Shu'aib

176. The people of Midyan disbelieved the messengers.

177. Their brother Shu'aib said to them, "Would you not be righteous?

178. "I am an honest messenger to you.

179. "Observe God and obey me.

180. "I do not ask you for any pay; my pay comes from God, Lord of the universe.

181. "Give the full measure when you trade, and do not be cheaters.

182. "And weigh with an equitable scale.

183. "Do not cheat the people out of their things, and do not corrupt the earth.

184. "Observe the One who created you and the multitudes before you."

185. They said, "You are simply bewitched.
186. "You are no more than a man like us, and we think you are a liar.
187. "Why do you not drop masses from the sky on us, if you are truthful?"
188. He said, "My Lord is the One who knows your works."
189. Since they disbelieved him, the retribution struck them on the day of the canopy; it was the retribution of a terrible day.
190. This should be a lesson, but most people are not to believe.
191. Surely, your Lord is the almighty, the most merciful.

The Guilty Isolated From Quran*

192. This is a revelation from the Lord of the universe.
193. Brought down by the honest Spirit (Gabriel).
194. It was placed into your heart (O Muhammad), to make you one of the warners.
195. It comes in clear Arabic tongue.*
196. It contains the same message as the previous scriptures.
197. Is it not a clue for them that it is recognized by the scholars of Israel?
198. If presented in Arabic to non-Arabic people;
199. they could not believe in it when recited to them.
200. This is the way we render it to the hearts of the wicked.
201. Consequently, they fail to believe, till the painful retribution strikes them.
202. And it only strikes them suddenly, when they least expect it.
203. Then they say, "Can we get a second chance?"
204. Did they not challenge our doom?
205. We may let them enjoy for years;
206. then what is promised to them afflicts them.
207. Their possessions can never help them.
208. We never destroy any community without sending warners.
209. They first remind them, for we are never unjust.
210. This Quran cannot be a revelation by the devils.
211. They neither would, nor could.
212. For they have been isolated from hearing.
213. You shall not call on any idol besides God, lest you join the doomed.
214. And warn the people closest to you.
215. And lower your wing for the believers who follow you.
216. If they disobey you, then say, "I disown your works."
217. And trust in the almighty, the most merciful.
218. He is the One who sees you when you pray in the night.

26:192-200. See 13-31, 17:45-46, 18:57, and 56:79.

26:195. See Appendix 3 for details as to why the Quran was revealed in Arabic.

219. And when you fall prostrate.
220. He is the Hearer, the knower.
221. Let me tell you upon whom the devils descend.
222. They descend on every wicked fabricator.
223. They appear to listen, and most of them are liars.
224. As for the poets, they are followed by the strayers.
225. Do you not notice that their loyalty constantly shifts?
226. And they utter what they do not necessarily do?
227. Excepted are those who believe and work righteousness, and commemorate God constantly, and steadfastly persevere when oppressed. As for the wicked, they will certainly find out how miserable their ultimate destiny is.

Sura 27:   The Ant (Al-Naml)

In the name of God, most gracious, most merciful

1. T.S.* These (letters) are miracles of this Quran; a profound scripture.
2. A guide and good news for the believers;
3. who observe the **salat** prayers, give the **zakat** charity, and are positively certain about the hereafter.
4. As for those who do not believe in the hereafter, we adorn their works in their eyes so that they continue to blunder.
5. They have deserved the worst retribution, and in the hereafter they will be the losers.
6. This Quran comes to you from One who is wise, omniscient.

Moses

7. Recall that Moses said to his family, "I just saw a fire, and I am going to check. I may bring you some of it to warm up."
8. But when he approached it, it was announced, "Blessed is this fire and its surroundings. Glory be to God, Lord of the universe."
9. "O Moses, this is I, God, the almighty, the wise.
10. "Throw down your staff." When he saw it move like a demon, he turned around and ran. "O Moses, do not be afraid; My messengers have nothing to fear.
11. "Even those who commit evil, but later substitute righteousness in place of evil; I am forgiving, merciful.
12. "Now put your hand in your pocket; it will come out white, without a blemish. Another one of nine miracles you shall show Pharaoh and his people, for they are wicked."
13. When our clear signs were presented to them, they said, "This is clever magic."
14. They thus disregarded them, and their souls were ridden with wickedness and pride. Therefore, note the consequences for the wicked.

David and Solomon

15. We gave David and Solomon knowledge, and they acknowledged, "Praise be to God, who blessed us more than many other believing servants."

27:1.   *These letters are part of the Quran's miraculous numerical code that proves that Quran is God's message to the world (see Appendix 1 and footnotes 10:1, 12:1, and 26:2).*

16. Solomon was David's heir, and he said, "O people, we have been endowed with the understanding of the birds' language; we have been blessed with all kinds of things; a profound grace."

17. Mobilized for Solomon were troops of jinns and humans, as well as the birds; all subjugated.

18. Once, when they approached a valley of ants, one ant said, "O you ants, go inside your homes, otherwise Solomon and his troops may crush you unintentionally."

19. He smiled in amusement from her statement, and prayed, "My Lord, direct me to appreciate the blessings You bestowed upon me and my parents, and to work righteousness that is pleasing to You, and admit me into Your mercy with Your righteous servants."

20. He inspected the birds and said, "How come I do not see the hoopoe? Why is he absent?

21. "I will certainly punish him severely, or sacrifice him, unless he shows me a valid excuse."

22. Not much later, the hoopoe came and said, "I found out something you do not know. I bring you important news from Sheba.

23. "I found a woman ruling them, who possesses all kinds of things, and a great mansion.

24. "I found her and her people worshiping the sun, instead of God. The devil has adorned their works for them, and diverted them from the path; they are misguided."

25. That is because they did not submit to God; the One who uncovers the secrets of the heavens and the earth, and knows what you conceal and what you declare.

26. God; there is no god except He; the Lord with the great throne.

27. Solomon said, "We will find out whether you told the truth, or lied.

28. "Take this message to them, then turn away and watch their response."

29. The Queen of Sheba said, "O my elders, I just received an honorable message.

30. "It is from Solomon, and it is **IN THE NAME OF GOD, MOST GRACIOUS, MOST MERCIFUL.***

31. "It says, 'Do not be too arrogant, and come to me as Muslims (submitters).' "

32. She said, "O you elders, advise me in this matter; I will not make a decision without your opinion."

33. They said, "We possess tremendous power and great influence. The final decision is yours. What is your command?"

34. She said, "Whenever the kings invade a community, they corrupt it and humiliate the dignified people thereof; this is what they usually do.

35. "I will send them a gift, then see what the messengers bring back."

36. When they came to Solomon he said, "Are you giving me money? What God bestowed upon me is far better than what He bestowed upon you. It is you who may be impressed by such a gift.

37. "Go back (and tell them) we will mobilize against them formidable troops. We will banish them in humiliation and disgrace."

38. Solomon said to his troops, "Which of you can bring her mansion to me, ahead of their arrival here?"

39. A demon from the jinns said, "I can bring it to you before you stand up. I am capable and honest."

40. But the one who possessed knowledge from the scripture said, "I can bring it to you while you blink your eyes." When he saw it placed before him, he said, "This is grace from my Lord, in order to test me and show whether I turn appreciative or unappreciative. Those who are appreciative are appreciative for their own good. As for those who are not appreciative, my Lord is in no need, generous."

41. He then said, "Remodel the inside of her mansion, and let us see if she will be guided, or fail to follow the guidance."

42. When she arrived, she was told, "Is this your mansion?" She said, "This is exactly like it." We knew in advance what she was going to do, and we were already Muslims.

43. The idol worship had kept her from the right guidance, and thus, she belonged with the disbelieving people.

27:30.   This verse represents a significant part of the Quran's numerical miracle; the physical, touchable, and examinable miracle that proves that Quran is a divine scripture. The reader knows by now that the foundation of the Quran's miraculous numerical code is the 19-letter statement "BISM ALLAH ARRAHMAN ARRAHEEM" (in the name of God, most gracious, most merciful). Every sura opens with this statement, except one, namely, sura 9. Since the Quran consists of 114 suras (19x6), the absence of "Bismillah" from sura 9 would upset the intricate and delicate balance of this divine system. Since this miraculous code must be perfect, we find that the missing **"Bismillah"** statement is compensated for in this sura, verse 27:30. Thus, while the **"Bismillah"** is missing from sura 9, we find two **Bismillah's** in sura 27. This makes the total frequency of this important statement 114, a multiple of 19. Equally miraculous is the fact that the total number of suras from sura 9, where the **"Bismillah"** is missing, through sura 27, where we find two **Bismillahs**, is exactly 19 suras. This proves to us that the specific order of suras as we know it today is divinely revealed.

44. She was told, "Go inside the mansion." When she saw its interior, she thought it was a pond, and uncovered her legs." Solomon said, "This is made of reflective crystal." (When she realized that it was her mansion, moved and remodeled,) she said, "My Lord, I have wronged my soul. I submit, together with Solomon, to God, Lord of the universe."

Saalih

45. We sent to Thamood their brother Saalih, saying, "You shall worship God." But they divided themselves into two feuding parties.
46. He said, "O my people, why do you challenge me to bring doom, instead of prosperity? If only you turn to God for forgiveness, you will attain mercy."
47. They said, "You and your followers are a bad omen for us." He said, "Your omen rests only with God, and you are being put to the test."
48. There was a gang of nine in the city, who were corrupt and never did any good.
49. They said, "Let us swear by God that we eliminate Saalih and his people, then say to his heirs that we never witnessed their demise, and that we are truthful."
50. They thus schemed their schemes, but we also schemed our scheme, while they did not perceive.
51. Note the consequences of their scheming; we utterly destroyed them and their people.
52. Their homes became empty ruins, because of their wickedness. This should be a lesson for those who know.
53. We saved those who believed and worked righteousness.

Lot

54. Also Lot (was sent) to his people, saying, "How could you commit such an abomination before your eyes?
55. "You practice sex with the men, instead of the women! Indeed, you are ignorant people."
56. The only response from his people was their saying, "Banish Lot and his followers from your town; they wish to be holy."
57. We then saved him and his family, but not his wife; we condemned her with the doomed.
58. We showered them a certain shower (of stones); a miserable shower, after being forewarned.

God Alone Worthy of Worship

59. Say, "Praise be to God, and peace be on His servants whom He chose. Is God better, or the idols they set up?"

60. Who is it that created the heavens and the earth, and sent down water from the sky? We grow with it gardens full of beauty. You could not possibly initiate the trees thereof. Is it another god besides God? Indeed, they are people who deviate.

61. Who is it that made the earth habitable, and placed rivers and stabilizers therein, and created a barrier between the two seas? Is it another god besides God? Indeed, most of them do not know.

62. Who is it that answers the distressed who implore Him, relieves adversity, and makes you inheritors of the earth? Is it another god besides God? Rarely do you take heed.

63. Who is it that guides you in the darkness of land and sea? Who is it that sends the winds with good omen and mercy from His hands? Is it another god besides God? Most exalted is God, over any partnership.

64. Who is it that initiates the creation, then repeats it? Who is it that provides for you from the heaven and the earth? Is it another god besides God? Say, "Show us your proof, if you are truthful."

65. Say, "None knows the future in the heavens and the earth except God; nor do they perceive the manner or the time of their resurrection."

66. Indeed, their knowledge about the hereafter is nil. They are even doubtful thereof. Indeed, they are totally blind thereto.

Belief in the Hereafter: The Greatest Obstacle

67. Those who disbelieve would say, "After becoming dust, do we and our ancestors come back to life?

68. "This was promised to us, and to our ancestors before us. This is but history from the past."

69. Say, "Travel the earth and note the consequences for the guilty."

70. Do not grieve over them, and do not be annoyed by their schemes.

71. They say, "Where is the doom you threaten, if you are truthful?"

72. Say, "You are already suffering some of the doom you ask for."

73. Indeed, your Lord is gracious towards the people, but most of them are not appreciative.

74. Your Lord is fully aware of whatever their hearts conceal, and whatever they declare.

75. There is nothing in the heaven and the earth that is not recorded in a manifest record.

76. This Quran informs the children of Israel about many things that they dispute.

77. It is a guide and mercy for the believers.

78. Your Lord is the one who will judge them according to His law. He is the almighty, the omniscient.
79. Therefore, put your trust in God; you are following the manifest truth.
80. You can never make the dead hear, nor the deaf hearken when they turn around to flee.
81. Nor can you guide the blind who stray. You can make none hear, except those who believe in our revelations, and decide to submit.
82. Once they deserve the final judgment, we will produce for them a creature from the earth who will speak to them, saying that the people did not firmly believe in our scripture.*
83. And the day will come when we summon from every community a group of those who rejected our revelations; they will totally submit.
84. Once they are assembled, God will say, "Did you not reject My scripture, even before examining it, or what is it that you did?"
85. They will then incur the final judgment, because of their wickedness, and they will utter nothing.
86. Did they not see how we designed the night for their rest, and the day lighted? This provides proofs for people who believe.
87. When the day comes and the horn is blown, horrified will be everyone in the heavens and the earth; but not those whom God wills. All will come to Him submissively.

A Quranic Scientific Marvel

88. When you look at the mountains, you may think that they are standing still. But they are moving in the same manner as the clouds. Such is the creation of God, who perfected everything. Surely, He is fully cognizant of everything you do.
89. Those who work righteousness are repaid manyfold, and they are perfectly secure from the horror of that day.
90. As for those who work evil, they will be forced into the hellfire. Are you not paid for what you used to do?
91. I was simply commanded to worship the Lord of this town, the town He made sacred. To Him belongs everything. I was commanded to be a Muslim (submitter).
92. And (I was commanded) to read the Quran. Thus, whoever is guided is guided for his own good, and those who stray, tell them, "I am no more than a warner."
93. And say, "Praise God; He will show you His signs until you recognize them." Your Lord is never unaware of anything you do.

27:82. *Strong evidence points at "the computer" as the "creature" predicted in this verse. Through the decoding of the Quran's numerical miracle (see Appendix 1), the computer speaks to the world that this is God's message and that the people have discarded it.*

Sura 28: History (Al-Qaṣaṣ)

In the name of God, most gracious, most merciful

1. T.S.M.*
2. These (letters) constitute miracles in this profound scripture.*
3. We relate to you herein some history of Moses and Pharaoh; the truth for people who believe.
4. Indeed, Pharaoh was a tyrant on earth, who divided the people into castes. He enslaved a group of them, slaughtering their sons and sparing their daughters. He was really wicked.
5. We wanted to rescue the oppressed, make them leaders, and make them the inheritors.
6. We wanted to establish them on earth, and to show Pharaoh, Haamaan, and their troops exactly what they feared.
7. We inspired Moses' mother, saying, "Keep on nursing him, and whenever you fear for his life, throw him into the river without any fear or worry. We will return him to you, and will make him one of the messengers."
8. Pharaoh's people picked him up, only to become their enemy and a source of grief for them. That is because Pharaoh, Haamaan, and their troops were sinners.
9. Pharaoh's wife said, "What a joy for me and you; do not kill him. He may be useful to us; we may even adopt him." They had no idea.
10. Moses' mother's mind was getting so terrified that she almost gave away her relationship to him. But we strengthened her heart, in order to make her confident.
11. She said to his sister, "Trace him." She watched him from afar, while they did not perceive.
12. Then we forbade for him all the nursing mothers. His sister said, "I know people who can raise him for you, and take good care of him."
13. We thus returned him to his mother, causing her to rejoice, and alleviating her grief. We let her know that God's promise is truth. However, most people do not know.
14. When he grew up and matured, we endowed him with wisdom and knowledge. We thus reward the righteous.

28:1.   The meaning of these letters is explained in detail in Appendix 1.

28:2.   This verse informs us that the Quranic initials in verse 28:1, together with the Quranic initials in 28 other suras, represent miracles in this Quran. It is significant that this particular expression is used **EXCLUSIVELY** in conjunction with Quranic initials (see 10:1, 12:1, 13:1, 15:1, 26:2, 27:1, 31:2).

15. Once he entered the city in disguise, and found two men fighting, one from his clan (Hebrew), the other from his enemy (Egyptian). The Hebrew implored him for help against the Egyptian. Moses punched the Egyptian, killing him. He said, "This is the devil's work; surely, he is an ardent, misleading, enemy."

16. Moses said, "Lord, I have wronged my soul; forgive me." God forgave him, for He is the forgiver, the merciful.

17. Moses said, "Lord, You have indeed blessed me, and I pledge never to support the sinners."

18. The next morning he visited the city, fearful and watchful. The same Hebrew he had helped the day before implored him again for help. Moses said, "You are really a trouble maker."

19. And when he started to strike their common enemy, he said, "O Moses, do you want to kill me as you killed another man yesterday? You really want to be a tyrant on earth, not a righteous person."

20. A man came from the other side of the city, saying, "O Moses, the people are plotting to kill you; you better get out. This is my sincere advice to you."

21. Moses fled, fearful and watchful, saying, "Save me, Lord, from the oppresive people."

22. As he headed towards Midyan, he said, "May my Lord guide me in the right path."

23. When he reached Midyan's water, he found a crowd watering, and noticed two women standing on the side. He said, "What is your problem?" They said, "We cannot water until the crowd disperses; our father is an old man."

24. He watered for them, then turned to rest in the shade, saying, "Lord, I am in dire need for any provisions You may send me."

25. Soon, one of the two women came to him walking shyly. She said, "My father invites you to pay you for watering us." When he went to him and told him his story, he said, "Do not worry, you are safe here from the oppressive people."

26. One of the women said, "Hire him father, for he is a good one to hire. He is strong and honest."

27. He said, "I wish to offer you one of my daughters in marriage, in return for your working for me eight pilgrimages (years). If you complete ten, it would be voluntary on your part. I do not want to be harsh on you. You will find me, God willing, fair."

28. Moses said, "(I accept this agreement) between me and you. Whichever period I choose to fulfill will be acceptable to you. God attests to our agreement."

29. Moses fulfilled the interim, and as he traveled with his family, he noticed a fire at the slope of Mount Toor (Sinai). He said to his family, "Wait for me here. I just saw a fire; maybe I can bring news or some fire to warm you up."

30. When he reached it, he was called from the right side of the valley, where the bush was burning: "Moses, this is I, God, Lord of the universe."

31. Then he was told to throw down his staff. When he saw it moving like a demon, he turned around and fled. "Moses, come back, and have no fear. You are perfectly safe.

32. "Put your hand in your pocket; it will come out white, without a blemish. Gather your confidence, for these are only two of the proofs you will take from your Lord to Pharaoh and his elders. They are wicked people."

33. Moses said, "Lord, I killed one of them, and I fear lest they kill me.

34. "Also, my brother Aaron is more eloquent than I. Send him with me for support. I am afraid they may disbelieve me."

35. God said, "We will strengthen you with your brother, and provide you both with authority. They can never harm you. With our signs, you two and all those who follow you will be victorious."

36. When Moses went to them with our profound miracles, they said, "This is no more than fabricated magic. We have never heard of this since our ancient ancestors."

37. Moses said, "My Lord knows best who is bringing the true guidance from Him, and will be the ultimate winner. Surely, the wicked never succeed."

38. Pharaoh said, "O people, I never knew of any other god for you except me. Burn the clay, O Haamaan, and build a tower for me. Maybe I can take a look at the God of Moses. I think he is a liar."

39. He and his troops were oppressive tyrants on earth. They were unjust, and totally mindless of their returning to us.

40. Consequently, we punished him and his troops, and threw them into the sea. Therefore, note the consequences for the wicked.

41. We made them imams who lead their people to the hellfire, and on the day of resurrection, they will not be helped.

42. We accursed them in this life, and on the day of resurrection they will be despised.

43. We gave Moses the scripture, after destroying the previous generations, to serve as enlightenment for the people, and guidance and mercy, that they may take heed.

44. You were not present at the Western slope when we gave Moses the commandments, nor were you a witness.

45. We established many generations who received no scripture for a long time. Nor were you residing with the people of Midyan, reciting for them our revelations. But we did send messengers.

46. Nor were you at the slope of Al-Toor (Mount Sinai) when we called. This is indeed mercy from your Lord, that you may warn people who received no warner before you; perhaps they take heed.

47. Now, if a disaster strikes them because of their own deeds, they cannot say, "Our Lord, had You sent a messenger to us, we would have followed Your commandments, and would have been believers."

Quran: God's Message to the World

48. However, when the truth came to them from us, they said, "If only we could see the same thing as that given to Moses (we will then believe)." Did they not disbelieve in what was given to Moses? They said, "(The Torah and the Quran are) two magics that support one another, and we reject them both."*

49. Say, "Show me a book from God that provides more guidance than them. I will follow it, if you are truthful."

50. If they fail to respond to you, then know that they only follow their opinions. And who is more astray than one who follows his own opinions, without guidance from God. God does not guide the wicked.

51. We have certainly delivered the message to them, that they may take heed.

52. Those who truly studied the previous scriptures will believe in this.

53. When (this Quran is) recited to them, they would say, "We believe that this is the truth from our Lord. We have been, according to it, Muslims."

54. These will be given double the recompense because of their steadfastness, and because they repel evil with righteousness, and from our provisions to them, they give to charity.

55. And when they encounter vain talk, they ignore it, saying "We are responsible for our work, and you are responsible for your work. Peace be on you, we have no desire to befriend the ignorant."

Only God Guides

56. You cannot guide those you love. God is the one who guides whomever He wills, for He is fully aware of those who deserve the guidance.

57. (The pagans also) said, "If we follow your guidance, we will be persecuted throughout the land." Did we not establish for them a sacred shrine that is perfectly secure, with all kinds of provisions donated to it from us? Indeed, most of them do not know.

58. Many a community we destroyed when they turned unappreciative. Here are their ruins that were abandoned, except a few; we were the inheritors.

28:48. *The Jews abandoned the Torah in favor of the Mishnah and Gemara, while the Muslims abandoned the Quran in favor of* **Hadith** *and* **Sunna.**

59. Your Lord never destroys any community, unless He sends in the midst thereof a messenger who recites our revelations for them. We never destroy any community unless its people are wicked.

60. Whatever you possess is the material of this life, and its vanities. What God possesses is far better, and eternal; do you not understand?

61. Is one whom we promised a good promise that is sure to come, equal to one who enjoys the temporary vanities of this life, then is forcibly gathered on the day of resurrection?

62. On that day, He will call upon them saying, "Where are those idols you set up besides Me?"

63. Those who have deserved the judgment would say, "Our Lord, these are the ones we misled. We only misled them because we ourselves were misled. We now disown them and surrender to You; they were not worshiping us."

64. They will be told, "Call upon your idols (to help you)." They would call upon them, but they will not respond. They will then see the retribution, and they will wish that they had been guided.

65. On that day, God will call on them, saying, "How did you respond to the messengers?"

66. They will be so stunned by the news on that day, that they will not ask any questions.

67. As for him who repents, believes, and works righteousness, he will be with the winners.

68. Your Lord creates whatever He wills, and chooses. None else can do the choosing. God be glorified; He is most exalted, above any partnership.

69. And your Lord is fully aware of anything they hide in their chests, and anything they declare.

70. And He is the One God; there is no god except He. To Him belongs all praise in the first and in the hereafter. All kingship belongs to Him, and to Him you ultimately return.

71. Say, "If God caused the night to become eternal for you until the day of resurrection, which god, other than God, can bring you light? Do you not hear?"

72. Say, "If God caused the daylight to become eternal for you until the day of resurrection, which god, other than God, can bring you a night for your rest? Do you not see?"

73. It is mercy from Him that He created the night and day, so you can rest after seeking his bounties, that you may be appreciative.

74. The day will come when God calls on them, saying, "Where are the idols you had set up besides Me?"

75. Then we will summon from each community a witness, and say, "Show us your proof." They will then realize that all truth belongs to God, and the idols they had invented will abandon them.

Qaroon

76. Qaroon was a member of Moses' clan, but he oppressed them. We endowed him with so much wealth, the keys of his treasures were almost too heavy for the strong men. His people used to tell him, "Do not be so vain, for God dislikes those who are vain."

77. "And use God's blessings to you in seeking the hereafter, without necessarily neglecting your share in this life. And be charitable as God has been charitable towards you. Do not corrupt the earth, for God dislikes the corruptors."

78. He said, "I accomplished this through my cleverness." Did he not know that God has destroyed generations before him, who were more powerful, and more numerous? The guilty need not be asked about their sins.*

79. One day, he went out in full splendor, and those who care about the materials of this world said, "Oh, we wish we were as lucky as Qaroon. He is really fortunate."

80. Those who possessed knowledge said, "Woe to you; God's rewards are far better for those who believe and work righteousness. None attains them except the steadfast."

81. Subsequently, we caused the earth to swallow Qaroon and his mansion. No army could help him against God, nor was he ever to win.

82. Those who wished to be in his place the day before said, "It seems that God is the only one who increases the provision for anyone, or withholds it. If it were not for God's grace towards us, He could have caused the earth to swallow us too. It seems that the disbelievers never succeed."

83. We have reserved the abode of the hereafter for those who do not seek exaltation in this life, or corruption. The ultimate victory belongs to the righteous.

84. Whoever works righteousness receives credit for more, while those who work evil are punished only for the evil they commit.

85. Surely, the one who decreed the Quran for you, will bring you back at a predetermined time. Say, "My Lord is fully aware of those who follow the right guidance, and those who have gone astray."

86. You never expected to receive the scripture, but it is mercy from your Lord. Therefore, do not be defender of the disbelievers.

87. Nor shall you be diverted from the revelations of God, after being revealed to you. You shall invite others to come to your Lord, and never fall into idol worship.

88. You shall never call on any other god besides God. There is no god except He. Everything perishes except His countenance. To Him belongs all the command, and to Him you will be returned.

28:78.   See 55:39-41 and Appendix 10

Sura 29: The Spider (Al-'Ankaboot)

In the name of God, most gracious, most merciful

1. A. L. M.*
2. Do the people think that they will be left to say, "We believe," without being put to the test?
3. We have tested the generations before them, for God must distinguish those who are truthful from those who are liars.
4. Or, do those who commit evil think that they will get away from us? How wrong is their notion!
5. If anyone is looking forward to the meeting with God, such predetermined audience will certainly come to pass. God is the hearer, the omniscient.
6. Whoever strives is only striving for his own good; God is in no need for anyone.
7. Those who believe and lead a righteous life, we will certainly remit their sins, and reward them manyfold for their works.
8. We enjoined the humans to honor their parents. However, if they exhort you to idolize besides Me what you do not recognize, then do not obey them. To Me alone is your final return, then I alone will inform you of everything you had done.
9. Those who believe and lead a righteous life, we will certainly admit them with the righteous.
10. Among the people there are those who say, "We believe in God," but if they ever suffer in the cause of God, they equate the people's persecution with God's retribution. And when victory comes from your Lord, they say, "We were with you." Is God not fully aware of the people's innermost thoughts?
11. God will certainly distinguish the believers and the hypocrites.
12. Those who disbelieved would say to the believers, "Follow our path, and we will carry your sins." They can never carry any of their sins; they are liars.

29:1. *These letters constitute a significant part of the Quran's miraculous numerical code, and physically and indisputably prove that the Quran is God's message to the world. The meaning of these Quranic initials remained a divinely guarded secret until discovered in the course of this very translation. See Appendix 1 for details.*

13.   Indeed, they will carry their own loads, in addition to other loads besides their loads, and they will be held answerable, on the day of resurrection, for all their inventions.*

14.   We have sent Noah to his people, and he lived among them one thousand years less fifty,* then the flood annihilated them because of their wickedness.

15.   We delivered him and those who accompanied him in the ark, and we set this up as a lesson for the world.

16.   And Abraham went to his people, saying, "Worship God and observe Him. This is better for you, if you only knew."

17.   What you idolize besides God are idols of your creation. Whatever idols you set up possess no provision for you. Therefore, seek the provisions only from God, and worship Him alone, and be appreciative of Him. To Him you will be returned.

Role Of the Messenger

18.   If you disbelieve, so did many generations before you. The messenger's sole mission is to deliver (the message).

19.   Do they not see how God initiates the creation, then repeats it? This is easy for God to do.

20.   Say, "Travel the earth and see how the creation was started. God will also initiate the recreation in the hereafter. God is omnipotent."

21.   He punishes whomever He wills, and showers mercy upon whomever He wills. To Him you are finally turned over.

22.   You can never escape, on earth or in the heaven, nor do you have any lord or supporter besides God.

23.   Those who disbelieved in God's revelations, and in meeting Him, have despaired from My mercy; they have deserved painful retribution.

24.   The only response from Abraham's people was their saying, "Kill him, or burn him." But God saved him from the fire. These should be lessons for people who believe.

25.   Abraham said, "You keep on idolizing these idols only to maintain each others' friendship in this life. However, on the day of resurrection you will disown each other, and curse one another. Your final abode is hell, and you will find no supporters."

---

*29:13.   There are literally hundreds of "**Hadiths**" that "guarantee" salvation, regardless of one's deeds. These include for example the recitation of specific portions of Quran a specific number of times. The inventors of these lies will certainly perish in hell.*

29:14.   See footnote 7:142.

26. Among the believers was Lot. He said, "I will flee to my Lord; He is the almighty, the wise."

27. And to Abraham we granted Isaac and Jacob, and we endowed his descendants with prophethood and the scripture. We gave him his recompense in this life, and in the hereafter he will be with the righteous.

28. And (we sent) Lot to his people, saying, "You commit such an abomination; no one else has committed this.

29. "You practice sex with the men, commit highway robbery, and work evil in your society." The only response his people gave him was, "Bring God's doom, if you are truthful."

30. He said, "My Lord, grant me victory over these wicked people."

31. And when our messengers went to Abraham with the good news (of Isaac's birth), they said, "We will destroy that community (of Sodom), for the people therein are wicked."

32. Abraham said, "But Lot lives there." They said, "We are fully aware who lives there. Certainly, we will save him and his family, but not his wife; she is doomed."

33. And when our messengers went to Lot, they were mistreated, and he was embarrassed in their presence. But they said, "Have no fear, nor worry; we will save you and your family except your wife; she is doomed.

34. "We will smite this community with disaster from the sky, due to their wickedness."

35. We have left some of the ruins thereof as a profound lesson for those who understand.

36. To Midyan we sent their brother Shu'aib. He said, "O my people, worship God, seek the last day, and do not corrupt the earth."

37. Because they disbelieved him, the quake struck them, leaving them dead in their homes.

38. Similarly, 'Aad and Thamood; you have seen their ruins. The devil had adorned their works in their eyes and diverted them from the path, despite all the warnings to them.

39. Also Qaroon, Pharaoh, and Haamaan. Moses went to them with clear signs, but they were too arrogant and could not get away with it.

40. Each of these we punished for their sins. Some we afflicted with a violent storm, some were struck by the quake, some were swallowed by the earth, and some we drowned. It is not God who wronged them; it is they who wronged themselves.

41. The example of those who set up idols besides God is like those who take refuge in the female spider's home. The least trustworthy home is that of the female spider, if they only knew."*

42. God knows that the idols they set up besides Him are powerless, while He is the almighty, the wise.

43. We cite these examples for the people, and only the knowledgeable can appreciate them.

44. God is the one who created the heavens and the earth,truthfully; this is a lesson for the believers.

45. You shall recite what is revealed to you of the scripture,* and observe the **Salat** prayers. For **Salat** protects from falling in sin and evil and is the means for remembering God, which is even greater. God is fully aware of everything you do.

46. Do not argue with the people of the scripture except in the best manner, unless they treat you unjustly. And say, "We believe in what was sent down to us, and what was sent down to you; our God and your God is one and the same; to Him we submit."

47. We have revealed to you this scripture; and those who received previous scripture shall believe in this. Some of them do believe; and only the disbelievers will ignore our revelations.

48. You (Muhammad) never studied previous scripture, nor are you capable of writing one. In that case, the falsehood seekers may have reason to doubt.

49. Indeed, these revelations are clear in the chests of those who possess knowledge. Only the wicked disregard our revelations.

Muhammad Performed No Miracles*

50. They said, "How come no miracles were sent down to him from his Lord?" Say, "The miracles come only from God, and I am no more than a warner."

51. Is it not enough of a miracle that we sent down to you this scripture, which is being recited to them? Indeed, it is a mercy and a message for those who believe.

29:41-43. Those who are knowledgeable in entomology know that the black widow spider kills her mate after mating. Thus, the spider web is really a death trap for the male. Note that the spider mentioned in verse 41 is female. Verse 43 states that only the knowledgeable can appreciate such an example. These entomological facts were not known at the time of Quran's revelation.

29:45. This proves that the Quran was revealed to each one of us, and that we were all represented by the prophet Muhammad when he received the Quran. See 18:27-28, 33:21, 42:51, and Appendix 11.

29:50. Those who idolize the prophet against his wishes claim that he performed a long list of miracles. The Quran, however, which narrates the miracles of many prophets, teaches us that Muhammad did not perform any miracles. Those who love and respect the prophet, love him and respect him as he is.

52. Say, "God suffices as a witness between me and you. He is fully aware of everything in the heavens and the earth. Those who believe in falsehood and disbelieve in God are the real losers."

53. They challenge you to bring doom upon them. If it were not for a predetermined decision, the retribution would have come to them immediately. However, it will surely come suddenly, when they least expect it.

54. They challenge you to bring doom, though hell is actually surrounding the disbelievers.

55. The day will come when retribution will overwhelm them; from above them, and from beneath their feet. God will then say, "Suffer (the consequences of) your works."

Move Away, If You Have To

56. O My servants who believed, My earth is spacious, so worship Me alone.

57. Everyone will taste death, then to us you will be returned.

58. Those who believe and work righteousness, we will assign them to mansions in Paradise, with flowing streams; they abide therein forever; what a beautiful recompense for the workers.

59. They remained steadfast and trusted in their Lord.

60. Any creature that possesses no provision, God provides for it as well as for you. He is the hearer, the omniscient.

The Idol-Worshipers Believe in God

61. If you ask them, "Who created the heavens and the earth, and subdued the sun and the moon," they will answer, "God." How come they deviate?

62. God is the only one who increases the provision for whomever He chooses among His servants, or reduces it. God is fully aware of all things.

63. If you ask them, "Who sends down water from the sky, to revive dead land," they will answer, "God." Say, "Praise be to God." Indeed, most of them do not understand.

64. This life is no more than vanity and play, while the abode of the hereafter is the real life, if they only knew.

65. When they ride a ship, they sincerely implore God, totally devoted to Him. But as soon as He saves them to the shore, they set up idols.

66. Let them disbelieve in what we have given them, and let them enjoy. They will surely find out.

67. Do they not see that we appointed a sacred sanctuary for them, while the people around them are never safe? Would they still believe in falsehood and deny God's blessings?

68. Who is more wicked than one who invents lies about God, or rejects the truth when it comes to him?* Is hell not well deserved by the disbelievers?

69. As for those who strive towards us, we will surely guide them to our paths. God is always with the righteous.

---

*29:68. The advocates and followers of "**Hadith**" and/or "**Sunna**" are committing both evils; they reject the Quran's assertions that it is complete and perfect (6:19, 38, 114), and invent lies about God when they claim that "**Hadith**" and "**Sunna**" are divine revelations.*

Sura 30:   The Romans (Al-Room)

In the name of God, most gracious, most merciful

1.   A. L. M.*
2.   The Romans will be defeated.
3.   Throughout the land. After being defeated, they will win.
4.   Within a few years. Such is God's decision, both in the first time and the second time. The believers will then rejoice.
5.   With God's victory. He grants victory to whomever He wills. He is the almighty, the wise.
6.   This is the promise of God; and God never breaks His promise, but most people do not know.
7.   They recognize only the visible part of this world, while disregarding the hereafter.
8.   Why do they not reflect on themselves? God did not create the heavens and the earth, and everything between them, except for a specific purpose, and for a specific period. However, most people disbelieve in meeting their Lord.
9.   Did they not travel the earth and see the consequences for those before them? They possessed more power, and developed the earth and built on it even more than these have built. Their messengers went to them with profound signs. It was never God who wronged them; it was they who wronged themselves.
10.   The consequences were evil for those who committed evil; they rejected God's revelations and ridiculed them.
11.   God initiates the creation, and He repeats it, then to Him you will finally return.
12.   When the Hour comes, the guilty will be stunned.
13.   None of their idols can intercede on their behalf; they will even disown their idols.
14.   When the Hour comes, they will be divided.
15.   As for those who believed and worked righteousness, they enjoy Paradise.
16.   But those who disbelieved and rejected our revelations and the meeting of the hereafter, they will be committed to retribution.

30:1.   See Appendix 1 for details of the miraculous numerical code of Quran, and the meaning of these letters.

Signs of God

17. You shall glorify God when you retire at night, and when you get up in the morning.
18. He is worthy of all praise, in the heavens and the earth; in the evening, and when you rest at noon.
19. He produces the live from the dead, and the dead from the live. Just as He revives the land that had been dead, you will be resurrected.
20. Among His signs is that He created you from dust, then you became multiplying humans.
21. Among His signs is that He created for you spouses from among you, in order to find harmony together, and created love and kindness to join you together. These are lessons for people who reflect.
22. Among His signs is the creation of the heavens and the earth, and the variations in your languages and colors. These are signs for all the people.
23. Among His signs is your sleep during the night, and your work to seek His bounties during the day. These are signs for people who hear.
24. Among His signs is the lightning that He shows you to instill both fear and hope; He sends down water from the sky to revive a land that has been dead. These are signs for people who understand.
25. Among His signs is the fact that the heaven and the earth stand at His disposal. When He calls upon you, from the earth you will come out.
26. To Him belongs everyone in the heavens and the earth; all subservient to Him.
27. He is the one who initiates the creation, and repeats it; this is the easiest thing for Him. To Him belongs the highest similitude in the heavens and the earth; He is the almighty, the wise.

Monotheism: Natural Instinct

28. God cites herein an example from among you; would you share your assets with your servants, to the extent that you become equal, and to the extent that you respect them as they respect you now? We thus explain the revelations for those who understand.
29. Indeed, the wicked follow their own opinions, without knowledge. Can anyone guide those misguided by God? No one can help them.
30. Therefore, you shall devote yourself completely to the religion of monotheism. This is the natural instinct that God implanted into the people.* Nothing can change such creation of God. This is the perfect religion, but most people do not know.

30:30.   God gathered all the people and had them bear witness that He is the Lord. See 7:172.

31. You shall all submit to God, beware of Him, observe the **salat** prayers, and never fall into idol worship.
32. Do not be with those who divided their religion into sects; each party satisfied with what they have.*
33. When adversity touches the people, they implore their Lord and submit to Him. But as soon as He relieves them with His mercy, some of them set up idols besides their Lord.
34. Let them disbelieve in what we have given them, and let them temporarily enjoy themselves; they will surely find out.
35. Have we given them any commandment that supports the setting up of idols?
36. When we bless the people with mercy, they rejoice therewith, and when adversity afflicts them, as a consequence of their own deeds, they become dejected.
37. Do they not realize that God is the only one who increases the provision for whomever He wills, and reduces it? These are lessons for people who believe.
38. Therefore, you shall give the relative his right, and the needy, and the alien. This is better for those who seek the pleasure of God; they are the winners.
39. The usury you practice may increase the people's money, but it earns nothing at God, while the charities you practice, seeking only the pleasure of God, are multiplied manyfold.
40. God is the one who created you; He is the one who provides for you; He is the one who puts you to death; and He is the one who resurrects you. Can any of your idols do any of these? God be glorified; He is high above any idols they set up.
41. Corruption has prevailed throughout the land and sea, due to the people's work. Therefore, He makes them suffer the consequences of their works, that they may return.
42. Say, "Travel the earth and see the consequences for those before you." The majority of them were idol-worshipers.
43. Therefore, you shall devote yourself to the perfect religion, before a day comes that is inevitable. On that day, the people will be stunned.

30:32. The only reason the Muslims are divided into various sects is that some of them advocate other than the Quran; specifically, "**hadith**" and "**sunna**" as sources of law. The Quran calls these people idol worshipers, as we see in verse 31. Throughout the Quran, we are reminded that we shall adhere to Quran, the whole Quran, and nothing but the Quran. Ironically, those who claim to love the prophet, yet disobey him by inventing and advocating "**hadith**" and "**sunna**," are disowned by the prophet (see 6:159 and 25:31).

44. Whoever disbelieves causes his own detriment, and those who work righteousness do so for their own good.

45. God bestows His grace upon those who believe and work righteousness, while those who disbelieve are displeasing Him.

46. Among His signs is the sending of winds with good omen, showering you with His mercy, and allowing the ships to run by His command to seek His bounties, that you may be appreciative.

47. We have sent messengers before you to their people with profound signs, then we punished the rebellious. (As for those who believe,) I have made it a duty upon Myself to give victory to the believers.

48. God is the one who sends the winds to stir up clouds, spreads them throughout the sky as He wills, then makes them condense into rain and pours it down upon whomever He wills, that they may rejoice.

49. Before it was sent down to them, they had despaired.

50. Note the results of God's mercy and how He revives land that had been dead. He will thus resurrect the dead; for He is omnipotent.

51. Had we sent upon them a yellow sandstorm, they would have continued to disbelieve.

52. You can never make the dead hear, nor can you make the deaf hear once they turn away.

53. Nor can you guide the blind out of their straying. You can make none hear, except those who believe in our revelations and totally submit.

54. God is the one who created you weak, then He makes you grow stronger, then he makes you feeble and gray. He creates whatever He wills. He is the omniscient, the omnipotent.

No Time Between Death and Resurrection*

55. On the day of resurrection, the sinners will swear that they had lasted one hour. That is how wrong they were.

56. Those who possessed knowledge and faith will say, "You have lasted in God's record until the day of resurrection. This is the day of resurrection, but you did not know."

57. On that day, no excuse will be accepted from the wrongdoers, nor will they be asked to apologize.

58. We have cited for the people all kinds of examples in this Quran. However, even if you show them a miracle, the disbelievers will say, "You are falsifiers."

59. Thus does God seal the hearts of those who do not know.

60. Therefore, be patient, for God's promise is true, and do not be intimidated by those who possess no faith.

30:55. *The period between death and resurrection will feel like a one-night sleep (see 2:259, 18:19 and 25, and Appendix 14).*

Sura 31: Luqmaan

In the name of God, most gracious, most merciful

1. A.L.M.*
2. These (letters) are the miracles of this book of wisdom.*
3. A guide and mercy for the pious;
4. who observe the **salat** prayers and **zakat** charity, and are absolutely positive about the hereafter.
5. They have followed the guidance from their Lord; they are the winners.

Quran versus Hadith*

6. Some people uphold vain **hadith** in order to divert others from the path of God without knowledge, and to create a mockery out of it. These have deserved humiliating retribution.
7. When our revelations are recited to them, they turn away in arrogance, as if they never heard them; as if their ears are deaf. Promise them painful retribution.
8. As for those who believe and work righteousness, they have deserved the gardens of bliss.
9. They live in them forever; this is the truthful promise of God, He is the almighty, the wise.
10. He created the heavens without visible pillars, and placed stabilizers on the earth to prevent it from aberrating, and He spread all kinds of creatures therein. And we send down water from the sky, to grow all kinds of beautiful plants.
11. Such is the creation of God; show me what their idols have created. Indeed, the wicked are totally astray.

Luqmaan's Wisdom

12. We have endowed Luqmaan with wisdom, for he was appreciative of God. Whoever is appreciative is appreciative for his own good. As for the unappreciative, God is in no need; He is worthy of all praise.

31:1. See Appendix 1 for details of the Quran's miraculous numerical code involving these letters.

31:2. This expression is used exclusively in conjunction with Quranic initials.

31:6-7. The Quran teaches us that those who advocate **hadith** are false Muslims who have disobeyed the prophet and rejected God's revelations (See 6:112-116, 18:109-110, and Appendices 11, 15, 16, and 17).

13. Luqmaan said to his son as he enlightened him, "O my son, do not set up any idol besides God; idol worship is a gross offense."*

14. We enjoined the human being to honor his parents; his mother bore him as he got heavier and heavier, and cared for him for two years until weaning. You shall be appreciative to Me and to your parents; to Me is the ultimate destiny.

15. However, if they exhort you to set up idols besides Me, do not obey them. But continue to treat them nicely. You shall follow the path of those who submit to Me. To Me is your ultimate return, then I will inform you of everything you did.

16. "O my son, even if your deed is as small as a mustard seed, placed inside a rock or anywhere in the heavens or the earth, God will bring it. God is compassionate, cognizant.

17. "O my son, observe the **salat** prayers, advocate righteousness and forbid evil, and stay steadfast in the face of adversity; this is the real strength.

18. "Do not be arrogant, nor shall you walk in pride; God does not love the boastful, the arrogant.

19. "Be humble as you walk, and lower your voice; the ugliest voice is that of the donkey."

Be Appreciative of God

20. Do you not see that God put in your service everything in the heavens and everything on earth? He showers you with His bounties, obvious and hidden. Yet some people argue about God without knowledge, nor guidance, nor divine scripture.

21. And when they are told, "Follow what God has sent down," they say, "We follow only what we found our parents following." What if the devil is leading them to the hellfire?

22. Anyone who submits himself to God, and maintains piety, has gotten hold of the strongest bond. The ultimate end of all things is with God.

23. As for those who disbelieve, do not be saddened by their disbelief. To us is their ultimate return, then we will inform them of everything they did. God is fully aware of the innermost convictions.

24. We may let them enjoy temporarily, then commit them to a terrible retribution.

25. If you ask them who created the heavens and the earth, they will say, "God." Say, "Praise God;" most of them do not know.

31:13.   Idol worship is defined as a "gross offense," rather than a sin. It is far worse than any sin. The Quran teaches us that God forgives "all" sins (see 31:53), while idol worship is the only unforgivable offense (see 4:48, 4:116, and 5:72).

26. To God belongs everything in the heavens and the earth; God is bounteous, praiseworthy.

27. If all the trees on earth were made into pens; and the ocean, multiplied sevenfold, supplied the ink, God will never run out of words.* God is almighty, wise.

28. Your creation, and your resurrection, is like the creation and resurrection of one person.* God is hearer, seer.

29. Do you not realize that God merges the night into the day and merges the day into night? He subdued the sun and the moon, each running for a predetermined life span. God is cognizant of everything you do.

30. This is to show that God is truth, and whatever they idolize besides Him is falsehood, and that God is the most high, the great.

31. Do you not realize that the ships roam the sea carrying God's bounties, in order to show you some of His signs? These are signs for everyone who is steadfast, appreciative.

32. When overwhelming waves surround them, they implore God sincerely. But as soon as He saves them to the shore, some of them revert. Only unappreciative betrayers discard our revelations.

33. O people, beware of your Lord, and reverence the day when no father can help his son, nor a son can help his father. God's promise is true; therefore do not be distracted by this life, and do not be distracted by deceivers.

34. God is the only one who knows about the Hour: He is the one who sends down the rain; He knows the contents of every womb. Meanwhile, no one else knows what happens tomorrow, nor in which land he will die. God is omniscient, cognizant.

31:27. Yet some people claim that the Quran is not complete. This verse teaches us that God has given us all the words we need; He did not run out of words. Those who seek other than Quran as a source of law, flatly reject God's revelations (see also 18:109).

31:28. Once you design and perfect the original (master copy), the copies are easy to make.

Sura 32: Prostration (Al-Sajdah)

In the name of God, most gracious, most merciful

1. A.L.M.*
2. The revelation of this scripture is, without a doubt, from the Lord of the universe.*
3. Do they say that he made it up? Indeed, it is the truth from your Lord, to warn people who received no warner before you, that they may be guided.
4. God is the one who created the heavens and the earth, and everything between them in six days, then assumed all authority. You have none besides Him as a lord or intercessor; would you take heed?
5. He controls everything from the heaven to the earth, through a distance where one day is equivalent to one thousand of your years.
6. Such is the knower of all secrets and declarations; the almighty, the merciful.
7. He perfected everything He created, and started the creation of man from clay.
8. Then He continued his reproduction through a certain lowly liquid.
9. Then He perfected him and blew into him from His soul. He gave you the hearing, the eyes, and the minds; yet rarely are you appreciative.
10. They said, "After we vanish into the soil, do we get recreated?" Indeed, they disbelieve in meeting their Lord.
11. Say, "The angel of death that is assigned to you will terminate your life, then to your Lord is your ultimate return."
12. If you could only envision the guilty, bowing their heads, when they meet their Lord; they will say, "Our Lord, now we see and we hear. Send us back and we will work righteousness; now we are positive."
13. Had we willed, we could have given guidance to everyone. But it is already predetermined that I fill hell with jinns and humans all together.

32:1.   See Appendix 1 for details of the Quran's secret numerical code. These Quranic initials constitute a significant part of the Quran's miracle. The Quran came to the world 1400 years ago and stood on its own without any supporting evidence that it is a divine scripture. This 1400-year-old secret has been unveiled in the course of this translation.

32:2.   This verse tells us the meaning or significance of the first verse, i.e., these letters prove that the Quran is the word of God. This kind of statement invariably follows the Quranic initials throughout the Quran. In retrospect, our Creator has been telling us the meaning of these "mysterious" letters since the revelation of Quran.

14. Suffer the consequences of ignoring this day; for we ignore you now. Suffer the eternal retribution because of what you did.

15. The only people who truly believe in our revelations are those who, when reminded thereof, submit immediately;* they fall prostrate and praise the glory of their Lord without hesitation.

16. Their bodies forsake the beds in favor of worshiping their Lord, out of reverence and hope, and they spend (in charity) from our provisions to them.

17. No soul knows what is kept hidden for them of joy, as a reward for their work.

18. Is one who is a believer the same as one who is wicked? They are not equal.

19. As for those who believe and lead a righteous life, they have deserved the eternal abode of Paradise as a recompense for their work.

20. But those who worked evil, their abode is hell; whenever they try to get out of it, they will be returned to it and told, "Suffer the retribution of hell that you used to deny."

21. We afflict them with some retribution in this life, that they may reform.

22. Who is more wicked than one who is reminded of his Lord's revelations, then disregards them? We will certainly punish the guilty.

23. We have given Moses the scripture, stating, "You shall have no doubt about meeting God," and we made it a guide for the children of Israel.

24. We appointed **imams** from among them, who guided in accordance with our commandments, because they maintained steadfastness and upheld our scripture.

25. Your Lord is the one who judges them on the day of resurrection, regarding their disputes.

26. Does it ever occur to them how many generations we have annihilated before them? They have walked in their ruins. These are profound lessons; do they not hear?

27. Do they not realize that we drive the water to barren land and produce plants that feed them and their animals? Do they not see?

28. They say, "Where is this victory, if you are truthful?"

29. Say, "On the day of victory, it will be useless for the disbelievers to believe; no longer will they be respited."

30. Therefore, disregard them and wait; they too have to wait.

32:15.   *The true believers submit to the Quran without question and accept it as the **only** source of jurisprudence. See Appendices 15, 16, and 17.*

Sura 33:   The Allies (Al-Aḥzaab)

In the name of God, most gracious, most merciful

1. O you prophet, observe God, and do not obey the disbelievers or the hypocrites. God is omniscient, wise.
2. Follow what is revealed to you from your Lord; God is cognizant of everything you do.
3. You shall trust in God; for God suffices as guardian.

Forsake Traditions

4. God did not give any human two hearts. Nor did He make your wives, whom you estrange, forbidden for intercourse as if they were your mothers.* Nor did He make your adopted children your own. These are your inventions. God speaks the truth, and He guides to the right way.
5. You shall give your adopted children names that preserve their relationship to their real parents. This is more equitable in the sight of God. If you do not know their parents, then treat them as family members. You commit no sin if you make unintentional mistakes; you are responsible for your real intentions. God if forgiver, merciful.
6. The prophet is closer to the believers than themselves, and his wives are like mothers to them. The relatives shall be given priority, in accordance with God's scripture, ahead of the other believers and immigrants. But you shall maintain kindness towards all of them. These are written commandments of the scripture.
7. We have made a covenant with all the prophets; with you, and with Noah, Abraham, Moses, and Jesus the son of Mary. We made a solemn covenant with them.
8. That God rewards the truthful for their truthfulness, and has prepared for the disbelievers a painful retribution.

The Battle of the Allies*

9. O you who believe, remember God's blessing upon you when the troops came to you. We sent upon them a storm and invisible soldiers. God is seer of everything you do.

33:4. *A previously prevalent expression in the Arabic language was to estrange a wife by saying that she is like the husband's mother (as far as intercourse is concerned), without giving her the freedom of divorce.*

33:9. *This is the battle where the Muslims dug a ditch around Yathrib (Medina). The disbelievers were hit with a violent storm and had to disperse without victory.*

10. They converged upon you from above you, and from below you, and you became utterly frightened; you lost your confidence in God.

11. The believers were really tested then and were shaken up violently.

12. That is when the hypocrites and the doubtful were exposed and said, "What God and His messenger promised us is false."

13. Some of them even said, "O people of Yathrib,* you have no chance to win; let us give up." Some of them asked the prophet's permission to give up, saying, "Our homes are vulnerable," even though they were not vulnerable. All they wanted was to flee.

14. If the enemy were to invade from every direction, and they were asked to betray the believers, they would readily cooperate.

15. They had vowed to God that they will never flee, and they are responsible for such a vow.

16. Say, "Fleeing will never save you from death or from getting killed, eventually. You can only last a while longer."

17. Say, "Afterwards, who will protect you from God, if He decides to punish you or pardon you?" They can never find, besides God, any Lord or supporter.

18. God is fully aware of the hinderers among you, and those who tell their comrades, "Stay with us;" they are not willing to strive, except rarely.

19. They are stingy towards you; and when war erupts, you see them looking at you with terrified eyes, as if they were about to die. Once the war is over, they scold you with sharp tongues. They are too stingy to offer help, for they never really believed. Therefore, God nullifies their works, and this is easy for God to do.

33:13.   The ancient name of Medina.

*33:21.   This verse refers specifically to the prophet's confidence in God's support and victory. It is placed right in the middle of the story of the Al-Ahzaab battle, where the believers were truly shaken up and thought that Islam was finished. However, there is no harm in generalizing the verse and considering the prophet a good example for all of us. The prophet's example is set by the fact that he upheld the Quran, and nothing but the Quran (see 5:48, 49 and 7:73-75). Those who idolize the prophet forget that to love, respect, and obey the prophet is to worship God alone and uphold the Quran, the whole Quran, and nothing but the Quran. They invented a whole set of actions, which they called **sunna**, and attributed them to the prophet. The prophet will be the first to disown them on the day of judgment. Moreover, the abusers of this verse reveal their ignorance of Quran. They are not aware that this verse is repeated almost word for word in reference to Abraham (see 60:4 and 6).*

20. They thought that the allies may come back and wished they were scattered throughout the desert, checking on you from afar. If they happened to be with you, they would not fight, except rarely.

21. The messenger of God is a good example for you; for any of you who truly seek God and the hereafter and commemorate God frequently.*

22. As for the believers, when they saw the allies, they said, "This is what God and His messenger had promised us; God and His messenger are truthful." The prospect of war actually augmented their faith and their submission.

23. Among the believers, there are those who fulfill their vows to God. Some of them give up their lives, while the others stand ready; they never waver.

24. God will recompense the truthful for their truthfulness, and punish the hypocrites if He wills, or redeem them. God is forgiver, merciful.

25. God repelled the disbelievers with their rage; they gained nothing, and He spared the believers any fighting; God is powerful, almighty.

26. And He embarrassed the people of the scripture who allied themselves with the disbelievers, and He threw terror into their hearts. Some of them you killed, and some you took as captives.

27. He made you inherit their land, their homes, their properties, and lands that you had never set foot on. God is omnipotent.

Instructions to All Women*

28. O you prophet, say to your wives, "If you seek this life and its vanities, I can let you enjoy and allow you to go amicably.

29. "But if you seek God, His messenger, and the abode of the hereafter, then God has prepared for the righteous among you a great reward."

30. O wives of the prophet, if any of you commits a gross sin, the retribution will be doubled for her. This is easy for God to do.

31. If any of you maintains obedience to God and His messenger, and works righteousness, we will double the reward for her; we have prepared for her a generous recompense.

32. O wives of the prophet, you are not the same as other women, if you maintain righteousness. Do not speak so softly that a person with a doubtful heart may misunderstand your motive; you shall speak righteousness.

33:28-35. *Any home where the Quran is preached is the same as the prophet's home. The responsibility is doubled when any person receives the message. Thus, receiving the message can be a great blessing, or a disasterous curse, depending on one's response, i.e., heeding or not heeding. Obviously, the sin is a greater offense when committed by a person who knows, as compared to the one who does not know.*

33. Let your homes be your base, and forsake the permissiveness of the days of ignorance. You shall observe the **salat** prayers and **zakat** charity, and obey God and His messenger. God thus wishes to remove all impurity from you, O people of the shrine,* and to thoroughly purify you.

34. You shall heed what is recited in your homes of God's revelations and wisdom. God is compassionate, cognizant.

35. The Muslim men and the Muslim women, the believing men and the believing women, the obedient men and the obedient women, the truthful men and the truthful women, the steadfast men and the steadfast women, the reverent men and the reverent women, the charitable men and the charitable women, the fasting men and the fasting women, the chaste men and the chaste women, and the men and women who commemorate God frequently; God has prepared for them forgiveness and a great recompense.

Muhammad the Man versus Muhammad the Messenger*

36. No believing man or believing woman would voice any objection when God and His messenger decree a commandment. Anyone who disobeys God and His messenger has gone astray.

37. Thus, you said to the one endowed by God and by you, "Keep your wife, and observe God," while hiding in yourself what God wanted you to declare. You thus feared the people, instead of fearing God. Then, when Zeid (Muhammad's adopted son) was completely through with his wife, we had you marry her. This was done to establish the law that the believers can marry the divorced wives of their adopted sons. God's command must be carried out.

38. The prophet should not be embarrassed by what God decrees for him. This has always been God's system. The command of God is an obligatory duty.

39. For those who deliver God's messages, fear Him only, and never fear anyone else, God suffices as rewarder.

33:33.   See 11:73.

33:36-37.   These verses teach us that Muhammad the man is not different from any other man; he makes mistakes. Throughout the Quran, we see that Muhammad the man makes mistakes (see 4:79, 9:117, 17:73-74, 33:37, 40:66, 61:1, 80:1-10, and 94:7), while Muhammad the messenger utters only the perfection of Quran (53:3). Those who idolize the prophet claim that he never made mistakes. Thus, they flagrantly deny the truthfulness of God almighty and flatly refuse to believe the Quran. In verses 36 and 37, we see Muhammad the man disobey Muhammad the messenger.

40. Muhammad is not the father of any of you; he is a messenger of God, and the final prophet. God is fully aware of all things.

41. O you who believe, you shall commemorate God as much as you can.

42. Glorify Him day and night.

43. He and His angels honor you, in order to lead you out of the darkness into the light; He showers His mercy upon the believers.*

44. Their greeting on the day they meet God is, "Peace;" He has prepared for them a generous recompense.

45. O you prophet, we have sent you as a witness, a bearer of good news, and a warner.

46. And a caller towards God, by His leave, and a guiding beacon.

47. Give good news to the believers, that they will receive from God a great bounty.

48. Do not obey the disbelievers and the hypocrites, and disregard their insults. Put your trust in God; God suffices as a guardian.

49. O you who believe, when you marry the believing women, if you divorce them before touching them, then they owe you no interim.* You shall pay them a compensation, and let them go amicably.

50. O you prophet, we have permitted for you your wives, to whom you paid a dowry, and those who are rightly lawful for you from among the daughters of your uncles, and the daughters of your aunts who immigrated with you, and any believing woman who forfeits the dowry only for the prophet, if the prophet wishes to marry her. However, forfeiture of the dowry for the prophet may not apply to any other believer. We have already established the obligations for them towards their wives, and the women they can legally marry. In this way, you will not suffer any embarrassment. God is forgiver, merciful.

51. You may shun any of them, or accept any of them, if you wish; or you may accept one you had shunned previously. This will please them, and they will accept the dowry you give them. God is fully aware of your intentions; God is omniscient, clement.

52. You are not permitted to marry the women beyond these limits; nor shall you substitute any of them, even if you admire their beauty. Only those you can legally marry are permitted. God is watching all things.

33:43. These are the same words as those applied to the prophet in 33:56, a verse that is widely abused by those who idolize the prophet against his will.

33:49. See 2:228.

General Etiquette

53. O you who believe, do not enter the prophet's homes, unless you have permission to eat, and do not wait there expecting an invitation. But if you are invited, then you may enter. Once you finish eating, then leave; do not carry on a conversation. This used to hurt the prophet, and he was too embarrassed to tell you. But God does not shy away from the truth. When you ask his wives for something, ask them from behind a barrier. This is purer for your hearts and their hearts. You should beware of hurting the messenger of God. Do not marry any of his wives after him (divorced or widowed),* for this would be a blasphemy.

54. Whether you declare anything or conceal it, God is fully aware of all things.

55. The women commit no error by (dressing comfortably) in the presence of their fathers, their sons, their brothers, the sons of their brothers, the sons of their sisters, the women, and their servants. They shall observe God; for God witnesses all things.

56. God and His angels honor the prophet;* O you who believe, you shall honor him and regard him as he should be regarded.

57. Those who insult God and His messenger are cursed by God in this life and in the hereafter; He has prepared for them a humiliating retribution.

58. Those who insult the believing men and the believing women, without justification, have incurred a blasphemy and a gross sin.

Women Shall Dress Modestly

59. O you prophet, tell your wives and your daughters, and the believing women to lengthen their garments. Thus, they will be recognized and will not be insulted. God is forgiver, merciful.

33:53.   Verse 4:22 prohibits us from marrying any woman who was previously married to our fathers. Because marriage involves some very private behavior, God decreed this law to preserve respect for our fathers. Similarly, the prophet was a fatherly figure to all the believers of his generation. To preserve respect for the prophet and for the message he preached, God decreed a similar law regarding the prophet's wives.

33:56.   God and His angels honor and regard every believer. Note the similarity of Arabic words in 33:43. This is the verse that is used by satan most frequently to lead the believers into the trap of idol worship. To love and honor the prophet Muhammad or any other prophet is to worship God alone and to follow and uphold God's scripture as the only source of law.

60. Unless the hypocrites, those whose hearts are diseased, and the skeptics of the town refrain (from insulting the believers), we will order you to fight them until they move away.

61. Otherwise, they shall be condemned wherever they go; they shall be taken and executed.

62. This is the same system of God as given to those before you, for God's system is never changeable.

63. The people ask you about the Hour; say, "Only God knows about it." You may not realize it, but the Hour may be very close.*

64. God has cursed the disbelievers and has prepared for them hell.

65. They abide therein forever; they will find no ally or supporter.

66. On the day when their faces turn about the hellfire, they will say, "We wish we obeyed God and obeyed the messenger."

67. They will say, "Our Lord, we obeyed our masters and elders, and they misguided us.

68. "Our Lord, give them double the retribution, and curse them a mighty curse."

69. O you who believe, do not be like those who insulted Moses, then God absolved him of everything they said; he was honorable in the sight of God.

70. O you who believe, beware of God and speak only righteousness.

71. He will then correct your works and forgive your sins. Whoever obeys God and His messenger has triumphed a great triumph.

Only The Humans Are Free To Choose

72. We had offered the responsibility to the heavens and the earth and the mountains, but they refused to accept it and were afraid thereof. But the human being accepted it; surely, he was wrong, ignorant.*

73. For God will punish the hypocrite men and women, and the idol-worshiping men and women. And God will redeem the believing men and women; God is forgiver, merciful.

33:63. *The time from now to the day of resurrection equals, for all practical purposes, the time that is left of anyone's life. For people who will die within the next hour, the "hour" (of resurrection) is less than one hour away from them. See 30:55.*

33:72. *In view of the general human plague of idol-worship, and the fact that the vast majority of people are condemned to hell (see, 12:103 and 106), the chance that any particular individual will make it to heaven is practically nil. See also 32:13 and 36:7.*

Sura 34: Sheba (Saba')

In the name of God, most gracious, most merciful

1. Praise be to God, to whom belongs everything in the heavens and the earth, and to Him belongs all praise in the hereafter; He is the wise, the cognizant.

2. He knows everything that goes into the earth and everything that comes out of it, and everything that comes down from the sky and everything that climbs into it; He is the merciful, the forgiver.

3. Those who disbelieved said, "The hereafter will never come to pass." Say, "Yes indeed, by my Lord; it will certainly come to pass." He is the knower of all secrets; not an atom's weight is hidden from Him, be it in the heavens or the earth; not even smaller than that, nor larger, except in a profound record.

4. God rewards those who believe and work righteousness with forgiveness and a generous recompense.

5. As for those who challenge our revelations, they have deserved painful retribution.

6. Those who possess knowledge realize that what was sent down to you from your Lord is the truth, and that it guides to the path of the almighty, the praiseworthy.

7. The disbelievers said, "Let us show you a man who claims that after you disintegrate completely, you will be recreated.

8. "He either invented a lie about God, or he must be crazy." Indeed, those who disbelieve in the hereafter are condemned to retribution and total loss.

9. Do they not see (all the marvels) in front of them and behind them, in the heaven and the earth? If we wish, we can make the earth swallow them, or drop on them masses from the sky. This is a lesson for every obedient servant.

David and Solomon

10. We have endowed David with blessings from us, "O mountains, serve him," and the birds, and we softened the iron for him.

11. Now you can make useful things and control the way they fit. You shall work righteousness; for I see everything you do.

12. To Solomon we subdued the wind that traveled for a month back and forth, and we caused a spring of black oil to gush out for him. We subdued the jinns to work at his disposal, by God's leave. Any of them who deviated, we condemned him to the retribution of hell.

13. They made anything he wanted, including niches, statues, deep pools, and heavy pots. You shall work to show your appreciation, O David's family. Only a few of My creatures are appreciative.

14. When we terminated his life, (the jinns) did not realize that he had died until an earthly creature* tried to eat his staff. When he fell down, the jinns realized that if they really knew the secrets, they would not have continued to labor.

Sheba

15. Sheba lived in a marvelous palace with two gardens, one to the right and one to the left. Eat from the provisions of your Lord, and be thankful to Him. You have good land, and a forgiving Lord.

16. But they turned away, and consequently, we poured upon them a disasterous flood. We thus replaced their two gardens with gardens that grew only thorny cactus, bitter fruit, and a few edible plants.

17. We thus punished them because they disbelieved; do we punish other than the disbelievers?

18. Then we placed between them and the blessed communities a number of stations that we made accessible. Travel therein night and day in complete safety.

19. But (they were unappreciative;) they said, "Our Lord, let us travel long distances (without stopping in any stations)," thus creating inconvenience to themselves. Consequently, we turned them into history and broke them apart. These are lessons for everyone who is steadfast, appreciative.

20. Satan found them readily fulfilling his expectations, and they followed him, except a few believers.

21. He never had any power over them. But we thus distinguish those who believe in the hereafter, from those who are doubtful. Your Lord is in full control of all things.

Worship God, And Do Not Idolize Anyone

22. Say, "Call upon the idols you set up besides God. They do not possess an atom's weight in the heavens or the earth. Nor do they own any partnership therein, nor is any of them a helper of God."

23. Intercession is useless at Him, except on behalf of those already saved.* Once their hearts settle down and they are asked, "What did your Lord say?" They will answer, "The truth. He is the most exalted, the great."

34:14. Could be a goat or a sheep.

34:23. See Appendix 7.

24. Say, "Who provides for you from the heavens and the earth?" Say, "God," and, "Only one side is guided, either we or you; the other side is totally astray."

25. Say, "You are not responsible for our sins, nor are we responsible for what you do."

26. Say, "Our Lord will gather us together, then He will judge between us equitably. He is the final judge, the omniscient."

27. Say, "Prove to me that the idols you set up are partners of God." Never! He is the one God; the almighty, the wise.

Muhammad Sent To All The People

28. We have sent you to all the people; a bearer of good news, as well as a warner. But most people do not know.

29. They say, "Where is that doom, if you are truthful?"

30. Say, "You have a predetermined time; and you can never delay it by one hour, nor advance it."

31. And the disbelievers say, "We will not believe in this Quran, or in the previous scriptures." If you could only envision the wicked when they face their Lord; they will blame each other. Thus, the followers will say to the leaders, "If it were not for you, we would have believed."

32. The leaders will say to the followers, "It is not us who diverted you from the guidance when it came to you; it is you who were guilty."

33. The followers will say to the leaders, "It was your scheming, night and day, that directed us to disbelieve in God and set up idols to rank with Him." They will be grief stricken when they see the retribution. We will tie chains around the necks of those who disbelieved. Are they not equitably punished for their works?

34. Whenever we sent a warner to any community, the leaders therein would say, "We disbelieve in the message you bring."

35. And they say, "We possess enough wealth and children; we will never be punished."

36. Say, "My Lord is the one who provides for whomever He wills, and He withholds." But most people do not know.

37. It is not your wealth or your children that bring you closer to us. Only those who believe and work righteousness are rewarded manyfold for their works; they are secure in their homes.

38. As for those who challenge our revelations, they are condemned to retribution.

39. Say, "My Lord is the one who provides for whomever He chooses, or withholds it from him." Whatever you spend in charity, He multiplies it; He is the best provider.

40. On the day when He gathers them all, He will say to the angels, "Did these people idolize you?"

41. They will say, "Glory be to You; You are our Lord, not them." Instead, they idolized the jinns, and most of them were believers therein.*

42. Today, you possess no power to benefit or harm one another. We will say to the wicked, "Suffer the retribution of hell that you used to deny."

43. When our clear revelations are recited for them, they say, "This is a man who wants to divert you from the religion of your parents." They also say, "This is fabricated falsehood." And the disbelievers say, when the truth comes to them, "This is obvious magic."

44. We did not give them scriptures to study, nor did we send to them a warner before you.

45. Others before them have disbelieved; and although we gave them less than one-tenth of this, when they disbelieved My messengers, how terrible was My retribution!

46. Say, "I exhort you to do one thing: that you totally submit to God in pairs, or as individuals, then reflect. Your friend is not crazy; he only alerts you to evade terrible retribution."

47. Say, "I have not asked you for any wage. My wage comes from God; He witnesses all things."

48. Say, "My Lord presents the truth; He is fully aware of all secrets."

49. Say, "The truth has come, while falsehood can neither initiate anything nor repeat it."

50. Say, "If I go astray, I go astray to my own detriment; and if I am guided, it is because I follow the revelations of my Lord; He is hearer and very close."

51. If you could envision them as terror strikes; they cannot escape then and will be readily seized.

52. They will say, "We now believe in this," but it will be too late.

53. They had already disbelieved; and when they believe in the unseen after it becomes manifest it will be much too late.

54. They will be isolated from everything they like, just like the previous generations of their kind. They had harbored too much doubt.

34:41. When we fail to worship God alone, we are in effect worshiping the devil. (See 36:60.)

Sura 35: Initiator (Faatir)

In the name of God, most gracious, most merciful

1. Praise be to God, initiator of the heavens and the earth. He appoints
    ، angels as messengers with wings; two, three, and four. He adds to the
    creation whatever He wills. God is omnipotent.

2. When God showers mercy upon the people, none can stop it; and if He
    withholds it, who can release it? He is the almighty, the wise.

3. O people, be appreciative of God's favors upon you. Is there any creator,
    other than God, who provides for you from the heavens and the earth?
    There is no god except He; how could you deviate?

4. If they disbelieve you, messengers before you have been disbelieved. To
    God everything returns.

5. O people, God's promise is true. Therefore, do not be distracted by this
    life; nor shall you be distracted from God by any deceiver.

6. The devil is your enemy, so count him as one. He leads his allies to be
    deservers of hell.

7. Those who disbelieve have deserved terrible retribution, and those who
    believe and lead a righteous life have deserved forgiveness and a great
    recompense.

8. What if one's evil work is adorned for him, until he thinks it is righteous?
    God thus misleads those who deserve it,* and guides those who deserve
    guidance. Therefore, do not be terribly saddened over them. God is fully
    aware of all their works.

Dignity Only With God

9. God is the one who sends the winds, to stir up clouds, then we drive them
    to dead land and restore life to the dead soil. Such is the resurrection.

10. If anyone wants dignity, all dignity belongs with God. To Him ascends
    the good words, and He exalts the righteous work. As for those who
    scheme evil, they have deserved terrible retribution; their scheming is
    utterly detrimental to them.

11. God is the one who created you from dust, then from a drop, then He
    made you mates. Not a single female becomes pregnant or gives birth
    without His knowledge. Nor does anyone live a long life or a short one
    except in accordance with a profound record. This is easy for God to do.

35:8. *God is the only one who knows our innermost convictions, and He
knows those of us who deserve to be sent astray. Based on our real
convictions, God goes out of His way to guide us or mislead us. See Appendix
12.*

12. The two seas are not the same; this one is sweet and fresh, while the other is salty and undrinkable. But from both of them you eat tender meat, and extract jewels to wear. And you see the ships traveling therein, seeking His bounties, that you may be appreciative.

13. He merges the night into the day, and merges the day into the night; He subdued the sun and the moon, each running for a specific period. Such is God, your Lord. To Him belongs all kingship. Any idols you set up besides Him possess not as much as a seed.

14. If you implore them, they cannot hear you; even if they hear you, they cannot answer your prayers. On the day of resurrection, they disown your idol worship. None can inform you like a cognizant one.

15. O people, you are the ones who need God, while God needs no one; He is worthy of all praise.

16. If He wills, He can get rid of you and substitute a new creation.

17. This is not too difficult for God.

18. No soul will bear the load of another, and when a burdened soul implores for help, nothing can be unloaded, not even by a close relative. None will heed your warnings except those who reverence their Lord in their privacy, and observe **salat**. Anyone who purifies himself, does so for his own good. To God is the ultimate destiny.

19. The blind and the seer are not the same.

20. Nor is darkness and the light.

21. Nor the shade and the heat.

22. Nor the living and the dead. God is the one who can make anyone hear; you cannot be heard by those in the graves.

23. You are no more than a warner.

24. We have sent you with the truth as a preacher and a warner; every community receives a warner.

25. If they disbelieve you, those before them also disbelieved. Their messengers went to them with clear signs, the Psalms, and enlightened scripture.

26. Then I punished those who disbelieved; how terrible was my punishment!

27. Do you not see that God sends down water from the sky to produce fruits of various colors? The mountains show white and red streaks of different shades; and the ravens are black.

28. Also, the people, the animals, and the livestock are of different colors. This is why the servants of God who truly reverence Him are the knowledgeable. God is almighty, forgiving.

29. Those who recite God's scripture, observe the **salat** prayers, and give to charity from our provisions to them, secretly and publicly, seek a trade that never loses.

30. God will fully recompense them and shower them with His grace; He is forgiving, appreciative.

31. What we revealed to you of scripture is the truth, confirming all previous scriptures. God is fully cognizant of His servants, seer.

32. Then we pass on the scripture to our servants whom we choose. Some of them wrong their souls, others waver, while others are eager to work righteousness in accordance with God's will; this is the great triumph.

33. They have deserved the gardens of Eden, where they are adorned with bracelets of gold and pearls, and their clothes therein are made of silk.*

34. They will say, "Praise be to God, who removed our sorrows; our Lord is forgiving, appreciative.

35. "He placed us in this eternal abode, out of His grace. Never do we tire therein, nor do we suffer."

36. As for those who disbelieve, they have deserved the fire of hell; they are neither finished therein by death, nor is the retribution commuted for them. We thus requite every disbeliever.

37. They will scream therein, "Our Lord, if you take us out, we will work righteousness instead of what we used to do." Did we not give you a lifetime? None of you took heed when the warner came to you. Therefore, you have deserved this; the wicked have no helper.

38. God is the knower of all the secrets in the heavens and the earth; He is fully aware of the innermost convictions.

39. He is the one who made you inherit the earth, and anyone who disbelieves, disbelieves to his own detriment. The disbelief of the disbelievers incurs a great loss for them.

40. Say, "About the idols that you set up besides God; show me what on earth did they create. Do they own a share of the heavens? Did we give them a scripture that preaches idol worship? Indeed, the wicked promise each other nothing but illusions.

41. It is God who holds the heavens and the earth, lest they vanish. If anyone else held them, they would surely vanish. He is clement, forgiving.

42. They swore by God, solemnly, that if a warner had gone to them, they would have been better guided. But when a warner did go to them, he only increased their aversion.

43. This was due to their arrogance and evil schemes. The evil schemes only backfire against the schemers. Can they expect anything but the fate of previous generations? You will never find any change in God's system; you will never find any alteration in God's system.

44. Did they not travel the land and see the consequences for those before them? Although they were even stronger; nothing can escape from God in the heavens or the earth. He is omniscient, omnipotent.

35:33. *See Appendix 4 for details of this allegorical description.*

45. If God were to punish the people immediately for their actions, He would not leave a single creature on earth. But He respites them for a predetermined period. Once their time is up, then God is seer of His servants.

Sura 36: Y. S. (Ya Seen)

In the name of God, most gracious, most merciful

1. Y.S.*;
2. and this Quran that is full of wisdom;
3. (prove that) you (Muhammad) are one of the messengers.*
4. Advocating the right path.
5. (And prove that this is) a revelation from the almighty, most merciful.
6. To warn people whose parents were never warned; they are unaware.
7. It is already predetermined* that the majority of people will not believe.
8. Consequently, we chain their necks to their chins, and thus they are forced (into the direction they chose).
9. And we place a barrier in front of them and a barrier behind them, so they can never see.
10. Therefore, it is the same for them; whether you warn them or not, they will not believe.
11. You can only warn those who heed the message and reverence God most gracious in their privacy. Promise these forgiveness and a generous recompense.
12. We will surely resurrect the dead; we have recorded everything they had done in their life, as well as the post-mortem consequences. Everything is kept in a profound record.

Perennial Human Plague

13. Cite for them the example of a community who received the messengers.
14. We sent to them two, and they disbelieved them, then we supported them with a third. They said, "We are messengers to you."
15. They said, "You are no more than mortals like us, and God most gracious did not reveal anything to you. You are liars."
16. They said, "Our Lord knows that we are messengers to you.
17. "Our sole function is to deliver the profound message."
18. They said, "We consider you bad omen for us. Unless you refrain, we will surely stone you; you will suffer painful retribution at our hands."

36:1-5. *The miraculous numerical code associated with the Quranic initials, such as Y. S. here, proves that Muhammad was indeed a messenger of God (see also 13:43), and that the Quran is a divine revelation (see Appendix 1 for details).*

36:7. *This does not imply lack of freedom in our choice. It is simply a statement of fact as witnessed by God, who knows the future.*

19. They said, "You are the bad omen for yourselves, now that you have been reminded. Indeed, you are transgressors."
20. A man came from the far side of the city saying, "O my people, follow the messengers.
21. "Follow those who do not ask you for any wage; they are guided.
22. "Why shouldn't I worship the one who created me, and to Him is your final return?
23. "Shall I idolize besides Him idols that, if God most gracious willed any harm for me, their intercession will be useless, and they can never save me?
24. "If I do this, I would be totally astray.
25. "I have believed in your Lord; please listen to me."
26. He was told, "Enter paradise," and he said, "I wish my people knew,
27. "how my Lord has forgiven me, and how he has honored me."
28. We did not send down troops from the sky against his people; we did not need to.
29. All we needed was one blow, whereupon they became dead.
30. How sorry is the condition of the people! Whenever a messenger comes to them, they ridicule him.
31. Do they not see how many generations we annihilated before them, and how they never return to them?
32. All of them will be brought before us.
33. A sign for them is the dead land that we revive and produce from it grains for their food.
34. And we create in it gardens of date palms and grapes, and we cause springs to gush out.
35. This is to provide them with food from the fruits thereof, as well as what they cook with their hands. Would they be appreciative?
36. Glorified be the One who created all kinds of plants, as well as the people, and things they do not know.
37. Another sign for them is the night; we strip the day therefrom, whereupon they are in darkness.
38. And the sun running in a specific orbit. Such is the design of the almighty, the omniscient.
39. And we designed the moon to appear in stages, until it reverts to a thin curve.
40. The sun never catches up with the moon, nor does the night prematurely overtake the day. Each floats in its own orbit.
41. Another sign for them is that we carried their ancestors in the loaded ark.
42. Then we created similar vessels for them to ride.
43. Whenever we will, we can drown them, without a chance to scream or get saved.
44. It is mercy from us that we assign for them a predetermined life span.

45. Yet, when told, "Beware of your past and future, that you may attain mercy,"

46. And when every kind of sign is presented to them from their Lord, they turn away in aversion.

47. And when told, "Give to charity from God's provisions to you," the disbelievers would say to the believers, "Shall we feed those who can be fed by God, if He so wills? You are completely wrong."

48. And they say, "When will that promise come to pass, if you are truthful?"

49. All they see is one blow that strikes them as they feud.

50. They will not have a chance to utter a will, nor can they come back to their people.

51. And when the horn is blown, they scramble out of the graves to face their Lord.

52. They will then say, "Woe to us; who raised us from death? This is what God most gracious had promised. The messengers were right."

53. It takes only one blow, whereupon they are brought before us.

54. On that day, no one will be wronged in the least. You are not repaid, except for what you have done.

Heaven and Hell*

55. Those who deserved heaven on that day will be happily involved.

56. They, and their spouses, will enjoy the shade as they relax on their couches.

57. They will have fruits therein, and everything they wish.

58. Peace will be their greeting from the Lord most merciful.

59. And be marked on that day, O you guilty.

60. Did I not make a covenant with you, O children of Adam,* that you shall not worship the devil, for he is your ardent enemy?

61. That you shall worship Me alone to remain on the right path?

62. Indeed, he misled multitudes of you. Did you not possess any intelligence?

63. This is Gehenna that has been promised to you.

64. Burn in it today, because of your disbelief.

36:55-65.   Heaven and hell are described in allegorical terms throughout Quran (see 2:25-26). The Quran is aimed at all levels of education, culture, and mental capacity. See Appendix 4.

36:60.   See 7:172

The Video Tape*

65. On that day, we will seal their mouths, and their hands will speak to us, and their feet will testify about everything they had done.
66. Whenever we will, we cover up their eyes, so they miss the path by failing to see.
67. Whenever we will, we freeze them in the situation they choose; they can neither progress nor go back.
68. Anyone we allow to survive long enough, we revert them to weakness. Do they not understand?
69. We did not teach him (Muhammad) any poetry, nor should he. This is a profound message; a profound Quran.
70. To warn those who are alive, and to condemn the disbelievers.
71. Do they not realize that we created for them, with our hands, the livestock that they own?
72. We subdued the animals for them, so they ride some and eat some.
73. They derive various benefits therefrom, as well as drinks. Would they not be thankful?

Your Idols Can Never Help You*

74. Yet, they set up idols besides God to be of help to them.
75. But they can never help; instead, they become subjugated soldiers of their idols.
76. Do not be saddened by their utterances. We are fully aware of everything they conceal and everything they declare.
77. Does the human being realize that we created him from a tiny drop, then he turns into a defiant opponent?
78. He asks us a question, forgetting his initial creation, and says, "Who can resurrect the bones after having decayed?"
79. Say, "Resurrecting them will be the One who initiated them the first time. Of every creation, He is fully aware."
80. He is the One who turns the green trees into fuel for you.
81. Is it not possible for the One who created the heavens and the earth to create them again? Yes indeed, He is the creator, the omniscient.
82. His only command to have anything done, is to say, "Be," and it is.
83. Therefore, glorified be the One who possesses the kingship over all things, and to Him you ultimately return.

36:65.   God invented the video recorder in order to give us an idea how our hands and feet will testify on the day of judgment. See 42:21 and Appendix 10.

36:74-75.   Muhammad, Jesus, Mary, the saints, and all the idols possess no power to benefit or harm anyone. See 6:50, 7:188, 10, 49, 11:31, 60:4, 72:21 and Appendix 7.

Sura 37: The Columns (Al Ṣaaffaat)

In the name of God, most gracious, most merciful.

1. By the angels who will arrange the people in columns.
2. And gather them together.
3. And those who recite the message.
4. Your God is one.
5. The Lord of the heavens and the earth, and everything between them, and Lord of the easts.
6. We have adorned the lowest heaven* with the shining planets.
7. And sealed it against every rebellious devil.*
8. Thus, they cannot spy on the high society; they get shot from every side.
9. They will be defeated, then suffer eternal retribution.
10. Any of them that charges into the outer limit is followed by a piercing projectile.
11. Ask the people then; are they more powerful than some of our creations? We created them from soft clay.
12. While you marvel, they ridicule.
13. When they are reminded, they take no heed.
14. Whenever they see a miracle, they resort to mockery.
15. They say, "This is only magic.
16. "After we die and turn to dust and bones, are we resurrected?
17. "Even our old ancestors?"
18. Say, "Yes, you will be forced."
19. It will be one nudge, whereupon they get up, looking.
20. They will say, "Woe to us; this is the day of judgment."
21. This is the day of decision, that you used to deny.
22. Gather the wicked, and their spouses, and the idols.
23. That they set up besides God. Lead them to the path of hell.
24. Stop them, and ask,
25. Why do you not help one another?
26. They finally submit on that day.
27. They will come to each other, asking.
28. They will say, "You used to come to us from the right side."
29. They will say, "It is you who were not believers.

37:6. See Appendix 5. Our immediate universe, with all the countless billions of stars and planets is the smallest and innermost of seven heavens.

37:7. The outer limit of our heaven is not penetrable by anything except the angels.

30. "We had no power to force you. It is you who were transgressors.
31. "We have deserved our Lord's judgment; we have deserved the suffering.
32. "We misguided you, for we were misguided."
33. They will share the retribution on that day.
34. This is what we do to the sinners.
35. When told, "There is no god, except the one God," they turned arrogant.
36. They said, "Shall we leave our idols for the sake of a crazy poet?"
37. In fact, he brought the truth, and confirmed the messengers.
38. You have deserved painful retribution.
39. You only pay for what you did.
40. As for the servants of God, who are totally devoted to Him.
41. They have deserved a recognized reward.
42. Such as fruits and a great honor.
43. In the gardens of bliss.
44. On furnishings side by side.
45. Passing among them are cups of pure drink.
46. Clear and delicious for the drinkers.
47. No pollution mars it, and they are never deprived of anything.
48. With them will be magnificent companions;
49. As carefully protected as eggs.

The People In Heaven Visit The People in Hell*

50. They will come to each other asking.
51. One of them would say, "I used to have a friend,
52. "who used to say, 'Do you believe this?
53. 'After we die and turn to dust and bones, do we come back?' "
54. (God) will say, "Take a look."
55. He looks, and sees his friend in the depth of hell.
56. He then says to him, "By God, you almost caused me to fall.
57. "If it were not for my Lord's blessing, I would have been with you.
58. "Do you still think that when we die
59. "the first death, everything ends and we never get punished?"

37:50-59. *Immediately after resurrection and the manifested physical appearance of the almighty God and the angels, all people will be automatically stratified into four ranks, the highest being the closest to God. These four initial ranks are the high heaven, the lower heaven, the purgatory, and hell. Eventually, God's mercy will merge the purgatory into the lower heaven. The three final groups will be separated by barriers. The inhabitants of any rank can only move downward to visit lower rank(s), but no one will be able to move upward beyond his rank. Those closest to God, i.e., in the highest rank, will have access to any other stratum. See Appendix 10 for details.*

60. This is indeed the greatest triumph.
61. This is what everyone should strive for.
62. Is this better, or the tree of bitterness?
63. We have made it a retribution for the wicked.
64. It is a tree that grows at the bottom of hell.
65. Its fruits like the heads of devils.
66. They eat therefrom until their bellies are full.
67. Then they will add a drink of lava.
68. Then they return to hell.

Do Not Blindly Follow Your Parents

69. They had found their parents astray.
70. And readily followed their footsteps.
71. The majority of previous generations were similarly astray.
72. We had sent to them warners.
73. Note the final end for those who were warned.
74. Only the devoted servants of God are saved.

Noah and Abraham

75. Noah implored us, and we are the best responders.
76. We saved him and his family from the great disaster.
77. We made him and his family the survivors.
78. And preserved his history for the later generations.
79. Peace be upon Noah, throughout history.
80. We thus reward the pious.
81. He was one of our believing servants.
82. We drowned the others.
83. Similar to him was Abraham.
84. He came to his Lord wholeheartedly.
85. He said to his father and his people, "What is this you worship?
86. "Is it false gods, besides God, that you want?
87. "Do you not think of the Lord of the universe?"
88. He looked at the stars.
89. Then said, "I give up."
90. They ignored him.
91. He went to their idols saying, "Would you like to eat?
92. "Why don't you answer me?"
93. He then destroyed them.
94. They came to him furious.
95. He said, "How could you worship what you carve?
96. "While God created you and everything you make."
97. They said, "Build a great fire for him."

98. They wanted to hurt him; but we made them the losers.
99. He said, "I will turn to my Lord; He will guide me.
100. "My Lord, grant me righteous children."
101. We promised him a clement son.*
102. When he grew up and started to accompany him, he said, "My son, I see in a vision that I must sacrifice you. What do you think?"
He said, "Father, do whatever is enjoined upon you. You will find me, God willing, patient."
103. When they both submitted, and he turned him down on his forehead,
104. We called him, "O Abraham!
105. "You have fulfilled the vision." We thus reward the pious.
106. It was indeed an exacting test.
107. We ransomed him with a great offering.
108. And preserved his history for the following generations.
109. Peace be upon Abraham.
110. We thus reward the pious.
111. He was one of our believing servants.
112. We gave him the good news of Isaac, to be a righteous prophet.
113. We blessed him and Isaac. Among their descendants some are pious and some are wicked.

Moses and Aaron

114. We also blessed Moses and Aaron.
115. We delivered them and their people from the great disaster.
116. We supported them and made them the winners.
117. We gave them enlightening scripture.
118. We guided them in the straight path.
119. And preserved their history for the following generations.
120. Peace be upon Moses and Aaron.
121. We thus reward the pious.
122. They were of our believing servants.

Elias

123. Elias was one of the messengers.
124. He said to his people, "Would you turn to righteousness?
125. "Do you worship an idol and leave the almighty creator?
126. "God is your Lord, and the Lord of your ancestors."
127. They disbelieved him and were doomed.

37:101. This is Ishmael. According to the Bible (Genesis 16:16, 21:1-5, and 22:1-3), Ishmael was Abraham's only son for fourteen years. Isaac comes later in 37:112.

128. Only the devoted servants of God are saved.
129. We preserved his history for the following generations.
130. Peace be upon Elias' followers.
131. We thus reward the pious.
132. He was one of our believing servants.

Lot

133. Lot was one of the messengers.
134. We saved him and all his family;
135. Except the old woman; she was doomed.
136. Then we destroyed the others.
137. You can travel and see their ruins by day,
138. And by night. Would you then understand?

Jonah

139. Jonah was one of the messengers.
140. He fled to the loaded ship.
141. He rebelled and deserved distress.
142. Consequently, the fish swallowed him, as he complained.
143. If it were not that he repented.
144. He would have stayed in his belly until the day of resurrection.
145. We threw him out into the desert, exhausted.
146. We grew for him an edible tree.
147. Then we sent him to a hundred thousand people, or more.
148. They believed, and we let them enjoy their lives.

Blasphemies Against God

149. Consult them; does your Lord have daughters, while they have sons?
150. Did we create the angels as females? Did they witness?
151. They make up other blasphemies and say,
152. "God has begotten a son!" They are liars.
153. Did He prefer daughters over sons?
154. What is wrong with you? How do you make those statements?
155. Would you not take heed?
156. Do you have any proof?
157. Show me your scripture, if you are truthful.
158. They even invented a relationship between Him and the jinns. But the jinns know that they are subservient.
159. God be glorified; high above their claims.
160. Only the devoted servants of God are saved.
161. You and the idols you worship.

162. Do not bother Him in the least.
163. It is the idol worshipers who will burn in hell.
164. Each one of us (angels) has a recognized position.
165. It is we who will arrange them in ranks.
166. It is we who glorify Him.
167. They used to say,
168. "If we receive a message, like those before us,
169. "We would be devoted servants of God."
170. They disbelieved therein, and consequently, they will find out.
171. Our decree has already been issued to our servant messengers.
172. They will always be victorious.
173. Our soldiers will always be winners.
174. Therefore, disregard them for awhile.
175. Watch them, and they will be watching.
176. Are they in a hurry to see our retribution?
177. Once it comes to their area, what a miserable day it will be; they have been warned.
178. Just leave them alone for awhile.
179. Watch them, and they will be watching.
180. Glory be to your Lord; the Lord who possesses all power; over and above anything they claim.
181. And peace be upon the messengers.
182. Praise be to God, Lord of the universe.

Sura 38: Ṣ. (Ṣaad)

In the name of God, most gracious, most merciful

1. Ṣ.*, and the Quran that contains the message.
2. Those who disbelieve are plunged in pride and defiance.
3. Many a generation before them we annihilated; they called for help, but to no avail.
4. They wondered that a warner should come from among them. The disbelievers said, "He is a magician; a liar.
5. "Does he want to make the gods one god? This is really strange."
6. Their elders advised, "Carry on, and stay loyal to your gods. This is what we want.
7. "We never heard of this before. This is a fabrication.
8. "Did he, out of all us, receive the message?" Thus, they are doubtful about My message. They have not tasted My retribution yet.
9. Do they possess the treasures of your Lord's mercy? He is the almighty, the grantor.
10. Do they possess the dominion of the heavens and the earth, and everything between them? Then let them exalt themselves.
11. Their forces will always be defeated, no matter how numerous.
12. Disbelieving before them were the people of Noah, 'Aad, and Pharaoh the powerful.
13. Also Thamood, the people of Lot, and the (Midyanites) dwellers of the wood. These are the allies.
14. All of them disbelieved the messenger, and thus incurred retribution.
15. As for these, all they need is one blow, from which they never recover.
16. They said, "Our Lord show us the doom, before the day of reckoning?"
17. You shall be patient in the face of their utterances, and remember our servant David the resourceful; he was obedient.

David

18. We subdued the mountains in his service, day and night.
19. Also, the birds were mobilized to serve him.
20. We strengthened his kingship and bestowed upon him wisdom and correct judgment.
21. Have you noted the opponents who climbed into his sanctuary?

38:1. This Quranic initial occurs in three suras, namely 7, 19, and 38. The total frequency of occurrence of this letter in the three suras is 152 (19 x 8). See Appendix 1 for details of the Quran's miraculous numerical code.

22. When they entered, David was frightened, but they said, "Have no fear; we are just feuding against one another. Can you judge between us equitably and without bias? Guide us to the right way.

23. "This man is my brother, and he owns ninety-nine sheep, while I own one sheep. Yet he asked me to give him my sheep, and insisted."

24. David said, "He has wronged you by asking to mix your sheep with his sheep. Those who mix their properties usually transgress against one another, except for those who believe and lead a righteous life; these are rare." David thought that we disliked his judgment, and he asked his Lord for forgiveness as he bowed down; he totally submitted.

25. We forgave him and reserved for him a reward and a beautiful abode.

26. O David, we have appointed you a king on earth, so judge between the people equitably. Do not follow the ego, lest it diverts you from the path of God. Those who deviate from the path of God will suffer severe retribution. They disregarded the day of reckoning.

27. We have not created the heavens and the earth and everything between them in vain. This is what the disbelievers think. Consequently, they will suffer in hell.

28. Shall we treat those who believe and do righteous works like those who corrupt the earth? Shall we treat the righteous like the wicked?

29. We revealed to you this blessed scripture for them to study it carefully, and for those who possess intelligence to take heed.

Solomon

30. We granted to David Solomon, a good servant; he totally submitted.

31. One evening he became preoccupied with his beautiful horses.

32. Then he said, "I loved the material things more than the remembrance of my Lord, until they disappeared behind a barrier."

33. He asked to have them brought back, then he bid farewell to all of them after rubbing their legs and necks.

34. We thus put Solomon to the test. We placed in his dominion material wealth, but he submitted to God.

35. He said, "My Lord, forgive me, and grant me a kingship never to be attained by anyone else. You are the grantor."

36. We subdued the wind to run at his disposal and to bring rain wherever he wanted.

37. Also, the devils were subjugated as builders and divers.

38. Many others were bound in his service.

39. These are our provisions; you can donate or withhold without limits.

40. We have reserved for him a reward and a beautiful abode.

Job

41. Recall our servant Job; he called his Lord saying, "The devil has afflicted me with disease and suffering."

42. (We said,) "Strike the ground with your foot. A spring will provide you with healing as well as a cool drink."

43. We restored his family for him and multiplied them, as mercy from us, and a lesson for those who possess intelligence.

44. We told him, "Whenever you make a covenant, do not violate it." We found him steadfast; a good servant and a repenter.

Abraham And Descendants

45. Recall our servants Abraham, Isaac, and Jacob. They were resourceful and possessed vision.

46. We blessed them with a special blessing, being mindful of the final abode.

47. They were among our chosen righteous people.

48. Recall also Ishmael, Elisha, and Dhalkifl; all were pious.

49. This is a message; the righteous have deserved a beautiful destiny.

50. The gardens of Eden will be wide open for them.

51. Relaxing therein, they will enjoy many fruits and drinks.

52. With them will be the most magnificent spouses.

53. This is promised for you on the day of reckoning.

54. Our provision to you will never end.

55. As for the transgressors, they have deserved a terrible destiny.

56. Hell, wherein they burn; what a miserable abode!

57. They will suffer therein, with boiling lava and bitter food.

58. Also, other kinds, equally bad.

59. Here is another group to be condemned with you. They will not welcome them and will burn together in hell.

60. They will say, "You are not welcome either; you are the ones who misled us; what a miserable fate!"

61. They will say, "Our Lord, double the punishment of hell for those who misguided us and led us into this."

62. They will also say, "How come we do not see people we had considered wicked?

63. "We used to ridicule them, and we diverted our eyes from them."

64. It is an established truth that the people of hell will feud with each other.

Satan Determined To Mislead Us

65. Say, "I am only a warner; there is no god except God, the One, the most powerful.

66. "The Lord of the heavens and the earth, and everything between them; the almighty, the forgiving."
67. Say, "This is a great event.
68. "But you are heedless thereof.
69. "I have no information that the heavenly society ever feuded.
70. "I have been inspired that I am no more than a manifest warner."
71. Your Lord said to the angels, "I am creating a human from clay.
72. "Once I perfect him and blow into him from My soul, you shall fall prostrate before him."*
73. All the angels fell prostrate.
74. But not Satan; he was arrogant, and thus he became a disbeliever.
75. God said, "O Satan, what prevented you from prostrating before My creation; are you too arrogant; or much too high?"
76. He said, "I am better than he; You created me from fire and created him from clay."
77. He said, "Then you must get out, for you are rejected.
78. "You have deserved My curse till the day of judgment."
79. He said, "My Lord, respite me till the day of resurrection."
80. God said, "You are respited,
81. "Until the specified time."
82. He said, "I swear by Your majesty that I will mislead them all.
83. "Except Your servants who are absolutely devoted to You alone."
84. He said, "The truth is, and I utter only truth,
85. "I will fill hell with you and all those who follow you."
86. Say, "I do not ask you for a wage; I am not an imposter.
87. "This is a message to all the people.
88. "You will surely find out after awhile."

38:72.   See Appendix 6.

Sura 39: The Throngs (Al-Zumar)

In the name of God, most gracious, most merciful

1. This is the revealed scripture from God, the almighty, the wise.
2. We have revealed to you this scripture truthfully. Accordingly, you shall worship God alone and devote your worship absolutely to Him.
3. To God alone shall be the worship. Those who set up idols besides Him say, "We idolize them to bring us closer to God."* God will judge between them regarding their disputes. God never guides any liar, disbeliever.
4. If God wanted to get a son, He could have chosen whomever He willed. God be glorified; He is the One, the supreme.
5. He created the heavens and the earth truthfully. He rolls the night over the day and rolls the day over the night.* He subdued the sun and the moon, each to last a predetermined life span. He is the almighty, the forgiving.
6. He created you from one person, then made from him his mate. He sent down to you eight kinds of livestock. He creates you in your mothers' wombs, creation after creation, in three stages of darkness.* Such is God your Lord, to whom belongs all kingship. There is no god except He; how could you deviate?
7. If you disbelieve, God is in no need of you, and He dislikes for His servants disbelief. But if you are appreciative, then He is pleased for you. No one is responsible for anyone else's sins. To your Lord is your final return; then He will inform you of everything you did. He is fully aware of the innermost intentions.
8. When adversity touches the human being, he implores his Lord in total submission. But as soon as He bestows a blessing upon him, he forgets his previous submission and sets up idols to divert others from the path of God. Say, "Enjoy your heathenism temporarily, for you have deserved hell."

39:3. This is exactly what the worshipers of Muhammad and/or the saints say. They think that the invention of **sunna** and the establishment of **hadith** as a source of jurisprudence, and the other forms of idolizing the prophet will bring them closer to God. See Appendices 7, 8, and 11.

39:5. The expression used here, taken from the noun that means "ball" (yukawwir), cannot be used unless the planet earth is generally ball-shaped, a fact that was not known at the time of Quranic revelation.

39:6. The three stages of darkness probably are the dark period before birth, the dark period inside the womb, and the dark period in the grave.

9. As for the one who meditates through the night, prostrating and worshipping, conscious of the hereafter, and seeking mercy from his Lord; are those who know equal to those who do not know? Indeed, only those who possess intelligence take heed.

10. Say to My servants who believe, "You shall maintain righteousness towards your Lord. Those who are pious in this life will reap the credit therefor, and God's earth is spacious. The steadfast will be fully repaid without limits."

Muhammad An Example

11. Say, "I was commanded to worship God and devote the worship absolutely to Him alone.

12. "I was commanded to be the first to submit."

13. Say, "I fear, if I disobey my Lord, the retribution of a terrible day."

14. Say, "I worship God, and I devote my worship absolutely to Him alone.

15. "You may idolize whatever you wish besides Him." Say, "Such losers lose their souls and their families on the day of resurrection, and this is the real loss."

16. They have deserved masses of fire above them and masses of fire below them. God thus instills fear into His servants. O My servants, you shall reverence Me.

17. Those who avoid idol worship and totally submit to God, deserve to be congratulated. Therefore, congratulate My servants.

18. They listen to any views, then follow the best thereof. These are the ones guided by God; these are the ones who possess intelligence.

19. If anyone has already deserved retribution, can you save them from hell?

20. As for those who reverence their Lord, they have deserved mansions upon constructed mansions and flowing streams. This is God's promise; and God never breaks His promise.

21. Do you not realize that God sends down water from the sky, then directs it to springs throughout the earth, then produces plants of various colors, turning yellow as they grow, then He turns them into hay? This is a reminder for the intelligent.

22. The one whose chest is made wide open to Islam is the one who had followed the guidance from his Lord. But woe to those whose hearts are hardened against the message of God; they are in total loss.

23. God sent down the best **hadith,*** a scripture that is consistent, and describes both ways (to heaven and hell). The skins of those who reverence their Lord shudder therefrom, then their skins and their hearts soften and readily receive God's message. This is God's guidance; He guides with it whomever He wills. But the one who is misguided by God can never be guided.

24. That is the one who will face terrible retribution on the day of resurrection. The wicked will be told, "Suffer (the consequences of) your works."

25. Others before them have disbelieved and, consequently, the retribution came to them when they least expected.

26. God made them taste the humiliation in this life; and the retribution in the hereafter is far worse, if they only knew.

Quran: Sufficient Source of Jurisprudence

27. We have cited for the people in this Quran every kind of example, that they may take heed.

28. A Quran in Arabic, without ambiguity, that they may attain salvation.

29. God cites the example of a man with partners who contradict one another and a man who relies on one consistent source; are they the same?* Praise be to God; the majority do not know.

30. You will surely die, and they will surely die.*

31. Then, on the day of resurrection, you will blame one another before your Lord.

39:23. Although the blasphemy against the prophet called *"hadith"* did not appear until 250 years after the prophet's death, God obviously knew about it in advance. Therefore, it is appropriate to leave this word (**hadith**) without translation (see Appendices 11, 15, 16, and 17).

39:29. When the Muslims abandoned the Quran as their source of law, they plunged into perennial arguments and became divided partners. They argue about the "prophet's **hadith**," which is authentic and which is not. They argue about the various opinions; is Imam Shafei correct or Imam Hanbali; was Abu Bakr supposed to be the first Caliph, or was Ali? Ironically, the prophet is the first to disown those who claim to love him (see 6:159). Similarly, Jesus will be the first to disown those who "love him very much" and call him "God" or "son of God."

39:30. In other words, do not idolize Muhammad. He is a human like you. Leave the invented lies that you call **sunna** and **hadith**, and come back to the Quran.

32. Who is more wicked than one who lies about God and rejects the truth when it comes to him?* Is hell not well deserved by the disbelievers?

33. As for those who are truthful and follow the truth, they are the righteous.

34. They will enjoy everything they wish at their Lord. This is the well-deserved reward for the pious.

35. God will remit their bad deeds and reward them manyfold for their good deeds.

36. Is God not sufficient for His servant? Yet they frighten you with the (powerless) idols they had set up besides Him.* Whomever God misleads will have no guide.

37. And whomever God guides, none can mislead him. Is God not almighty, Lord of retribution?

You May Believe In God And Still Go To Hell *

38. If you ask them, "Who created the heavens and the earth?" they would say, "God." Say, "What about the idols you set up besides Him? If God wanted to hurt me, can they prevent Him? And if He wanted to bless me, can they stop His blessing?" Say, "God suffices for me; in Him the trusting put their trust."

39. Say, "O my people, work in your best way, and so will I; you will surely find out.

40. "(You will find out) which of us incurs humiliating retribution and abides in eternal suffering."

41. We have revealed to you the scripture for the people, bearing the truth. Thus, whoever is guided is guided for his own good, and if one goes astray, it is to his own detriment. You are not their advocate.

42. God puts the souls to rest at the time of death and at the time of sleep.* He seizes the one that is decreed to die, and lets the other one go until the predetermined time. These are lessons for people who reflect.

43. Did they find intercessors besides God? Say, "Even though they possess no power, nor understanding?"

39:32. Those who claim that **hadith** is divine revelation are lying about God and, at the same time, rejecting the truth of Quran (see 6:19, 38, and 114).

39:36. Those who idolize the prophet give you the impression that Muhammad will put you in hell or take you out of heaven if you do not follow the lies attributed to him, known as "**hadith**" and/or "**sunna**."

39:38. Unless you worship God ALONE, your worship is null and void (see 39:45, 39:65, 40:10-12, and 40:83-85).

39:42. See Appendix 14.

44. Say, "All intercession belongs to God.* To Him belongs the dominion of the heavens and the earth, and to Him you will be returned."

The Great Criterion*

45. When God alone is advocated, the hearts of those who do not believe in the hereafter shrink with aversion. But when idols are mentioned besides Him, they rejoice.

46. Say, "O God, initiator of the heavens and the earth, knower of all secrets and declarations; You alone judge Your servants regarding their differences."

47. If the wrongdoers possessed everything on earth, and even twice as much, they will readily offer it to spare them the terrible retribution on the day of resurrection. They will find out from God what they never expected.

48. The evils they committed will become obvious to them, and the very things they had ridiculed will cause their doom.

49. When the human being is touched by adversity, he turns to us imploring; but when we bless him, he says, "I attained this through my cleverness." These are all tests, but most of them do not know.

50. Others before them have uttered the same. Consequently, the material they acquired never helped them.

51. They were doomed because of the evils they committed. Similarly, the wicked among this generation will be doomed for the evils they commit; they can never escape.

52. Do they not realize that God is the one who increases the provision for anyone, or reduces? These are lessons for people who believe.

39:44. See Appendix 7. Neither Muhammad, nor Jesus, nor the saints, nor any idol possesses the power to intercede. All intercession belongs to God. See also 2:255, 6:51, 6:70, 10:3, 19:87, 22:28, 32:4, and 40:18.

*39:45. This is the classic test that shows us whether we really believe in the hereafter or simply deceive ourselves. A perfect example is footnote 39:44 above; those who disbelieve in the hereafter will dislike it. With many people, if you speak of God alone, they dislike you; but if you speak of God and Muhammad, e.g., Quran and **hadith**, they become happy and satisfied. This is characteristic of false Muslims, as we learn from this verse and from 6:112-116.*

God Forgives All Sins*

53. Say to My servants who exceeded the limits, "Never despair of God's mercy; God forgives all sins; for He is the forgiver, the merciful."

54. You shall be obedient to your Lord and totally submit to Him, before the retribution comes to you, then you find out it is too late to be helped.

55. You shall uphold the honorable revelations from your Lord, before the retribution comes to you suddenly when you least expect it.

56. Otherwise, you may say, "How miserable I am for being heedless of God, and for being one of the mockers."

57. Or say, "Had God guided me, I would have been righteous."

58. Or say when it sees the retribution, "If given another chance, I will be righteous."

59. Indeed, My revelations had come to you, but you rejected them, you turned arrogant, and you became a disbeliever.

60. On the day of resurrection, you will see the faces of those who lied about God darkened with misery.* Is hell not the right place for the arrogant?

61. God will save those who worked righteousness because of their fortunate decision. No harm will ever touch them, nor will they grieve.

God Alone Worthy of Worship

62. God is the creator of all things; in full control of all things.

63. To Him belongs all kingship in the heavens and the earth. Those who reject the revelations of God are losers.

64. Say, "Do you enjoin me to idolize others besides God, O you fools?"

65. It has been revealed to you (Muhammad), and to those before you, that if you ever fall into idol worship,* all your works will be nullified, and you will be a loser.

66. Therefore, you shall worship God alone, and be thankful.

67. They never valued God as He should be valued. The whole earth is within His fist on the day of resurrection, and the heavens are folded in His right hand. God be glorified; He is the most high, far above any idols.*

39:53. According to Quran, idol worship is not a sin; it is a category by itself; it is the only unforgivable offense (see 4:48, 116 and 31:13). The whole purpose of our creation is to worship God ALONE and never idolize anything or anyone besides Him.

39:60. This is an Arabic proverb that has nothing to do with the color of the skin.

39:65. The idols listed throughout Quran include the prophets, saints, representations (statues), spouses, children, and material possessions.

39:67. See Appendix 5.

The Day Of Resurrection

68. The horn was* blown, and everyone in the heavens and the earth, except whomever God willed, was struck dead. Then it was blown another time, whereupon they were all up, looking.

69. The earth then shined with the light of its Lord. The record was set up, the prophets and the witnesses were brought, and everyone was judged equitably. No one was wronged.

70. Everyone was then repaid for their works, for God is fully aware of everything they did.

71. Those who disbelieved were herded to hell in throngs. When they arrived, and the gates thereof were opened, the guardians of hell said to them, "Did you not receive messengers from among you who recited the revelations of your Lord and warned you about this day?" They said, "Yes, indeed, but the word of doom had been decreed against the disbelievers."

72. It was said, "Enter the gates of hell, wherein you abide forever. What a miserable abode for the arrogant!"

73. As for those who had observed their Lord, they were led to Paradise in throngs. When they arrived, and the gates were opened, the guardians of heaven said, "Peace be upon you. You are the fortunate ones. Enter therein forever."

74. They said, "Praise be to God, who fulfilled His promise to us, and made us inherit the earth and enjoy Paradise as we please." What a beautiful reward for the workers!

75. You will see the angels floating around the throne, glorifying and praising their Lord. Judgment has been issued among the people equitably; they will all declare, "Praise be to God, Lord of the universe."

39:68. *These verses are written in the past tense because they narrate events that actually did take place in the future -- our future. As far as God is concerned, our future is past, since the dimension of time does not apply to the almighty. See Appendix 10.*

Sura 40: Forgiver (Ghaafir)

In the name of God, most gracious, most merciful

1. H.M.*
2. (These two letters prove that) the revelation of this scripture is from God, the almighty, the omniscient.
3. Forgiver of sins, acceptor of repentance, strict in imposing retribution, and most powerful; there is no god but He; to Him is the final destiny.
4. None argues against the revelations of God except those who disbelieve; do not be deceived by their apparent success in this world.
5. Rebelling before them were the people of Noah and communities after them. Every generation persecuted their messenger, seeking to neutralize him, and they argued with falsehood to make it dominate the truth. But I overtook them; how terrible was My retribution!
6. Thus, the word of your Lord is predetermined that the disbelievers have deserved hell.

Believers Enjoy The Privilege Of Forgiveness

7. Those who serve the throne, and all those around it, praise the glory of their Lord, and believe in Him, and ask forgiveness for those who believe. "Our Lord, Your mercy and knowledge encompass all things. Therefore, forgive those who repent and follow Your path, and spare them the agony of hell.
8. "Our Lord, admit them into the gardens of Eden that You promised for them and the righteous among their ancestors, their spouses, and their descendants. You are the almighty, the wise.
9. "And protect them from falling in sin; whomever You protect from sin, You have endowed with mercy on that day. This is the great triumph."

Worship God ALONE

10. Those who disbelieved will be told, "God's abhorrence towards you is even greater than your abhorrence towards yourselves; because you were invited to belief, but you chose to disbelieve."

40:1.   These two Quranic initials occur in the next seven consecutive suras. The frequency of occurrence of the letter "H" in the seven suras is 280, and the frequency of occurrence of the letter "M" in the seven suras is 1829; making the total occurrence of the two letters 2109, a multiple of 19. Thus, like all Quranic initials, these two letters conform to the miraculous numerical code of Quran. (See Appendix 1.)

11. They will say, "Our Lord, you have given us two deaths and two lives;* we now confess our sins. Is there any way out?"

12. This is because when invited to worship God alone, you disbelieved, but when idols were mentioned besides Him, you believed.* Alas, the judgment has been decreed by God, the most exalted, the great.

13. He continuously shows you His signs, and sends down from the sky provisions for you. Only those who submit will take heed.

14. Therefore, you shall worship God, devoting your worship absolutely to Him alone, even if the disbelievers dislike it.

15. He is the grantor of the high ranks; the possessor of all authority. He dispatches inspiration to whomever He chooses among His servants, in order to warn about the day of audience.

16. That is the day when all will be exposed; nothing of them will be hidden from God. To whom does kingship belong on that day? To God alone; the one; the most powerful.

17. On that day, every soul will be paid for whatever it did. No injustice on that day. God's reckoning is quick.*

18. Warn them about the inevitable day, when the hearts will be terrified and helpless. The wicked will have no friend or intercessor to be obeyed.

19. He knows what the eyes cannot see and what the chest hides.

20. And God judges equitably, while the idols they set up possess no power to judge anything. God is the hearer, the seer.

21. Did they not travel the earth and find out about the generations before them? They were even stronger and left a greater legacy. But God punished them for their sins, and nothing could protect them from God.

22. That is because their messengers used to go to them with profound revelations, but they disbelieved. Consequently, God punished them, for He is powerful, most strict in imposing retribution.

Moses

23. We sent Moses with our miracles and manifest authority.

40:11. *We were dead, then brought into this life, then we die, then we get resurrected for the eternal life of the hereafter. (See 2:28).*

40:12. *This is exactly what the majority of "Muslims" have fallen in. Thus, if you ask them to worship God alone, i.e., uphold the Quran alone, they disbelieve. But when you mention God and Muhammad, i.e., the Quran and "hadith," they believe. (See 5:22).*

40:17. *The reckoning on the day of judgment will be instantaneous and automatic. See Appendix 10.*

24. To Pharaoh, Haamaan, and Qaaroon. But they said, "A magician; a liar."

25. And when he showed them the truth from us, they said, "Slay the sons of those who believe with him, and spare their daughters." Thus, the schemes of the disbelievers are always evil.

26. Pharaoh said, "Let me kill Moses, and let him implore his Lord. I fear lest he alters your religion or spreads corruption on earth."

27. Moses said, "I seek refuge in my Lord, and your Lord, from the arrogant who disbelieves in the day of reckoning."

28. A believing man among Pharaoh's people who was hiding his belief said, "Do you want to kill a man just for saying, 'My Lord is God,' despite the miracles he showed you from your Lord? If he is a liar, that is his problem. But if he is truthful, then you benefit from the promises he had given you. God does not guide any transgressor, liar.

29. "My people, today you have kingship and dominance on earth. But who will support us against God's doom if it comes?" Pharaoh said, "You shall follow only what I point out for you; I guide you in the right path."

30. The one who believed said, "My people, I fear for you a day like the days of the parties;

31. "like the example of Noah's people, 'Aad, Thamood, and those after them. God does not wish any hardship for the people.

32. "O my people, I fear for you the day of summoning.

33. "That is the day when you will flee, but you will have no protector from God. Whomever God sends astray will have no guide.

34. "Joseph had come to you with clear signs, but you continued to doubt his message. When he died, you said, 'God will not send another messenger after him.' " God thus misguides the transgressors, the doubtful.

35. For they dispute the revelations of God without any basis. This is abhorred by God and those who believe. God thus seals the hearts of every arrogant tyrant.

36. Pharaoh said, "O Haamaan, build for me a tower, that I may reach high.

37. "The height of the heavens, that I may look at the God of Moses. I think he is a liar." Thus was the evil work of Pharaoh adorned in his eyes, and he was thus prevented from following the path. Pharaoh's schemes were condemned.

38. The one who believed said, "My people, follow me and I will guide you in the right path.

39. "O my people, this life is only temporary; while the hereafter is the eternal abode.

40. "Whoever commits a sin is punished for the same, but whoever works righteousness, male or female, while believing, these have deserved Paradise. They enjoy provisions therein without limits.

41. "My people, I only invite you to salvation; while you invite me to hell.
42. "You invite me to be unappreciative of God, by setting up powerless idols besides Him; while I invite you to the One that is almighty, forgiver.
43. "There is no doubt that what you advocate has no basis in this life, nor in the hereafter, that our ultimate return is to God, and that the transgressors will end up in hell.
44. "You will remember everything I told you, and now I leave everything up to God. God fully sees all the people."
45. God protected him from the consequences of their evil work, while Pharaoh's people suffered terrible retribution.
46. The hellfire is shown to them day and night;* then, on the day of resurrection, admit Pharaoh's people into the worst punishment.
47. As they argue with each other in hell, the followers will say to the leaders, "We were your followers, can you spare us some of this hell?"
48. The leaders will say, "We are in this together; God has judged the people."
49. Those in the fire will say to the guardians of hell, "Call upon your Lord to commute our retribution for one day."
50. They will say, "Did you not receive messengers with clear revelations?" They will say, "Yes, indeed." They will say, "Then call (as much as you want); the disbelievers' calls are in vain."

Victory For The Believers

51. We will surely give victory to our messengers, and to those who believe, both in this life and on the day the witnesses are raised.
52. That is the day when the wicked will not be excused; they have deserved the curse, and a miserable abode.
53. We have given Moses the guidance and made the children of Israel inherit the scripture.
54. A guidance and a message for those who possess intelligence.
55. Therefore, be patient, for God's promise is truth; ask forgiveness for your sin, and praise and glorify your Lord night and day.
56. Those who dispute God's revelations without any basis are so full of arrogance, they cannot accept them. You shall seek refuge in God (from this condition); He is the hearer, the seer.

40:46. *The period of death, no matter how long, passes like one night of sleep. During that night, our dreams go on as happy dreams or nightmares, depending on our degree of righteousness at death. See Appendix 14.*

Creation of the Universe More Complex than the Creation of Man*

57. Indeed, the creation of the heavens and the earth is greater than the creation of people, but most people do not know.

58. The blind is not the same as the seer, nor are those who believe and work righteousness the same as the sinners. Rarely do you take heed.

59. The Hour is coming; no doubt about it; but most people do not believe.

60. Your Lord says, "Pray to Me, and I will answer your prayers. As for those who are too arrogant to worship Me, they will be committed to hell."

61. God is the one who made the night for your rest and the day visible. God is most generous towards the people, but most people are thankless.

62. Such is God your Lord; the creator of all things. There is no god except He; how could you deviate?

63. Only those who disregard God's revelations will deviate.

64. God is the one who made the earth for your settlement and the sky a structure; He designed you a perfect design and provided for you good things. Such is God your Lord; most exalted is God, Lord of the universe.

65. He is the eternally living; there is no god except He. You shall worship Him, devoting the worship absolutely to Him alone. Praise be to God, Lord of the universe.

Muhammad Worshiped Idols Before The Message*

66. Say, "I was stopped from worshiping the idols you worship besides God when the clear revelations came to me from my Lord. I was ordered to submit completely to the Lord of the universe."

67. He is the one who created you from dust, then from a drop, then from a clot, then He brings you out as an infant, then you reach full strength, then you become old, though some of you die earlier. You attain a predetermined life span, that you may understand.

40:57. Our immediate universe, the smallest and innermost among seven universes, contains a billion galaxies, a billion trillion stars, and countless trillions of planets. All these heavenly bodies move precisely in their specific orbits without crashing into each other.

40:66. It is valuable education to understand the mentality of the idol worshipers in order to effectively preach to them later. Those who idolize the prophet, exactly like those who idolize Jesus, refuse to believe the truth about the prophet. See also 6:56 and 93:7. As a human being, the prophet passed through the stages that each of us passes through towards perfection, i.e., the worship of God alone. (See 18:110 and 41:6.) The Arabic word "naha" indicates the termination of something that was actually taking place (See 2:192-193, 4:171, 8:38-39, 19:46, 26:116, 26:167, and 36:18).

68. He is the one who controls life and death; to have anything done, He simply says to it, "Be," and it is.

69. Have you noted those who dispute God's revelations and how they totally deviate?

70. They have rejected the scripture and what we sent with our messengers. Therefore, they will surely find out.

71. The shackles will be around their necks, and they will be dragged by the chains.

72. In Gehenna, and then in the hellfire; they will burn.*

73. They will be told, "Where are the idols you had set up

74. "besides God?" They will say, "They have abandoned us. When we implored them, we were imploring nothing." Thus does God mislead the disbelievers.

75. This is because you were satisfied on earth with other than the truth. You only wanted to play.

76. Enter the gates of hell, wherein you abide forever. What a miserable abode for the arrogant!

77. Therefore, be patient, for God's promise is truth. Whether we show you some of the retribution we promise them, or terminate your life before then, they ultimately return to us.

78. We have sent messengers before you; some we told you about, and some we did not tell you about. No messenger was to bring any judgment, except by God's leave. Whenever God's judgment comes, the truth is established, and the advocates of falsehood perish.

79. God is the one who made the livestock for you, to ride some and eat some.

80. You derive other benefits from them and satisfy many needs. You ride them, and you ride the ships.

81. He shows you His marvels; which of God's marvels can you deny?

82. Did they not travel the land and see the consequences for those before them? They used to be greater in number and in power, and they established more structures on earth. But their material achievements did not help them.

Evil Satisfaction With Inherited Knowledge

83. When their messengers went to them with clear revelations, they were satisfied with the knowledge they had. The very things they ridiculed caused their doom.

40:72.   See 19:71, 55:43-44, and Appendix 10

84. Then, when they saw our retribution, they said, "Now we believe in God ALONE, and we reject the idols we had set up."

85. But alas, their belief is no longer useful, once they see our retribution. This is God's system that is never changeable. The disbelievers are always losers.

Sura 41: Elucidated (Fuṣṣilat)

In the name of God, most gracious, most merciful

1. H. M.*
2. (These two letters prove that) this revelation is from God most gracious, most merciful.
3. A scripture whose verses have been elucidated in an Arabic Quran,* for those who know.
4. A bearer of good news, as well as a warner. But most people turn away, and thus, they fail to hear.
5. And they said, "Our hearts are protected from your views, our ears are deaf, and a barrier separates us and you. Do what you want, and we will do what we want."

Do Not Idolize Muhammad

6. Say, "I am a human being like you, who received inspiration that your God is the one God. Therefore, you shall be totally devoted to Him alone, ask Him for forgiveness, and woe to the idol worshipers.*
7. Who do not observe the **zakat** charity, and disbelieve in the hereafter.*

41:1. See footnote 40:1.

41:3. See footnote 41:44 and Appendix 3.

*41:6. In the two Quranic statements that describe the prophet as a human being (see also 18:110), we note that both verses close by enjoining us from idolizing the prophet. Obviously, God is fully aware of the human disease that led the Jews to invent the Mishnah (oral) and Gemarah (traditions) of Talmud to overtake the Torah, and the Christians to invent the trinity, and the Muslims to idolize Muhammad by inventing "**hadith**" (oral) and "**sunna**" (traditions) to overtake the Quran.*

*41:7. What we utter through our lips does not necessarily reflect what our hearts really believe. (See 16:22). In order to show us whether we believe or disbelieve in the hereafter, God has established the test of "**hadith**" as stated in 6:112-116. He allowed enemies of the prophet to fabricate "**sunna**" and "**hadith**" and attributed them to the prophet. As stated in 6:113, those who accept "**hadith**" and/or "**sunna**" do not believe in the hereafter as they claim. But those who reject all "**hadith**" and all "**sunna**" and accept the Quran, the whole Quran, and nothing but the Quran as their source of religious guidance and law, are the true believers (see also 25:30-31).*

8.   As for those who believe and work righteousness, they receive a well-deserved recompense.

9.   Say, "You disbelieve in the One who created the earth in two days, and you set up idols to rank with Him, though He is the Lord of the universe."

10. He placed stabilizers on earth, blessed it, and designed all provisions for it in four days to cover all needs.

11. Then He turned to the sky while it was still gas and said to it and to the earth, "Come into existence, willingly or unwillingly." They said, "We come willingly."

12. He thus established them as seven heavens (or universes) in two days, and established for each heaven its own laws. And we adorned the lowest heaven with lamps and established an unpenetrable barrier around it. Such is the design of the almighty, the omniscient.*

13. If they still turn away, then say, "I warn you lest you get struck as the people of 'Aad and Thamood were struck."

You Shall Not Worship Except God*

14. The messengers who came before them and after them said, "You shall not worship except God." They said, "Had God willed, He could have sent down angels. Therefore, we reject what you are sent with."

15. As for 'Aad, they were tyrants on earth without justice, and they said, "Who is more powerful than we?" Did they not realize that God, who created them, is more powerful than they? They discarded our revelations.

16. Consequently, we sent upon them devastating wind for a few miserable days that afflicted them with humiliating retribution in this life. The retribution of the hereafter is far more humiliating, and no one can help them.

17. As for Thamood, we guided them, but they chose blindness instead of guidance. Consequently, humiliating retribution struck them, because of what they did.

18. We saved those who believed and maintained righteousness.

19. The day will come when the enemies of God are gathered into the hellfire; they will be forced.

41:12.   See Appendix 5.

41:14.   The commandment, "You shall worship God," is not complete, since people can worship God and still go to hell, as stated in 23:85-89. The complete commandment is, "You shall worship God alone," or, "You shall not worship except God." The First Commandment, therefore, is a negative commandment, **"YOU SHALL NOT WORSHIP EXCEPT GOD."**

All Our Works Recorded*

20. When they arrive, their hearing, their eyes, and their skins will bear witness to everything they did.

21. They will say to their skins, "Why did you bear witness against us?" They will say, "God made us speak up, for He makes everything speak up." He is the one who created you the first time, and to Him you ultimately return.

22. You could never avoid being witnessed by your own hearing, your eyes, and your skins. In fact, you thought that God was unaware of many things you did.

23. Such is your thinking about your Lord, and it was utterly detrimental to you. This is why you turned losers.

24. No matter how long they survive, the hellfire is their inevitable destiny; and no matter what kind of excuse they offer, they are not excused.

25. We appoint companions for them, who entice them continuously. They are condemned along with their kinds of jinns and humans. They are real losers.

The Disbelievers Violate Quran

26. Those who disbelieve say, "Do not listen to this Quran, and distort it, that you may prevail."

27. Consequently, we afflict them with severe retribution, and punish them for their evil works.

28. Such is the retribution deserved by the enemies of God. Hell will be their eternal abode, for disregarding our revelations.

29. The disbelievers will say, "Our Lord, show us those who misled us among the jinns and the humans, in order to trample them under our feet and debase them.

Happiness In This World Guaranteed For the Believers

30. Those who say, "Our Lord is God," then maintain righteousness, the angels descend upon them saying, "You have nothing to fear, nor will you grieve. We deliver to you good news that Paradise awaits you.

31. "We are your protectors in this life, as well as in the hereafter. You will have anything you desire therein; you will have anything you ask for.

41:20-22. *The invention of the video recording systems brings to mind the closest idea about the day of reckoning. We will view our lives from birth to death (see also 36:65). While the disbelievers cannot edit their audio/video record, the believers enjoy this advantage through repentance. Repentance edits out all our sins, and thus, they will not exist on the record.*

32. "This is the position assigned to you by God, the forgiver, most merciful."
33. Who is better than one who invites others to come to God, works righteousness, and says, "I am a submitter (Muslim)."
34. The righteous deed is not the same as the evil deed. You shall counter the evil deed with the best possible response, so that the one who used to be your enemy may become a close friend.
35. None attains this except those who steadfastly persevere; none attains this except those who are extremely fortunate.
36. Whenever the devil approaches you, you shall seek refuge in God. He is the hearer, the omniscient.
37. Among His signs are the night and day, and the sun and moon. Do not fall prostrate before the sun or the moon; you shall fall prostrate before the one God who created them, if you really worship Him.
38. If they are too arrogant (to prostrate), those (honorable angels) at your Lord glorify Him night and day, without tiring.
39. Among His signs is that you see the land still, then as soon as we send down water, it vibrates with life. The one who revived it can certainly revive the dead. He is omnipotent.

Blaspheming Against Quran

40. Those who manipulate our revelations are not hidden from us. Is one who is destined for hell the same as one who comes secure on the day of resurrection? Do whatever you choose to do; He fully sees everything you do.
41. They reject this message when given to them, though it is a profound scripture.
42. No falsehood can ever enter it, in the past or in the future; for it is a revelation from God, most wise, praiseworthy.

Language Is No Barrier

43. What is said to you was said to messengers before you. Surely, your Lord possesses forgiveness, as well as painful retribution.

44. Had we made it a non-Arabic Quran, they would have said, "Why did it come down in that language?" Whether it is non-Arabic or Arabic, say "For those who believe, it is a beacon and a healing (regardless of their language).* As for those who do not believe, they will be deaf and blind to it; as if they are being called from afar.

45. We have given Moses the scripture, and it too was disputed. If it were not for a predetermined decision by your Lord, they would have been judged immediately. They are in great doubt thereof.

46. Whoever works righteousness does so for his own good, and whoever commits evil does so to his own detriment. Your Lord is never unjust towards the people.

47. Only He knows the time of resurrection; not a fruit emerges from its sheath, nor a female bears a fetus or gives birth, without His knowledge. The day will come when He calls upon them, "Where are the idols you had set up besides Me?" They will say, "We hear; but there is no witness among us."

48. Thus, whatever they idolize will abandon them, and they will find no refuge.

Submission Required Under All Circumstances

49. The human being never tires from imploring for bounties. But when afflicted with adversity, he becomes despondent, desparate.

50. When we endow him with mercy from us, after adversity had afflicted him, he says, "I deserve this; I do not believe in resurrection; even if returned to my Lord, I will find better things." We will certainly inform the disbelievers of everything they had done. We will let them suffer terrible retribution.

51. When we endow man with a blessing, he becomes heedless and turns away; but when adversity touches him, he implores loudly.

Quran's Miracles To Be Revealed

52. Say, "What if it is really from God, and you disbelieve therein? Who is worse than those who oppose it?"

41:44. *We are told here that the only prerequisite to fully understand the Quran is sincerity of faith. The Quran will be placed into the hearts of sincere believers, regardless of their language. On the other hand, those who are not sincere will be rendered incapable of understanding the Quran, even if they are the highest scholars of Arabic linguistics. The Quran is not like any other book (see 17:45-46 and 18:57), and God is the only teacher thereof (see 55:1-2, 75:19 and Appendices 3 and 17).*

53. We will show them our miracles in the horizons and within themselves, until it becomes evident that this is the truth. Is your Lord not sufficient as witness to all things?

54. Indeed, they harbor doubts about meeting their Lord, and He is fully aware of everything.

Sura 42:   Consensus (Al-Shoora)

In the name of God, most gracious, most merciful

1.   H. M.*
2.   'A. S. Q.*
3.   This is what is revealed to you and to those before you from God, the almighty, the wise.
4.   To Him belong everything in the heavens and the earth. He is the most high, the great.
5.   The heavens almost shatter out of reverence for Him, and the angels praise the glory of their Lord and ask forgiveness for those on earth. Indeed, God is the forgiver, most merciful.
6.   Those who set up idols besides Him, God is in full charge of them; you are not their advocate.
7.   We have revealed to you this Quran in Arabic, to warn the central town and all around it, and to warn about the day of gathering, which is inevitable. Consequently, some will deserve heaven and some will deserve hell.
8.   Had God willed, He could have made you one congregation. But He admits whomever He wills into His mercy, while the wicked have no lord or supporter.
9.   Why should they set up idols besides Him, when God is the Lord? He is the one who resurrects the dead, and He is omnipotent.
10.   Anything you dispute among yourselves will be ultimately judged by God. Such is God, my Lord; in Him I trust, and to Him I submit.
11.   He is the initiator of the heavens and the earth. He created for you mates, from among you, and also for the animals, in order to multiply. Nothing equals Him; He is the hearer, the seer.
12.   To Him belongs the keys of the heavens and the earth. He increases the provision for whomever He wills, or reduces it. He is omniscient.

42:1.   See footnote 40:1.

42:2.   When the reader counts the Arabic letters 'Ayn, Seen, and Qaf, in this sura, he will find their total frequency of occurrence 209, a multiple of 19. Thus, it conforms to the Quran's secret numerical code. The letter Q has a special characteristic. There is only one other sura that is initialed with this letter, namely sura 50, which is entitled "Q." The frequency of occurrence of the letter Q in each of these suras is exactly the same, 57, despite the difference in length of the two suras. For details of this Quranic miracle, see Appendix 1.

Only One Religion

13. He has decreed for you the same religion decreed for Noah, and what is revealed herein, and what was decreed for Abraham, Moses, and Jesus. You shall uphold the one religion, and do not be divided. It is simply too difficult for the idol worshipers to accept what you advocate. God is the one who brings towards Him whomever He wills; He guides towards Himself those who submit.

14. They became divided after the knowledge had come to them, due to sheer jealousy. If it were not for a predetermined decision by your Lord, they would have been judged immediately. Even those who inherited the scripture continued to harbor doubts.

15. You shall preach and uphold this scripture as commanded, and do not follow their wishes. And say, "I believe in all the scriptures revealed by God, and I am commanded to treat you amicably, God is our Lord and your Lord; we have our deeds and you have your deeds. There is no argument between us and you. God will gather us together; to Him is the ultimate destiny."

16. Those who argue about God, after being declared, their argument is nullified at their Lord; they have deserved wrath and retribution.

17. God is the one who revealed this scripture truthfully and equitably. For all you know, the Hour may be very close.*

18. Challenging it are those who do not believe in it. But those who believe are concerned about it, and recognize that it is the inevitable truth. Indeed, those who are doubtful about the Hour are totally astray.

19. God is most compassionate towards His servants, providing as He wills. He is the most powerful, the almighty.

20. Anyone who seeks the harvest of the hereafter, we multiply his harvest. But anyone who seeks the harvest of this world, we will give him therefrom, while receiving no share in the hereafter.

The Idol Worshipers Invent Laws

21. They follow idols who decree for them religious laws never authorized by God.* If it were not for the predetermined decision, they would have been judged immediately. The wicked have deserved painful retribution.

42:17.   *See Appendix 14. The hour of resurrection is only as far from us as the end of our individual lives in this world.*

42:21.   *A typical example is shown in footnote 24:1-2. The idol worshipers refuse to accept God's laws and follow instead laws attributed to their idols, including the prophet and the various saints and imams. When God alone is advocated as the only source of jurisprudence, they become uncontrollably upset (see 17:46, 39:45, 40:10-12, and 40:84).*

22. You will see the wicked frightened by their own works, knowing that the consequences are unavoidable. As for those who believed and led a righteous life, they will be in gardens of Paradise where they have anything they wish. This is the greatest achievement.

23. Such is the good news that God offers to His servants who believe and work righteousness. Say, "I do not ask you for any wage; I ask that each of you regard his own relatives.*" Whoever produces a righteous work, we multiply it for him manyfold. God is forgiver, appreciative.

24. If they claim that you fabricated some lies and attributed them to God, then God is able to seal your heart, erase any falsehood, and reestablish the truth with His words. He is fully aware of the innermost intentions.*

25. He accepts the repentance of His servants and pardons the sins. He is fully aware of everything you do.

26. He responds to those who believe and work righteousness and increases His blessings to them, while the disbelievers have deserved painful retribution.

Why God Controls Provisions

27. If God were to increase the provisions for His servants, they would transgress; this is why He sends it down in exact measure, as He wills. He is fully cognizant of His servants' needs, seer.

28. He is the one who sends down the rain when they despair and spreads His mercy. He is the only Lord, the praiseworthy.

29. Among His signs is the creation of the heavens and the earth and the creatures He spread in both of them. He is able to gather them together, when He so wills.

30. Any disaster that hits you is the result of your own works, and He overlooks much more.

31. There is no escape for anyone, and you have none besides God as Lord and supporter.

32. Among His signs are the ships that roam the sea like flags.

33. If He wills, He can halt the winds, leaving them standing still. These are signs for everyone who is steadfast, appreciative.

34. Or, He may cause them to drown as a consequence of their deeds; but He overlooks much.

35. Those who dispute our revelations will find out that they have no basis.

42:23. If everyone regards his own relatives, we will all be taken care of.

42:24. We are told here that even if the prophet erred or unintentionally distorted the Quran, God would have corrected any distortion. God is omnipotent, and He has guaranteed the integrity of Quran forever (see 15:9 and 17:73-75).

36. Whatever you possess is the temporary material of this life. What God possesses is far better and everlasting, for those who believe and trust in their Lord.

37. And they avoid gross evil and sins, and whenever provoked, they forgive.

38. They respond to their Lord, and observe the **salat** prayers. Their affairs are decided by consensus among them, and from our provisions to them they donate.

39. When injustice befalls them, they defend themselves until victory.

40. They counter aggression with an equivalent response. However, those who pardon and conciliate receive a better reward from God; God is never unjust.

41. If one avenges an injustice, he shall not be blamed.

42. To be blamed are those who inflict injustice upon the people and resort to aggression without provocation. These have deserved painful retribution.

43. If one resorts to patience and forgiveness, this reflects true strength.

44. Whomever God misguides will find no protector, and you will see them, as they face the retribution saying, "Can we get another chance?"

45. You will see them facing it humiliated and debased; looking and trying to evade it. Those who believed will say, "The real losers are those who lost their souls and their families on the day of resurrection. Indeed, the wicked have deserved eternal retribution."

46. They will have no allies to support them against God. Whomever God misguides will find no path.

47. You shall respond to your Lord, before a day comes which is inevitable. You will have no refuge on that day, nor could you deny anything.

Sole Function Of The Messenger

48. If they turn away, we have not sent you as their guardian. Your sole mission is to deliver this message. Whenever we endow the humans with mercy from us, they turn joyful, but when adversity befalls them, as a consequence of their own deeds, they turn unappreciative.

49. To God belongs the dominion of the heavens and the earth. He creates whatever He wills. He grants whomever He wills daughters and grants whomever He wills sons.

50. He may have the males and the females get married, yet keep them sterile. He is omniscient, omnipotent.

God Communicates With Us

51. It is not possible for a human to communicate with God except through inspiration, or behind a barrier, or through a messenger to whom He reveals whatever He wills. He is most high, wise.

52.   We thus revealed to you an inspiration from us declaring our
      commandments. Previously, you had no idea what the scripture was, or
      what faith was. But we made this scripture a beacon to guide whomever
      we will. Indeed, you guide to a straight path.
53.   This is the path of God, who possesses everything in the heavens and the
      earth. To God all matters ultimately return.

Sura 43: Vanity (Al-Zukhruf)

In the name of God, most gracious, most merciful

1. H. M.*
2. And this manifest scripture.
3. We have made it an Arabic Quran, that you may understand.*
4. It is recorded with us in the master record, honorable and full of wisdom.
5. Shall we simply ignore the fact that you are transgressors?
6. We sent many a prophet to previous generations.
7. Whenever a prophet went to them, they ridiculed him.
8. Consequently, we annihilated stronger people than these, and this is a lesson from the past.

Worshipping God Not Enough*

9. If you ask them, "Who created the heavens and the earth," they would say, "The almighty, the omniscient."
10. He is the one who made the earth for your habitation and established for you roads therein, that you may be guided.
11. He is the one who sends down water from the sky, in exact measure, and revives dead land therewith. You will thus be raised.
12. He is the one who created all kinds, and made the ships, as well as certain animals for you to ride.
13. As you mount their backs, you shall appreciate the blessings of your Lord and say, "Glory be to the one who subdued this for us; we could not subdue it ourselves.
14. "We ultimately return to our Lord."
15. Yet, they set up idols from among His servants. Indeed, the human being is unappreciative.
16. Others claim that He chose daughters among His creation, while giving them sons.
17. Yet, when one of them is given news that he has begotten a daughter, his face becomes darkened with misery.

43:1.   See footnote 40:1.

43:3.   The word "you" in this verse refers to all the people on earth, regardless of their language. Careful research, involving most major languages on earth, has revealed that Arabic is the most suitable language for writing statutes. See Appendix 3 for details.

43:9-22.   See footnote 41:14.

18. For the girl is brought up to be beautiful, not to help him in war.
19. They claimed that the angels, who are servants of God most gracious, are females. Did they ever witness their creation? Their blasphemy will be recorded, and they will be questioned.
20. They also said, "If it is the will of God most gracious, we would not idolize them." Indeed, they have no basis for idol worship; they only invent.
21. Did we give them any scripture that advocates idol worship?

Do Not Follow Your Parents Blindly

22. What they said was, "We found our parents doing this, and we simply followed their footsteps."
23. Thus, whenever we sent a warner to any community, the leaders said, "We found our parents following a religion, and we are following their footsteps."
24. The messenger would say, "What if I showed you better guidance than that of your parents?" They said, "We reject whatever you bring."
25. Consequently, we punished them. Note the consequences for the rejectors.
26. Abraham said to his father and his people, "I disown your idols.
27. "I worship only the one who created me and guides me."
28. His example is set up for those who come after him, that they may return.*
29. I have allowed these people and their parents to enjoy themselves until the truth came to them, and a clarifying messenger.
30. But when the truth came to them, they said, "This is magic, and we reject it."

God Chooses His Messenger

31. They said, "How come this Quran was not revealed through a prominent man from either town?"
32. Are they the ones who distribute the mercy of your Lord? We assign to them shares in this life, raising some of them above others, in order to use the services of one another. However, the mercy from your Lord is far better than any materials they hoard.

43:28. The lesson of Abraham is prominently detailed throughout the Quran. He grew up in an idol-worshipping community, and without receiving any education, he looked at the universe around him and discovered God (see 6:75-79). Similarly, no one has any excuse for not discovering and worshipping God alone. Like Abraham, we are all born with the knowledge of God as a natural instinct. (See 7:172).

The Materials Of This World Are Nil

33. If it were not that all the people may become disbelievers, we would have granted every disbeliever a mansion with silver roofs and tall stairs.

34. Any many gates and luxurious furniture.

35. And numerous vanities. All these are the materials of this world. But the hereafter is reserved at your Lord for the righteous.

36. Anyone who neglects the message of God most gracious, we appoint a devil to be his constant companion.

37. Then the devils keep them away from the path, and make them think that they are guided.*

38. Then, when they come to us, each will say to his devil, "I wish you were as far from me as the distance between the two easts. What a miserable companion!"

39. On that day, there will be no consolation in being together in hell.

40. You cannot make the deaf hear, nor can you guide the blind, nor can you guide those who are totally astray.

41. Whether we let you die before it or not, we will sooner or later punish them.

42. We may let you see the doom we promised them. We are in total control over them.

43. Therefore, you shall uphold what is revealed to you, for you are in the right path.

44. This is a message for you and your people, for which you will be answerable.

45. Study the history of all the messengers before you; did we ever allow any idols to be set up besides God most gracious?

The Lesson From Moses

46. For example, we sent Moses with our miracles to Pharaoh and his people saying, "I am sent by the Lord of the universe."

47. When he showed them our miracles, they laughed at them.

48. Every sign we showed them was greater than the previous one; as we afflicted them with plagues, that they may return.

49. They said, "O you magician, call upon your Lord to relieve our plagues; we will then follow the guidance."

50. But when we relieved their plagues, they broke their vows.

51. Pharaoh announced, "O my people, do I not possess the kingdom of Egypt and these rivers flow beneath me? Do you not see?

43:36-37. *Those who neglect the Quran in favor of "**hadith**" and/or "**sunna**" (which are lies attributed to the prophet), believe that they are rightly guided. (see Appendices 11, 15, 16, and 17.)*

52. "Which one is better, me or this one who is lowly and can hardly speak?
53. "Why does he not receive a treasure of gold or bring the angels with him as assistants?"
54. Pharaoh thus duped his people and made them obey him; they were wicked.
55. Because they opposed us, we avenged and drowned them all.
56. We set them up as examples for the others.
57. And when the son of Mary was cited as an example, your people rebelled.
58. They said, "Which is better, worshipping our idols, or worshipping Jesus (as the Christians do)?" They used his example to argue with you. Indeed, they are contentious.*
59. Jesus is no more than a servant whom we blessed. We made him an example for the children of Israel.
60. Had we willed, we could have sent angels to reside with you on earth.
61. He was sent to provide you with knowledge relevant to the Hour, "You shall not be doubtful, and follow me; this is a straight path.
62. "Let not the devil repel you; for he is your ardent enemy."
63. When Jesus came with miracles, he said, "I bring you wisdom and clarifications of some disputes. Beware of God, and obey me.
64. "God is my Lord and your Lord; you shall worship Him. This is a straight path."
65. But the various parties disputed among themselves. Therefore, woe to the wrongdoers from the retribution of a painful day.
66. Are they waiting until their end comes suddenly when they least expect it?
67. The close friends on that day will become enemies, except for the righteous.
68. O My servants, do not worry about anything today; nor shall you grieve.
69. They believed in our revelations and totally submitted.
70. Enter Paradise, you and your spouses, and rejoice.
71. Trays made of gold will be passed around for them, and cups. They will have anything their souls desire or their eyes wish. They abide therein forever.
72. This is Paradise that you inherit because of your works.
73. You will have many fruits therein from which you eat.
74. As for the guilty, they will abide forever in hell.
75. They will never be reprieved and will be confined therein.
76. It is not us who wronged them; it is they who wronged themselves.

*43:58. The Muslims who deviated from Quran and advocated other sources of law, such as the invented "**hadith**" and/or "**sunna**," are not any better than those who idolize Jesus, as stated in this verse. Deviating from the Quran constitutes disobedience of the prophet and idolizing him against his will (see 25:30-31).*

77. They will call, "O Malik (guardian of hell), let your Lord finish us." But he will say, "You will last forever.

78. "We have given you the truth, but most of you disliked the truth."

79. Have they planned a certain plan? We also plan. Did they think that we could not hear their secret conspiracies?

80. Indeed, our messengers are with them, recording.

81. Say, "If God most gracious had a son, I will be the first to believe."*

82. Glory be to the Lord of the heavens and the earth, Lord of the throne; He is high above their claims.

83. Let them blunder and play, until they meet the day that is promised to them.

84. He is the one God in the heaven and the one God on earth; He is the wise, the omniscient.

85. Most exalted is the one who possesses the dominion of the heavens and the earth and everything between them. Only He knows when the Hour will come. To Him you ultimately return.

There Will Be No Intercession*

86. The idols they set up besides Him possess no power to intercede, unless their intercession coincides with the truth, and unless they are aware thereof.

87. Ironically, when you ask them who created them, they would say, "God." Why then did they deviate?*

88. They will be declared as disbelievers.

89. Therefore, disregard them and say, "Peace," for they will eventually find out.

43:81.   If God indeed had a son, who would object? It simply happens to be an untruth, and a blasphemy.

43:86.   See Appendix 7 for details.

43:87.   See footnote 23:84.

Sura 44: Smoke (Al-Dukhan)

In the name of God, most gracious, most merciful

1. H. M. *
2. And this profound scripture.
3. We have revealed the Quran in a blessed night, that we may warn.*
4. In it, every matter of wisdom is explained.
5. This is our decision; we are to send messengers.
6. This is mercy from your Lord; He is the hearer, the omniscient.
7. He is the Lord of the heavens and the earth, and everything between them, if you only believe.
8. There is no god except He; the one who controls life and death; your Lord and the Lord of your ancestors.
9. Indeed, they are doubtful, heedless.

Before The End Of The World*

10. Watch for the day when the sky brings overwhelming smoke.
11. It will envelope all the people and will be painful.*
12. Our Lord, remove this suffering from us; we now believe.
13. How come they remember now, when an honest messenger had come to them?
14. But they ignored him and said, "He is well educated, but crazy."
15. We will relieve the retribution a little bit, but soon after you will revert.

44:1.   See footnote 40:1.

44:3.   The Quran was revealed into Muhammad's heart all at once (see 2:185, 17:1, 53:1-18, and 97:1), and released through his mouth over a period of 23 years (see 17:106).

44:10.   This is one of the signs that must be fulfilled before the end of the world. The other signs include the appearance of a creature who will exhort the people to believe (27:82), the splitting of the moon (54:1), and the discovery of Quran's secret numerical code (74:30-37), and the invasion by Gog and Magog (18:94-99 & 21:96). Three of these signs appear to have been fulfilled, namely, the decoding of the Quran's secret, the violation of the moon in 1969, and the appearance of the "creature," i.e., the computer (see footnote 27:82).

44:11.   The famous Haley's comet drags a tail of cyanogen gas that is about 3 million miles long. If this tail passes close enough to the earth's gravity, it can easily envelope the whole earth with cyanogen gas. Our next close encounter with Haley's comet will take place in mid-1986, then every 75 years thereafter.

Smoke (Al-Dukhan) 44:16-43   345

16. However, on the day we strike the final stroke, we will effect retribution.
17. In the past, we tested the Pharaoh's people by sending an honorable messenger to them.
18. (He said,) "You shall heed Me, O servants of God. I am an honest messenger to you.
19. "Do not be too arrogant to worship God. I bring to you profound miracles.
20. "I seek refuge in my Lord and your Lord, lest you stone me.
21. "If you do not wish to believe, then just leave me alone."
22. He then prayed to his Lord that, "These are evil people."
23. (He was told,) "Then move during the night, together with My servants. You will be pursued.
24. "You will cross the sea in a hurry, while their troops will drown."
25. Thus, the Pharaoh's people left gardens and springs.
26. And crops and nice homes.
27. And blessings that they enjoyed.
28. We made other people inherit them.
29. Neither the heaven nor the earth wept for them; they were no longer respited.
30. We thus delivered the children of Israel from the humiliating persecution.
31. From Pharaoh, the oppressive tyrant.
32. We chose them knowingly from among the people.
33. We showed them many miracles, thus making the test more exacting for them.

Resurrection Will Come

34. These people say,
35. "There is only one death, and we never rise.
36. "Bring back our ancestors, if you are truthful."
37. Are they better than the people of Tubba', and others before them? We destroyed them for their sins.
38. We have not created the heavens and the earth and everything between them in vain.
39. We created them for a specific purpose,* but most people do not know.
40. The day of decision awaits them all.
41. On that day, no friend will avail his friend in any way; no one can be helped.
42. Only those who have attained mercy from God; for He is the almighty, most merciful.
43. The tree of bitterness.

44:39. See Appendix 6.

44. Will provide food for the sinner.
45. Like molten rocks, it will boil in their bellies.
46. Like bubbling lava.
47. Take him and throw him into the depth of hell.
48. Then pour upon his head the painful lava.
49. Suffer; you used to be so haughty and so honored.
50. This is what you doubted.
51. As for the righteous, they will be in a secure abode.
52. In gardens and springs.
53. They wear silk and velvet, and will be neighbors.
54. We will join them with magnificent spouses.
55. They will enjoy every kind of fruit; they will be safe and secure.
56. Never again will they taste death, after the first death, and God protects them from the agony of hell.*
57. This is the blessing from your Lord; this is the great triumph.
58. We made this Quran easy to understand through your tongue, that they may take heed.*
59. Then wait in anticipation; they too will wait.

44:56. The inhabitants of heaven will be able to visit their friends and relatives in hell, without suffering any harm. See 37:51-59.

44:58. See 41:44 and Appendix 3.

Sura 45: Humbled (Al-Jaathiyah)

In the name of God, most gracious, most merciful

1. H. M.*
2. The revelation of this scripture is from God, the almighty, the wise.
3. Throughout the heavens and the earth, there are signs for the believers.
4. And in your creation, and the creatures He produces, there are signs for those who are certain.
5. Also, the alternation of night and day, the provisions that God sends down from the sky to revive dead land, and the manipulation of the winds; all these are signs for people who understand.

The Inventors and Followers Of "**Hadith**" Doomed

6. These are God's revelations that we recite for you with the truth; which **hadith**,* besides the revelations of God, do they believe?
7. Woe to every inventor, guilty.
8. He hears God's revelations recited to him, then insists on his way arrogantly, as if he never heard them.* Promise him painful retribution.
9. When he hears our verses, he takes them in vain. These have deserved humiliating retribution.
10. Hell awaits them. Nothing they possess will help them, nor will the idols they set up besides God. They have deserved terrible retribution.
11. This is the guidance, and those who reject the revelations of their Lord have deserved the retribution of a painful curse.
12. God is the one who subdued the sea for you, that the ships may roam therein by His command and seek His bounties; you should be appreciative.
13. He subjugated for you everything in the heavens and on earth, all from Him. These are signs for people who reflect.

45:1.   See 40:1.

45:6.   See footnote 39:23. "Hadith" is no more than inventions by enemies of the prophet, as stated in 6:112-116, 25:30-31, and 45:7, aimed at repelling the people from God's way and from the Quran (see 31:6).

*45:8.   God teaches us throughout the Quran that the Quran is complete, fully detailed, and shall be the only source of law. But those who advocate **hadith** and **sunna** refuse to accept these verses; they have failed the test and proved to be false muslims (see 6:112-116, 25:30-31, and Appendix 15).*

14. Ask the believers to forgive those who do not expect the days of God. He is the one who judges the people for whatever they do.

15. Whoever works righteousness does so for his own good; and whoever commits evil does so against his soul. Ultimately, you will be returned to your Lord.

16. We have given the children of Israel the scripture, wisdom, and prophethood, and we endowed them with good provisions, and we set them apart from all the people.

17. We gave them clear commandments, but they disputed after the knowledge had come to them, out of sheer jealousy among themselves.

18. Then we decreed the commandments for you. You shall follow this, and not the opinions of those who do not know.

19. They can never help you against God's will. The wicked are allies for each other, while God befriends the righteous.

20. This (Quran) provides the people with enlightenment, guidance, and mercy for those who attain certainty.

21. Do the people who work evil expect to be treated like those who believe and work righteousness? Could they be the same in life and death? Wrong indeed is their expectation.

22. God created the heavens and the earth for a specific purpose, to repay every soul for whatever it did, without the least injustice.

23. What do you think of one who idolizes his own ego? God sends him astray, seals his hearing and his heart, and places a veil on his eyes. Who can guide him thereafter? Would you not take heed?

24. They said, "There will be only this life; we live and die, and only time causes our death." They have no basis for saying this; they only conjecture.

25. When our clear revelations are recited to them, their only argument is, "Bring back our ancestors, if you are truthful."

26. Say, "God grants you life, then He puts you to death, and He will gather you on the day of resurrection." There is no doubt about it, but most people do not know.

27. To God belongs the dominion of the heavens and the earth. On the day resurrection takes place, the advocates of falsehood will be the losers.

28. You will see every congregation humbled; every congregation will be invited to view its record.* Today you get paid for everything you did.

29. This is our record pronouncing the truth about you. We have recorded everything you did.

30. As for those who believe and work righteousness, their Lord will admit them into His mercy. This is the greatest triumph.

45:28.   See footnote 41:20-21 and Appendix 10.

31. Those who disbelieved will be told, "Did you not hear My revelations recited to you, and you turned arrogant and guilty?

32. "When you were told that God's promise is truth, and that there is no doubt about resurrection, you said, 'We have no idea what resurrection is. We can only conjecture; we are not sure.' "

33. The wickedness of their work will become evident to them, and the very thing they mocked will cause their doom.

34. They will be told, "Today we forget you, just as you forgot this day. Your abode is hell, and no one can help you.

35. "This is because you had taken God's revelations in vain, and you were distracted by the first life." There will be no way out for them, nor will they be excused.

36. To God belongs all praise; Lord of the heàvens and Lord of the earth; Lord of the universe.

37. To Him belongs all majesty in the heavens and the earth; He is the almighty, the wise.

Sura 46: The Dunes (Al-Ahqaf)

In the name of God, most gracious, most merciful

1. H. M.*
2. (These letters prove that) this scripture comes from God, the almighty, the wise.
3. We have not created the heavens and the earth, and everything between them, except for a specific purpose, and for a specific life span. The disbelievers are heedless of all the warnings.
4. Say, "You set up idols besides God; show me what on earth did they create. Do they own any part of the heavens? Show me any previous scripture or established knowledge (that supports idol worship), if you are truthful."

The Righteous Idols*

5. Who is farther astray than those who idolize, besides God, people who cannot respond to them until the day of resurrection and are completely unaware of their idolization?
6. When the people are gathered (on the day of resurrection), they will become their enemies and will disown their idol worship.
7. When our clear revelations are recited for them, the disbelievers say about the truth, "This is obviously magic."
8. Otherwise, they would say, "He made it up." Say, "If I made it up, then you cannot protect me from God. He is fully aware of everything you scheme. He suffices as a witness between me and you. He is the forgiver, the merciful."

Muhammad Only Human

9. Say, "I do not bring anything new; I bring the same message as previous messengers. I have no idea what will happen to me or to you. I only follow the inspirations given to me. I am no more than a manifest warner."
10. Say, "What if this is from God, and you reject it?" A witness from the children of Israel has testified that it has been expected, and while he believed, you turned arrogant. God never guides the wicked people.

46:1.   See 40:1.

*46:5.   Such as Jesus, Mary, Muhammad, the saints, and the righteous imams.
See also 16:86.*

11. The disbelievers said of the believers, "If this message were any good, they would not have accepted it before us." Because they are not guided therewith, they say, "These are ancient fabrications."

12. Previously, the scripture of Moses was revealed as a guide and mercy, and this scripture confirms all previous scriptures. It is revealed in Arabic,* to warn the wicked and to give good news to the pious.

13. Those who say, "Our Lord is God," then maintain righteousness, have nothing to fear, nor will they grieve.

14. They have deserved Paradise, wherein they abide forever, as a reward for their work.

The Crucial Age Of Forty

15. We have enjoined man to honor his parents; his mother carried him arduously, gave birth to him arduously, then cared for him thirty months prior to weaning. By the time he grows up and reaches the age of forty, he should say, "My Lord, direct me to appreciate the blessings You have bestowed upon me and my parents, and to work righteousness that pleases You, and grant righteousness to my children. I have repented, and I totally submit to you."

16. It is from these that we accept the righteous works and overlook their sins. They have deserved Paradise; this is the truthful promise that is offered to them.

17. Then there is the one who defies his parents saying, "You mean to tell me that I will come back to life? What about those previous generations?" His parents plead to him in the name of God, "Woe to you, if you do not believe. God's promise is truth." But he insists, and says, "These are old tales."

18. It is these who are condemned to doom, along with others like them from the past generations of jinns and humans; these are the losers.

19. Each will be assigned ranks in accordance with their works; no one will suffer injustice.

20. The day will come when the disbelievers will be presented to hell, "You have wasted your material things in the first life and enjoyed them. Today you suffer humiliating retribution, since you were arrogant on earth, without justification, and you were wicked.

46:12. See footnote 41:44.

You Shall Not Worship Except God*

21. Remember the brother of Aad; he warned his people at the dunes, the same warnings given to those before him and after him, "You shall not worship except God. I fear for you the retribution of a horrible day."

22. They said, "Did you come to divert us from our idols? Show us the doom you threaten, if you are truthful."

23. He said, "Only God knows (when His judgment comes); I simply deliver the message entrusted to me. But I see that you are ignorant people."

24. When they saw the tornado heading towards their valley, they said, "This will bring us rain." Indeed, it is the punishment you asked for; violent wind with disasterous retribution.

25. It destroyed everything as commanded by its Lord. By morning, only their lifeless homes were seen. We thus punish the guilty people.

26. We had established them in the same way as we established you, and we gave them hearing, eyes, and minds. But their hearing, their eyes, and their minds did not help them, as a consequence of ignoring the revelations of God. The very thing they ridiculed was the cause of their doom.

27. We have annihilated many a community around you, after showing them signs, that they may repent.

28. How come the idols they had set up "to bring them closer to God" did not help them? In fact, they abandoned them. It was pure invention on their part.

Quran Is The Whole Message*

29. We summoned a group of jinns to you, to hear the Quran. When they came they said, "Listen," and when it was finished, they went to their people with the warning.

30. They said, "O our people, we heard a scripture that came down after Moses, confirming the previous scriptures. It guides to the truth and a straight path.

31. "O our people, you shall respond to God's call, and believe in Him. He will then forgive your sins and protect you from painful retribution."

46:21. As it turns out, the commandment, "You shall worship God," is not enough, since people can worship God and still go to hell. See footnote 41:14.

46:29-32. If there were anything else that the prophet preached besides Quran, the jinns would have reported it to their people. The Quran constitutes God's message, the whole message, and nothing but the message. See Appendix 15.

32. Anyone who fails to respond to God's message will never escape. Nor will he have friends to help him against God. These are totally astray.

33. Do they not realize that God, who created the heavens and the earth without getting tired, is able to resurrect the dead? Yes indeed; He is omnipotent.

34. The day will come when the disbelievers will be shown the hellfire; "Is this not the truth?" They will say, "Yes indeed, by our Lord." He will then say, "This is what you deserve for disbelieving."

35. Therefore, be patient, like all the messengers who possessed strength, and do not be eager to see their punishment. When the appointed day comes, and they see the retribution promised to them, it will seem as if they lasted one hour of the day. This is a declaration; is it not the wicked who are doomed?

Sura 47: Muhammad

In the name of God, most gracious, most merciful

1. Those who disbelieve and repel others from the path of God, God nullifies their work.

2. But those who believe, work righteousness, and believe in what was revealed through Muhammad, which is the truth from their Lord; God will remit their sins and restore their contentment.

3. That is because those who disbelieve follow falsehood, while those who believe follow the truth from their Lord. God thus cites the examples for the people.

4. Therefore, when you encounter in war those who disbelieve,* you shall strike their necks. Once you defeat them, you shall hold them captive until released amicably or ransomed at the end of war. Had God willed, He could have stopped them Himself. But He puts you to the test; those who readily strive for the cause of God, He will never waste their works.

5. He will guide them and restore their contentment.

6. He will admit them into Paradise, just as He promised them.

7. O you who believe, if you support God, He will support you and strengthen your foothold.

8. As for those who disbelieve, they have deserved misery, and God will nullify their works.

9. This is because they hated what God had revealed, and consequently, He neutralized their works.

10. Did they not travel the earth and see the consequences for those before them? God destroyed them, and all disbelievers will suffer the same fate.

11. This is because God is the Lord of those who believe, while the disbelievers have no lord.

12. God will admit those who believe and work righteousness into gardens with flowing streams. As for those who disbelieve, they temporarily enjoy and eat like animals, then hell is their ultimate destiny.

13. Many a town was stronger than the town that banished you (O Muhammad), but we destroyed them; they had no one to help them.

14. Is one who follows a proof from his Lord the same as one whose evil work is adorned in his eyes? These people are following their own opinions.

47:4.   *See the laws of war in 2:190.*

15. The allegory of Paradise that is promised for the righteous is one with rivers of unpolluted water, rivers of unchanged milk, rivers of delicious intoxicants, and rivers of filtered honey. They will have all kinds of fruits therein, as well as forgiveness from their Lord. Is this better, or those who last in hell forever, drinking molten lava that dissolves their intestines?

16. Some of them listen to you, but when they leave, they ask those who are knowledgeable, "What did he say?" God has sealed their hearts, and thus, they follow their own opinions.

17. As for those who are guided, God augments their guidance and grants them their righteousness.

18. Are they waiting until the Hour comes to them suddenly? Its signs and conditions have already come.* What will they do about this reminder as it comes to them?

19. Therefore, you shall recognize no god except the one God, and ask forgiveness for your sins and for the believing men and women. God is fully aware of your course and your ultimate destiny.

20. Those who believe look forward to the revelation of any sura. But when a straight forward sura is revealed, wherein fighting is decreed, you see those with doubtful hearts looking at you as if they were dying. They have deserved to be exposed.

21. Obedience and righteous utterances are expected of them. Thus, when a decision is made, if they show faithfulness towards God, it will be better for them.

22. Is it your intention that as soon as you leave, you will corrupt the earth and mistreat your relatives?

23. It is these whom God curses by deafening their ears and blinding their eyes.

24. Why do they not study and heed the Quran? Are their hearts locked up?

25. Those who turned back and fled, after the guidance had been pointed out to them, the devil has duped them and enticed them.

26. They had said to those who dislike God's message, "We will obey you in some instances." God is fully aware of their secrets.

27. This is why when the angels put them to death, they will beat them on the faces and the rear ends.

28. They had followed what angers God and disliked to please Him. Consequently, He nullifies their works.

29. Did those with doubtful hearts expect that God will never expose their hatefulness?

30. If we will, we can show them to you, and let you recognize them by their marks. You can recognize them by the way they talk. God is fully aware of all your works.

47:18. *See footnote 44:10.*

We Must Be Put To The Test

31. We will certainly put you to the test until we distinguish the strivers among you who remain steadfast, and to test your behavior.
32. Those who disbelieved, repelled from the path of God, and opposed the messenger after the guidance had been clarified for them, never harm God in the least; He will nullify their works.
33. O you who believe, obey God, and obey the messenger,* and do not nullify your works.
34. Those who disbelieved, repelled from the path of God, and died as disbelievers, God will never forgive them.
35. You shall never waver nor surrender, for you will be victorious; God is with you and will never fail to reward you for your works.
36. This life is no more than play and vanity. If you believe and work righteousness, God will give you your rewards, instead of asking you for money.
37. If He asks you to donate in excessive amounts, you may turn stingy, and hatred may prevail among you.
38. Here you are being exhorted to spend in the cause of God, and some of you turn stingy. Those who turn stingy are stingy against their souls. God is rich, while you are poor. IF YOU TURN AWAY, GOD WILL SUBSTITUTE OTHER PEOPLE IN YOUR PLACE, AND THEY WILL NOT BE LIKE YOU.*

47:33. To obey God and the messenger is to uphold the Quran, the whole Quran, and nothing but the Quran. The invention of **hadith** and/or **sunna** to distort and even supersede the Quran represents the height of disobience to God and the messenger. See 6:112-116, 25:30-31, and Appendix 11.

47:38. The so-called muslims throughout the "Muslim world" have abandoned the Quran **en masse** and failed the **hadith** test (see 6:112, 116 and 25:30-31). It seems that a process of substitution is taking place now according to this statement. Islam is being reestablished in the English-speaking world, after being restored to its pristine purity.

In the name of God, most gracious, most merciful

1. We have endowed you with a great bounty.
2. Whereby God forgives your past and future sins, completes His blessings upon you, and guides you in a straight path.
3. And God will grant you a great victory.
4. He is the one who placed calm into the hearts of the believers, in order to strengthen their faith. To God belongs all the forces in the heavens and the earth. God is omniscient, wise.
5. Whereby, God admits the believing men and women into gardens with flowing streams; they abide therein forever. And He remits their sins. This is the great triumph from God.
6. He will punish the hypocrite men and women, and the idol worshipping men and women, for they harbor evil thoughts about God. Evil will backfire against them; God is angry with them, curses them, and has prepared for them hell; a miserable destiny.
7. To God belong all the forces of the heavens and the earth; God is almighty, wise.
8. We have sent you (Muhammad) as a witness, a bearer of good news, as well as a warner.
9. In order that you (people) believe in God and His messenger, and honor God, reverence God, and glorify Him day and night.
10. Those who make a vow with you are making a vow with God; God's hand is over their hands. Therefore, anyone who violates his vow, does so to his own detriment, and anyone who fulfills his vow to God, God will grant him a great recompense.
11. Those bedouins who stay behind (when you mobilize for war) would say, "We were preoccupied with our business and our families, so forgive us." They utter with their tongues what is not in their hearts. Say, "Who can prevent God, if He wanted to harm you or benefit you?" Indeed, God is fully cognizant of everything you do.
12. You had expected that the messenger and the believers would never return to their families, and this was affirmed into your hearts. You had harbored bad thoughts, and you did so maliciously.
13. If anyone refuses to believe in God and His messenger, we have prepared for the disbelievers hell.
14. To God belongs the dominion of the heavens and the earth. He forgives whomever He wills and punishes whomever He wills. God is forgiver, merciful.

15. Those who stayed behind would say, when you reap the spoils of war, "Let us join you," seeking to change the words of God. Say, "You cannot join us, for this is what God had said." Then they might say, "You must have been envious of us." Indeed, they hardly understand.

16. Say to the bedouins who stay behind, "You will be asked to fight people who are very powerful until you win or they embrace Islam. If you obey, God will grant you a good reward. But if you refuse as you did previously, then God will punish you a painful punishment."

17. The blind is not to be blamed; the handicapped is not to be blamed; and the ill is not to be blamed. Anyone who obeys God and His messenger, God will admit him into gardens with flowing streams, and anyone who refuses, God will commit him to painful retribution.

18. God was pleased with the believers as they made a vow with you under the tree. He thus confirmed what was in their hearts. Consequently, He sent down calm upon them and rewarded them victory to be attained.

19. Also, many spoils to be earned; God is almighty, wise.

20. God promised you many spoils that you will earn; He thus advances some rewards for you in this life. God withheld the people's hands from harming you, and made this a sign of support for the believers. God guides in a straight path.

21. As for the other group that you could not defeat, God neutralized them. God is omnipotent.

22. If the disbelievers ever fight you, they will turn around and flee; they will find no ally or supporter.

23. This is God's system that has always prevailed. God's system is never changeable.

24. He is the one who kept their hands off of you and kept your hands off of them in the valley of Mecca, after granting you victory over them. God is seer of everything you do.

25. It is they who disbelieved and barred you from the Sacred Mosque and prevented your offerings from reaching their destination. If it were not for believing men and women you did not even know, you would have assaulted them, then regretted such action. God admits into His mercy whomever He wills. Had they reverted, we would have punished the disbelievers among them a painful punishment.

26. While the disbelievers stirred up their old fanaticism; fanaticism of the days of ignorance; God sent down calm upon His messenger and the believers, and He blessed them with righteousness, as they rightly deserved. God is fully aware of all things.

27. God fulfilled the vision of His messenger saying, "You will enter the Sacred Mosque by God's leave, and you will cut your hair (as you observe the rituals of pilgrimage). You will have no more fear. He knows what you never knew, and thus, He now grants you a great victory soon to be attained."

Islam Will Prevail

28. He is the one who sent His messenger with the guidance and the religion of truth, to make it prevail over all religions. God suffices as witness.

29. Muhammad is a messenger of God; those who truly follow him are stern against the disbelievers, but compassionate among themselves. You see them bowing and prostrating, seeking grace from God and His pleasure. Their marks are on their faces from prostration. Such is their description in the Torah, while their allegory in the Injeel (the Gospel) is like a plant that germinates, grows stronger, then becomes erect and pleases the farmer. God thus enrages the disbelievers. God promises the believers who work righteousness forgiveness and a great recompense.

Sura 49: The Dwelling (Al-Ḥujuraat)

In the name of God, most gracious, most merciful

1. O you who believe, do not take God and His messenger for granted; beware of God; God is hearer, omniscient.

Etiquette

2. O you who believe, do not raise your voices above the voice of the prophet,* nor shall you shout at him as you shout at one another, lest you nullify your works without perceiving.

3. Those who lower their voices at the messenger of God are the ones whose hearts are rendered righteous by God. They have deserved forgiveness and a great recompense.

4. As for those who call you from outside your dwelling, most of them do not understand.

5. Had they waited until you came out, it would have been better for them. God is forgiver, merciful.

Investigate Rumors

6. O you who believe, when a wicked person brings you any news, you shall investigate, lest you hurt others through ignorance, then regret what you have done.

7. And know that God's messenger is among you;* if he obeyed you in many things, you would have made things too difficult for yourselves.* But God inspired you to love belief and beautified it in your hearts. And He inspired you to abhor disbelief, wickedness, and rebellion. These are the rightly directed ones.

8. This is grace from God, and a blessing. God is omniscient, wise.

49:2.   *In order for the student to benefit from the teacher, the student must respectfully pay attention and observe certain etiquette. See the student/teacher behavior of Moses and his teacher in 18:66-82.*

49:7.   *God's messenger is fully represented by Quran, the whole Quran, and nothing but the Quran.*

49:7.   *There is a human tendency, with help from satan, to impose more hardship as a sign of piety. Thus, some people invariably go too far in prohibiting foods that are perfectly lawful (see Appendix 13), or imposing additional duties that were never decreed. The Quran teaches that such practices are tantamount to idol worship.*

9. If two groups of believers fight each other, you shall reconcile them. If one of them aggresses, then you shall fight the group that aggresses until it returns to God's law. Once they return, you shall reconcile them equitably and be just. God loves those who are just.

10. The believers are brothers, and you shall reconcile between your brothers. You shall observe God, that you may attain mercy.

11. O you who believe, no people shall mock other people, for they may be better than they; nor shall women mock other women, for they may be better than they. Do not defame each other, nor ridicule any names. It is repugnant to practice wickedness after acquiring faith. Those who refuse to repent are wicked.

12. O you who believe, you shall avoid suspicions; even a little bit of suspicion is sinful. You shall not spy, nor shall you backbite each other. Does any of you like to eat the flesh of his dead brother? You certainly abhor this. You shall observe God, for God is redeemer, merciful.

13. O people, we created all of you from the same male and female (Adam and Eve), and we made you into nations and tribes in order to recognize each other. The best among you is the most righteous.* God is omniscient, cognizant.

Islam versus Iman*

14. The nomads said, "We are **Mu'mins** (believers)." Say, "You are not **Mu'mins** yet; rather, you should say that you are Muslims, until **Iman** (faith) enters your hearts." If you obey God and His messenger, God will never fail to recompense you. God is forgiver, merciful.

Definition of Mu'min

15. The **Mu'mins** (believers) are those who believe in God and His messenger, and harbor no doubts whatsoever. They strive with their monies and their lives in the cause of God. These are the truthful.

16. Say, "Are you informing God about your religion; when God knows everything in the heavens and the earth? God is fully aware of all things."

49:13. The only criterion that renders any person better than another is righteousness. Color, knowledge, wealth, physical appearance, social status, family lineage, etc. do not necessarily make any person better than another.

49:14. A person who believes in God and His messenger, in accordance with this Quran, is a Muslim for as long as he harbors occasional doubts and questions. Once he gets rid of all doubts in his heart, then he is a **Mu'min** (believer). Therefore, a **Mu'min** is higher in rank than a Muslim.

17. They act as if they are doing you a favor by embracing Islam; say, "You are not doing me any favor by embracing Islam. God is the one who did you a great favor by guiding you to the faith, if you are sincere."

18. God knows the secrets of the heavens and the earth. God is seer of everything you do.

Sura 50: Q

In the name of God, most gracious, most merciful

1. Q,* and the glorious Quran.
2. Yet, they are still doubtful that a warner should come to them who is one of them.* The disbelievers say, "This is really strange.
3. "After we die and turn to dust? This is impossible."
4. We are fully aware when the earth consumes any of them; for we keep an accurate record.
5. Indeed, they rejected the truth when it came to them. Consequently, they are afflicted with confusion.
6. Do they not see the sky above them; how we constructed it and beautified it, without any flaw?
7. And we constructed the earth, distributed stabilizers therein, and we grew all kinds of beautiful plants.
8. This is to enlighten and remind every obedient person.
9. We send down from the sky blessed water, to produce gardens and food grains.
10. And tall palms with clustered fruits.
11. To provide for the people. And we revive with it dead land. Thus will be the resurrection.

Miraculous Numerical Code

12. Rebelling before them were the people of Noah, the dwellers of Rass, and Thamood.
13. Also, Aad, Pharaoh, and the brethren* of Lot.

50:1. See footnote 42:1 and Appendix 1.

50:2. Despite the miracle imbedded in the letter Q and throughout the glorious Quran, they are still doubtful.

*50:13. The people who disbelieved Lot are mentioned in the Quran 12 times, namely in 7:80; 11:70, 74, 89; 22:43; 26:160; 27:54,56; 29:28; 38:13; 50:13, and 54:33. Consistently, these people are called "**Qawm**," with a single exception. In this sura (Q), the people who disbelieved in Lot are called "**Ikhwan**." The reader can easily see that if the word "**Qawm**" was used here, as is customary throughout the Quran, the frequency of occurrence of the letter "Q" in this sura would become 58 instead of 57. The number 58 is not divisible by 19, it will not equal the 57 "Q's" in the other Q-initialed sura (sura 42), and the total number of "Q's" in the two suras would not equal the number of suras in the Quran (114). In other words, the whole numerical system collapses if the word "**Qawm**" is used instead of "**Ikhwan**." This demonstrates the fact that every word, indeed every letter, in Quran is divinely designed beyond human ability.*

14. And the dwellers of the woods, and the people of Tubba'. They all disbelieved the messengers, and therefore, My retribution was inevitable.

15. Was creating you the first time too difficult for us? Is this why they doubt resurrection?

16. Since we created the human being, we are fully aware of his innermost thoughts. We are closer to him than his jugular vein.

17. The two angels, at right and at left, record everything he does.

18. Not a single utterance he utters without a vigilant watcher.

19. Then the intoxication of death finally comes. This is what you tried to evade.

The Day of Judgment*

20. The horn is blown; this is the promised day.

21. Every soul came, along with a herder and a witness.

22. You used to be mindless of this; but today we removed your veil, and thus, your memory is (as strong as) steel.

23. His companion said, "Here is his detailed record."

24. Throw into hell every stubborn disbeliever.

25. He was an opponent of righteousness; transgressor, and doubtful.

26. He set up besides God another god. Therefore, throw him into severe retribution.

27. His companion said, "Our Lord, I did not mislead him; he is the one who went astray."

28. God said, "Do not feud in front of Me; I have already advanced sufficient warnings to you.

29. "Nothing can be changed now;* I am never unjust towards the people."

30. On that day, we will ask hell, "Did you have enough?" and it will say, "Can I have more?"

31. Paradise will be presented to the righteous, very close.

32. This is what has been promised for every steadfast submitter.

33. They have reverenced God most gracious in their privacy, and submitted to Him wholeheartedly.

34. Enter it in peace; this is the day of eternity.

50:20-29. These verses are written in the past tense because they are actual happenings that took place on the day of judgment. Since the day of judgment is future as far as we are concerned, it is described to us as witnessed by God.

50:29. Our condition at resurrection is irreversible. We end our life here with a soul that is strong, well fed, and well developed (as a result of heeding God's message), or a soul that is weak, shrunk, and undeveloped (as a result of disregarding God's message). God is never unjust, since he left our spiritual growth and development completely up to us. See Appendix 10.

35. They have deserved whatever they wish therein, and we have even more.

We Should Learn From The Past

36. We annihilated generations before them who were stronger and more civilized. Could they escape?

37. This should be a lesson for anyone with a heart or one who listens and bears witness.

38. We have created the heavens and the earth and everything between them in six days, and no fatigue ever touched us.

39. Therefore, be patient in the face of their utterances, and praise the glory of your Lord before sunrise and before sunset.

40. Glorify Him during the night, and in prostration.

41. Beware of the day when the caller calls from a near place.

42. When they hear the truthful blow; this is the day of resurrection.

43. It is we who give life and death, and to us is the ultimate destiny.

44. On that day, the earth will crack everywhere and give rise to them. This gathering is easy for us to do.

45. We are fully aware of what they say, while you can never force them. Therefore, remind with the Quran* those who reverence My warning.

50:45.   *The prophet's message is the Quran, the whole Quran, and nothing but the Quran. (See also 6:19.)*

Sura 51: The Winds (Al-Dhaariyaat)

In the name of God, most gracious, most merciful

1. By the blowing winds,
2. carrying clouds,
3. and bringing bounties,
4. to be distributed by command.
5. What is promised to you is truth.
6. Judgment is sure to come.
7. Despite the perfectly created sky,
8. you dispute the truth.
9. However, deviating are those who are supposed to deviate.
10. Woe to the falsifiers.
11. Who are heedless in their blunders.
12. They ask, "When is the day of judgment?"
13. That is the day when they suffer in hell.
14. Taste your retribution; this is what you defiantly challenged.
15. As for the righteous, they have deserved gardens and springs.
16. They receive their Lord's blessing, in return for their works.
17. Rarely did they sleep the whole night.
18. At dawn, they used to implore for forgiveness.
19. A portion of their monies was set aside for the needy and deprived.
20. In the earth there are signs for those who are certain.
21. Even within yourselves; do you not see?
22. In the heaven is your provisions and everything that is promised to you.
23. By the Lord of the heaven and the earth, this is as real as the fact that you speak.

Lessons From The Past

Abraham

24. Have you noted the narration about Abraham's honorable guests?
25. When they entered, they said, "Peace," and he said, "Peace to you strangers."
26. He then asked his family to prepare a fattened calf.
27. He offered it to them, but they did not eat.
28. He became wary of them. They said, "Do not be afraid," and they gave him good news of a knowledgeable son.
29. His wife came in astonishment, pointing at her face and saying, "I am a sterile old woman."
30. They said, "Your Lord said thus. He is the most wise, the omniscient."

Sodom And Gomorrah

31. Abraham said, "Where are you going, O messengers?"
32. They said, "We are being dispatched to guilty people.
33. "We are to shower them with stones of clay.
34. "Marked at your Lord for the transgressors."
35. We then delivered all the believers.
36. We found only one house of muslims (submitters) therein.
37. We set it up as a lesson for anyone who fears the painful retribution.

Moses

38. There are lessons to be learned from Moses. We sent him to Pharaoh with manifest authority.
39. But he turned away arrogantly and said, "Either a magician or a crazy man."
40. Consequently, we took him and his troops and threw them into the sea, even though he was apologizing.

'Aad And Thamood

41. There are also lessons to be learned from 'Aad. We sent upon them disasterous winds.
42. Whatever it passed by was left as dead as an old corpse.
43. Also, Thamood were told, "Enjoy yourselves for awhile."
44. They rebelled against the command of their Lord. Consequently, the lightning struck them as they looked.
45. They never got up thereafter, and there was nothing to protect them.
46. Before them, the people of Noah were wicked.

Humans And Jinns Created To Worship God Alone

47. We constructed the heaven with our hands, and we keep expanding it.
48. We spread the earth, and we are the best pavers.
49. Of everything, we created a pair, that you may take heed.
50. Therefore, you shall flee to God; I am sent to you by Him as a manifest warner.
51. You shall not set up another god besides God; I am sent to you by Him as a manifest warner.
52. Consistently, when a messenger went to the previous generations they said, "Magician or crazy."
53. Do they inherit this behavior from their ancestors? Indeed, they are trangressors.
54. If you turn away from them, you will not be blamed.

55. You shall continue to remind them; for the reminder benefits the believers.
56. I have not created the jinns and the humans except to worship Me alone.*
57. I do not need any provision from them, nor do I need them to feed Me.
58. God is the one who provides; the one who possesses all power, the omnipotent.
59. Those who commit evil will be doomed like their previous counterparts were doomed. Therefore, they should not hasten to challenge our doom.
60. Woe to those who disbelieve, from the day that is promised to them.

51:56.   The whole idea behind creating us is to show the angels that a creature who never sees God is capable of reaching God and worshipping Him alone. When one of the angels, namely satan, entertained rebellious ideas despite the fact that he saw God and knew well that He was the absolute master, God decided to show the angels that a creature who never sees God is capable of worshiping God alone (See Appendix 6).

Sura 52: Mount Sinai (Al-Toor)

In the name of God, most gracious, most merciful

1. By Mount Sinai.
2. And the scripture that is recorded.
3. And published on paper.
4. By the frequented shrine.
5. With its high ceiling.
6. By the vast ocean.
7. The retribution from your Lord is a reality.
8. Nothing can stop it.
9. That is the day when the heaven will violently thunder.
10. The mountains will be erased.
11. Woe on that day to the rejectors.
12. Who are heedless and playing.
13. On that day, they will be herded to the fire of hell.
14. This is the fire that you used to deny.
15. Is this magic, or do you not see?
16. Burn therein, whether you can or cannot stand it, you have no other choice. You are paying for what you did.
17. As for the righteous, they have deserved gardens of bliss.
18. They enjoy what their Lord bestows upon them. Their Lord has spared them the agony of hell.
19. Eat and drink with blessings, in return for what you did.
20. They relax on rows of furnishings, and we join with them magnificent spouses.*
21. Those who believed and whose children followed them in belief, we will reunite them with their children. We never deprive them of any work they had done. Every person is ransomed in accordance with his work.
22. We supply them with fruits and meats that they desire.
23. They will share drinks that never run out and are never polluted.
24. Serving them will be servants like precious pearls.
25. They will converse with each other.
26. They will say, "We used to be humble among our people.
27. "Then God showered us with His blessings and spared us the agony of ill winds.
28. "We used to implore Him; He is the benign, the merciful."

52:20.   See Appendix 4, detailing these allegorical descriptions of heaven and hell.

29. Therefore, you shall continue to remind the people, for you are never doubtful about your Lord's message, nor are you crazy.

30. They may say, "He is a poet; let us just ignore him until he is dead."

31. Say, "Keep on waiting; I am waiting along with you."

32. Is it their dreams that lead them to this, or is it wickedness?

33. Do they say that he made this up? They simply cannot believe.

34. Let them show us a "**hadith**" (narration) like this, if they are truthful.

35. Were they created out of nothing? Could they be the creators?

36. Did they create the heavens and the earth? Indeed, they are never certain.

37. Do they possess the treasures of your Lord? Are they in control?

38. Do they have a stairway that enables them to listen to us? Let their listener show his evidence.

39. Does God have daughters, while you have sons?

40. Are you asking them for a wage, so they are burdened thereby?

41. Do they know the future and record it?

42. Is it obstruction that they seek? The disbelievers only hinder themselves.

43. Do they have a god other than God? God be glorified, over and above any idols they set up.

44. When they see masses about to fall from the sky, they would say, "Dense clouds."

45. Therefore, disregard them until they meet their day of doom.

46. On that day, their schemes will never help them; nothing will protect them.

47. The wicked actually suffer retribution in this life, without realizing it.

48. You shall steadfastly persevere in preaching the message of your Lord. You are in our eyes. And praise the glory of your Lord when you get up.

49. Glorify Him during the night, and at dawn, as the stars fade away.

Sura 53: The Star (Al-Najm)

In the name of God, most gracious, most merciful

1. By the falling star.*
2. Your friend is neither astray, nor a liar.
3. He does not speak on his own.*
4. This is a divine inspiration.
5. A teaching from a mighty one.
6. The possessor of omnipotence, who assumed (all authority).
7. From the highest horizon,
8. He came closer, by moving downwards.*
9. Until He became as close as possible.*
10. He then revealed to His servant what He revealed.
11. The mind did not imagine what it saw.
12. Are you doubtful of what he sees?
13. He saw him in another descent.
14. At the ultimate point.
15. That is where the abode of paradise is located.
16. The ultimate point was then overwhelmed.
17. The eyes did not waver or imagine things.
18. He actually saw great marvels of his Lord.

53:1-18. These verses describe the process by which the Quran was revealed into Muhammad's heart. Although the revelation process was completed during one night (see 17:1, 44:3 and 96:1), the release of such revelation spanned 23 years (see 17:106). The release process was effected by Gabriel taking over Muhammad's body then uttering a number of verses. During the release process, Muhammad himself was unconscious. When he came to, he asked the revelation writers about the new Quranic verses.

53:3. This is one of the most abused verses in Quran. Those who fell into satan's trap and idolized the prophet against his will, claim that this statement applies to everything the prophet uttered; and not the Quran alone. Using this crutch, they proceeded to invent an endless number of lies and attributed them to the prophet. Thus, they defiantly, disobey God and the prophet. However, as stated in 6:112-116, this is God's will in order to use the **hadith** and/or **sunna** to distinguish the true muslims from the false muslims. See Appendix 11. It should be noted that this particular expression is very common in all the scriptures (see Deuteronomy, 18:19; Gospel of John, 12:49 & 16:130).

53:8. See Appendix 10.

53:9. See footnote 7:143.

Idol Worshipers Never Sure

19. What about Allat and Al-Uzza?*
20. Also Manat, the third one?
21. So you have sons, while He has daughters?
22. This is indeed an unjust distribution.
23. They are only names that you invented; you and your ancestors. God never placed any power in them. They follow conjecture and their own opinions, when the sure guidance had come to them from their Lord.
24. What is it that the human being wants?
25. God possesses both the hereafter as well as this world.
26. Even the angels of heaven cannot intercede on behalf of anyone. Only if it coincides with God's decision.*
27. Those who do not believe in the hereafter may assign to the angels female names.
28. They have no basis for such a claim; they only follow conjecture. Conjecture is no substitute for the truth.
29. Therefore, stay away from those who disregard our message and seek only the material of this world.
30. This is the extent of their knowledge. Your Lord is fully aware of those who deviate from His path, and He is fully aware of those who are guided.
31. To God belongs everything in the heavens and the earth. He will requite the evildoers only for their deeds, and reward the righteous manyfold.
32. For the righteous avoid gross sins and transgressions, except minor offenses, and your Lord is full of forgiveness. He is fully aware of you. He is the one who created you from the earth, then reproduced you as embryos in your mothers' wombs. Therefore, you do not need to exalt yourselves; He is fully aware of the righteous.
33. What about the one who turns away?
34. Who rarely gives to charity, and then complains?
35. Does he possess knowledge of the future; does he see?
36. Did he not know about Moses' scripture?
37. And Abraham who fulfilled?
38. (They taught) that no burdened soul can bear the burdens of another.
39. And that every human being is responsible for what he does.
40. And that everything he does will be witnessed.

53:19. These are female names of the two most popular idols of the pre-Muhammad era. Allat is their feminine name for Allah. The idol worshipers claimed that those idols were the daughters of God.

53:26. There will be no intercession on the day of judgment. See Appendix 7 for details.

41. Then he is fully repaid therefor.
42. And that to your Lord is the final destiny.
43. And that He is the one who makes you happy or miserable.
44. And that He is the one who controls death and life.
45. And that He is the one who created both kinds, male and female,
46. from a drop of semen.
47. And that He will effect the recreation.
48. And that He is the one who makes you rich or poor.
49. And that He is the Lord of the glowing star.
50. And that He is the one who annihilated ancient 'Aad.
51. Also Thamood; He wiped them out.
52. Before that, He annihilated Noah's people. They were more wicked and more sinning.
53. And He destroyed the sinners (of Sodom and Gomorrah).
54. They were completely overwhelmed.
55. Which of your Lord's marvels can you deny?
56. This is a warning like the previous warnings.
57. The inevitable has drawn near.
58. No one besides God can relieve it.
59. Are you wondering about this message?
60. Are you laughing, instead of crying?
61. Are you stubborn?
62. You shall fall prostrate before God, as you worship.

Sura 54: The Moon (Al-Qamar)

In the name of God, most gracious, most merciful

1. When the Hour approaches, the moon will split.*
2. Yet, whenever they see a sign, they turn away saying, "This is real magic."
3. They disbelieve and follow their own opinions and what they could physically sense.
4. They have received enough knowledge to set them straight.
5. Great wisdom (has come to them), but the warnings seem to be useless.
6. Therefore, leave them alone. The day will come when the caller calls them to something terrible.
7. Their eyes will be humbled as they come out of the graves, like swarms of locusts.
8. Obeying the caller, the disbelievers will say, "This is a difficult day."
9. Before them, the people of Noah have disbelieved. They disbelieved our servant and said, "Crazy." He was rejected.
10. He implored his Lord, "I have been humiliated; give me victory."
11. Whereupon, we opened the gates of the sky, pouring water.
12. Springs gushed out from the earth. The waters met according to predetermined judgment.
13. We carried him on (a craft) of wood and nails.
14. It ran under our watchful eyes, as a reward for the rejected messenger.
15. We set it up as a lesson; is there anyone who wishes to learn?
16. How (terrible) was My retribution and warnings?
17. We have made the Quran easy to remember; is there anyone who wishes to learn?*
18. 'Aad disbelieved; how (terrible) was My retribution and warnings?
19. We sent upon them violent wind, on a day of continuous misery.

54:1. *As frequently observed, the Quranic language is often in the past tense, indicating a prediction that is sure to come, or rather, an event that actually took place and was witnessed only by God, the only witness of our future. The storytellers, who were unfamiliar with the Quranic linguistics, invented numerous stories about a miracle performed by Muhammad, whereby he allegedly caused the moon to split. The flagrant contradictions among these stories testify to the false nature of "hadith." The most "reliable" book of hadith, namely Bukhari, reports two versions of the alleged miracle, one in Mecca and one in Mina. In another book of hadith, it is reported that one-half of the moon fell down and was found in the courtyard of Ali's house!!! The violation of the moon already took place by the landing of the humans in 1969. See also 44:10.*

54:17. *See Appendix 17.*

20. It tossed the people as if they were decaying palm trees.
21. How (terrible) was My retribution and warnings?
22. We have made the Quran easy to remember; is there anyone who wishes to learn?
23. Thamood rejected the warnings.
24. They said, "Shall we follow a man like us? We will then be wrong and stupid.
25. "Was he chosen out of all of us to receive the message? He is a flagrant liar."
26. They will find out tomorrow who the flagrant liar is.
27. We sent the camel as a test for them. Just watch them and be patient.
28. Tell them that the water shall be shared between them at specific times.
29. They consulted their leader, and after receiving the message, he slaughtered (the camel).
30. How (terrible) was My retribution and warnings.
31. We sent upon them one strike, whereupon they became like harvested hay.
32. We have made the Quran easy to remember; is there anyone who wishes to learn?
33. The people of Lot rejected the warnings.
34. We showered them with rocks, except Lot's family; we saved them at dawn.
35. That was a blessing from us. We thus reward the appreciative.
36. He had warned them of our strike, but they doubted the warnings.
37. They negotiated with him about his guests; we had blinded their eyes. They have deserved My retribution and warnings.
38. On the following morning, they were hit by devastating retribution.
39. They have deserved My retribution and warnings.
40. We have made the Quran easy to remember; is there anyone who wishes to learn?
41. Pharaoh's people received the warnings.
42. They rejected all our signs and, consequently, we punished them as an almighty, omnipotent can punish.
43. Are your disbelievers any better than those? Did you receive a pardon in the scriptures?
44. Do they say, "We will be victorious?"
45. Indeed, they will be defeated; they will flee.
46. The Hour awaits them. The Hour will be far worse and more devastating.
47. The guilty ones are in total loss and stupidity.
48. The day will come when they are dragged into the hellfire forcibly. They have deserved the agony of retribution.
49. We have created everything in exact measure.

50. Whatever we will is done within the blink of an eye.
51. We have destroyed your counterparts; is there anyone who wishes to learn?
52. Everything they did is recorded in the scriptures.
53. Everything, small or large, is written down.
54. The righteous have deserved gardens and streams.
55. They occupy an honorable position, at the omnipotent King.

Sura 55: Most Gracious (Al-Rahmaan)

In the name of God, most gracious, most merciful

1. God most gracious.
2. The one who teaches the Quran.*
3. The one who created the human being.
4. The one who taught him how to distinguish (right from wrong).
5. The sun and the moon created as timing devices.
6. The stars and the trees prostrate.
7. He raised the heaven and established the balance.
8. You shall not transgress when you weigh.
9. You shall be equitable when you weigh; do not cheat when you trade.
10. He made the earth for all the people.
11. With fruits and palms with sheaths.
12. With food grains and flowers.
13. Which of your Lord's marvels can you two deny?*
14. He created the human from clay like the potter's.
15. And created the jinns from blazing fire.
16. Which of your Lord's marvels can you two deny?
17. Lord of the two easts and the two wests.
18. Which of your Lord's marvels can you two deny?
19. He separates the fresh water from the salt water.
20. Between them is a barrier they cannot surmount.*
21. Which of your Lord's marvels can you two deny?
22. From the two seas, you extract pearls and coral.
23. Which of your Lord's marvels can you two deny?

55:2. *The Quran is a book unlike any other book; every aspect of it is surrounded by invisible forces. Our creator teaches us that the Quran is attainable exclusively by those who sincerely seek the knowledge therein. The insincere are hopelessly barred from getting one word correctly out of Quran (see 17:45-46, 18:57, and 56:79). In direct opposition to Quran, those who idolize the prophet claim that we need the "hadith" in order to teach us the Quran. This verse and others throughout the Quran clearly state that only God is the teacher of Quran (see 41:44 and 75:19). The inventors and followers of "hadith" are defying the Quran's consistent assertion that our source of religious knowledge shall be the Quran, the whole Quran, and nothing but the Quran. See Appendix 15.*

55:13. *This sura is specifically directed to the two kinds of creatures who possess the freedom of choice, namely the humans and the jinns.*

55:20. *See footnote 25:53.*

24. He controls the ships that roam the sea like flags.
25. Which of your Lord's marvels can you two deny?
26. Everyone on earth will perish.
27. Only the presence of your Lord will continue; He is the possessor of majesty and honor.
28. Which of your Lord's marvels can you two deny?
29. Everyone in the heavens and the earth implore Him. Everyday He is in full control.
30. Which of your Lord's marvels can you two deny?
3ŀ. We will deal with both of you, the two entities (humans and jinns).
32. Which of your Lord's marvels can you two deny?
33. O you jinns and humans, if you can penetrate the outer limits of the heavens and the earth, then penetrate. You can only penetrate when given authority.
34. Which of your Lord's marvels can you two deny?
35. You will be bombarded with masses of fire and molten metal, and you can never succeed.
36. Which of your Lord's marvels can you two deny?

The Day Of Resurrection*

37. When the sky is torn asunder and becomes like rosy paint.
38. Which of your Lord's marvels can you two deny?
39. On that day, neither a human nor a jinn will be asked about his sins.*
40. Which of your Lord's marvels can you two deny?

Hell

41. The guilty will be recognized by their looks;* they will be taken by the feet and forelocks.
42. Which of your Lord's marvels can you two deny?
43. This is the hell that the guilty used to deny.
44. They will circulate between hell and a terrible agony.*

55:37-78. See Appendix 10 for detailed descriptions.

55:39-41. There will be no need to ask anyone about his or her actions in this life. The righteous believers will appear strong and well developed, while the disbelievers will appear small, shrunk, and underdeveloped. See Appendix 10.

55:44. The inhabitants of hell are the farthest from God on the day of judgment. Knowing that heaven is close to God, they will leave hell and sneak into the area closer to God. But because they are not sufficiently prepared to come close to God (see 7:143), they will suffer terribly in the presence of God and will flee back to hell, and so on forever (see Appendix 10).

45. Which of your Lord's marvels can you two deny?

The Higher Heaven

46. For those who reverence the glory of their Lord, there will be two paradises.*
47. Which of your Lord's marvels can you two deny?
48. With abundant vegetation.
49. Which of your Lord's marvels can you two deny?
50. Two springs run freely therein.
51. Which of your Lord's marvels can you two deny?
52. They will have two kinds of every fruit.
53. Which of your Lord's marvels can you two deny?
54. They will relax on furnishings lined with silk, while the fruits of the two gardens are brought near.
55. Which of your Lord's marvels can you two deny?
56. They will have magnificent spouses therein; never before touched by any human or jinn.
57. Which of your Lord's marvels can you two deny?
58. They will look like gems and corals.
59. Which of your Lord's marvels can you two deny?
60. Is the reward of righteousness anything but the best blessings?
61. Which of your Lord's marvels can you two deny?

The Lower Heaven

62. Below these two gardens, there will be two lower gardens.*
63. Which of your Lord's marvels can you two deny?
64. Side by side.
65. Which of your Lord's marvels can you two deny?
66. There will be two wells to be pumped.
67. Which of your Lord's marvels can you two deny?
68. There will be fruits, date palms and pomegranate.
69. Which of your Lord's marvels can you two deny?

55:46. A paradise for the humans and a different paradise for the jinns.

55:62. There will be a high heaven, which is closest to God, and below it a lower heaven, then hell, which is the farthest from God. Note how the allegorical description of the high heaven is represented by "flowing" water, while the lower heaven's water needs pumping; the high heaven contains all kinds of fruits, while the lower heaven contains a limited number of fruits; the spouses in the high heaven are with the inhabitants, while those in the lower heaven have to go looking for spouses. See Appendices 4 and 10 for details, and sura 56.

70. There will be beautiful creatures therein.
71. Which of your Lord's marvels can you two deny?
72. Spouses that are kept in the tents.
73. Which of your Lord's marvels can you two deny?
74. Never did a human touch them before, nor a jinn.
75. Which of your Lord's marvels can you two deny?
76. They relax on green furnishings and beautiful carpets.
77. Which of your Lord's marvels can you two deny?
78. Most exalted is the name of your Lord; the possessor of all majesty and honor.

Sura 56: The Inevitable (Al-Waaqi'ah)

In the name of God, most gracious, most merciful

1. When the inevitable comes to pass.
2. No force can prevent it from coming.
3. It will lower (some people) and exalt (others).
4. The earth will be shaken up.
5. The mountains will disintegrate.
6. They will disappear into thin air.
7. You will be stratified into three classes.
8. The righteous people will be in good fortune.
9. And the wicked people will be in misery.

The High Heaven

10. And those who are far ahead will be far ahead.
11. They will be the closest (to God).
12. In the gardens of bliss.
13. Multitudes from the early generations.*
14. But only a few from the later generations.
15. On sturdy furnishings.
16. They will relax in rows facing each other.
17. Serving them will be immortal servants.
18. With cups, pitchers, and pure drinks.
19. They are never diverted therefrom nor deprived.
20. With fruits of their choice.
21. And meat of birds that they desire.
22. And magnificent spouses.
23. Like precious pearls.
24. This is the recompense for their works.
25. They will hear no vain talk therein, nor sins.
26. Only utterances of peace, peace.

The Lower Heaven

27. As for the inhabitants of the right side, they will be on the right side.

56:13.   *The early generations of muslims were characterized by following the Quran, the whole Quran, and nothing but the Quran. Two hundred fifty years after the prophet, "hadith" and "sunna" appeared, followed by the various schools of jurisprudence. This marked the progressive deterioration of the "Muslim" nation.*

28. They will enjoy lush orchards.
29. And fresh fruits.
30. And abundant shade.
31. And water to be poured.
32. And many fruits.
33. Always in season.
34. And exalted furnishings.
35. We raise spouses for them.
36. Never previously touched.
37. Magnificent companions.
38. Exclusively reserved for inhabitants of the right side.
39. Multitudes from the early generations.
40. And multitudes from the later generations.*

Hell

41. As for the inhabitants of the left, they will be on the left.
42. In ill winds and retribution.
43. In shade that actually burns.
44. Never cool, never tolerable.
45. They used to be spoiled.
46. They insisted on the great blasphemy.
47. They used to say, "After we die and become dust and bones, do we get resurrected?
48. "Even our early ancestors?"
49. Say, "The early generations and the late generations.
50. "Will be gathered together on a predetermined day.
51. "Then you, O strayers and disbelievers,
52. "will eat from the trees of bitterness.
53. "You will fill your bellies therefrom.
54. "Then you will top it with lava.
55. "You will ingest drinks of humiliation."
56. Such is their position on the day of judgment.
57. We created you; if you could only believe.
58. Do you see the semen you produce?
59. Is it you who create it, or are we the creators?*
60. We have designed death for you, and nothing can prevent us;
61. from substituting others in your place and establishing what you do not know.

56:40. *Because all the humans who die as children will be assigned to the lower heaven, the proportion from each generation is about the same.*

56:59. *See Appendix 9 for explanation of the plural tense.*

62. You know all about the first creation, if you could only remember.
63. Do you see what you plant?
64. Are you the ones who grow it, or are we?
65. If we will, we can turn it into useless hay, then you will complain:
66. "We have lost.
67. "We are deprived."
68. Do you see the water you drink?
69. Is it you who pour it down from the clouds, or is it we?
70. If we will, we can make it undrinkable. Would you then be thankful?
71. Do you see the fire you ignite?
72. Did you create its tree, or did we?
73. We made it a reminder, and to benefit those who travel.
74. You shall glorify the name of your Lord, the great.

The Honorable Quran

75. I swear by the positions of the stars.
76. And it is an awesome oath, if you only knew.
77. This is an honorable Quran.
78. In a perfectly preserved book.
79. None can touch it, except the righteous.*
80. It is a revelation from the Lord of the universe.
81. Are you then evading this message?
82. Do you make it your share that you reject it?
83. Your soul will reach your throat some day.
84. You will then look around.
85. We are closer to it (your throat) than you are, but you cannot see.
86. If you do have any power,
87. you should reclaim your soul, if you are truthful.
88. Thereafter, if he is one close to Me,
89. then happiness, flowers, and gardens of bliss.
90. And if he belongs with those on the right,
91. then peace to you, from those on the right.
92. But if he is one of the rejectors; the strayers,

56:79. *The Quran is by no means a regular book. Only the sincere seekers of the truth will be allowed to understand it (see 41:44). The insincere will be prevented from acquiring any knowledge from the Quran (see 17:46, 18:57, and Appendix 17). In fact, those who are prevented by God from learning the Quran claim that this verse means that no one can physically "touch" the Quran unless he satisfies certain ablution requirements. Obviously, this distortion is a clever satanic plot to prevent people from studying God's message to them. Our salvation is in reading, studying, and heeding the Quran.*

93.   then the abode of retribution.
94.   and burning hell.
95.   This is the inevitable truth.
96.   You shall glorify the name of your Lord, the great.

Sura 57: Iron (Al-Hadeed)

In the name of God, most gracious, most merciful

1. Glorifying God is everything in the heavens and the earth. He is the almighty, most wise.
2. To Him belongs the dominion of the heavens and the earth. He controls life and death. He is omnipotent.
3. He is the first and the last, the outermost and innermost. He is fully aware of all things.
4. He is the one who created the heavens and the earth in six days, then assumed all authority. He knows everything that enters the earth, and everything that comes out of it, and everything that descends from the sky and everything that ascends into it. He is with you wherever you may be. God is seer of everything you do.
5. To Him belongs the dominion of the heavens and the earth. God is in full control of all things.
6. He merges the night into the day and merges the day into the night. He is fully aware of the innermost thoughts.
7. You shall believe in God and His messenger, and spend from the bounties He entrusted to you. Those among you who believe and spend in charity have deserved a great recompense.
8. Why should you not believe in God, when the messenger invites you to believe in your Lord. He has taken a covenant from you,* if you are believers.
9. He is the one who reveals to His servant clear revelations, in order to take you out of the darkness into the light. God is compassionate towards you, merciful.
10. Why should you not spend in the cause of God, when God is the one who owns the heavens and the earth? Not equal to the rest are those who spend before the victory, and strive. They occupy higher ranks than those who spend after the victory, and strive. For both, God promises happiness. God is fully cognizant of everything you do.
11. Who would lend God a loan of righteousness, so that He multiples it for him and grants him a generous reward?
12. The day will come when you see the believing men and women with their light radiating in front of them and on their right. Rejoice today in gardens with flowing streams. They abide therein forever. This is the great triumph.

57:8. *See 7:172.*

13. On that day, the hypocrite men and women will say to those who believed, "Look towards us, that we may derive some of your light." They will be told, "Go back and seek some light elsewhere." A barrier will be placed between them, with a gate that separates mercy on one side from retribution on the other side.

14. They will call upon them, "Were we not with you?" They will say, "Yes indeed; but you cheated your souls, hestitated, harbored doubts, and became distracted by wishful thinking,* until God's judgment came. You were diverted from God by the deceivers.

15. "Today, no ransom is acceptable from you, nor from those who disbelieved. Your abode is hell; it is now your ally and your miserable destiny."

16. Is it not time for the believers to wholeheartedly submit to this message of God and the truth that He revealed herein?* Do not be like those who received previous scriptures, then their hearts became hardened by the passage of time; many of them are wicked.

17. Know that God is the one who revives the land after it had died. We explain the revelations for you, that you may understand.

18. The charitable men and women, who have loaned God a loan of righteousness, will be paid manyfold; they receive a generous recompense.

19. Those who believed in God and His messengers are the truthful ones. Together with the martyrs, they receive their recompense and their light from their Lord. As for those who disbelieved and rejected our revelations, they have deserved hell.

20. Know that this life is temporary play, waste, vanity, boasting among yourselves, and hoarding of monies and children. It is like rain that produces plants that please the disbelievers, then grow and turn yellow, then blow away as hay. In the hereafter, there will be either terrible retribution, or forgiveness from God and pleasure. This life is no more than a temporary illusion.

---

*57:14.   One example of such wishful thinking is found in the blasphemy against the prophet called "**hadith**." The advocates of "hadith" entertain the idea that by simply uttering, "There is no god except God," one is guaranteed salvation. See 10:90.*

57:16.   It takes time and effort for the believers to reach total submission and complete acceptance of Quran. This is manifested in the fact that the majority of Muslims at any given time do not accept the fact that all they need is the Quran, the whole Quran, and nothing but the Quran.

21. You shall compete in attaining forgiveness from your Lord and a paradise whose width encompasses the heaven and the earth; it awaits those who believe in God and His messengers. This is God's grace that He bestows upon whomever He wills; God possesses unlimited grace.

Profound Fact*

22. Anything that happens on earth, or to you, is already recorded in a record before the creation. This is easy for God.

23. Knowing this, you should not grieve over anything you miss, nor should you be proud of anything you attain. God does not love any arrogant show-off,

24. who is stingy and exhorts the people to be stingy. If anyone turns away, then God is in no need; worthy of all praise.

25. We have sent our messengers with clear revelations, and we sent down with them the scripture and the law, to spread justice among the people. We also sent down the iron, wherein there is great strength and many benefits for the people. All this, to distinguish those who support God and His messengers in good faith. God is most powerful, almighty.

26. We sent Noah and Abraham and entrusted their descendants with prophethood and the scripture; some of them are guided, while the majority are wicked.

27. Subsequent to them, we sent other messengers, then we sent Jesus, the son of Mary. We gave him the Injeel (Gospel), and we placed in the hearts of his followers kindness and mercy. As for the hermitism that they invented, it was never decreed for them. They were only asked to uphold God's commandments, but they did not uphold the commandments as they should. Consequently, while we will grant the believers among them their due recompense, the majority are wicked.

28. O you who believe, you shall observe God and believe in His messenger; He will then double His mercy upon you, grant you a light with which you advance, and forgive you. God is forgiver, merciful.*

29. The followers of previous scriptures shall realize that they do not monopolize God's grace and that all grace is in God's hand; He bestows it upon whomever He wills. God possesses unlimited grace.

57:22. *Each one of us has the video tape of his or her life, from birth to death, already recorded before birth. What, then, is the purpose of our existence? Do we have any choice? For the answers, see Appendices 6 and 12.*

57:28. *This verse teaches us that the Christians and Jews who reach a conviction to believe, honor, and heed this divine message will receive double the reward; a special blessing.*

Sura 58: The Debate (Al-Majaadalah)

In the name of God, most gracious, most merciful

1. God has heard the woman who debated with you about her husband and complained to God. God heard your discussion; God is hearer, seer.

2. Those among you who estrange their wives, as if they were their mothers, are doing wrong. They should not be treated as if they were their mothers. Their mothers are only those who gave birth to them. Indeed, they utter evil and a falsehood.* God is pardoner, forgiver.

3. Those who estrange their wives in this manner, then reconcile, shall expiate by freeing a slave before they resume intercourse. This is to admonish you. God is cognizant of everything you do.

4. If you cannot find a slave to free, then you shall fast two consecutive months before resuming intercourse, and those unable to fast shall feed sixty poor persons. This is for you to believe in God and His messenger. These are God's laws; and the rejectors have deserved painful retribution.

5. Those who oppose God and His messenger are doomed like those before them who were doomed. We have revealed clear revelations, and the disbelievers therein have deserved painful retribution.

6. The day will come when God resurrects them, then informs them of everything they had done. God has recorded it, while they forgot. God witnesses all things.

7. Do you not realize that God knows everything in the heavens and the earth? No three people can meet in secrecy without Him being the fourth, nor five without Him being the sixth, nor less than this, nor more, without Him being there. Then, on the day of resurrection, He will inform them of everything they did. God is fully aware of all things.

8. Those who are prohibited from conspiracy, then go back to it, conspiring sinfully, maliciously, and in defiance of the messenger; and when they come to you, they greet you not with God's greeting, and say to themselves, "Let us see if God will punish us for what we say;" their only destiny is hell wherein they burn; what a miserable destiny!

9. O you who believe, if you have to confer secretly, you shall not confer to commit sin, transgression, and disobedience to the messenger. You may confer only to work righteousness and piety. Beware of God, for you will be gathered before Him.

58:2. A common statement by Arabian husbands who wanted to punish their wives was, "You are as forbidden to me in intercourse as my mother."

10. Conspiracy is from the devil, only causing problems to those who believe; though he cannot harm them against the will of God. In God the believers shall trust.

11. O you who believe, if you are asked to make room for others to sit down with you, you shall make room, that God may make room for you. If you are asked to leave, you shall leave. God raises those among you who believe and those who attain knowledge to higher ranks. God is fully cognizant of everything you do.

12. O you who believe, if you wish to confer with the messenger, you shall give away a charity before you confer with him. This is better for you and more purifying. If you cannot afford it, then God is forgiver, merciful.

13. If you had failed to give to charity before your conference and you repented thereafter, then you shall observe the **salat** prayers and **zakat** charity and obey God and His messenger. God is cognizant of everything you do.

14. There are those who ally themselves with people who have angered God; they neither belong with you, nor with them; and they deliberately swear lies.

15. God has prepared for them severe retribution. Evil indeed is what they did.

16. They use their oaths as a cover to repel others from the path of God. Consequently, they have deserved humiliating retribution.

17. Never will their monies or children help them against God. They have deserved hell; wherein they abide forever.

18. On the day when God resurrects them, they will swear to Him, just as they swear to you, and they will think they have some basis. Indeed, they are liars.*

19. The devil possessed them and persuaded them to neglect God's message. These are the party of the devil, and the party of the devil are losers.

20. Those who oppose God and His messenger are the lowliest.

21. God has decreed, "I, and My messengers, will always win." God is powerful, almighty.

58:18.   *The majority of believers are only lip-service believers (see 12:106). Their hearts do not believe, and they do not even know it (see 16:22). In order to show us whether we are true believers or false believers, God allowed the invention of "**hadith**" and "**sunna**" to serve as a test. Thus, the true believers will obey God and His messenger and accept the Quran only as their source of religious instruction, while the false believers will be attracted to "**hadith**" and "**sunna**" as additional sources (see 6:112-116). These false believers swear now, and all the way through the day of judgment, that they are believers (see 6:21-23).*

Run For Your Life

22. You will not find people who believe in God and the last day befriending
     those who oppose God and His messenger, even if they were their own
     parents, or children, or siblings, or family. God places faith into their
     hearts, as He supports them with inspiration. He will admit them into
     gardens with flowing streams, wherein they abide forever. God is pleased
     with them, and they are pleased with Him. These are the party of God,
     and the party of God are winners.

Sura 59: Exodus (Al-Hashr)

In the name of God, most gracious, most merciful

1. Glorifying God is everything in the heavens and the earth; He is the almighty, most wise.
2. He is the one who banished the disbelievers among the followers of previous scripture in mass exodus. You never expected them to leave, and they thought that their castles could protect them from God. But God came to them whence they never expected and threw terror into their hearts. Thus, they deserted their homes on their own accord. You shall learn from this, O you who possess vision.
3. Even if God did not decree exodus for them, He would have punished them in this life anyway. Additionally, they have deserved the retribution of hell.
4. This is because they opposed God and His messenger. For anyone who opposes God, God is strict in imposing punishment.
5. Whatever you tear down or leave standing during war is in accordance with God's will. He thus defeats the wicked.
6. Any spoils of war that God bestows upon His messenger, it is not your horses or equipment that earned them. God is the one who sends His angels against whomever He wills; God is omnipotent.
7. The spoils of war that God bestows upon His messenger from the banished inhabitants of the town shall go to God and the messenger, in the form of charity to the relatives, the needy, and the alien. In this way, it will not be monopolized by the rich among you. Any gained spoils that the messenger gives you, you shall accept, and whatever he forbids you, you shall leave. Beware of God; God is strict in imposing punishment.*
8. The spoils shall also go to the poor immigrants who were evicted from their homes and deprived of their properties in seeking God's grace and pleasure and supporting God and His messenger. These are the truthful.

59:7. The ignorant who idolize the prophet abuse this verse more than any other verse in Quran. Although we are enjoined throughout the Quran to obey God and the prophet, these ignorant people use this verse out of context to say, "Any instructions attributed to the messenger you shall follow, and whatever he forbids you, you shall leave." All it takes is to read the verse in order to realize that they take it out of context. But this is God's way to expose their ignorance. Ironically, they are the first to disobey the prophet by accepting other than the Quran as their source of law. See Appendix 11.

9. And those who had established their homes and their faith previously readily welcome the immigrants who come to them. They find no hesitation in their hearts to give them what they need. They even prefer them over themselves, even though they themselves may be in need. Anyone who is spared the stingy nature of himself, these are the winners.

10. As for the immigrants who came later to Islam, they say, "Our Lord, forgive us and forgive those who preceded us to Islam. Remove from our hearts any hatred towards the believers. Our Lord, you are compassionate, most merciful."

11. The hypocrites said to their allies who disbelieved among the followers of previous scripture, "If you are banished, we will go with you; we will not obey anyone against you; if you are fought against, we will support you." God bears witness that they are liars.

12. If they do get banished, they will not go with them, and if they are fought against, they will not support them. Even if they supported them, they will turn around and flee; they will never attain victory.

13. Indeed, they fear you a lot more than they fear God. This is because they do not comprehend.

14. They will not fight you together unless protected in formidable castles or behind walls. Their power among themselves seems impressive, and you would think they are united. But in their hearts they are divided. This is because they do not understand.

15. Just like those before them, they will suffer the consequences of their work; they have deserved painful retribution.

16. They are like the devil who says to the human being, "Disbelieve." Then, when he disbelieves, he says, "I have nothing to do with you; I fear God, Lord of the universe."

17. The consequence for both of them is eternal hell. This is the requital for the wicked.

18. O you who believe, beware of God, and let each of you examine what he or she has advanced for the coming day. You shall observe God, for God is cognizant of everything you do.

19. Do not be like those who forgot God, so He made them forget their own souls. These are the wicked.

20. Not equal are those who have deserved hell and those who have deserved heaven. Those who have deserved heaven are the winners.

Awesomeness Of Quran

21. If we revealed this Quran to a mountain, you will see it trembling, crumbling, out of reverence for God. We cite these examples for the people, that they may reflect.

22. He is the one God; there is no god except He, the knower of secrets and declarations; He is the most gracious, most merciful.

23. He is the one God; there is no god except He, the king, the sacred, the peace, the faithful, the supreme, the almighty, the powerful, the dignified. God be glorified, over and above anything they idolize.

24. He is the one God, the creator, the initiator, the designer; to Him belong the most beautiful names. Glorifying Him is everything in the heavens and the earth; He is the almighty, the wise.

Sura 60: The Tested Woman (Al-Mumtaḥanah)

In the name of God, most gracious, most merciful

1. O you who believe, do not take My enemies and your enemies as allies, offering them friendship when they have disbelieved in the truth that came to you. They persecute the messenger and you, only because you believe in God, your Lord, and strive for My sake and My pleasure. If you secretly befriend them, I am fully aware of everything you conceal and everything you declare. If any of you does this, he has strayed off the right path.

2. Whenever they encounter you, they reveal their enmity and hurt you with their hands and their tongues, and want you to disbelieve.

3. Your relatives and your children can never help you. The day of resurrection will keep you apart. God is seer of everything you do.

4. A good example* has been set for you by Abraham and those with him. They said to their people, "We disown you and the idols you set up besides God. We reject you, and you will see from us nothing but enmity and opposition, until you believe in God alone." The only exception was Abraham's utterance to his father, "I will ask forgiveness for you, but I have no power to protect you from God." Our Lord, we trust in You; we submit to You; to You is the final destiny.

5. "Our Lord, protect us from persecution by those who disbelieve; and forgive us, our Lord; You are the almighty, most wise."

6. A good example* has been set for you by them; this is for anyone who seeks God and the last day. If anyone turns away, then God is in no need; He is worthy of all praise.

7. God may substitute friendship between you and your enemies in place of animosity. God is omnipotent; God is forgiver, merciful.

60:4 & 6. *The reader should note that the Arabic words that describe Abraham here as a "good example" (Uswah Hasanah) are exactly the same words used to describe Muhammad in 33:21. Because of the ignorance of the idol worshipers who have set up the prophet as an idol against his will, they are not aware of this verse. The Quran teaches us that Abraham is the source of all religious practices in Islam (see Appendix 8). Similarly, they remember verse 33:56 and forget verse 33:43.*

Fight Only The Aggressors

8. God does not forbid you from befriending those who did not fight you because of religion and did not banish you from your homes. You shall befriend them and be equitable towards them. God loves the equitable.

9. God enjoins you from befriending those who fought you because of religion, banished you from your homes, and banded together in order to banish you. You shall not befriend them, for those who befriend them are wicked.

10. O you who believe, if believing women come to you seeking refuge from the disbelievers, you shall test them. God is fully aware of their faith. If you find that they are sincere believers, then you shall not return them to the disbelievers; they are not lawful for them in marriage; nor is it lawful for the pagan men to marry them. You shall pay back to the disbelievers whatever dowry they had paid. You commit no error by marrying them, provided you give them their due dowry.* Do not stay married to disbelieving women; you may ask for the dowry you had paid them, and they may ask for whatever they spent. This is God's law to judge between you. God is omniscient, most wise.

11. If any of your women forsake you and join the disbelievers, then you may ask for compensation, and compensate the forsaken husbands for whatever they spent. You shall observe God, in whom you believe.

12. O you prophet, when the believing women come to you vowing that they will never set up idols besides God, nor steal, nor commit adultery, nor kill their children, nor invent any falsehood, nor disobey any of your righteous orders, then you shall accept their vow, and ask God to forgive them. God is forgiver, merciful.

13. O you who believe, do not befriend people with whom God is angry. They are hopelessly doomed in the hereafter, like disbelievers who are already in the grave.

60:10. See verse 4:24.

Sura 61: The Column (Al-Ṣaff)

In the name of God, most gracious, most merciful

1. Glorifying God is everything in the heavens and the earth; He is the almighty, most wise.
2. O you who believe, why do you utter what you do not do yourselves?
3. Most abominable in the sight of God is uttering what you do not do.
4. God loves those who strive in His cause united as one column, like the bricks in one wall.
5. Moses said to his people, "O my people, why do you insult me, even though you know that I am God's messenger to you?" As a consequence of their disunity, God disunited their hearts. God never guides the wicked people.
6. Jesus, the son of Mary, said, "O children of Israel, I am God's messenger to you, confirming the Torah and predicting that a messenger will come after me whose name is highly praised." Now that he has come to them with profound revelations, they said, "This is obviously magic."
7. Who is more evil than one who invents lies about God, while being invited to Islam? God does not guide the wicked.
8. They wish to extinguish God's light with their mouths. But God insists upon completing His light, in spite of the disbelievers.
9. He is the one who sent His messenger with the guidance and the religion of truth to make it prevail over all religions, despite the idol worshipers.

The Most Profitable Trade

10. O you who believe, let me inform you of a trade that saves you from painful retribution.
11. You shall believe in God and His messenger, and struggle in the cause of God with your properties and your lives. This is the best for you, if you only knew.
12. In return, He will forgive your sins and admit you into gardens with flowing streams and good homes in the gardens of Eden. This is the great triumph.
13. In addition, you attain something else you love; support from God and immediate victory. Congratulate the believers.
14. O you who believe, be supporters of God like the disciples of Jesus, son of Mary. When he said to them, "Who are my supporters towards God?" the disciples said, "We are God's supporters." Thus, some of the children of Israel believed, and some disbelieved. We supported those who believed against their enemies, until they became victorious.

Sura 62: Friday (Al-Jumu'ah)

In the name of God, most gracious, most merciful

1. Glorifying God is everything in the heavens and the earth; He is the king, the sacred, the almighty, the most wise.

2. He is the one who raised among the gentiles a messenger to recite His revelations for them, sanctify them, and teach them the scripture and wisdom. Before this, they had gone astray.

3. Others among them refused to join. He is the almighty, the wise.

4. This is God's grace; He bestows it upon whomever He wills. God possesses unlimited grace.

5. The example of those who were given the Torah, then failed to study it, is that of a donkey carrying great works of literature. Miserable indeed is the example of those who reject God's revelations.* God never guides the wicked people.

6. Say, "O you who are Jewish, if you claim that you are God's chosen, to the exclusion of all other people, then you should long for death; if you are truthful."

7. They never long for it, because of what their hands have committed. God is fully aware of the wicked.

8. Say, "The death that you flee from will inevitably catch up with you. Then you will be turned over to the knower of all secrets and declarations; He will inform you of everything you did.

Friday Prayer Decreed

9. O you who believe, when the **salat** prayer is announced on Friday, you shall hasten to the commemoration of God, and leave all business. This is better for you, if you only knew.*

10. Once the **salat** prayer is finished, you shall spread through the land, seek God's bounties, and continue to commemorate God frequently, that you may succeed.

11. Yet, when they see business or entertainment, they rush to it and leave you standing. Say, "What God possesses is far better than the entertainment and the business; God is the best provider."

62:5. *Those who are given the Quran, then turn to any other sources for religious guidance, reject God's assertion that the Quran is complete and perfect (see 6:19, 38, 114, and Appendix 15). This example is here to serve a specific purpose; the Jews abandoned the Torah and invented the Talmud, while the Muslims abandoned the Quran and invented the "**hadith**."*

62:9. *The commandment is directed to all the believers, and not only the men as claimed by the blasphemous inventions known as **Hadith**.*

Sura 63: The Hypocrites (Al-Munaafiqoon)

In the name of God, most gracious, most merciful

1. The hypocrites come to you and say, "We bear witness that you are the messenger of God." God knows that you are His messenger, and God bears witness that the hypocrites are liars.*
2. They use their oaths to deceive and to repel others from the path of God. Evil indeed is what they do.
3. They have believed, then disbelieved. Consequently, their hearts were sealed and, consequently, they cannot understand.
4. When you see them, you may be impressed by their appearance; and when they speak, you hear their voice. But they are like wooden logs. They think that every cry is intended against them. Beware of them. God curses them, for they have deviated.
5. When they are told, "Come, let the messenger of God ask forgiveness for you," they turn their heads away, repulsed by their arrogance.
6. Whether you ask forgiveness for them or do not ask forgiveness for them, God will not forgive them. God does not guide the wicked people.
7. They are the ones who say, "Do not give any charity to those who follow the messenger of God, that they may abandon him." To God belongs the treasures of the heavens and the earth, but the hypocrites do not understand.
8. They say, "If we return to the city, the powerful will displace the weak therefrom." All dignity and power belong to God, and to His messenger and the believers; but the hypocrites do not know.

Do Not Be Distracted By Business And/Or Family

9. O you who believe, do not be distracted by your business and your children from the commemoration of God. Those who do this are losers.
10. And spend (in charity) from what we provided for you, before death comes to the one of you and then say, "My Lord, if you postpone this for a short while, I will be charitable and righteous."
11. God never postpones the end for any soul, once the predetermined time has come. God is cognizant of everything you do.

63:1. *Even though the hypocrites are uttering a truth, God calls them liars. This teaches us that we must reject all the fabrications attributed to the prophet under the name of "hadith," even if such "hadith" narrates a truth. The fabrication of "good hadith," is the bait that Satan uses to cover a deadly hook (see 6:112-116 and Appendices 11, 15, and 16).*

Sura 64:   Mutual Blaming (Al-Taghaabun)

In the name of God, most gracious, most merciful

1. Glorifying God is everything in the heavens and the earth; to Him belongs all kingship; to Him belongs all praise; He is omnipotent.
2. He is the one who created you, yet some of you disbelieve and some believe. God is seer of everything you do.
3. He created the heavens and the earth, truthfully, and He designed you in perfect design. To Him is the final destiny.
4. He knows everything in the heavens and the earth; He knows everything you conceal and everything you declare. God is fully aware of the innermost thoughts.
5. Did you not receive the history of those who disbelieved in the past? They suffered the consequences of their decision and deserved painful retribution.
6. This is because their messengers went to them with clear revelations, but they said, "Human beings to guide us?" Thus, they disbelieved and turned away. God does not need them; God is in no need, worthy of all praise.
7. The disbelievers claim that they will not be raised. Say, "Yes indeed, by my Lord, you will be resurrected and informed of everything you had done." This is easy for God.
8. Therefore, you shall believe in God and His messenger, and the light that we sent down (Quran). God is cognizant of everything you do.

The Day of Mutual Blaming

9. The day will come when He gathers you on the day of gathering; that is the day of mutual blaming. Anyone who believes in God and works righteousness, God will remit his sins and admit him into gardens with flowing streams; they abide therein forever. This is the great triumph.
10. As for those who disbelieved and rejected our revelations, they have deserved hell as their abode. What a miserable destiny!
11. No disaster strikes except in accordance with God's will. Anyone who believes, God will guide his heart. God is fully aware of all things.
12. You shall obey God and obey the messenger.* If you turn away, then our messenger's only duty is to deliver (the message).

64:12.   *The enemies of the prophet took advantage of this commandment and flagrantly abused it (see 6:112 and 25:30-31). Thus, they invented a whole set of religious teachings that suit their traditions and desires and attributed them to the prophet, then demanded that everyone follow them instead of, or besides, the Quran (see Appendices 11, 15, and 16).*

13. God; there is no god except He; in God the believers shall trust.

Your Monies And Families Are A Test

14. O you who believe, your spouses and your children could be enemies of yours; beware of them. If you pardon, forget, and forgive, then God is forgiver, merciful.

15. Your monies and children constitute a test, and God possesses a great recompense.

16. Therefore, you shall observe righteousness towards God as much as you can. You shall hearken, obey, and spend (in charity) for your own good. Those who overcome their natural stinginess are the winners.

17. If you lend God a loan of righteousness, He will multiply it for you manyfold and forgive you. God is appreciative, clement.

18. He is the knower of secrets and declarations; the almighty, the wise.

Sura 65:   Divorce (Al-Talaaq)

In the name of God, most gracious, most merciful

1. O prophet, when you divorce the women, you shall observe their divorce interim, and count the interim.* Beware of God, your Lord, and do not evict them from their homes, nor shall they leave on their accord (during the interim), unless they commit a proven adultery. These are God's laws. Anyone who transgresses God's laws commits injustice against his own self. You never know, God may allow certain things to happen.

2. Once they fulfill their interim, then you may allow them to stay in your household amicably,* or let them depart amicably. You shall have two equitable witnesses among you witness the divorce agreement, and monitor such agreement as witnessed. This shall be heeded by those who truly believe in God and the last day. Whoever observes righteousness towards God, He will create an exit for him,

3. and provide for him whence he never expects. Anyone who trusts in God, God will suffice him. God always carries out His decisions. God has laid down the plans for everything.

4. As for the women who have reached menopause, if you have any doubts, their interim shall be three months. As for those who do not menstruate because of pregnancy, their interim lasts until they give birth. Whoever observes righteousness towards God, God will make everything easy for him.

5. This is God's command that He sent down to you. Anyone who reverences God, God will remit his sins and multiply his recompense.

6. You shall continue to provide the same housing for the divorcees as you would provide for yourselves. You shall not harass them by reducing their housing privileges. If they are pregnant, you shall provide for them until they give birth. If they nurse the infant for you, you shall pay them. You shall maintain the amicable relations among you. If you disagree, you may hire a nursing mother.

7. The rich shall spend from his bounties, and the poor shall spend in accordance with what God has given him. God never burdens anyone beyond what He has given him. God may substitute wealth in place of poverty

---

65:1.   The divorce interim is three menstruations. Thereafter, the divorcee may remarry (see 2:228).

65:2.   A divorcee may choose to stay within the ex-husband's household to take care of her children, or because she has no other place to go.

You Shall Heed God's Law

8. Many a community rebelled against God's law and against His messengers. Consequently, we held them strictly responsible and afflicted them with a terrible retribution.

9. Thus, they suffered the consequences of their decision, and their final end was disasterous.

10. God has prepared for them severe retribution. Therefore, you shall observe righteousness, O you who showed intelligence and believed. God has sent this message for you.

11. He has sent a messenger to recite for you God's profound revelations. Thereby, He leads those who believe and work righteousness out of the darkness into the light. Anyone who believes in God and works righteousness, God will admit him into gardens with flowing streams. They abide therein forever. God showers him with the best blessings.

12. God is the one who created seven heavens and the same of the earth. The decisions flow between them. You shall know that God is omnipotent and that He is fully aware of all things.

Sura 66: Prohibition (Al-Tahreem)

In the name of God, most gracious most merciful

1. O prophet, why do you prohibit what God had permitted for you, just to please your wives? God is forgiver, merciful.
2. God has decreed for you the laws dealing with your oaths. God is your Lord; He is the omniscient, most wise.
3. The prophet entrusted some of his wives with a secret, but one of them divulged it, and God informed the prophet thereof. He then told her part of the information, and disregarded part. She said, "Who informed you?" He said, "I was informed by the knower, the cognizant."
4. If the two of you repent to God, then your hearts have hearkened; but if you band together against the prophet, then God is his ally, and so is Gabriel, and the righteous believers; even the angels are his allies.
5. If he divorces you, then his Lord may substitute wives who are better than you; muslims, faithful, obedient, repentant, worshipping, devoted, be they virgin or previously married.
6. O you who believe, spare yourselves and your families the hellfire, whose fuel is people and rocks. Guarding it are angels who are stern and powerful. They never disobey any order from God; they do whatever they are commanded to do.
7. O you who disbelieve, do not apologize today. You are punished only for what you did.
8. O you who believe, repent to God a sincere repentance. Your Lord will then remit your sins and admit you into gardens with flowing streams. The day will come when God will not forsake the prophet and those who believed with him. Their light will flow ahead of them and to their right. They will say, "Our Lord, perfect our light for us, and forgive us; You are omnipotent."
9. O prophet, strive against the disbelievers and the hypocrites, and be stern against them. Their abode is hell; what a miserable destiny!

Spouses May Disagree

10. God cites as examples of disbelievers the wife of Noah and the wife of Lot. They were under two of our righteous servants, but they betrayed them. Consequently, they could not protect their wives at all from God. The wives were told, "Enter the hellfire along with the others."

11. And God cites as an example of the believers the wife of Pharaoh. She said, "My Lord, build an abode for me in paradise, and save me from Pharaoh and his evil work; save me from the wicked people."

12. Also Mary, the daughter of Imran; she guarded her chastity, so we blew into her from our spirit. She upheld the commandments of her Lord and His scriptures, and she was obedient.

Sura 67:   Kingship (Al-Mulk)

In the name of God, most gracious, most merciful

1.   Most exalted is the one who possesses all kingship; He is omnipotent.

The Sole Purpose Of Creation*

2.   He is the one who created death and life, in order to test you and distinguish the righteous among you; He is the almighty, the forgiver.

3.   He is the one who created seven heavens in layers. You never see a flaw in the creation of God most gracious. Keep looking; do you see any flaw?

4.   Then look again and again; your eyes will come back stumped and conquered.

5.   We have adorned the lowest heaven with lamps,* and we placed projectiles therein to shoot the devils; we prepared for them the retribution of burning.

6.   Those who disbelieve in their Lord will suffer the retribution of hell; a miserable destiny.

7.   When they are thrown therein, they will hear its furor as it fumes.

8.   It almost explodes from rage; whenever a group is thrown therein, the guardians will ask them, "Did you not receive a warner?"

9.   They will say, "Yes indeed, a warner had come to us, but we disbelieved and said, 'God did not reveal anything. You are totally astray.' "

10.   They also said, "Had we hearkened or understood, we would not have deserved hell."

11.   They will thus confess their sins; woe to those who have deserved hell.

12.   Those who reverence their Lord in their privacy have deserved forgiveness and a great recompense.

13.   Whether you conceal your utterances or declare them, God is fully aware of the innermost thoughts.

14.   Should He not know, since He is the one who created? He is the benign, the cognizant.

15.   He is the one who subdued the earth for you. Roam its corners and eat from His provisions. Before Him you will be ultimately gathered.

16.   Did you guarantee that the one in heaven will not cause the earth to crush you as it quakes?

17.   Did you guarantee that the one in heaven will not send violent wind upon you? Is this not sufficient warning?

67:2.   See Appendix 6

67:5.   See Appendix 5.

18. Others before them have disbelieved; how terrible was My retribution!

19. Do they not see the birds flying above them, none can stop them except God most gracious? He is the seer of all things.

20. Where are those soldiers who can support you against God most gracious? The disbelievers are really deceived.

21. Where are those who can provide for you, if God withheld His provisions? Indeed, they have plunged deep into transgression and aversion.

22. Is one who walks forcibly humiliated better guided; or one who walks straight on the right path?

23. Say, "He is the one who initiated you and gave you the hearing, the eyes, and the brains; rarely are you appreciative."

24. Say, "He is the one who spread you through the earth, and before Him you will be gathered."

25. They say, "When will this promise come to pass, if you are truthful?"

26. Say, "The knowledge thereof is only with God. I am no more than a warner."

27. When they see it coming, the faces of those who disbelieved will be miserable. They will be told, "This is what you asked for."

28. Say, "What if God decided to destroy me and those who follow me, or to have mercy on us, who is there to protect the disbelievers from painful retribution?"

29. Say, "He is God most gracious; we believe in Him, and trust in Him. You will find out which of us is really wrong."

30. Say, "What if your water sinks deeper and deeper; who can bring you fresh water?"

Sura 68: The Pen (Al-Qalam)

In the name of God, most gracious, most merciful

1. N,* and the pen, and everything they write.
2. You (Muhammad) are not unappreciative of your Lord's blessings.
3. And you will receive a well deserved recompense.
4. And you are endowed with a great character.
5. You will see, and they will see,
6. which of you is deceived.
7. Your Lord is fully aware who is straying off His path and who is guided.
8. You shall not obey the rejectors.
9. They wish that you deviate, so they can deviate.
10. Nor shall you obey any lowly swearer.
11. Who backbites and creates discord among the people.
12. A forbidder of charity; a transgressor, a sinner.
13. Besides all this, he is greedy and unappreciative.
14. Despite the blessings of money and children,
15. when our revelations are recited to him, he says, "Tales from the past."
16. We will brand him on the nose.
17. We have put them to the test, the same as the owners of the garden who swore with certainty that they will harvest the next morning.
18. They had no doubts.
19. However, a tornado from your Lord wiped it out while they slept.
20. By morning, it was like empty sticks.
21. When they got up, they called on each other;
22. to go harvest their crop.
23. As they went, they thought,
24. "None of us will be poor as of today."
25. They were so sure.
26. But when they saw it, they said "We were wrong.
27. "We have been deprived."
28. The most righteous among them said, "Did I not tell you to worship?"
29. They said, "Glory be to our Lord. We were really wrong."
30. They started to blame each other.
31. They said, "Woe to us, we were transgressors."
32. "Maybe our Lord will give us a better one. We now turn to our Lord."

68:1. *This is the only N-initialed sura. This letter occurs in this sura 133 times, or 19 x 7. See Appendix 1 for details of the Arabic test of the Quran's miraculous numerical code.*

33.   Such was their punishment; and the retribution of the hereafter is far worse, if they only knew.

34.   The righteous have deserved the gardens of bliss at the Lord.

35.   Shall we treat the submitters like the guilty?

36.   What is wrong with you? How do you judge?

37.   Do you have another book that you apply?

38.   One that gives you anything you want?*

39.   Did you take certain pledges from us to be fulfilled on the day of resurrection? This is your wishful thinking.

40.   Ask them who guarantees anything for them.

41.   Do they have idols (who will help them)? Let them call their idols, if they are truthful.

42.   The day will come when everything will be exposed; they will be required to fall prostrate, but they will be unable.

43.   Their eyes will be humbled and disgrace will envelope them. They had been asked to fall prostrate when they were able.

44.   Let Me deal with the rejectors of this **hadith** (narration); we will lead them on without them ever realizing it.

45.   I encourage them and lead them on. My scheme is formidable.

46.   Are you asking them for a wage that burdens them?

47.   Do they know the future and manipulate it?

48.   You shall be steadfast in upholding your Lord's commandments, and do not be like the one who called from confinement inside the fish (Jonah).

49.   If it were not for a blessing from his Lord, he would have been ejected into the wilderness.

50.   But his Lord redeemed him and counted him with the righteous.

51.   Those who disbelieve show their ridicule when they look at you. As they hear the message, they say, "He is really crazy."

52.   Though it is truly a message for all the people.

68:38. Those who blasphemed against the prophet by inventing "hadith," can find anything they want in "hadith." They strongly defend and uphold "hadith" because it conveniently fits their traditions and personal desires.

Sura 69:   The Reality (Al-Ḥaaqqah)

In the name of God, most gracious, most merciful

1. The reality.
2. What a reality!
3. Do you have any idea what the reality is?
4. Thamood and 'Aad disbelieved in the shocker.
5. As for Thamood, they were destroyed by the overwhelming (quake).
6. While 'Aad were destroyed by violent, miserable wind.
7. God sent it upon them for seven nights and eight days, ceaselessly. You could see the people tossed around like decaying palm trunks.
8. Can you find any trace of them?
9. Pharaoh, others before him, and the communities (of Sodom and Gomorrah) committed evil.
10. They disobeyed the messenger of their Lord. Consequently, God afflicted them with a devastating retribution.
11. When the flood water rose, we carried you in the ark.
12. We made it a lesson for you, and every alert ear will hearken.

The Day Of Resurrection

13. When the horn is blown once.
14. And the earth and the mountains are carried off and crushed in one blow.
15. That is when the inevitable day will come to pass.
16. The heaven will shatter into fragments.
17. The angels will be all around. Above them, eight will carry the throne of your Lord.
18. On that day, you will be exposed; nothing will be hidden.
19. As for the one who receives his record in his right hand, he will say, "Here is my record; read it.
20. "I expected to be held accountable."
21. He has deserved a happy life.
22. In an exalted garden.
23. Where the fruits are within reach.
24. Eat and drink happily because of your works in the past days.
25. As for the one who receives his record in the left hand, he will say, "I wish I never received my record;
26. "I wish I never found out.
27. "I wish my death was permanent.
28. "My money cannot help me now.
29. "All my power is gone."

30. Take him and tie him up.
31. Then burn him in hell.
32. Then in a chain that is seventy arms long, wrap him up.
33. He refused to believe in God, the great.
34. He did not advocate feeding the poor.
35. Consequently, he has no ally.
36. And no food, except the bitter variety.
37. Only the sinners eat therefrom.
38. I solemnly swear by the things you see.
39. And the things you do not see.
40. This is the utterance of an honorable messenger.
41. It is not the utterance of a poet; however, rarely do you believe.
42. Nor is it the utterance of a soothsayer; rarely do you take heed.
43. It is a revelation from the Lord of the universe.
44. If he ever made up any utterances and attributed them to us,
45. we would immediately punish him,
46. and stop the revelation to him.
47. None of you can protect him then.
48. This is a reminder for the righteous.
49. We fully realize that some of you are rejectors.
50. It is but a curse that afflicts the disbelievers.
51. This is the absolute truth.
52. Therefore, you shall glorify the name of your Lord, the great.

Sura 70: The Heights (Al-Ma'aarij)

In the name of God, most gracious, most merciful

1. A questioner questioned the inevitable retribution.
2. For the disbelievers, nothing can stop it.
3. It will come from God, who possesses the highest heights.
4. The angels and the spirit climb to Him in a day that equals fifty thousand years.
5. Therefore, be patient, a gracious patience.
6. They see it far away.
7. While we see it close.
8. On that day, the heaven will be like lava.
9. The mountains will be like wool.
10. No friend will care about his friend.
11. When they see each other, the guilty will wish to ransom himself with his own children.
12. And his spouse and siblings.
13. And his tribe that raised him.
14. And all the people on earth, if it would save him.
15. No use; there will be hell.
16. Eager to burn.
17. It will summon anyone who turned away and fled.
18. Those who hoarded and were stingy.
19. The human being is naturally emotional.
20. When adversity touches him, he becomes despondent.
21. And when good fortune is his share, he becomes stingy.
22. Not so the worshipers, who observe the **salat** prayers.
23. They continuously observe their **salat** prayers.
24. Part of their monies is an assigned right.
25. For the needy and deprived.
26. They believe in the day of judgment.
27. They are wary of their Lord's retribution.
28. The retribution of their Lord is never taken for granted.
29. They maintain their chastity.
30. Only with their spouses, or what rightly belongs to them, they have intercourse.
31. Anyone who seeks anything beyond this, these are the transgressors.
32. They keep their trust and fulfill their vows.
33. They are equitable when testifying as witnesses.
34. They consistently observe their **salat** prayers.
35. They have deserved to be honored in Paradise.

36. Why do the disbelievers watch you from afar?

37. Then flee to the right and to the left.

38. How could any of them expect to enter the garden of bliss?

39. Never; we created them and they know from what.

40. Being the Lord of the easts and the wests, we are able

41. to substitute better people in their place; we are never helpless.

42. Thus, let them blunder and play, until they meet the day that awaits them.

43. That is the day when they come out of the graves in a hurry, as if rushing to the altars.

44. Their eyes will be disgraced, and humiliation will envelope them. This is the day that was promised to them.

Sura 71: Noah

In the name of God, most gracious, most merciful

1. We sent Noah to his people: "You shall warn your people, before painful retribution comes to them."
2. He said, "O my people, I come to you as a warner.
3. "You shall worship God, work righteousness, and obey me.
4. "God will then forgive your sins and respite you for a predetermined life span. When the interim designated by God is complete, nothing can delay it, if you only knew."
5. He later said, "Lord, I have preached to my people night and day.
6. "But my preaching only increased their fleeing.
7. "Whenever I exhorted them to seek Your forgiveness, they placed their fingers in their ears, covered themselves with their clothes, and insisted on their arrogance.
8. "Then I preached to them loudly.
9. "I preached to them publicly, and I preached to them privately.
10. "I said, 'Ask forgiveness from your Lord; He is forgiving.
11. 'He will then shower you with generous rain.
12. 'And supply you with money and children; and grant you gardens and rivers.' "
13. Why do you not wish to reverence God?
14. He is the one who created you in stages.
15. Do you not realize that God created seven heavens in layers?
16. He placed the moon therein as a light and the sun as a lamp.*
17. God is the one who germinated you from the earth, just like plants.
18. Then He will return you to it, then resurrect you.
19. God is the one who made the earth habitable for you.
20. That you may establish roads therein.
21. Noah said, "Lord, they disobeyed me and followed one who is corrupted by his money and his children.
22. "They schemed evil schemes.
23. "They said, 'Do not abandon your idols; do not abandon Wadd, or Suwa', or Yaghooth, or Ya'ooq, and Nasr.'
24. "They misguided many people. (My Lord,) do not increase the wicked except in straying."
25. Because of their transgressions, they were drowned and destined for hell. They had none to help them against God.
26. Noah said, "Lord, do not leave on earth a single disbeliever.

71:16.   *See footnote 25:61.*

27. "If You leave any of them, they only mislead Your servants and give birth to evil disbelievers.
28. "My Lord, forgive me, and my parents, and anyone who enters my home as a believer, and all the believing men and women. As for the wicked, do not increase them except in loss."

Sura 72: The Jinns (Al-Jinn)

In the name of God, most gracious, most merciful

1. Say, "It was revealed to me that a group of jinns listened, then said, 'We have heard a wonderful Quran.

2. 'It guides to righteousness, so we believed in it and will never set up idols besides our Lord.

3. 'He is the most high; our one and only Lord; never did He have a spouse, nor a son.

4. 'It was the fool among us who used to utter such blasphemies about God.

5. 'We never thought that the humans and the jinns could utter lies about God.

6. 'Some human beings used to seek benefits from jinn beings, but they only gave them problems.

7. 'They thought, just like you thought, that God will not resurrect anyone.

8. 'And we tried to touch the heaven, but we find it full of mighty guards and projectiles.

9. 'We used to sneak therein to listen; now, anyone who listens is immediately pursued by a projectile.

10. 'And we have no idea whether those on earth are destined for disaster or if their Lord plans something good for them.

11. 'Some of us are righteous and some are less than righteous. We follow various paths.

12. 'We know that we can never escape from God or flee from Him.

13. 'When we heard the guidance, we believed therein. Anyone who believes in his Lord shall fear no adversity nor hardship.

14. 'Among us are Muslims, and among us are compromisers.' " Those who submit are the ones who found guidance.

15. As for the compromisers, they will be fuel for hell.

16. If they steadfastly remain on the right path, we will bless them with abundant water.

17. We thus test them. Anyone who disregards the message of his Lord, God commits him to lasting retribution.

18. The mosques belong to God; do not call on anyone else besides God.*

19. When the servant of God advocated the worship of God alone, they almost unanimously opposed him.

72:18. *God and all His messengers preached that we shall forget about Muhammad, Moses, Jesus, Abraham, and anyone else and worship God alone (see 39:45, 40:12, 84-85, the Bible's Book of Deuteronomy, 6:4, and the Gospel of Mark, 12:29-30.)*

The Prophet's Teachings

20. Say, (O Muhammad), "I worship only my Lord; I never set up any idols besides Him."

21. Say (O Muhammad), "I have no power to harm you or benefit you."

22. Say, (O Muhammad), "No one can protect me from God, nor can I find any refuge besides Him.

23. "My sole mission is to deliver the declaration from God and His messages." Anyone who disobeys God and His messenger has deserved the fire of hell, wherein they abide forever.

24. When they see what is promised to them, they will find out who is weaker in power and lesser in number.

25. Say, "I have no idea how soon or how far is that which is promised to you."

26. Only God is the knower of the future; He lets no one else acquire such knowledge.

27. Only the messengers that he chooses may be given certain information concerning the past or the future.*

28. This is to make sure that they have delivered the messages of their Lord. He is fully aware of what they accomplish, and He is in full control of all things.

72:27.   *For example, Joseph was told of some future events (12:15), and Moses' mother was told that her infant will be returned to her, and that he will be a messenger of God (28:7).*

Sura 73: Wrapped Up (Al-Muzzammil)

In the name of God, most gracious, most merciful

1. O you wrapped up.
2. Get up to worship during the night, except a little.
3. Half of it or a little less.
4. Or a little more; and recite the Quran frequently.
5. We will deliver to you a heavy message.
6. The meditation at night is more effective and more powerful.
7. During the day you have a lot of time for business.
8. You shall commemorate the name of your Lord and come ever closer to Him.
9. He is the Lord of the East and the West; there is no god except He; therefore, you shall trust in Him.
10. And be patient in the face of their utterances, and disregard them amicably.
11. Let Me handle the rejectors, who have been endowed with many bounties. Respite them a little.
12. We have severe retribution and a hell.
13. And bitter food and painful retribution.
14. The day will come when the earth and the mountains are shaken. The mountains will turn into fluffy piles.
15. We have sent a messenger as a witness among you, just as we sent to Pharaoh a messenger.
16. Pharaoh disobeyed the messenger, and consequently, we punished him severely.
17. If you disbelieve, how could you evade a day so terrible that it makes the infant gray haired?
18. The sky will disintegrate on that day. This is His inevitable promise.
19. This is a reminder; whoever wills shall seek a path to his Lord.

20. Your Lord knows well that you stay up close to two-thirds of the night,
     sometimes half of it, sometimes one-third of it. Also, some of those who
     follow you do the same. God has designed the night and the day, and He
     knows that you cannot do this every night. He pardons you; therefore,
     you shall recite what you can of the Quran. He knows that some of you
     may be ill; others may be traveling in search of God's bounties; others
     may be striving in the cause of God. Therefore, recite what you can of it,
     observe the **salat** prayers* and give the **zakat** charity, and lend God a loan
     of righteousness. Whatever good you advance on behalf of your souls,
     you will find it at God far better and multiplied manyfold. You shall ask
     God for forgiveness; God is forgiver, most merciful.

73:20.   *The enemies of the prophet and the storytellers invented a* **hadith**
stating that **salat** *was decreed in heaven during the ninth year at Mecca. This
verse in this very early sura proves that* **salat** *was a familiar expression. The*
salat *prayers, as well as all religious practices of Islam were passed down to us
from Abraham, generation after generation (see 2:135; 3:67, 68, 95; 16:23,
21:73; and Appendix 8).*

Sura 74: The Hidden Secret* (Al-Muddath-thir)

In the name of God, most gracious, most merciful

1. O you hidden secret.
2. Come out and warn.
3. Glorify your Lord.
4. Remove your cover.
5. Condemn evil.
6. You (people) shall not ask for more and more.
7. Persist in the service of your Lord.
8. When the trumpet is blown.
9. That will be a difficult day.
10. For the disbelievers, it will not be easy.
11. Let Me deal with the one I had created as an individual.
12. I provided him with a lot of money.
13. Also, children to witness.
14. I made life easy for him.
15. Yet, he is always greedy for more.
16. Never; he was too stubborn to accept our revelations.
17. I will punish him, increasingly.
18. He reflected and pondered.
19. Woe to him, he really pondered.
20. Then woe to him, he pondered again and again.
21. Then he looked (at the Quran).
22. Then he frowned and complained.
23. Then he turned away in arrogance.
24. He said, "This is but old magic.
25. "This is man-made."
26. I will commit him to suffering.
27. And what suffering.
28. Thorough and efficient.
29. It will be obvious to all the people.
30. On it are nineteen.

74:1-56.   In retrospect, now that the secret numerical code of Quran has been unveiled, we see clearly that this whole sura deals with this miraculous code. This code has been hidden for 1400 years; it is based on the number 19 (verse 30); it provides the perfect answer for those who claim the Quran is man-made (verse 25), and it is an overwhelming miracle (verse 35) that is physical, touchable, examinable, and utterly indisputable (see Appendix 1 for details).

31. We appointed angels to be guardians of hell.* And we appointed this number (19) to serve as a punishment for the disbelievers; and to assure those who received previous scripture (that this is a divine book); and to strengthen the faith of the believers;* and to remove all traces of doubt from the hearts of those who received previous scripture, as well as the believers; and to expose the hypocrites and the disbelievers, for they will say, "What did God mean by this example?" God thus misleads whomever He wills and guides whomever He wills. No one knows the actual number of your Lord's soldiers except He. This is simply a reminder for the people.

One Of The Greatest Miracles

32. Indeed, by the moon.
33. By the night as it passes.
34. By the morning as it shines.
35. This is one of the greatest miracles.
36. A warning for the people.
37. Based on this, you can either advance or choose to regress.
38. Every soul is accountable for what it did.
39. Except the people of righteousness.
40. As they enjoy Paradise, they will ask.
41. About the guilty,
42. "What led you into the suffering?"
43. They will say, "We were not among those who observed the **salat** prayers.
44. "Nor did we feed the poor.
45. "We blundered with those who blundered.
46. "We disbelieved in the day of judgment.
47. "Until certainty came to us."
48. Consequently, the intercession of any intercessors will never help them.
49. Why are they so averse to the reminder?
50. Like speeding asses.
51. Fleeing from a lion.
52. It seems as though each one of them wants to receive the scripture individually (from God).*

74:31. *This expression provided the earlier generations with a temporary interpretation for the number 19 of verse 30. We are given here five functions of the 19-based code of Quran: (1) a rebuttal against the disbelievers; (2) to assure the Jews and Christians that Quran is God's message to them; (3) strengthen the faith of the believers (see 2:260); (4) remove all doubt from the hearts of the Jews, Christians, and Muslims; and (5) expose the doubters, the hypocrites, and disbelievers; they will say, "So what."*

53. They do not fear the hereafter.
54. Indeed, this is a reminder.
55. Whoever wills, let him take heed.
56. None can take heed except in accordance with God's will. He is the source of righteousness; He is the source of forgiveness.

74:52. God is the teacher of His scripture. However, the Quran informs us here that this is done through human teachers. Thus, one man, namely Muhammad, was chosen to receive Quran then deliver it to the world (see also 18:17).

Sura 75: Resurrection (Al-Qiyaamah)

In the name of God, most gracious, most merciful

1. I swear by the day of resurrection.
2. And by the soul that continuously blames.
3. Does the human being think that we cannot recollect his bones?
4. We can even reconstruct the tip of his finger.*
5. The human being tends to believe only what he sees in front of him.
6. He asks, "What is the day of resurrection?"
7. When the vision is sharpened.
8. And the moon is turned off.
9. And the sun and the moon crash.
10. The human being will say on that day, "Where is the escape?"
11. There will be no escape.
12. To your Lord will be the only refuge on that day.
13. The human being will be informed on that day of everything that caused him to advance or regress.
14. Everyone will be his own judge.*
15. No excuses will be accepted.

Muhammad Only Delivers Quran

16. Do not move your tongue (O Muhammad) to hasten this revelation.
17. We are in charge of putting it together into Quran.
18. Once we recite it, you shall follow this Quran.
19. Then, it is we who will explain it.*
20. Indeed, you (people) love this fleeting life.
21. And you ignore the hereafter.
22. Some faces on that day will be happy.

75:4. *This revelation came down hundreds of years before it became known that each of us has unique fingerprints.*

75:14. *See also 17:14 and Appendix 10.*

75:19. *The enemies of the prophet who invented "hadith" and/or "sunna" claim that their fabrications are needed to explain the Quran. Obviously, they are ignorant of this verse. God is the only one who explains the Quran, as He places it into the hearts of sincere believers, regardless of their language or level of education (see 41:44 and 55:1-2). Note that the verse number is 19, a significant link with the Quran's miraculous numerical code (see also 6:19, 38, 114; 20:114; and Appendix 10).*

23. Looking at their Lord.
24. Other faces on that day will be miserable.
25. Realizing that they are doomed.
26. Indeed, the time will come when it (the soul) reaches the throat.
27. It will be said, "Is there any reliever?"
28. He will realize that the separation is imminent.
29. One leg will lay next to the other leg.
30. To your Lord, on that day, is the destination.
31. He was neither charitable, nor did he observe the **salat** prayers.
32. He disbelieved and turned away.
33. He was arrogant among his people.
34. You should not have done that, you should not.
35. Indeed, you should not have done it, you should not.
36. Does the human being think that he will be left unaccountable?
37. Was he not a drop of ejected semen?
38. Then he became a clot, and God created and perfected him?
39. God created them in two kinds, male and female.
40. Is He not able to resurrect the dead?

Sura 76: The Human (Al-Insaan)

In the name of God, most gracious, most merciful

1. Did the human being go through a period of time when he was nothing?
2. We have created the human from a drop, in stages, in order to put him to the test. We made him hearer and seer.
3. We showed him the path, then he is either appreciative or unappreciative.
4. We have prepared for the disbelievers chains, and shackles, and hell.
5. As for the righteous, they will drink from cups wherein balm is mixed.
6. From a spring that the servants of God fully control.
7. They fullfill their vows and reverence a day that is extremely difficult.
8. They donate the food, despite their love thereof, to the needy, the orphan, and the captive.
9. We feed you only in obedience to God; we require no recompense or thanks.
10. We fear from our Lord a day that is full of trouble and misery.
11. God will spare them the misery of that day and will grant them happiness and joy.
12. He will reward them for their steadfastness; Paradise and silk.
13. Relaxing on the furnishings therein, they do not see any sun heat or bitter cold.
14. The shade will cover them and the fruits within reach.
15. Passing among them will be silver bowls and translucent cups.
16. Translucent, though made of silver. They rightly deserved them.
17. They enjoy drinks wherein spices are mixed.
18. From a spring therein named **"Salsabeel."**
19. Serving them will be immortal servants; when you see them, you will think they are scattered pearls.
20. And when you see, you will see ecstacy and a great dominion.
21. Their garments will be of green velvet and silk; they will be adorned with silver bracelets; their Lord will grant them pure drinks.
22. This is the recompense you have deserved; for your works are appreciated.
23. We have revealed to you this Quran; a revelation from us.

76:23-24. These are clear orders that we shall uphold God's laws as stated in the Quran, the whole Quran, and nothing but the Quran. Those who rely on additional sources of law, such as invented "hadith" and/or "sunna," disbelieve in the Quran's assertions that it is perfect and complete (see 6:19, 38, 112-116; 25:30-31; and Appendix 15).

24. You shall steadfastly uphold the laws of your Lord, and do not obey any guilty one or disbeliever among them.

25. You shall commemorate the name of your Lord, day and night.

26. During the night, fall prostrate before Him. Glorify Him throughout many nights.

27. These people love the fleeting life and ignore a heavy day that awaits them.

28. We created them, gave them strength, and, if we will, we can substitute others in their place.

29. This is a reminder; whoever wills shall follow a path to his Lord.

30. Whatever you will is in accordance with God's will. God is omniscient, most wise.

31. He admits whomever He wills into His mercy. As for the wicked, He has prepared for them a painful retribution.

Sura 77: Dispatched (Al-Mursalaat)

In the name of God, most gracious, most merciful

1. By the dispatched (angels), in succession.
2. Who stir up violent winds.
3. And spread clouds everywhere.
4. And distribute the rain.
5. And deliver messages.
6. Good news as well as warnings.
7. What is promised to you will come to pass.
8. The stars will be turned off.
9. The heaven will be torn.
10. The mountains will be wiped out.
11. The messengers will be summoned.
12. On the specific day.
13. That is the day of judgment.
14. Do you have any idea what the day of judgment is?
15. Woe, on that day, to the disbelievers.
16. Did we not eliminate the ancestors?
17. Then we made others follow them?
18. This is what we do to the guilty.
19. Woe, on that day, to the disbelievers.
20. Did we not create you from a lowly liquid?
21. Then we placed it in a protected repository.
22. For a specific period.
23. We designed everything; we are the best designers.
24. Woe, on that day, to the disbelievers.
25. Did we not make the earth habitable?
26. Accommodating both the living and the dead.
27. We placed huge stabilizers therein, and we gave you fresh water to drink.
28. Woe, on that day, to the disbelievers.
29. Go to what you used to deny.
30. Go to a shade with three layers.
31. It provides no coolness, nor does it spare you any heat.
32. The sparks it emits are as big as mansions.
33. They will look as yellow as the camels.
34. Woe, on that day, to the disbelievers.
35. That is the day when they need not speak.*
36. No permission will be given to them to even apologize.

77:35.   See also 36:65, 41:21, 55:41, and Appendix 10.

37. Woe, on that day, to the disbelievers.
38. This is the day of judgment; we have gathered you together with the previous generations.
39. If you have any power to do anything, then show Me your power.
40. Woe, on that day, to the disbelievers.
41. The righteous have deserved shade and springs.
42. And all the fruits they desire.
43. Eat and drink happily, in return for your works.
44. We thus reward the righteous.
45. Woe, on that day, to the disbelievers.
46. Eat and enjoy for a short while; you are guilty.
47. Woe, on that day, to the disbelievers.
48. When told, "Bow down (in **salat**)," they do not bow down.
49. Woe, on that day, to the disbelievers.
50. Which **hadith**, besides this, do they believe in?

Sura 78: The Event (Al-Naba')

In the name of God, most gracious, most merciful

1. What are they questioning?
2. The great event.
3. About which they dispute.
4. Indeed, they will find out.
5. Then, they will really find out.
6. Did we not make the earth habitable?
7. And the mountains stabilizers?
8. We created you male and female.
9. We made the sleep for your rest.
10. We made the night a cover.
11. We made the day for business.
12. We built above you seven formidable heavens.
13. We made a bright lamp.
14. We send down from the clouds pure water.
15. To produce grains and vegetation.
16. And dense gardens.
17. The day of judgment is predetermined.
18. That is the day when the horn is blown, whereupon you come in throngs.
19. The heaven will be opened into many gates.
20. The mountains will be wiped out, as if they were a mirage.
21. Hell is inevitable.
22. For the transgressors, it will be the final abode.
23. They stay in it for ages.
24. They never taste coolness in it, nor a drink.
25. Only lava and bitter food.
26. This is their just retribution.
27. They did not expect any reckoning.
28. They have rejected our revelations.
29. Everything they had done we recorded in a record.
30. So taste, we will only increase your retribution.
31. The righteous have deserved a reward.
32. Gardens and grapes.
33. And magnificent spouses.
34. And pure drinks.
35. They will not hear any vain talk or lies.
36. This is the recompense from your Lord; a well deserved gift.
37. He is the Lord of the heavens and the earth, and everything between them; the most gracious; no one abrogates His decisions.

38. On that day, the spirit and the angels will stand in a row; none will speak unless permitted by God most gracious, and utter only what is right.

39. That is the inevitable day. Therefore, whoever wills shall follow the path to his Lord.

40. We have warned you of imminent retribution. The day will come when every person sees what his hands had advanced, and the disbelievers will say, "I wish I were dust."

Sura 79: The Snatchers (Al-Naazi'aat)

In the name of God, most gracious, most merciful

1. By those (angels) who snatch (the souls of the guilty).
2. By those (angels) who gently seize (the souls of the righteous).
3. By those (angels) who float downward.
4. By those (angels) who are ever eager.
5. To carry out the commands.
6. The day will come when the quake will quake.
7. Followed by the inevitable.
8. Some hearts, on that day, will be terrified.
9. Their eyes will be disgraced.
10. They used to say, "Do we get recreated from the grave?
11. "After becoming rotten bones?"
12. They said, "This is an impossible recurrence."
13. But it will take only one call.
14. Whereupon they rise.
15. Have you received the history of Moses?
16. His Lord called him in the sacred valley Tuwa.
17. Go to Pharaoh; for he has transgressed.
18. Tell him, "Would you not purify yourself?
19. "Let me guide you to your Lord. You shall be humble."
20. He then showed him the great miracle.
21. But he disbelieved and rebelled.
22. He turned around in a hurry.
23. And sent announcers to summon (the magicians).
24. He said, "I am your supreme Lord."
25. Consequently, God committed him to retribution in the hereafter, as well as in the first life.
26. This is a lesson for the reverent.
27. Are you more difficult to create than the heaven that He built?
28. He raised its masses and perfected it.
29. He made its night dark and its morning visible.
30. Thereafter, He made the earth egg-shaped.*
31. He produced therefrom its water and its pasture.

79:30.   Before the discovery that the planet earth is egg-shaped, the readers of Quran interpreted the Arabic word "Dahaaha" in many different ways. In retrospect, this is one of the Quran's great scientific miracles. Millions of Arabic speaking people today still use the original Arabic word for egg, namely, "Dahhy."

32. And He placed the mountains.
33. And provisions for you and your animals.
34. Then, when the great event comes to pass.
35. The human being will remember everything he had done.
36. Hell will be shown to everyone who sees.
37. For the transgressor.
38. Who preferred the first life.
39. Hell will be the abode.
40. For the one who appreciated the greatness of his Lord and controlled his lusts.
41. Heaven will be the abode.
42. They ask you about the Hour.
43. You have no way of knowing it.
44. Only your Lord controls its destiny.
45. You only warn those who appreciate it.
46. The day they see it, they will feel as if they lasted one night or one day (in this life).

Sura 80: He Frowned* ('Abasa)

In the name of God, most gracious, most merciful

1. He (Muhammad) frowned and turned away.
2. When the blind man came to him.
3. How do you know? He may attain salvation.
4. Or he may take heed and benefit from heeding.
5. As for the rich man.
6. You gave him your attention.
7. You could not guarantee his guidance.
8. The one who came to you eagerly.
9. And he is reverent.
10. You ignored him.
11. Indeed, this is a reminder.
12. Whoever wills shall take heed.
13. It is recorded in an honorable scripture.
14. Exalted and pure.
15. Written by the hands of scribes.
16. Who are honorable and righteous.
17. Woe to the human being; he is most unappreciative.
18. What did God create him from?
19. From a tiny drop He created him and designed him.
20. Then He pointed out the path for him.
21. Then He put him to death, into the grave.
22. When He wills, He will resurrect him.
23. If only the human could fulfill the commandments.
24. The human being should consider his food.
25. We poured the water generously.
26. Then we split the soil.
27. And grew grains therein.
28. And grapes and pasture.
29. And olives and date palms.
30. And dense orchards.
31. And fruits and vegetables.

80:1. *Despite the Quran's assertion that Muhammad is a human being like any of us (see 18:110, 33:37, and 41:6), those who idolize the prophet against his will adamantly refuse to believe that he made any mistakes. The Quran, however, demonstrates the humanity of Muhammad, as well as that of Noah, Moses, Jonah, and other prophets, by relating the errors they have committed (see 11:46, 28:15, 33:37, 66:1, and 68:48).*

32. Provisions for you and your animals.
33. Then, when the blow comes.
34. That is the day when the person will flee from his own brother.
35. From his mother and his father.
36. From his wife and children.
37. Each person will worry about his own neck.
38. Some faces will be, on that day, happy.
39. Joyful and rejoicing.
40. Other faces, on that day, will be covered with misery.
41. Doom will overwhelm them.
42. Such are the wicked disbelievers.

Sura 81: The Rolling (Al-Takweer)

In the name of God, most gracious, most merciful

1. When the sun is rolled away.
2. And the stars crash.
3. And the mountains are removed.
4. And the reproduction is halted.
5. And the beasts are gathered.
6. And the oceans are set aflame.
7. And the souls are coupled (with their bodies).
8. The girl buried alive will be asked.
9. For what crime was she killed?
10. The records will be opened.
11. The sky will be torn.
12. Hell will be ignited.
13. Heaven will be presented.
14. Every soul will find out what it brought.
15. I swear by the stars.
16. By the moving constellations.
17. By the night as it falls.
18. By the morning as it comes to life.
19. This is the utterance of an honorable messenger.
20. Supported by the mighty possessor of the throne, with authoritative foundation.
21. To be obeyed and trusted.
22. For your friend is not crazy.
23. He has received it at the high horizon.*
24. He is not withholding any prophecies.
25. This is not the utterance of a rejected devil.
26. Which way will you go?
27. This is a message for all the people.
28. For those of you who will to go straight.
29. Whatever you will is in accordance with the will of God, Lord of the universe.

81:23.   See 17:1 and 53:1-18.

Sura 82: The Shattering (Al-Infitaar)

In the name of God, most gracious, most merciful

1. When the sky shatters.
2. And the planets disperse.
3. And the oceans explode.
4. And the graves are opened.
5. Every soul will find out what caused it to advance and what caused it to regress.
6. O human being, what diverted you from your honorable Lord?
7. He created you, designed you, and perfected you.
8. In the shape that He chose, He constructed you.
9. Indeed, you deny the judgment.
10. Guards are assigned to protect you.
11. They are honest recorders.
12. They know everything you do.
13. The righteous have deserved bliss.
14. While the wicked have deserved hell.
15. They will burn therein on the day of judgment.
16. They can never evade it.
17. Do you have any idea what the day of judgment is?
18. Again, do you have any idea what the day of judgment is?
19. That is the day when no soul will have any power to help another soul, and all decisions, on that day, will be made by God.

Sura 83: The Cheaters (Al-Mutaffifeen)

In the name of God, most gracious, most merciful

1. Woe to the cheaters.
2. Who, when taking the measures from the people, get a full measure.
3. But when giving the measure or the weight to the people, they cheat.
4. Do they not expect to be resurrected?
5. On a great day.
6. That is the day when the people will rise before the Lord of the universe.
7. Indeed, the record of the wicked will be lowly.
8. Do you have any idea how lowly?
9. It is a numbered record.
10. Woe, on that day, to the disbelievers.
11. Who disbelieved in the day of judgment.
12. None disbelieves therein except the sinful transgressor.
13. When our revelations are recited for him, he says, "Tales from the past."
14. That is because their hearts have been shielded by their own sins.*
15. Consequently, they will be veiled, on that day, from their Lord.
16. Then they will burn in hell.
17. Then they will be told, "This is what you used to deny."
18. As for the record of the righteous, it will be exalted.
19. Do you have any idea how exalted?
20. It is a numbered record.
21. It will be attained by those who are close to Me.
22. The righteous have deserved bliss.
23. Watching, as they relax on furnishings.
24. You recognize in their faces the radiance of happiness.
25. They will be given drinks of pure nectar.
26. Sealed with musk. This is what any competitors should compete for.
27. Mixed in it will be perfume.
28. From a spring exclusively reserved for those close to Me.

The Believers Ridiculed

29. The guilty used to laugh at those who believed.
30. When they passed by them, they poked each other.
31. When they talked with each other, they mocked them.

83:14. Each time a sinner sins, a thin layer of invisible shield (see 17:45) falls around the heart. Gradually, the number of thin layers becomes so strong that no guidance can penetrate into the heart (see 39:23).

32.   Whenever they saw them, they said, "These people are way off.

33.   "No angels are assigned to accompany them."

34.   Today, those who believed will be laughing at the disbelievers.

35.   As they relax on furnishings, they will watch.

36.   Are the disbelievers paying for what they did?

Sura 84: The Splitting (Al-Inshiqaaq)

In the name of God, most gracious, most merciful

1. The time will come when the sky is split asunder.
2. It will submit to its Lord and expire.
3. The earth will be leveled.
4. It will throw its contents, as it erupts.
5. It will submit to its Lord and expire.
6. O you human being, you are irreversibly moving towards your Lord, until you meet Him.
7. As for the one who receives his record in his right hand.
8. His reckoning will be easy.
9. He will return to his people in joy.
10. As for the one who receives his record behind his back.
11. He will declare remorse.
12. He will burn in hell.
13. He used to be proud among his people.
14. He thought that he is never held accountable.
15. Yes indeed, his Lord sees him.
16. By the token of the glowing sunset clouds.
17. By the night as it spreads.
18. By the moon as it rises.
19. You pass from stage to stage.
20. Why then do they not believe?
21. When the Quran is recited to them, they do not submit.
22. The disbelievers are those who reject it.
23. God is fully aware of what they think.
24. Promise them painful retribution.
25. As for those who believe and work righteousness, they receive a well deserved recompense.

Sura 85: The Constellations (Al-Burooj)

In the name of God, most gracious, most merciful

1. By the sky with its constellations.
2. By the promised day.
3. By the witness and the witnessed.
4. The people of the canyon were doomed.
5. They set up a flaming fire.
6. They sat around it.
7. Watching the believers burn.
8. They persecuted them simply because they believed in God, the almighty, the praiseworthy.
9. To Him belong the heavens and the earth; and God witnesses all things.
10. Those who persecute the believing men and women, then fail to repent, have deserved the retribution of hell; they have deserved the agony of burning.
11. Those who believe and work righteousness have deserved gardens with flowing streams; this is the great triumph.
12. The blow of your Lord is severe.
13. He is the one who initiates and resurrects.
14. He is the forgiver, the compassionate.
15. Possessor of the glorious throne.
16. Doer of anything He wills.
17. Did you receive the history of the troops?
18. Pharaoh and Thamood?
19. Those who disbelieve are rejecting (the truth).
20. God is completely surrounding them.
21. Indeed, this is a glorious Quran.*
22. In a protected record.

85:21.   What can we say to describe the Quran or emphasize the importance of studying and heeding it, when the almighty Himself describes it as glorious, honorable, and great (see 15:87, 50:1, and 56:77).

Sura 86: The Bright Star (Al-Ṭariq)

In the name of God, most gracious, most merciful

1. By the token of the sky and Al-Taariq.
2. Do you know what Al-Taariq is?
3. The bright star.
4. Every person is well guarded.
5. The human being should reflect on his own creation.
6. He was created from ejaculated liquid.
7. Issuing from between the spine and the viscera.
8. Certainly, God is able to resurrect him.
9. The day will come when all secrets become known.
10. No one will have any power or helpers.
11. By the sky that returns the water.
12. By the earth that cracks (to produce plants).
13. This is a decisive message.
14. It is not vain talk.
15. They plot and scheme.
16. But so do I.
17. Therefore, disregard the disbelievers for a short while.

Sura 87: The Most High (Al-A'la)

In the name of God, most gracious, most merciful

1. Glorify the name of your Lord, the most high.
2. He created and perfected.
3. He designed and guided.
4. He produces the pasture.
5. Then He turns it into light hay.
6. We will recite for you, so do not forget.
7. Everything is in accordance with God's will. He knows what is declared and what is hidden.
8. We will make things easy for you.
9. So remind; the reminder may be useful.
10. The reverent will take heed.
11. But the wicked will evade it.
12. He will burn in the great fire.
13. He will neither die therein nor stay alive.
14. Winner is the one who turns righteous.
15. Who commemorates the name of his Lord by observing the **salat** prayers.
16. Indeed, the people give priority to this life.
17. While the hereafter is far better and everlasting.
18. This is the same as in the previous scriptures.
19. The scriptures of Abraham and Moses.

Sura 88: The Overwhelming (Al-Ghaashiyah)

In the name of God, most gracious, most merciful

1.   Did you receive a description of the overwhelming?
2.   Some faces, on that day, will be humiliated.
3.   Laboring and exhausted.
4.   Burning in a blazing fire.
5.   Drinking from a boiling spring.
6.   They will have no food, except from one source.
7.   That never fills, nor satisfies any hunger.
8.   Other faces, on that day, will be happy.
9.   Satisfied with their works.
10. In exalted Paradise.
11. You never hear in it any nonsense.
12. In it, a flowing spring.
13. In it, exalted furnishings.
14. And drinks within reach.
15. And cushions in rows.
16. And vast carpets.
17. Do they not reflect on the camels; how they were created?
18. And the sky; how it was raised?
19. And the mountains; how they were constructed?
20. And the earth; how it was spread?
21. You shall remind. You are no more than a reminder.
22. You have no power over them.
23. As for the one who turns away and disbelieves.
24. God will commit him to terrible retribution.
25. To us is their ultimate return.
26. Then we will hold them accountable.

Sura 89: Dawn (Al-Fajr)

In the name of God, most gracious, most merciful

1. By the dawn.
2. By the ten nights.
3. By the even and the odd.
4. By the night as it moves on.
5. This is a formidable oath, for those who understand.
6. Do you not see what your Lord did to 'Aad?
7. Iram, the city with pillars.
8. There was nothing like it anywhere.
9. Also Thamood, who carved rocks in the valley.
10. And Pharaoh with the troops.
11. They all transgressed in the land.
12. They spread corruption.
13. Consequently, your Lord poured upon them terrible retribution.
14. Your Lord is ever watchful.
15. Consider the human being; when his Lord puts him to the test by endowing him and blessing him, he says, "My Lord has endowed me."
16. But when He puts him to the test by reducing his provision, he says, "My Lord has humiliated me."
17. No; (it is not your Lord who humiliates you.) It is you who do not regard the orphan.
18. Nor do you exhort each other to feed the poor.
19. You unlawfully consume the (orphan's) inheritance.
20. You love money too much.
21. Indeed, the earth will be demolished; totally crushed.
22. As your Lord comes,* together with the angels in row after row.
23. Hell will be brought forth on that day. The human being will then remember, and what a remembrance!
24. He will say, "Oh I wish I had prepared for my (eternal) life."
25. On that day, the retribution is worst.

89:22. *Our immediate universe, including the earth and a billion trillion stars in the lowest heaven (see Appendix 5), cannot stand the physical presence of God. Thus, our world will end simply by God's coming on the day of judgment (see 7:143 and Appendix 10).*

26. The confinement is absolute.*
27. As for you, secure and content soul.
28. Come back to your Lord, satisfied and satisfying.
29. Enter with My servants.
30. Enter My paradise.

89:26. *The inhabitants of hell will be confined to the lowest stratum; the farthest from God. They will not be able to exist beyond the limit that separates them from heaven (see Appendix 10 for details).*

Sura 90: The Town (Al-Balad)

In the name of God, most gracious, most merciful

1. I swear by this town.
2. Wherein you reside.
3. By the one that gives birth and the one that is born.
4. We have created the human being to attain a certain accomplishment.
5. Does he think that no one controls him?
6. He boasts, "I spent so much money."
7. Does he think that no one sees him?
8. Did we not give him two eyes?
9. A tongue and two lips?
10. We showed him the two paths.
11. He should choose the formidable path.
12. Do you know what the formidable path is?
13. The freeing of slaves.
14. Or feeding at the time of difficulty.
15. An orphan who is related.
16. Or a poor person who is despondent.
17. In addition, there shall be belief and you shall exhort one another to be steadfast; exhort one another to be compassionate.
18. These have deserved happiness.
19. As for those who reject our revelations, they have deserved misery.
20. They have deserved confinement in hell.

Sura 91: The Sun (Al-Shams)

In the name of God, most gracious, most merciful

1. By the sun and its heat.
2. By the moon that follows it.
3. By the day and its brightness.
4. By the night and its darkness.
5. By the sky and Him who built it.
6. By the earth and Him who spread it.
7. By the soul and Him who designed it.
8. He taught it what is bad and what is good.
9. Winner is the one who purifies it.
10. And loser is the one who diminishes it.
11. Thamood transgressed and disbelieved.
12. When a poor man among them was sent.
13. The messenger of God said to them, "This is God's camel; you shall let her drink."
14. They disbelieved him and slaughtered her. Their Lord condemned them because of their sins and wiped them out.
15. Yet, those who came after them remain heedless.

Sura 92: The Night (Al-Layl)

In the name of God, most gracious, most merciful

1. By the night as it gets dark.
2. By the day as it gets bright.
3. By Him who created the male and the female.
4. Your works are of various kinds.
5. As for the one who is charitable and righteous.
6. Who upholds the scripture.
7. We will direct him towards happiness.
8. But the one who is stingy and arrogant.
9. And rejects the scripture.
10. We will direct him towards misery.
11. His money will never help him, once he falls.
12. It is us who guide.
13. To us belong the last, as well as the first.
14. I have warned you of a blazing hell.
15. Burning therein are the wicked.
16. Who disbelieved and turned away.
17. Spared from it is the righteous.
18. Who gives his money in charity.
19. Expecting nothing in return.
20. Seeking only his Lord, the most high.
21. He will certainly rejoice.

Sura 93: The Forenoon (Al-Duhaa)

In the name of God, most gracious, most merciful

1. By the forenoon.
2. By the night as it covers.
3. Your Lord did not foresake you, nor does He hate you.
4. The hereafter is what really counts, not this life.
5. Your Lord will bless you, until you are pleased.
6. Did He not find you (O Muhammad) an orphan, and He gave you shelter?
7. Did He not find you astray,* and He guided you?
8. Did He not find you poor, and He made you rich?
9. Therefore, you shall not mistreat the orphan.
10. Nor shall you despise the poor.
11. And speak up of your Lord's blessings.

93:7. See footnote 40:66.

Sura 94: Cooling the Temper (Al-Sharh)

In the name of God, most gracious, most merciful

1. Did we not cool your temper?*
2. Did we not remove your burden?
3. That had burdened your back?
4. Did we not bless you with an exalted message?
5. Even with difficulty, there will be relief.
6. With difficulty, there will be relief.
7. Therefore, whenever possible, you shall work hard.
8. Attaining closeness to your Lord.

94:1. See also 3:159, 20:25, and 26:13.

Sura 95: The Fig (Al-Teen)

In the name of God, most gracious, most merciful

1. By the fig and the olive.
2. By Mount Sinai.
3. By this holy land.
4. We have created the human in the best design.
5. Then we reverted him to lowliest of the lowly.
6. Except those who believe and work righteousness; they enjoy a well deserved recompense.
7. After all this, why do you still reject faith?
8. Is God not the wisest of the wise?

Sura 96: The Clot (Al-Alaq)*
First Sura Ever Revealed

In the name of God, most gracious, most merciful

1. Read, in the name of your Lord who created.
2. He created man from a clot.
3. Read, your Lord is the most honorable.
4. He teaches by means of the pen.
5. He teaches man what he never knew.
6. Indeed, the human being transgresses.
7. Whenever he becomes rich.
8. To your Lord is the final return.
9. What do you think of one who forbids.
10. A person from praying?
11. Is it not better that he follows the guidance?
12. And advocates righteousness?
13. If he chooses to disbelieve and turn away.
14. Does he not realize that God sees?
15. Indeed, unless he refrains, we will seize him by the forelock.
16. The forelock that is rejecting and sinful.
17. Let him call the idols he used to implore.
18. We will call the guardians of hell.
19. You shall not obey such a person. Instead, you shall fall prostrate and come closer.

96:1-19.   *This is the first sura ever revealed, and it occupied a special position in the Quran's secret numerical code (see Appendix 1 for details). As part of the secrecy of this code, which is based on the number 19, this sura is placed in position number 19 from the end of Quran. The first words brought by Gabriel to the prophet Muhammad, namely verses 1-5 of this sura, are exactly 19 (Arabic) words. When we count the Arabic letters that make up these 19 words, we find them 76 (19 x 4). And when we count the total number of letters in the whole sura, we find them 285 (19 x 15). The reader will also note that the sura consists of 19 verses.*

Sura 97: Power (Al-Qadr)

In the name of God, most gracious, most merciful

1. We have revealed this Quran in the night of power.*
2. Do you know what the night of power is?
3. The night of power is better than a thousand months.
4. The angels and the spirit (Gabriel) descend therein, with permission from their Lord, to carry out every command.*
5. Peaceful it is, until the rising of the dawn.

97:1. *See footnote 17:1.*

97:4. *Every believer who sincerely fasts during the month of Ramadan and observes a perfect month of righteousness and devotion witnesses the "night of power" by the end of Ramadan. The angels visit such a person and fulfill his or her dearest wishes (see 2:186).*

Sura 98: The Proof (Al-Bayyinah)

In the name of God, most gracious, most merciful

1. Those who disbelieved among the followers of previous scriptures, as well as the idol worshipers, will never believe, even after the proof has come to them.
2. A messenger from God, reciting sacred scripture.
3. Wherein there are valuable commandments.
4. Those who received previous scripture became divided after the proof did come to them.
5. All that is enjoined upon them is to believe in God, to devote the worship to Him alone, and to observe the **salat** prayers and **zakat** charity. This is the perfect religion.
6. Those who disbelieved among the followers of previous scripture, as well as the idol worshipers, will abide in hell forever. They are the worst creatures.
7. Those who believe and work righteousness are the best creatures.
8. Their recompense is with their Lord; gardens of Eden with flowing streams; they abide therein forever. God is pleased with them, and they are pleased with Him. This is the reward for those who reverence their Lord.

Sura 99: The Quake (Al-Zalzalah)

In the name of God, most gracious, most merciful

1. When the earth is quaked by its (final) quake.
2. When the earth erupts and issues its loads.
3. The human being will then say, "What is happening?"
4. On that day, it will explain.
5. That the Lord had commanded it.
6. On that day, the people will come out in throngs, to be shown their works.
7. Whoever does an atom's weight of righteousness will see it.
8. And whoever does an atom's weight of evil will see it.

Sura 100: The Runners (Al-'Aadiyaat)

In the name of God, most gracious, most merciful

1. By the speedy runners.
2. Who ignite sparks.
3. And invade at morning.
4. Spreading terror into the enemy.
5. Invading the heart of their land.
6. The human being is unappreciative of his Lord.
7. He bears witness to that.
8. He loves material wealth too much.
9. Does he not realize that those in the graves will be revived?
10. And the innermost secrets will be declared?
11. Their Lord is fully cognizant of everything they do.

Sura 101: The Shocker (Al-Qaari'ah)

In the name of God, most gracious, most merciful

1. The shocker.
2. What a shocker!
3. Do you have any idea what the shocker is?
4. That is the day when the people rise like multitudes of moths.
5. The mountains will be like fluffy wool.
6. As for him whose weights are heavy.
7. He will live a happy life.
8. As for him whose weights are light.
9. His destiny is lowly.
10. Do you know what it is?
11. The burning hell.

Sura 102: Hoarding (Al-Takaathur)

In the name of God, most gracious, most merciful

1. You remain preoccupied with hoarding.
2. Until you go to the graves.
3. Indeed, you will find out.
4. Yes indeed, you will find out.
5. If you could only find out now.
6. You would envision hell.
7. You would envision it with the eye of certainty.
8. You will be asked about your hoarding.

Sura 103: The Afternoon (Al-'Asr)

In the name of God, most gracious, most merciful

1. By the token of the afternoon.*
2. The human being is in total loss.
3. Except those who believe and lead a righteous life, and exhort each other to uphold the truth, and exhort each other to be steadfast.

103:1. The Quran pays tribute to various times of day (see 89:1, 92:1-2, and 93:1-2) in order for us to reflect. The alternation of night and day represents a great cosmic design.

Sura 104: The Backbiter (Al-Humazah)

In the name of God, most gracious, most merciful

1. Woe to the backbiter, the slanderer.
2. Who collects money (in this way),* and hoards it.
3. As if his money will make him immortal.
4. Indeed, he will be thrown into devastating doom.
5. Do you know what devastating doom?
6. God's flaming hellfire.
7. It burns them inside out.
8. They will be confined therein.
9. In long rows.

104:1-2.   *Often people backbite their fellow workers and slander them to their supervisors, in order to attain a promotion or a raise. They rise on the corpses of their fellow workers.*

Sura 105: The Elephant (Al-Feel)

In the name of God, most gracious, most merciful

1. Have you noted what your Lord did to the people of the elephant?
2. Did He not frustrate their plans?
3. He sent upon them airborne multitudes.
4. Showering them with sandstone rocks.
5. He made them like chewed up hay.

Sura 106: Quraish

In the name of God, most gracious, most merciful

1. Quraish should have cherished (this message).
2. The way they cherished the journeys of the winter and the summer.
3. They shall worship the Lord of this shrine.
4. The one who fed them after hunger, and gave them security after fear.

Sura 107: Charity (Al-Ma'oon)

In the name of God, most gracious, most merciful

1. Do you know who is the rejector of faith?
2. The one who neglects the orphan.
3. And never advocates the feeding of the poor.
4. Therefore, woe to those who observe the **salat** prayers.
5. While heedless of their **salat**.
6. They only show off.
7. And are averse to charity.

Sura 108: Bounty (Al-Kawther)

In the name of God, most gracious, most merciful

1. We have given you many bounties.
2. In appreciation, you shall worship your Lord, and be charitable.
3. Your enemy, henceforth, will be the loser.

Sura 109: The Disbelievers (Al-Kaafiroon)

In the name of God, most gracious, most merciful

1. Say, "O you disbelievers.
2. "I do not worship what you worship.
3. "Nor are you worshipping what I worship.
4. "Nor will I ever worship what you worship.
5. "Nor will you ever worship what I worship.
6. "To you is your religion, and to me is my religion."

Sura 110: Help (Al-Nasr)*
Last Sura Ever Revealed

In the name of God, most gracious, most merciful

1. When God's support comes and victory.
2. You will see the people embracing God's religion in great numbers.
3. You shall praise the glory of your Lord, and ask Him forgiveness; He is the redeemer.

110:1-3. Because this is the last sura ever revealed, it participates in the Quran's miraculous numerical code. This sura consists of exactly 19 Arabic words. The reader will note that the first revelation also consisted of 19 words (see 96:1).

Sura 111: Thorns (Al-Masad)

In the name of God, most gracious, most merciful

1. Doomed are the schemes of Abee-Lahab,* and he is doomed.
2. His money and his material accomplishments will never help him.
3. He will burn in the flaming hellfire.
4. And his wife, the evil bearer.
5. Will have a rope of thorns around her neck.

111:1. *One of the prophet Muhammad's uncles.*

Sura 112: Absoluteness (Al-Ikhlaas)

In the name of God, most gracious, most merciful

1. Say, "He is God; the only one.
2. "The absolute God.
3. "He never begets, nor was He ever begotten.
4. "There is none that equals Him."

Sura 113: Daybreak (Al-Falaq)

In the name of God, most gracious, most merciful

1. Say, "I seek refuge in the Lord of daybreak.
2. "From the evils among His creation.
3. "From the evils of darkness as it falls.
4. "From the evils of the troublemakers.
5. "And from the envious who envies."

Sura 114: The People (Al-Naas)

In the name of God, most gracious, most merciful

1. Say, "I seek refuge in the Lord of the people.
2. "The King of the people.
3. "The God of the people.
4. "From the evils of the sneaky whisperer.
5. "Who whispers into the hearts of the people.
6. "Be he of the jinn kind or the humankind."

LESSONS FROM QURAN

QURAN: THE FINAL SCRIPTURE
(Authorized English Version)

Translated From The Original By:
Rashad Khalifa, Ph.D.

Appendices 1-19

APPENDIX I

Secret Quranic Proof Unveiled: An Historical Landmark

In the name of God, most gracious, most merciful

Verse 88 of sura 17 states that: "If the humans and the jinns banded together to produce a Quran like this, they will surely fail, no matter how much assistance they lend one another." This impossibility to produce a similar Quran could not refer to the literary excellence of Quran, since many human beings have already produced great works of literature in every language. There had to be other features in Quran that render it impossible to imitate.

The unveiling of the Quran's miracle after the era of Muhammad is indicated in verse 20 of sura 10.

The existence of a secret proof in the Quran is implied in 25:4-6 and 13:43. The verses in sura 25 state: "The disbelievers claimed that this Quran is a fabrication invented by Muhammad, assisted by other people. Indeed, they have committed a blasphemy and a falsehood. They also said that this Quran is merely tales from the past, dictated to him day and night. Say, 'This was sent down by the One who knows the **SECRETS** in the heavens and the earth.'" And verse 43 of sura 13 states: "The disbelievers say that you (Muhammad) are not a messenger. Say, 'God suffices as witness between me and you, together with those who attain knowledge of the Quran.'"

The Quran was revealed to the world some 600 years after Christ and stood on its own without physical proof for 1400 years. It was the will of God, the author of Quran, that the secret Quranic proof shall await an era of mathematical sophistication, when the people can both understand and appreciate the miraculous intricacy of this proof. Electronic computers were needed to unveil an extremely sensitive system, where the alteration of a single letter in Quran causes total collapse of the system. Figure 1 shows a computer printout of the simple frequency of the letter "Q" (Qaf) in every sura, and Figure 2 shows the frequency of the letter "N" (Noon) throughout Quran. The reader will note that the Quran is uniquely characterized by the existence of "mysterious" alphabet letters, the Quranic initials, in a number of suras. The letter "Q", for example, prefixes two suras, namely suras 42 and 50. As shown in the computer printout, the frequency of occurrence of the letter "Q" in the two suras is 57 and 57. The frequency of occurrence of the letter "N" in the single N-initialed sura, namely sura 68, is 133. The reader may note here that there is a common denominator in the frequency of occurrence of the letter "Q" in suras 42 and 50, and the letter "N" in sura 68. The common denominator in 57 and 133 is "19," 57 = 19 × 3 and 133 = 19 × 7. The significance of this fact will become apparent as the reader examines the details of this miracle and finds that "19" is the common denominator for all the Quranic initials, without exception.

Since Quran is God's message to all the people, regardless of their level of education or cultural sophistication, the literary style of Quran encompasses a wide range of simplicity as well as complexity. Similarly, the Quran's proof spans a wide range of simplicity and complexity that renders it fully appreciable by the illiterate student of Quran as well as the most educated scholar.

The Simple Facts

1. The first verse in Quran, namely "In the name of God, most gracious, most merciful," consists of 19 Arabic letters.

2. Every word in this verse is repeated throughout Quran a number of times that is consistently a multiple of 19. Thus, the first word "Ism = name" is found in Quran exactly 19 times. The second word "Allah = God" is mentioned 2,698 times (19 × 142). The third word, "Al-Rahmaan = most gracious," is mentioned 57 times (19 × 3). The fourth word, "Al-Raheem = most merciful," is found in Quran 115 times. This number is not a multiple of 19. But, we note that there is one "Al-Raheem" word in Quran that refers specifically to the prophet Muhammad and not to God (verse 128 of sura 9). Since the first verse is in the name of God, we must exclude the word referring specifically to the prophet. Thus, the frequency of occurrence of "Al-Raheem" as an attribute of God is 114, 19 × 6.

It should be noted that although the opening statement, "In the name of God," is found at the opening of every sura (except sura 9), only the very first verse is assigned a number. Therefore, the count of words shown here includes only the first opening statement. Also, we note that all the Arabic letters of **"Basmalah"** (verse 1 of sura 1) belong to the same group as the Quranic initials, known as the light letters, except for the first letter "B".

Although this simple fact is an extremely minute component of the Quran's numerical miracle, the respected American journal, **Scientific American**, referred to it as "an ingenious study of Koran." (September 1980, pages 22-24.) Come to think of it, this fact alone is sufficient to prove the divine source of Quran. If we take all the man-made books in the world, how many will exhibit this unique phenomenon? How many books will show their opening statement consisting of an "x" number of letters and every word in the statement repeated throughout the book a multiple of "x"?

3. The Quran consists of 114 suras (19 × 6).

4. The opening statement, "In the name of God," is found at the beginning of every sura, except one, namely sura 9. This means that this crucial statement is repeated in Quran 113 times, just one short of the 6 multiples of 19. However, we discover that one sura, namely 27, contains two such statements. Sura 27 opens with the statement "In the name of God, most gracious, most merciful," then we find the statement repeated in verse 30. Verse 30 of sura 27 (30 + 27 = 57 = 19 × 3) refers to the queen of Sheba's statement that she had received a letter from Solomon, and that the letter is "In the name of God, most gracious,

most merciful." Thus, the total occurrence of the Quran's opening statement is 114 (19 × 6).

5.   Not only is the absence of **Basmalah** (the opening statement) from sura 9 compensated in sura 27, but we find that the number of suras from sura 9 to sura 27 is 19. In other words, to find the missing **Basmalah** from sura 9, you have to count 19 suras, then you find the extra **Basmalah** in sura 27.

6.   In sura 27, the number of words between the opening **Basmalah** and the **Basmalah** of verse 30 is 342 words (19 × 18).

7.   The first sura ever revealed, i.e., sura 96, is placed in Quran in position number 19 from the end. This point, in addition to point 5 above, prove that the written sequence of suras as we know it today was divinely inspired.

8.   The first Quranic revelation, namely the first 5 verses of sura 96, consist of exactly 19 words.

9.   The 19 words of the first Quranic revelation contain 76 letters (19 × 4).

10.   The first sura revealed, sura 96, consists of 19 verses.

11.   The number of alphabet letters that make up sura 96 is 285 letters (19 × 15).

12.   The last Quranic revelation, namely sura 110, consists of exactly 19 words.

13.   There is a whole sura about this secret numerical code entitled "The Hidden Secret," namely sura 74. In this sura, God informs us that if anyone claims that the Quran is man-made (verse 25), God will prove to him otherwise by the number 19 (verse 30).

14.   The Quran states that the number 19 will serve five functions: (1) to disturb the disbelievers; (2) to assure the good Jews and Christians that Quran is indeed a divine scripture; (3) to strengthen the faith of the believers; (4) to remove any lingering doubt in the hearts of the Muslims, Christians, and Jews that the Quran is God's message to the world; and (5) to expose the hypocrites, who are indifferent to this overwhelming Quranic miracle.

15.   God informs us that His numerical code is "one of the greatest miracles." (Verse 35 of sura 74.)

16.   In the sequence of revelation of Quran, which is different from the written sequence, the 19 letters of "Basmala" (verse 1 of sura 1) were revealed immediately following the number 19 mentioned in Quran (verse 30 of sura 74).

The Intricate Facts

The 16 facts mentioned above are simple, physical, and can be easily appreciated by anyone, regardless of education. There is absolutely no opinion or conjecture in those facts. In other words, no one is saying, "In my opinion, the opening statement of Quran consists of 19 letters and the number of suras is 114." Every single fact listed here is physical, touchable, examinable, and indisputable. Although the facts mentioned above are more than sufficient to prove that Quran can never be man-made; that it is God's message to the world, the greater portion of this physical evidence is embedded in the "mysterious" letters known as "Quranic Initials."

We find exactly half the Arabic alphabet, 14 letters, participating in the make-up of exactly 14 different sets of Quranic initials, and these initials prefix 29 suras. The 14 letters are Alif, Ha, Ra, Seen, Saad, Ta, 'Ayn, Qaf, Kaf, Lam, Meem, Nun, Ha, and Ya. The 14 sets of initials are Qaf, Nun, Saad, Ta Ha, Ya Seen, Ta Seen, Ha Meem, Alif Lam Meem, Alif Lam Ra, Ta Seen Meem, 'Ayn Seen Qaf, Alif Lam Meem Ra, Alif Lam Meem Saad, and Kaf Ha Ya 'Ayn Saad. The 29 suras that begin with Quranic initials are suras numbered 2, 3, 7, 10, 11, 12, 13, 14, 15, 19, 20, 26, 27, 28, 29, 30, 31, 32, 36, 38, 40, 41, 42, 43, 44, 45, 46, 50, and 68. These Quranic initials are unique to the Quran; they are not found in any other book in history, anywhere in the world. You will see that these Quranic initials have a consistent and direct relationship to the number 19, the letters of BISMILLAHIR RAHMANIR RAHIM. To begin with, 14 letters participate in forming 14 sets of initials, and these are found in 29 suras. When you add 14 + 14 + 29, you find the total 57, 19 × 3.

Now, let us examine each of the Quranic initials individually:

1. **The Quranic Initial "Q" (Qaf):**

This single-lettered Quranic initial is found in two suras, namely sura Qaf (No. 50) and sura Al-Shoora (No. 42). As shown in the computer printout of Figure 1, the letter "Q" occurs 57 times (19 × 3) in both suras.

Please note that sura 42 is more than twice as long as sura 50. Not only do we find that the only suras initialed with the letter Qaf contain the same number of Qafs, and that this number is a multiple of 19, but also when we add the total number of Qafs in these two suras, we find that the total 114 (19 × 6), equals the total number of suras in Quran. Thus, if the initial "Qaf" (Q) stands for "Quran," this factual observation tells us that the 114 suras constitute the Quran, the whole Quran, and nothing but the Quran.

An illustration of the miraculous intricacy of this Quranic mathematical system is in order. Looking at sura Qaf, verse 13, for example, we find it a short verse which is usually recited without any special attention. But, it contains a most profound demonstration of how every word, indeed every letter in Quran is divinely designed, calculated, and carefully placed. This short verse says, "'Aad, Pharaoh, and the brethren of Lot." The people of Lot are mentioned in Quran 12 times (7:80; 11:70, 74, 89; 22:43; 26:160; 27:54, 56; 29:28; 38:13; 50: 13; and 54:33) and they are consistently referred to as "Qawm Lot," with only one exception; in sura Qaf they are called "Ikhwan." It is readily obvious that the use of the word "Qawm" or "Ikhwan" determines the number of occurrences of the letter "Qaf" (Q). Thus, had the word "Qawm" been used in sura Qaf instead of the word "Ikhwan," the number of occurrences of the letter "Qaf" (Q) would have been 58, a number that is not a multiple of 19; and a number that will not match the number of "Qaf's" (Q's) in the sister sura where the initial Qaf occurs;

The Absolute Frequency of Occurrence of the Letter Qāf
(Q) in All Suras of the Qur'an; in Ascending Order.

CHAPTER	Q	ق	
CXI	0	--------	Al-Masad (Thorny Fibers)
CV	0	--------	Al-Fīl (The Elephant)
CVIII	0	--------	Al-Kawthar (Bounty)
CVII	0	--------	Al-Ma'ūn (Food for Charity)
CX	0	--------	Al-Nasr (Support)
CIX	1	--------	Al-Kafirūn (The Disbelievers)
CVI	1	--------	Quraish (The Quraish Tribe)
CXII	1	--------	Al-Ikhlāṣ (Absoluteness)
CIII	1	--------	Al-'Aṣr (The Afternoon)
CIV	1	--------	Al-Humaza (The Niggardly)
CXIV	1	--------	Al-Nas (Mankind)
XCIV	1	--------	Al-Sharḥ (Delight)
I	1	--------	Al-Fatiḥa (The Opener)
XCIII	2	--------	Al-Duhā (The Forenoon)
LXXXII	3	--------	Al-Infitār (The Disinitigration)
C	3	--------	Al-'Adiyāt (The Runners)
CII	3	--------	Al-Takāthur (Hoarding)
XCV	3	--------	Al-Tīn (The Fig)
XCVII	3	--------	Al-Qadr (Power)
LXXXVIII	3	--------	Al-Ghāshiya (Overwhelming)
XCVIII	4	--------	Al-Bayyina (The Evidence)
CI	4	--------	Al-Qāri'a (The Shocker)
XCIX	4	--------	Al-Zalzala (The Quake)
XCII	5	--------	Al-Layl (The Night)
LXXXV	6	--------	Al-Burūj (The Constellations)
LXXXVII	6	--------	Al-A'Lā (The Most High)
CXIII	6	--------	Al-Falaq (Daybreak)
LXXXI	8	--------	Al-Takwīr (The Folding)
XCVI	8	--------	Al-'Alaq (The Hanging Clot)
LXXXVI	9	--------	Al-Ṭāriq (The Bright Star)
LXXXIX	10	--------	Al-Fajr (Dawn)
XCI	10	--------	Al-Shams (The Sun)
XC	10	--------	Al-Balad (Hometown)
LXXIX	11	--------	Al-Nazi'āt (The Soul Snatchers)
LXXXIII	13	--------	Al-Muṭaffifīn (The Cheaters)
LXXX	13	--------	'Abasa (He Frowned)
LXII	14	--------	Al-Jumu'a (Friday)
LXIV	14	--------	Al-Taghābun (Requital)
LXXVI	15	--------	Al-Insān (Man)
LXXXIV	15	--------	Al-Inshiqāq (The Splitting)
LXX	16	--------	Al-Ma'ārij (Infinite Heights)
LXXVIII	17	--------	Al-Naba' (The News)
LIII	17	--------	Al-Najm (The Star)
LXVI	17	--------	Al-Taḥrīm (Prohibition)
LXXVII	18	--------	Al-Mursalāt (The Wended Winds)
LXI	19	--------	Al-Ṣaff (The Column)
LXXI	21	--------	Nūh (Noah)
LXVIII	21	--------	Al-Qalam (The Pen)
LV	22	--------	Al-Raḥmān (The Compassionate)
LXIII	23	--------	Al-Munāfiqūn (The Hypocrites)
LXXIII	24	--------	Al-Muzzammil (Wrapped Up)
LXXII	25	--------	Al-Jinn (The Jinns)
LXXIV	25	--------	Al-Muddathir (Bundled Up)

(Continued)

The Frequency of Occurrence of the Letter Nūn (N) in Each Sura. The Suras are Arranged in Ascending Order.

CHAPTER	N ن	
CXII	2	Al-Ikhlāṣ (Absoluteness)
CV	3	Al-Fīl (The Elephant)
CVI	4	Quraish (The Quraish Tribe)
CXI	5	Al-Masad (Thorny Fibers)
XCII	5	Al-Duhā (The Forenoon)
CVIII	6	Al-Kawthar (Bounty)
CIII	6	Al-'Aṣr (The Afternoon)
CIV	6	Al-Humaza (The Niggardly)
CX	6	Al-Naṣr (Support)
CXIII	6	Al-Falaq (Daybreak)
XCIX	7	Al-Zalzala (The Quake)
XCVII	9	Al-Qadr (Power)
XCI	9	Al-Shams (The Sun)
XCIV	9	Al-Sharḥ (Delight)
CIX	10	Al-Kāfirūn (The Disbelievers)
CXIV	10	Al-Nās (Mankind)
CI	11	Al-Qāri'a (The Shocker)
I	11	Al-Fātiḥa (The Opener)
CII	11	Al-Takāthur (Hoarding)
C	11	Al-'Ādiyāt (The Runners)
CVII	12	Al-Ma'ūn (Food for Charity)
LXXXVII	14	Al-A'lā (The Most High)
LXXXVI	17	Al-Ṭāriq (The Bright Star)
XCV	18	Al-Tīn (The Fig)
XCII	23	Al-Layl (The Night)
LXXXVIII	24	Al-Ghāshiya (Overwhelming)
LXXXII	24	Al-Infiṭār (The Disintegration
LXXXIX	24	Al-Fajr (Dawn)
XCVI	25	Al-'Alaq (The Hanging Clot)
XC	25	Al-Balad (Hometown)
LXXXV	29	Al-Buruj (The Constellations)
LXXXI	31	Al-Takwīr (The Folding)
LXXXIV	32	Al-Inshiqāq (The Splitting)
LXXX	34	'Abasa (He Frowned)
XCVIII	35	Al-Bayyina (The Evidence)
LXXIX	47	Al-Nāzi'āt (The Soul Snatchers)
LXII	49	Al-Jumu'a (Friday)
LXXV	53	Al-Qiyāma (Resurrection)
LXXIII	58	Al-Muzzammil (Wrapped Up)
LXXI	61	Nūḥ (Noah)
LXXVIII	62	Al-Naba' (The News)
LXIV	67	Al-Taghābun (Requital)
LXXVII	68	Al-Mursalāt (The Wended Winds)
LXIII	70	Al-Munāfiqūn (The Hypocrites)
LXXXIII	71	Al-Muṭaffifīn (The Cheaters)
LXIX	74	Al-Ḥāqqa (Retribution)
LXI	77	Al-Ṣaff (The Column)
LXXIV	79	Al-Muddathir (Bundled Up)
LXX	81	Al-Ma'ārij (Infinite Heights)
LXXVI	87	Al-Insān (Man)
LXV	95	Al-Talāq (Divorce)
LXVI	99	Al-Taḥrīm (Prohibition)
LXVII	100	Al-Mulk (Kingship)

478

(Continued)

and the total number of "Qaf's" will not match the total number of suras in Quran. In other words, the whole system collapses as a result of altering one letter. During the last 1400 years, if one word containing the letter Qaf, such as "Qawm, Yaqoolu, Qad, etc." was added, deleted, or altered in sura Qaf or sura Al-Shoora, this elaborate mathematical code would have simply disappeared.

2. The Quranic Initial "N" (Noon):

This initial is found in one sura, namely sura Al-Qalam (No. 68). When we count the number of occurrences of this letter in this sura, we find the total 133, a multiple of 19. Again, it is readily evident that the alteration of one word containing the letter "Noon" (N) would have caused this phenomenon to disappear. And, once again, the reader can appreciate the fact that this Quranic miracle is physical, examinable, and indisputable.

3. The Quranic Initial "S" (Saad):

This letter is found as an initial in sura 7 (Al-A'raaf), sura 19 (Maryam), and sura 38 (Saad). Adding up the number of occurrences of the letter Saad in these three suras, we find the total is 152, also a multiple of 19.

4. The Quranic Initials Y.S. (Ya Seen):

These two letters occur in sura 36, entitled Y.S. The letter "Y" occurs in this sura 237 times, and the letter "S" occurs 48 times. This makes the total frequency of the two letters in this sura 285, a multiple of 19.

5. The Quranic Initials H.M. (Ha Meem):

These two letters occur as initials in seven consecutive suras, namely 40 through 46. The frequency of occurrence of the letter "H" in the seven suras is 64, 48, 53, 44, 16, 31, and 36, respectively. The frequencies of the letter "M" in the seven suras are 380, 276, 300, 324, 150, 200, and 225, respectively. This makes the grand total of the two letters in the seven suras 2,147, a multiple of 19.

6. The Quranic Initials 'A.S.Q. ('Ayn Seen Qaf):

This set of initials constitutes verse 2 of sura 42. When we count the letter 'Ayn in this sura, we find it 98, while the letter "S" is found 54 times, and the letter "Q" 57 times (see also section 1 above). This makes the total frequency of occurence of the three letters in this sura 209, or 19 × 11.

7. The Quranic Initials A.L.R. (ALif Lam Ra):

This set of Quranic initials is found in five suras, namely 10, 11, 12, 14, and 15. As the reader notes, each set of Quranic initials is characterized by a unique relationship with the number 19. This particular set is found to occur in multiples of 19 in each individual sura initialed with A.L.R. Thus, the frequency of occurrence of the three letters in sura 10 is 1319, 913, and 257, respectively. This makes the total occurrence of the three letters in this sura 2489, or 19 × 131. Strangely, we find that the three letters total exactly the same in sura 11, though the frequency of the individual letters is different. We find that A, L, and R occur in sura 11 at frequencies of 1370, 794, and 325, respectively, totalling 2489 (19 × 131). In sura 12, the three letters are found in frequencies of 1306, 812, and 257, respectively, totalling 2375 (19 × 125). Sura 14 contains the three letters at frequencies of 585, 452, and 160, totalling 1197 (19 × 63). In sura 15, the three letters are found in frequencies of 493, 323, and 96, totalling 912 (19 × 48).

8. The Quranic Initials A.L.M. (Alif Lam Meem):

This set of Quranic initials is found in suras 2, 3, 29, 30, 31, and 32. The total frequency of occurrence of these letters is a multiple of 19 in each of these suras independently. Thus, sura 2 contains the letters A, L, and M in frequencies of 4502, 3202, and 2195, respectively. This adds up to a total of 9899 which is 19 × 521. Sura 3 contains 2521 of the Arabic letter "A", 1892 of the letter "L", and 1249 of the letter "M". This makes the total for the 3 initials 5662 (19 × 298). Sura 29 contains 774 A's, 554 L's, and 349 M's; totalling 1672, or 19 × 88. For sura 30, the frequencies of occurrence of the Arabic letters A, L, and M are 544, 393, and 317, respectively. The total of the 3 letters in this sura is 1254 (19 × 66). In sura 31 the frequencies are 347, 297, and 173, totalling 817 (19 × 43). The last sura in this group contains 257 A's, 155 L's, and 158 M's, totalling 570 (19 × 30).

9. The Quranic Initials A.L.M.Ṣ. (Alif Lam Meem Ṣaad):

These initials are found in sura 7 at frequencies of 2529, 1530, 1164, and 97, totalling 5320, or 19 × 280. Note the interlocking relationship of the letter "Ṣaad" with sura 38, and the letters A.L.M. of suras 2,.3, 29, 30, 31, and 32.

10. The Quranic Initials A.L.M.R. (Alif Lam Meem Ra):

This set of Quranic initials prefixes sura 13, and the grand total of A, L, M, and R in this sura is 1482, a multiple of 19. The letter "A" is found in a frequency of 605, the frequency of occurrence of the initial "L" is 480; for the letter "M", it is 260, and the letter "R" occurs in this sura 137 times.

11. The Quranic Initials K.H.Y. 'A.Ṣ. (Kaf Ha Ya 'Ayn Ṣaad):

This five-lettered set of Quranic initials occurs in sura 19. The letter "K" is found in this sura 137 times, the letter "H" 175 times, the letter "Y" 343 times, the letter, " 'A" 117 times, and the letter "Ṣ" occurs 26 times. Thus, the total frequency of occurrence of the five letters is 798, 19 × 42.

12. The Interlocking Initials Ha (H), Ṭa Ha (ṬH), Ṭa Seen (ṬS), and Ṭa Seen Meem (ṬSM):

An intricate interlocking system makes this group of Quranic initial unique. The suras covered by this system are 19 (Ha), 20 (Ṭa Ha), 26 (Ṭa Seen Meem), 27 (Ṭa Seen), and 28 (Ṭa Seen Meem). Details of the numbers involved are shown in the computer printout below. The grand total of these initials in their suras is 1767 or 19 × 93.

It should be noted that all counts are based on the original Quranic Arabic, as found in Quranic printings strictly adhering to the original. The reader, by now, appreciates the fact that the slightest alteration in one word, indeed one letter, utterly destroys this miraculous system. For example, point number 9 of the simple facts listed above states that the first Quranic revelation (19 words) consisted of 76 letters (19 × 4). This first revelation contains two words of الانسـن , which means "the human being." Some printings of the Quran use the conventional Arabic الانسان , rather than the Quranic

Arabic الإنسـن . The reader who consults a printing that does not conform to the original Quranic Arabic will find that the first revelation consists of 78 letters, which is wrong.

Another example is noteworthy. The letter "Noon"(N) of sura 68, verse 1, is spelled out into three alphabet letters نون. The new printings of Quran have dropped this spelling and usually write down the single letter "N". Thus, if the reader consults a Quranic printing that does not spell out the letter "N" into "Noon", will have a deficiency of 1 in the total frequency of "Noon" in sura 68. It should be noted that this is the only letter that is spelled out in the original, and it is the only Quranic initial that stands by itself without interacting or interlocking with the other initials.

THE TOTAL FREQUENCY OF OCCURRENCE OF THE QURANIC INITIALS HA (H), TTA (T), SEEN (S), AND MEEM (M) IN CHAPTER 19 (HA), CHAPTER 20 (TTA HA), CHAPTER 26 (TTA SEEN MEEM), CHAPTER 27 (TTA SEEN), AND CHAPTER 28 (TTA SEEN MEEM)

	HA	TTA	SEEN	MEEM
CHAPTER 19	175	–	–	–
CHAPTER 20	251	28	–	–
CHAPTER 26	–	33	94	484
CHAPTER 27	–	27	94	–
CHAPTER 28	–	19	102	460
	426	107	290	944

GRAND TOTAL OF THE 5 INITIALS = 426+107+290+944 = 1767 = 19X93

Quranic Numbers

Since the Quranic evidence is based on the numerical code just presented, it was thought that the numbers mentioned in Quran may also be involved. Indeed, a Muslim scholar from Homs, Syria (Sidqi Al-Baik) reported that the Quran contains 285 numbers, and 285 = 19 × 15. When all 285 numbers mentioned in Quran are added up, the total is 174591, a multiple of 19. As if this is not enough, when we remove all repetitions, we find the total is 162146, also a multiple of 19.

Quran Proves the Miracles of Moses and Jesus

Since Quran is God's final message to the world, it is only logical that it should be preserved intact, protected from the slightest distortion, and set up as a confirmation for all previous scriptures (see 15:9 and 5:48). Not only does the Quran prove Muhammad as a messenger of God, but it also provides the first physical proof of the miracles performed by Jesus, Moses, Solomon, and all the prophets. For example, none of us witnessed Moses when he threw down his staff and it turned into a serpent; none of us witnessed the parting of the Red Sea; none of us witnessed the virgin birth of Jesus. But when the world receives such statements in Quran, supported by physical proof that every letter is a divine truth, then those miracles of Moses and Jesus become physically proven facts.

What God Says About This Quranic Miracle

There is no greater acknowledgement of this Quranic miracle than God's own words in sura 74, verse 35. The Quran's numerical code is described in this verse as "one of the greatest miracles." The objective reader will readily agree with the Almighty.

In retrospect, we now realize that sura 74, entitled "The Hidden Secret," refers to the Quran's numerical code. We find that God most gracious, informs us that anyone who claims that Quran is man-made (verse 25), will be proven wrong by means of the number 19 (verse 30). Furthermore, we are told in verse 31 that this secret code was placed in Quran to perform five different functions:
   (1)   To disturb the disbelievers;
   (2)   To prove to the Christians and Jews that Quran is a divine scripture;
   (3)   To augment the belief of the Muslims who already believe that Quran is a divine scripture (see 2:260);
   (4)   To remove all traces of doubt from the hearts of Jews, Christians, and Muslims, regarding the divine source of Quran; and
   (5)   To expose the hypocrites and disbelievers, for they will be indifferent or averse.

Also, in retrospect, we discover that God has been telling us the meaning of the Quranic initials since the revelation of Quran. Almost invariably, the Quranic initials are followed by a statement to the effect that God is the author of Quran. More specifically, eight suras describe the Quranic initials as "the miracle of Quran." (See 10:1, 12:1, 13:1, 15:1, 26:2, 27:1, 28:2, and 31:2.)

Why 19?

The theme of Quran is that we shall worship God, the ONE God, alone, and never idolize anyone or anything else. The whole message of Quran centers around the ONE God, and it was discovered that 19 = ONE.

Before the invention of numbers, people in the ancient times used the alphabet to express numbers. Thus, the first ten letters of the Arabic alphabet, in their original order, are as follows:

$\mathbf{1}$ = 1, $\underline{\smile}$ = 2, ζ = 3, $\mathbf{3}$ = 4,

$\clubsuit$ = 5, $\mathbf{9}$ = 6, $\mathbf{j}$ = 7, ζ = 8,

$\mathbf{b}$ = 9, and $\mathcal{S}$ = 10.

The Arabic word for ONE is وَحِد , consisting of $\mathbf{9}$ = 6, $\mathbf{1}$ = 1,
ζ = 8, and $\mathbf{3}$ = 4. By adding the numerical value of these four letters (6 + 1 + 8 + 4), we find the total 19. Therefore, 19 = واحــد = ONE.

The role of the number 19 seems to have universal dimensions. As it turns out, the sun, the moon, and the earth, as created and designed by the author of Quran, are lined up in a specific orientation once every 19 years. Thus, in the Jewish traditions, the Jewish lunar year is adjusted every 19 years, when the sun, the moon, and the earth are aligned in that specific orientation. It seems that the cosmos is declaring, "God is ONE." Consult the Jewish Encyclopedia (Encyclopedia Judica) under "Calendar."

After carefully reflecting on this overwhelming Quranic miracle, the reader will fully appreciate the statement in verse 21 of sura 59, "If we reveal this Quran to a mountain, you will see it trembling, crumbling, out of reverence for God."

Some readers may legitimately say, "Asking me to count these vast Quranic numbers is the same as asking me to count the stars." To accommodate all the readers who wish to check every aspect of this great miracle, the frequency of occurrence of the Quranic initials has been made available on a "verse by verse" basis. The full details, verse by verse, are published in a separate book entitled "The Computer Speaks: God's Message to the World." The book is available from Islamic Productions International, 739 East 6th Street, Tucson, Arizona 85719, U.S.A. With the verse by verse details, any reader can easily spot-check any verse or verses to verify the accuracy of all counts. The reader does not need to check whole suras to confirm the truth.

APPENDIX 2

We Made the Quran Easy to Memorize

Verse 1 of sura 11 informs us that the Quran's numerical code involves two distinct miraculous feats; the design of every letter in Quran according to a numerical system, and the simultaneous composition of an extraordinary literary work. You may be able to control the numerical distribution of alphabet letters when you write, but the literary quality of such work will be adversely affected by numerical restrictions.

The extraordinary control of alphabetical distribution throughout Quran is manifested in the fact that Quran is made easy to memorize. The title of this Appendix is repeated in sura 54, verses 17, 22, 32, and 40.

As it turns out, every letter in Quran is positioned in such a way as to remind us of the next expression or the next verse. God created us and knows how our brains work. Without even realizing it, the person who memorizes Quran is helped by an intricate audio system as he utters the sounds of Quranic words. To illustrate, I will cite here two examples:

1. In sura 2, verses 127, 128, and 129 end up with two names of God each. Verse 127 ends with the names "Assamee' Al-'Aleem" السميع العليم (the hearer, the omniscient), verse 128 ends with "Attawwab Arraheem" التواب الرحيم (the redeemer, most merciful), and verse 129 ends with "Al-Azeez Al-Hakeem" العزيز الحكيم (the almighty, most wise). Normally, if this were a regular book, a person who memorizes these verses would mix the six names and confuse the positioning of one or more of them. Not so in the Quran. We find that the words of these three verses (like all words in Quran) are designed so as to make it virtually impossible to confuse or mix up these names of God. Thus, ahead of the words "Assamee' Al-'Aleem السميع العليم " of verse 27, we find a reminding bell with a prominent "S س " and " 'Ayn ع ," that remind us that the divine names to follow must be "Assamee' Al-'Aleem." The reminding bell in this verse is the word Ismaa'eel (Ishmael). The reader will note that this word is peculiarly removed from its natural place and brought closer to the ending of the verse, thus effecting a sure reminder. The normal Arabic composition for this verse would be, "As Abraham and Ishmael raised the foundations of the shrine . . ." But the Quranic composition places the word "Ishmael" closer to the end of the verse, in order to remind us of God's names "Assamee' Al-'Aleem." The Quranic composition, which is in perfect literary style despite this rearrangement, is like this: "As Abraham raised the foundations of the shrine with Ishmael . . ."

In verse 128, we find the reminding bell strategically placed ahead of God's names "Attawwab Arraheem التواب الرحيم " in the word "Tubb تب " (redeem). Since the word Arraheem follows the word Attawwab throughout Quran, the person who memorizes the Quran will automatically remember "Arraheem" as the word to follow "Attawwab." the Quran contains nine such expressions, i.e., "Attawwab Arraheem" (see 2:37, 2:54, 2:128, 2:160, 4:16, 4:64, 9:104, 9:118, and 49:12). There is only one "Tawwab" word that is followed by "Hakeem" (24:10).

In verse 129, the two names "Al-Azeez, Al-Hakeem" are strategically preceded by a powerful reminding bell, namely the word "Yuzakkeehim يزكيهم" prominently displaying the two letters "Z" and "K".

2.   Another example is found in verses 176, 177, and 178 of sura 3. These three verses end up with the words "Azaabun 'Azeem عذاب عظيم," "'Azaabun Aleem عذاب اليم," and "'Azaabun Muheen عذاب مهين," respectively. Three different adjectives for the word "'Azaabun," which means "retribution." If this were a regular book, the person who memorizes these verses would confuse and mix the three adjectives. Not so in Quran. We find powerful reminding bells that tell us which adjective will follow. Thus, in verse 176, the reminding bell is the word "Hazzan حظا," which is strategically located so as to remind us that the last word in the verse is "'Azeem عظيم." In verse 177, the reminding bell is the word "Eemaan ايمان," which tells our brain that the adjective to be used is "Aleem اليم." In verse 178, the adjective "Muheen مهين" is made utterly unforgettable by four reminding bells repeating the two letters "H" and "M" throughout the verse.

These are just two examples, but the Quran is similarly designed throughout so as to make it easy to remember; not only remember the contents of the verse, but also the subsequent verse. See, for example, the Arabic ending of verse 3:173 and the beginning of 174, the ending of verse 4:52 and the beginning of 53, the ending of 4:61 and the beginning of 62, and the ending of verse 18:53 and the beginning of 54.

APPENDIX 3

Why was the Quran Revealed in Arabic?

Sura 41, verse 44, teaches us that the Quran had to come down in some language and that if it was in Japanese, the disbelievers will say, "Why was it revealed in Japanese?" The same verse teaches that the language of God's scripture is immaterial; that God will put it in the hearts of sincere believers, regardless of their tongue. On the other hand, the disbelievers and insincere believers will be rendered totally blind and deaf to it, even if they were the greatest scholars of Arabic linguistics (see also 17:45-46 and 18:57).

During my work as a United Nations (UNIDO) technical expert, I had a chance to compare the efficiency of virtually all languages of the world. As it turned out, Arabic proved to be the most efficient, especially in regards to the writing of statutes. A simple and clear example is the word "they" in the English language. When we say "they," we could be talking about either a group of men or a group of women, or a mixture of men and women, or two males or two females. This problem does not exist in Arabic; there is a word for the group of men, "Hum هـم ," there is a word for the group of women "Hunna هن ," there is a word for the two "Humaa هما," there is a word for the two males, "Haazaani هذان ," and there is a word for the two females, "Haataaniهاتان

In Arabic, the verbs and adjectives can selectively and unmistakably refer to males, or females, or two people, or more than two people. The efficiency of the Arabic language can be illustrated by the word "Qaalataa قالتا"(28:23), which requires four English words, "The two women said." These characteristics of the Arabic language are extremely important in the writing of laws and statutes, which exist abundantly throughout Quran, a statute book. A case in point is the laws of marriage, divorce, and inheritance. For example, verse 233 of sura 2 states that a divorcee cannot remarry until an interim of three menstruations is fulfilled. If pregnancy occurs, then the divorcee must inform the husband, and if the husband wishes to reconcile, the wife should forsake her personal wishes and reconcile with the husband. The verse almost exclusively uses the feminine language, except where it comes to the husband's wishes. We find that one word stands out in the masculine, namely the word "**araadoo** (they wish)." No other language in the world can effectively state this divine law, without using an excessive number of words.

Another important possibility for choosing Arabic as the Quran's language is the fact that the words "he" and "she" do not necessarily imply gender. Thus, when the Quran refers to God as "He," this does not at all imply that God is "male." God be glorified; He is not male, nor female : above gender. The Arabic language refers to the "the door" as masculine, "the window" as feminine, the "book" as masculine, and the "house" as masculine, even though we know that these things are neither male nor female. On the other hand, when the English language refers to God as "He," this creates the subconscious impression that God is male. Together with the reference to God as "Father," a satanic idea is reinforced, namely that God is either the man Jesus or the "father" of Jesus. Needless to say, these are blasphemous and disasterous impressions.

APPENDIX 4

Heaven and Hell

The descriptions of heaven and hell throughout Quran are given in allegorical terms, as stated in 2:24-26, 13:35, and 47:15. The reality of heaven and the reality of hell are beyond our wildest imaginations. We are told in 2:26 that heaven and hell, as described in Quran, are in the same proportion to the real thing as a mosquito compared to you. In verses 13:35 and 47:15, we find the description preceded by the word "**mathal** مشـل ," which means allegory. Linguistically, this word is not needed at all, if the description of heaven and hell were not allegorical. These verses will be perfect and make complete sense, linguistically, without the word "**mathal**." Obviously, the word is needed because the descriptions of heaven and hell throughout Quran are allegorical.

APPENDIX 5

Greatness of God

Verse 67 of sura 39 states that the people could never value God's greatness. The verse tells us that all seven heavens are "folded in God's hand." The Quran teaches us that our universe is the lowest, smallest, and innermost of seven "heavens" or "universes," and that we can never penetrate beyond the borders of our universe (see 41:12, 55:33, 67:5, and 72:8-12). It has been scientifically established that our universe contains a billion galaxies, a billion trillion stars, and countless trillions of planets (see 40:57 and 79:27-30). Some of the galaxies within our "small" universe are millions of light years away.

If we can imagine going on a space odyssey where we leave the planet earth, then exit the solar system with its millions of miles distances, its 12 major planets, hundreds of satellites, and thousands of minor planets or asteroids, comets, and meteors, then we leave our Milky Way Galaxy, try not to lose sight of our planet Earth (the solar system is a small component of the Milky Way Galaxy). The whole planet Earth, when we look at it from the outer limits of the Milky Way, is like a speck of dust in a standard size room. Let us go on to the outer limits of our universe. Looking from that point, the Milky Way will be like a speck of dust in a large room. Can you imagine the submicroscopic size of our planet Earth in this vast universe?

Our universe is the smallest and innermost of seven universes created by God. The second universe, or "heaven" as referred to in this translation, is necessarily much larger than our universe. The third layer, or universe, or heaven, is, of course, larger than the second, and so on to the seventh universe. Try to envision the vastness of the seven universes and the infinitesimal size of the planet Earth. On that tiny planet lived such creatures as yourself, Jesus, Mary and Muhammad. How significant are any of these as a component of this vast creation of God?

Verse 67 of sura 39 informs us that all seven universes are folded in God's right hand. Such is the greatness of God.

APPENDIX 6

Why Were We Created?

In the beginning, there was God and nothing else. Then God created the angels to carry out certain tasks not fit for the almighty, or tasks where the presence of God is utterly devastating (see 7:143). However, one of the archangels who was given vast power and authority, namely Satan, started to develop haughty ideas. He thought he was powerful enough to be a partner of God. Since these ideas were simply internal thoughts, none of the angels were aware of Satan's outrageous haughtiness. God, of course, was fully aware (see 2:30). There were two choices to defuse Satan's coup: (1) banish Satan from angelhood, and (2) expose Satan's rebellion before effecting retribution. It was the will of the Almighty to expose Satan first. Without exposing Satan, the angel population would have wondered, "Why did God banish Satan, when he did nothing wrong?"

In order to expose Satan as a haughty rebel, God decided to create a creature from clay, namely Adam. Then He asked the angels to fall prostrate before Adam (see 2:34). They all fell prostrate; but not Satan. Thus, Satan was exposed as a rebel, and this was one purpose for creating us.

It was certainly too much of a blasphemy on the part of Satan to entertain such rebellious ideas. The angels see God and KNOW that He is the Lord of the universe. Yet, one of them developed haughty and rebellious ideas, and this was too much indeed. Consequently, God wanted to show the angels a creature who submits completely to God, without ever seeing Him. And this is the second purpose behind creating us. Now that Satan has been exposed and punished, the only purpose of our life is to discover God, reach Him, and come to the conclusion that He alone is king and master, without ever seeing Him. When you thus fulfill the purpose of your life, God is proud of you. He tells the angels, "Look at this creature of Mine; he never saw Me, yet he discovered Me, recognized Me, and totally submitted to Me." It follows that any human being who makes it, fulfills the purpose of his or her life, and totally submits to God, is better than the angels. A creature who submits to God without ever seeing Him certainly deserves more credit than a creature who sees God and knows beforehand that He is the absolute Lord. The purpose of our creation is spelled out simply and clearly in verse 56 of sura 51, "I did not create the humans and the jinns except to worship Me." The humans are Adam's descendants, while the jinns are Satan's descendants.

Some people ask, "Why did God create me, put me through this misery, and demand that I worship Him?" The fact is that we were not forced into this situation. The Quran teaches us that we were given a choice, and we decided, each one of us, that we wanted to undergo the test (see 7:172 and 33:72). On the other hand, the choice of happiness or misery, both in this life and the hereafter, is completely and absolutely up to us. We can choose to be perfectly happy or utterly miserable (see 10:62-64 and 20:124).

APPENDIX 7

The Myth of Intercession

One of Satan's most effective tricks to dupe the people into idol worship is the myth of intercession. Thus, many Christians believe that Jesus will serve as an intercessor for them at God, and many Muslims believe that Muhammad will intercede on their behalf. These beliefs have led both the Christians and the Muslims into idolizing Jesus, Muhammad, Mary, in addition to hundreds of saints.

The Quran teaches us consistently that, for all practical purposes, there will be no intercession on the day of judgment. As a statement of fact, we learn from Quran that everyone in heaven will inevitably wish that his or her beloved family and friends were also in heaven. This kind of "intercession" will be effective only if it happens to coincide with God's decision. In other words, if you implore God, on the day of judgment, to admit your mother into heaven, your intercession will work if your mother was already saved. If, on the other hand, your mother was not among the saved, then your intercession will be in vain. The Quran vividly illustrates these facts by setting the prophets themselves as examples. Thus, the prophet Muhammad's uncle is condemned in Quran (sura 111), and the prophet can never intercede on his behalf. Muhammad is told clearly in Quran that he cannot intercede on behalf of sinners (see 9:80). Abraham's father is similarly condemned, and God's chosen friend, Abraham (see 4:125), cannot intercede on his behalf (see 9:114). Noah's intercession on behalf of his son is rejected (see 11:45). Two wives of two prophets, namely Noah and Lot, cannot be helped by their husbands (see 66:10).

Specifically, we are told that the prophets' intercession is useful only if their wishes happen to coincide with God's decision (see 21:28). Furthermore, we are told in the same verse that the prophets themselves are worried about their own necks. See also 2:48,123,254,255; 6:51,70,94; 7:53; 10:3; 19:87; 20:109; 21:28; 26:100; 30:13; 32:4; 36:23; 39:44; 40:18; 43:86; 53:26; and 74:48.

APPENDIX 8

Abraham: Founder of Islam

One of the prevalent myths is that Muhammad was the founder of Islam. The Quran, however, informs us that Abraham was the first user of the word "Islam" (submission), that he is the one who called us "Muslims" (submitters) (see 22:78), and he is the first recipient of all the religious duties practiced by the Muslims today. We learn from Quran, in no uncertain terms, that Muhammad was a follower of Abraham (see 16:123).

Although the Quran repeatedly states that it is perfect, complete, and needs no supporting materials (6:19, 38 and 114), Satan uses the religious duties in Islam to confuse those who are ignorant of Quran. Satan asks them, "If the Quran is complete and perfect, where in Quran can we find descriptions of the **salat** prayers?" This same question is used to dupe multitudes of people into seeking false sources of jurisprudence, such as **hadith** and/or **sunna**. To reject God's assurances that Quran is complete (see 6:115) and seek other sources of religious regulation amounts to idol worship (see 18:57 and 42:21).

The Quran clearly states that all religious duties in Islam were originally revealed through Abraham, then transmitted to us generation after generation. This is why we find the Quran instructing us to uphold "previous revelations" (see 2:4), at the very beginning of Quran. Specifically, we find the **salat** prayers and **zakat** charity revealed to Abraham in 21:73. The fasting of Ramadan was originally given to Abraham (2:183), then modified when given to Muhammad (see footnote 2:187). The **Hajj** pilgrimage was specifically revealed through Abraham in 22:26-27.

We find that the pre-Muhammad Arabia was practicing **salat** prayers (8:35), and that the very early revelations of Quran were talking about **salat** and **zakat** as well-known practices (see 73:20). The storytellers, who used to be the major form of entertainment, invented a most unreasonable story about the prophet Muhammad receiving and bargaining about **salat**. The story emanated from ignorance and misunderstanding of 17:1 (see footnote 17:1). See also 2:127-128, 2:135, 3:68, 3:95, 4:125, 16:123, 21:73, 22:27, and 22:78.

APPENDIX 9

God's Plural Tense Throughout Quran

In the English speaking world, where the trinity doctrine is prevalent, some people become intrigued by God's usage of the plural tense throughout Quran. The oneness of God is never in question anywhere in Quran (see 2:133, 2:163, 4:171, 5:73, 6:19, 9:31, 12:39, 13:16, 14:48, 14:52, 16:22, 16:51, 18:110, 21:108, 22:34, 37:4, 38:65, 29:4, 40:16, 41:6, 112:1, and the end of Appendix 1). The plural tense is used consistently when the action involves the angels, rather than God alone. For example, the revelation of Quran was effected with Gabriel's participation (see 2:97). When talking about Quranic revelations, therefore, the plural is used to acknowledge Gabriel's role. Similarly, whenever the plural is used, we know that the angels have participated, and that God credits the angels for their participation. On the other hand, in situations where God alone is the doer, we find the Almighty using the singular. For example, when God spoke to Moses, there was no angelic mediation, and we find God speaking in the singular (see 20:12-15). The act of worship is directed, singularly, to God alone (see 12:14 and 51:56).

APPENDIX 10

The Day of Resurrection

The believer in Quran is never in the dark. We are given, direct from our creator, reliable information dealing with the purpose of our creation, who we are, what we are, why we are, and where we are going. The believer of Quran knows, for example, how this world will end and the signs that must be fulfilled before the end comes. This very translation is one such sign. The discovery of the Quran's miraculous secret numerical code (Appendix 1), after 14 centuries of continuous work, is proclaimed in 74:35 as one of the signs that must be fulfilled before the end of the world. The other signs are the splitting of the moon (54:1), the smoke that will envelope the world (44:10), the creature that will speak to the people (27:82), and the invasion by Gog and Magog (18:94-99). Before the day of resurrection comes, these prophecies must be fulfilled.

Vivid descriptions of the end of the world are given in 55:37-78, 56:1-56, 69:13-37, 75:6-15, 78:17-40, 82:1-19, and 89:21-30. The Quran teaches us that this world will end when God simply "comes" (see 89:22), since our world cannot stand the presence of God (see 7:143). One may ask, "Does this mean that God is not here now?" And the answer is, "Yes. God is not here now." We learn from Quran that God's work on earth is done through the angels, and that our universe cannot stand the presence of God. Through remote control, however, God is closer to you than your jugular vein (50:16). Through remote control, God runs and controls every minute detail in our world, including the number of blood cells in your veins; not a leaf falls without His knowledge and control (6:59).

Since our universe and our present bodies cannot stand the presence of God (7:143), a process of substitution will take place (14:48). A new earth and new heavenly bodies will replace the present earth and heavenly bodies. The new sky will be rose colored, instead of today's blue (55:37). We will be given new bodies; bodies that will last forever, without deteriorating. The size and/or looks of our bodies will depend on our response to God's message. Those who responded positively, heeded the message, and carried out the commandments, will be given strong, healthy, and well developed bodies. They themselves have developed their own bodies through such prescribed exercises as the **salat** prayers, **zakat** charity, fasting, pilgrimage, and the righteous works. As for those who did not heed God's message and failed to exercise and develop their souls, they will be given weak, shrunken, and miserable bodies. We learn from Quran that the differences in looks between the righteous and unrighteous will be so profound that the guilty will not even be asked, "What did you do wrong?" Verses 39-41 of sura 55 teach us that the guilty will be recognized by their looks, and that there will be no need to ask them about their sins.

We are told that, initially, everyone will go to hell; and this includes Jesus, Moses Muhammad, Mary, and Noah (see 19:71). This is God's decree that must be carried out as 19:71 informs us. Why? You cannot fully appreciate heaven unless you see what hell looks like. Your enjoyment of heaven will multiply manyfold when you know hell. Additionally, being in hell initially is an integral part of the mechanism of resurrection. On the day of resurrection, we will derive our nourishment, sustenance, and happiness in the presence of God. The absence of God is hell. Thus, we will be resurrected, all of us, simultaneously (see 18:99, 36:51, 39:68, 69:13, and 78:18). Once we are raised, we will all be in hell since God has not yet appeared (19:71). Then, God and the angels come (89:22), whereupon the stars crash into one another (82:1-2), and the sun, moon, earth, and the planets shatter. God then creates a new earth and new heavens that are capable of bearing His presence (14:48).

When God appears on the day of resurrection, we will be automatically stratified into four different classes. This stratification will take place automatically and instantaneously (2:202, 3:19, 3:199, 5:4, 6:62, 6:165). Those among us who failed to heed God's message and do not possess strong enough souls will not stand the presence of God. Thus, when God comes, they will flee to the lowest and farthest layer, namely hell. Those among us who heeded God and carried out His commandments will possess strong souls and new strong bodies. They will immensely enjoy the presence of God. They will be stratified into the layer closest to God, namely the high heaven (55:46-62 and 56:10-27). Those among us who did not develop as much as the occupants of the high heaven, and also those who die as children, or were not mentally sound in this life, will be stratified into the lower heaven (55:62 and 56:27-40). The differences between the high heaven and the low heaven are spelled out allegorically in sura 55. We note that the high heaven contains springs that gush out and flow (55:50), while the low heaven contains wells that require pumping (55:66). The beautiful companions in the high heaven readily come to the occupants, while those in the low heaven must go searching for them (55:72). These allegorical comparisons teach us that there are vast differences between the high heaven (closest to God) and the low heaven (farther from God) (see 17:21).

There will be people who developed just enough to be spared hell. Their works in this life caused their souls to grow and develop just enough to keep them outside the borderline of hell. But they will be too weak to climb into the borderline of the low heaven. They cannot stand to be any closer to God. The area between hell and the low heaven, where these people are placed initially is known as "Al-A'raaf," translated here as "Purgatory." Eventually, God's mercy will allow those in the purgatory to enter the low heaven, and the purgatory will be permanently annexed into the low heaven (7:46-49).

We learn from Quran that the inhabitants of hell (farthest place from God) will recognize that the nourishment, sustenance, and indescribable happiness can be attained only in the presence of God. Consequently, they will actually sneak into the low heaven. But, as they come closer to God, they will suffer even more because of their weak, shrunken, and unprepared souls. They will then run back to hell. Being so hopelessly miserable in hell, away from God, they will try again to sneak into heaven, and so forth. They will spend eternity circulating between hell and the worse suffering when they sneak into heaven. This is presented vividly in 55:43-44.

The Quran teaches us that the inhabitants of each layer can only move downward, farther from God, and not upward. In fact, the inhabitants of heaven will move down to hell and visit their friends and relatives there (37:51-57).

Once the Almighty comes, on the day of resurrection, and we are automatically stratified into the ranks we have chosen, we will then find out why we are assigned a particular rank or position. Each one of us will be given an audio-video record of his or her life on earth (17:13-14). Every minute detail of our life in this world, from birth to death will be in our record (18:49). Each one of us will be his own judge (17:14). This record, showing three dimensional, real life images, and even exposing our innermost thoughts, is described throughout the Quran (36:65, 41:20-21).

The Mechanism of Worship

We learn from Quran that the extent of our development in this life determines our eternal rank in the real life, the hereafter. When we "believe," this constitutes the first step towards salvation. Belief alone by no means suffices. Pharaoh sincerely believed in God as he was dying. But his belief did not help him one bit (see 10:91). We have to "do" something that causes our souls to grow and develop. Just as our bodies need nutrition to grow and develop, so do our souls. Unfortunately, the vast majority of people spend their lives feeding, clothing, housing, and caring for their bodies, while neglecting their souls. Then, when the time of separation comes, they become shocked; they have wasted their time and effort caring for something they shed and throw away into the soil.

The food needed to grow and develop our souls is prescribed in Quran and includes **salat**, **zakat**, fasting, **hajj** pilgrimage, and carrying out the commandments. These religious duties were prescribed for our growth and development; God does not need our worship. Because our souls are literally a small part of God (15:29, 32:9 and 38:72). when we do anything that has to do with God, our souls grow in leaps and bounds. Every time you observe a **salat** prayer, something happens to you that makes you vastly different from a person who did not observe **salat**. While our bodies grow to 5 to 7 feet tall, the growth of our souls is in much larger scales (17:29). Every righteous work that is done with God in mind (see 4:124, 16:97, and 20:75 and 112) increases the size and "weight" of our souls (see 7:8, 23:102, and 101:6). Those who are righteous, i.e., they are honest, truthful, and charitable, but do not believe in God, or are idolizing anyone besides God, are only wasting their time and effort (see 3:116-117). Those who fail to develop their souls will end up weak, shrunken, and "weightless" on the day of resurrection (see 18:105). We are provided with criteria that show us whether our souls are grown enough or not enough. The religious duties in Islam are designed to strengthen the soul, the eternal entity, and make it dominate the body, the vanishing entity, Thus, the first **salat** prayer is due every morning before sunrise. At this time of day, the body wants to sleep, while the soul "needs" to get up for the morning nutrition. If the person forces the body to get up for **salat**, the soul will grow a little stronger. Eventually, the soul will be so strong that the body stops resisting and becomes obedient to the soul, the real you. Therefore, the degree of resistance that your body gives you at dawn is one criterion that shows you the degree of your growth. Similarly, when we fast during the month of Ramadan, we are telling the body, "You are not going to eat or drink until sunset." Initially, the body will resist, but as the soul grows and develops, the body stops resisting. In practicing the **zakat** charity, we take from the body its beloved money and give it away to the poor. The extent of the body's resistance to the acts of worship provides us with a measure of our soul's strength.

APPENDIX 11

Role of the Prophet

The Prophet's sole mission was to deliver Quran, the whole Quran, and nothing but Quran (see 3:20, 5:48-50, 5:92, 5:99, 6:19, 13:40, 16:35, 16:82, 24:54, 29:18, 42:48, and 64:12). It is an historical fact that the prophet Muhammad instructed his followers to take from him only Quran, and nothing but Quran, as evidenced by the fact that the first two centuries of Islam witnessed no "**Hadith.**" Ironically, this historical fact is recorded in some of the most prominent books of **Hadith.** The document on page 504 shows a **Hadith** reported in the book of Muslim, where the Prophet is reported to have said, "Do not write from me except Quran. Anyone who wrote anything else shall erase it." The same document shows that Imam Ahmad Ben Hanbal, the most strict imam of jurisprudence, reported in his **"Is-haah"** that this order by the Prophet was never changed. Iman Ben Hanbal reports the following **hadith.** "After the death of the Prophet and all four successors, the Khalifas Abu Bakr, Umar, Uthman, and Ali, the head of the Muslim nation was Mu'aawiyah. One time the famous revelation writer Zeid Ben Thaabit, also known as the Prophet's secretary, was visiting Mu'aawiyah. During the conversation, Zeid mentioned something the Prophet had said. Mu'aawiyah liked the story and ordered someone to write it down. But Zeid said, 'The Prophet ordered us not to write anything from him except Quran.' Mu'aawiyah then ordered the story erased." Thus, the early Muslims, for 250 years, obeyed the Prophet and respected his wishes. The first disobedience of the Prophet was committed by Bukhaary, who was born some two centuries after **Hijrah.**

Satan's pledge to mislead the believers (see 7:16, 15:39, and 38:82) proved successful against the Jews, Christians, and Muslims. Thus, a few centuries after Moses, the "scholars" of Israel invented the Mishnah (oral) and Gemarah (traditions) to constitute Talmoud and replace the Torah. Today, the Jews follow the Talmoud instead of God's divine scripture. The same thing happened to the Muslims. A few centuries after Muhammad, the "scholars" of Islam invented **"Hadith"** (oral) and **"Sunna"** (traditions) to replace Quran. Today, the Muslims follow the **Hadith** and **Sunna** instead of Quran (see 24:1-2). The first person to complain from this blasphemy will be the prophet Muhammad on the day of judgment (please see 25:30-31). This incredible parallel between the Jews and the Muslims explains the prevalence of Moses and Israel throughout Quran.

A few centuries after Jesus, the "scholars" of Christianity met in the conferences of Nicene and invented the trinity. Today, the trinity is the basic doctrine followed by the Christians, in total defiance of the Bible's truth. The Bible preaches clearly that Jesus is not God (see the Gospel of Mark 10:18 and 15:34), and that he was simply a messenger of God (see John 5:24, 8:40, 8:42, and Revelation 1:1). Consult any encyclopedia under "Nicene."

« السابع - النهى عن كتابة غيرِ القرآن »

عَنْ أَبِى سَعِيدٍ الْخُدْرِىِّ رَضِىَ اللهُ عَنْهُ قَالَ : قَالَ رسُولُ اللهِ صَلَّى اللهُ عَلَيْهِ وَسَلَّمَ : «لَاتَكْتُبُوا عَنِّى شَيْئاً سِوَى الْقُرْآنِ . مَنْ كَتَب شَيْئاً سِوَى الْقُرْآنِ فَلْيَمْحُهُ »[1] .

(احمد ج ۱ ص ۱۷۱ ومسلم)

عَنْ عَبْدِ الْمُطَّلِبِ بْنِ عَبْدِ اللهِ قَالَ : [دَخَل زَيْدُ بْنُ ثَابِتٍ رَضِى اللهُ عنْهُ عَلَى مُعَاوِيةَ رَضِىَ اللهُ عَنْهُ ، فَحَدَّثَهُ حَدِيثاً ، فَأَمَرَ إِنْسَاناً أَنْ يَكْتُب . فَقَالَ زَيْدٌ : إِنَّ رسُولَ اللهِ صَلَّى اللهُ عَلَيْهِ وَسَلَّمَ نَهَى أَنْ نَكْتُب شَيْئاً مِنْ حديِثِهِ ، فَمحَاهُ] .

(أحمد ج ۱ ص ۱۹۲)

As it turns out, God willed that these false sources of jurisprudence must be invented, including the Mishnah, the Gemarah, the trinity, the **Hadith**, and **Sunna** (see 6:112). Why did God allow these fabrications? Verse 113 of sura 6 gives us the answer. A person may grow up in an environment that teaches, "If you are a good person, you must believe in God, the day of judgment, and heaven and hell." Consequently, this person may grow up confessing belief in God and the hereafter. But deep inside, his or her heart may be unconvinced. the Quran describes these people by saying, "Their hearts are denying" (16:22). Furthermore, the Quran teaches that such people are not aware of their hearts' denial; they actually believe that they are believers (see 6:22-24). Up until the day of judgment, and even as they face their creator, they will continue to deny that they have fallen into idol worship. To distinguish the true believers from the false believers, and to prove to us that our faith is genuine or false, God willed the invention of false doctrines. We learn from Quran that "every prophet will have enemies who will fabricate fancy statements (**hadith**) and attribute them to the prophet" (6:112 and 25:31). The false believers will be attracted to the false inventions and will accept them as sources of religious instruction (6:113). They will reject God's scripture, even though it is "fully detailed" (6:114).

There is no doubt that we must obey God and the messenger. But, the identity of the messenger is confused by the false believers. They identify the messenger with the false teachings invented by his enemies. However, the true identity of the Prophet is defined in Quran (5:48-50 and 17:73-75). We are told that the messenger is fully represented by Quran, the whole Quran, and nothing but Quran (see also 6:19, 38 and 114).

To justify their attraction to the false teachings, the followers of **hadith** claim that the Quran is too difficult to understand, and the Prophet's "**hadith**" is needed to explain the Quran. The fact is that the Quran is a lot easier to understand than the majority of **hadith**. However, because they reject the Quran's assurances that it is complete and perfect (6:38, 114, and 115), God makes the Quran inaccessible to them (please see 18:57). Furthermore, God tells the Prophet not to utter anything other than Quran itself, when it comes to "explanation" of Quran (see 20:114 and 75:16), and that God Himself will explain the Quran (41:44 and 75:19).

In order to justify their attraction to **hadith** and **sunna**, the false Muslims claim that these blasphemous inventions are divine revelations. However, the Quran teaches us that God's revelations will be perfectly protected from the slightest distortions (15:9), and that no falsehood will ever mar them (41:42). It is well known that the vast majority of **hadith** and **sunna** are recognized by the **hadith** advocates themselves as false. Therefore, **hadith** does not fulfill this criterion and could not possibly be divine revelation.

The false Muslims consistently abuse Quran, take it out of context, and reveal their ignorance. One of their favorite statements is: "What the messenger gives you, you shall take; and what he forbids you, you shall abstain from." They are seemingly unaware that this statement is not even a verse. It is part of verse 7, sura 59, which is grossly taken out of context. Another favorite quotation to justify their idol worship against the Prophet's will is verse 56 or sura 33. They are ignorant of the fact that verse 43 of the same sura accords the same honor to every believer, not just the Prophet. Finally, they misrepresent verse 3 of sura 53, "He does not speak on his own." Those who are knowledgeable read the whole sura and discover that this statement refers to Quran, and nothing but Quran.

Because God is fully aware of the human plague of idol worship, He enjoined us from idolizing the Prophet. In the two verses that describe the Prophet as "as human being like you," we note that each verse closes by warning us against idolizing the Prophet (18:110 and 41:6). Furthermore, Muhammad was instructed to inform us that he is absolutely powerless to even benefit or harm himself (7:188, 10:49, and 72:21), let alone benefit us. He was told to inform his followers that he does not know the future, nor was he an angel (6:50). We are told that Muhammad's only miracle was the Quran (29:50-51), and that Muhammad the man committed many mistakes (40:66, 66:1, 80:1-10, and 93:7); he even disobeyed Muhammad the messenger (33:37). The prophet Muhammad is told that if he ever fell into idol worship all his works would be nullified, and he would end up in hell (17:39 and 39:65). All the prophets, and all the people for that matter, were told the same thing (21:29). The Prophet was even too powerless to guide anyone (see 2:272 and 28:56).

Upon reading these divine truths, those who idolize Muhammad will undoubtedly lose their temper. They have rejected God's revelation, and consequently, God blinds them and blocks them out (17:45-46 and 18:57). Similarly, when you tell the average Christian that Jesus was not God, he or she will accuse you of blasphemy against Jesus. The average Christian believes that he or she loves Jesus, while those who recognize Jesus' truth are accused of opposing him. However, just as Jesus will disown those who love him "too much," (5:116), Muhammad will disown those who claim to love him (25:30-31).

APPENDIX 12

Predestination

We are absolutely free to choose belief in God or disbelief; this is God's decree throughout Quran (18:29, 25:57, 73:19, 74:37, 74:55, 76:29, 78:39, 80:12). Even before creation, the human being was given a choice as to submitting to God or to acquire the freedom of choice (33:72). However, because God is God, He happens to know exactly what choice each of us is going to make. As the reader notes from Appendix 6, God did not create us to see what we will do. Rather, He created us to show the angels that a creature who never sees God is capable of submitting totally to God. Not only did God know the path each of us will take, He even recorded everything before creation (57:22). Thus each of us had his or her life recorded on something like a video tape from birth to death, even before we were created (17:13). Predestination, therefore, is a fact as far as God is concerned, not as far as we are concerned. Since we do not know the future, we are completely free to believe or disbelieve.

Once we make a decision, however, God goes out of His way to augment our decision. For as long as we shun the guidance and try to stay away from God, He deliberately keeps us away. On the other hand, if we decide to seek Him and heed His message, He creates the circumstances that augment our guidance. See 2:26, 7:146, 10:9, 10:99-101, 13:27, 14:27, 28:56, and 36:10.

APPENDIX 13

Dietary Prohibitions

Imagine yourself hosting some of your favorite people. You invite them to dinner at your place; you go to the market and buy the best possible ingredients; and you spend extra money, time, and effort to prepare a sumptuous meal. But when your guests sit at the table, they turn their noses up; they don't like your food. How will you feel?

The Quran teaches us that God is extremely displeased with those who prohibit anything that is not **specifically** prohibited in Quran (16:112-116). We are told that the acceptance of any prohibitions not specifically mentioned in Quran amounts to unforgivable idol worship (6:142-152). The absolute specificity of Quranic prohibitions is best illustrated in verses 145 and 146 of sura 6. We learn from these two verses that when God wants to prohibit the meat of any animal, He prohibits the meat, specifically, and not the fat (6:145). And when He wants to prohibit the fat of any animal, He specifically prohibits the fat, and not the meat (7:146). The Quran specifically prohibits four animal products:

(1) Animals that die of themselves, without any human interference;
(2) Running blood (free blood, as compared to blood trapped in the meat);
(3) The "meat" of pigs; and
(4) Animals sacrificed in the name of other than God.

Any other prohibitions are satanic inventions and represent the setting up of some idol besides God. If you worship God alone, you follow His instructions alone. (See 2:173, 5:3, 6:142-152, and 16:112).

APPENDIX 14

Death

Death is a great mystery to most people. Not so for the students of Quran. The Quran tells us exactly what death is like. Thus, we learn that death is exactly like sleeping; complete with dreams. The period between death and resurrection, no matter how long, passes like one night of sleep (see 2:259, 6:60, 10:45, 16:21, 18:11, 19, 25, and 30:55). Most, if not all the people, never know that they have died. They will be utterly surprised on the day of resurrection.

What makes death easily understandable is the fact that we already experienced death. The period from creating our souls (7:172) to the moment of our birth, which is probably millions of years, was a period of death (see 2:28 and 40:11). The way you feel about this first death is exactly identical to the second and final death, with one exception. Because of the experiences we go through in this life, the second death is characterized by dreams. These will be joyous and happy dreams or horrible nightmares, depending on the way you led your life (see 40:46).

APPENDIX 15

Quran: All You Need

The words of Quran speak in verse 64 of sura 19, saying, "We have come down to bring the commandments of your Lord. He fully controls everything we deal with, past, present, and future, and your Lord is never forgetful." God did not forget to tell us, for example, how to sleep. Nor did He run out of words (please see 18:109 and 31:27). Yet, the inventors of **hadith, sunna,** and other false doctrines insist upon decreeing and legislating everything we do; for example, a specific way to sleep. Self-appointed **sunna** advocates roam the Prophet's mosque in Medina, Saudi Arabia, and beat up the exhausted travelers who dare to sleep the wrong way. The Quran teaches us that anything that is left out was left out on purpose, and we are completely free to handle it. God wants us to sleep in any way we wish (see 5:101). The inventors of **hadith** and **sunna** came up with voluminous books of etiquette and false regulations. The Quran promises them terrible retribution (see 6:21, 6:93, 6:144, 10:17, 11:18, 18:15, and 29:68).

Throughout the Quran, we are told that nothing else is needed (6:19,38,114; 20:114 and 75:19). In fact, to resort to anything besides Quran as a source of religious regulation is tantamount to idol worship (17:46). The true believers follow Quran, the whole Quran, and nothing but Quran. See also 15:90-96.

APPENDIX 16

Hadith and the Quran's Secret Code

When I discovered the Quran's secret numerical code, between the years 1968 and 1981, I became a popular speaker around the world. The Muslims everywhere were naturally glad to hear about the miraculous composition of Quran. But, when the Quran's miraculous code physically proved that **Hadith** and **Sunna** are false doctrines, and that we shall uphold Quran, the whole Quran, and nothing but the Quran, my popularity plummeted. The idol worshipers rejected ALL my work and even threatened my life and tried to assassinate my character. The computerized study of the Quran's numerical code generated physical, indisputable proof, showing the following:

1. That the Quran is complete, perfect, and shall be the sole source of religious statutes and commandments;

2. that **Hadith, Sunna**, and regulations made up by various "imams" are all false doctrines sponsored by Satan, though in accordance with God's will; and

3. that these false doctrines are permitted by God as a necessary test to distinguish the true believers from the false believers; the true believers will uphold Quran, the whole Quran, and nothing but Quran.

For an effective test, the Quran often places crucial doctrines in the middle of a long verse. As the reader knows by now, it was the will of God to keep the Quran's numerical code a hidden secret for 14 centuries (see 15:87 and sura 74). The reader also notes from Appendix 1 that the Quran's code is founded on the number 19. As stated in 74:25-30, anyone who doubts the divine source of Quran will be proven wrong by the number 19.

I will present to the reader here the Quranic statements about the completeness of Quran and their connection with the secret numerical code.

1. There is a statement in Quran where God "testifies" in the strongest terms that Quran was the only thing given to Muhammad for delivery to the people of every generation, and that those who seek any other sources (such as **hadith, sunna**, or imams' opinions) are idol worshipers. This powerful statement is found in sura 6, and the reader will note the verse number is **19**.

2. مَا فَرَّطْنَا فِي الكِتٰبِ مِــن شَــيء "We did not leave anything out of this book." This statement tells us that nothing was left out of Quran; that we need nothing else; that Quran is all we need. Not only does this statement consist of **19** Arabic letters, but also we find it in verse **38 (19 × 2)** of sura 6.

3. أنزل اليكم الكتٰب مفصلا "He sent down to you this book fully detailed and fully explained." This statement clearly

informs us that we do not need anything else besides Quran to either augment it or explain it. Not only does this statement consist of **19** Arabic letters, but also we find it in verse **114 (19 × 6)** of sura 6.

4. A statement in sura 20 instructs the Prophet not to utter anything related to Quran, other than Quran itself. Significantly, we find this statement in verse **114.**

5. Similar statements are found in sura 75, where the Prophet is instructed, in no uncertain terms, not to utter anything related to Quran, unless it is the Quran itself, and that the Prophet (and of course his followers) shall follow Quran, the whole Quran, and nothing but Quran. These profound statements close with God's declaration that He alone will explain the Quran (not Muhammad); that He alone will put the truth of Quran in the hearts of the believers (See 55:1-2), regardless of their mother tongue (see 41:44). The reader will note that this divine declaration is in verse **19** of sura 75.

6. Finally, the Quran contains four similar statements saying, in effect, "We have cited in this Quran all the necessary examples." The clear message is that we do not need anything else besides Quran. These four statements are found in 17:89, 18:54, 30:58, and 39:27. It would seem that these statements broke the pattern we witness in the previous five points, namely, that the statements dealing with completeness of the Quran carry numbers that are multiples of **19.** But the reader notes that the verse numbers of these almost identical statements are 89, 54, 58, and 27. When we add the four numbers we discover that the total is **228 (19 × 12).**

Despite these indisputable, physical proofs that the Quran is complete and perfect, and that seeking any other sources besides Quran is idol worship (6:19), the advocates of **hadith** and **sunna** (worshipers of Muhammad) will probably increase in defiance and the belligerency. They will continue to reject Quran and try very hard to prove that it is not complete. Why? This is what the Quran teaches us (see 5:64, 68; 17:41, 60, 82).

APPENDIX 17

Quran: Unlike Any Other Book

The Quran is God's message to the world, and He has pledged to protect it from the slightest distortion (see 15:9 and Appendix 1). Thus, the Quran is surrounded by invisible forces that guard and even correct any distortion that might touch it (see 13:39, 41:42, and 42:24). Verse 24 of sura 42 informs us that even if the prophet Muhammad had made an error in delivering Quran, be it deliberate or unintentional, God would have erased the wrong and substituted the correct words. This pledge holds true forever (13:39).

Moreover, we learn that not everyone can readily receive Quran; only those worthy of guidance are given the Quran. Verses 45 and 47 of sura 17, and verse 57 of sura 18 inform us that those who do not deserve the guidance will be blocked out and actively prevented from understanding Quran. Verses 45 and 46 of sura 17 say, "When you read Quran, we will place an invisible shield on those who do not believe in the hereafter. We will block out their hearts to prevent them from understanding it, and we will place deafness in their ears. And when you advocate the worship of God ALONE and the Quran ALONE, they will turn away in aversion." Therefore, those who refuse to accept the Quran ALONE as a source of religious regulations are completely isolated, by God Himself, from Quran. Verse 57 of sura 18 is even more profound. This verse states that: "those who reject the Quranic truth (such as the completeness of Quran) will be completely prevented from Quran, because of their wickedness. Consequently, no matter what you do to guide them, they will never be guided." As profound as the Quran's numerical code is, the idol worshipers actually attacked it and accused me of "mental deficiency." That is why God has rendered them blind. And this is exactly what the Quran states in 7:146 and 13:31. These verses teach us that no matter what kind of miracle they see in Quran, they will be prevented by God from appreciating it. Verse 31 of sura 13 states that even if the Quran caused mountains to move, or caused the dead to speak, or the earth to break apart, they will not appreciate. Is it any wonder, then, that the idol worshipers could not appreciate the physical miracles of the Quran's code?

Because of the invisible forces associated with Quran, the Quran is readily attainable by the sincere believers (see 41:44) and impossible to acquire by those who do not deserve it (39:9-11 and 56:79).

APPENDIX 18

Satan: Fallen Angel

Before the beginning, there was God and nothing else. Then God created the angels to serve Him and carry out certain chores in areas that cannot stand the manifested presence of God (see, for example, 7:143). One of the archangels who was given special powers and authority became ridden with pride, to the extent that he wanted to be a partner of God. Satan (Ibless, in Arabic) was the archangel. Only God knew what was in Satan's head (2:30). There were two choices for dealing with this blasphemy; God could have banished or punished Satan for his rebellious thoughts, or He could have exposed him first. The first choice would have left the rest of the angels puzzled. They would have wondered why God treated Satan in that manner when he had done nothing wrong. It was the second choice (exposing Satan first) that was decided. Thus, God created a creature from a lowly material, clay, and ordered the angels to fall prostrate before the new creature (Adam). That was the test that exposed Satan as a haughty rebel.

The Quran clearly confirms all previous scripture regarding the identity of Satan as a fallen angel. However, due to ignorance of the Quranic language, and due to Satan's own interference, some people deny that Satan was ever an angel. They thus deny the overwhelming and straightforward statements of Quran which affirm Satan's previous angelhood. The confusion arose from a misunderstanding of verse 50 in sura 18. Instead of understanding the Quranic expression كان من الجن to mean "became one of the jinns," some people took it to mean "was one of the jinns." Obviously, these people are not aware that the word كان throughout Quran means "became," and not "was," as commonly used in the common Arabic. This becomes clear if we look at this word in another verse that involves Satan, namely verse 34 of sura 2. This verse states that: "We said to the **angels**, 'Fall prostrate before Adam,' and they fell prostrate, except Satan; he refused, turned arrogant, and he **became** a disbeliever." Clearly, the expression كان من الكافرين means "**became** a disbeliever," since Satan obviously was not created a disbeliever.

The reader will readily note that the order to fall prostrate was directed specifically to "**the angels**." We find this repeated in Quran seven times (2:34, 7:11, 15:28, 17:61, 18:50, 20:116, and 38:71). If Satan was not an angel, then he was never required to fall prostrate, and consequently, he never disobeyed God.

It should be noted here that the biggest source of confusion for those who refuse to believe Quran is the blasphemy against the prophet known as **hadith** (see 6:112 and 25:31). The inventors of **hadith**, inspired by Satan, stated that the angels were created from light. No where in Quran do we find that the angels were created from light. Since the Quran states that Satan was created from fire (7:12, 15:27, 38:76, and 55:15), those deceived by **hadith** refuse to put Satan in the same category as the angels.

Another source of confusion is the general belief that angels do not disobey God. This happens to be true in the sense that an angel is an angel for as long as he does not disobey God. Once an angel disobeys God, he is no longer an angel; he becomes a jinn.

There are two types of creatures on earth who are undergoing the test, namely, the humans and the jinns. The humans are descendants of Adam, and the jinns are descendants of Satan. Both Adam and Satan sinned, and both were banished to the lowest universe. (2:36).

APPENDIX 19

The Bible's Preview of Muhammad

Despite the disastrous human interference in the holy writings of the Torah and the Gospel, as admitted by the Bible's publishers, the scriptures still contain a goodly portion of the original truth. So much so that those who truly believe and follow the Bible, even in its present form, will certainly be guided to Islam (Qur'an 2:121). Those who honestly follow the teachings of Moses and Jesus (may God bestow blessings and peace upon them), even in their current state, will be led to the completion and fulfillment of what their creator expects of them. This has been the experience of many free-minded followers of the Bible. One such example is the author of this article. As a former ordained Christian minister, Sulaymān Shāhid Mufassir recounts the biblical guidance which led him to the light of Islam.

THE BIBLE contains a vivid preview of the person and mission of Muḥammad (peace be upon him) that is so distinct and unmistakable that many a sincere Jew and Christian was happy to accept him as the prophet when he appeared. But over the subsequent centuries of theological antagonism, preceded and accompanied by the editing, rewriting and dogmatizing of portions of the scriptural record, that written portrait has become obscured as with a thick layer of dust. When the centuries-old encrustations of dogma and sectarian hermeneutics are removed, many well-known, little understood verses of the Bible serve as signposts for the serious scholar.

The Role of the Bible

Muslims believe that the original Torah and Gospel were revealed by Almighty God. When Jesus began to call the Jews to return to sincere and devoted service to God, the Torah of Moses had been subjected to serious instances of careless copying and dogmatic editing, but he confirmed in his preaching whatever remained intact of the divine revelation. He said, "Do not suppose that I have come to abolish the Law (Torah) and the prophets; I did not come to abolish, but to complete. I tell you this: so long as heaven and earth endure, not a letter, not a stroke, will disappear from the Law until all that must happen has happened"(1). The essence of the Torah was confirmed in the Gospel. Six hundred years after the Gospel, when it had similarly suffered through careless copying and editing, Muḥammad resumed the prophetic mission and confirmed whatever had remained of both the Torah and the Gospel. He received from God the clarified book, the Qur'an, which would be protected forever from error and distortion, and which would therefore *serve* as the protector or *the ultimate reference* (muhaimin) of all previous revelations(2).

The Bible does not now contain the Torah and Gospel as they were divinely revealed. Biblical scholars themselves have recognized the human nature and composition of the book(3). However, we may expect to find within its pages some portion of the Torah and the Gospel, although careful study is necessary in order to make the message comprehensible(4). An amazing feature of the Bible, even in its present form, is that it indicates the divine revelation would progress through a number of message-bearers or prophets and be completed finally in one man, one particular prophet whose message would be so comprehensive and whose mission would be so universal that no further prophets would ever be needed.

It is easy for God to speak with distinction of things thousands of years prior to their occurrence, but impossible for man to do so. According to the Old Testament, the faithfulness of Abraham was given special reward by a covenant or promise to bless all mankind through his descendants. His line would be distinguished by divine guidance and prophecy. "By Myself have I sworn, saith the Lord, because thou hast done this thing, and hast not withheld thy son, thine only son, that in blessing I will bless thee, and in multiplying I will multiply thy seed as the stars of the heaven, and as the sand which is upon the seashore . . . and in thy seed shall all the nations of the earth be blessed, because thou hast hearkened to My voice"(5).

The Bible is the record, primarily, of God's favor to Abraham's second son Isaac, in whose line came Moses and Jesus, peace be upon them. But what about the first-born of Abraham, Ishmael?

The Genesis story about the turning out of Ishmael and his mother, Hagar, the Egyptian servant woman of Sarah, due to Sarah's jealousy in being unable to bear the first son of Abraham, is an early example of Hebrew chauvinism, full of contradictory elements(6). In effect, Genesis closes the door on Hagar and Ishmael; from henceforth only Isaac and Sarah matter. But God's promise to Abraham was not biased. When He made the "everlasting covenant" with the family of Abraham, Isaac was not even in the picture. Ishmael was his only son and God declared: "As for Ishmael, I have heard thee; behold I have blessed him . . . twelve princes shall he beget, and I will make him a great nation"(7).

514

Double Honor due to Ishmael's Line

The writers of Genesis wrongly attempted to make it appear that Ishmael would receive an inferior blessing because his mother was a servant woman, but Isaac, being the son of the free woman, would inherit the glory of the first-born son. In so doing, they disregarded the clear family laws of the Torah. According to this law, the rights of the first-born son are not invalid due to the social status of his mother. This applied especially in polygamous marriages such as that of Abraham(8). Man's social prejudices do not in any way dictate the favor of God. According to the Torah:

כִּי־תִהְיֶיןָ לְאִישׁ
שְׁתֵּי נָשִׁים הָאַחַת אֲהוּבָה וְהָאַחַת שְׂנוּאָה
וְיָלְדוּ־לוֹ בָנִים הָאֲהוּבָה וְהַשְּׂנוּאָה
וְהָיָה הַבֵּן הַבְּכֹר לַשְּׂנִיאָה: וְהָיָה בְּיוֹם
הַנְחִילוֹ אֶת־בָּנָיו אֵת אֲשֶׁר־יִהְיֶה לוֹ

לֹא יוּכַל לְבַכֵּר אֶת־בֶּן־הָאֲהוּבָה
עַל־פְּנֵי בֶן־הַשְּׂנוּאָה הַבְּכֹר: כִּי אֶת־
הַבְּכֹר בֶּן־הַשְּׂנוּאָה יַכִּיר לָתֶת לוֹ פִּי
שְׁנַיִם בְּכֹל אֲשֶׁר־יִמָּצֵא לוֹ כִּי־הוּא
רֵאשִׁית אֹנוֹ לוֹ מִשְׁפַּט הַבְּכֹרָה:

"If a man has two wives, one loved and the other unloved (i.e., slighted or socially despised due to inferior social status), and both the loved and the unloved have borne him sons, but the first-born is the son of the unloved wife, when he wills his property to his sons, he may not treat as first-born the son of the loved one in disregard of the son of the unloved one who is older. Instead he must accept the first-born, the son of the unloved one, and allot him a double portion of all he possesses; since he is the first fruit of his vigor, the birthright is his due"(9).

But the Bible disregards this fair principle and gives throughout the "double portion" of honor to Isaac, the second son and makes it actually appear that the "birthright" is his (Cf. Genesis 17:21: "but My covenant will I establish with Isaac, whom Sarah shall bear ..."). This makes the "Torah" of the Bible a contradictory law. By right, the *double honor* and the birthright belong to the line of Ishmael, and the "unloved" social status of his mother detracts from this not at all.

Ishmael's descendants came to be known as Arabs, a term which, in Hebrew, meant those who inhabited the *'arabah* or desert (10). It is not a coincidence that of the twelve sons of Ishmael (Genesis 25:12-16) the one mentioned most prominently is Qaydar (*Qedar* in Hebrew). In some Bible verses, Qaydar is synonymous with the Arabs in general(11). This is an important indication that the line of Qaydar was marked by God for a unique purpose, to bring forth the one whose life and work would bring "a double portion" of honor to the house of Ishmael.

The nature of this twofold honor begins to be revealed in the Old Testament book of Isaiah. There are many brilliant parables and prophecies in Isaiah which concern the fulfillment of God's promise to bless all mankind through the family of Abraham. Christians believe that some of these accounts relate to the gentle but forthright mission of Jesus as the Messiah. But the 42nd chapter of Isaiah is distinct because it points, not to the Hebrew, but to the Arab branch of Abraham's family. Here Isaiah points out a chosen "Servant of the Lord" who would have a prophethood to all mankind, unlike the Hebrew prophets whose mission was limited to Israel. God's spirit would guide him and he would establish justice on earth. He would not rule as a loud or boisterous demagogue. Unlike the brief ministry of Jesus, this prophet would serve long enough to "set right in the earth," to actually establish a society or community based on truth and justice. He would be "a light of the nations." What is most startling about this particular servant of the Lord is that he, alone, is *identified with Qaydar* in verse 11.

הֵן עַבְדִּי אֶתְמָךְ־בּוֹ ׳
בְּחִירִי רָצְתָה נַפְשִׁי
נָתַתִּי רוּחִי עָלָיו
מִשְׁפָּט לַגּוֹיִם יוֹצִיא:
לֹא יִצְעַק וְלֹא יִשָּׂא ²
וְלֹא־יַשְׁמִיעַ בַּחוּץ קוֹלוֹ:
קָנֶה רָצוּץ לֹא יִשְׁבּוֹר ³
וּפִשְׁתָּה כֵהָה לֹא יְכַבֶּנָּה
לֶאֱמֶת יוֹצִיא מִשְׁפָּט:
לֹא יִכְהֶה וְלֹא יָרוּץ ⁴
עַד־יָשִׂים בָּאָרֶץ מִשְׁפָּט
וּלְתוֹרָתוֹ אִיִּים יְיַחֵלוּ:

כֹּה־אָמַר הָאֵל ׀ יְהֹוָה ⁵
בּוֹרֵא הַשָּׁמַיִם וְנוֹטֵיהֶם
רֹקַע הָאָרֶץ וְצֶאֱצָאֶיהָ
נֹתֵן נְשָׁמָה לָעָם עָלֶיהָ
וְרוּחַ לַהֹלְכִים בָּהּ:
אֲנִי יְהֹוָה קְרָאתִיךָ בְצֶדֶק ⁶
וְאַחְזֵק בְּיָדֶךָ
וְאֶצָּרְךָ וְאֶתֶּנְךָ לִבְרִית עָם
לְאוֹר גּוֹיִם:
יִשְׂאוּ מִדְבָּר וְעָרָיו ¹¹
חֲצֵרִים תֵּשֵׁב קֵדָר
יָרֹנּוּ יֹשְׁבֵי סֶלַע
מֵרֹאשׁ הָרִים יִצְוָחוּ:

"Here is My servant, whom I uphold, My chosen one in whom I delight, I have bestowed My spirit upon him, and he will make justice shine on the nations. He will not call out or lift his voice high, or make himself heard in the open market. He will not break a bruised reed, or snuff out a smouldering wick; he will make justice shine on every race, never faltering, never breaking down, he will plant justice on earth, while coasts and islands wait for his teaching. Thus speaks the Lord Who is God, He Who created the skies and stretched them out, Who fashioned the earth and all that grows in it, Who gave breath to its people, the breath of life to all who walk upon it: I, the Lord, have called you with righteous purpose and taken you by the hand; I have formed you and appointed you to be a light to all peoples, a beacon for the nations ... Let the wilderness and its towns rejoice, and the villages of the tribe of Kedar (Qaydar)"(12).

This prophecy could apply to none of the Hebrew prophets. Even Jesus made it plain that his mission was far from being universal, saying: "I am not sent but unto the lost sheep of the house of Israel"(13). His calling was limited and it was the later Gentile converts, not Jesus, who gave Christianity its inclusive nature. Nor was Jesus or any of the Hebrew prophets related in any way to "Kedar" (Qaydar). In promising a great prophet from the Arabs, Isaiah was merely amplifying the prophecy made previously by Moses. God revealed to Moses that a prophet would arise from the *brothers* of the Hebrews — the Arabs, who were children of the brother of Isaac, Ishmael — who would command world-wide attention and obedience:

נָבִיא אָקִים לָהֶם מִקֶּרֶב אֲחֵיהֶם
כָּמוֹךָ וְנָתַתִּי דְבָרַי בְּפִיו וְדִבֶּר אֲלֵיהֶם
אֵת כָּל־אֲשֶׁר אֲצַוֶּנּוּ: וְהָיָה הָאִישׁ
אֲשֶׁר לֹא־יִשְׁמַע אֶל־דְּבָרַי אֲשֶׁר יְדַבֵּר
בִּשְׁמִי אָנֹכִי אֶדְרֹשׁ מֵעִמּוֹ:

"I will raise them up a Prophet from among their brethren, like unto thee, and will put My words in his mouth, and he shall speak unto them all that I shall command him. And it shall come to pass, that whosoever will not hearken unto My words which he shall speak in My name, I will require it of him"(14). This prophet would have to be "like unto thee (Moses)," who was founder, leader and exemplar of a community of believers, one whose mission would last long enough to achieve cohesive, concrete results.

The Gospel Preview: The Paraclete

The Gospel of Jesus brought into sharper focus the identity of the one who would fulfill the promise to make the line of Ishmael a great nation. In the Gospel of John — a New Testament book which is not the Gospel of Jesus and which may be considered as representing only in general terms portions of Jesus' teaching — Jesus informs his close companions that his work among them was drawing to conclusion, but God would send someone else after a time to carry forward the prophetic movement. This someone, however, would be the last of the prophets.

JOHN 14:16, 17:

καὶ 16
ἐγὼ ἐρωτήσω τὸν πατέρα, καὶ ἄλλον παράκλητον
δώσει ὑμῖν, ἵνα μένῃ μεθ' ὑμῶν εἰς τὸν αἰῶνα, τὸ 17
πνεῦμα τῆς ἀληθείας

"And I will pray the Father, and He shall give you another Comforter, that he may abide with you forever, even the spirit of truth"(15).

JOHN 16:13, 14:

> ὅταν δὲ ἔλθῃ ἐκεῖνος, τὸ πνεῦμα 13
> τῆς ἀληθείας, ὁδηγήσει ὑμᾶς εἰς πᾶσαν τὴν ἀλή-
> θειαν· οὐ γὰρ λαλήσει ἀφ' ἑαυτοῦ, ἀλλ' ὅσα ἄν
> ἀκούσῃ λαλήσει, καὶ τὰ ἐρχόμενα ἀναγγελεῖ ὑμῖν.
> ἐκεῖνος ἐμὲ δοξάσει

"When he, the spirit of truth is come, he will guide you unto all truth; for he shall not speak of himself; but whatsoever he shall hear (from God), that shall he speak, and he will show you things to come. He shall glorify me"(16).

In Jesus' written portrait of the last messenger he is called the "Comforter," which represents the word *parakletos* in the Greek New Testament. More precisely, *parakletos* means an advocate, one who pleads the cause of another, one who counsels or advises another from deep concern for the other's welfare(17). *Parakletos* would designate one who would be considered the "Mercy for all creatures", *Rahmatun lil 'ālamīn* (Qur'an 21:107). He would be the counsellor who would "lead forth those who believe and do righteous deeds from the depths of darkness into light" (Qur'an 65:11), the true advocate who would be *harīsun 'alaykum* (Sura Al-Tawba); *genuinely solicitous* for the welfare of humanity, pleading their case with God and showing them the sure way of return to the favor of the divine Judge.

THE GREEK WORD "PARACLETE" (Ho Parakletos):

ὁ παράκλητος

However, some scholars believe that what Jesus said in his own language of Aramaic represents more closely the Greek word *periklytos*, which means the Admirable or Glorified One. *Periklytos* corresponds to the word *Muhammad* in Arabic(18). There are several proven cases of similar word substitutions in the New Testament. There are also several instances of another possibility, the possibility that the Greek text originally had *both* words, *parakletos* and *periklytos*, and due to the similarity of spelling and close proximity to one another in the sentence, one got left out by the copyists. In such case the Greek text would have read: ΚΑΙ ΑΛΛΟΝ ΠΑΡΑΚΛΗΤΟΝ ΤΟΝ ΠΕΡΙ-ΚΛΥΤΟΣ ΔΩΣΕΙ ΥΜΙΝ instead of the present reading: ΚΑΙ ΑΛΛΟΝ ΠΑΡΑΚΛΗΤΟΝ ΔΩΣΕΙ ΥΜΙΝ that is, "and He will give you another Counsellor, the Admirable One," instead of the present reading, "and He will give you another Counsellor." Such mistakes occurred in copying because the ancient texts had all the letters written close together. The eye of the copyist could easily pass over a word similar in spelling or close in position(19).

When Jesus declares of this coming prophet-counsellor that he would "abide with you forever," he shows that there would be no need for additional prophets to succeed him. He would be the last one. He would lead mankind "unto all the truth"(Greek: πᾶσαν τὴν ἀλη θειαν· "to the whole truth," "to every aspect of the truth."); there would be no necessity for anyone to come with additional truth. Indeed, there would be no more additional truth, in the general sense, to bring. So truthful and trustworthy would he be that he could be called *Al-Amîn*, or as the Greek text of John 16:13 says, τὸ πνεῦμα τῆς ἀληθείας, "the spirit of truth," one of whom it could be said: "He has brought them the Truth." (Qur'an 23:70).

The term "spirit" here does not mean that the coming prophet would be other than human. In New Testament Greek, this word has also been applied to an inspired *person*, "the possessor of a spiritual communication" or revelation. The one who becomes overwhelmed with a divine revelation is himself termed a "spirit"(20). The "spirit of truth" would be the person who would possess a spiritual communication, that is, a divine revelation, and whose life and conduct and character would be marked to an extreme degree by devotion to the truth. This is why the next sentence of the verse containing this expression says: "He will guide you unto all truth; for he shall not speak of himself, but whatsoever he shall hear (from God), that shall he speak." (John 16:13). This person would receive the revelation of truth from God and these words alone would constitute the message, not his own opinions or the writings of his companions. His message or revelation would be first and foremost and literally the Word of God. Note that this corresponds exactly to what God revealed to Moses about the prophet who would come from among the "brothers" of the Hebrews: "I ... will put My words in his mouth, and he shall speak unto them all that I shall command him." (Deuteronomy 18:18).

A more striking point is the similarity between the divine mission given to Moses, Jesus and the Spirit of Truth (Muḥammad) as bearers of a single thread of Revelation from God. By comparing Deuteronomy 18:15, 17-19; John 12:49; 16:12-13; and Qur'an 73:15, one observes that despite the thousands of years involved and the disastrous human interference in the Bible, the words describing these three personalities are almost identical. Therefore, the (original) Torah, Gospel and the Qur'an have One Source and reveal the same Truth, which is Eternal.

It cannot be overlooked that Jesus gives a unique requirement that would help to identify the last prophet: "He shall glorify me." (John 16:14). If anyone had come claiming to be this prophet, but did not give due honor to Jesus as prophet and Messiah, he would be the wrong one. As a nation, the Jews rejected Jesus. At the same time, this prophet to come would not be a follower of Jesus, that is, a Christian, because Jesus said that this prophet would reveal things of which Jesus himself was unaware. If Jesus had brought "all the truth," there would have been no need for him to single out someone else who would come with all the truth. Likewise, since this prophet would bring all the truth he would have to be the last one, the seal of the prophets. Therefore, we would have to look for someone who, like Abraham in whose line he would come, would be neither Jew nor Christian but would believe in God. Unlike the Jews as a whole, he would "glorify" Jesus by insisting that Jesus was a true messenger of God and by acknowledging that Jesus was the true Messiah. But the teaching of this prophet would come from God Himself. As a revelation from God, the message of this last prophet would confirm what God had revealed previously by means of the original Torah and the original Gospel, *but his message would be no mere plagiarized copy*, no "condensed edition" of either the Torah or the Gospel. God Almighty had said, "I ... will put My words in his mouth," and it is proper that these words would agree with previously revealed words of the One and Same God. "Whatsoever he shall hear (from God), that shall he speak."

The one reference at John 14:26 which seeks to identify the coming prophet as "the Holy Ghost" or Spirit is the only one like it in the entire Bible. It is obviously the addition of some editor of the Gospel of John who sought in his own way to explain who he thought the "spirit of truth" was. But this indefensible exegesis simply contradicts what Jesus is reported to have said elsewhere in John. According to other verses he indicated clearly that the prophet or "Paraclete" would not come until Jesus' own mission was finished. The holy spirit — the angel of revelation — was active already, both before and during the ministry of Jesus, delivering God's revelations to His prophets and assisting them. (See Psalms 51:11; Matthew 3:16; 4:1, etc.). This strange "Holy Ghost" interpretation gained currency only after Christians began to look upon God as a "Trinity," with the "Holy Ghost" being an aspect of it. Neither the word Trinity nor its concepts can be found anywhere in the Bible. The Paraclete would be a man, not a ghost, because the same word is applied to Jesus himself at 1 John 2:1:

παράκλητον ἔχομεν πρὸς τὸν πατέρα, Ἰησοῦν Χριστὸν δίκαιον·

"We have a Paraclete (Advocate, Counsellor) with the Father, Jesus Christ, the righteous one." Jesus had been a "paraclete" to the Jews and his followers so considered him, but the Paraclete to come after Jesus (John 14:16) would be for all people, all places and all times.

The Greek text at John 14:16 which foretells the coming of "another Paraclete" is so specific that even the word "another" has significance. In English, "another" may mean "one more of the *same* kind" or "one more of a *different* kind." It is important to know which meaning Jesus had in mind, because if he meant "one more of a *different* kind" that would mean the Paraclete would perhaps be a spirit and the current Christian interpretation has some merit. But if he meant "one more of the *same* kind," then this is positive proof that the Paraclete would be just like Jesus was: a man, a human being, a prophet, NOT a spirit. Which did Jesus mean? The Greek text of the New Testament gives the verdict clearly because it uses the word *allon,* which is the masculine accusative form of *allos*: "ANOTHER OF THE *SAME* KIND." The Greek word for "another of a different kind" is *heteros,* but the New Testament does not use this word at John 14:16. Clearly, then, the Paraclete would be "ANOTHER OF THE *SAME* KIND" as Jesus, or as Moses said, "Like unto me": a MAN, not a spirit.

Detail of the Revelation

We can now begin to put together the complete "picture" which emerges from the Bible and come up with a very specific, graphic portrait of the messenger whose prominent characteristics are twofold: (1) He would be the last one and (2) he would be universal. According to the information given in the Old and New Testaments, this prophet would:

  i. be firm but merciful
 ii. establish a community based on justice
iii. be a light for all the nations
 iv. be associated with Qaydar;

(All based on Isaiah 42:1-11)

  v. be a descendant of Ishmael, a "brother" to the Hebrews
 vi. fulfill the promises made to Abraham and Ishmael to
     a. serve as a blessing to all the nations
     b. establish the Arabs as a "great nation"
     c. inherit the "double portion" of honor;
vii. receive revelation directly from God;
     (All based on Genesis 17:20; 22:16-18; Deuteronomy 21:15-17)

viii. come after Jesus' mission was ended
  ix. comfort and counsel mankind (paraclete), for which he would be known as the praised one (periclyte)

x. be outstanding for his truthfulness

xi. receive words directly from God

xii. deliver "all the truth," the whole truth

xiii. have a ministry of lasting effect

xiv. glorify Jesus.

(All based on John 14:16, 17 and 16:13, 14)

To refine these points for still clearer focus, the last prophet would differ from all the others in at least three vital aspects:

(1) He would have a universal mission

(2) He would be the seal of the prophets

(3) He would be an Arab, and of the 12 sons of Ishmael, he would have to come in the line of Qaydar.

This is the witness of the Bible, which cannot be accused of being "influenced" by the Qur'an or by the Sīrah (the Prophet Muhammad's traditions).

Would it be possible for any *one man* to fit this "picture" completely? Unless he could fulfill all the requirements, he would not be the prophet promised by the scriptures. The possiblity for any one man to meet all these criteria, purely by chance, is inconceivable. It would be impossible also for anyone to cause himself deliberately to meet them all. For example, who can control the question of who his ancestors will be? For the sake of argument, let us suppose that an Arab wanted, of his own desire, to be this prophet. But he could have descended from any of the other 11 sons of Ishmael. Perhaps he would have wanted to curry the favor or support of his own tribe, and thus he would have preached tribalism or nationalism rather than universalism. Or perhaps he would never even think of mentioning Jesus in his message, or would have agreed with the Jews that Jesus was but an imposter and troublemaker. Perhaps he would die before gaining a following or establishing a cohesive community. There are too many possibilities for anyone to consciously control all the criteria presented in the Bible for identifying the last prophet. Then there is the problem that the Bible was not translated into Arabic until the tenth century C.E., so *no Arab living before the year 1000 would have had the opportunity to examine the written text of the Bible in his own language*(21). Only God Almighty could have caused all these diverse elements necessary to come to fruition in one specific human being.

The fact is that one man, and only one man did answer to all the proper conditions, namely, Muhammad b. 'Abdullāh, may God grant him blessings and peace. The preview of him in the Torah and the Gospel is clear and undeniable, despite the errors and dogmatism of some copyists of the scripture.

Genealogical Table from Abraham to Muḥammad

(may God bestow peace and blessings upon them)

Abraham (Ibràhim)··················was father of

Ishmael (Ismail)···················· "   "   "

Kedar (Qaydar)···················· "   "   "

'Adnān···························· "   "   "

Ma'add···························· "   "   "

Nizār····························· "   "   "

Muḍar····························· "   "   "

Ilyās······························ "   "   "

Mudrikah·························· "   "   "

Khuzaimah························ "   "   "

Kinānah·························· "   "   "

Al-Naḍr·························· "   "   "

Mālik···························· "   "   "

Quraysh (Fihr)···················· "   "   "

Ghālib···························· "   "   "

Lu'ayy··························· "   "   "

Ka'ab···························· "   "   "

Murrah··························· "   "   "

Kilāb···························· "   "   "

Quṣayy··························· "   "   "

'Abd Manāf························ "   "   "

Hāshim·························· "   "   "

'Abdul Muttalib···················· "   "   "

'Abdullāh························· "   "   "

MUHAMMAD

(See Genesis 25:12-16, and *Muhammad the Holy Prophet* by H. G. Sarwar, pp. 10, 11)

---------------------------| Note added in proof: |---------------------------

The following is a direct photo-copy from page 567 of *The Gospel of John, A Commentary*, by Rudolf Bultmann, German Christian theologian, 1971, The Westminster Press, Philadelphia, U.S.A. (A translation of the German edition of 1964, *Das Evangelium des Johannes.*) It shows that the views of this well-known Christian scholar are identical with the views expressed on page 6 of this article.

> *The Paraclete therefore is a parallel figure to Jesus himself*; and this conclusion is confirmed by the fact that the title is suitable for both (14.16: . . . καὶ ἄλλον παρακλ. δώσει ὑμῖν).[1]
>
> It is clear from 14.16 that the source taught that there were two sendings of two Paracletes, Jesus and his successor, the one following the other.
>
> [1] W. Michaelis (Coniect. Neotest. XI 1947, 147–162) tries to avoid this conclusion by taking ἄλλον (14.16) pleonastically: "There will be another one too, and as Paraclete (or, 'that is to say, the Paraclete')". Even if that is correct, there would still be two messengers, two parallel figures; but I Jn. 2.1 confirms that the Evangelist applies the title "Paraclete" to Jesus.

Footnotes

1. Matthew 5:17, 18 in the *New English Bible.*
2. Sura Al-Maida, verses 44-48.
3. Curt Kuhl, *The Old Testament: Its Origin and Composition* (London, 1961), pp. 47, 51, 52.
4. James Hastings, *Dictionary of the Bible* (New York, 1963), pp. 340, 567-569.
5. Genesis 22:16-18, Jewish Publication Society's version, 1955. Note that the son of sacrifice (Dhabīhullāh) is stated to be the *only* son of Abraham. Recent Jewish translations change this to read the "favored son" of Abraham. However, the Hebrew text says *yehideka,* which is a noun form of *yahīd. Yahīd* in Hebrew corresponds with *wahīd* in Arabic and has the same meaning: "sole, single, only, only one." (*Shilo Hebrew Dictionary,* p. 83.). The reference thus must be to Ishmael, not Isaac, since Isaac was never the sole or only son of Abraham. However, some Jewish commentators, while admitting that *yehideka* means "only son," twist the meaning to make it refer to Isaac by saying that Ishmael was illegitimate, so Isaac was the only real son of Abraham. But the Torah of the Bible nowhere says that Ishmael was illegitimate. Rather, it says, "And Sarah Abraham's wife took Hagar her maid, the Egyptian, and gave her to her husband Abraham *to be his wife.*" (Genesis 16:3) Since Hagar became the second WIFE of Abraham, Ishmael could not have been "illegitimate." A man does not bear illegitimate children from his wife! Further, God says of Ishmael, "*I have blessed him . . .* and will make him a great nation." (Genesis 17:20) In Genesis 17:23, 25 and 26, we read: "And Abraham took Ishmael HIS SON . . . and Ishmael HIS SON was thirteen years old, when he was circumcised . . . In the selfsame day was Abraham circumcised, and Ishmael HIS SON." At the very last, when Abraham had passed away, the Bible says: "And his sons Isaac AND ISHMAEL buried him in the cave of Machpelah." (Genesis 25:9) The Bible is explicit that Ishmael was fully the son of Abraham and by no means illegitimate!
6. E. A. Speiser, *Genesis* (New York, 1964), The Anchor Bible, vol. I, pp. 156,157.
7. Genesis 17:4-10, 20.
8. Hastings, *op. cit.,* p. 626.
9. Deuteronomy 21:15-17, from *The Torah,* Jewish Publication Soceity, 1962.
10. Hastings, *op. cit.,* p. 47.
11. See Jeremiah 2:10; Ezekiel 27:21; Isaiah 60:7; Song of Solomon 1:5.
12. Isaiah 42:1-6, 11, *New English Bible.*
13. Matthew 15:24.
14. Deuteronomy 18:18, 19.
15. John 14:16, 17.
16. John 16:13, 14. It may be argued that Jesus was speaking for the benefit of his contemporaries, who died at least 500 years before Muhammad (pbuh). But many are the examples in the New Testament wherein Jesus, though speaking with his immediate followers, actually addresses his remarks to different generations in a future time. For example, see Matthew 16:27, 28. Jesus talks about Judgment Day but says: "Verily I say unto you, There be some standing here, which shall not taste of death, till they see the Son of Man coming in his kingdom." And at Matthew 24:3, 34, while speaking about the Last Day, he declares, "Verily I say unto you, This generation shall not pass, till all these things be fulfilled" Obviously, *those disciples* with Jesus then did not live to see either Judgment Day or the Second Coming of Jesus, neither of which has even yet occurred. *Jesus' words, though given to his contemporaries, had reference primarily to a time far distant in the future.* When Jesus says "I say unto YOU," he means his followers in the general sense, i.e., "you my people". Jesus is identifying in John 14 and 16 the Last Prophet for the benefit of his followers who would be living when he appeared.
17. Joseph H. Mayfield, *Beacon Bible Commentary* (Kansas City, 1965), vol. VII, p. 168.

18. Hastings, *op. cit.*, p. 14. Note the striking similarity between the two words *parakletos* and *periklytos* in Greek:

παρακλητος   περικλυτος

The consonants are exactly the same, the difference is only in the vowels, increasing the possibility of substituting one word for the other or omission of the one through careless copying.

19. For example, compare the many restorations of words and phrases made on the basis of ancient manuscripts, which were omitted from the standard New Testament text, as found in *The Emphatic Diaglott* of B. Wilson.

20. Reverend Thomas S. Green, *A Greek-English Lexicon to the New Testament*, 26th ed. (London n. d.), p. 149. As examples, see usual Christian interpretation of 1 Corinthians 2:10; 2 Thessalonians 2:2 or 1 John 4:1-3.

21. Hastings, *op. cit.*, p. 105. cf. Qur'an, sura Al-Nahl verse 103.

Principal References

1. Green, Thomas S. *A Greek-English Lexicon to the New Testament*. London: Samuel Bagster & Sons, Ltd. n.d.

2. Hastings, James. *Dictionary of the Bible*. New York: Charles Scribner's Sons, 1963.

3. Kuhl, Curt. *The Old Testament: Its Origins and Composition*. London, Oliver and Boyd, 1961.

4. Mayfield, Joseph H. "John," *Beacon Bible Commentary*, vol. VII. Kansas City: Beacon Hill Press, 1965.

5. *The Interpreter's Bible*, vol. VII. New York: Abingdon Press, 1951.

*The author is a former ordained Christian minister. His series of lectures, *Biblical Studies from a Muslim Perspective* is being published by The Islamic Center in Washington, D.C.

Index

Arrogance, 2:34, 87; 4:172-173; 5:82; 6:93; 7:13, 36, 40, 48, 75, 76, 88, 133, 146, 206; 10:75; 16:22, 23, 29, 49; 21:19; 25:21; 28:39; 31:7; 32:15; 35:43; 37:35; 38:74-75; 39:59; 40:27, 35, 56, 60, 76; 41:15, 38; 45:8, 31; 46:10, 20; 63:5; 71:7; 74:23.

Arrows, 5:3, 90.

Ascend, 6:125; 15:14; 32:5; 34:2; 35:10; 57:4; 70:4.

Ascension, of Muhammad, 17:1, 60; 53:1-18.

Assassination, 2:61, 87, 91; 3:21, 112; 4:92-93, 157; 5:32, 70; 6:151; 8:30; 17:33; 25:68; 28:20; 29:24.

Assurance, 2:260; 3:126; 5:113; 8:10.

Astronomy, 2:22, 29, 164, 255; 3:190; 7:54, 185; 9:36; 10:3, 6, 101; 11:7; 12:105; 13:1; 14:48; 15:14, 16; 17:44, 99; 18:51; 21:32, 104; 22:65; 23:17; 25:59, 61; 30:22; 31:10; 32:4; 33:72; 34:2, 3, 9, 22; 35:41; 36:40; 37:6; 39:67; 40:57, 64; 41:11-12; 44:10; 46:33; 50:6; 51:7, 47; 52:9, 44; 55:7, 33, 37; 57:4; 65:12; 67:3-5; 69:16; 70:8; 71:15; 72:8; 73:18; 77:9; 78:19; 79:27; 81:11; 82:1; 84:1; 85:1; 88:18. Big Bang Theory, 21:30.

Atheism, 7:136, 146, 179, 205; 10:7, 29; 16:108; 18:28; 21:97; 30:7.

Atom, 4:40; 10:61; 34:3, 22; 99:7-8.

Atonement, 2:184, 196; 4:92; 5:89, 95; 57:15; 58:3, 4.

Attire (see clothes, modesty)

Author, of Quran, see Appendix 1, 2:23, 41, 91, 97, 99, 159, 174, 176, 285; 3:3, 4, 7; 4:47, 105, 113, 136, 140, 166, 174; 5:48, 49; 66, 67, 68, 104; 6:92, 114, 155; 7:3, 196; 8:41; 10:94; 11:1, 14; 12:2; 13:1, 37, 19; 14:1; 15:9; 16:44, 64, 89, 101, 102; 17:82, 105, 106; 18:1; 19:64; 20:2, 4, 113; 21:10, 50; 22:16; 24:1, 34, 46; 25:1, 6; 26:192, 193; 28:87; 29:47, 51; 31:21; 32:2; 34:6; 36:5; 38:29; 39:1, 2, 23, 41, 55; 40:2; 42; 42:15, 17; 44:3; 45:2; 46:2; 47:2, 9; 56:80; 58:5; 64:8; 65:10; 69:43; 76:23; 97:1.

Aversion, 2:83; 3:23; 6:35; 8:23; 9:76; 17:41, 46; 21:24; 25:60; 35:42; 39:45; 67:21.

Awesomeness, of Quran, 2:2; 15:9, 87; 17:88; 36:2; 39:28; 41:42; 50:1, 56:77.

Azar, Abraham's father, 6:74.

Baby, girls killed, 16:58, 59; 81:8.

     Jesus, 3:47; 19:19-34.

     Moses, 20:39, 40; 26:18.

Backbiting, prohibited, 49:12; 104:1.

Bakkah, Mecca conformed to miraculous code, 3:95.

Banking, see Hoarding, Usury.

Barrier, invisible, 17:45, 7:46; 18:94; 19:17; 33:53; 36:9; 41:5; 42:51.

Battle, 3:123; 9:25; 33:9, 22.

Bedouin, 9:90, 97-101; 12:100; 33:20; 48:11, 16; 49:14.

Bee, 16:68.

Beggar, 2:177, 273; 51:19; 70:25; 93:10.

Betray, 4:105, 107; 8:27, 58, 71; 22:38; 66:10.

Betting, prohibited, 2:219; 5:90-91.

Bible, confirmed, 2:41, 89, 91, 97, 101; 3:3, 50, 81; 4:47; 5:43-48; 6:92; 35:31; 37:37; 46:12, 30; 61:6.

Cooperation, 3:103, 200; 5:2; 8:46; 18:28; 61:4; 90:17; 103:3.

Corruption, 2:11, 12, 27, 30, 60, 205, 251; 5:32, 33, 64; 7:56, 74, 85, 86, 103, 127; 8:73; 10:91; 11:85, 116; 12:73; 13:25; 17:4; 18:94; 21:22; 23:71; 26:152, 183; 27:14, 34, 48; 28:4, 77, 83; 29:36; 30:41; 38:28; 40:26; 47:22; 89:12.

Courage, 2:150, 243, 244; 3:173; 4:77, 95; 5:3, 24, 44, 54; 9:5, 13, 18, 46, 83, 86, 90; 33:37, 39.

Courtesy, 2:178, 229, 237, 262, 264; 4:19-22, 86; 16:125; 17:23-38, 53; 23:96; 24:27-29, 58; 29:46; 31:17-19; 33:53; 41:34; 49:2.

Covenant, with Israel, 2:40, 63, 83, 84, 93; 3:183; 4:154, 155; 5:12, 13, 70; 7:169.
    with others, 2:27, 124, 125, 177; 3:76, 81, 187; 4:21, 90, 92; 5:7, 14; 6:152; 7:172; 8:56, 72; 9:1, 4, 7, 75; 13:20, 25; 16:91, 95; 17:34; 20:115; 23:8; 33:7, 23; 36:60; 48:10; 57:8; 70:32.

Covet, you shall not, 4:32; 15:88; 20:131; 28:82.

Cow, 23:67-71; 6:144, 146; 12:43, 46.

Cowardice, (see Courage).

Creation, of man, 2:21, 30:38, 228; 4:1; 6:2; 7:11, 12, 189; 15:26, 28, 33; 16:4; 18:37; 19:67; 20:55; 22:5; 23:12; 24:45; 25:54; 30:20, 21, 40, 54; 31:28; 32:7; 35:11; 36:36, 77; 37:96; 38:71, 76; 39:6; 49:13; 50:16, 38; 51:49, 56; 53:45; 55:3, 14, 15; 56:57; 71:14; 75:38; 76:2, 28; 77:20; 78:8; 80:18-19; 82:7; 86:6; 92:3; 95:4; 96:1, 2.

    of the heavens and the earth, 2:29; 6:1, 73, 101, 102; 7:54, 185; 9:36; 10:3, 6; 11:7; 13:2, 16; 14:19, 32; 15:85; 16:3, 5, 8, 48, 81; 17:99; 20:4; 21:16, 33; 22:73; 23:17, 91; 24:45; 25:2, 3, 59; 27:6; 29:44, 61; 30:8; 31:10, 25; 32:4; 36:71, 81; 37:11; 38:27; 39:5, 38, 62; 40:62; 41:9, 37; 43:9; 44:38; 45:22; 46:3, 33; 54:49; 57:4; 59:24; 64:3; 65:12; 67:3, 14; 71:15.

    Jesus, John, & Isaac, 3:39, 49, 59; 5:110; 11:71, 72; 19:7, 49; 21:72, 89, 90; 29:27; 37:112.

Creature, 2:164; 6:38; 8:22, 55; 11:6, 56; 16:49, 61; 22:18; 24:45; 27:82; 29:60; 31:10; 34:14; 35:28, 45; 42:29; 45:4.

    the computer, 27:82 (see the book entitled, "The Computer Speaks: God's Message to the World," published by Islamic Productions, 739 East 6th Street, Tucson, Arizona 85719, U.S.A.)

Criminal Justice, 2:178, 179, 194, 283; 4:15, 135; 5:8, 32, 33, 38, 45; 17:33; 22:30; 24:1-2, 4, 6, 13; 25:72.

Criterion, 17:46; 39:45; 40:12.

Crucifixion, 4:157; 5:33; 7:42; 12:41; 20:71; 26:49.

Cure, 10:57; 16:69; 17:82; 26:80; 41:44.

Curse, 2:88, 89, 159, 161; 3:61, 87; 4:46, 47, 52, 93, 218; 5:13, 60, 64, 78; 7:38, 44; 9:68; 11:18, 60, 99; 13:25; 15:35; 17:60; 24:7, 23; 28:42; 29:25; 33:57, 61, 64, 68; 38:78; 40:52; 47:23; 48:6.

Darkness, 2:17, 19, 20, 257; 5:16; 6:1, 39, 59, 63, 97, 122; 10:27; 13:16; 14:1, 5; 21:87; 24:40; 27:63; 33:43; 35:20; 39:6; 57:9; 65:11.

Daughter, 3:36; 4:11, 23, 176; 6:100; 11:78, 79; 15:71; 16:57, 58; 17:40; 28:27; 33:50, 59; 37:149, 153; 42:49; 43:16; 52:39; 53:21; 66:12; 81:8.

40, 55; 34:43; 37:17, 69, 85, 102; 43:22-26, 29; 44:36; 56:48; 58:22; 60:4; 80:35.

Favoritism, 4:135; 5:8, 42; 58:22.

Fear, 2:150; 3:173; 4:77, 5:3, 44; 9:13, 18; 33:37, 39.

Feast, 5:113, 114; 12:31.

Festival, 20:59.

Fetus, see Abortion.

Fig, 95:1.

Fighting, see War.

Fingerprint, 75:4.

Fire, see Hell.

Fish, 5:96; 7:163; 68:48.

Flood, 7:133; 11:40-44; 23:27; 29:14.

Food, see Prohibitions.

Forbid, see Prohibitions.

Forgiveness, 2:221; 3:135; 4:48, 64, 116, 137, 168; 8:38; 9:80, 114; 19:47; 39:53; 42:37; 45:14; 47:34; 60:4; 63:6.

Fornication, see Adultery.

Fractions, 2:237; 4:11, 12, 25, 176; 8:41; 73:3, 20.

Freedom of Choice, 18:29; 33:72; 41:40; 73:19; 74:37, 55; 76:3, 29; 78:39; 80:12; 81:28.

Friday, 62:9.

Funeral, 9:84.

Gabriel, 2:87, 97, 98, 253; 5:110; 16:102; 19:17; 26:193; 66:4; 70:4; 78:38; 97:4.

Gambling, 2:219; 5:3, 90, 91.

Garden, see also Heaven, 2:265, 266; 6:99, 141; 13:4; 17:91; 18:32, 33, 35, 39, 40; 23:19; 25:8, 10; 26:57, 134, 147; 34:15, 16; 36:34; 44:25; 50:9; 68:17; 71:12; 78:16.

Garland, 5:2, 97.

Garlic, 2:61.

Garment, see Clothes.

Gas, 4:43; 5:6; 41:11; 44:10.

Gentile, 3:20, 75; 7:157, 158; 62:2.

Germination, 2:261; 15:19; 22:5; 71:17; 80:27.

Girl, see Daughter.

Glorify, 2:30; 3:41; 7:206; 13:13; 15:98; 17:44; 19:11; 20:33, 130; 21:20, 79; 24:36, 41; 25:58; 32:15; 33:42; 38:18; 39:75; 40:7, 55; 41:38; 42:5; 48:9; 50:39, 40; 52:48, 49; 56:74, 96; 57:1; 59:1, 24; 61:1; 62:1; 64:1; 68:28; 69:52; 76:26; 87:1; 110:3.

Gluttony, 6:141; 7:31.

God, 2:255; 3:2; 24:35; 59:22-24; 112:1-3.

Gog and Magog, 18:94; 21:96.

Gold, 3:14, 91; 9:34; 18:31; 22:23; 35:33; 43:53, 71.

Goliath, 2:249-251.

Gomorrah, see Sodom.

Gospel, 3:3, 48, 65; 5:46, 47, 66, 68, 110; 7:157; 9:111; 48:29; 57:27.

Grain 2:261; 6:59, 95, 99; 21:47; 31:16; 36:33; 50:9; 55:12.

Grave, 5:31; 9:84; 22:7; 35:22; 60:13; 80:21; 82:4; 100:9; 102:2.

Greed, 6:152; 7:85; 11:85; 17:35; 26:181.

Greeting, 4:86; 10:10; 14:23; 24:27, 61; 25:75; 33:44.

Grief, 2:38, 62, 112, 262, 274, 277; 3:139, 153, 170, 176; 5:41, 69; 6:48; 7:35; 9:40, 92; 10:62, 65; 12:13, 84, 86; 15:88; 16:127; 19:24; 20:40; 21:103; 27:70; 28:7, 13; 29:33; 31:23; 33:51; 35:34; 36:76; 41:30; 43:68; 46:13; 58:10.

Guardian, 4:6; 13:11; 82:10; 83:33; 86:4.
       of Hell, 43:77; 66:6; 74:31; 96:18.

Haamaan, 28:6, 8, 38; 29:39; 40:24, 36.

Hadith, false sayings attributed to Muhammad, 6:112-116; 25:30-31.

Hand, 2:79, 195, 249; 3:26; 4:43, 77; 5:6, 11, 28, 33, 38, 64, 94; 6:7, 93; 7:108, 124, 195; 8:70; 9:14, 52; 11:70; 12:31, 50; 17:29; 20:22, 71; 23:88; 24:24, 40; 26:33, 49; 27:12; 28:32; 36:35, 65, 71, 83; 38:44, 75; 39:67; 48:10, 20, 24; 57:29; 59:2; 60:2; 67:1; 80:15; 111:1.

Haroot and Maroot, 2:102.

Harvest, 6:141; 12:47.

Hate, 35:39; 40:10.

Healing, 10:57; 16:69; 17:82; 26:80; 41:44.

Heart, 2:74, 97, 204, 225, 260, 283; 3:103, 126, 151, 154, 159; 6:46; 7:101, 179; 8:10-12, 24, 70; 9:117; 10:74; 13:28; 15:12; 16:106; 18:28; 22:32, 46; 24:37; 26:89, 149, 200; 28:10; 30:56; 33:4, 5, 10, 32, 51, 53; 37:84; 39:45; 40:18, 35; 42:24; 45:23; 47:24; 48:4, 12; 50:33, 37; 57:27; 64:11; 66:4; 79:8.

Heaven, see Eternity.

Hebrew, 2:104; 4:46.

Heifer, 2:67-71 (see also Cow).

Heir, 2:180-182, 233, 240; 4:11-12, 19, 176; 19:6; 21:89; 27:16.

Hell (see Eternity).

Hoarding, 9:34, 35; 104:2.

Holy, 5:21; 20:12; 59:23; 62:1; 79:16.

Honesty (see Cheat).

Honey, 16:69; 47:15.

Honor (see Dignity).

Hood, the prophet, 7:65-72; 11:50-60; 26:123-140; 46:21-26.

Horn, 6:73; 18:83-95, 99; 20:102; 23:101; 27:87; 36:51; 39:68; 50:20; 69:13; 78:18.

Horse, 3:14; 8:60; 16:8; 59:6; 17:64.

Hour, 6:31, 40; 7:34, 187; 10:45, 49; 12:107; 15:85; 16:61, 77; 18:21, 36; 19:75; 20:15; 21:49; 22:1, 7, 55; 25:11; 30:12, 14, 55; 31:34; 33:63; 34:3,, 30; 40:46, 59; 41:50; 42:17, 18; 43:61, 66, 85; 45:27, 32; 46:35; 47:18; 54:1, 46; 79:42.

Hunain, battle of, 9:25-27.

Hunger, 2:155; 16:112; 20:118; 88:7; 106:4.

Hunt, 5:1, 2, 94, 95, 96.

Hurricane, 13:31; 17:68; 29:40; 54:34; 67:17; 69:7.

Husband, 2:102, 230, 232; 4:12, 20; 9:24; 13:23; 16:72; 24:6; 33:4; 40:8.

Jacob, 2:132, 133, 136, 140; 3:84; 5:163; 6:84; 11:71; 12:6; 12:38, 68; 19:6, 49, 58;
    21:72; 29:27; 38:45.
Jail, 12:25, 32, 33, 35, 36, 39, 41, 42, 100; 26:29.
Jealousy, 2:90, 213; 3:19; 42:14; 45:17.
Jesus, 2:87, 136, 253; 3:45, 52, 55, 59, 84; 4:157, 163, 171; 5:46, 78, 110, 112, 114,
    116; 6:85; 19:34; 33:7; 42:13; 43:63; 57:27; 61:6, 14.
Jews, 2:113, 120; 3:67; 5:18, 51, 64, 82; 9:30.
Jinn, 6:100, 112, 128, 130; 7:38, 179; 15:27; 17:88; 18:50; 27:10, 17, 39; 28:31;
    34:12, 14, 41; 41:25, 29; 46:18, 29; 51:56; 55:15, 33, 39, 56, 74; 72:1, 5, 6.
Job, 4:163; 6:85; 21:83, 84; 38:41-44.
John the Baptist, 3:39; 6:85; 19:7, 12; 21:90.
Jonah, 4:163; 6:87; 10:98; 37:140; 68:48-50.
Joseph, 6:84; sura 12; 40:34.
Judgment (see Day).
Jugular Vein, 50:16; 56:85.
Kaabah, 2:125, 127, 142-150, 158; 3:96, 97; 5:2, 95, 97; 8:35; 11:73; 22:26, 29, 33;
    33:33; 52:4; 106:3.
Kiblah, or Giblah (see Kaabah).
Killing, 2:178, 179; 4:29, 92; 5:32; 6:151; 17:31, 33.
King, 2:246, 247; 5:20; 12:43, 50, 54, 72, 76; 18:79; 20:114; 23:116; 27:34; 54:55;
    59:23; 62:1; 114:2.
Koran (see Quran).
Kosher, 3:93; 4:160; 6:146; 16:118.
Lamp, 24:35; 25:61; 33:46; 41:12; 67:5; 71:16; 78:13.
Language, irrelevant to understanding Quran, 41:44.
Lard, see footnote 6:145-146.
Law, 2:178; 4:60, 65; 5:38, 42-50; 13:41; 24:1, 2, 4, 51; 33:36.
Left, 7:17; 16:48; 18:17, 18; 34:15; 50:17; 56:41; 69:25; 70:37.
Lending, 2:245, 282, 283; 5:12; 57:11, 18; 64:17; 73:20. See also Debt.
Letter, 27:30.
Letters, alphabet (see Appendix 1).
Life, twice, 2:28; 40:11.
Light, 2:17, 257; 4:174; 5:15, 16, 44, 46; 6:1, 91, 122; 7:157; 9:32; 10:5; 13:16;
    14:1, 5; 24:35, 40; 25:61; 33:43, 46; 35:20; 39:22, 69; 42:52; 57:9, 12, 13, 19,
    28; 61:8; 64:8; 65:11; 66:8; 71:16.
Lightning, 2:19, 20, 55; 4:153; 13:12, 13, 31; 30:24; 41:13, 17; 51:44.
Liquor (see Alcohol).
146; 18:14.
Loss, 2:155; 3:186, 4:119; 6:31, 140; 7:9, 53; 10:45; 11:21, 22; 18:103; 22:11;
    23:103; 39:15; 40:78, 85; 42:45; 45:27; 57:22; 103:2.
Lot, 6:86; 7:80; 11:70, 74, 77, 81, 89; 15:59, 61; 21:71, 74; 22:43; 26:160, 161, 167;
    27:54, 56; 29:26-33; 37:133; 38:13; 50:13; 54:33, 34; 66:10.
Love, 5:82; 16:125; 17:53; 23:96; 29:25; 30:21; 41:34; 42:23; 60:7.
Luqman the prophet, 31:12, 13.
Lust, 3:14; 4:37; 7:81; 19:59; 27:55.

Mosque, 2:114, 144, 149, 150, 187, 191, 196, 217; 5:2; 7:29, 31; 8:34; 9:7, 17-19, 28, 107, 108; 17:1, 7; 18:21; 21:25; 22:40; 48:25, 27.

do not call on anyone but God, 72:18.

Mosquito, 2:26.

Mother, 4:11, 23; 5:17, 75, 116; 7:150; 16:78; 19:28; 20:38, 40, 94; 23:50; 24:61; 28:7, 13; 28:10; 31:14; 33:4; 39:6; 46:15; 53:32; 58:2; 80:35.

Mountain, 7:143, 171; 13:31; 27:88; 33:72; 59:21.

Muhammad, 3:144; 6:112, 18:110; 25:30, 31, 33:1, 21, 37, 40, 45, 56; 40:66; 41:6; 66:1; 80:1.

Murder, 2:61, 72, 85, 87, 91; 3:21, 112, 183; 4:29, 92, 93, 157; 5:27-32, 70; 6:140, 151; 7:127, 141, 150; 8:30; 17:31, 33; 18:74; 20:40; 25:68; 26:14; 29:9, 19, 20, 33; 29:24; 40:25-28; 60:12; 81:9.

Muslim, 2:128, 132, 133, 136; 3:52, 64, 67, 80, 84, 102; 5:111; 6:163; 7:126; 10:72, 84, 90; 12:101; 15:2; 16:89, 102; 21:108; 22:78; 27:31, 38, 43, 81, 91; 28:53; 29:46; 30:53; 33:35; 39:12; 41:33; 43:69; 46:15; 51:36; 66:5; 68:35; 72:14.

Neighbor, 4:36.

Night, of revelation of Quran, 2:185; 17:1; 44:3; 97:1.

Nineteen, 74:30, see Appendix 1 and the book, "The Computer Speaks: God's Message to he World," published by Islamic Productions.

Noah, 3:33; 4:163; 6:84; 7:59, 69; 9:70; 10:71; 11:25, 32-48, 89; 14:9; 17:3, 17; 19:58; 21:76; 22:42; 23:23; 25:37; 26:106, 116; 29:14; 33:7; 37:75, 79; 38:12; 40:5, 31; 42:13; 50:12; 51:46; 53:52; 54:9; 57:26; 66:10; 71:1, 21, 26.

Oath, 2:224, 225; 3:77; 5:53, 89, 108; 6:109; 9:12; 16:38, 91, 92, 94; 24:53; 35:42; 58:16; 63:2; 66:2.

Obedience, 2:285; 3:32, 100, 132, 149; 4:13, 34, 59, 69, 80; 5:92; 6:116, 121; 8:1, 20, 46; 9:71; 18:28; 20:90; 24:47, 51-56, 25-52; 29:8; 31:15; 33:1, 66, 67, 71; 43:54; 47:33; 48:16, 17; 49:7, 14; 58:13; 64:12, 16; 68:10; 96:19.

Olive, 95:1.

Orphan, 2:83, 177, 215, 220; 4:2, 3, 6, 8, 10, 36, 127; 6:152; 8:41; 17:34; 18:82; 59:7; 76:8; 89:17; 90:15; 93:9; 107:2.

Palace (see Mansion).

Paradise (see Eternity).

Parents, 2:83, 180, 215; 4:7, 33, 36, 135; 6:151; 14:41; 17:23; 19:14; 27:19; 29:8; 31:14; 46:15; 71:28.

Patriarch, 2:136, 140; 3:84; 4:163; 5:12; 7:160.

Peace, 2:208; 4:90, 91, 94; 5:16; 6:127; 8:61; 10:25; 25:63; 28:55; 39:29; 43:89; 47:35; 59:23; 97:5.

Pen, 31:27; 68:1; 96:4.

Penalty, 5:89, 95.

Persecution, 2:191, 193, 217; 8:39; 85:10.

Pharoah, 2:49, 50; 3:11; 7:103-141; 8:52-54; 10—75-90; 11:97; 14:6; 17:101, 102; 20:24, 43, 60, 78, 79; 23:46; 26:11, 16, 23, 41, 44, 53; 27:12; 28:3-9, 32, 38; 29:39; 38:12; 40:24-46; 43:46, 51; 44:17, 31; 50:13; 51:38; 54:41; 66:11; 69:9; 73:15, 16; 79:17; 85:18; 89:10.

Pilgrimage, 2:189, 196, 197; 3:97; 9:3; 22:27; 28:27.

Plagues, 7:130-133.

Planets, 6:76; 12:4; 37:6; 82:2; 85:1 (see also Constellation, Star).

Poets, 21:5; 26:224; 36:69; 37:36; 52:30; 69:41.

Polygamy, 4:3, 129.

Poor, 2:83, 177, 184, 215; 4:8, 36; 5:89, 95; 8:41; 9:60; 17:26; 18:79; 24:22; 30:38; 59:7; 68:24; 69:34; 74:44; 89:18; 90:16; 107:3.

Pork, 2:173; 5:3; 6:145; 16:115.

Prayer (see Salat).

Predestination, 57:22.

Pregnancy, 2:228; 3:6; 13:8; 22:5; 31:34.

Pride, 2:34; 4:172, 173; 6:93; 7:36, 40; 16:22, 23, 29; 25:21; 28:39, 74; 38:74; 39:59; 40:56; 41:38; 45:31; 46:20; 74:23.

Priests, 5:82; 6:138.

Prison (see Jail).

Privacy, 24:58, 59.

Profanity, 4:148; 49:11.

Promise, 2:268; 3:194; 4:95, 120; 5:9; 7:44; 9:68, 72, 114; 14:22; 16:97; 17:64; 19:61; 20:86, 124; 22:72; 24:55; 28:61; 33:22; 36:52; 40:8; 48:29; 57:10; 65:3, 4.

Proof (see Appendix 1).

Prophet, 3:39, 68, 161; 6:112; 8:67; 9:117; 19:30, 41, 49, 51-56; 22:52; 25:31; 33:6, 28, 45, 56; 43:6; 49:2; 66:1 (see also Muhammad).

Prostitution, 24:33.

Psalms, 3:184; 4:163; 16:44; 17:55; 35:25; 54:43.

Purgatory, 7:46-48.

Quails, 2:57; 7:160; 20:80.

Quake, 7:78, 91, 155; 22:1; 29:37; 73:14; 79:6; 99:1.

Queen, of Sheba, 27:22; 34:15.

Quran, 2:185; 4:82; 5:48, 101; 6:19, 38, 114; 7:204; 9:111; 10:15, 37, 61; 12:3; 13:31; 15:1, 87, 91; 16:98; 17:9, 41, 45, 46, 60, 78, 82, 88, 89, 106; 18:54; 20:2, 114; 25:30, 32; 27:1, 6, 76, 92; 28:85; 30:58; 34:31; 36:2, 69; 38:1; 39:27; 41:3, 26, 44; 42:7; 43:3, 31; 46:29; 47:24; 50:1, 45; 54:17, 22, 32, 40; 55:2; 56:77; 59:21; 72:1; 73:4, 20; 75:17-19; 76:23; 84:21; 85:21.

Rabbi, 5:44, 63; 9:31, 34.

Racism, 4:1; 49:13.

Ramadan, 2:185.

Rank, 2:253; 3:163; 4:95; 6:83, 132, 165; 8:4; 9:20; 12:76; 17:21; 20:75; 43:32; 46:19; 58:11.

Raven, 5:31; 35:27.

Recitation, of Quran, 10:61; 18:27; 27:92; 29:45; 35:29.

Reckoning (see Judgment).

Reconciliation, 2:182, 224; 4:128; 49:9, 10.

Record, 6:59; 8:68; 10:61; 11:6; 17:13, 58; 18:49; 20:52; 22:70; 27:75; 34:3; 35:11; 39:69; 50:4; 57:22; 83:7, 9, 18, 20.

Recorders, 82:10-12.

Redeem (see Repentance).

Refrain (see Stop).

Regret, 4:73; 6:27; 18:42; 25:27, 28; 33:66; 43:38; 69:25, 27; 78:40; 89:24.

Relatives, 2:83, 177, 180; 4:7, 8, 33, 36; 5:106; 8:41; 9:113; 16:90; 17:26; 24:22; 26:214; 30:38; 35:18; 42:23; 59:7.

Religion, 2:256; 3:19, 83; 9:29, 33, 122; 10:105; 12:40; 22:78; 30:30, 43; 39:2, 3; 40:14, 65; 42:13, 21; 48:28; 60:8; 61:9; 98:5; 107:1; 110:2.

Remission, of sin, 3:193, 195; 4:31; 5:12, 65; 8:29; 29:7; 39:35; 48:5; 64:9; 65:5; 66:8.

Remorse (see Regret).

Repentance, 4:17, 18; 9:104; 39:53; 66:8.

Reproach, 2:261, 262.

Resurrection, 2:56; 6:29, 36, 60; 7:14; 11:7; 15:36; 16:21, 38, 84, 89; 17:49, 79, 89, 98; 18:12, 19; 19:33; 22:5-7; 23:16, 37, 82, 100; 26:87; 27:65; 30:56; 31:28; 36:52; 37:16, 144; 38:79; 56:47; 58:6, 18; 64:7; 72:7; 83:4.

Retaliation, 2:178, 179; 17:33.

Revelation (see Inspiration).

Ridicule, 2:15, 212; 4:140; 5:57, 58; 6:5, 10; 11:8, 38; 15:11; 16:34; 18:56, 106; 21:36, 41; 23:110; 25:41; 26:6; 30:10; 31:6; 36:30; 37:14; 38:63; 39:48, 56; 40:83; 43:7; 45:33, 35; 46:26; 49:11.

Rumor, do not repeat unless verified, 4:83; 24:11-17; 49:6.

Sabbath, only for Jews, 2:65; 4:47, 154; 7:163; 16:124.

Sacrifice, Ishmael, 37:107.

          during pilgrimage, 2:196; 5:2, 97; 48:25; 108:2.

Saint, 4:69; 5:75; 12:46; 19:41, 56; 57:19.

Satan, 2:34; 7:11; 15:31, 32; 17:61; 18:50; 20:116; 26:95; 34:20; 38:74, 75.

Saul, 2:247.

Schism (see Division).

Scientific Miracles, 6:125; 10:5, 92; 25:61; 27:88; 71:16; 79:30.

Secret, hidden in Quran, the numerical code, 10:20; 13:43; 25:4-6 (see Appendix 1).

Sects (see Division).

Security, 2:125; 3:154; 4:83; 6:81, 82; 24:55.

Siblings, 4:11, 12, 23, 176.

Sickness (see Illness).

Sister (see Siblings).

Skin, 4:56; 16:80; 22:20; 39:23; 41:20, 21, 22.

Slander (see Rumor).

Slaughter, 5:4; 6:118, 119; 22:26.

Slavery, abolished (see Abolition).

Sleepers, of Ephesus, 18:9-25.

Smoke, 41:11; 44:10.

Sodom (see Lot).

Solomon, 2:102; 4:163; 6:84; 21:78-81; 27:15-18, 30, 36, 44; 34:12; 38:30, 34.

Son, 4:11; 5:27; 11:42; 21:91; 31:13.

Sonship, of Jesus, 2:116; 4:171; 6:101; 10:68; 18:4; 19:35, 88-92; 21:26; 23:91; 25:2; 43:81; 112:3.

Spider, ch. 29.

Spouse, 2:102, 228-240; 3:15; 4:3, 11, 12, 20, 23; 9:24; 13:23, 38; 16:72; 30:21; 33:37; 35:11; 39:6; 42:11; 43:70; 58:1.

Squander 4:6.

Stealing (see Law).

Suicide, 4:29; 6:151; 17:33.

Sun, 2:258; 6:78, 96; 7:54; 10:5; 12:4; 13:2; 14:33; 16:12; 17:78; 18:17, 86, 90; 20:130; 21:33; 22:18; 25:45; 27:34; 29:61; 31:29; 35:13; 36:38, 40; 39:5; 41:37; 50:39; 55:5; 71:16; 75:9; 76:13; 81:1; 91:1.

Supersede, 5:48.

Surety, 2:283.

Surrender, 47:35.

Suspicion, sinful, 49:12.

Swear, 4:148; 17:53.

Syngogue, 22:40.

Teacher, 18:17, 66.

Temple, 22:40.

Temporary, 2:36; 3:14, 185, 197; 4:77; 7:24; 10:70; 17:117; 28:60; 40:39; 42:36; 43:35; 57:20.

Temptation, 2:36; 3:155; 4:60, 120; 5:90, 91; 7:20, 27, 200, 201; 8:11, 48; 14:22; 16:63; 17:64; 20:120; 41:36; 47:25; 59:16.

Test, 67:2.

Throne, 7:54; 9:129; 10:3; 11:7; 13:2; 17:42; 20:5; 21:22; 23:86, 116; 25:59; 27:23, 26; 32:4; 39:75; 40:7; 43:82; 57:4; 69:17; 81:20; 85:15.

Thunder, 13:13.

Torah, 3:3, 48, 50, 65, 93; 5:43, 44, 46, 66, 68, 110; 7:157; 9:111; 48:29; 61:6; 62:5.

Travel, 2:184, 185, 283; 4:43; 5:6; 9:42; 18:62; 34:19.

Treasure, 11:12; 18:82; 25:8; 26:58; 28:76.

Treaty, 4:90, 92; 8:72.

Trinity, 4:171; 5:73.

Uncle, 4:23; 24:61; 33:50.

Unity, 3:103, 105; 6:159; 8:46; 30:32; 42:13.

Usury (see Interest).

Veil, 6:25; 17:46; 18:57; 24:31; 41:5.

Vicegerent, 2:30; 38:26.

Videotape, 17:13; 36:65.

Vision, 12:43; 17:60; 37:106; 48:27.

Wandering, Jews, 5:26.

War, 2:190-194; 8:161.

Whipping, 24:2, 4.

Widow, 2:234, 240.

Will, 2:180, 240; 4:11, 12, 176; 5:106.

Wine (see Alcohol).

This is the ONLY scripture in existence, with a built-in physical, examinable, and indisputable proof that it is God's message to the world.

First authorized English version of Quran (see footnote 1:1).

First English rendering by a Muslim whose mother tongue is Arabic.

First scriptural writing since Muhammad to purge out all the superstitions, traditions, customs, and idol worship and restores Quran and Islam to their original pristine purity.

Never before was the Quran so clearly presented to the world.